'This is an impressive addition to the research literature on philanthropy, one which takes a broad view of the nature of philanthropy and its demographic and geographic reach. It both challenges and expands prevailing views.'
— Jenny Onyx, Emeritus Professor, University of Technology Sydney, Australia

'This collection provides a comprehensive and important reference volume on the changing nature of philanthropy. It will be valuable reading to anyone interested in this field.'
— Patrick M. Rooney, Professor of Economics and Philanthropic Studies, Indiana University, USA

'This rich compendium of research findings and reflection gives us multiple perspectives on the "old-new" concept of philanthropy. It focuses on current practices and dilemmas whilst constantly reminding us about historical roots and the diversity of international and national experience.'
— Margaret Harris, Emeritus Professor, Aston Business School, UK

'A desk-side publication for all scholars and practitioners wanting a comprehensive reference to critical understandings of contemporary philanthropy.'
— Professor Myles McGregor-Lowndes, Australian Centre for Philanthropy and Nonprofit Studies, Australia

T0360969

The Routledge Companion to Philanthropy

Philanthropy – the use of private resources for public purposes – is undergoing a transformation, both in practice and as an emerging field of study.

Expectations of what philanthropy can achieve have risen significantly in recent years, reflecting a substantial, but uneven, increase in global wealth and the rolling back of state services in anticipation that philanthropy will fill the void. In addition to this, experiments with entrepreneurial and venture philanthropy are producing novel intersections of the public, nonprofit and private spheres, accompanied by new kinds of partnerships and hybrid organisational forms. *The Routledge Companion to Philanthropy* examines these changes and other challenges that philanthropists and philanthropic organisations face.

With contributions from an international team of leading contemporary thinkers on philanthropy, this *Companion* provides an introduction to, and critical exploration of, philanthropy. It discusses current theories, research and the diverse professional practices within the field from a variety of disciplinary perspectives. *The Routledge Companion to Philanthropy* is a rich and valuable resource for students, researchers, practitioners and policymakers working in or interested in philanthropy.

Tobias Jung is Senior Lecturer in Management at the School of Management, University of St Andrews, UK. He is a founding member of the UK's Centre for Charitable Giving and Philanthropy (CGAP) and a former Governor and Trustee of the St Katharine and Shadwell Trust and London's East End Community Foundation.

Susan D. Phillips is Professor of Philanthropy and Nonprofit Leadership in the School of Public Policy and Administration at Carleton University, Canada. From 2005–2014 she served as Director for the School and in 2013 she founded and continues as Supervisor of Canada's only graduate program in Philanthropy and Nonprofit Leadership.

Jenny Harrow is Professor of Voluntary Sector Management, Cass Business School, City University London, UK. She is founding Co-Director of the Centre for Charitable Giving and Philanthropy, funded by the UK's Economic and Social Research Council (ESRC) from 2008–2014.

Routledge Companions in Business, Management and Accounting

Routledge Companions in Business, Management and Accounting are prestige reference works providing an overview of a whole subject area or sub-discipline. These books survey the state of the discipline including emerging and cutting edge areas. Providing a comprehensive, up to date, definitive work of reference, Routledge Companions can be cited as an authoritative source on the subject.

A key aspect of these Routledge Companions is their international scope and relevance. Edited by an array of highly regarded scholars, these volumes also benefit from teams of contributors which reflect an international range of perspectives.

Individually, Routledge Companions in Business, Management and Accounting provide an impactful one-stop-shop resource for each theme covered. Collectively, they represent a comprehensive learning and research resource for researchers, postgraduate students and practitioners.

Published titles in this series include:

The Routledge Companion to Philanthropy

Edited by Tobias Jung, Susan D. Phillips
and Jenny Harrow

LONDON AND NEW YORK

First published 2016 by Routledge

2 Park Square, Milton Park, Abingdon, Oxfordshire OX14 4RN

52 Vanderbilt Avenue, New York, NY 10017

Routledge is an imprint of the Taylor & Francis Group, an informa business

First issued in paperback 2019

British Library Cataloguing in Publication Data
A catalogue record for this book is available from the British Library

Library of Congress Cataloging in Publication Data
Names: Jung, Tobias, editor. | Phillips, Susan (Philanthropy researcher) editor. | Harrow, Jenny, editor.
Title: The Routledge companion to philanthropy / edited by Tobias Jung, Susan Phillips, Jenny Harrow. Other titles: Companion to philanthropy
Description: New York : Routledge, 2016. |
Series: Routledge companions in business, management and accounting | Includes bibliographical references and index.
Identifiers: LCCN 2015027123| ISBN 9780415783255 (hardback) | ISBN 9781315740324 (ebook)
Subjects: LCSH: Charities.Classification: LCC
HV40 .R6846 2016 | DDC 361.7–dc23
LC record available at http://lccn.loc.gov/2015027123

ISBN: 978-0-415-78325-5 (hbk)
ISBN: 978-0-367-86660-0 (pbk)

Typeset in Bembo
by Cenveo Publisher Services

Contents

Contents

Contents

Figures

Tables

Contributors

Frank Adloff, Professor, Institut für Soziologie, FAU Erlangen-Nürnberg, Erlangen, Germany

Kelly Albertson, Founder and CEO, Virtueocity, Inc., North Carolina, USA

Aisha Faleh Al-Thani, Member of the Supreme Education Council of Qatar, Founder of Doha Academy, Chair of the Board of Patrons of the World Congress of Muslim Philanthropists, Qatar

Helmut Anheier, President, Dean, Academic Director and Professor, Sociology Department, Hertie School of Governance, Centre for Social Investment, Heidelberg University, Berlin, Germany

Putnam Barber, Senior Advisor, Nancy Bell Evans Center on Nonprofits and Philanthropy, Evans School of Public Affairs, University of Washington, Washington, USA

René Bekkers, Royal Netherlands Academy of Arts and Science (KNAW)/Van der Gaag Stichting Extraordinary Professor Social Aspects of Prosocial Behaviour, and Director, Centre for Philanthropic Studies, Vrije Universiteit, Amsterdam, Netherlands

Lucy Bernholz, Visiting Scholar, Centre for Philanthropy and Civil Society, Stanford University, Stanford, USA

Elizabeth Branigan, Senior Lecturer and Program Director, Faculty of Business and Law, Swinburne Centre for Social Impact, Swinburne University of Technology, Hawthorne, Australia

Oonagh B. Breen, Senior Lecturer, Sutherland School of Law, University College Dublin, Dublin, Ireland

Calum M. Carmichael, Director and Associate Professor, School of Public Policy and Administration, Carleton University, Ottawa, Canada

Jim Clifford, OBE, Partner and Director of BWB Advisory and BWB Impact, Bates Wells Braithwaite London LLP, London, United Kingdom

Hugh Cunningham, Emeritus Professor, School of History, University of Kent, Kent, United Kingdom

Jacques Defourny, Director and Professor, Centre d'Economie Sociale Department of Economics, HEC Management School, Université de Liège, Liège, Belgium

Gemma Donnelly-Cox, Assistant Professor, Business & Administration Studies, School of Business, Trinity College Dublin, Dublin, Ireland

Sharon Eng, Adjunct Associate Professor, Faculty of Business and Government, University of Canberra, Canberra, Australia

Íñigo García-Rodriguez, Researcher, Business Economics, Universidad Autònoma de Madrid, Spain

Jillian Gordon, Lecturer, Adam Smith Business School, University of Glasgow, Glasgow, United Kingdom

Peter Grant, Lecturer, Centre for Charity Effectiveness, Faculty of Management, Cass Business School, City University London, London, United Kingdom

Femida Handy, Professor, School of Social Policy and Practice, University of Pennsylvania, Pennsylvania, Philadelphia USA

Jenny Harrow, Professor and Co-Director, Centre for Charitable Giving and Philanthropy, Cass Business School, City University London, London, United Kingdom

Charles Harvey, Visiting Professor, Entrepreneurial Philanthropy Research Group, Hunter Centre for Entrepreneurship, Strathclyde Business School, University of Strathclyde, Glasgow, United Kingdom

John Healy, Adjunct Professor, Centre for Nonprofit Management, School of Business, Trinity College Dublin, Dublin, Ireland

Tessa Hebb, Director, Carleton Centre, School of Public Policy and Administration, Carleton University, Ottawa, Canada

Sally Hibbert, Associate Professor, Nottingham University Business School, Nottingham University, Nottingham, United Kingdom

Emily Jansons, Manager of Corporate Social Responsibility and Global Community Outreach, SkyPower Global, Toronto, Canada

Tobias Jung, Senior Lecturer, School of Management, University of St Andrews, St Andrews, United Kingdom

Naim Kapucu, Program Coordinator and Professor, Public Administration graduate and doctoral programs, School of Public Administration, University of Central Florida, Florida, USA

Michael D. Layton, Research Fellow, Alternativas y Capacidades, A.C., Mexico City, Mexico

Diana Leat, Visiting Professor, Cass Business School, City University London, London, United Kingdom

Sean MacKinnon, Lawyer & Risk Management Consultant, Euler Hermes, North America Toronto, Ontario, Canada

Mairi Maclean, Professor and Director of Research, Newcastle University Business School Newcastle University, Newcastle upon Tyne, United Kingdom

Debra Mesch, Director, Women's Philanthropy Institute, and Eileen Lamb O'Gara Chair of Women's Philanthropy, Indiana University Lilly Family School of Philanthropy, Indianapolis, USA

Michael Moran, Lecturer, Faculty of Business and Law, Swinburne University of Technology, Hawthorne, Australia

Shauna Mottiar, Senior Lecturer, School of Built Environment and Development Studies, University of KwaZulu-Natal, Durban, South Africa

Hanna Shaul Bar Nissim, The Paul Baerwald School of Social Work and Social Welfare, Hebrew University of Jerusalem, Jerusalem, Israel

Mvuselelo Ngcoya, Senior Lecturer, School of Built Environment and Development Studies, University of KwaZulu-Natal, Durban, South Africa

Marthe Nyssens, Professor Economics School of Louvain, Catholic University of Louvain, Centre de Recherches Interdisciplinaires Travail, Etat, Société, Louvain-la-Neuve, Belgium

Andrea Pactor, Associate Director, Women's Philanthropy Institute, Indiana University Lilly Family School of Philanthrophy, Indianapolis, USA

Cathy Pharoah, Co-Director, Centre for Charitable Giving and Philanthropy, Cass Business School, City University London, London, United Kingdom

Susan D. Phillips, Professor and Supervisor, Philanthropy and Nonprofit Leadership Graduate Program, School of Public Policy and Administration, Carleton University, Ottawa, Canada

Hillel Schmid, Emeritus Professor, The Paul Baerwald School of Social Work and Social Welfare, The Center for the Study of Philanthropy in Israel, Hebrew University of Jerusalem, Jerusalem, Israel

Eleanor Shaw, Professor and Department Head, Hunter Centre for Entrepreneurship, Strathclyde Business School, University of Strathclyde, Glasgow, United Kingdom

M. **Elena Romero-Merino**, Associate Professor, Department of Economic and Business Administration, Business Administration Graduate Program, Universidad de Burgos, Burgos, Spain

Mark Sidel, Doyle-Bascom Professor, University of Wisconsin Law School, University of Wisconsin-Madison, Madison, USA

Natalie Slawinski, Assistant Professor, Faculty of Business Administration, Memorial University Newfoundland, St Johns, Canada

David Horton Smith, Research and Emeritus Professor, Department of Sociology, Boston College, Chestnut Hill, USA

Steven Rathgeb Smith, Executive Director American Political Science Association, and Associate Professor, Evans School of Public Affairs, University of Washington, Seattle, USA

Ekkehard Thümler, Project Director, Centre for Social Investment, Heidelberg University, Heidelberg, Germany

Severine Thys, Research Assistant, Centre d'Economie Sociale Department of Economics, HEC Management School, Université de Liège, Liège, Belgium

Georg von Schnurbein, Director and Associate Professor, Center for Philanthropy Studies, University of Basel, Basel, Switzerland

Richard D. Waters, Associate Professor, School of Management, University of San Francisco, San Francisco, USA

Acknowledgements

Mirroring the saying cited in the chapter by Shauna Mottiar and Mvuselelo Ngcoya that 'one finger cannot pick up a grain', compiling a *Companion to Philanthropy* is necessarily a work of many hands. Without their support and help, this book would not have come to fruition. While it is impossible to thank everyone who has contributed, either directly – via hands-on assistance, providing resources or food for thought – or indirectly – through encouragement, humour and patience – there are a number of individuals and organizations that warrant our special thanks.

First and foremost, we would like to thank our families, especially, Hannah, Percy and Charlie (Tobias); Brian (Susan); and Stephen (Jenny), who bore with us over the course of this long project, and accepted the editorial requirement of numerous evenings and weekends locked away with computer screens, pens, paper and pages of manuscripts.

Second, a special thanks goes to everyone who has helped to support the bringing together of this volume. The contributors have brought a wealth of insights, expertise and original research that provide the basis for this work, and we thank them for their patience with the length of the process. Our thanks for the superb research assistance by graduate students in Carleton University's School of Public Policy and Administration (SPPA), Laurel Carlton (now Manager, Office of the President, Community Foundations of Canada), and Cara-Lynn Janzen, and by the Centre for Charitable Giving and Philanthropy's (CGAP) Margaret Busgith. Our thanks also to Paloma Raggo and Amanda Clark, Philanthropy and Nonprofit Leadership graduate program, SPPA, for their helpful comments on drafts of the first and final chapter; to our students at both Carleton and St Andrews who 'test drove' a number of the chapters; and to the many other colleagues – they know who they are – who provided advice and a second reading of various chapters.

The support provided by Routledge and its editorial team has been outstanding. Here, a special mention needs to be made of Natalie Tomlinson, editor on the business and management list, and Nicola Cupit, who provided invaluable guidance, remaining calm and patient in the light of our expanding timescales. At Routledge, thanks also go to David Varley and Alexander Krause, whose advice and leadership was instrumental at the inception stages of this *Companion*.

Third, we would like to acknowledge the support provided by our respective institutions, the School of Management at the University of St Andrews, the School of Public Policy and Administration at Carleton University and the School of Social Policy and Practice, University of Pennsylvania (where a visiting fellowship for Susan enabled her contributions to completion), and the Centre for Charitable Giving and Philanthropy (CGAP) at Cass Business School, City University London, where this project began. As part of this, the UK's Economic and Social Research Council (ESRC) and the Social Sciences and Humanities Research Council of

Canada (SSHRC) have been instrumental in repeatedly funding and supporting our research. Such resources have been essential to shaping our thinking on, and knowledge of, philanthropy, and to developing invaluable networks across academia, policy and practice.

Finally, we would like to thank the Association for Research on Nonprofits and Voluntary Action (ARNOVA), the International Society for Third Sector Research (ISTR), and the International Research Society for Public Management (IRSPM) which, as part of their conference programs, allowed us to hold a series of roundtable discussions with contributors and colleagues, the content of which further informed and shaped the direction of this volume.

Part I
Setting the scene

Foreword

Helmut Anheier

As philanthropic action, locally and globally, increases and alters in complexity and scope, there is a strong need for a better understanding of contemporary philanthropy. What are philanthropy's multiple facets, trajectories and ambitions? How is philanthropy developing and changing? What are its risks and rewards? These questions are among some of the diverse and important issues addressed by this *Routledge Companion to Philanthropy*.

This *Companion* recognizes and demonstrates the spread of philanthropy scholarship: it offers reflection, admiration and critical engagement with philanthropy as a vital area of practice and scholarship. To this end, it provides both theoretical and empirical insights on which we are able to further build, amend, refresh – and sometimes discard – our understanding and perceptions of philanthropic actions and organizations. Chapters, such as those on philanthropy's historical growth, institutional patterns, effectiveness and legitimacy, ensure that our awareness of rationales, routines and reputations affecting the 'why', 'where', 'for whom' and 'how' of philanthropy in its various guises is increased. Simultaneously, the contributions on non-Western perspectives, the policy-philanthropy nexus, and the 'dark side' challenge some of the popular conceptions of philanthropy as 'the love of humanity'. To highlight the learning implications and the contexts within which we need to understand, interpret and challenge philanthropy, the scholarly contributions are supplemented with illustrative vignettes that demonstrate implications for, and lessons from, the practice of philanthropy.

The variety of philanthropic models and movements, practices and philosophies, trophies and testing grounds discussed in this *Companion* show how fine-grained philanthropy scholarship has become over recent years. Neither trite descriptions of portentous philanthropic journeys, nor carping assertions of its self-serving nature help the field. Instead, philanthropy theory and practice is enhanced when the various facets of philanthropy discourses and practices are acknowledged and examined: searching for definitiveness and clarity go hand-in-hand with seeking diversity and managing ambiguity. This is where this *Companion* excels. The Editors have brought together a group of international authors from a diverse set of disciplines.

Collectively, they take our knowledge on philanthropic actors and activities forward; they extend the scholarly conversations concerning philanthropy, its actors, activities and promises, all of which are fundamental of civil society and central to the contemporary recasting of the public, private and nonprofit spheres. The Editors and Contributors will value your own contribution to further extending and examining the philanthropy arena: in this book they provide a basis on which you can build.

1

Introduction

A New 'New' Philanthropy: From Impetus to Impact

Susan D. Phillips and Tobias Jung

Philanthropy is increasingly being called upon to help solve some of the most serious social, economic and environmental issues of our times. To achieve impacts of this magnitude, many have argued that philanthropy needs to 'up its game' (Dean, 2013), that it should be renewed, even revolutionized (Cohen, 2014a). Combined with innovations from within philanthropy itself, such conjectures have led to a reimagining, recasting and rebranding of philanthropy, both as professional practice and as a field of academic research. Expectations of donors and volunteers, ideas about impact and 'social investment', new philanthropic tools and technologies, the nature and strategies of major philanthropic institutions, and philanthropy's relationships with the state and the market are all rapidly evolving. To differentiate these developments from a long tradition of philanthropic fashions and foibles, recent years have seen the emergence and use of various qualifiers: strategic, venture, entrepreneurial, catalytic, high impact, social change, and, simply, 'new' philanthropy.

The current appellation of 'new' is expressed in the ideas and ideals of 'philanthrocapitalism' (Bishop 2006; Bishop and Green 2008). This strongly resembles Andrew Carnegie's (1901) vision for a more scientific approach to philanthropy; it emphasizes innovation and focuses on the transfer and application of business strategies and market based models (Salamon, 2014). The assumption is that, in an almost 'laserlike' way (Bishop and Green 2014: 550), donors articulate clear goals and pursue evidence-based approaches (Brest, 2015) for achieving and measuring impact to address complex, 'wicked' problems. This is by no means the first time that philanthropy has been considered 'new' (Cunningham, Chapter 2). Furthermore, the turn towards business principles, and the veiled interests inherent therein, has not been without their critics (Edwards, 2008): so far, strategic philanthropy has 'failed to solve even one social problem once and for all, by penetrating to its root cause' (Schambra, 2013: NP). Consequently, in the current enthusiasm for a particular style of philanthropy, it is important not to fall under the spell of fashion. Instead, we need to embrace and understand the diversity that has always characterized philanthropy; it is currently making philanthropy even more varied in its ideas, expressions and institutions. This *Routledge Companion to Philanthropy* explores and reflects on this expanding richness of philanthropy in a manner that is international in scope and that is informed by, and intended to inform, research and practice.

The growing diversity of philanthropy

As three recent examples demonstrate, philanthropy occurs in ways that are big and modest, businesslike and community-first, strategic and spontaneous. Iconic of the power of institutionalized philanthropy is the part played by large foundations in aiding the City of Detroit emerge from bankruptcy in 2014. In order to save the City's impressive art collection from circling creditors, and to prevent thousands of city workers from losing their pensions or livelihoods, ten philanthropic foundations entered into an 'improbable arrangement' (Davey, 2014): they negotiated behind closed doors with unelected officials in which they flexed 'their political muscle to the limit' (Schambra, 2014: NP), put together a joint financial contribution of $366 million (Dolan, 2014), and strategically made their grants contingent upon particular outcomes. Although these foundations are playing a critical role in the future of a major city, their involvement has raised major questions about 'big' philanthropy: about its transparency, democratic accountability and its influence over public policy.

The bulk of philanthropy, however, occurs at much more modest scales, often rooted in community-based approaches that offer 'a meeting point where numerous expressions of giving, responsibility and solidarity can come together' (Hodgson, 2013a: 49). This is illustrated by the Waqfeyat al Maadi Community Foundation (WMCF) in Egypt. Established by a small group of community changemakers in a suburb of Cairo in 2007, WMCF aims to create sustainable sources of funding for building civil society in the area. It seeks to do so by reviving and modernizing the traditional Islamic concept of the *waqf* endowment (Herrold, 2015). Despite its small size, WMCF has quickly become a community hub, offering a variety of grants, loans and training, as well as arts, neighbourhood improvement and youth engagement programs. While it had navigated tricky political waters by being expressly apolitical, when several members of the Maadi community were shot during the 2011 Tahir Square protests, WMCF needed to assume new leadership responsibilities (Global Fund Community Foundation, 2011; El Daly, 2012), using its asset of community trust to become a source of education for democratic rights, while continuing to lessen the gap of rich and poor in its community.

Finally, social media has added a new degree of spontaneity to philanthropy by enabling more virtual forms of collective action. A prime illustration is the 'Ice Bucket Challenge' that went viral in the summer of 2014: millions of people across the globe having buckets of ice water dumped on them to raise money for amyotrophic lateral sclerosis (ALS), known as motor neurone disease (MND) in the UK. A host of pop stars and former politicians – from Bill Gates to Victoria Beckham and Mark Zuckerberg – took the challenge (Perez, 2014), and more than 2.4 million unique videos, viewed over 10 billion times by more than 440 million people were posted to Facebook (Facebook, 2014). This resulted in ALS/MND associations raising $US 220 million, 100 times their average annual revenue (O'Neil, 2015). Does this sort of 'viral philanthropy' represent a new approach for engaging the selfie generation? Does it promote a kind of slacktivism that represents the worst of philanthropy? Does such spontaneity countermand more strategic approaches?

To understand what lies ahead for an evolving, evermore diversified, philanthropy requires us to look beyond business–oriented, strategic approaches. The aim is not to dismiss them, as they have unquestionably taken hold on a large part of philanthropy's landscape, but to consider other ways in which philanthropy is responding to a changing environment. The following chapters examine this varied landscape. They provide a critical assessment of the history, recent developments and emerging challenges in the field of philanthropy, ranging from the 'big' to the community-based. Our volume is purposely international, with contributions by leading scholars from a wide range of countries and disciplines. The contributors address some of the major questions that the agents and critics of philanthropy are grappling with; they identify gaps in the extant knowledge base and suggest productive directions for future reflection and research. The volume's organizational logic is to move along a continuum of engagement: from the impetus and motivations for philanthropy, through its management in different institutional settings, to how its impact is being assessed.

This introductory chapter concentrates on exploring the developing trends of philanthropy in more depth. It makes the case that the unfolding changes are varied, and at times contradictory, and should compel creative thinking about how to shape philanthropy's future. Our starting point is a working definition of philanthropy that, rather than sentimentalizing it, can serve as a useful platform for social science research. We then offer a brief overview of recent trends in the inflows and distribution of philanthropy and provide a roadmap through the themes and structure of the 31 chapters and six 'vignettes' that follow.

Philanthropy: An expansive definition

Put simply and broadly, philanthropy is the use of private resources – treasure, time and talent – for public purposes. While this builds on Salamon's (1992: 10) definition as 'the private giving of time and values (money, security, property) for public purposes', it extends beyond gifts to embrace some of the new tools and practices of philanthropy. As Salamon (2014: 2) has argued more recently, there has been a 'massive explosion' in tools that fit under the umbrella of philanthropy. This is especially noticeable in relation to new forms of social investment and social entrepreneurship. Raising expectations of financial as well as social returns, the promise is to do good while doing well, a recurring theme in philanthropy's history (Jung and Harrow, 2015a). Furthermore, our definition does not limit philanthropy to acts of the affluent helping the less fortunate (Adam, 2004); in addition to financial contributions, it encompasses volunteering, collective action, and giving of creativity or other talents. As in the outskirts of Cairo, some of the most interesting and promising experiments are occurring in grassroots philanthropy where communities, often very disadvantaged ones, are working together in creative ways to advance economic, social and cultural development that they would neither describe as charitable giving nor as traditional volunteering (Knight, 2012; Kasper et al., 2014). Although our casting of philanthropy provides a broad platform on which to explore a wide range of motivations and actions, it is important to bear in mind that philanthropy remains a contested concept, particularly in its 'normative valence' (Daly, 2012: 545).

Our definitional stance contrasts with the popular perception of philanthropy as 'love of humanity'. This widely espoused notion was first set out in English in Samuel Johnson's *A Dictionary of the English Language*, published in 1755 (Sulek 2010; 2011); it is a loose translation from philanthropy's roots in ancient Greek. Unfortunately, it has perpetuated a normative dimension of benevolence. Even recent definitions, formulated for academic purposes, often retain an emotional and normative aspect. For example, Sulek (2010: 399), after extensive scholarly analysis of the concept's development, reaches a warm glow interpretation of 'love motivating the greater realization of human potential'. Similarly, Payton and Moody (2008: 30, 50) assert that the defining feature of philanthropy as 'voluntary action for the public good' is 'morality and moral action'. Such approaches are of limited use in social science research. They make it easy to ignore how philanthropy has been shaped across history by its intellectual, social and political contexts; how at different times philanthropy generated diverse sets of questions and answers regarding its purposes, values, and consequences. Of course, practices that we would call philanthropy are neither restricted to Western perspectives nor to European lineage (Mottiar and Ngcoya, Chapter 9), but it is this heritage that has largely shaped the contemporary assumptions about philanthropy that are represented, and challenged, in this volume.

Philanthropy: A concept of embedded dynamics

First appearing in the fifth century BC in the Greek play *Prometheus Bound*, 'philanthropy' is a compound of 'phílos', that which is beloved, dear and important, and 'ánthrōpos', a human being. In contrast to the emotion-laden – 'love of' – concept that has become so entrenched, McCully (2008: 3) argues that philanthropy is appropriately translated as 'caring about, seeking, and nourishing human potential', while Carmichael (2013a) suggests that it expresses a 'regard for' humankind. Initially referring to a manner in which certain gods of Greek mythology dealt with mortals, philanthropy necessarily implicated power relationships. However, it also involved reciprocity as it flowed through the social and civic networks of obligation and help that the ancient Greeks had cultivated (Carmichael, 2009). From the very beginning then, philanthropy involved value judgements; it was strategic and practical, oriented to solving collective problems. In essence, the gods were figuring out, and guiding, humanity's progression.

As philanthropy developed through Judeo–Christian and Islamic religions, it acquired a sense of obligation and duty, particularly in helping the deserving poor and downtrodden. The act of giving, frequently accompanied by the promise of 'reward in heaven' (van Leeuwen, 2012: 325), became as important as the gift. When the concept of philanthropy entered popular English use during the seventeenth century, it was imbued with altruistic motivations. In Victorian times, it was further constricted to refer primarily to charitable giving, an interpretation that has stuck to it. Nonetheless, as philanthropy had become secularized through Europe during the Enlightenment, it also became equated with both citizenship and community. A view that 'indiscriminate charity' simply perpetuated charity (Garrioch, 2004: 490) propelled an interest in helping the poor escape poverty through more comprehensive structural reforms and instilled a confidence in the ability of philanthropy to achieve this. Secular organizations, such as the *Société Philanthropique de Paris* in the late 1700s, declared philanthropic action to be a duty of a *citizen* – not just of a Christian (Cunningham, Chapter 2). Philanthropy also became an expression of both 'sensibility and sociability' (Garrioch, 2004: 496). It was the mark of a feeling person attuned to the world, a key means for the aspiring middle class to be integrated into the bourgeois (Adam, 2004: 14) and, particularly for women over the next century, a way of being part of a social community (Prochaska, 1980). While the power of philanthropy produced certain tensions between the aristocratic views of charity and its recipients, it also stimulated cooperative movements among the poor themselves, and led to alliances of the middle classes with the poor, in part as a means of justifying the former's social position (Prochaska, 1990).

The popular definition of philanthropy is also problematic in that it perpetrates a prominent misconception: that philanthropy exists in an entirely different sphere from business or government, that the intersections of private, public and philanthropic spheres that are now touted as 'new' have no antecedents. Yet, many of the early industrialists married their business acumen to their philanthropy (Lala, 2006; Harvey *et al.*, 2011). For example, the practice of '5 percent philanthropy', by which philanthropists invested in social housing for a below market return, was popular in Victorian England and later exported to the US (Tarn, 1973). Preceding twenty-first century developments in social finance, the proponents of five percent philanthropy believed that 'only the connection of philanthropy with market economy could solve the housing problem' (Adam, 2004: xxii). Similarly, the conventional narrative that the modern welfare state evolved in discreet stages – from control by the church, provision by secular charities, absorption by the state, and in the past few decades again privatized to charities and nonprofits – overlooks the various forms of a mixed economy of welfare by which philanthropy and state provision have long coexisted (Lewis, 1999; Harris and Bridgen, 2007; Jung and Harrow, 2015a). This is not to deny that there is much that is new and innovative in contemporary social finance and cross-sectoral collaborations. However, we need to look beyond benevolence in both past and present, to appreciate what is novel and how these experiments relate to and shape philanthropy's trajectories.

Another problem with the adoption of a normatively imbued perspective is that it conflates motives with action. By implying an inherent altruism, (Adloff, Chapter 3) this too often leads to a romanticized and sentimental discussion. While altruism is often a key motivation for philanthropic action, people may also give, volunteer or invest in public purposes for a variety of other reasons. On closer inspection, some of these might not be all that altruistic or noble: vanity, as a potential motive in celebrity philanthropy (Narapruet, 2011); profit and shareholder value, as contributing factors to corporate philanthropy (Gautier and Pache, 2015); the reduction of tax burdens, prominently illustrated in the debate about the legality of the UK's Cup Trust, which, while only spending £55,000 on charitable work over a two year period, claimed £46 million in tax relief (NAO, 2013); accessing and building beneficial social circles and networks (Odendahl, 1990); using power and influence to shape society, a recurring theme in philanthropy's involvement in education (Gasman and Drezner, 2008; Scott *et al.*, 2009; Ball and Junemann, 2011); or simply exerting control, where philanthropy obstructs meaningful social change (Arnove and Pinede, 2007), undermines uncomfortable policies and political debates (Brulle, 2014), and provides 'angry gifts' to vent civic discontent (Silber, 2012). Consequently, it is important to appreciate that philanthropy serves both a 'private, consumptive and expressive function' (Frumkin, 2006: 18), in which the donor is at the centre of analysis, and a 'public' one that has 'goals of change, innovation, redistribution and pluralism'. Frumkin (2006) is careful to make a further distinction. This differentiates between setting public goals and achieving them. Just as a definition useful for social science research needs to avoid the tautology of imputing motivations, it must also abstain from necessarily assuming positive outcomes from philanthropy.

Although philanthropy is directed towards public purposes, what constitutes the 'good' for the 'public' is defined, at least in the first instance, by the donor(s). Whether philanthropy succeeds in achieving any public benefit is therefore an open question, subject to empirical testing and, often considerable debate. This leads to questions of accountability and answerability to the public: what are the boundaries between private and public (Brody and Tyler, 2012)? To whom and how should the use of these private assets and their impact be accountable? On the one hand, philanthropy comes from private wealth – albeit not always accrued through honourable means – which people have chosen to donate for public purposes, rather than consume in other ways. On the other hand, and at a most basic level, these donors most likely received tax benefits so that taxpayers at large subsidized these contributions. The cloak of altruism, however, has somewhat shielded philanthropy from criticisms and closer scrutiny: how can we be overly critical of benevolence without undermining underlying honourable intentions? Although both philosophical and evidence-based critiques are alive, particularly of philanthrocapitalism (Edwards, 2008) and mega-foundations (Reich, 2013; Barkan, 2014), they have always been more marginal than mainstream. They are, however, beginning to assume a new vigour.

Finally, philanthropy needs to be disentangled from the concept of charity. Although related, if sometimes uncomfortably, from the time of the Enlightenment, and accentuated by the scientific approach advocated by Carnegie and his contemporaries in the late 1800s and early 1900s, philanthropy has tried to differentiate itself from charity (Bremner, 1956; Zunz, 2012). The distinction that has frequently been made is that philanthropy is more solution focused: it aims to address root causes rather than symptoms. Thus, charity involves more individualized giving to provide services or other assistance to those in need; it treats the manifestations of poverty, or ill health, or unemployment. Philanthropy, however, advocates for policy and social change, promotes self- or mutual-help, or addresses root causes (Gross, 2004; Frumkin, 2006; Hammack and Anheier, 2013). Charity also implies a measure of compassion and, particularly in its passage through the Victorian era, accumulated problematic associations of inequality: the more affluent helping the less fortunate. Perhaps the key distinction that can be made is that, in a number of jurisdictions, charity has legal status, whereas philanthropy does not. The legal concept of charity identifies a set of purposes deemed to be 'charitable' under common or statutory law that are used to legitimize and award to qualifying nonprofits significant tax benefits (O'Halloran, 2012; Harding *et al.*, 2014). Increasingly, however, even charities are trying to disassociate themselves from charity, preferring to be known through an alternative lexicon: public benefit, civil society, social profit, or similar terminology, often considered to be less weighted with limiting connotations.

Because this volume strives for a rigorous analytical assessment of philanthropy, without glossing over its potential pitfalls, we prefer an expansive but simple concept that can be used to interrogate motivations, practices and effectiveness. We do, however, appreciate the resulting challenge: this expansion opens a broad terrain to cover while the space available within this volume is necessarily limited. Consequently, although the contributions of time and talent are of similar importance to those of money, and the three are increasingly intertwined as people engage in fulsome ways with the organizations and causes they support, our chapters focus specifically on financial contributions rather than on volunteerism or other in kind uses of private resources. Bearing in mind the wider available and forthcoming literature on philanthropy, this is where we currently see the largest and most important gap in the knowledge-base on philanthropy. To prepare the basis for the more detailed analysis of why and how philanthropy is being reshaped provided throughout this *Companion*, the next section presents some basic information about the sources, inflows and distribution of philanthropy, and the demographic trends that are beginning to alter these.

The State of Philanthropy

Opinions differ dramatically on the current state of philanthropy. Bill and Melinda Gates (2013), reflecting on the international achievements of philanthropy in reducing extreme poverty and infant mortality, describe 'amazing progress', while recognizing there is still much to do. In contrast, Sir Ronald Cohen (2014b), founding chair of Big Society Capital, an independent organization set up by the UK's Cabinet Office with the aim to grow the British social investment market, laments the 'sorry state' of philanthropy: it has too great a focus on giving, rather than on achieving social outcomes; its timelines are too short; it is of too limited scale; and it pays inadequate attention to growth. Could they both be right in their assessment of the field? That depends on how one views evolving trends, particularly in individual giving as the dominant source of philanthropy.

The sources of philanthropy

The financial contributions of philanthropy originate from four primary sources: living individuals; estates and bequests from individuals; foundations which, as permanent endowments were created by individuals and their families; and corporations, including corporate foundations. While some authors argue for three categories, seeing foundations as a giving vehicle for individuals, estates and corporations (Frumkin, 2006: 24), this seems inappropriate. Not only do foundations have a permanency and life of their own, but in many countries, data on giving by foundations are treated as distinct, and separated from, individual and corporate giving. As such, foundations warrant to be in a category of their own. Increasingly, a fifth category is emerging, encompassing large institutions, such as pension and other investment funds, that are central players in a range of market-based social finance, and mission-related investment tools, which serve a public purpose while delivering some rate of financial return (Nicholls 2010; Bugg-Levine and Emerson, 2011; Salamon, 2014:7). Among these categories individuals are by far the most important source. Across developed countries, they provide about three-quarters of total contributions, compared to around 15 percent from foundations, eight percent from bequests, and five percent from corporations (Anheier, 2014; Giving USA 2014). Such data, however, always represent only a partial picture of overall philanthropy. This has mainly to do with the ways in which contributions are recorded and administered. For instance, while only a quarter of Canadian tax filers claim any tax benefits on their giving, 85 percent of the population reported that they had made a charitable donation in 2010 (Department of Finance Canada, 2015: 37).

Philanthropic contributions can be made directly, or through various intermediaries that facilitate philanthropic giving and investment (Frumkin, 2006: 24). Among these intermediaries are: federated funders that collect donations and are responsible for distributing them to specific organizations and causes (e.g. United Ways and Jewish federations); Donor Advised Funds (DAFs) that are analogous to savings accounts, administered by community foundations or commercial financial institutions, to which donors contribute (receiving tax benefits) and retain direction over when, how much and to which causes and organizations grants will be made; and other types of pooled trusts or funds, such as impact-investing funds. In addition to, and often accompanied by volunteer time or pro bono services, philanthropic contributions may take the form of cash, securities, tangible items (e.g. art, automobiles, real estate), and a new, and evermore complex, array of social investment instruments (e.g. equities, bonds and low interest loans). Within this burgeoning 'philanthropy industry', a wide range of professionals play increasingly important roles: from traditional wealth managers, financial and gift planners, lawyers and accountants, to the emerging breed of dedicated 'philanthropy wealth advisors'. The recipients of any largesse may be 'individuals', 'charities' or 'public benefit' organizations legally recognized as such by the state, or other types of nonprofits, social enterprises and new forms of low-profit limited liability entities.

The sustainability, pluralism and redistribution of philanthropy

In contemporary debates and practices, philanthropy is usually assessed in two primary ways. The first of these focuses on philanthropy's impact(s) on donors: what are individual effects, such as enhanced mental and/or physical well-being (Aknin *et al.*, 2013; Dunn *et al.*, 2014; Helliwell *et al.*, 2015) and what are wider, collective outcomes, such as creating a shared culture of giving, civic engagement and trust (Walzer, 1990; Warren, 2011; Kemmis, 2014)? The second way examines what philanthropy achieves in terms of benefit to others: what are its consequences for society as a whole, particularly in serving a redistribution function? A primary consideration in the creation of a shared culture is the extent to which philanthropic participation is widely spread across a community or population. Its ability to deliver positive societal benefits depends on aggregate levels and their sustainability, and on how it is distributed. Does it in fact make a positive difference, serve redistributive purposes, and go to causes where it can achieve the most good? These are not simple questions – neither in theoretical nor in empirical terms – and they are at the heart of a growing debate about the relative merits of pluralism versus impact (Reich, 2013). In relation to this, scholars approaching the field from an explicit or implicit Marxist or Neo-Marxist perspective often cast philanthropy as simply unacceptable, as co-option, as social control by elites (Fisher, 1983; Roelofs, 2003; Arnove and Pinede, 2007; Parmar, 2012). While critical engagement with the underlying issues of philanthropy's nature, resources, power and voice are of the utmost importance, it is equally important to be pragmatic: negating a role for, and denying the importance of a healthy philanthropy runs counter to the aims of our volume. What then do recent trends in individual giving suggest about philanthropy's sustainability, breadth of participation and distribution?

Aggregate levels, sustainability and pluralism

Philanthropy is an important source of revenue for the nonprofit sector, not only in amounts, but because it may be less restrictive than government funding committed to service provision. As an international average, philanthropy (from all sources) has been estimated to represent between 12 percent (Salamon *et al.*, 2003: 29) and 23 percent (Salamon *et al.*, 2013: 5) of the total income of the nonprofit sector. The variation in percentage is partly dependent on reliability of the data. Official figures of domestic giving are frequently underestimated as they can exclude non-receipted donations, informal giving and remittances sent internationally through diaspora communities, and numbers on international philanthropy vary greatly due to difficulties in obtaining reliable data. Nevertheless, distinctive regional and country-specific patterns are evident. For instance, in the US, the share of the third sector's total revenue that comes from philanthropy is about 13 percent (McKeever and Pettijohn, 2014), while in the UK it is 23 percent (Keen, 2014), and in Brazil 42 percent (Salamon *et al.*, 2013). In addition, the relative importance of philanthropy as a revenue source increases when only the 'core' sector is included, absent the big para-public charities such as hospitals, universities and schools. In the Canadian context, Lasby (2011) shows that when these para-public institutions are removed from analysis of charities, the share of revenue from donations and fundraising for the 'typical' medium-sized charity increases from a sector average of 10.8 percent to 30.5 percent, albeit with variations across subsectors.

When measured in absolute terms, the aggregate levels of philanthropy are impressive but, once again, these numbers need to be treated with caution. In the US, aggregate annual philanthropy is worth more than $335 billion (Giving USA, 2014), the highest of any country. Compared internationally, country-specific patterns of giving vary substantially (Wiepking and Handy, 2015). While other high income countries also have high aggregate levels of giving as a percentage of gross domestic product (GDP), the incidence of giving across the population neither simply aligns with national wealth nor with countries we usually associate with philanthropy. For instance, the CAF Global Index of Giving (2014: 11) reports that only six of the countries in the top 20 givers – as indexed by a composite of the percentage of the population helping strangers, volunteering and donating money – are members of the G20, the world's largest economies. Considering only the incidence of donating money (not the aggregate amounts given or other forms of engagement), the countries ranked in the top ten on this measure are: Myanmar (91 percent of the population donated) reflecting the Theravada Buddhist traditions of alms giving; Malta (78 percent); Thailand (77 percent); UK and Ireland (74 percent); Canada (71 percent); Netherlands and Iceland (70 percent); USA (68 percent); Australia and Indonesia (66 percent). The explanations offered for regional differences, albeit with no definitive agreement, include: cultural norms, national wealth and its distribution, overall tax rates, tax incentives for charitable giving and the much debated questions as to whether large welfare states crowd out private giving, partly because nonprofits with greater government support might reduce their fundraising efforts (Andreoni and Payne, 2010; Wiepking and Handy, 2015).

In terms of sustainability, aggregate philanthropy as a percentage of GDP and as a percentage of household income has been remarkably stable over time in most developed countries (NCVO/CAF, 2012). Looking to the future of philanthropy and civic engagement, Putnam

(2000) famously made a less than optimistic prediction based on cohort effects. His case was that a long 'civic generation', who entered adulthood during the depression and Second World War, were inclined by their core values and upbringing to be much more engaged and philanthropic than any other cohort; that their passing would reduce overall social capital: younger generations would literally be 'bowling alone', and contributing much less to society (Reed and Selbee, 2001).

At least across the Anglo-Saxon countries, the trend over recent years might seem to support Putnam's thesis. Fewer numbers of people are carrying the bulk of giving and volunteering (Phillips and Smith, Chapter 13; CAF, 2012). With fewer contributors, overall giving levels only remain stable as a result of larger gifts by High Net Worth (HNW) individuals, defined in the US as those earning more than $200,000 per year. In some cases, these gifts have been very large: those over $1 million increased by almost 50 percent in 2013 over the previous year (Coutts, 2014). Over 125 of the world's billionaires have signed on to the 'Giving Pledge'. Started by Warren Buffet and Bill and Melinda Gates, they commit to dedicating the majority of their wealth to philanthropy (Giving Pledge, 2015). This increased reliance of philanthropy on HNW donors does not imply the affluent are on average more generous. On the contrary, as a percentage of their income, the amounts donated by middle and lower income households are two to three times the share of the affluent (Cowley *et al.*, 2011: 3). This is reflected in the Giving Pledge of Warren Buffett. Promising to donate 99 percent of his entire wealth – estimated to be around $71 billion in May 2015 (Forbes 2015) – to philanthropy he writes:

> measured by dollars, this commitment is large. In a comparative sense, though, many individuals give more to others every day ... my family and I will give up nothing we need or want by fulfilling this 99% pledge ... Moreover, this pledge does not leave me contributing the most precious asset, which is time.
>
> *(Buffett, ND)*

At present, a major philanthropic role is played by those born between 1946 and 1964, commonly referred to as the 'Boomers'. This demographic cohort is responsible for 43 percent of all individual giving in the US, and those over 65 account for 35 percent of all giving in the UK, as compared to 25 percent in 1978 (Cowley *et al.*, 2011; Pharoah, 2011: 72). With the passing of the Boomers, a massive intergenerational transfer of wealth is projected. For the US alone, this is estimated to be $58 trillion over the next 55 years, leading to predictions of a 'golden age' for philanthropy (Havens and Schervish, 2014: 27). Changes in giving patterns, however, are not waiting for Boomer bequests.

With considerable wealth in the hands of younger entrepreneurial HNW households, and with the age of 65 described as the new 50 (Rabin, 2014), changes in giving patterns are quickly emerging in ways that weaken Putnam's cohort hypothesis. HNW donors, particularly younger ones, have distinctive preferences for giving. For the most part, their wealth has been earned, not inherited; they are educated, entrepreneurial, global, and they expect results (Bank of America, 2012; BNP Paribas, 2014). For some, the creation of large pools of capital while still in their 30s or 40s often means that they are very conscious of their social responsibilities. According to US data, a very high percentage of HNW households give (98 percent) and also volunteer (75 percent) (US Trust, 2014). These self-made people are 'intentional about and engaged in their giving' (quoted in Cohen, 2014a: NP), very likely to be 'hands-on' with their contributions (volunteering as well as giving, running their own foundations or setting up DAFs), and looking to social *investing* not simply giving. As one philanthropic advisor observes, they are asking 'what else you can do besides write a check or write a check that clears after you're dead?' (Knowledge@Wharton, 2013: NP). The good news for recipient organizations is that HNW individuals, unlike governments or foundations tend to be 'operating fund philanthropists', willing to support operating costs or making their support unrestricted (Cohen, 2014a).

In terms of aggregate levels, then, the future for philanthropy looks promising and, assuming the absence of major recessions, may bring several decades of significant increases. Notwithstanding our earlier point that philanthropy data systematically underestimate those who give in small amounts without filing tax claims, in terms of breadth of participation that may bring widely distributed societal benefits, the increased concentration could be read as problematic. Concerns about its diversity might be diminished, however, when we look to the ways that participation in philanthropy is being reshaped by the involvement of women and Millennials (those born between 1980 and 2000) and, globally, by changing geographies of wealth.

A new pluralism? Changing patterns of participation

Women have become significant players in philanthropy, well beyond their roles in joint, household decision-making about giving. They have entered the global workforce in record numbers, are better educated than ever, and a significant proportion are in a position of making substantial gifts in their own right (TD Bank, 2014; US Trust, 2014;). Mesch and Pactor explore the differences in their approaches to philanthropy in Chapter 5, making a convincing case that women have the potential to transform philanthropy. Although significant inequalities still exist between women in developed and developing countries, globally, their empowerment and engagement is already reshaping civil society.

The Millennial generation is a second force of change. Refuting dire predictions based on generational theory, they are carving out directions for philanthropy that are quite different from those of their parents and grandparents. The Millennials are the largest, most diverse, and most connected, cohort in history, representing currently about a third of the global population, and, by 2025, about 75 percent of the global workforce (Deloitte, 2014). The stereotype of this youngest of adult cohorts is that they are disengaged: that they are lounging in the basement on Mom and Dad's sofa, playing video games, and are more interested in Facebook than in getting out in the 'real' community. This image is misleading. While, as digital natives, they are highly connected and know how to build their own 'personal brands' using social media (Pew Research Centre, 2010), but they are 'less entitled and more cynical than' popularly perceived (Gara, 2013). They value authenticity, want to 'solve real problems' with systemic solutions, look to corporations for leadership in social change, and are themselves entrepreneurial with business-inspired approaches (Johnson Center on Philanthropy, 2013; Roberts, 2014). They are less devout than previous generations, but, particularly for younger women, any lack of religious affiliation is by no means inhibiting their philanthropy (Women's Philanthropy Institute, 2014). Although their contributions may still be relatively small due to limited financial means, the Millennials are already active donors, with 87 percent in the US reporting that they gave to a nonprofit in 2014, and 47 to 57 percent indicating they volunteered, rates higher than any other generation (Achieve, 2014; Nielsen, 2014). They are also much more likely to use online tools without requiring tax receipts; indeed, 62 percent prefer to make donations via their mobile phones (Rover and Loeb, 2013). They like to support causes rather than specific organizations (Achieve, 2014), particularly education, poverty prevention and the environment (Nielsen, 2014), and want hands-on experience and a voice in the organizations they support, expecting these organizations to be transparent about results including failures (Johnson Center on Philanthropy, 2013; Rover and Loeb, 2013). Such preferences seem poised to forge new intersections of giving, volunteering and activism, and add momentum to the movement for impact and transparency.

A third set of drivers for greater pluralism in philanthropy are more culturally diverse populations and the changing geography of wealth. Immigrants and ethnic minorities have frequently been discounted as being too poor or insular in their own cultural communities to be taken seriously in philanthropy. Although relatively little is known about the philanthropic patterns of immigrants and cultural minorities (and there are differences across groups), a recent Canadian study found that multicultural immigrants who have become well established in their adopted country donate at well above average rates, and do so for all types of organizations, not just ones specific to their own culture or local community (Norris, 2012). The same applies to more recent immigrants. While they may not yet have acquired a degree of affluence, they are often still sending remittances to their homelands and, as shown by a UK study they are 42 percent more likely to donate to domestic charities than is the general population (Pharoah and McKenzie, 2013).

Notwithstanding that inequalities with the Global North are still significant, an emerging geographical shift of influence is also occurring due to the rise of the middle class in the Global South. As an overall percentage of the population considered middle class, those residing in the Global South rose from 26 percent in 1990 to 58 percent in 2010 (UNDP, 2013: 14). This is expected to increase to 80 percent by 2030, reflecting changing patterns of economic development and sheer population numbers in these emerging economies (UNDP, 2013: 14). With the right public policies in place to encourage this new global middle class to give at the same modest rate as the UK (0.4 percent of household income), $US 224 billion would be available annually (CAF, 2013: 3), thereby changing opportunities for both domestic and transnational philanthropy. In addition, the super-rich (those with assets of more than $100 million) are expected to increase to 86,000 in 2016, a rise of 37 percent in five years (Kharas, 2010), with the greatest growth of this new wealth concentrated in Asia. Their philanthropy tends to seek the 'best innovations and the most effective institutions wherever they find them' (CAF, 2014: 21) while maintaining cultural affinities with their countries of origin and preferences for social investment methods (Newland et al., 2010). In short, this shifting geography of philanthropy is likely to generate both new intra-regional and transborder patterns that promise to be quite different from the remittances or international relief that moved mainly 'from West to East and from North to South' (CAF, 2013: 5).

The distribution of philanthropy

The final criterion for assessing philanthropy is how it is distributed, and specifically whether its use has positive outcomes. The emphasis on impact, at least in its more directive forms, is encountering resistance from those who favour the pluralism that has been embedded in philanthropic policy. For the pluralists, donor choice in how to direct their private resources is paramount. They argue that the diversity of donors and the pluralism of their personal preferences results in support for services and causes that neither the state nor the market would fund. This is expressed in the well-known government (Weisbrod, 1975) and market failure theories (Hansmann, 1980). A sharply contrasting position is taken by the 'effective altruism' perspective, prominently associated with Australian moral philosopher Peter Singer and Facebook co-founder Dustin Moskovitz and his wife Cari Tuna. Mirroring and at times replicating the discourse on scientific and strategic philanthropy, effective altruism is based on a consequentialist philosophical worldview and attempts to apply 'evidence and reason to working out the most effective ways to improve the world' (Singer, 2015: 5). Rather than basing giving on emotions and valuing personal preferences, effective altruism promotes using results-based evidence to determine the most worthwhile causes – those with the greatest benefit in a utilitarian sense – which lean to reducing extreme poverty in developing countries, while eschewing support for art and culture (Matthews, 2015). Absent the normative, utilitarian philosophy, there is unquestionably a growing and broadly based international interest among philanthropic stakeholders in better measurement and communication of impact.

Giving patterns by both individuals and foundations, however, reveal a spotty record on redistribution and systems change to help the most disadvantaged groups in society (Pharoah, Chapter 4; LaMarche, 2014). By far the bulk of individual giving – over a third in the US, Canada and Australia – goes to religion with negligible amounts to public policy advocacy (Phillips and Smith, Chapter 13). Among HNW donors, the most popular causes are higher education, the arts and religion, with the largest donations going to education and religion or to their foundations (Coutts 2014; US Trust, 2014). How many HNW households will ultimately direct their donations is still an open question, especially as DAFs are the fastest growing destination for their contributions (CF Insights, 2012: 5; Giving USA, 2014). Collectively, DAFs hold $US 45 billion, substantially more than the world's largest foundation, the Bill and Melinda Gates Foundation. They have been criticized for their lack of transparency, and questions over how much they actually pay out each year have been aired, although among those held by community foundations the annual payout rates are higher than those of most philanthropic foundations (Council on Foundations, 2009: 2). Whether they are part of the solution or part of the problem of achieving greater impact is uncertain.

The coincidence of demographic trends, new technologies, the movement for impact and an increasing norm of professionalism is creating a new set of tensions for philanthropy. On the one hand, technology is facilitating spontaneous giving and activism on a large scale, particularly by a younger demographic. The power of social media for mobilizing collective action has been well demonstrated in important political episodes – from the Arab Spring to the Occupy Movement. The small group of friends who first challenged each other to donate to a charity of their choice by tossing buckets of ice water over their heads had no expectations of their little fundraising scheme going viral as an international phenomenon (Sifferlin, 2014). Although online methods still account for a very small amount of charitable fundraising, online giving rose by almost 14 percent in 2013 and is being used by a widening demographic (Blackbaud, 2014: 2). At the same time philanthropy is becoming more professionalized, growing in employment, and requiring more sophisticated and diverse set of skills. The role of the professional advisors to potential philanthropists has acquired greater saliency, particularly with the projected vast transfer of wealth occurring over the next decade. The extent and nature of the specific counsel these advisors provide might significantly alter philanthropy action. Wealth planning has, however, not yet stepped up to the demand: while nine out of ten wealth advisors said they discuss philanthropic giving with their clients, only about half of their HNW clients recall having such conversations (US Trust, 2013, BMO *et al.*, 2015). Consequently, whether they will broaden or narrow the distribution of philanthropy remains to be seen.

Within this context, the *Routledge Companion to Philanthropy* aims to provide a window into assessing some of these unfolding changes in philanthropy – from their impetus through to their implementation – and to anticipate the kinds of research questions and needs they will generate.

From impetus to implementation: A guide through the *Companion's* major themes

The *Companion* is organized to consider the spectrum of philanthropy and to critique the theories, extant research and diverse professional practices from a variety of disciplinary perspectives. At the end of each chapter, the authors have been asked to assess the current state of the research and identify important directions for future research on the topic. The chapters are organized into six sections, each of which addresses a major aspect of philanthropy in a logic that flows from the high level questions of the contexts and motivations for philanthropy to more operational matters of the management of philanthropy. Each section begins with a short 'vignette', written from personal experience, that provides a concrete illustration of some of the issues.

Impetus: What propels philanthropy?

The first section examines the historical roots, religious influences and myriad of personal motivations that propel philanthropy. The opening story of Zita Cobb, as told by Natalie Slawinski, is an illustration of how personal experience and place shape choices in philanthropy, and of how big its aspirations for social change can be. In spite of her humble beginnings growing up on a remote island off the northeast coast of Canada whose economy was sustained by fishing (until its collapse), Zita had a very successful career in the high-tech industry, retiring young as a multimillionaire and devoting her time to her philanthropic project. Her aspiration is to restore the economic vitality of Fogo Island in a way that maintains its cultural integrity. She is doing so through creation of an artist-in-residency program to generate a new geo-tourism industry that she hopes could be a model for rural communities worldwide. Like so many entrepreneurs-turned-philanthropists, Zita is taking a very hands-on approach, directing the work herself rather than making passive gifts to charities and is using the tools of business that she had used so successfully in her professional career.

Although what motivates specific people to be philanthropic may be idiosyncratic, deriving from a mix of personal experience and place as for Zita Cobb, two forces have had a pervasive and enduring influence as an impetus for philanthropy – historical context and religion. In an overview of the history of philanthropy, Hugh Cunningham encourages us to think like geologists, uncovering different strata of assumptions, traditions and institutions that have been laid down on top of each other. In looking back more than a thousand years and considering connections to class, gender and civil society, Cunningham notes that philanthropy has been reinvented and declared 'new' on many occasions, and some of the initiatives that we currently think of as recent inventions, such as social enterprise, in fact have old, and often religious, roots.

Complementing the Greek mythological perspective of Prometheus as the 'father' of philanthropy, religion has been cast as 'the mother of philanthropy' (Moe, 1961: 141). From Abrahamic traditions, covering Judaism, Islam and Christianity, to Dharmic worldviews, including Hinduism, Buddhism and Sikhism, and Taoic perspectives, such as Taoism and Confucianism, religion has always provided philanthropic values, obligations, practices and structures. Thus, in Taoic outlooks we can find the notions of *ren* (benevolence), *yi* (righteousness), *shi* (giving) and *shu* (reciprocity) which, taken together, point to the requirement of acting for those in need and the importance of reciprocal and supportive relationships (Pan-chiu and Lee, 2002). Within Dharmic positions, similar sentiments are expressed through the concept of *dana*. Forming part of one's religious responsibilities, or *dharma*, *dana* highlights and stresses the importance of practicing and cultivating unconditional generosity as a path to perfection (Sugirtharajah, 2001). These in turn resemble the expectations of Abrahamic approaches expressed in ideas such as *tzedakah* in Judaism, the expectation to help those in need (Tobin, 2010), or *zakat* in Islam, the obligation of alms-giving as an act of worship that both channels doing good and provides a path to purity, comprehension of material responsibility, and an enhanced sense of spirituality (Elsanousi, 2010; Esposito, 2010). Quite often, even the specifics of appropriate philanthropic acts resemble each other: Judaism refers to 'tithing', Sikhism to 'dasvand', both focus on providing 'a tenth' to those in need.

Given this proximity of religion and philanthropy, it is unsurprising that the nexus between faith, fortune and furnishing gifts has long attracted scholarly attention (Ilchman *et al.*, 1998; Berger, 2006; Hall, 2006; Schervish and Whitaker, 2010; Vaidyanathan *et al.*, 2011; Ward, 2013). In spite of a growing secularization in many countries, a key predictor of the likelihood that someone will be an active giver or volunteer remains regular attendance at faith services (Bekkers and Wiepking, 2011), and a greater share of individual giving still goes to religion than any other type of organization or cause. As such, rather than being considered separately, religion is a theme that is returned to, and touched upon, within a number of the topics covered by subsequent chapters.

The section then turns to understanding the variety of personal motivations that propel philanthropy, approaching this first from a social theory and then an empirical perspective. Frank Adloff interrogates how social theory has treated altruism, making the case that neither altruism nor self-interest are adequate explanations for motivating philanthropy. Rather, meso- and macro-level factors, such as the social networks, culture, and institutional contexts in which philanthropy is embedded play important parts. For instance, whether civil society organizations are actively and effectively involved in fundraising and make good 'asks' influences how people respond. Cathy Pharoah tackles the question of motivations in a different way, drawing on recent empirical studies of both endogenous motivations and demographic factors that predict philanthropic behaviour. Giving, argues Pharoah, needs to be understood as an action 'within both private and public spheres, within donors' intentions, as well as within their public circumstances'. This dual embeddedness makes giving behaviours relatively resistant to change, at least over the short term. Recognizing that giving takes multiple forms, she synthesizes current research: there is no single explanation for why people give, rather a mix of reasons are generally involved. In terms of demographic factors, income is of course positively correlated with a propensity to give, but even more so is education; being older, married, and female also increases the likelihood of donating. In considering where donations go, Pharoah is critical of philanthropy's relatively poor record on redistribution and of public policy attempts to make it more so, noting that instead these have been 'aimed at reinforcing private passions rather than at meeting publicly-identified needs'.

A force that is changing the status quo of philanthropy is the role of women. In Chapter 5, Debra Mesch and Andrea Pactor discuss gender differences, noting that women give and volunteer more than men: they vary in their motivations for giving and exhibit different giving patterns. In particular, women are more likely to give when they see evidence that the gift will make a difference, are more likely to actively engage with and do great due diligence on the organizations they are considering supporting, looking to impacts not just administrative overheads and other simplistic indicators of financial efficiency (TD Bank, 2014). Consequently, the fundraising approaches that work for men may not work for women.

A range of intermediaries are involved in translating philanthropic intent into action: people give because they are asked, as the Ice Bucket Challenges so vividly demonstrated. In Chapter 6, Sally Hibbert links research on motivations to the mechanisms and messaging of philanthropic asks. Hibbert shows how a charity's brand, portrayal of the need and beneficiaries, social comparisons and the method and timing of requests significantly influence how much and how often people contribute, and how they explain their reasons for doing so. She speculates that as communication technologies shift from being one-way – from charities to donors – towards a dialogue among charities, donors and a variety of other stakeholders, new opportunities are being created for donors to be more active decision makers and influencers on the patterns and practices of philanthropy.

The changing geographies and scales of philanthropy

Place has always mattered in philanthropy, and is becoming simultaneously more and less important. On the one hand, community-based and indigenous approaches, which are necessarily rooted in specific cultures and locales, are putting renewed significance on place. On the other hand, the internationalization of ideas about philanthropy, increased transborder flows and the scaling up of projects to a global level are reducing the significance of geographic boundaries. This duality is illustrated in the vignette by Emily Jansons and Femida Handy about two of India's leading philanthropists who are indicative of how the country's new wealth is changing traditional approaches to philanthropy. Both Rohini Nilekani and the creators of the Dasra foundation, Deval Sanghavi and Neera Nundy, acquired most of their wealth outside the country, and brought international models of both philanthropy and business to the ways in which they structured their giving in India. While they initially followed the traditional tendency of India's philanthropists to be controlling and operational by creating their own institutions, in part due to the challenges of finding existing organizations capable of handling the scale of funding they sought to contribute, they soon developed more collaborative approaches, such as giving circles designed to empower community-based organizations.

René Bekkers examines the relevance of place with a reminder that philanthropic traditions and practices differ greatly from one place to another, and that stable regional patterns are consistently found in comparative cross-national research. Bekkers assesses alternative hypotheses that explain these strong regional differences, but also offers an important caution. In Europe, for example, the countries of the north-west that have relatively high GDPs and less Catholic cultural backgrounds are shown to have higher levels of engagement in philanthropy than poorer, historically Catholic countries of the south. Rather than dwelling on these differences, Bekker's main point is to advise prudence in ascribing and explaining regional patterns due to data and measurement issues, making the case for much better quality data to advance comparative research.

One implication of geographical differences is that assumptions as to what constitutes philanthropy need to be understood in cultural context, extending beyond the concepts employed in developed countries. This is well represented by the wide range of experiments in community and indigenous philanthropy that are revitalizing the connection of philanthropy to place (Hodgson, 2013b; Knight and Milner, 2013; Kasper *et al.*, 2014). 'Community' (sometimes referred to as 'horizontal') philanthropy refers to individuals and community-based organizations working together to help themselves, with a view to creating enduring assets and promoting community empowerment and social justice. In his overview of emerging practices of community philanthropy, Michael D. Layton observes how little academic research exists in this area, with most of the recent case studies produced or commissioned by foundations and other funders of these practices. It is thus difficult to empirically assess the claims that community philanthropy empowers both communities and donors and that it has an enduring impact. The complementary chapter by Shauna Mottiar and Mvuselelo Ngcoya discusses an example of indigenous philanthropy, the concept of *ubuntu* as practiced in South Africa. As a worldview that promotes a dynamic process of interdependence based on reciprocity and cooperation, *ubuntu* rests on a premise of abundance rather than scarcity and, contrary to popular perceptions of indigenous approaches, is quite formalized and ritualized in its structures and practices.

The section then turns to the gaining momentum of the internationalization of giving and investing. Hillel Schmid and Hanna Shaul Bar Nissim examine the various streams of transborder flows of private capital that collectively are significantly greater than the Official

Development Assistance provided by governments and are growing rapidly (Adelman *et al.*, 2013). Although mega-donors – such as the Bill and Melinda Gates Foundation that is shaping an international agenda for public health and the Open Society Foundation through which George Soros has been pursuing policy transfer aimed at strengthening emerging democracies – are important players, the greatest growth is among diasporas where ethnic groups of migrants send money, as well as making in kind contributions of their time and knowledge, to peoples and organizations in their homelands. Support of humanitarian aid and disaster relief is the other main contributor to an internationalized philanthropy, as examined by Naim Kapucu. While natural disasters have long been times when people respond with sympathy and financial contributions, Kapucu shows how the variety of actors and influences in these responses are becoming more complicated, particularly with the use of social media and the involvement of celebrities, resulting in huge differences of which events command significant resources and which are overlooked. How do we account for the US $750 million in private donations raised in just five weeks to help victims of the 2010 Haiti earthquake while only $25 million went to supporting victims of the 2010 Pakistan floods (Polgreen, 2010)? The answer is not that 30 times more people were affected by the Haitian earthquake than those who suffered in Pakistan.

With both more place-based *and* more globalized philanthropy, a new set of challenges arises for public policy and regulatory regimes that still pay little attention to the potential for enabling philanthropy on a global scale or the implications of international regulatory competition. These issues are taken up in Part IV.

The private-public divide: Philanthropy as a bridge?

Philanthropy has an ambivalent relationship with the state, one that at certain times and locales is complementary and constructive, and at other times tense and uncertain (Jung and Harrow 2015a). At a basic level, government has a duty to protect the public from fraud, for instance from unethical fundraisers or charities used as illegal tax shelters. Although recent surveys from several countries reveal that the public still places a great deal of trust in the nonprofit and philanthropic sector, they increasingly want to know where the money goes and what difference it makes in terms of outcomes (Ipsos Mori, 2010; Muttart Foundation, 2013; Edelman, 2015). To what extent can, or should, governments require reporting and attempt to regulate transparency, and how is this feasible when philanthropy crosses borders (Phillips, 2013)? How much transparency is too much (Tyler, 2013)? As governments turn to philanthropy to complement or substitute for reduced public funding of services – whether to bail out insolvent cities such as Detroit or catalyze bigger societies as in England – the balance of responsibilities and associated accountabilities have become more complex. This relationship is further complicated when mega-donors give billions of dollars to 'fix' public education or cure specific diseases, thereby bypassing government and established public policy priorities (Nickel and Eikenberry, 2009). The problem with most philanthropy, however, is not that it is overly ambitious in its aspirations for social change, but not ambitious enough (Reich, 2013; LaMarche, 2014). Some governments have chosen to be quite directive in channeling the distribution of charitable giving by offering differential tax benefits for particular causes, notably the alleviation of poverty, or have established their own funds to incentivize social innovation (Carmichael, 2013b; Phillips and Smith, 2014). Alternatively, those who support the case that philanthropy is inherently private and democratizing in its own right prefer to let the proverbial thousand flowers bloom, absent overly directive public policy.

Part IV examines the issues at the intersection of the public sector *and* philanthropy, and of public policy *for* philanthropy. First, Diana Leat shows how 'muddy' such relationships can be with her account of the disastrous floods in Queensland Australia in late 2010 and early 2011, when governments and the insurance industry used philanthropic institutions for both public benefit and self-interest. The question of whether philanthropy is willing to become a substitute for shrinking public funding is explored by John Healy and Gemma Donnelly-Cox. Notwithstanding the current popularity of a high-engagement and high-impact approach, in which philanthropists strategically set their own priorities, Healy and Donnelly-Cox argue that philanthropy still perceives its role as complementary to the state. Philanthropists see themselves as 'increasing efficiency in public and charitable provision through a competency in developing and testing innovative ways to address social problems', not as 'the palliative provision of public goods'. Furthermore, there is neither consistent evidence that a shrinking state necessarily produces expanded philanthropy, nor that increased public spending crowds out philanthropy. Healy and Donnelly-Cox note, however, that the current relationship between most governments and philanthropy is not a stable, harmonious accord because public policy expectations of philanthropy seldom concur with philanthropy's expectations of itself.

The discussion then turns to three components of public policy for philanthropy: incentives for potential donors to contribute private resources; regulation of how these resources are raised; and determination of which kinds of causes and civil society organizations are subsidized through tax systems as eligible recipients of philanthropy. Focusing on the Anglo-Saxon cluster of countries, Susan D. Phillips and Steven Rathgeb Smith argue that the policy and regulatory regimes governing philanthropy have always been place-bound, conceiving of philanthropy as a domestic phenomenon and seeing little need to position tax incentives or other regulations so as to align or be competitive with other jurisdictions. In analyzing the 'problem' for philanthropy policy, they posit that most of these countries have experienced policy drift, with an occasional intervention of partisan politics, resulting in growing divergence of their policy regimes. This theme of divergence is reinforced in other chapters.

As Oonagh Breen observes, government oversight of fundraising may be designed with quite different objectives in mind. These range from high level goals of enhancing donor education and preserving public confidence in charities, through more operational issues of ensuring charities effectively manage the funds they receive, to the very targeted goal of preventing fraud due to deceptive fundraising practices or outright embezzlement. Given this mix of goals and the different points at which fundraising can be regulated (before, during or after solicitations are made), fundraising regulation is taking quite different forms, involving voluntary codes, sector certification and other self-regulation models, soft law, state/sector co-regulation and new statutory regimes. As Breen notes, however, the growth of cross-border giving and emergence of an innovative array of automated banking and online giving platforms, which do not respect geographic boundaries, makes such regulation an uphill task for regulators.

This international pattern of policy diversity is reinforced by Calum M. Carmichael in his examination of the awarding of tax privileges to nonprofits that benefit from philanthropy. Assessing the theoretical rationales and actual practices for such tax privileges across eight countries, he finds that the existence of such privileges (exemption from income tax, elimination of output tax, or subsidization of cash contributions) is almost universal. In addition, governments are maintaining a role in determining their distribution and use. However, the underlying rationales and the actual types of benefits differ greatly, as do the extent to which eligible organizations are able to engage in advocacy or business activities.

Policy divergence is further amplified in the ways in which emerging economies are beginning to create or modernize their approaches to philanthropy. Reviewing policy developments in Asia, specifically China and India, Mark Sidel shows how such policy reform is enveloped by a continuing tension of an interest in facilitating philanthropy and a desire to control and constrain it, particularly foreign funding that supports nonprofit advocacy (Moore and Rutzen, 2011). Although giving is growing throughout Asia, the associated tax incentives are still very limited, and the regulatory barriers to the formation of associations, registration as 'public benefit' organizations, and fundraising remain high, with recently tightened constraints on overseas giving. Sidel predicts expansion of self-regulation, in part to prevent greater government control, and increased cooperation between governments and the philanthropic and nonprofit sectors, while noting that the hurdles to well functioning and coherent regulatory regimes in the region are significant.

This section concludes with a look at what David Horton Smith, Sharon Eng and Kelly Albertson call the 'darker' side of philanthropy. Smith and colleagues concentrate on three types of 'deviant' behaviour: from the perfectly legal (but in their view unethical) to the criminal. They note how difficult it has been for public policy to mitigate or prevent such behaviours. The first type of deviant behaviour is associated with private foundations that enable wealthy elites to shelter wealth from taxation, pay excessive compensation to their trustees or waste large amounts of money on ineffective philanthropy. The second occurs in the context of transnational humanitarian aid, when non-governmental organizations (NGOs) of the Global North are more attuned to pleasing their Northern donors than working effectively with their Southern partners. The third example involves the illegal action of financing terrorist activities, either intentionally through charities that act as 'fronts' or, without the donors' knowledge, through opaque webs of interconnected organizations. Although some readers might dispute their argument and evidence, the chapter serves as a reminder that debates about the ethics of philanthropy are a lively component of the state of the art.

The institutions and expressions of philanthropy

How the impetus for philanthropy is realized occurs through a variety of institutional expressions, which are examined in Part V. This section begins with the more traditional forms, private and community foundations. It then considers the various ways in which philanthropy is being combined with other institutional logics, particularly its intertwining with entrepreneurialism and the corporate sector. The section concludes with a critique of the unfolding paradigm shift from philanthropy to 'social investment'. The growing hybridity of institutional forms is highlighted by Aisha Faleh Al-Thani's vignette of Reach Out to Asia (ROTA), a charity affiliated with the Qatar Foundation that promotes youth education and that is working at the shifting intersections of governments and business in a manner which is both international and community-centred.

Since their rise in the 1800s (Hammack and Anheier, 2013), 'private' foundations – entities with permanent endowments with grantmaking capacity for public purposes – have been the mainstay of institutionalized philanthropy. Their economic significance is impressive: the 100 largest foundations in the US and the UK are estimated to have assets of more than $100 billion, making grants of about $10 billion annually (Pharoah, 2011: 27–28). Over the past decade, foundations have gained popularity among donors who seek control, visibility and longevity for their philanthropy, although the vast majority of foundations are small. Diana Leat assesses the changing role of foundations by first clarifying terminology, which differs across countries, leading us through the distinctions between 'private' and 'family' foundations and between grantmaking and operating foundations. Although foundations tend to assume a character that reflects ideas about philanthropy at the time they were created – for example as 'gift-givers', or as 'scientific' – Leat argues that important changes are occurring in how foundations see themselves, and how they are assessed by the public. This new self-perception is as changemakers, rather than supporters of services, and has an affinity for market models to achieve social change and roles that extend beyond grantmaking. Indeed, many foundations are choosing to be more operational, hiring their own staff to lead projects rather than entrusting these to grantees. As Leat observes, they 'talk less about their money and more about their other resources (reputation, convening power, independence, knowledge etc.)'. They are also taking a greater interest in business, not just as a means of problem-solving but as 'a locus of power', and are crafting new ways of working across the private, public and nonprofit sectors. A consequence of their interest in results is that the benefits of operating in perpetuity are being questioned: perhaps their money can work faster and better by spending out over a fixed period rather than dribbling out four or five percent of an endowment forever (Klausner, 2003).

The model of a community foundation, which was 'invented' in Cleveland USA, celebrated its 100th anniversary in 2014, and has become a global phenomenon with their numbers almost doubling over the past 15 years (Community Foundation Atlas, 2014). A community foundation differs from its private counterpart in two important ways: its endowment is aggregated from multiple sources (including individuals, governments, corporations and private foundations) through ongoing fundraising, and its work is centred on the locale in which it is situated (Graddy and Morgan, 2006; Ostrower, 2007). Community foundations thus face the dual challenges, and potential paradox, of being philanthropy-led and community-responsive. Jenny Harrow, Tobias Jung and Susan D. Phillips examine the global diffusion of community foundations, noting that quite different norms and approaches have taken hold in different places. With both advantages and limitations of being place-based, community foundations have developed leadership tools and capacities beyond grantmaking; in particular, many are situating themselves as knowledge hubs about, and for, their communities. An important issue that will shape their future is the role of DAFs whose popularity has soared over the past decade, growing at more than 10 percent annually and currently constituting more than 50 percent of the assets held by most community foundations (CF Insights, 2012: 5). DAFs present a tradeoff between flexibility for donors, which may increase the likelihood of giving, and reduced discretion for community foundations in determining how they are used. Their popularity means that community foundations are increasingly competing with private foundations and with financial institutions that also offer DAFs. As a result, professional advisors to philanthropists have assumed much greater significance as navigators through this increasingly crowded landscape.

Taking up this theme of rapidly evolving intersections across sectors, Steven Rathgeb Smith traces how hybridization has resulted in a broader array of philanthropic tools, including DAFs, program-related investments, social impact bonds, and other forms of social finance, and produced new grantmaking strategies, broader networks of intersectoral collaboration and new hybrid institutions. Such hybridization creates new issues of risk, and presents complicated dilemmas regarding mission, transparency and accountability. This more diverse philanthropic universe, argues Smith, highlights the ill-fit of government regulatory approaches and points to an increased need for self-regulation in this sector.

The grafting of entrepreneurship onto philanthropy is a primary source and outcome of the new hybridity. Venture philanthropy, which has a preference for market-oriented tools to make strategic investments in nonprofits so as to achieve high social returns, rose to prominence in the 1990s and has been championed by successful private sector entrepreneurs. This brand of philanthropy is by no means new, however. Jillian Gordon, Charles Harvey, Eleanor Shaw and Mairi Maclean remind us that a hundred years earlier its pioneer, Andrew Carnegie (who was deeply offended by being considered a 'robber baron'), had put his entrepreneurial talent and not just his money into his philanthropic projects. Fast-forwarding to the philanthropy of HNW entrepreneurs in the UK, Gordon and her colleagues find that they, like Carnegie, view philanthropy as a mechanism 'to invest excess wealth to orchestrate social change on a large scale through application of their business know-how', aiming for measurable results as a return on their investments. Gaining access to the elite world of such aspirations is not automatic, though, and the chapter demonstrates how these hyper-agents exercise their cultural and social capital acquired through their power in the corporate domain, using networks that seamlessly span business, politics, government and philanthropy.

Venture philanthropy is generally assumed to align with social entrepreneurship, both in choice of philanthropic tools and desired outcomes. Jacques Defourny, Marthe Nyssens and Severine Thys question this presumption of convergence because it depends on how social enterprise is defined according to three distinct schools of thought. Social enterprise, alternatively, is conceived with an emphasis on earned-income strategies, on social innovation and outcomes, or in the European school as a mix of economic, social and participatory governance mechanisms. From their European perspective, Defourny and colleagues point out that neither venture philanthropy nor social enterprise necessarily means seeking market incomes and that the appropriate tools depend in part on the life stage of the supported organizations: approaches that work for a start-up may be quite different when scaling up or achieving long term sustainability. When the emphasis is on innovation and outcomes, the funded organizations are more likely to be hybrids that have secured a mix of resources to support their social mission. In this context, entrepreneurial philanthropy works best when it is only one type of funding, working in collaboration with various stakeholders, and making efforts to appraise overall performance and social value in a manner that grasps the net effect of the investment.

Ekkehard Thümler argues something bigger, of which venture philanthropy is a symptom, is transforming this field, although its full consequences are not yet clear. He claims that financialization, with its discourse of social investment is redirecting philanthropy just as finance reshaped the economy. By financialization, Thümler is referring to more than the marketization of services and use of market-based instruments. Investment with the expectation of a future return is the dominant instrument of financialization. This necessarily creates means by which uncertainty can be converted to risk assessment and investments can be valued and traded. Third party rating agencies arise to support such valuation and exchanges are established to trade investments, leading to the standardization and globalization of investments, and ultimately reconfiguration of power relationships. As philanthropy is being transformed from unconditional gift-giving to social investment, new actors and activities such as pooled funds and impact investments have been created, and the measurement of social return on investment (SROI) has become a major preoccupation. Although Salamon (2014) has extolled the benefits of this new diversity of tools, Thümler is much less optimistic, calling on scholars to pay much more attention to understanding the drivers and consequences of such sweeping financialization.

Finally, hybridity is manifest through the blending of the logics of social, environmental and economic value within the corporate sector. Corporate philanthropy, defined as the allocation of company funds to support worthy projects, is a relatively small contributor to the revenues of the nonprofit sector, but new forms of corporate involvement are increasingly important in a more hybrid world. In recent years, corporations have become much less likely to think of, and make their contributions as, *philanthropy;* instead, these are being integrated into corporate social responsibility (CSR) and 'common shared value' (Porter and Kramer, 2011). Michael Moran and Elizabeth Branigan trace this evolution and the theories that have underpinned it, showing how it constitutes a new institutional logic. Even the once laggard firms now routinely report on their social and environmental activities, have established units to oversee their responsibility programs and tend 'to genuinely believe that their philanthropic and CSR activities are core to business and beneficial to society'. The challenge, then, is not convincing the corporate sector that CSR is good for their bottom-line, but to figure out how it can be well executed with effective civil society and public sector partners to deliver better outcomes.

The management of philanthropy: Opening boxes

The management of philanthropy has been described as a 'black box' (Diaz, 1999) to which scholarly research has paid little attention or has been unable to secure access to foundations and other philanthropic institutions (for exceptions see Orosz, 2007; Silk and Lintott, 2011). More emphatically, Jung and Harrow (2015b) describe philanthropic management as a Pandora's box – attractive on the outside but capable of unleashing unanticipated and detrimental consequences unless handled with care. The chapters of Part VI examine different aspects of the management of philanthropy, and collectively point to five major trends that are altering professional practice and accelerating the need to better understand philanthropic management. First, the heightened expectations that philanthropy can deliver 'innovative miracles' (Leat, 2006: 30), particularly through new entrepreneurial approaches, means that good governance is more important than ever. Second, governance and strategic planning is occurring in an increasingly networked context, making the management of relationships (for fundraising, grantmaking and community leadership) essential. A third factor is that philanthropy has developed a range of new financial and non-financial instruments that extend beyond gift-giving and grantmaking. Fourth, technology is rapidly changing, indeed disrupting, many aspects of philanthropy. The final theme running through all the chapters, starting with the vignette by Jim Clifford of successful use of SROI for a UK children's charity, is an expectation that impact will be demonstrated. What difference have we made, and how do we know?

Existing research on governance systems for both foundations and the nonprofits they fund is underdeveloped and impractical, so argue M. Elena Romero-Merino and Íñigo García-Rodriguez. Although there is no uniformly optimal way to configure a governance system, the literature has taken an overly normative approach, providing checklists and inventories that imply a 'right' way in governance. In addition, the dominance of resource dependency theories has produced a limiting focus on financial performance, and the sparse empirical evidence is overwhelming from the US which may not translate well elsewhere. In questioning the influence that funders exercise in the promotion of good governance and monitoring practices of the recipient nonprofits, Romero-Merino and García-Rodriguez suggest that only major public sector funders have any significance effect.

Exploring the interaction between good governance and effective strategic planning in the context of grantmaking, Peter Grant reflects that the way in which Ostrower (2004: 4) articulated the problem a decade ago is still very relevant. Foundations tend to define effectiveness in very general terms, with considerable variation across different funders; they often forget about their own internal workings as a funder. Grant's case is that foundations need to better clarify and specify what they believe it means to be effective, paying greater attention to three aspects of philanthropic management. The first is the quality of recruitment, for both board members and staff, which is a particular issue for family foundation as senior salaried roles often go to junior family members. Second, as foundations look 'beyond grantmaking' to other ways in which they add value and serve as changemakers, they need to build stronger capacity for these other functions. Third, most foundations struggle to assess results due to limited expertise and absence of quality data, and their boards often abdicate their roles in such efforts. Ultimately, Grant questions the entire value of the top-down strategic approach currently advocated as part of the impact agenda, citing the danger that strategic plans become ends in themselves and foundations fail to manage the stakeholder and internal relationships that are so vital to this approach.

The complementary chapter by Richard D. Waters examines these relationships from the perspective of nonprofits, focusing on the management of fundraising. Applying a communications lens, Waters contends that we should not view fundraising with a focus on solicitations, but as a means of creating and cultivating mutually beneficial relationships. As it has become more sophisticated and professionalized, fundraising is making good use of research to determine which occasional donors can be converted to sustained, major or bequest givers, but needs to pay more attention to the main success factor – the ability to build solid relationships and keep donors involved with the organization.

Lucy Bernholz demonstrates how nonprofits are both using – and being used by – data and technology. She makes the case that in the new sharing economy, individuals are the center of gravity. Individuals (and organizations) can readily amass data from a variety of sources, aggregate and repurpose it or manage their own brands through various social media. But, people are also constantly creating data. In understanding how innovation occurs and diffuses, Bernholz distinguishes between established institutions which tend to apply new technologies to solve pre-defined problems faster or more cheaply (the 'core'), and new entrants (the 'edge') which use the technologies to redefine the problem in the first place. The dynamic between the two is a mix of competition and cooperation, and when combined become a third force to change the entire sector – which 'is precisely the moment we've reached in philanthropy'. Data and technology have clearly changed fundraising and giving practices, facilitated the rise of micro-volunteering, aided mobilization for collective action, and created the ability to tell better stories. The truly disruptive nature of technology that comes from the edges, however, is only beginning to be felt (Bernholz, 2015). Some of the edges to watch, suggests Bernholz, are the hackers capable of mashing and repurposing data, new kinds of philanthropic advisors who can readily make themselves experts, rating organizations, and peer-to-peer networks (such as giving circles) that can seamlessly learn, compare, give, rally and give feedback, all generated by and evolving around individuals.

The final three chapters take up the themes of impact and accountability, including the new impact toolkit, questions of measurement and broader issues of accountability. Tessa Hebb and Sean Mackinnon take a critical look at some of the new methods, collectively labelled as 'impact investing', that strive to align assets with missions in meaningful and measurable ways, generate positive social and/or environmental impacts, as well as financial returns to the investor and inject substantial new private capital into the nonprofit sector. From a management perspective, the investment-driven paradigm that replaces a grantmaking mentality fundamentally alters the relationship between philanthropic organizations and the recipients of their investments. 'Rather than seeing themselves as defined solely by the good works they undertake and in turn seeking others prepared to support their mission, recipient organizations begin to see their economic, social and environmental impacts as assets. They ask "who else values these results?"' (Hebb with MacKinnon, Chapter 29). Within a foundation, the firewall between its granting and investing (i.e. expanding the endowment) activities is dissolved, replaced by a continuum of alternative tools that range from an emphasis on 'impact first' to 'finance first'. As a new asset class estimated to be worth $1 trillion over the next ten years (JP Morgan, 2011), impact investing is having global effects and the challenge is quickly shifting from there being a lack of capital for investment to the absence of a supply of civil society organizations capable and willing to take up the investment opportunities. To fully realize the potential of this capital, Hebb argues the need for governments to modernize their regulatory regimes.

An enduring question for philanthropy is 'what constitutes success'? There might be a reasonably straightforward answer when a philanthropic project has modest goals and a short time frame. When philanthropy has aspirations to produce solutions to complex problems of global proportions, involving many partners and a variety of instruments, the answer is by no means simple. It raises even more fundamental questions: for what, to whom and how should philanthropic institutions be accountable? Georg von Schnurbein reviews the state-of-the-art of impact measurement by assessing the drivers, complexity of measurement, and implications for the funder–grantee relationship. As funders become more operationally engaged in realizing impact, von Schnurbein argues that the philanthropic relationship has shifted 'from a paternalistic, financial exchange to a partnership structure in which the funder is investor, consultant, and collaborator'. Again, the theme of collaboration surfaces as von Schnurbein asserts that the path to better measurement of success runs through more effective cooperation among funders, nonprofits and other partners.

Accountability entails more than measurement, as Jenny Harrow discusses in the final chapter of this section. She situates accountability in a broad sense, as both rule-based and negotiated and as comprising four facets: transparency by giving an account; responsibility through fixing problems; responsiveness by linking actions to community needs and values; and impact by linking action to results. The current preoccupation of accountability as results-based, impact-oriented has favoured rule-based over negotiated styles and it pushes philanthropy towards time-limited social interventions from which it can exit when the problem at hand, albeit often an exceedingly complex problem, is deemed to be 'solved'. Central to accountability in all its forms is professionalism of this sector, which Harrow argues is hard pressed to deliver meaningful accountability.

Getting personal, looking forward

The final section reinforces two key themes of the *Companion* – that philanthropy is not confined to millionaires and mega-foundations, and that it is undergoing significant change. In a personal reflection on his own giving, Putnam Barber provides the important reminder that all of us can be philanthropists, if only in modest ways. He offers advice relevant to any potential philanthropist: examine your motives, have a strategy rather simply being responsive, ask questions before giving, look to outcomes, and do not be taken in by the simple idea that the lower a nonprofit's operating expenses the more efficient or worthy it is. Indeed this popular heuristic is 'damagingly misleading' to good practices of philanthropy.

The concluding chapter by Susan D. Phillips and Tobias Jung looks beyond the current version of new philanthropy to speculate on the disruptive forces – philanthropy's equivalent of Uber (the software company that has turned the taxi business on its head and left governments scrambling for regulatory responses) – that may be on the horizon.

Conclusion: Is there a case for another new philanthropy?

The model of philanthropy currently branded as new and strategic – one that seeks to tackle big issues, takes impact seriously, makes use of a diversity of social finance and philanthropic tools and embodies an entrepreneurial spirit – has been around for about a decade, although aspects of it are anything but new. The attraction to entrepreneurial approaches is no longer confined to the big philanthrocapitalists who have been its greatest proponents; the search for impact has become an overarching mantra for philanthropy. This is highlighted by the creation of a new asset class of impact investments and by surveys which show that four out of five donors say they pay attention to impact, although only a fraction of them actually use such information to make decisions about their giving (Bagwell *et al.*, 2013). Notwithstanding that a strategic, impact-oriented approach has generated enormous confidence in what philanthropy can do, it also has its limits, as illustrated by many of the chapters in this volume. It does a particular disservice when it obscures the vitally important, yet more modest versions of philanthropy that place community first or that occurs as simple acts: from putting money in the collection plate or spontaneously buying cookies from canvassing Girl Guides. Given that the search for more innovative and impactful philanthropy is likely to continue for some time, the *Companion* argues the need to look beyond a single 'solution' or model to understand the multi-faceted nature of philanthropy and changes that are occurring in it.

Philanthropy is not waiting to be revolutionized but is already undergoing substantial redesign. Part of this is intentional; some of it is the result of being pulled – willingly or not – in new directions by external forces. These forces include the growing significance of women and Millennials as philanthropists, the rapid expansion of the middle class in the Global South and engagement of established immigrants across many countries, and the effects of technology, digital innovation and big, open data. As a result, philanthropy is becoming transnational, creative in the vehicles for giving and community mobilizing, and transparent as never before.

Philanthropic institutions are not only being pushed, but are remodeling themselves with expanded capacities for leadership and relationship management, and are equipped with a variety of new tools. New types of hybrid organizations, informal giving circles and community-based movements have generated greater diversity, expanding opportunities for engagement and increasing the ability to work at different scales. Philanthropy's relationships with both the public and private sectors are also in flux. Many governments have developed an 'enchantment' with philanthropy as a means of filling the voids of shrinking government spending on public services (Harrow and Jung, 2011: 1051), and philanthropic institutions and nonprofits are responding with innovation and with resistance (Milbourne, 2013). The tension of the boundaries and accountabilities between the private and the public that has long been at the core of philanthropy has taken on new saliency. Corporations, too, are carving out new relationships with nonprofits as they realign their philanthropy with strategic business priorities (Council on Foundations, 2012).

Some of these factors are already slowly moving philanthropy in different, albeit somewhat predictable, ways. But, philanthropy is also likely to be unexpectedly disrupted by its own Uber equivalents that are, by their very nature, less predictable and not incremental. The reason to expect such disruption is rooted in the emergence of a sharing economy in which relationships are more peer than power driven, and in which engagement and collaboration are fundamental. While not replacing more strategic, entrepreneurial–oriented approaches, such collaboration would further extend the repertoire of philanthropic tools, and implicate a different role for the state beyond thinking of philanthropy as a substitute for reduced public spending.

Does philanthropy need to up its game? With the potential of the vast amounts of money that are being unlocked by intergenerational transfers, the talent and treasure that Millennials and others are ready to contribute, the changing geographies of affluence and the potential for more coordinated approaches to addressing seemingly intractable problems, current practices are undoubtedly under pressure. Is philanthropy up for the challenge? That is the focus of the chapters that follow.

Acknowledgement

The authors thank Paloma Raggo, Assistant Professor, School of Public Policy and Administration (SPPA), Carleton University for her careful reading and constructive comments on a draft of this chapter. The diligent research assistance of SPPA graduate students, Laurel Carlton and Cara-Lynn Janzen, is greatly appreciated. The 2014 research paper by Erin O'Neil, a student in Carleton University's Master of Philanthropy and Nonprofit Leadership, provided a source of some of the ideas and references in the discussion of Millennials. The opportunity to spend a term as Visiting Fellow at the School of Social Policy and Practice (SP2), University of Pennsylvania provided Susan Phillips with a collegial environment for work on this chapter; particular thanks to Professors Femida Handy and Chao Guo.

References

Achieve. (2014) *2014 millennial impact report: Millennial usability testing*. Indianapolis, IN: Achieve Inc.

Adam, T. (2004) Philanthropy and the shaping of social distinctions in nineteenth-century U.S., Canadian and German Cities. In T. Adam (ed.). *Philanthropy, patronage and civil society: Experiences from Germany, Great Britain and North America*. Bloomington, IN: Indiana University Press, 1–20.

Adelman, C., Spantchak, Y., Norris, J., and Marano, K. (2013) *The index of global philanthropy and remittances*. Washington, DC: Hudson Institute, Center for Global Prosperity.

Aknin. L. B., Barrington-Leigh, C. P., Dunn, E. W., Helliwell, J. F., Burns, J., Biswas-Diener, R., Kemeza, I., Nyende, P., Ashton-James, C. E., and Norton, M. I. (2013) Prosocial spending and well-being: Cross-cultural evidence for a psychological universal, *Journal of Personality and Social Psychology*, 104(4): 635–52.

Andreoni, J. and Payne, A. A. (2010) *Is crowding out due entirely to fundraising? Evidence from a panel of charities*. Cambridge, MA: National Bureau of Economic Research.

Anheier, H. K. (2014) *Nonprofit organizations: Theory, management, policy*, 2nd ed. London: Routledge.

Arnove, R. and Pinede, N. (2007) Revisiting the 'Big Three' foundations, *Critical Sociology*, 33(3): 389–425.

Bagwell, S., de Las Casas, L., van Poortvliet, M., and Abercrombie, R. (2013) *Money for good: Understanding donor motivation and behaviour*. London: NPC.

Ball, S. J. and Junemann, C. (2011) Education policy and philanthropy—The changing landscape of English educational governance, *International Journal of Public Administration*, 34(10): 646–61.

Bank of America. (2012) *The 2012 Bank of America study of high net worth philanthropy*. Boston, MA and Indianapolis, IN: Bank of America and Indiana University.

Barkan, J. (2014) How to criticize 'big' philanthropy effectively, *Dissent*, 9 April. www.dissentmagazine. org/blog/how-to-criticize-big-philanthropy-effectively [Accessed 2 March 2015].

Bekkers, R. and Wiepking, P. (2011) Who gives? A literature review of predictors of charitable giving: Part One: Religion, education, age and socialisation, *Voluntary Sector Review*, 2(3): 337–65.

Berger, I. E. (2006) The influence of religion on philanthropy in Canada, *Voluntas*, 17: 115–32.

Bernholz, L. (2015) *Philanthropy and the social economy: Blueprint 2015*. New York, NY: Foundation Center.

Bishop, M. (2006) The birth of philanthrocapitalism, *The Economist*, 23 February, 6.

———. and Green, M. (2008) *Philanthrocapitalism: How the rich can save the world*. New York: Bloomsbury Press.

———. (2014) Part B: Who gains? In L. M. Salamon (ed.). *New frontiers of philanthropy: A guide to the new tools and new actors that are reshaping global philanthropy and social investing*. New York, NY: Oxford University Press, 549–61.

Blackbaud. (2014) *Charitable giving report: How nonprofit fundraising performed in 2013*. Charleston, SC: Blackbaud.

BMO Harris Private Banking, Canadian Association of Gift Planners, GIV3 and Philanthropic Foundations of Canada. (2015) *The philanthropic conversation: Understanding philanthropic advisors' approaches and high net worth individuals' perspectives*. Toronto, ON: GIV3.

BNP Paribas. (2014) *Individual philanthropy index*. New York, NY: Forbes Insight.

Bremner, R. H. (1956) Scientific philanthropy, *Social Science Review*, 30(2): 168–73.

Brest, P. (2015) Strategic philanthropy and its discontents, *Stanford Social Innovation Review*, April 27. www. ssireview.org/up_for_debate/article/strategic_philanthropy_and_its_discontents [Accessed 20 May 2015].

Brody, E. and Tyler, J. (2012) *How public is private philanthropy? Separating reality from myth*. New York, NY: The Philanthropy Roundtable.

Brulle, R. J. (2014) Institutionalizing delay: Foundation funding and the creation of U.S. climate change counter-movement organizations, *Climatic Change*, 122(4): 681–94.

Buffett, W. (No Date) My Philanthropic Pledge, www.givingpledge.org/pdf/pledge-letters/Buffett_ Letter.pdf [Accessed 25 May 2015].

Bugg-Levine, A. and Emerson, J. (2011) *Impact investing: Transforming how we make money while making a difference*. San Francisco: Jossey-Bass.

CAF – Charities Aid Foundation. (2012) *Mind the gap: The growing generational divide in charitable giving – a research paper*. London: CAF.

———. (2013) *Future world giving: Unlocking the potential of global philanthropy*. London: CAF.

———. (2014) *World giving index 2014: A global view of giving trends*. London: CAF. www.cafonline.org/docs/ default-source/about-us-publications/caf_wgi2014_report_1555awebfinal.pdf [Accessed 8 February 2015].

Carmichael, C. (2009) Managing munificence: The reform of naval finance in classical Athens, *Historical Methods*, 42(3): 83–96.

———. (2013a) Lecture, Foundations of Philanthropy, Philanthropy and Nonprofit Leadership Program, Carleton University, July. Ottawa, Canada, Unpublished.

———. (2013b) Doing good better? The differential subsidization of charitable contributions, *Policy and Society*, 29(3): 201–17.

Carnegie, A. (1901) *The gospel of wealth and other timely essays*. New York, NY: The Century Company.

CF Insights (2012) *Do more than grow. Realizing the potential of community foundation donor-advised funds*. Council on Foundations.

Cohen, R. (2014a) How the other half gives: Philanthropy from high net worth individuals, *Nonprofit Quarterly*, 18 November. www.nonprofitquarterly.org/philanthropy/25182-how-the-other-half-gives-philanthropy-from-high-net-worth-individuals.html [Accessed 2 May 2015].

Cohen, Sir R. (2014b) Revolutionising philanthropy – Impact investing. Presentation to the Lord Mayor's Leadership Programme, 23 January. London: Cass Business School. www.ronaldcohen.org/sites/default/files/26/Sir%20Ronald%20Cohen%20Mansion%20House%20Speech%2023JAN14.pdf [Accessed 4 January 2015].

Community Foundation Atlas. (2014) *Dimensions of the field: An indepth analysis of the community foundation movement*. www.communityfoundationatlas.org/facts/#analysis [Accessed 10 May 2015].

Council on Foundations. (2009) *Donor Advised Funds provide the majority of grant funds awarded by communiy foundations*. New York, NY: Council on Foundations.

———. (2012) *Increasing impact, enhancing value: A practitioners guide to leading corporate philanthropy*. New York, NY: Council on Foundations.

Coutts. (2014) *Coutts million dollar donor report*. www.philanthropy.coutts.com/en/reports/2014/executive-summary.html [Accessed 8 April 2015].

Cowley, E., McKenzie, T., Pharoah, C., and Smith, S. (2011) *The new state of donation: Three decades of household giving to charity 1978–2008*. London: Centre for Charitable Giving and Philanthropy, Cass Business School.

Daly, S. (2012) Philanthropy as an essentially contested concept, *Voluntas*, 23(3): 535–57.

Davey, M. (2014) Finding $816 million, and fast, to save Detroit, *New York Times*, 7 November. www.nytimes.com/2014/11/08/us/finding-816-million-and-fast-to-save-detroit.html [Accessed 10 January 2015].

Dean, M. (2013) UK philanthropy needs to up its game, *The Guardian*, 15 October. www.theguardian.com/society/2013/oct/15/uk-philanthropy-up-game [Accessed 9 January 2015].

Deloitte. (2014) *Big demands and high expectations: The Deloitte Millennial study*. London: Deloitte Touche Tohmatsu Limited. www2.deloitte.com/content/dam/Deloitte/global/Documents/About-Deloitte/gx-dttl-2014-millennial-survey-report.pdf [Accessed 20 May 2015].

Department of Finance Canada. (2015) *Tax expenditures and evaluations*. Ottawa, ON: Department of Finance Canada.

Diaz, W. A. (1999) The behavior of grantmaking foundations. In H. K. Anheier and S. Toepler (eds.). *Private funds, public purpose*. New York, NY: Kluwer Academic.

Dolan, M. (2014) In Detroit bankruptcy, art was key to the deal, *The Wall Street Journal*, 7 November. www.wsj.com/articles/in-detroit-bankruptcy-art-was-key-to-the-deal-1415384308 [Accessed 9 January 2015].

Dunn, E., Aknin, L., and Norton, M. (2014) Prosocial spending and happiness: Using money to benefit others pays off, *Current Direction in Psychological Science*, 23(1): 41–7.

Edelman. (2015) *Edelman trust barometer 2015 – Annual global survey*. New York, NY: Edelman Global Network.

Edwards, M. (2008) Philanthropy –Whose canvas?, *Alliance*, 13(3): 51.

El Daly, M. (2012) From Maadi to Tahrir Square: Waqfeyat al Maadi Community Foundation walked the road for Egypt's liberty, development and social justice. Paper presented to the International Society for Third Sector Research. Sienna, Italy.

Elsanousi, M. A. (2010) Islamic philanthropy. In D. F. Burlingame (ed.) *Philanthropy in America*, Vol II. Santa Barbara, CA: ABC-CLIO Inc.

Esposito, J. L. (2010) *Islam: The straight path*, 4th edition. Oxford: Oxford University Press.

Facebook. (2014) The Ice Bucket Challenge. *Facebook Newsroom*. www.newsroom.fb.com/news/2014/08/the-ice-bucket-challenge-on-facebook/ [Accessed 10 January 2015].

Fisher, D. (1983) The role of philanthropic foundations in the reproduction of hegemony, *Sociology*, 17(2): 206–33.

Forbes. (2015) The richest person in every state – Warren Buffett. www.forbes.com/profile/warren-buffett/ [Accessed 26 May 2015].

Frumkin, P. (2006) *Strategic giving: The art and science of philanthropy*. Chicago: Chicago University Press.

Gara, T. (2013) Truth about millennials: Less entitled and more cynical than you think. *Wall Street Journal*, 6 June. www.blogs.wsj.com/corporate-intelligence/2013/06/06/truth-about-millennials-less-entitled-and-more-cynical-than-you-think/ [Accessed 12 January 2015].

Garrioch, D. (2004) Making a better world: The enlightenment and philanthropy. In M. Fitzpatrick, P. Jones, C. Knellwolf, and I. McCalman (eds.). *The Enlightenment World*. London: Routledge, 486–501.

Gasman, M. and Drezner, D. (2008) White corporate philanthropy and its support of private Black colleges in the 1960s and 1970s, *International Journal of Educational Advancement*, 8: 79–92.

Gates, B. and M. (2013) Bill and Melinda Gates annual letter. www.gatesfoundation.org/who-we-are/resources-and-media/annual-letters-list/annual-letter-2013 [Accessed 10 May 2015].

Gautier, A. and Pache, A.-C. (2015) Research on corporate philanthropy: A review and assessment, *Journal of Business Ethics*, 126: 343–69

Giving Pledge. (2015) Frequently Asked Questions. www.givingpledge.org/faq.aspx [Accessed 25 May 2015]

Giving USA. (2014) *The annual report on philanthropy for the year 2013*. Indianapolis, IN: Giving USA Foundation and Indiana University Lilly Family School of Philanthropy.

Global Fund for Community Foundations. (2011) 'Nothing really made it easy except that things got complicated': The story of the Waqfeyat al Maadi Community Foundation. www.globalfundcommunityfoundations.org/latest-news/2011/10/31/nothing-really-made-it-easy-except-that-things-got-complicat.html [Accessed 10 January 2015].

Graddy, E. L. and Morgan, D. L. (2006) Community foundations, organizational strategy, and public policy, *Nonprofit and Voluntary Sector Quarterly*, 35(4): 605–30.

Gross, R. A. (2004) Giving in America: From charity to philanthropy. In L. J. Friedman and M. D. McGarvie (eds.). *Charity, philanthropy and civility in American history*. Cambridge: Cambridge University Press, 29–48.

Hall, P. D. (2006) Religion, philanthropy, service and civic engagement in twentieth century America. In A. C. Brooks (ed.). *Gifts of time and money: The role of charity in America's Communities*. Lanham, MD: Rowman & Littlefield.

Hammack, D. C. and Anheier, H. K. (2013) *A versatile American institution: The changing ideals and realities of philanthropic foundations*. Washington, DC: The Brookings Institution.

Hansmann, H. (1980) The role of nonprofit enterprise, *Yale Law Journal*, 89: 835–901.

Harding, M., O'Connell, A., and Stewart, M. (2014) Introduction: Theoretical and comparative perspectives on not-for-profit law. In M. Harding, A. O'Connell, and M. Stewart (eds.). *Not-for-profit law: Theoretical and comparative perspectives*. Cambridge: Cambridge University Press.

Harris, B. and Bridgen, P. (2007) Introduction: The 'mixed economy of welfare' and the historiography of welfare provision. In B. Harris and P. Bridgen (eds.). *Charity and mutual aid in Europe and North America since 1800*. London: Routledge, 1–18.

Harrow, J. and Jung, T. (2011) Philanthropy is dead; Long live philanthropy? *Public Management Review*, 13(8): 1048–56.

Harvey, C., Maclean, M., Gordon, J., and Shaw, E. (2011) Andrew Carnegie and the foundations of contemporary entrepreneurial philanthropy, *Business History*, 53(3): 425–50.

Havens, J. J. and Schervish, P. G. (2014) *A golden age of philanthropy still beckons: National wealth transfer and potential for philanthropy, Technical report*. Boston, MA. Boston College, Center on Wealth and Philanthropy.

Helliwell, J. F., Huang, H. and Wang, S. (2015) The geography of world happiness. In J. F. Helliwell, R. Layard, and J. Sachs (eds.). *World happiness report 2015*. New York: Sustainable Development Solutions Network, 12–41.

Herrold, C. E. (2015) Giving in Egypt: Evolving charitable traditions in a changing political economy. In P. A. Wiepking and F. Femida (eds.). *The Palgrave handbook of global philanthropy*. Hampshire, UK: Palgrave Macmillan.

Hodgson, J. (2013a) Building something new for the future, *Alliance Magazine*, 18(1): 18.

Hodgson, J. (2013b) *The case for community philanthropy: How the practice builds local assets, capacity, and trust—and why it matters*. Flint, MI: Charles Stewart Mott Foundation, Aga Khan Foundation, Global Fund for Community Foundations and Rockefeller Brothers Fund.

Ilchman, W. F., Katz, S. N., and Queen, E. L. (eds.). (1998) *Philanthropy in the world's traditions*. Bloomington, IN: Indiana University Press.

Ipsos Mori. (2010) *Public trust and confidence in charities*. London: Charity Commission.

Johnson Center for Philanthropy. (2013) *#Nextgen donors, respecting legacy, revolutionizing philanthropy.* Grand Rapids, MI: Johnson Center for Philanthropy at Grand Valley State University.

JP Morgan. (2011) *Impact investing: An emerging asset class.* New York, NY: JP Morgan, Rockefeller Foundation and GIIN.

Jung, T. and Harrow, J. (2015a) Philanthropy, the state and public goods. In O. P. Guerrero and P. Wilkins (eds.). *Doing public good? Private actors, evaluation and public value.* Comparative Policy Evaluation, Volume 23, Transaction Publishers.

——. (2015b) New development: Philanthropy in networked governance – treading with care, *Public Money and Management,* 35(1): 47–51.

Kasper, G., Marcoux, J., and Ausinheiler, J. (2014) *What's next for community philanthropy.* San Francisco, CA: Monitor Institute.

Keen, R. (2014) *Charities, social action and the voluntary sector.* London: Library, House of Common, UK.

Kemmis, D. (2014) *Philanthropy and the renewal of democracy: Is it time to step up our game?* New York. Kettering Foundation.

Kharas, H. (2010) *The emerging middle class in developing countries, Working paper no. 285,* Paric: OECD Development Centre.

Klausner, M. (2003) When time isn't money. *Stanford Social Innovation Review,* 1(1): 51–9.

Knight, B. (2012) *The value of community philanthropy: Results of a consultation.* Washington, DC and Flint, MI: Aga Khan Foundation and Charles Stewart Mott Foundation.

Knight, B. and Milner, A. (2013) *What does community philanthropy look like.* Flint, MI: Charles Stewart Mott Foundation.

Knowledge@Wharton. (2013) The new philanthropists: More sophisticated, more demanding – and younger. Philadelphia, PA: Wharton Business School, University of Pennsylvania.

Lala, R. M. (2006) *Creation of wealth: The Tatas from the 19th to the 21st Century.* New Delhi: Penguin Books.

LaMarche, G. (2014) Democracy and the donor class. *Democracy: A Journal of Ideas,* 34(fall). www.democracyjournal.org/34/democracy-and-the-donor-class.php?page=all [Accessed 10 April 2015].

Lasby, D. (2011) What T3010 data tell us about charity financing. *The Philanthropist,* 24(2): 155–60.

Leat, D. (2006) Grantmaking foundations and performance measures: Playing pool? *Public Policy and Administration,* 21(3): 25–37.

Lewis, J. (1999) The voluntary sector in the mixed economy of welfare. In D. Gladstone (ed.). *Before Beveridge: Welfare before the welfare state.* London: Institute of Economic Affairs, 10–17.

McCully, G. (2008) *Philanthropy reconsidered: Private initiatives – public good –quality of life.* Bloomington, IN: AuthorHouse.

McKeever, B. S. and Pettijohn, S. L. (2014) *The nonprofit sector in brief 2014: Public charities, giving and volunteering.* Washington, DC: The Urban Institute.

Matthews, D. (2015) You have $8 billion. You want to do as much good as possible. What do you do? *Vox,* 24 April. www.vox.com/2015/4/24/8457895/givewell-open-philanthropy-charity [Accessed 26 April, 2015].

Milbourne, L. (2013) *Voluntary sector in transition: Hard times or new opportunities?* Bristol: Policy Press.

Moe, H. A. (1961) Notes on the origin of philanthropy in Christendom, *Proceedings of the American Philosophical Society,* 105(2): 141–4.

Moore, D. and Rutzen, D. (2011) Legal framework for global philanthropy: Barriers and opportunities, *International Journal of Not-for-Profit Law,* 13(1–2): 5–41.

Muttart Foundation. (2013) *Talking about charities.* Edmonton, AB: Muttart Foundation.

NAO – National Audit Office. (2013) *The cup trust.* Report by the Comptroller and Auditor General. HC 814 Session 2013–14 4 December 2013. London: National Audit Office.

Narapruet, O. (2011) Celebrity philanthropy: Reassessing fame for civil society, *Social Space,* (1): 62–7.

NCVO/CAF. (2012) *UK giving 2012.* London, National Council of Voluntary Organisations and Charities Aid Foundation.

Newland, K., Terrazas, A., and Munster, R. (2010) *Diaspora philanthropy: Private giving and public policy.* Washington, DC, Migration Policy Institute.

Nicholls, A. (2010) The institutionalization of social investment: The interplay of investment logics and investor rationalities, *Journal of Social Entrepreneurship,* 1(1): 70–100.

Nickel, P. M. and Eikenberry, A. M. (2009) A critique of the discourse of marketized philanthropy, *American Behavioral Scientist,* 57(7): 974–89.

Nielsen. (2014) *Millennials – Breaking the myths.* New York, NY: The Nielsen Company.

Norris, D. (2012) *Donational patterns of the multicultural population: Some evidence from Geodemography.* Toronto, ON: Environics.

Odendahl, T. (1990) *Charity begins at home: Generosity and self-interest among the philanthropic elite.* New York, NY: Basic Books.

O'Halloran, K. (2012) *The profits of charity.* Oxford: Oxford University Press.

O'Neil, M. (2015) At ALS Association, fundraising success begets fundraising success, *Chronicle of Philanthropy,* 8 January. www.philanthropy.com/article/At-ALS-Association/152003 [Accessed 25 February 2015].

Orosz, J. L. (2007) *Effective foundation management: 14 challenges of philanthropic leadership – and how to outfox them.* Lanham, MD: Altamira Press.

Ostrower, F. (2004) *Foundation effectiveness: Definitions and challenges.* Washington, DC, The Urban Institute.

———. (2007) The relativity of foundation effectiveness: The case of community foundations, *Nonprofit and Voluntary Sector Quarterly,* 36(3): 521–27.

Pan-chiu, L. and Lee, P. (2002) Traditions of giving in Confucianism, *Alliance Magazine,* 7(1): 13–14.

Parmar, I. (2012) *Foundations of the American Century.* New York, NY: Columbia University Press.

Payton, R. L. and Moody, M. P. (2008) *Understanding philanthropy: Its meaning and mission.* Bloomington, IN: Indiana University Press.

Perez, S. (2014) The Ice Bucket Challenge, by the numbers. *techcrunch.com,* 3 September. www.techcrunch.com/2014/09/03/the-ice-bucket-challenge-by-the-numbers/ [Accessed 9 February 2015].

Pew Research Center. (2010) *Millennials: A portrait of generation next.* Washington, DC: Pew Research Center.

Pharoah, C. (2011) Private giving and philanthropy – Their place in the Big Society. *People, Place and Policy Online* 5(2): 65–75.

Pharoah, C. and McKenzie, T. (2013) *Giving back to communities of residence and of origin.* London: Centre for Charitable Giving and Philanthropy, Cass Business School.

Phillips, S. D. (2013) Shining light on charities or looking in the wrong place? Transparency and co-regulation in Canada, *Voluntas,* 24(3): 881–905.

———. and Smith, S. R. (2014) A dawn of policy convergence? Third sector policy and regulatory change among the 'Anglo-Saxon' cluster, *Public Management Review,* 16(8): 1141–63.

Polgreen, L. (2010) The special pain of a slow disaster, *New York Times,* 10 November. www.nytimes.com/2010/11/11/giving/11AID.html?_r=0 [Accessed 8 February 2015].

Porter, M. and Kramer, M. R. (2011) Creating shared value, *Harvard Business Review,* 82(1/2): 62–77.

Prochaska, F. K. (1980) *Women and philanthropy in 19th century England.* Oxford: Oxford University Press.

———. (1990) Philanthropy. In F. M. L. Thompson (ed.). *The Cambridge social history of Britain, 1750–950, Volume 3 – social agencies and institutions.* Cambridge, UK: Cambridge University Press, 357–94.

Putnam, R. D. (2000) *Bowling alone: The collapse and revival of American community.* New York, NY: Simon and Schuster.

Rabin, S. (2014) *Age of opportunity: Putting the ageing society of tomorrow on the agenda of the voluntary sector today.* London, UK: NPC.

Reed, P. B. and Selbee, L. K. (2001) The civic core in Canada: Disproportionality in charitable giving, volunteering, and civic participation, *Nonprofit and Voluntary Sector Quarterly,* 30(4): 761–80.

Reich, R. (2013) Forum: What are foundations for? *Boston Review,* 1 March. www.bostonreview.net/forum/foundations-philanthropy-democracy [Accessed 25 February 2015].

Roberts, D. (2014) Millennials have big faith in big business. Surprised? *Fortune,* 19 September. www.fortune.com/2014/09/19/millennials-big-business/ [Accessed 20 January 2015].

Roelofs, J. (2003) *Foundations and public policy: The mask of pluralism.* Albany, NY: State University of New York Press.

Rover, M. and Loeb, P. (2013) *The next generation of Canadian giving: The charitable habits of generations Y, X, Baby boomers and civics.* Toronto, ON: Blackbaud. www.hjcnewmedia.com/nextgencanadiangiving2013/downloads/The_Next_Generation_of_Canadian_Giving_2013.pdf [Accessed 23 February 2015].

Salamon, L. M. (1992) *America's nonprofit sector: A primer.* New York, NY: The Foundation Center.

———. (ed.). (2014) *New frontiers of philanthropy: A guide to the new tools and new actors that are reshaping global philanthropy and social investing.* New York, NY: Oxford University Press.

———., Wojciech Sokolowski, S,. and List, R. (2003) *Global civil society: An overview.* Baltimore: Johns Hopkins Center for Civil Society Studies.

———., Wojciech Sokolowski, S., Haddock, M., and Trice, H. S. (2013) *The state of global civil society and volunteering: Latest findings from the implementation of the UN Nonprofit Handbook.* Baltimore, MD: Center for Civil Society Studies, Johns Hopkins University. www.ccss.jhu.edu/wp-content/uploads/downloads/2013/04/JHU_Global-Civil-Society-Volunteering_FINAL_3.2013.pdf [Accessed 17 April 2015].

Schambra, W. (2013) The problem of strategic philanthropy, *Nonprofit Quarterly*, 12 August. www.non-profitquarterly.org/philanthropy/22729-the-problem-of-strategic-philanthropy.html [Accessed 20 February 2015].

——. (2014) Foundations offering to bail out Detroit may regret their decision, *Chronicle of Philanthropy*, 24 January. www.philanthropy.com/article/Foundations-Offering-to-Bail/153763 [Accessed 21 February 2015].

Schervish, P. G. and Whitaker, K. (2010) *Wealth and the will of God*. Bloomington, IN: Indiana University Press.

Scott, J., Lubienski, C., and DeBray-Pelot, E. (2009) The politics of advocacy in education, *Educational Policy*, 23(1): 3–14

Sifferlin, A. (2014) Here's how the ALS Ice Bucket Challenge actually started, *Time*, 18 August. www.time.com/3136507/als-ice-bucket-challenge-started/ [Accessed 14 January 2015].

Silber, I. F. (2012) The angry gift: A neglected facet of philanthropy, *Current Sociology*, 60: 320–37

Silk, R. D. and Lintott, J. W. (2011) *Managing foundations and charitable trusts*. Hoboken, NJ: John Wiley & Sons.

Singer, P. (2015) *The most good you can do. How effective altruism is changing ideas about living ethically*. New Haven, CO: Yale University Press.

Sugirtharajah, S. (2001) Traditions of giving in Hinduism, *Alliance Magazine*, 6(3): 17–20.

Sulek, M. (2010) On the classic meaning of philanthropia, *Nonprofit and Voluntary Sector Quarterly*, 39(3): 385–408.

——. (2011) On the modern meaning of philanthropy, *Nonprofit and Voluntary Sector Quarterly*, 39(2): 193–212.

Tarn, J. N. (1973) *Five percent philanthropy: An account of housing in urban areas between 1840 and 1914*. Cambridge: Cambridge University Press.

TD Bank. (2014) *Time, treasure, talent: Canadian women and philanthropy*. Toronto, ON: TD Bank.

Tobin, G. A. (2010) Jewish philanthropy in American Society. In D. F. Burlingame (ed.). *Philanthropy in America*, Vol II. Santa Barbara, CA: ABC-CLIO Inc.

Tyler, J. (2013) *Transparency in philanthropy: An analysis of accountability, fallacy and volunteerism*. Washington, DC: The Philanthropy Roundtable.

United Nations Development Programme (UNDP). (2013) *The rise of the South: Human progress in diverse world*. Human Development Report 2013. New York, NY: UNDP.

US Trust. (2013) *The US Trust study of the philanthropic conversation: Understanding advisor approaches and client expectations*. Boston, MA: US Trust in partnership with the Philanthropic Initiative. www.newsroom.bankofamerica.com/sites/bankofamerica.newshq.businesswire.com/files/press_kit/additional/US_Trust_Study_of_the_Philanthropic_Conversation_2013.pdf [Accessed 10 March 2015].

US Trust and Lilly Family School of Philanthropy. (2014) *The 2014 US Trust Study of high net worth philanthropy*. Boston, MA and Indianapolis, IN: US Trust and Lilly Family School of Philanthropy, Indiana University.

Vaidyanathan, B., Hill, and Smith, C. (2011) Religion and charitable financial giving to religious and secular causes: Does political ideology matter? *Journal for the Scientific Study of Religion*, 50(3): 450–69.

van Leeuwen, M. H. D. (2012) Giving in early modern history: Philanthropy in Amsterdam in the Golden Age, *Continuity and Change*, 27(2): 301–43.

Walzer, M. (1990) *The civil society argument*. Gunnar Myrdal Lecture. Stockholm: University of Stockholm.

Ward, J. P. (2013) *Culture, faith and philanthropy: Londoners and provincial reform in early modern England*. Basingstoke: Palgrave Macmillan.

Warren, M. E. (2011) Civil society and democracy. In M. Edwards (ed.) *Oxford handbook of civil society*. Oxford: Oxford University Press, 377–90.

Weisbrod, B. A. (1975) Toward a theory of the voluntary nonprofit sector in a three-sector economy. In E. Phelps (ed.). *Altruism, morality and economic theory*. New York, NY: Russell Sage Foundation, 171–95.

Wiepking, P. and Handy, F. (eds.). (2015) *The Palgrave handbook of global philanthropy*. Hampshire, UK: Palgrave Macmillan.

Women's Philanthropy Institute. (2014) *WomenGive 14: New research on women, religion and giving*. Indianapolis, IN: Lilly Family School of Philanthropy, Indiana University. www.philanthropy.iupui.edu/files/research/womengive14_final.pdf [Accessed 8 March 2015].

Zunz, O. (2012) *Philanthropy in America*. Princeton: Princeton University Press.

Part II

The roots of and impulses for philanthropy

Vignette: The Roots and Impulses for Philanthropy

(G)Local philanthropy

Local ideas, global potential – The Shorefast Foundation

Natalie Slawinski

Zita Cobb's philanthropy grows out of a concern for the future of Fogo Island – a ruggedly beautiful, remote island in the North Atlantic with a unique distinction. During the existence of the satirical Flat Earth Society of Canada in the late 1970s and early 1980s, the group, composed of published authors, poets and philosophers, declared Fogo Island to be one of the four corners of the earth: they had discovered that from Brimstone Head, a massive rock forming part of the island's northwestern coastline, one could spot 'the Edge' (Colombo, 1984).

A philanthropist's roots

Zita Cobb comes from humble beginnings. The only girl of seven children, she was born on Fogo Island in 1958. At the time, Fogo Island was predominantly a subsistence economy. Most residents engaged in fishing and sealing. Cobb's family was no different; they struggled to carve out an existence on the island. When she was five, Cobb was diagnosed with tuberculosis. As a result, she was sent away to a sanatorium for a year, separated from her family. This experience contributed to turning her into a fiercely independent and self-reliant person.

By the time she was a teenager, the economic situation on the island had become worse. With fishery in decline, Cobb's father insisted she leave for the mainland of Canada to pursue a better life. He told Cobb, 'the only difference between us down here starvin' to death and them up there going to the opera, whatever that is, is they have an education and we don't'.

At age 17, following her parents' advice, Cobb left for Ottawa to pursue a business degree. It would be thirty years before she moved back home again. During that time, Cobb built a very successful career in the high tech industry. As the Vice President of Strategy at JDS Uniphase, she helped grow the company into a large multinational operating in the field of fiber optics. At the height of her career, she was reportedly the third highest paid female executive in North America (Bartlett, 2008), and she retired in 2001 a multimillionaire. Following her retirement, she spent the next several years sailing the world and engaging in philanthropic work in Africa. In 2006, she returned to Fogo Island.

The challenge

Settled in the seventeenth century, Fogo Island and nearby Change Islands are rich in culture and tradition that revolved around the cod fishery. These small islands of 284 and 27 square kilometers respectively can be reached by ferry from Farewell, Newfoundland – itself a remote community. Mirroring trends in many rural communities in the Canadian province of Newfoundland and Labrador, the population in this area had been declining continuously over the past decades. Developments, such as the Canadian government's imposed moratorium on cod fishing in 1992, had accelerated this trend; many Newfoundlanders could no longer earn their living off the sea. They were forced to leave their communities in search of jobs elsewhere. As such, the population in this area had declined by almost half since the 1950s and, in 2011, the population of Fogo Island rested around 2,200, while Change Islands had a mere 200 residents. Although the majority of the remaining residents, as in many other small outport communities in Newfoundland, still made their living from fishing, now relying on species other than cod, increasingly, the fishery could no longer sustain the population of Fogo Island and Change Islands. Zita Cobb became determined to find a way to reverse this trend. She hoped that alternative economic drivers could be identified and developed. The challenge was to create enough jobs to reverse the trend of outmigration. This new employment had to be meaningful. It also had to complement and fortify the culture and traditions of the islands while leaving the smallest environmental footprint possible.

The Shorefast Foundation

To achieve this vision of 'cultural and economic resilience for Fogo Island and Change Islands', Cobb founded the Shorefast Foundation with two of her brothers. The name 'shorefast,' which describes a tether that joins a cod trap to the shore, was chosen as it provides a metaphor for the importance of place and tradition in communities. Cobb's biggest fear was that Fogo Island would suffer from a 'flattening of culture' as residents continued to leave the Island in search of work. She also worried about the homogenizing side of globalization, and how Fogo Island might start to resemble other North American communities if franchises started to appear. Her goal was to 'help us remain shorefast on our rock', and she believed that Fogo Island was a special place that has much to offer its residents and visitors.

To this end, the Shorefast Foundation turned to geotourism and art. Geotourism was seen as an economic driver that could potentially create enough meaningful jobs to keep people from moving away. It refers to 'tourism that sustains or enhances the geographical character of a place – the environment, heritage, aesthetics, food, culture & wellbeing of local people' (Tourtellot, 2010: NP). Art was equally important to Shorefast's vision because, as Cobb explains, 'art engages our senses and our reason, and contributes to the critical thinking needed to resist being culturally flattened'. Bearing this in mind, Shorefast developed an artist residency program designed to attract high-caliber artists from around the world to Fogo Island; given that Fogo Island is a unique destination with much to offer but was missing some of the bases for attracting affluent tourists, the Foundation also undertook to build necessary tourism infrastructure. Newfoundland-born, world-renowned architect, Todd Saunders designed the plans for four stunning artist studios and a luxury five-star Inn that have drawn international attention.

Funding for the Shorefast Foundation's initiatives came mainly from Cobb's personal wealth and from the provincial and federal governments, which each contributed $5 million CDN. While the initial estimate to build the artist studios and the Inn came in at $16 million CDN, it had since risen to close to $30 million by 2012. Most of the additional costs were the result of Shorefast's uncompromising commitment to social and environmental ideals. Getting the Inn right was critical to all of Shorefast's other initiatives: as a social enterprise, it would provide the revenue necessary to fund Shorefast's social mission to build economic and cultural resilience on the Island.

Using an enterprising approach

Although Shorefast was officially registered as a charitable organization, Cobb decided to run the Foundation as a social enterprise: to use business principles to achieve the Foundation's social goals. Two initiatives in particular were designed with social entrepreneurship in mind. The first was the business assistance fund, a one million-dollar fund designed to provide funding and business coaching to entrepreneurs on Fogo and Change Islands. The second initiative, and the one on which the whole Shorefast model hinged, was the Fogo Island Inn. One hundred percent of all surpluses generated by the Inn would belong to the community.

As with most social enterprise approaches, balancing social, environmental and economic goals presented a significant challenge. This challenge was especially salient in constructing the Inn. While a modern design, the 40,000 square foot, four-story building was built with stilts supporting one part of the structure. These stilts pay homage to the traditional architecture of the area, but also reduce the physical disturbance of the building on the land. The Inn is clad in wooden clapboard with more than one hundred floor-to-ceiling windows providing views of the rugged North Atlantic Ocean. In addition, it has public spaces for the community, including an art gallery, library and cinema. Designed with the people of Fogo Island in mind, it highlights an important point: the participation of the community in Shorefast's projects is critical for the success of its goals.

A significant issue in building the Inn was finding skilled tradespeople and construction workers. With a deep commitment to creating employment on the Islands, the Shorefast Foundation hired a number of local residents, but due to the shortage of workers and specific skills, it was forced to hire workers from other parts of Newfoundland, Canada, and the world. This contributed significantly to increased construction costs. Another challenge was the substantial expense associated with building an environmentally-friendly Inn. While five-star hotels normally cost $200,000 per room to build, the Fogo Island Inn well exceeded that number, largely as a consequence of keeping its environmental footprint to a minimum. For example, the Foundation installed solar panels on the roof of the building to lower its carbon footprint. To conserve the town's water supply, they installed a 117-gallon cistern that collects rainwater used for flushing toilettes and other water-intensive activities that do not require potable water. This solution allows the Inn to reduce its water consumption by 70 percent, compared to a traditional building of the same size. Although these decisions increased initial capital costs, Cobb is convinced that the long-term savings and environmental benefits will be substantial.

Ultimately, Cobb's greatest concern was that either too few or too many visitors would come to Fogo Island. If too few tourists come, not enough revenue will be generated to support employment and Shorefast's other programs, including the artist residency program. On the other hand, if too many come, the culture of Fogo Island and the natural environment could be negatively affected. Already, the international media attention drawn by the Shorefast Foundation was attracting large numbers of tourists to the Island, creating longer wait times to catch the ferry.

Lessons learnt

Attracting visitors, including affluent tourists, to a remote island in the North Atlantic is no small feat. However, Cobb is convinced that Fogo Island has much to offer, including spiritual well-being. As she explains,

> you cannot, even if you wanted to, escape or deny the existence of the earth and the forces of the earth. It presses upon you and then it makes you a little bit more human and when that happens it connects you, I think, better to other human beings. So just being able to reorient and reconnect is really the gift that I think this place gives you.

Cobb is also confident that she had assembled a strong executive team of individuals passionate about Shorefast's goals. Many of these individuals had significant business experience and had worked internationally in a variety of industries. Cobb herself had decades of management experience and was determined to master the art of running a social enterprise, working hard to overcome the many tensions and challenges that emerged along the way. She is very involved in running the Foundation, working 16 hour days to lead its work, while giving numerous media interviews and jet-setting around the world to promote the Foundation and its goals.

There have been many lessons learned along the way for Cobb. These include the need to find the 'right speed and scale' for the Foundation's activities. For example, the Inn took much longer to build than Cobb anticipated, but she learned to accept that the pace on Fogo Island was different from that in the corporate world. She also learned the importance of deep community engagement, for without the community's strong support and involvement, Shorefast's efforts would surely fail. But perhaps the biggest challenge of all was trying to operate a social enterprise within an institutional and policy environment that was ill-equipped to handle such newer forms of enterprise that did not fit neatly into for-profit or nonprofit categories. Social enterprise was a widely defined, newly evolving phenomenon and the guidelines from a taxation, legal and accounting perspective were complex. Cobb and her team recognized yet again that they would need to find 'new ways with old things' in order to meet their mandate under these constraints and to emerge as a model of social enterprise that other communities could follow.

Reflections

Zita Cobb hopes that the Shorefast Foundation will reverse the trend of outmigration while building economic and cultural resilience on Fogo Island and Change Islands. She believes that rural communities are important repositories of cultural and environmental knowledge and 'ways of knowing'. Consequently, these communities need to find sustainable futures. As she explains,

> Newfoundland and Labrador epitomizes the plight of the rural community. It's a place that has always been defined by its small communities, scattered along the rugged coastline and where the people have for hundreds of years lived from the resources of the sea, deeply entangled with the natural world. They're remote places, sometimes unforgiving places but in a time when humanity is losing its intimacy with the earth, they are important places that have much to give.

Despite the many challenges, including some objections from the community, the Shorefast Foundation is not only creating jobs, but breathing new life into the communities on Fogo Island

and Change Islands. There is a strong sense of optimism for the future, and an entrepreneurial spirit is beginning to blossom. Several businesses, including a high-end restaurant and a day-care facility, have opened their doors, and an increasing number of tourists are visiting the Islands.

Cobb is thinking big about Fogo Island, but also about rural communities around the world. She hopes that Shorefast's work on Fogo Island could become 'a world model for rural economic transformation'. From the beginning, she was thinking about the power of the specific to inform the universal. According to Cobb, every place is unique, and Fogo Island could help other communities uncover and leverage their own uniqueness. While she has large aspirations, she worries that time is running out as cultures around the world are being flattened and lost: she is working hard to ensure Fogo Island and Change Islands will not suffer this same fate.

Notes

The author wishes to thank Bradley Hookey for his research assistance.

References

Bartlett, S. (2008) *The Grit and the Courage: Stories of Success in an Unforgiving Land*. St. John's, NL, Canada: Creative Publishers.

Colombo, J. R. (1984) *Canadian Literary Landmarks*. Ontario: Hounslow Press.

Tourtellot, J. (2010) *About Geotourism*. National Geographic Center for Sustainable Development. http:// travel.nationalgeographic.com/travel/sustainable/about_geotourism.html [Accessed 1 June 2015].

2

The multi-layered history of Western philanthropy

Hugh Cunningham

Historians increasingly write about philanthropy as a gift relationship. Alan Kidd (1996: 184), for example, describes philanthropy as

> non-commercial social transfers of wealth, material objects or non-material assistance rendered in forms that are culturally meaningful and that generate moral relationships between individuals or groups such as solidarity, dependence, legitimacy, and reputability.

The history of philanthropy, however, is not simply a history of giving, far less one of giving only by the rich; it requires us to examine the various sides of the relationship. This brings it into close engagement with many other branches of history: class, gender, national identity and empire, religion and missions, poor relief and welfare, wealth and taxation, civil society. All these, and others, touch on philanthropy.

In this synopsis, I argue that historians of philanthropy need to think like geologists. Stop the clock at any time, say 1850 in Europe, and you will find strata, or layers, of philanthropic giving accumulated on top of each other. The philanthropy of the past leaves its material record, its buildings, its legal documents, its charitable gifts, its assumptions and practices, in layer after layer. The present adds a topsoil of the latest projects, but the lower layers continue to exercise their influence, sometimes in the form of outcrops from earlier ages of giving.

The strata of philanthropy

First stratum: Ancient Greece

Excavators of the first stratum focus on ancient Greece and seize on Aristotle (384–322 BCE), who wrote that to give money 'to the right person, in the right amount, at the right time, with the right aim in view, and in the right way – that is not something anyone can do, nor is it easy' (Aristotle, 2000: 35). Twenty-first-century philanthropists love to quote this: philanthropy, it seems to say, is not easy, but to engage in it has the sanction of ancient wisdom. In fact Aristotle was exploring how to achieve a mean between wastefulness and stinginess; for him the truly virtuous person, in the words of Roger Crisp, 'is unlikely to stir himself to help the vulnerable' (Aristotle, 2000: xviii).

The Greek word *philanthropia* originally referred to the relationship of the gods to humans; it came to be applied to rulers who were generous to their subjects, and then to the wealthy more generally. It incorporated the notion of a return, *philanthropon*, from the recipients in the form of honours heaped on the donor: it was a form of gift exchange, a quid-pro-quo (Hands, 1968: 35–7; 80). Often, it referred to a relationship between wealthy individuals, indicative of a cast of mind as much as the conferring of a gift. The fourth century philosopher Themistius, for example, thought it 'ridiculous … to attest to love of mankind in a weaver or a carpenter who has a mean dwelling, and scarcely leaves his house through weariness and lack of leisure' (Finn, 2006: 215). Philanthropy was given a new twist by early Christians, but, as a term, it soon disappeared from view before re-emerging in the late eighteenth century.

Second stratum: Early Christianity

The second stratum is made up of the teachings of the Bible and of the early Christian Fathers, of their interpretation from the twelfth century onwards, and of the medieval world of giving. At their root was a sense of justice, that the poor should be relieved by the rich. The Christian Fathers argued that all property belonged to all men. According to the preachings of the influential theologian Basil of Casesarea (329–379 CE), if God was the great philanthropist, Christians should imitate 'God's *philanthropia* by both taking pity and sharing things out and being generous with favours' (Finn, 2006: 236). In the Middle Ages, from the centres of intellectual activity in Paris, Rome and Bologna, ideas and teachings about giving circulated throughout Europe, progressively simplified as they descended the social scale. The stress was on the obligations of the rich. In the words of Robert of Flamborough's thirteenth century penitential *Liber Poenitentialis*, 'whoever does not receive guests in his home, as God has ordained, nor give alms, if he makes no amends by bread and water for an equivalent period, let him do penance' (Rubin, 1987: 62). Alms giving was itself a form of penance. As Bartholomew of Exeter pointed out: 'alms extinguish sins' (Rubin, 1987: 64). The poor should know, it was said in the mid-twelfth century, 'that in alms they receive the sins of men, and also that they can reciprocate by offering prayers in return' (Rubin, 1987: 83). The pressure to give was heightened by the growing belief from the later twelfth century in purgatory as the place where most people would go, and suffer, after death. The length of time to be spent in purgatory, and the degree of suffering to be undergone, could be lessened by prayer: '[m]en of property were expected to give to the church and to the poor, during life and at death, both to justify their inequitable status in the social hierarchy and to buy prayers for their own souls' (Rosenthal, 1972: 8). Mary of Bassingbourn, for example, gave an endowment in 1301 to an Augustinian priory which had to maintain four regular canons to pray for Mary's soul and for the souls of her two husbands and her parents, but in addition she provided for an almshouse for seven poor and infirm men and for distributions of food to 1,000 poor people on three occasions every year (Rubin, 1987: 249).

If there was an obligation to give, it was also increasingly argued that it should be done with discrimination. Early systematic teachings of canon law, as illustrated by the Summa *'Elegantius in iure divino'* (c. 1169), asserted that

> In almsgiving there should be distinction between people. You had better give to your own than to strangers, to the sick rather than to the healthy, to ashamed rather than aggressive beggars, to the have-not rather than to him that has, and amongst the needy, first to the just and then to the unjust. That is ordered charity.
>
> *(Rubin, 1987: 70)*

The distinction between the deserving and the undeserving poor, with a long and unfinished history ahead of it, was in place. From the thirteenth century onwards there was particular merit, it was felt, in giving to the shame-faced poor, those who had fallen into poverty from previous comfort. The donor's motives, however, as much as the worthiness of the recipient, gave merit to an act of giving (Rubin, 1987).

The experience of Italian cities helps to capture the scale and reach of late medieval charity. It was 'chiefly intended for the respectable, the innocent, and the holy' (Pullan, 1988: 181). Hospital building had taken off in the twelfth and thirteenth centuries. By 1383, there were twenty-one in Genoa alone, some housing and caring for the elderly, others foundling hospitals for abandoned babies. Confraternities, perhaps best seen as mutual aid self-help organizations, began to proliferate in the fourteenth and fifteenth centuries. By 1521, Venice had at least 120 small confraternities and five large ones. In the middle years of the fifteenth century, cities began to build great hospitals, partly to bring some coherence and order to a charitable world where there were too many institutions with overlapping missions. They also began to develop the micro-credit schemes known as Monti di Pietà, making small loans to the worthy poor (Pullan, 1988).

Third stratum: The Middle Ages

The third stratum originated in the later Middle Ages and was dominant until the late nineteenth century. The socio-economic fact underlying it was the existence of poverty among a substantial proportion of the population. Finding that about one-third of the population of mid-eighteenth century Florence applied for public poor relief, a percentage similar to that in England, Peter Laslett (1988: 164) concluded that 'Everything points to the existence within European traditional societies of a sizeable block of the population looking to the collectivity to get by'. In famines or epidemics, one-third of the population might rise to half (Pullan, 1988: 178). Some of this poverty was of a kind prominently known to the Middle Ages: the poverty of the elderly, of widows, of the sick, of children. On top of this, there was poverty among men of working age. In face of the endemic problem of poverty, the belief that the poor were closer to Christ than the rich was less frequently voiced. On the contrary, it was their idleness, their fecklessness, their immorality, which impressed itself. Extensive poor relief strategies were adopted, and charity became inextricably bound up with them.

In the administration of poor relief, the distinction between private donations and state funding, so fundamental to modern thinking, made little sense. 'The mixed economy of welfare', the phrase widely used by historians to describe both the source of funding and the agency of control in poor relief measures, draws attention to the blurring of boundaries. In England, '[m]any private gifts and bequests were administered directly by local officials' (McIntosh, 1988: 212). The innovation in England at the beginning of the seventeenth century of taxing people to pay for poor relief was sometimes described as charity; the Poor Law and the Charitable Uses Act both, and not coincidentally, date from 1601. In Italy, the words for poor relief and charity were used interchangeably (Cavallo, 1998: 110). The Société Philanthropique de Bruxelles (1828) was founded by private initiative, subsidized by local government, and had the mayor of Brussels as its president (Dekker, 1998: 133–4). No one could say where the private ended and the public began.

Poor relief could be granted for a variety of reasons, some of them far from obviously philanthropic. Marco van Leeuwen (1994) has argued that there was a 'logic of charity'. On the part of elites, and the same might also be said of the bourgeoisie, poor relief could help to: regulate the labour market; stabilize the social order; avert turmoil; reduce the risk of infection; civilize the poor; affirm their own status; forward a career and a web of patronage; and promote one's own salvation. Sandra Cavallo (1991) has stressed, with special reference to Turin, that giving was often a way of deepening the ties of family and of patronage, and thereby of exercising power. There was nothing new in this. In fifteenth century Florence, 'charity and patronage became almost indistinguishable' (Henderson, 1994: 424). It was no accident that there was increasing emphasis on confining eligibility for charity to those born in a particular city. In the rituals that accompanied giving, there was a high quotient of symbolic action that reinforced a particular notion of social order, and giving was marked by much rivalry between institutions, social actors and power blocs. Need, in any kind of objective measurement, did not determine the level or direction of charity. The poor had to use a range of survival strategies, including pawning, migration, begging, prostitution, crime, revolt, formation of mutual societies and accepting poor relief; turning to charity was by no means the first avenue they explored, nor did it ever enjoy exclusive preference.

Charity, then, was a site where power was exercised and negotiated, the poor being the weaker party but not without some bargaining strength. The poor knew that they needed to adopt special forms of words and body language if they wanted help. Letters had to be written for entry to almshouses, a letter-writer perhaps employed to undertake the task. For example, a Joan Young, applying for admission to the almshouse at Bruton in Somerset, described herself as

> a very indigent disconsolate widow full of years and necessities almost blind and impotent unable to get a penny towards her subsistence widowed with nothing but misery and sadness [who] unless supported by the hand of charity will necessarily perish.
>
> *(Hindle, 2004: 160)*

It ticked the right boxes: moving and at the same time mildly threatening to those who might be tempted not to lift the hand of charity (Hindle, 2004: 160).

From around 1520, an international movement for welfare reform can be identified across Europe (Davis, 1987: 51–2). As part of this, and of fundamental importance, there was a decisive shift from charitable action initiated and controlled by the church to one where laymen were the dominant force. This did not mean that Christianity ceased to be a vital force in the world of charity, rather, that charity shifted its focus from giving to religious causes to attending to 'the secular needs of humanity', and that laymen were conspicuous in its funding and organization (Jordan, 1959: 17). As Cissie Fairchilds (1976: 21) has expressed it, 'the merchants of almost every major town in Western Europe began in the late fifteenth and early sixteenth centuries to establish new charities, which they, and not the Church, would control'. Brian Pullan (1988: 200), while stressing continuity from the past, has described this as a 'new philanthropy', the first of a number of 'new philanthropies'. The central text of this new approach was *De Subventione Pauperum*. Written in 1526 by the Spanish humanist Juan Luis Vives, this two-volume tract on the private and public relief of poverty was initially addressed to the Consuls and Senate of Bruges, but soon enjoyed Europe-wide renown. While Vives' argument for a stronger role for secular authorities in welfare reform challenged the authority of the Church, the tract simultaneously provided an acceptable theological grounding for his argument, as well as practical guidance on how to approach such reform (Spicker, 2010). For example, in the first chapter of his second volume Vives noted how 'The young children of the poor are villainously brought up, they [mothers] and their sons lying outside the churches or wandering round begging' (Cunningham, 2005: 116). The perceived solution to the problem was to place these children in institutions. Sometimes existing hospitals for poor or abandoned children were taken over and measures to improve discipline enacted, usually with the provision of education for the brighter ones. In due course, the boys might be apprenticed, and dowries paid for the girls. This was

Christian humanism in action, instilling discipline, offering the possibility of advancement, lay-controlled, but suffused with a religious ethos, whether Protestant or Catholic (Cunningham, 2005: 116–17).

This third stratum is often associated with the Protestant Reformation of the sixteenth century. In the historiography of philanthropy, the Protestant/Catholic divide was until the 1960s the focus of attention. Thereafter, social historians downplayed the divide, pointing to similar responses between Protestants and Catholics to what was seen as an extended economic and social crisis that pre-dated the Reformation. Recently, however, the distinctiveness, both of Protestant attitudes and actions and of Counter-Reformation responses, has been urged. Luther, it is argued, preceded Vives in proposing radical reforms in the administration of relief. He was particularly critical of Catholic mendicant orders and religious confraternities whose voluntary poverty displaced attention from the real poverty of the poor. Nuremberg and other towns in Germany had already poor relief reforms in place in the early 1520s. The attempt to eliminate begging and to make a clear distinction between the deserving and the undeserving all bear the mark of Protestant thinking and action (Grell, 1997: 45–9). Protestant thinking about the poor, moreover, spread rapidly across national boundaries, often carried by refugees. In London, the Dutch Reformed and other churches became 'not only a model for English Puritans, but were widely admired by those within the Church of England who had little sympathy for Calvinism' (Grell and Cunningham, 1997: 9).

In Protestant countries, the predominant catechism made it clear that good works did not contribute to salvation, but should be seen as a sign of thankfulness to God (Ben-Amos, 2008: 246–7). Sensitive to criticism that they had dismantled Catholic forms of charity, Protestants responded in part by their approach to giving, in part by ceremonies of extravagant praise for benefactors (Archer, 2002; Ben-Amos, 2008). For example, Jordan (1959: 250–1) celebrated the levels of giving in Protestant England up to 1660. Although his figures have subsequently been revised downwards, there is no denying the scale of giving, nor its focus on poor relief, either directly, or indirectly by promoting education or schemes of social rehabilitation; it amounted to at least three-quarters of all giving.

In Catholic countries, following the Council of Trent and the ideals of the Counter-Reformation it embodied, the lead was taken by the Church. Faced with very similar social problems to those in countries that had turned Protestant, numerous orders of monks and nuns set about the task of promoting public morality, of Christianizing the masses, and of distributing food to the deserving. Grell and Cunningham (2002: 3) have concluded that in the Reformation and Counter-Reformation

> The Northern, Protestant, countries came to be characterised by schemes predominantly initiated by local and central governments, while the southern, Catholic, parts of Europe in particular witnessed a reinvigoration of confessional institutions and the creation of new lay and clerical orders dedicated to the poor and the sick.

Early modern charity was proud to be in the public eye. It was urban and it was promoted as an adornment of any town or city. It was an inducement to the poor to migrate from the countryside – only England, with its parish-based poor law from the beginning of the seventeenth century, offered much help to the rural poor. Once the poor, and particularly their children, became inmates of institutions, they became enmeshed in a philanthropic world which was dependent for funds and reputation on public display. Funerals, certainly in Catholic countries, became the major sites of display. In Paris, the children of the key institutions were, as Ariès (1981: 165–8) put it, 'specialists in death'; in Castile, the Colleges of the Niños de la

Doctrina, which housed, clothed and fed poor boys, taught them reading and writing, and instructed them in Christianity, also required them to accompany funeral processions, their presence there, amongst other things, a means of raising money (Martz, 1983).

Fourth stratum: Associations

Over the course of the roughly 350 years (1520–1870) during which charity and poor relief were virtually coterminous, there emerged three distinctive new strata with a long life ahead of them. The first, our fourth stratum, originated in England in the late seventeenth and eighteenth centuries. Historians in the early twentieth century described what happened as 'associated philanthropy'. Instead of there being a multiplicity of individual one-off acts of giving, people came together to promote a cause they believed in: they formed societies, they funded themselves through annual subscriptions from members, the latter having the right to elect the governors of the charity; they published annual reports. These initiatives in organizational form bore a similarity to the contemporaneous development of financial institutions in the City of London, especially joint-stock companies. The causes they were drawn to in the late seventeenth century were the establishment of charity schools, the provision of employment, in part through the building of workhouses, and the formation of Societies for the Reformation of Manners. If, from one angle, they look like an outpouring of organized Christian zeal, from another they seem primarily concerned with social control. The same could be said of a key development of the eighteenth century: the establishment of hospitals. A concern for health had to fight for prominence against a range of other purposes, that it was thought a hospital could serve. These are neatly encapsulated in the title of a sermon delivered in 1746: 'Hospitals and Infirmaries Considered as Schools of Christian Education for the Adult Poor: and as a Means Conducive Towards a National Reformation in the Common Peoples' (Fissell, 1991: 84).

These new subscription charitable organizations can be seen as initiating what is now often described as the 'voluntary' or 'nonprofit' sector. The promoters of all these efforts were dominantly from the mercantile class, with men like Thomas Coram of Foundling Hospital fame and Jonas Hanway, being the mainspring behind many later initiatives. Retiring early from business, they devoted themselves to the public good. They received due recognition, Coram a portrait by Hogarth, Hanway a memorial in Westminster Abbey (Andrew, 1989). The new hospitals described themselves as 'voluntary'. They were carving out a role for themselves that was independent of both state and church, and they were run by unpaid volunteers. Even doctors who worked in them did so without receiving any fee, though the prestige and networking that accrued to them was often more than adequate compensation.

More importantly, the hospitals received no money directly from the state, though some from Poor Law Guardians who sent patients to them. They were, it can be argued, laying the foundations of 'civil society'.

Civil society was also evident in Hamburg where the establishment of the General Poor Relief in 1788 was the outcome of over twenty years of reforming effort. It reinvigorated the campaign against begging, it looked for ways to get paupers back into work, but above all it was marked by a recognition that, as Johann Georg Büsch (1801), a leading political theorist in late eighteenth century Germany, put it, 'the common man earns too little to live on' (cited in Lindemann, 2002: 138). A growing city like Hamburg, its population swollen by migrants whose livelihoods were dependent on the ups and downs of global trade, required, 'a restructuring of charity', 'a new type of philanthropy', one that was responsive to the need to get workers who fell ill back into work. Poor relief began to extend beyond paupers (Lindemann, 2002). The emphasis was on providing medical relief in the home with domiciliary visits to the poor by doctors and other volunteers, themselves inspired by humanitarianism and a service ethic. The ideas and practices generated in Hamburg spread to other German towns, and although the escalating expense led to much debate on the merits of the system, domiciliary visiting of the poor remained a crucial element of philanthropic action through the nineteenth century (Lindemann, 2002). Given powerful backing by French philanthropist and philosopher Joseph Marie de Gérando in his 1820 examination of charitable activity, *Le Visiteur du Pauvre*, it was 'adopted as the standard mould of nineteenth century voluntary charity' (Woolf, 1986: 104). Initiatives in one town soon spread. If Hamburg provided a template for a new philanthropy in the late eighteenth century, there were others equally prominent in the nineteenth century. Notable examples included the Scottish city of Glasgow under the reforming impact of Thomas Chalmers in the 1830s and 1840s, and the German town Elberfeld from the mid-century onwards. Both built on the Hamburg model, dividing up the city into welfare districts, emphasizing personal supervision of recipients and the removal of any right to relief.

Fifth stratum: Re-emergence of 'philanthropy'

The fifth stratum becomes identifiable towards the end of the eighteenth century: it ceases to be anachronistic to write about 'philanthropy'. Francis Bacon in the early seventeenth century had equated what 'the Grecians call *philanthropia* with 'goodness ... affecting of the weal of men', but the word only became widely used with the Enlightenment (Sulek, 2010: 194–5). Like the revolution to come, it was French, and it reflected a powerful strand of anti-clericalism in French society, a strong critique of existing charities, and an optimistic belief that in a well-ordered society human beings would throw off the chains, both physical and psychical, that restricted them. The background to it was a collapse in donations through wills to existing charities, and increasing socio-economic pressures (Jones, 1982). The foundation of the Société Philanthropique de Paris in 1780, though it had little impact in its first five years, was a landmark. In a 1787 manifesto, it declared that philanthropic activity was the main duty of a citizen (Duprat, 1993: 68). Hitherto, charitable giving had been incited by the belief that it was a duty incumbent on Christians. Now it became, as it remains, the mark of true citizenship. The Société Philanthropique was not a total break with the past, far from it: it became in the nineteenth century the repository of conservative attitudes. Nevertheless, this late eighteenth century moment effectively marks the beginning of 'philanthropy' as something which might be distinguished from 'charity'.

Philanthropy crossed the Channel from France to England in the 1780s. The first person in England to be described as a philanthropist was John Howard who toured, and reported on, prisons and similar institutions in Britain and Europe, urging reform. In 1786, he became 'John Howard, the philanthropist', seen as a lover of humankind, more famous for the 42,033 miles that he calculated he had traveled than for any money he might have given. It was in the 1780s, too, that Robert Young, long-resident in France, returned to his native England, and was there instrumental in founding the Philanthropic Society to reform young criminals or those in danger of becoming so. For many years, it looked as if philanthropy would be located on the left of the political spectrum. '[E]very philanthropist should be a reformer', wrote the Unitarian George Dyer (1795: 35–6), echoed by the historian Graham John Barker-Benfield (2003: 73) for whom 'from the latter eighteenth century, reform and philanthropy were nearly interchangeable'. Mutualist societies wore the philanthropic label. The Philanthropic Society of House Carpenters and Joiners in Newcastle in 1812, for example, was a mutual aid society, dedicated 'upon all just occasions to assist and support each other'. In 1818, the first attempt to form a union of all trades unions was called 'The Philanthropic Hercules' (Postgate, 1923: 19, 33).

This radicalism of philanthropy soon died away. Philanthropy began to align itself with the dominant social and economic ideology of the time, political economy. Political economists preached market solutions to social problems. They were above all concerned that wages should be determined by the market. Earning a living through wages was fundamental both to a successful economy and to personal morality. Charity in its old forms, political economists argued, undermined that, and political economists were hard to ignore. In England in 1824, one writer reflected on the impact that political economy had made:

> To convince the public, twenty or thirty years ago, of the goodness of a charity, it was sufficient to shew that the objects relieved were in a state of real distress.... But now, that the circumstances are more generally known, on which the condition of the labouring classes depends, all former reasonings on the subject of charity ... are invalidated.... The condition of the labouring classes with regard to the necessaries and comforts of life, is evidently determined by the rate of wages.
>
> *(Coats, 1973: 99)*

Nothing did more harm, it was said in 1815, than 'the misplaced benevolence of the charitable and humane' (Coats, 1973: 121).

This was an attack on charity and on that much-heralded eighteenth century virtue, 'benevolence'. In the 1820s, claims were made for 'philanthropy' as the means by which political economy could set bounds to unlimited charity. Teaching the poor 'the knowledge of the laws which regulate wages', it was said, '... depends in a great measure upon the exertions of enlightened philanthropists' (Coats, 1973: 113). Thirty years later, the message was still being drummed home: once the principles of political economy were firmly established, 'our kindly impulses ... will cast off the lazy shape of charity, and rise into the attitude and assume the garb of true philanthropy' (Coats, 1973: 88). Philanthropy and political economy, it seemed, were to be allies against 'the lazy shape of charity'. By the 1860s, however, there were mutterings about 'a misguided and sanguine philanthropy', about philanthropy being 'misdirected' (Coats, 1973: 454–5). Philanthropy seemed to be no better than the charity or benevolence from which it was trying to emancipate itself.

If nagging doubts had entered some parts of the philanthropic world by mid-century, other parts of it proclaimed confidence in what they were doing. Inheriting from the Enlightenment a belief in the transformative power of well-run institutions, they focused their attention on the young, and in particular on young males who seemed likely to go astray. Criminality and its prevention lay at the heart of much early philanthropy: in George Eliot's novel *Middlemarch: A Study of Provincial Life*, set in the 1830s, it is said of Mr. Casaubon that 'he doesn't care much about the philanthropic side of things; punishments, and that kind of thing' (Eliot, 1965: 77). It was a feature of this concern with crime and punishment that it was international in nature. The Philadelphia Society for Alleviating the Miseries of Public Prisons, formed in 1786, was closely linked through Benjamin Rush, Founding Father of the US, with people with similar concerns in England, notably the Quaker doctor and philanthropist, John Coakley Lettsom, and the aforementioned prison reformer John Howard. By personal correspondence, which then found its way into friendly newspapers, reformers on one side of the Atlantic kept themselves informed of initiatives on the other. The London Society for the Improvement of Prison Discipline, formed in 1816, was open about its indebtedness to Philadelphia. The men involved in these exchanges had wide interests, extending, for example, to opposition to slavery, and they were filled with enthusiasm for what Rush called 'the extension of the empire of humanity'. William Allen, another Quaker, was a central figure in these international networks, publishing

The Philanthropist, a periodical designed to 'stimulate to virtue and active benevolence' (Lloyd and Burgoyne, 1998).

This tradition of sharing experience and good practice was given a Continental European dimension with the foundation of the Rauhes Haus, or 'rough house', near Hamburg by Johann Hinrich Wichern in 1833. This was aimed at providing shelter and support for poor boys. The Rauhes Haus, in its turn, inspired the foundation in France in 1840 of the agrarian colony of Mettray, near Tours. Dutch, English and Belgian philanthropists flocked to Mettray and copied it. This 'philanthropic tourism' (Dekker, 1998), was a notable feature of philanthropy in the first half of the nineteenth century. Across Europe, though in different forms in different countries, there was 'a firm conviction that *their* nation could be transformed by means of philanthropy' (Dekker, 1998).

The degree of faith in the reforming potential of institutions is best exemplified in the building of asylums in the US after 1830. By 1850, there were twenty-seven public and private institutions caring for children in New York State. In the country as a whole, the seventy-seven private orphanages of 1851 had increased to 613 by 1880, with a further 474 founded over the ensuing twenty years. By then, there was a counter-blast to placing children in particular in what came to be described as 'barracks'. Americans coined the word 'institutionalized' to describe a child who was 'mechanical and helpless from the effect of asylum life' (Cunningham, 2005: 150). What followed in response were in part attempts to improve domestic institutions, to organise them on a smaller scale, but also in part a new major experiment in social engineering, the emigration of children from the environment of the city to the countryside, that countryside often being on the other side of the world: American East coast children were taken to the Mid-West, British children shipped to Canada and later to Australia (Cunningham, 2005: 148–52).

This belief, that children thrived only in the countryside, reflected another aspect of philanthropic change in the nineteenth century. Until then, it had been reasonably assumed that the prime purpose and function of philanthropy was to shift resources from the rich to the poor. By the middle of the nineteenth century, the target of philanthropy shifted from the poor to the town or city. Of course, the poor constituted a large part of the urban 'problem', but they were not the whole of it. Philanthropists began to think that they could best improve their societies by providing their cities with a civic infrastructure of public parks, art galleries, museums, concert halls and libraries. It was one of the attractions of this form of philanthropy that it escaped the censure of political economists; another that the benefactor's name often became attached to the donation. It was linked, too, to another novelty of nineteenth century philanthropy, an early example of what we now call 'social enterprise', the attempt to relieve housing problems by five percent philanthropy – an investment in building new apartment blocks for the respectable working class that would have the distinct attraction of bringing the donor a five percent return. This belief in the civilizing impact of cultural institutions, in his case libraries, reached its height in the work of the Scot who emigrated and made a fortune in the US, Andrew Carnegie.

In 1869, the English feminist, Josephine Butler, distinguished between feminine and masculine forms of philanthropy, the latter marked by 'large and comprehensive measures, organizations and systems planned by men and sanctioned by Parliament' (Simey, 1992: 78). If these masculine forms dominated publicity as they do much history, it was nevertheless the case that the distinctive feminine forms of philanthropy had profound social and political consequences. It was not simply that women vastly outnumbered men in charitable activity, important though that was: in 1893, it was estimated that half a million women in England worked 'continuously and semi-professionally' in philanthropy (Prochaska, 1980:224–5). Perhaps more significant in the long term, middle-class women found in philanthropy a space where they had a degree of autonomy and an ability to influence outcomes, creating what Kathleen McCarthy (2003) has described as 'parallel power structures' to those of men. In the US, the outcome was that welfare measures focused on the needs of women and children rather than, as in Europe, of men.

Sixth stratum: Global missionary philanthropy

If philanthropy at its outset was secular in outlook, this was not to last. Christians were soon attracted to the ambition and optimism that inspired philanthropy and brought their own distinctive approach to the aim of regenerating society. Whereas secular philanthropists predominantly focused their attention on home soil, evangelical Christians had the world in their sights: this forms the sixth stratum. There were earlier forerunners, not least in Latin America, but it was from the late eighteenth century onwards that 'global missionary philanthropy' (Twells, 2008) came close to being a reality. The long-standing sense that relief to the poor should be prioritized on those born and bred in the locality gave way, not without controversy, to a belief that there was both an opportunity and a duty to bring the benefits of Christianity and civilization to the 'heathen' overseas. Which should come first, Christianity or civilization, was much debated, but that the two were intimately connected was not in doubt. Missions gained a previously lacking legitimacy by adopting some of the optimistic language of the Enlightenment and of philanthropy: the Bible, according to a Dutch pamphlet of 1801, contained 'the true grounds and rules of civilization' and knowledge of it had to be spread by Protestant Europeans, 'the principal members of the great household of humanity' (van Eijnatten, 2000). In Britain, simultaneously forging an empire, the 1790s was an important decade: the Baptist Missionary Society sent a mission to India in 1792, the London Missionary Society set itself up in Tahiti, Tongatapu and Marquesas in 1796, and, by the end of the decade, the Methodists and the Church Missionary Society were in West Africa. The British initiative was soon taken up by Protestants in other countries, Americans, Germans, Danes, Swedes and Norwegians. The Roman Catholic Church, battered by the assaults on it in the French Revolution, was slower in the field, but by the 1830s was making its mark (Neill, 1986: 214, 335–8). It is arguable that Christian missions form no part of philanthropy, but the counter-argument, that out of funds that came primarily from the West, they were expanding education and health, as well as proselytizing, is a powerful one. Missions were 'diverting much of [Britain's] charity to religious causes overseas' (Porter, 1999: 244). In the twentieth century, particularly after the Second World War, secular versions of global philanthropy set themselves up alongside the missionary ones.

Seventh stratum: Philanthropy as gap filler

A seventh stratum in the history of philanthropy surfaced in the later nineteenth century, eventually disconnecting the intimacy of the link between philanthropy and poor relief. The state, it began to be argued with increasing force, was better placed than philanthropy to resolve the social and cultural problems that beset so many lives. If philanthropy in the nineteenth century had to pitch itself in relation to political economy, by the twentieth century, it was doing so also in relation to the state. In the nineteenth century, the mixed economy of welfare had allowed a growth of both state and philanthropic initiatives. Neither was without criticism, what the British called 'grand-motherly legislation' as much as philanthropy. What was new by the end of the century was that the state was poised to intrude into areas that had hitherto been the preserve of philanthropy. Philanthropy, it was argued, was patchy in its coverage, condescending in its attitudes and with insufficient resources for the scale of the problems thrown up by urban and industrial society. Many rejected it on democratic and socialist grounds. If the political economists who had so scared philanthropists can be seen as on the right of the political spectrum, those who championed the role of the state were on the left. A pincer movement was strangling philanthropy, or at least many forms of it.

The intrusion of the state deeply worried many who were closely engaged in the relief of poverty. In retrospect, however, the emergence of a new way of coping with poverty was as striking as the expanding role of the state. Across the western world, there spread an understanding of the circumstances that produced poverty and of a means of diminishing it. The risks associated with stages of the life cycle, unemployment and ill-health could be calculated, insurance could be taken out to mitigate them. Legislation often made insurance compulsary. Who paid for the insurance differed widely, but normally employees, employers and the state all contributed.

The outcome was that philanthropy as the solution to poverty was seen as playing a role secondary to, and separate from, the state. The public/private divide, impossible to disentangle for most of philanthropy's centuries, now came to be thought of central importance. Philanthropy might pioneer new approaches for the state later to adopt, it might try to fill the gaps which the state did not cover, it might, and increasingly did, run services on behalf of, and financed by, the state, but it was not, and no longer aspired to be, the lead actor. Some people began to ask whether it had any future role. Others, like Elizabeth Macadam in Britain (1934), talked up a 'new philanthropy' consisting of a partnership between statutory and voluntary services. The history of philanthropy was written as a prelude to the history of the welfare state, a perhaps well-meaning but insufficient attempt to cope with social problems that were beyond its capacity. This was largely a European discussion and diagnosis.

Eight stratum: Big philanthropic foundations

Across the Atlantic, fueled by vast fortunes, a new kind of philanthropy was born, an eighth stratum. It was the age of foundations (Leat, Chapter 18; Harrow et al., Chapter 19), established, in the words of one of them 'for the improvement of mankind'. The Carnegie, John D. Rockefeller Sr., the John D. Rockefeller Jr., the Edward Harkness, the Russell Sage Foundations were all founded in the early twentieth century, all aiming, as Frederick Gates, Rockefeller Sr.'s advisor, put it, on giving wholesale, not retail (Sealander, 2003: 221). Emancipated by their wholesale approach from having to grapple with individual poverty, or indeed with poverty at all, they were free to aim at the eradication of disease or the improvement of agricultural yields. There were 27 foundations in the US by 1915, over 200 by 1930 (Zunz, 2011: 22). Linking up with progressive reformers, they believed that the solution to deep-rooted problems lay in science and research, not in giving directly to the poor. The beneficiaries of their largesse were likely to be universities and research institutes, especially in the social sciences.

Ninth stratum: 'New' philanthropy

The ninth and final stratum in the history of philanthropy to date emerged with the criticism of welfare states that started in the 1970s and grew with exponential speed from the 1980s onwards. It coincided with a marked increase in inequality, and in the relative wealth of the very rich. High taxation levels disappeared as entrepreneurs argued that they were a disincentive to investment, risk-taking and hard work. The resulting superfluity of ready money in the pockets of high net worth (HNW) individuals gave a new confidence to philanthropists that they had a role to play and the money with which to play it. Another 'new philanthropy' was born. Some of its propagandists, lauding 'philanthrocapitalism', saw it as capable of solving the world's most deep-rooted problems, a happy marriage of capitalism's efficiency and entrepreneurship applied to disease and poverty, to higher education and the arts (Bishop and Green, 2008).

Concluding remarks

The history of philanthropy has too often been written in an either/or way. Either as something to celebrate and take inspiration from, or as a cautionary tale of man's – and it is almost entirely reported as a male story – over-optimistic hopes of what could be achieved, not unmixed with a degree of vanity and self-promotion. A geological approach helps to free us from the either/or approach. It suggests that strata laid down centuries ago still work their influence; it draws attention to the ways in which philanthropy is constantly claiming novelty, while often only reverting to old models and ways of thinking. Its history is as much circular and repetitive as progressive and linear, not least because there is only a limited number of ways of trying to resolve poverty and the problems associated with it, and they are likely to recur, or run alongside each other. How do you distinguish between the deserving and undeserving? Can residential institutions help people or do they simply institutionalize them?

A geological approach highlights the indeterminate boundaries of philanthropy. The word itself gained currency only in the late eighteenth century, and what it signified changed considerably in the period since then, and has never been fixed. The nine strata I have identified could be extended. I have written nothing about giving by the poor to the poor which, it was widely attested in the nineteenth century, was much more significant than that of the rich to the poor (Prochaska, 1980: 42–3). I have not explored the interrelations between philanthropic imperatives and religious beliefs occurring within, and impacting upon, the West which are derived from faiths other than Christianity (Robbins, 2006; Singer, 2013). Nor have I elaborated on what Zunz (2011) calls 'mass philanthropy', represented by March of the Dimes in the US, small giving by the mass of the population. All these different strata, however, have one thing in common: they are all forms of gift relationships that continue to exert influence in numerous ways and across different contexts on the sometimes contentious and sometimes contended understandings of philanthropy in the West.

Notes

An earlier version of this chapter was presented as an Occasional Paper at the Centre for Charitable Giving and Philanthropy (CGAP), Cass Business School, City University London.

References

Andrew, D. T. (1989) *Philanthropy and Police: London Charity in the Eighteenth Century*, Princeton, NJ: Princeton University Press.

Archer, I. W. (2002) 'The Charity of Early Modern London,' *Transactions of the Royal Historical Society*, 12: 223–44.

Ariès, P. (1981) *The Hour of our Death*, London: Allen Lane.

Aristotle (2000) *The Nicomachean Ethics*, translated and edited by Roger Crisp, Cambridge: Cambridge University Press.

Barker-Benfield, G. J. (2003) 'The Origins of Anglo-American Sensibility,' in L. J. Friedman and M. D. McGarvie (eds.) *Charity, Philanthropy and Civility in American History*, Cambridge: Cambridge University Press, 71–89.

Ben-Amos, I. K. (2008) *The Culture of Giving: Informal Support and Gift Exchange in Early Modern England*, Cambridge: Cambridge University Press.

Bishop, M. and Green, M. (2008) *Philanthrocapitalism: How the Rich Can Save the World and Why We Should Let Them*, London: A & C Black.

Cavallo, S. (1991) 'The Motivations of Benefactors: An Overview of Approaches to the Study of Charity,' in J. Barry and C. Jones (eds.) *Medicine and Charity Before the Welfare State*, London: Routledge, 46–62.

Cavallo, S. (1998) 'Charity as Boundary Making: Social Stratification, Gender and the Family in the Italian States (Seventeenth-Nineteenth Centuries),' in H. Cunningham and J. Innes (eds.) *Charity, Philanthropy and Reform From the 1690s to 1850*, Basingstoke: Macmillan, 108–29.

Coats, A. W. (ed.) (1973) *Poverty in the Victorian Age*, Vol. III, Charity, Farnborough: Gregg International Publishers.

Cunningham, H. (2005) *Children and Childhood in Western Society Since 1500*, Harlow: Longman.

Davis, N. Z. (1987) *Society and Culture in Early Modern France*, Cambridge: Polity.

Dekker, J. J. H. (1998) 'Transforming the Nation and the Child: Philanthropy in the Netherlands, Belgium, France and England, c. 1780–c.1850,' in H. Cunningham and J. Innes (eds.) *Charity, Philanthropy and Reform from the 1690s to 1850*, Basingstoke: Macmillan, 130–47.

Duprat, C. (1993) *Le Temps des Philanthropes*, Tome 1, Paris: Éditions du C. T. H. S.

Dyer, G. (1795) *A Dissertation on the Theory and Practice of Benevolence*, London, 1795.

Eliot, G. (1965) *Middlemarch*, Harmondsworth: Penguin.

Fairchilds, C. C. (1976) *Poverty and Charity in Aix-en-Provence 1640–1789*, Baltimore: Johns Hopkins University Press.

Finn, R. (2006) *Almsgiving in the Later Roman Empire: Christian Promotion and Practice 313–450*, Oxford: Oxford University Press.

Fissell, M. E. (1991) *Patients, Power, and the Poor in Eighteenth-Century Britain*, Cambridge: Cambridge University Press.

Grell, O. P. (1997) 'The Protestant Imperative of Christian Care and Neighbourly Love,' in O. P. Grell and A. Cunningham (eds.) *Health Care and Poor Relief in Protestant Europe 1500–1700*, London: Routledge, 43–65.

Grell, O. P. and Cunningham, A. (1997) 'The Reformation and Changes in Welfare Provision in Early Modern Northern Europe,' in O. P. Grell and A. Cunningham (eds.) *Health Care and Poor Relief in Protestant Europe 1500–1700*, London: Routledge, 1–42.

——. (2002) 'Health Care and Poor Relief in 18th and 19th Century Northern Europe,' in O. P. Grell, A. Cunningham, and R. Jütte (eds.) *Health Care and Poor Relief in 18th and 19th Century Northern Europe*, Aldershot: Ashgate, 3–14.

Hands, A. R. (1968) *Charities and Social Aid in Greece and Rome*, London: Thames and Hudson.

Henderson, J. (1994) *Piety and Charity in Late Medieval Florence*, Oxford: Clarendon Press.

Hindle, S. (2004) *On the Parish? The Micro-Politics of Poor Relief in Rural England c. 1550–1750*, Oxford: Clarendon Press.

Jones, C. (1982) *Charity and Bienfaisance: The Treatment of the Poor in the Montpellier Region 1740–1815*, Cambridge: Cambridge University Press.

Jordan, W. K. (1959) *Philanthropy in England 1480–1660*, London: George Allen & Unwin.

Kidd, A. J. (1996) 'Philanthropy and the "Social History Paradigm",' *Social History*, 21(2): 180–92.

Laslett, P. (1988) 'Family, Kinship and Collectivity as Systems of Support in Pre-Industrial Europe: A Consideration of the "Nuclear-Hardship" Hypothesis,' *Continuity and Change*, 3(2): 153–75.

Lindemann, M. (2002) 'Urban Charity and the Relief of the Sick Poor in Northern Germany, 1750–1850,' in O. P. Grell, A. Cunningham, and R. Jütte (eds.) *Health Care and Poor Relief in 18th and 19th Century Northern Europe*, Aldershot: Ashgate, 136–54.

Lloyd, K. and Burgoyne, C. (1998) 'The Evolution of a Transatlantic Debate on Penal Reform, 1780–1830,' in H. Cunningham and J. Innes (eds.) *Charity, Philanthropy and Reform From the 1690s to 1850*, Basingstoke: Macmillan, 208–27.

Macadam, E. (1934) *The New Philanthropy: A Study of the Relation Between the Statutory and Voluntary Social Services*, London: George Allen & Unwin.

McCarthy, K. D. (2003) 'Women and Political Culture,' in L. J. Friedman and M. D. McGarvie (eds.) *Charity, Philanthropy and Civility in American History*, Cambridge: Cambridge University Press, 179–97.

McIntosh, M. K. (1988) 'Local responses to the poor in late medieval and Tudor England,' *Continuity and Change*, 3(2): 209–45.

Martz, L. (1983) *Poverty and Welfare in Habsburg Spain: The Example of Toledo*, Cambridge: Cambridge University Press.

Neill, S. (1986) *A History of Christian Missions*, London: Penguin.

Porter, A. (1999) 'Religion, Missionary Enthusiasm, and Empire,' in A. Porter (ed.) *The Oxford History of the British Empire, Vol. III. The Nineteenth Century*, Oxford: Oxford University Press, 222–46.

Postgate, R. (1923) *The Builders' History*, London: The National Federation of Building Trade Operatives.

Prochaska, F. K. (1980) *Women and Philanthropy in Nineteenth-Century England*, Oxford: Clarendon Press.

Pullan, B. (1988) 'Support and Redeem: Charity and Poor Relief in Italian Cities from the Fourteenth to the Seventeenth Century,' *Continuity and Change*, 3(2), 177–208.

Robbins, K. C. (2006) 'The Nonprofit Sector in Historical Perspective,' in R. Steinberg and W. W. Powell, *The Nonprofit Sector: A Research Handbook*, Yale: Yale University Press, 13–31.

Rosenthal, J. T. (1972) *The Purchase of Paradise*, London: Routledge & Kegan Paul.

Rubin, M. (1987) *Charity and Community in Medieval Cambridge*, Cambridge: Cambridge University Press.

Sealander, J. (2003) 'Curing Evils at Their Source: The Arrival of Scientific Giving,' in L. J. Friedman and M. D. McGarvie (eds.) *Charity, Philanthropy and Civility in American History*, Cambridge: Cambridge University Press, 217–39.

Singer. A. (2013) 'Giving Practices in Islamic Societies,' *Social Research: An International Quarterly*, 80(2), 341–58.

Simey, M. (1992) *Charity Rediscovered: A Study of Philanthropic Effort in Nineteenth-Century Liverpool*, Liverpool: Liverpool University Press.

Spicker, P. (ed.) (2010) *The Origins of Modern Welfare Reform*, Oxford: Peter Lang.

Sulek, M. (2010) 'On the Modern Meaning of Philanthropy,' *Nonprofit and Voluntary Sector Quarterly*, 39(2): 193–212.

Twells, A. (2008) *The Civilising Mission and the English Middle Class, 1792–1850: The "Heathen" at Home and Overseas*, Basingstoke: Palgrave Macmillan.

van Eijnatten, J. (2000) 'Civilizing the Kingdom: Missionary Objectives and the Dutch Public Sphere around 1800,' in P. N. Holtrop and H. McLeod (eds.) *Missions and Missionaries*, Woodbridge: The Boydell Press, 65–80.

van Leeuwen, M. H. D. (1994) 'Logic of Charity: Poor Relief in Preindustrial Europe,' *Journal of Interdisciplinary History*, xxiv(4): 589–613.

Woolf, S. (1986) *The Poor in Western Europe in the Eighteenth and Nineteenth Centuries*, London: Methuen.

Zunz, O. (2011) *Philanthropy in America: A History*, Princeton: Princeton University Press.

3

Approaching philanthropy from a social theory perspective

Frank Adloff

Why do we give? This question points to the human capacity to give in general, as well as to the reasons, conditions, and motives for giving in different societal and historical contexts. To explore possible answers, this chapter examines philanthropy through a social theory lens. Moving from the micro to the macro level, the chapter begins with examining predominant theories of giving and discusses how an interactionist approach, and a stronger focus on emotions, can overcome some of the shortcomings of traditional perspectives. After highlighting the importance of organization and structure for philanthropy, the chapter draws on insights from Germany and the US to provide a historical-comparative perspective on philanthropic foundations and the wider socio–cultural contexts within which philanthropy has developed. The chapter concludes with some critical reflections on the state of theorizing about, and within, philanthropy.

Before setting out, it is important to clarify that throughout this chapter philanthropy is perceived broadly, as covering selfless, pro-social forms of action in which an actor A gives something, a gift, to another actor B free of charge (Boulding, 1981). Actor A incurs costs; actor B benefits. A key aspect of this definition is that it does not insist on philanthropic or altruistic motives, thus avoiding the tautology of automatically attributing altruistic actions, that is actions that benefit others, to altruistic motives.

The Micro Level

Most of the literature on philanthropy dichotomizes possible motives for charitable giving into theories that view voluntary giving of money as an altruistic act, and into approaches defining it as self-serving (Halfpenny, 1999). The latter, individualist-utilitarian position, explains society in terms of concurrent actions of self-interested actors; the former, normativist social theory perspective, focuses on powerful supra-individual values and the norms to which individuals adhere. This theoretical divide has had a major impact on the social sciences. Featuring already in paradigmatic form in the writings of Thomas Hobbes and Jean Jacques Rousseau, it has remained essentially unchanged. As a consequence, twentieth century sociology entered into what might be called a division of labour with economics: the latter examines economic action on the basis of rationalist and individualist models, while much of sociology pursues a collectivist and normativist approach to the non-economic domain of society. This theoretical dichotomy, however, appears to lead to intellectual stalemate rather than theoretical or empirical advancement.

Economic theory, rational choice and self-serving actors

Based on the idea of maximizing utility, theories of rational choice assume that an actor is selfish: he or she cannot make a donation without receiving something in return (Blau, 1964; Kolm, 2000). If one assumes that charitable giving makes no sense in economic terms, that it always involves greater expenditure than income, then such behaviour would have to be considered non-rational, and hence beyond the remit of neoclassical economic theory. Since economists have considered this to be unsatisfactory, the usual way to overcome this dilemma has been to broaden the theoretical definition of 'utility'. This is either done by quasi-empirical claims that helping others procures psychological rewards for the giver, or by integrating third-party utility into the giver's own utility in purely formal terms, making such altruistic behaviour part of the giver's utility function, i.e. integrating it in the conceptualization of the desirability of different actions, goods and services to the giver and the perceived benefits they provide.

The problems with this approach are obvious: if one acknowledges the existence of non-rational action, one drastically restricts the explanatory scope of economic models. If the concept of utility is generously broadened, the theory becomes too general and potentially tautologous. If all actions serve the maximization of utility, where utility may consist of income, prestige, moral integrity, altruistic self-sacrifice, or whatever else, then the theory is no longer capable of falsifying distinctions: it is always both true and meaningless (Etzioni, 1988). It thus appears questionable whether philanthropy can be described, analytically or empirically, in terms of the model of self-interested and rational action: charitable giving, donations and philanthropic foundations all have characteristics that cannot be explained in economic terms. In an economic sense at least, the actors derive no clear, unambiguous benefit from charitable giving or making donations.

It is therefore striking that current economic theory takes the existence of pro-social motives, like fairness and reciprocity, as well as negative, 'irrational', motives, like revenge, seriously. Experimental economy, an emerging school of thought that utilizes experiments to explore economic questions, uses game theory to study the existence of such forms of behaviour and to examine social preferences in standardized test settings (Fehr and Gächter, 2000; Fehr and Fischbacher, 2003; Safin et al., 2015). In doing so, it departs from the utility-based paradigm of neoclassical economy and moves towards classical sociological models that have always empha-sized the independent influence of values and norms on human action (Parsons, 1937). Beyond this, however, the question of the formation and evolution of preferences and meta-preferences (Taylor, 1985) remains open in economic theory. Preferences appear only as something given, as revealed preferences. In the light of these objections, it thus seems useful to take a closer look at social psychological and sociological models that do not follow the utilitarian paradigm.

Sociology, altruism and socialized norms

Given that being philanthropic is not a general requirement, that it involves economic sacrifices, and that philanthropic organizations may do more than what is legally required of them, the last couple of decades have seen a rediscovery of the long forgotten concept of altruism: the 'self-lessness' of the altruist being the opposite to the 'self-interest' of the egoist. Altruism, as a term and concept, was introduced into the emerging discipline of sociology in the mid-nineteenth century by Auguste Comte and then developed further by Emile Durkheim. Thereafter, the concept disappeared almost totally from academic discourse. It has only been since the 1970s that the idea has undergone a renaissance. This has been driven by three developments: the growing research interest in the motives and social backgrounds of 'rescuers', with its strong focus on people who saved others during the Holocaust (Oliner and Oliner, 1988); the idea of 'situational altruism' in the context of bystander research (Brewster and Tucker, 2015); and a focus on understanding 'pure gifts' in the form of voluntary donations of blood to anonymous third parties (Niza et al., 2013). The latter, which can be traced back to the studies conducted by Titmuss (1997) on blood donation practices in Britain and the US, has exerted a particularly strong influence on research into charitable giving, foundations and the non-profit sector. A common objection to any altruism research is that altruistic behaviour leads to a positive self-image and other positive feelings towards oneself and is thus not free of egoism. It is, however, doubtful that such a consequence of altruistic behaviour also motivates such behaviour (Simmons, 1991).

What then constitutes altruism? A relatively narrow and useful definition is provided by Monroe (1994: 862), who defines altruism 'as behavior intended to benefit another, even when doing so may risk or entail some sacrifice to the welfare of the actor'. The emphasis here is on sacrifice, on a reduction in the extent of one's own welfare to the benefit of third parties. Most of the research into altruists who fulfil the requirement of self-sacrifice is based on developmental or social psychology and draws on the work of Piaget (1932) and Kohlberg (1984) and focuses either on the phases of moral development or on analyzing socialization processes to find out what makes the altruist an altruist. The question asked in these contexts is whether there is such a thing as an altruistic personality, or whether altruistic actions come about as a result of specific situations (Piliavin and Charng, 1990: 29). Findings from psychology indicate that personality traits distinguishing altruists from non-altruists do exist. On average, for example, altruists tend to display more confidence in others (Piliavin and Charng, 1990: 33) than non-altruists. In general, however, any such distinguishing personality traits tend not to be strongly developed. In one social psychology study (Lee et al., 1999), just over 1,000 people were asked about their intentions to give to charity. The result was that past charitable giving and the giver's own role identity – measured according to the statement 'blood/money/time donation is an important part of who I am' (Lee et al., 1999: 281) – are the most important factors in generating an intention to give, although role models and interiorized norms can also play a significant part.

In recent years, the literature on altruism has been enriched by studies from evolutionary anthropology and primate research. This body of work indicates that donations that were not requested by the recipient, and that do not generate any benefit for the giver, are generally not found amongst primates. Other than with the exception of chimpanzees, who at times do display behavioural patterns that closely resemble this model, the predominant form of behaviour found amongst primates is reciprocal altruism, i.e. behaviour from which both parties benefit. As explanation for human altruism, however, reciprocal and kin altruism appear to be insufficient. First of all, evidence from evolutionary theory (Gintis et al., 2003; Bowles, 2006) indicates that human beings are more altruistic than primates because they are at the same time more warlike. Hostility to group outsiders and altruism seem to have relied on each other in the late Pleistocene. A second proposed differentiating factor between human and primate altruism is that humans are more capable of understanding the intentions of other people and seeing things from another's perspective (Tomasello, 1999). As a result, humans are perceived as possessing a greater capacity for empathy, resulting in so-called shared intentions, that is we pursue joint projects with a common aim. This also explains humans' greater sense of cooperation and fairness as compared with that shown by primates during experiments in captivity and observations in the wild. A third factor has been proposed by the American developmental psychologist Michael Tomasello (2009) who speaks of a natural, i.e. biological, human tendency towards altruism: barely socialized infants aged between one and three already show themselves to be very helpful and cooperative, and their motivation is intrinsic. This almost unreserved willingness to cooperate changes in the course of their ongoing socialization, shifting towards expectations of being rewarded for help or towards adaptation to the norms governing behaviour within their group.

This transition, from 'natural altruism' to a 'socialized state' based on group norms, brings us back to a sociology of charitable giving that enquires into the specific forms, functions, motives and consequences of such behaviour in modern societies. Consequently, there does not appear to be a need to further pursue the discussion surrounding altruism: provided the chosen definition is not overly broad, it is clear that not everyone who makes donations or engages in other kinds of charitable activity is a genuine altruist. Neither theories of self-interest nor theories of altruism provide a satisfactory answer to the question of the specific situational motives for charitable giving or the functioning and institutional conditions of the modern gift economy. Such a focus prominently fails to discuss issues around emotional identification, an idea central to interactionist theories. These try to provide an alternative approach that moves from attributing the act of giving to one or more motives, towards overcoming the dichotomy itself.

Interactionist perspectives on giving

Charitable giving and donations are usually not one-off acts. Instead, giving is socially embedded and frequently prompts a counter-gift. As such, it seems useful to pay attention to theories of interaction and reciprocity. As Marcel Mauss (1990) pointed out in his famous study on the function of gifts and reciprocity in archaic societies: giving, taking and reciprocating form a three-part cycle of actions. Pre-modern forms of giving, taking and reciprocating are the basic collective activities through which such societies reproduce themselves. Mauss emphasizes that reciprocal offering of gifts with the aim of establishing relationships rests simultaneously on voluntary and obligating aspects of giving, taking and giving back. Recent anthropological research has also shown that reciprocal behaviour is a universal feature of human cultures on the one hand, and that, on the other hand, there is a huge cultural and historical variety of interpretations as to what constitutes generosity and reciprocity (Caillé, 2000; Henrich et al., 2005). Therefore, if we wish to explain philanthropic behaviour, we first need a theory of cognitive and emotional identification. Such a model is based on the seemingly trivial insight that donors and creators of foundations often feel connected to other people, to their concerns or problems, either considering themselves as having a link and a duty to specific groups, or even being involved with these groups on a practical level through formal and informal networks.

The readiness to make donations and to become involved in charitable activities clearly depends on empathy and identification of, and with, the needs and sufferings of others. Such identification, referred to by social psychologist George Herbert Mead (1934) as role taking, i.e. the ability to put oneself in another's place, gives rise to an attitude of obligation: it is as if one was addressing oneself and taking on another person's ideas, interests, needs or feelings (Mead, 1930). This capacity for cognitive and emotional role taking, and the resulting feelings of obligation, develop in interactive contexts, primarily in close-knit social relations of care, family, friendship and community. As adults, we mostly participate in networks of social commitment because we are either motivated by people we know personally, or we are recruited and encourage by organizational networks, i.e. solicited. Once such commitments or a social network have been entered into, the related attitudes and motivations are reinforced. This means, that in the case of philanthropy, philanthropy is not constituted by individuals making altruistic decisions on their own. Instead, it implies that group processes give rise to civic identities whose influence can spread to larger contexts: interactions, groups and organizations thus 'create' philanthropy, civic altruism, and adherence to values based on identification.

It would, however, be naive to assume that such relations of interaction automatically lead to an increase in role taking and result in donations to strangers with whom the giver has no initial connection. Charitable giving to strangers, such as in cases of famine or disasters (Kapucu, Chapter 11), usually only becomes possible when a cognitive or emotional social connection to those people is established (Godbout and Caillé, 1998). In our globalized world, the media plays a major part in this process (Wenzel and Scholz, 2010); it is only through the media that we become aware of the need for such donations (Bekkers and Wiepking, 2011). While we still know far too little about what prompts us to identify with some people and not with others, questions of identity appear to play a central role: who are we when we make donations, with whom do we feel a connection?

Most donations are primarily self-referential and self-serving in that they benefit the structures and organizations with which one is directly or indirectly involved. As such, giving is accompanied by both taking and relations of more or less balanced or generalised reciprocity (Sahlins, 1972; Adloff, 2009): one gives and receives something in return. Donations to religious communities, schools and cultural institutions, for example, often have a self-serving dimension as they support organizations that are of direct benefit to the giver (Schervish and Ostrander, 1990; Schervish, 2000). Finally, there are status-related, publicly staged donations, such as charity galas and similar events, not only to display one's status but above all to legitimize it. It is well known, for example, that within a US context it is important to engage in regular acts of philanthropy in order to qualify as a legitimate member of the 'good society'. The attainment of reputation is thus another important motive for charitable giving (Collins and Hickman, 1991; Bekkers and Wiepking, 2011; Gordon et al., Chapter 21).

More indirect, and not so closely linked to expectations of reciprocity, on the other hand, are donations to organizations which then pass them on to groups further removed within society. Charities that collect donations usually take these differences in the giver's relationship to the meaning and purpose of his/her donation into consideration: they may offer moral gratification and public recognition, or involvement in decision-making processes, such as seats on advisory boards. When the interests and identificatory values of all parties involved in the process of social exchange, of giving and taking, coincide, when direct or indirect reciprocities take effect, this should increase the chances of a donation being made.

From cognition to emotions: Empathy and sympathy

While all of this appears as a useful starting point for understanding philanthropy, the literature on identification and charitable giving reveals a cognitivist bias. This is a prominent concern with both sociological theories and Mead's model of role taking. It therefore appears useful to construct processes of identification in a broader way. As Charles Horton Cooley (1902: 152) already pointed out in his notion of the 'looking glass self', adopting another person's point of view is always also an evaluative process: 'I assess myself as another sees me'. This, in turn, is associated with specific emotions. According to Cooley and many sociological theories of emotions (including Theodore Kemper, Jonathan Turner, Randall Collins and

Thomas Scheff), the emotions triggered by such evaluative role taking are pride and shame: pride in the case of positive self-evaluation, shame in the case of disdain and low esteem (Turner and Stets, 2006a).

Another question that arises is whether emotional comprehension and concurrence might also be necessary, or at least helpful, in the first step towards role taking, i.e. empathy. Empathy, too, is not purely cognitive: we can share and empathize with the emotional state of another person, or we can react emotionally to the emotions we perceive in another person. In this way, empathy can result either in sympathy or, if the suffering perceived in the other person seems unpleasant and frightening, in a situation of personal stress (Davis, 2006). When empathy finds expression as sympathy, it can engender action. In doing so, it follows a set of sequences based on specific emotional rules (Schmitt and Clark, 2006). For example, according to Western emotional norms, not everyone is entitled to sympathy: the ideal recipient of sympathy is simply the victim of bad luck and not responsible for any suffering in question. Particularly vulnerable individuals, like children, the elderly and the infirm, attract our sympathy (Cunningham, Chapter 2). This, in turn, has given rise to a sympathy market: sympathy entrepreneurs in the form of aid organizations use mass media to let the public know who merits sympathy; trustworthy sympathy brokers such as prominent public figures present the suffering group as being worthy of sympathy. This socio-emotional gift economy is meant to flow both ways: in most cases, one expects at least gratitude for a display of sympathy and a donation of support. If the help required is too arduous, futile, or not appreciated, then the tendency to feel sympathy quickly fades. An expectation of help that is too clearly formulated can also seriously interfere with the giver's voluntary transfer of sympathy, leading to negative reactions.

A central and fundamental motive for human actions is the protection and affirmation of one's own identity (Turner, 1987); the principal goal is to maintain ontological security and to deflect anxiety. If this succeeds, interactions elicit positive emotions; failure brings negative emotions such as fear, guilt, shame and anger. If one refuses to help, or behaves immorally, one's own moral identity is at stake. The resulting feelings of guilt and shame are particularly painful: either these are dissolved by means of moral actions, or they are pushed aside by defence mechanisms. Guilt does not preclude role taking, sympathy and help (Turner and Stets, 2006b). However, once a certain level of guilt is reached, defence mechanisms are to be reckoned with. Projection, displacement and attribution are frequent examples. In sociological terms, negative attribution, i.e. the externalization of negative emotions onto other social and cultural groups, is the most important defence mechanism (in turn preventing the provision of help). A specific instance of this would be the view that victims of an accident are in fact themselves to blame. Successful provision of aid, then, depends on a balanced system of: self-critical emotions such as guilt and shame; critical emotions directed towards others such as rage and anger; feelings relating to the suffering of others such as empathy and sympathy; and finally, emotions reflecting recognition of others such as gratitude and respect (Turner and Stets, 2006b).

This process of charitable giving points to a highly complex system of emotions and of cultural feeling rules (Hochschild, 1979) that either facilitate the process in a regulatory capacity or, in the case of imbalances, cause it to fail. Feelings of guilt and shame can play a positive role in the genesis of pro-social forms of action. If such feelings are not acknowledged, however, then such pro-social behaviour does not occur: examples include situations of public begging in cities, dramatically emotionalized calls for donations, or suffering individuals who appear too closely associated with one's own life situation. Acts of charitable giving clearly require a sufficient closeness to the recipient at the same time as a certain distance to protect against negative emotions.

The Meso Level

Fundraising and institutionalized philanthropy

Intermediary structures and organizations play an important role in explaining various forms of charitable giving. The requesting and raising of funds forms a separate behavioural category in addition to Mauss' cycle of giving, taking and reciprocating. From an institutional perspective, it can be argued that fundraising is an institutional and organizational precondition for personal giving. It provides: specific knowledge of potential needs for donations; knowledge of the organizations that collect donations; and the possibility of entering into contact with these organizations on a trust basis.

Although fundraising has only come to public attention in recent decades as a result of a tendency towards increased professionalization, it is an old social technique. For Europe, the roots of fundraising certainly lie in the religious domain. While believers in Greek and Roman times were already called on to make religious donations, the practice was perfected by Christians: while St Paul already collected donations for the community in Jerusalem, the golden age of church fundraising occurred in the Middle Ages, beginning in the twelfth century, where the amassed funds were used for a variety of purposes, such as the construction of churches and monasteries, funding religious orders and crusades, for bridge- and road-building, as well as for establishing and running various institutions and universities (Neuhoff, 2003; Cunningham, Chapter 2).

The underlying aim of fundraising is to: publicize a specific, historically variable, charitable cause; raise awareness of the issues involved; and, to stimulate focused readiness to provide aid, ideally leading to ongoing ties or support such as membership, regular sponsoring, etc. In this process, the social figure of the fundraiser serves as a mediator between the giver and the recipient of donation who must try to take the interests, motives and values of both parties into consideration. Over the past three or four decades, the work of fundraisers has become increasingly important: 'This act [fundraising] has now acquired an unprecedented level of legitimacy and explicitness, and in fact possesses its own structures of organisation and professionalisation – powerful ones' (Silber, 1998: 145). A prominent example of this are leading American universities where dozens of fundraising staff are employed with the task of acting as brokers and negotiating to establish what is the 'correct donation' in symbolic, legal and economic terms (Vogel and Kaghan, 2001). In many cases, the possibility of donating for a specified cause grants the donor a degree of participation. Publication of donors' names is one way of offering gratification in the form of recognition and prestige. An interesting aspect in this context is the special role played by mass media as fundraising instruments. Compared to other fundraising media, their capacity for agenda setting, emotional representation and, more generally, the construction of reality are of outstanding importance.

The centrality of the structure and organization of charitable giving is illustrated by empirical research conducted by sociologist Kieran Healy (2000). This was prompted by the fact that certain European countries have considerably higher percentages of blood donors than others. In Luxembourg, in the early 1990s, 14 percent of the adult population gave blood, compared to 44 percent in neighbouring France. Healy thus posed the rhetorical question: are the French more altruistic than the Luxembourgers? To demonstrate that this was not the case, he showed how differently structured institutional systems for donating blood reached different sections of the population and activated their readiness to give blood to differing degrees. The study found that it was not the motives of potential donors that varied from country to country, but the institutional settings: the way donors were recruited, the way the blood was collected, the way public relations were conducted. Bearing in mind that blood donations are usually requested by organizations rather than being proactively offered by individualism (Barman, 2007), the behaviour of potential blood donors can be organized by creating opportunities to give and a sense of duty to do so. Those who do not donate are not less altruistic; in most cases, they simply have not been asked.

These cursory remarks make clear that the modern gift economy would be simply unthinkable without institutionalized forms of requesting donations. This is a differentiated field within modern societies where emotional and moral ties are negotiated with the aim of awakening personal motivation, and converting these into binding and lasting support, thereby making it also more calculable for the receiving organizations.

Philanthropic foundations

Compared with the charitable giving practiced by people in the lower and middle income and wealth brackets, those who create philanthropic foundations, that is a specific legal institution typically created so as to put an endowment to (usually) charitable ends (Leat, Chapter 18), are usually motivated by two additional factors: a shaping influence and generativity. People who set up foundations want to make an impact on society, to preserve or change, to exert influence, to work for the common good – and to do so within a self-defined institutional framework beyond the duration of their own life. The 'eternal' foundation preserves something of its founder and his/her identity, long after his/her death.

If one examines a period of several decades, one can state that the creation of philanthropic foundations, unlike the charitable giving of lower and middle income groups, is especially active and extensive at those times when a specific scope for action opens up for philanthropic elites. Whereas it is possible to create structures of opportunity for charitable giving via established fundraising channels, the same does not apply for the setting up of foundations. The focus here is on motives of generativity and shaping conditions within society: which conditions favour the successful pursuit of such motives?

Comparative historical studies provide strong evidence for the notion that the creation of philanthropic foundations is driven less by demand than by supply (Adloff, 2010). In phases of major capital growth, the number of new foundations also increases. For example, in post-war Germany, it was not until the 1980s and 1990s that sufficient major fortunes had again been amassed to spark a wider setting up of foundations: capital growth among the wealthiest ten percent of the German population had been huge during the 1990s (Bergmann, 2004), and this correlates with the fact that roughly one third of all foundations in Germany were founded in the last 10 to 15 years. Furthermore, foundations are created at times when opportunities to shape society are open to philanthropic elites, i.e. especially in historical situations where the state gives these elites scope for action. Examples from the foundation sector in Germany and the US illustrate this theory.

Contrary to the widespread assumption of an American Exceptionalism, the German and American foundation sectors in the late nineteenth century were very similar (Adam, 2002, 2007): at this time, civic philanthropy was a widespread phenomenon on both sides of the Atlantic. Although the philanthropy of those years had its roots in a range of traditions in both countries, it was also genuinely modern: institutionalized philanthropy became a civic means of solving society's problems, especially the so-called social question. Those who set up foundations occupied spaces within public life, attempting to define the rules themselves: they built private governance structures that were nonetheless of public relevance. In Germany, this was often coordinated with local authorities and with a view to recognition from the state, and thus in some cases from the Kaiser. The organization and apparatus of the state was held in high esteem and philanthropy through foundations, coordinated or collaborating with the state, was not unusual. Prior to 1914, this approach formed the basis for strong private support for research, scholarship and institutions across Germany (Fuchs and Hoffmann, 2004). With World War I and the subsequent hyperinflation, this development came to an abrupt end. Thousands of foundations were dissolved, and the political and social tensions of the Weimar years unsettled the wealthy middle classes to such a degree that philanthropic activities shrank drastically.

In the US, following the onset of industrial prosperity around the turn of the century, an entirely new type of organization emerged around 1910: large philanthropic foundations set up by industrialists. In the spirit of an optimistic confidence in science and technology, philanthropy was equated with an attempt to get to the root of social problems (Sealander, 2003). Another contributing factor to this new philanthropic movement was the attempt to establish private institutional alternatives to 'impending state socialism'. The failure of progressivism left a great deal of scope for private initiatives that were progressive in content – medicine, social welfare, etc. – but that were not politically affiliated with it, and that rejected a greater role for the state (Karl and Katz, 1981).

However, following the expansion of state activity in the course of the New Deal of the 1930s, and especially from the 1950s onwards, American foundations, too, found themselves obliged to consult and collaborate more closely with the state (Sealander, 1997; Karl and Karl, 1999). In the 1950s, for example, the state became involved in funding for science and the arts. Networks linking foundations and government institutions took shape on domestic and international topics (Arnove, 1980; Anheier and Hammack, 2010; Krige and Rausch, 2012), allowing funding programs, such as the War on Poverty, to be coordinated. It is important, then, to dispense with the preconception that foundations in the US occupy a domain separate from the state. The activity of the large foundations from their origins around 1910 until far into the 1970s was marked by close ties with the state, either in that pioneering projects were later coordinated with the authorities, or in an advisory capacity. In these years, the American state was still held in higher esteem than has been the case since the 1980s.

Since the end of the 1980s, America's foundations have been obliged by public criticism and state pressure to improve their transparency, becoming actors displaying a greater degree of legitimacy and accountability. Especially the Tax Reform Act of 1969, which placed foundations under federal supervision, sets requirements for disclosure, restricts the scope for holdings in companies, and defines minimum annual payouts, led to a critical public perspective of foundations (Frumkin, 1999), of a kind that is still highly underdeveloped in Germany, especially as foundations there are still not obliged to publish annual reports (see Strachwitz in Keller, 2015).

From a historical viewpoint, no case can be made for a simple crowding out theory on the link between state activity and philanthropic foundations. State funding of the arts, for example, varies hugely between Germany and the US: in Germany, over 90 percent of the cultural sector's income comes from state sources, while in the US the figure is just over ten percent (Toepler, 1998: 156). In spite of this, and attributable to the prestige associated with it, arts funding tops the list of funding priorities for German foundations. Conversely, one can refer to the example of the social sector to show that relatively restrained social–political activity on the part of the state, as in the US, does not automatically lead to the setting up of foundations in a given field. Foundations, then, are not created and organized to fit demand.

Since the 1990s, Europe's philanthropic sectors have become increasingly dynamic: more foundations are being set up, often establishing a greater degree of autonomy from the state (Anheier and Daly, 2007). Upheavals in the system of corporatism and in the European welfare states are fostering this development, with new philanthropic elites freed from corporatist obligations acting as mediators and claiming a leadership role within society. We are seeing economic elites liberated from institutionally regulated and imposing social duties; at the same time they are taking on voluntary commitments in the form of corporate citizenship and the creation of foundations. Those likely to set up foundations constitute a sub-group among the wealthy members of society – i.e. those who aim for a shaping role within society and some degree of control over the funds donated – which combines individualism with an interest in the common good (Ostrower, 1995). Foundations and other forms of philanthropy can permit economic elites to bridge the divides between them and the political, social, religious, scientific and other sectors in order to exert an influence within these fields. Via philanthropic activities, someone occupying an economic elite position can also belong to the elite of the common good. Elites thus not only create foundations, foundations also create elites – elites of the common good. As we have seen, these elites may compete with the state or cooperate with it, and their commitment may imply forms of giving based either on solidarity or on hierarchy (Adloff, 2006; Jung and Harrow, 2015). This varies according to the macro level, the wider social and historical contexts.

The macro level

For some years now, philanthropy has been linked with the concept of civil society. A strong civil society, the argument goes, is also a guarantee for philanthropic activity. This view can be traced back to Alexis de Tocqueville (2000), who visited the USA during the 1830s, and claimed religion in the US had entered into a symbiotic relationship with political liberty. According to Tocqueville and his followers, republican and religious traditions of self-governance and virtuousness are responsible for America's exceptional customs, as free associations fill democracy with life and maintain it. Some years ago, Lipset (1996) returned to the notions of American Exceptionalism and the American Creed, originally formulated in the 1960s, tracing them back to Tocqueville and explicitly relating them to the field of philanthropy: 'The American Creed can be described in five terms: liberty, egalitarianism, individualism, populism, and laissez-faire. [...] These values reflect the absence of feudal structures, monarchies and aristocracies' (Lipset, 1996: 19). In this view, philanthropic institutions are considered as a concrete historical manifestation of America's system of values. Does this mean that philanthropy is, in real or ideal typical terms, an American concept?

Studies focusing on the US highlight that religiosity is a decisive, independent factor in influencing charitable actions and donations (Bielefeld et al., 2005). Those who go to church regularly, that is at least once a month, donate a portion of their income three times greater than people with weaker religious ties (O'Herlihy et al., 2006: 16). This holds when income and education are statistically controlled. In other countries, too, statistics demonstrate the influence of religiosity on civic engagement. This means that the high level of voluntarism in the US – 50 percent are involved in civic activities on a regular basis – can be attributed to the comparatively high degree of religiosity and church affiliation among Americans, a quarter of whom attend a church service every week. If membership of a religious community is statistically controlled, the rate of voluntary activity in the US is no longer higher than it is in most European states (Curtis et al., 1992, 2001); the same is true of charitable giving.

Clearly, religious traditions are particularly well suited to awakening and upholding charitable motives and values. The bulk of differences between the American and European levels of donating time and money could thus be due to the different levels of religiosity. High rates of civic activity and membership are generally observed in countries with great religious diversity and high levels of church autonomy (countries with a mix of faiths, but also predominantly

Protestant countries), that have a long democratic tradition and that are relatively wealthy (Curtis *et al.*, 2001: 801) – meaning northern and western Europe, the US, and Canada.

These differences with regard to religiosity, civic engagement and donations can also be attributed to cultural differences, as is customary in studies of political culture (Almond and Verba, 1963; Inglehart, 1997). In addition, it is important to stress structural and institutional differences that determine the framework for the different developments and historical patterns. Schofer and Fourcade-Gourinchas (2001) have shown how the level of voluntary membership in associations varies internationally, depending on how states and societies are constructed and interrelated. Institutionalized patterns of political sovereignty and organization correspond to different patterns of voluntary activity. As well as personal factors such as education, income and religious affiliation, the form of statehood and the degree of corporatism can be viewed as decisive factors influencing the form taken by charitable activity and civil society (Anheier and Daly, 2007). One can distinguish between autonomous, bureaucratized and centralized states, such as France and Germany, and weak, decentralized ones based more strongly on the idea of self-governance, such as the Anglo-Saxon countries. The level of corporatism is measured in terms of how strongly society is organized, putting Germany in the corporatist category in contrast to the US. These two structural factors explain much of the variation in the degree and form of voluntarism: strong states display a lower level of such activity and less new social movements; a society structured along corporatist lines favours memberships in traditional associations and organizations (such as unions). At the same time, recent years have seen a slight worldwide trend towards liberalization and a related increase in new forms of association: 'Certainly the worldwide diffusion of a powerful liberal vision, in which 'civil society' is regarded as the most important agent of such a successful democracy, is not irrelevant to this transformation' (Schofer and Fourcade-Gourinchas, 2001: 823). It can thus be claimed that the American – originally religiously influenced – culture of individualism, activism and voluntarism is being globalized and transported via the United Nations and other international bodies, spreading via diffusion and imitation (Meyer, 2009; Krige and Rausch, 2012). Especially American foundations are well-resourced, influential and high-prestige players and driving forces in the emerging global society (Vogel, 2006) which thus displays a strong American character.

Conclusion

To summarize, one can state that engaging in philanthropy depends on basic human abilities and practices: the ability to cooperate, to empathize, to share intentions and emotions with others, to give help and to act altruistically on behalf of others. But this always takes place within specific social contexts. Consequently, philanthropic activity also varies throughout history, finding expression in very different forms – it may be horizontally networked, binding people together in solidarity, but it may equally reproduce and represent hierarchies and distinctions of social status (Blau, 1964). Interaction on the level of face-to-face contacts must also be taken into account, as well as cultural, social and institutional frameworks.

In general terms, it is possible to identify social factors conducive to charitable giving (Bekkers and Wiepking, 2011): high levels of education within the population, involvement in social networks of charitable engagement, religiosity, mass media generation of cosmopolitan empathy and, finally, the organization of gift gathering in the form of fundraising. Although charitable giving and the creation of foundations are both one-sided transfers of resources, further distinction is necessary. Setting up a foundation requires large sums of money or other resources, but it must also be understood as an act of institution building. In most cases, charitable giving does not offer the same scope for structuring society. The creators of foundations are institution builders and hyperagents, capable of framing social relations in institutional form beyond the scope of their own lives (Schervish, 2006).

Societies with a strongly developed philanthropic sector usually possess free resources in the form of accumulated wealth. Philanthropic activity also depends on a positive climate within society, meaning both structures for the recognition of such activities and a certain culture of philanthropic competition among the county's elites. Greater transparency in the philanthropic sector can only encourage this. Finally, high levels of philanthropy in modern societies depend on philanthropic elites being granted scope for influencing society, either in competition or cooperation with the state – with the still unanswered question of the democratic legitimacy of such philanthropic elites posing a major problem in normative terms.

There are further questions challenging the current state of theorizing philanthropy. Up to now, the perspectives of various contributing disciplines, such as history, sociology, psychology, political science and philosophy, are rather unconnected; integration is still pending. Besides the already mentioned question of the legitimacy of wealth translating into social influence, more general issues of power differentials are of importance: from a postcolonial perspective the 'good intentions' of western charities, foundations and philanthropists can be ambivalent in their effects (Fassin, 2012) and it can be asked if they reproduce longstanding historical asymmetries and hegemonies (Roelofs, 2003; Parmar, 2012). Thus, how do local traditions and western globalized models of philanthropy relate? Furthermore, whereas we currently know a lot about western ideas and practices of philanthropy, research on philanthropic models in non-western cultures and regions is just emerging (Mottiar and Ngcoya, Chapter 9), but is greatly needed to better understand the plurality of philanthropic practices.

References

Adam, T. (2002) 'Transatlantic Trading: The Transfer of Philanthropic Models Between European and North American Cities During the Nineteenth and Early Twentieth Centuries', *Journal of Urban History*, 28: 328–51.

——. (2007) 'Stiften in Deutschen Bürgerstädten vor dem Ersten Weltkrieg: Das Beispiel Leipzig', *Geschichte und Gesellschaft*, 33(1): 46–72.

Adloff, F. (2006) 'Beyond Interests and Norms: Gift-Giving and Reciprocity in Modern Societies', *Constellations: An International Journal of Critical and Democratic Theory*, 13(2): 407–27.

——. (2009) 'What Encourages Charitable Giving and Philanthropy?', *Ageing and Society*, 29: 1185–1205.

——. (2010) *Philanthropisches Handeln: Eine Historische Soziologie des Stiftens in Deutschland und den USA*. Frankfurt/New York: Campus.

Almond, G. and Verba, S. (1963) *The Civic Culture*. Princeton, NJ: Princeton University Press.

Anheier, H. K. and Daly, S. (2007) *The Politics of Foundations: A Comparative Analysis*. London: Routledge.

Anheier, H. K. and Hammack, D. C. (eds.) (2010) *American Foundations. Roles and Contributions*. Brookings: Washington.

Arnove, P. (1980). *Philanthropy and Cultural Imperialism*. Indiana University Press: Indiana.

Barman, E. (2007) 'An Institutional Approach to Donor Control: From Dyadic Ties to a Field-Level Analysis', *The American Journal of Sociology*, 112(5): 1416–57.

Bekkers, R. and Wiepking, P. (2011) 'A Literature Review of Empirical Studies of Philanthropy: Eight Mechanisms that Drive Charitable Giving', *Nonprofit and Voluntary Sector Quarterly*, 40(5): 924–73.

Bergmann, J. (2004) 'Die Reichen werden Reicher – auch in Deutschland. Die Legende von den Moderaten Ungleichheiten', *Leviathan* 32(2): 185–202.

Bielefeld, W., Rooney, P., and Steinberg, K. (2005) 'How Do Need, Capacity, Geography, and Politics Influence Giving?', in A. C. Brooks (ed.) *Gifts of Time and Money: The Role of Charity in America's Communities*. Lanham, MD: Rowman & Littlefield.

Blau, P. (1964) *Exchange and Power in Social Life*. New York: Wiley.

Boulding, K. E. (1981) *A Preface to Grants Economics: The Economy of Love and Fear*. New York: Wadsworth.

Bowles, S. (2006) 'Group Competition, Reproductive Leveling, and the Evolution of Human Altruism', *Science*, 314: 1569–72.

Brewster, M. and Tucker, J. M. (2015) 'Understanding Bystander Behavior: The Influence of and Interaction Between Bystander Characteristics and Situational Factors', *Victims and Offenders: An International Journal of Evidence-based Research, Policy, and Practice*, 00: 1–27.

Caillé, A. (2000) *Anthropologie du Don : Le Tiers Paradigme*. Paris: Desclée de Brouwer.

Collins, R. and Hickman, N. (1991) 'Altruism and Culture as Social Products', *Voluntas*, 2(2): 1–15.

Cooley, C. H. (1902). *Human Nature and the Social Order*. New York: Charles Scribner's Sons

Curtis, J. E., Grabb, E. G., and Baer, D. E. (1992) 'Voluntary Association Membership in Fifteen Countries: A Comparative Analysis', *American Sociological Review* 57(2): 139–52.

———. (2001) 'Nations of Joiners: Explaining Voluntary Association Membership in Democratic Societies', *American Sociological Review*, 66(6): 783–805.

Davis, M. H. (2006) 'Empathy', in J.E. Stets and J.H. Turner (eds.) *Handbook of the Sociology of Emotions*. New York: Springer.

Etzioni, A. (1988) *The Moral Dimension: Toward a New Economics*. New York: Free Press.

Fassin, D. (2012) *Humanitarian Reason: A Moral History of the Present*. Berkeley/Los Angeles: University of California Press.

Fehr, E. and Gächter, S. (2000) 'Fairness and Retaliation: The Economics of Reciprocity', *Journal of Economic Perspectives*, 14(3): 159–81.

Fehr, E. and Fischbacher, U. (2003) 'The Nature of Human Altruism', *Nature*, 425: 785–91.

Frumkin, P. (1999) 'Private Foundations as Public Institutions: Regulation, Professionalization, and the Redefinition of Organized Philanthropy', in E. Condliffe Lagemann (ed.) *Philanthropic Foundations*. Bloomington: Indiana University Press.

Fuchs, E. and Hoffman, D. (2004). 'Philanthropy and Science in Wilhelmine Germany', in Thomas Adam (ed.) *Philanthropy, Patronage, and Civil Society: Experiences from Germany, Great Britain, and North America*. Bloomington, 103–19.

Gintis, H., Bowles, S., Boyd, R., and Fehr, E. (2003) 'Explaining Altruistic Behaviour in Humans', *Evolution and Human Behavior*, 24: 153–72.

Godbout, J. T. and Caillé, A. (1998) *The World of the Gift*. Montreal: McGill-Queen's University Press.

Halfpenny, P. (1999) 'Economic and Sociological Theories of Individual Charitable Giving: Complementary or Contradictory?', *Voluntas*, 10(3): 197–215.

Healy, K. (2000) 'Embedded Altruism: Blood Collection Regimes and the European Union's Donor Population', *The American Journal of Sociology*, 105(6): 1633–57.

Henrich, J., Boyd, R., Bowles, S., Camerer, C., Fehr, E., Gintis, H., McElreath, R., Alvard, M., Barr, A., Ensminger, J., Smith Henrich, N., Hill, K., Gil-White, F., Gurven, M., Marlowe, F. W., Patton, J. Q., and Tracer, D. (2005) '"Economic Man" in Cross-cultural Perspective: Behavioral Experiments in 15 Small-scale Societies', *Behavioral and Brain Sciences*, 28(6): 1–61.

Hochschild, A. (1979) 'Emotion Work, Feeling Rules, and Social Structure', *The American Journal of Sociology*, 85(3): 551–75.

Inglehart, R. (1997) *Modernization and Post-Modernization: Cultural, Economic and Political Change in 43 Societies*. Princeton, NJ: Princeton University Press.

Jung, T. and Harrow, J. (2015) 'Philanthropy, the State and Public Goods', in R. P. Guerrero O. and P. Wilkins (eds.) *Doing Public Good? Private Actors, Evaluation and Public Value*. Comparative Policy Evaluation Volume 23, Transaction Publishers.

Karl, B. D. and Katz, S. N. (1981) 'The American Private Philanthropic Foundation and the Public Sphere 1890–1930', *Minerva*, 19: 236–70.

Karl, B. D. and Karl, A. W. (1999) 'Foundations and the Government: A Tale of Conflict and Consensus', in C. T. Clotfelder and T. Ehrlich (eds.) *Philanthropy and the Nonprofit Sector in a Changing America*. Bloomington/Indianapolis: Indiana University Press.

Keller, E. (2015) 'The German Philanthropic Sector: A Conversation With Rupert Graf Strachwitz', *Philanthopic*, March 26.

Kohlberg, L. (1984). 'The Psychology of Moral Development: The Nature and Validity of Moral Stages' (Essays on Moral Development, Volume 2). Harper & Row.

Kolm, S. C. (2000) 'Introduction: The Economics of Reciprocity, Giving and Altruism', in L.-A. Gérard-Varet, S.-C. Kolm, and J. M Ythier (eds.) *The Economics of Reciprocity, Giving and Altruism*. London: Macmillan.

Krige, J. and Rausch, H. (eds.) (2012) *American Foundations and the Coproduction of World Order in the Twentieth Century*. Göttingen: Vandenhoeck and Ruprecht.

Lee, L., Piliavin, J. A., and Call, V. R. (1999) 'Giving Time, Money, and Blood: Similarities and Differences', *Social Psychology Quarterly* 62(3): 276–90.

Lipset, S. M. (1996) *American Exceptionalism: A Double Edged Sword*. New York: W.W. Norton.

Mauss, M. (1990 [1925]) *The Gift: The Form and Reason for Exchange in Archaic Societies*, trans. W. D. Hallis. New York/London: Norton.

Mead, G. H. (1930) 'Philanthropy from the Point of View of Ethics', in E. Faris, F. Laune and A. J. Todd (eds.) *Intelligent Philanthropy*. Chicago: University of Chicago Press.

——. (1934) *Mind Self and Society from the Standpoint of a Social Behaviorist*. C. W. Morris (ed.) Chicago: University of Chicago Press.

Meyer, J. W. (2009) *World Society: The Writings of John W. Meyer*. New York: Oxford University Press.

Monroe, K. R. (1994) 'A Fat Lady in a Corset: Altruism and Social Theory', *American Journal of Political Science*, 38(4): 861–93.

Neuhoff, K. (2003) 'Zur Geschichte des Gebens und Spendens, des Teilens und Stiftens in Deutschland', in Fundraising Akademie (ed.) *Fundraising: Handbuch für Grundlagen, Strategien und Instrumente*. Wiesbaden: Gabler.

Niza, C., Tung, B., and Martin, T. M. (2013) 'Incentivizing Blood Donation: Systematic Review and Meta-Analysis to Test Titmuss' Hypotheses', *Health Psychology* Vol. 32, No. 9, 941–9.

O'Herlihy, M. A., Havens, J. J., and Schervish, P. G. (2006) 'Charitable Giving: How Much, By Whom, and How?', in W. W. Powell and R. Steinberg (eds.) *The Nonprofit Sector: A Research Handbook*. New Haven: Yale University Press.

Oliner, S. P. and Oliner, P. M. (1988) *The Altruistic Personality: Rescuers of Jews in Nazi Europe*. New York: Free Press.

Ostrower, F. (1995) *Why the Wealthy Give: The Culture of Elite Philanthropy*. Princeton, NJ: Princeton University Press.

Parmar, I. (2012). *Foundations of the American Century*. Columbia University Press.

Parsons, T. (1968 [1937]) *The Structure of Social Action*. New York: Free Press.

Piaget, J. (1932) *The Moral Judgment of the Child*. Glencoe: The Free Press.

Piliavin, J. A. and Charng, H. W. (1990) 'Altruism: A Review of Recent Theory and Research', *Annual Review of Sociology*, 16: 27–65.

Roelofs, J. (2003). *Foundations and Public Policy: The Mask of Pluralism*. Albany, New York: State University of New York Press.

Safin, V., Arfer, K. B., and Rachlin, H. (2015) 'Reciprocation and Altruism in Social Cooperation', *Behavioural Processes*, 116: 12–16.

Sahlins, M. (1972) *Stone Age Economics*. Chicago: Aldine.

Schervish, P. G. (2000) 'The Modern Medici: Patterns, Motivations, and Giving Strategies of the Wealthy.' Paper presented at "What is 'New' About New Philanthropy?" University of Southern California Nonprofit Studies Centre, Los Angeles.

Schervish, P. G. (2006) 'The Moral Biography of Wealth: Philosophical Reflections on the Foundation of Philanthropy', *Nonprofit and Voluntary Sector Quarterly*, 35(3): 477–92.

Schervish, P. G. and Ostrander, S. A. (1990) 'Giving and Getting: Philanthropy as a Social Relation', in J. van Til (ed.) *Critical Issues in American Philanthropy. Strengthening Theory and Practice*. San Francisco: Jossey-Bass.

Schmitt, C. S. and Clark, C. (2006). 'Sympathy', in J. E. Stets and J. H. Turner (eds.) *Handbook of the Sociology of Emotions*. New York: Springer.

Schofer, E. and Fourcade-Gourinchas, M. (2001) 'The Structural Contexts of Civic Engagement: Voluntary Association Membership in Comparative Perspective', *American Sociological Review* 66(6): 806–28.

Sealander, J. (1997) *Private Wealth and Public Life. Foundation Philanthropy and the Reshaping of American Social Policy from the Progressive Era to the New Deal*. Baltimore: Johns Hopkins University Press.

——. (2003) 'Curing Evils at their Source: The Arrival of Scientific Giving', in L. J. Friedman and M. D. McGarvie (eds.) *Charity, Philanthropy, and Civility in American History*. Cambridge, MA: Cambridge University Press.

Silber, I. (1998) 'Modern Philanthropy: Reassessing the Viability of a Maussian Perspective', in W. James and N. J. Allen (eds.) *Marcel Mauss: A Centenary Tribute*. New York: Berghahn Books.

Simmons, R. G. (1991) 'Presidential Address on Altruism and Sociology', *The Sociological Quarterly*, 32(1): 1–22.

Taylor, C. (1985) 'What is Human Agency?', in *Human Agency and Language. Philosophical Papers*, Vol. 1. Cambridge, UK: Cambridge University Press.

Titmuss, R. M. (1997 [1980]) *The Gift Relationship: From Human Blood to Social Policy*, A. Oakley and J. Ashton (eds.). New York: New Press.

Tocqueville, A. de (2000 [1835/40]) *Democracy in America*. Chicago: University of Chicago Press.

Toepler, S. (1998) 'Foundations and Their Institutional Context: Cross-Evaluating Evidence from Germany and the United States', *Voluntas*, 9(2): 153–70.

Tomasello, M. (1999) *The Cultural Origins of Human Cognition*. Cambridge, MA: Harvard University Press.

——. (2009) *Why We Cooperate*. Cambridge, MA: MIT Press.

Turner, J. H. (1987) 'Toward a Sociological Theory of Motivation,' *American Sociological Review*, 52: 15–27.

Turner, J. H. and Stets, J. E. (2006a) 'Sociological Theories of Human Emotions', *Annual Review of Sociology*, 32: 25–52.

——. (2006b) 'Moral Emotions', in J. E. Stets and J. H. Turner (eds.) *Handbook of the Sociology of Emotions*. New York: Springer.

Vogel, A. (2006) 'Who's Making Global Civil Society: Philanthropy and US Empire in World Society', *British Journal of Sociology* 57(4): 635–55.

Vogel, A. and Kaghan, W. N. (2001) 'Bureaucrats, Brokers, and the Entrepreneurial University', *Organization*, 8(2): 358–64.

Wenzel, H. and Scholz, T. (2010) 'Die Medienvermittelte Teilhabe an Katastrophen', in F. Adloff, E. Priller and R. G. Strachwitz (eds.) *Prosoziale Motivation. Bedingungen des Spendens in interdisziplinärer Perspektive*. Stuttgart: Lucius & Lucius.

4

What motivates people to give their own private resources for the public good?

Cathy Pharoah

While the previous chapter has looked at some of the broader issues around giving and philanthropy, this chapter will focus in more detail on the question: why do we give away part of what we have? This question has intrigued people of different cultures, from diverse walks of life, and from numerous academic disciplines; it is assuming renewed significance in this time of widening global inequality. As governments increasingly roll back the state and seek to redefine the balance between individual and public responsibilities, there are growing expectations of the contribution which philanthropy might make (Harrow and Jung, 2011). In purely material and instrumental terms, private giving provides substantial financial support for a vast range of civil society activities and organizations which depend on it: it provides 11 percent of their income globally (Salamon *et al.*, 1999). Today, private giving is worth more than \$335 billion in the US (Giving USA, 2014), and over £18 billion per year from individuals, companies and charitable trusts in the UK (Pharoah, 2011a,b). It is therefore increasingly important to understand the philanthropic impulse and how it might be changing in a social environment of growing secularism, individualism, consumerism, and multiculturalism. This chapter highlights how research has found that giving is embedded in multiple social, personal and moral contexts; that the motivation to give is multi-faceted. It outlines the different ways in which that motivation has been addressed and interpreted in research, some of the key findings, and concludes with reflections on the challenges to donor motivation in today's increasingly complex and demanding environment for philanthropy.

The multiple private and public dimensions to giving

As outlined by Cunningham (Chapter 2), history presents many examples of how private philanthropy is embedded in the public and civic roles and responsibilities of donors. These include private donations raised in Ancient Greece for major public projects including walls, bridges and harbours, the long European tradition from the early middle ages of founding charitable hospices, hospitals and almshouses, often within religious contexts, and the more recent US philanthropic response to the 9/11 World Trade Center bombings (Kapucu, Chapter 11). In a comprehensive study of powerful elite US donors, Ostrower (1997: 113) analyzes how the private and public are meshed in the philanthropic rationale of powerful wealthy families in the US, writing that they 'defend a complex position that legitimates philanthropy … as (an institution) whose mission is 'public' but carried out under private auspices'. In a study of charitable family trusts in the UK (Pharoah, 2011a), some founders said that a collective sense of family public responsibility motivated private family philanthropy based on shared wealth, often derived from the family business. One said 'we share the same values around philanthropy, the same sense of our responsibilities as part of society and of the duty towards private money for public good' (Pharoah, 2011a: 61).

The meanings we attach to giving lie in the complex and multiple spaces we articulate between our private and public worlds. Payton (1996: ix) spells out the implications of this for understanding motivation when he comments that if the multiple personal, ethical and socio-political contexts of philanthropy are taken into account, it becomes clear that the notion of charity wears 'many faces', that 'the hunt for a single explanation is misguided'. Moreover, as historical commentators have highlighted, notions around the philanthropic impulse have changed and developed over time: '[t]he discussions of reasons why and how people should give are ancient and continuous' (Mullin, 2002: 12). Their complexity is well illustrated in Davis' (1996: 2) approach to historical gifts for the establishment of public hospitals and other great institutions: '[a]re (they) … power plays, penance for evils done, acts to ingratiate the doer with the gods, or expression of compassion at the plight of the indigent?'. In reality, such interpretations are neither alternative nor exclusive. Farsides (ESRC/NCVO, 2005: 10) argues that

> [j]ust as various people may have different reasons for acting in a certain way, an individual may behave in the same way for a variety of reasons on separate occasions … attempts to identify the key reasons for giving are unlikely to succeed.

Similarly, the study of routes to philanthropy amongst UK family foundation founders concluded that its development does not have a single motivation, but often results from a number of relevant events coming together, including life-events such as illness or bereavement, sudden wealth acquisition, seminal contact with charitable activities or other philanthropists, seeing a need or an opportunity, and wanting a life-change (Pharoah, 2011a). Exploring the impulse to give then is not about the search for a single trigger, but about uncovering the many, often co-existing factors, which may encourage general willingness to give, and prompt a specific gift.

Part of the complexity of understanding motivation is that giving not only straddles different aspects of our lives, but also encompasses many different kinds of behaviours: from the committed dropping of money into a church collection plate to the casual dropping of a coin or spare change into a street collecting tin; from a major gift to a cause with which the donor has deep personal, professional or social associations, to the gifting of large part of the donor's estate for general charitable purposes over which the donor will have little control. The giving of money can be spontaneous and one-off, regular or part of planned budgeting and expenditure, and can represent a very large or small part of our spending. Gifts of money can be made to those close to us, or to complete strangers, and can be anonymous or bring wide public recognition and reward. Moreover, as the Editors highlight in their introductory chapter, giving is not confined to money, but encompasses gifts of time, labour, food and many other gifts in kind. It should not be assumed that these different giving behaviours and their motivations come from the same social, psychological or moral spaces. In relation to the giving of the wealthy, for example, Ostrower (1997) argues that some major variations in the giving behaviour of elite donors are related to the internal social organization of the elite groups to which they belong.

Different disciplinary perspectives on giving

The multi-dimensional nature of both the impulse to give and of giving behaviours means that motivation has lent itself to study within many different disciplinary contexts, each bringing its own particular insights. Economists have explored how far giving can be explained in terms of addressing 'market failures', of self-interest in supporting services which we might need but which others, such as government, neglect. There has however been an increasing understanding that such purely 'instrumentalist' explanations for giving are insufficient (Adloff, Chapter 3), that self-interest could include the personal 'warm glow' experienced from the act of giving in itself (Andreoni, 1990; Kingma, 1997) or considerations of wider public benefit (Vesterlund, 2006). There is no doubt that peer effects require further examination (Bekkers, Chapter 7). Some biologists believe there is a 'gene' related to altruistic behaviour (Reuter *et al.*, 2010), with socio-biologists pointing out that altruism has a role in evolutionary advantage (Dawkins, 2006). Sociologists look at how the impulse to give is embedded in social meanings, norms and cultures, such as those around compassion or responsibility (Sprecher and Fehr, 2005), while social anthropologists regard gift-giving as absolutely central to the exchange and reciprocity relationships essential to any society (Mauss, 1954). Psychologists and others aim to understand how giving is related to our values, beliefs, attitudes and personal identity. Religious faith, as a source of the values which inspire giving, holds a central place in this research (Wuthnow, 1999; Wilhelm *et al.*, 2007). Others have explored the ways in which the impulse to give derives from generally pro-social helping or caring impulses which also lead to other forms of giving (Lee *et al.*, 1999). For philosophers and theologians, the motivation to give has both outward- and inward-facing aspects. On the one hand, prompted by, for example, a desire to achieve greater social justice, and, on the other, to achieve personal virtue and moral goodness (Schneewind, 1996). Marketing research tends to be more applied, studying how the ways in which we are asked influence whether – and how much – we give, or the most effective ways of evoking the passions or values which might prompt a gift. For example, Ford and Merchant (2010), amongst others, have highlighted the power of tapping into nostalgia; how the memory of what we have valued in the past can prompt a gift in the present. More recently, behavioural economics has placed a focus on how the framing or structuring of options for various kinds of payments affects our economic choices (Thaler and Sunstein, 2009), and how far people can be 'nudged' towards giving through, for example, options to give when they carry out basic daily financial transactions, such as using cash machines (ATM) or paying bills (UK Cabinet Office, 2011). But, while many different factors have been found to be related to giving, one of the main purposes of the study of motivation is to explore how, and how much, singly or in combination, various impulses and influences actually explain giving behaviour.

What determines our individual giving?

Most people have a fairly strong intuitive sense of what motivates themselves and others to give; they would not regard explanations such as 'seeing a need', 'wanting to help others', 'caring about the environment' or believing 'it's the right thing to do' as in any way complex. What is elusive about understanding giving is that we know so little about the extent to which such factors influence us, or their relative importance. How much do we care about the environment if this amounts to the occasional ad hoc gift to the World Wildlife Fund (WWF), a gift whose value might be considerably less than we can afford? How common is the belief that charity is a duty? Does it mean the same to everyone and how does it get translated into the many different ways of giving? In spite of the existence of the many different perspectives on giving outlined above, few studies have taken a multi-disciplinary approach to analyzing motivation. The vast majority of giving research takes as its starting-point that giving is a private, individual action to be explained in terms of individual characteristics and experiences. The individual person, or sometimes household, is the prime unit of study, with research variously exploring the relationships between the individual's giving behaviour and intrinsic determinants, like personal attitudes, beliefs, faith or values, or 'extrinsic' factors, such as age and economic status (Sargeant, 1999).

Internal factors influencing giving

Looking first at the internal factors which influence giving, this area of research has been less systematically tackled than the study of extrinsic factors, but is wide-ranging. In an extensive literature review of empirical studies aimed partly at informing fundraising, and including studies of the impact of particular marketing approaches or techniques, Bekkers and Wiepking (2007) identified key mechanisms influencing motivation as: the donor's awareness of need, concern for reputation, expected psychological benefits and values. Considerable experimental research has explored the effect of awareness of need on giving behaviour. It has generally found that the likelihood of a donation is positively related to degree of need (Levitt and Kornhaber, 1977). Awareness increases where donors know the potential beneficiaries of an organization (Radley and Kennedy, 1992; Polonsky et al., 2002). This might explain why people often give to organizations with which they are involved in other ways, such as through volunteering and serving on boards. The significant effect of awareness of need might explain why mass communications providing direct donor experience of the impact of international disasters, for example, can have such a significant role in motivating and shaping support (Kapucu, Chapter 11). Not all donors perceive need in the same way, however, and they are only likely to give where they believe that the beneficiaries are 'deserving', and have not been the architects of their own problems.

Moving from the donor's perceptions of external need to internal perceptions, research suggests that issues of reputation are important. When given the choice, people generally prefer their donations to be known by others (Andreoni and Petrie, 2004), and the trend towards wearing coloured ribbons, or wristbands, so-called 'conspicuous compassion', facilitates public recognition of support. Social pressure appears to work more strongly if people with whom the donor has a strong tie are present when they give, or make the request for a donation. Schervish and Havens (1997) found that people who are asked to give by a relative or friend donate a larger percentage of their income, and contributions to the US 'United Way' organizations, a movement focused on 'mobilising the power of communities' (United Way, 2015), are higher in communities with stable populations. The existing social status of both the donor and the fundraiser can enhance the value of approval, and research has suggested that a donation is more likely, and larger, when requested by a person of higher social status (Jackson and Latané, 1981; Vriens et al. 1998).

Studies of different kinds have looked at the personal psychological reward derived from helping other people, or the 'feelgood' factor. Studies within disciplines such as neuropsychology suggest that helping others produces positive psychological consequences or 'empathic joy' for the helper (Batson and Shaw, 1991) and also reinforces stronger self-image as, for example, being a generous person (Schlegelmilch et al., 1997). Halfpenny (1999) has argued that rational economic explanations based on the individual's attempt to maximize personal utility are irreconcilable with those of, for example, qualitative sociology, which involves making sense of why people give through understanding the framework of meanings in which they embed it. This is discussed further below. Other modifications to purely economic explanations were explored in a paper by Vesterlund (2006), drawing attention to the value of including other factors within economic studies, such as the potential influence of wider social norms or interactions with other donors, the effectiveness and impact of the recipient and the benefits of the gift. In general, authors agree that more detailed empirical studies of actual decision-making processes are needed to both test such hypotheses and to determine which factors take priority when people are involved in giving.

While some of our giving may be motivated by factors present at the point of giving, such as the particular portrayal of the beneficiary or whether others are making a gift, studies of values concern more general underlying attributes which promote positive attitudes towards giving. In studies of wealthy donors, a passionate belief in a specific cause has been identified as an important motivational factor (Lloyd, 2004). Strong relationships between various kinds of values and the likelihood of being a charitable donor have been found. These include: a belief in the importance of altruistic behaviour (Farmer and Fedor, 2001; Farsides, 2005; Bekkers and Schuyt, 2005) and the presence of generally pro-social values (Bekkers, 2006, 2007); the individual's endorsement of a moral principle of care (Bekkers and Wilhelm 2008); concern for social order and social justice (Todd and Lawson, 1999); or a sense of social responsibility (Amato, 1985; Reed and Selbee, 2002; Schuyt et al., 2004).

A crucial strand running through the history of the study of motivations to give, is the role of faiths, and their related beliefs and values. Both in the US and in the UK, for example, giving to religious causes represents a very large component of all individual charitable giving (Pharoah 2011b; Giving USA, 2014). Within this context, it is important to highlight that a major study of philanthropy within the world's great faith traditions identifies perceptions of giving as a duty or responsibility as a common thread, 'rooted in the ethical notions of giving and serving to those beyond one's family – (which) probably existed in most cultures and in most historical periods' (Ilchman et al., 1998: ix). Many empirical studies have noted the strong positive relationships between religious affiliation or involvement and giving, and also giving to religious causes (Independent Sector, 2002), and the impact of faith-based and spiritual values (Todd and Lawson, 1999). An extensive literature review of giving within religious contexts has concluded that its effects need to be understood as occurring at multiple levels, including: impact of faith on individual values; influence of particular religious norms, such as tithing or giving away a particular proportion of income; and the socio-political influence of particular religious groups or congregations on those who belong to them (Lincoln et al., 2008). While we very often interpret notions of giving in the context of an individual's personal morality (Sanghera, 2011), recent research has shown that amounts of giving are higher amongst donors living in communities with high degrees of religious or ethnic homogeneity, and are reduced in proportion to increases in diversity (Andreoni et al., 2011).

External factors influencing giving

Turning to the extrinsic determinants of giving, these have been studied largely through the substantial body of survey research with its focus on measuring whether, and how much, individuals give. This has readily lent itself to further in-depth study of the relationship between the giving behaviour of individuals or single households, and the demographic and socio-economic characteristics which appear to determine it, such as income and educational attainment (Reece 1979; Jones and Posnett, 1991a; Banks and Tanner, 1997; Clain and Zech, 1999; Yen, 2002; Carroll et al., 2005; Havens et al., 2006; Wilhelm et al., 2007; NCVO/CAF UK Giving 2005–2011 Editions; Cowley et al., 2011). These studies and annual surveys have robustly established some of the key parameters which determine individual giving. Their findings have proved to be remarkably consistent over time and geography. Research from the US has shown that strong positive relationships exist between both the likelihood of giving and the amounts given. Key factors include higher levels of income and wealth, higher educational achievement, older age, and being married. Research from the UK on thirty-year trends in household giving, drawing on data on household expenditure collected annually within the Living Costs and Food survey carried out by the Office of National Statistics, (Cowley *et al.*, 2011), establishes strong positive links between having received higher education, being employed and home ownership, and donating. Gender was also found important in this study, with households consisting of a higher proportion of adult women, and those with children, being more likely to donate. It is important to note, however, that the positive relationship between women's giving and children is reversed for charitable bequests. These are much more likely to be made by women without children (James, 2008). In addition to finding strong positive links between household income and expenditure and both likelihood and amount of giving, the study by Cowley *et al.* (2011) also found that these links have become even stronger over time. Similarly, the positive relationship between age and the likelihood of giving has strengthened over time. It finds that fewer households in the UK are giving now than in 1978, but that donors give more. Increases in both participation and donations among the richest ten percent of households over time mean that their average share of giving increased from 16 percent in the period 1978–82, to 22 percent in 2003–8. This suggests that philanthropy is increasingly becoming the preserve of older, better-educated and wealthier people. In the UK, the over-65s now account for over one-third of the value of all donations, compared with one-quarter in 1978. Growth in participation and donation size amongst older age groups contrasts with falling participation over the whole period for almost every other age band.

Echoing US findings on the strong link between higher levels of giving and higher income and wealth (Havens *et al.*, 2006), the UK research finds giving heavily skewed towards donors giving larger amounts, with the top 50 percent of households, ranked by donation size, accounting for 92 percent of all giving. This pattern has remained remarkably constant over the three decades of the study. Amounts given, however, are a poor indicator of generosity, and where poorer households do give, they are more generous. In the UK, giving comprises 3.6 percent of total spending among the poorest givers, compared to 1.1 percent amongst the richest. In spite of this contrast, there is little research on what motivates decisions on how much to give, though there is further discussion later in this chapter on factors which tend to lead to giving higher amounts. The proportion of expenditure given to charity by the wealthiest households increased during the 1980s, but this was at a time when their general share of wealth was increasing and the gap between rich and poor households was widening. It does not appear to have increased since that time. Over the last three decades, the value of giving has typically grown in times of economic growth, and has not fallen at the same rate as the economy during recessions. Overall, this study concluded that giving as a share of total spending has been remarkably stable over the last thirty years, and a recent update shows that average participation in and amounts given continued to remain from 2008–11 (McKenzie *et al.*, 2013). It seems, that despite considerable changes, philanthropy has neither increased nor declined in general importance over the last few decades. Findings on giving in Canada over the period 2007–10 confirm a similar picture, indicating that there has been little change in the proportion of people giving, or the amounts they give over this recent period (Statistics Canada, 2010). Perhaps, habits of giving are indeed relatively unchanging, or hard to change – a challenging message for fundraisers constantly inventive in the use of new technology and marketing approaches to prompt donations. 'Mental accounting', the theory that people treat money in different ways, and budget for different spending in different ways, has been put forward as a possible explanation by economic psychologists for the relatively constant amount devoted to giving. Research has suggested that we do indeed have a 'mental pot' for expenditure related to giving, as to other areas of expenditure (Walker and Pharoah, 2002). Wunderink (2002) finds in her research in the Netherlands that when donations are part of the donor's mental accounting system the average amount given is greater than for ad hoc donations, while Canadian research finds that this philanthropic pot is 'malleable' and open to influence by fundraising approaches (LaBarge and Stinson, 2013).

The role of incentives, such as tax reliefs of various kinds, the impact of changes to taxation, and the economic 'price' of the gift in motivating, and determining, changes in the level of giving, has been extensively studied within the US economic literature (Auten *et al.*, 2002). Summarizing four decades of US studies, Karlan and List (2007) concluded that it was difficult to make any strong conclusions on the impact of charitable tax reliefs or 'price' on giving. There has been little similar UK research. A study of the impact of tax reliefs on giving through covenant only, a method of committed long-term giving replaced by Gift Aid in 2000, however, found no substantive price effect on participation in, or the level of, giving: it queried the value of charitable tax reliefs almost two decades ago prior to their considerable and steady expansion in the UK (Jones and Posnett, 1991b). Smeaton *et al.*'s (2004) examination of the use of UK tax reliefs concluded that there was little evidence that amounts of donations were related directly to the, rather labyrinthine, rules of UK tax relief. Taking an international comparative perspective of the impact of tax rules on giving, research by Dehne *et al.* (2008) recently concluded that while many national governments do indeed consider charitable tax reliefs to play an important role in encouraging personal giving, the differences between national systems of tax reliefs make assessing their comparative effects very difficult. In a context of growing government interest in the extent to which financial behaviours can be influenced by the way in which incentives or offers are framed, Smith and Scharf's (2010) UK study concluded that a matched payment to a charity receiving a gift had greater impact on giving than a tax rebate to the donor.

Relative importance of different motivations

The previous paragraphs have illustrated not only the multi-faceted nature of motivation to give, but how different motivations may be present in any single act of giving. Bekkers and Wiepking (2007) conclude that the relative influence of different mechanisms on the motivation to give is still unclear. From their overview of motivation studies, they conclude that multiple motives are likely to operate simultaneously in any single act of giving, and, interestingly, that the mix of motives will differ over time, place, organizations, and donors. Few studies have addressed, or tried to measure, the relative relationships between the multiple intrinsic and extrinsic factors present when a decision to give is made, though a number of survey studies already reveal the value which such research approaches might have. For example, it has been shown that apparent variations in levels of giving between different religious denominations could be accounted for, not by any assumed differences in values or beliefs about giving, but by the traditions and beliefs surrounding the ways in which gifts are given or solicited themselves. According to this, Protestant congregations are more likely to give through traditions of tithing and annual pledges, whereas Catholic churches are more likely to raise funds through regular collections (Hoge and Yang, 1994; Zaleski and Zech, 1992). Relationships between different factors might change over a person's lifetime and changing circumstances. James (2008), for example, has shown the impact of life-events on charitable bequesting, and how changes to wills are related to experiences of illness, or the birth of children and grandchildren. Bequest decision-making may be analogous to visualizing the final chapter in one's autobiography (James and O'Boyle, 2014).

Social contexts which prompt giving

Many researchers believe, however, that a sole focus on the individual, and on individual characteristics, is insufficient to explain what motivates giving; they have turned their attention to social influences. Havens *et al.* (2006) highlight the importance of 'communities of participation', or groups and organizations in which the donor is involved, as predictors of the likelihood of charitable giving. They point out that many of the individual characteristics they studied are in practice proxies for the degree to which donors are engaged in society, or their 'network-based social capital'. For example, a college graduate probably has access to exclusive networks such as alumni or professional associations, each offering many opportunities for asking and giving. Moreover, while research has shown powerful relationships between giving and various socio-economic characteristics at the individual level, there is little research exploring why giving behaviour differs between those with apparently similar individual characteristics. For example, why do only about half of the wealthiest UK households give to charity? The explanation may lie in individuals' different social and family situations, and considerable, mainly US, research has explored the extent to which giving and philanthropy occur in contexts where they are embedded within family, social, cultural, business, religious or location-based structures. The research is disparate but reveals the importance of context. As mentioned above, Ostrower's (1997) work has highlighted the role of family and social networks in the giving of the wealthy, while other research has shown that decisions about charitable giving can be influenced and taken by both partners within families or households (Andreoni *et al.*, 2003; Burgoyne *et al.*, 2005; Yörük, 2010). The positive effect of cultural factors on local levels of giving, including the nature and history of activity by local authorities, has been highlighted by Wolpert (1988). Group effect was studied by Ma and Parish (2006) who found that making charitable gifts was used by members of an immigrant business community to gain advantage through strengthening their political position. That those involved in small religious groups or congregations adopted the norms of such groups in relation to altruistic behaviour and taking responsibility for others was shown by Wuthnow (1991). Other relevant research has highlighted how belonging to associations has a generally positive influence on wider civic engagement (Kwak, 2004), while Eikenberry (2009) has recently shown that belonging to social networks such as 'giving circles', whether formal or informal, promotes collective giving behaviour. The polarity between 'individualism' and 'collectivism' has been identified as a significant indicator of the differences between the social values and behaviours of different cultures (Schwartz, 2003), but there has been comparatively little study of the place of collective values, social structures and contexts in prompting philanthropy, or their effect on, for example, exclusiveness in participation, or the achievement of other non-charitable as well as charitable goals.

Elites and celebrities

An exception to the relative neglect of social influences lies within the detailed study of elite giving. Ostrower's (1997) study of the wealthy highlights the important influences of family, social, political, business and other public networks on donor choices, revealing that a high proportion of wealthy donors make gifts to organizations with which they already have a relationship, as a board member, or in a congregation. It showed that philanthropic activity bestowed social prestige and status within groups, confirming membership of an exclusive elite. This also operated within important social sub-groups such as, for example, Jewish subcultures. There is a multiplier effect, too, as donors hold multiple group identities and affiliations, and their status as an elite donor can also confer status in their other wider social circles of which they have or seek to gain membership (Gordon *et al.*, Chapter 21). Research in the UK has also found that the ideas and initiatives of peers, family, friends and colleagues can play a key role in how founders develop their philanthropic vision and mission, and that personal business, social and personal contacts have a significant role in opening up routes into philanthropy (Pharoah 2011a). Many founders identify projects to fund, or test out their ideas, amongst their colleagues and friends.

There are many important historic and geographical links between founders' and trustees' interests or experiences and their giving, such as Paul Hamlyn's seminal contact with the work of Jaipur Foot organizations (BMVSS) in India, which led to the Foundation's continuing interest in this region. Former Commonwealth links through business and other activities also influence the targeting of particular regions for support. Examples of this include the work of the Beit Trust in South Africa, and the Dulverton Trust in East Africa, both originally set up by families who made their fortunes in these regions, and are still dedicated today to helping to develop them. Growing globalism is seeing today's multi-national business activities continue to shape the international philanthropic interests of many major entrepreneurs. Many successful international entrepreneurs are only too aware of global inequalities, aiming to make a substantial contribution to development in the countries and communities from which they originated. George Soros, for example, has used the huge wealth amassed through global finance management to fund open society developments across Central and Eastern Europe, while the Khodorkovsky Foundation supports higher education amongst young Russians, and the Kusuma Trust UK, founded by Anurag Dikshit, aims to strengthen secondary and tertiary educational achievement in India. The giving of George Soros has been argued by some as representing a 'policy' rather than a 'philanthropic' transfer (Stone, 2010), highlighting issues of governance in relation to major international donations and their wider social, economic or political implications which are increasingly attracting attention (Parliamentary Select Committee on International Development, 2012).

For some, the faith and other value or cultural traditions within family, educational and wider community contexts provide important philanthropic role models or leadership. Several founders in Pharoah's (2011a) study referred to the significance of family background: as one said 'we were a family who gives'. Some founders came from backgrounds where they had direct experience of need, or had parents who saw exposure to need as an important part of family upbringing. One commented that 'involving them in voluntary work was the best thing my mother could ever have done ... my interest in philanthropy began right there, every young person should do this'. The reason for falling rates of giving participation amongst younger groups in the UK has been identified as a lack of parental or school example and motivation, and the Citizenship Foundation is funded to develop school curricula around charitable giving. Fundraising charities themselves have turned to celebrities as a new kind of elite model for giving, particularly for younger generations of donors. This carries risks. Shared involvement in supporting a common cause may make potential donors feel closer to a familiar and admired celebrity and give the impression that they can attract some of their glory. However, there is a danger that this may result in devaluing giving to lower-profile activities. It can lead to the commodification of philanthropy as just another item of consumption, or to the point where philanthropy becomes 'charitainment' (Driessens *et al.*, 2012). This can be damaging if fashions in celebrities, and causes, move on (Cooper, 2008). Moreover, if celebrity engagement in charity is trivialized, and its value seen as reputational rather than substantive in relation to a cause or to real social change, there is a risk of alienating potential donors, denigrating celebrity contributions and damaging the credibility of the cause. Recent examples where celebrities have lost their status, such as Jimmy Savile in the UK or Lance Armstrong in the US, resulted in the charities they set up being closed or losing donations. Association between powerful elites from entertainment, media, business or government worlds and charitable causes are risky: both sides stand to gain hugely from the relationship, but a good cause may lose significant donations as well as potential reputational risk if a high-status donor falls from grace, particularly in the spotlight of the media.

Public and private choices

Current government interest and policy development around philanthropy derive from a notion that the motivation towards private philanthropy could replace the need for the state to assume total responsibility for the provision of public welfare (Healy and Donnelly-Cox, Chapter 12; Phillips and Smith, Chapter 13). Research on philanthropic giving to the major charities and causes in the UK, however, shows marked contrasts in the way in which philanthropic and statutory funding is distributed across them (Pharoah 2011c). The majority of UK private giving, for example, supports the four causes of international development, cancer, animal welfare and religious causes associated with international development or general welfare. While international causes also attract a great deal of statutory funding, the others do not. Social welfare needs in the UK attract a much larger proportion of statutory than philanthropic funding, while in contrast health causes are much more dependent on philanthropy. Charitable giving for health at the local level appears particularly strong, with local hospices in the UK showing the fastest growth in giving of all local causes, raising funds on a par with many big national charities. Hospices offer the dedicated palliative care in small, intimate and homely contexts which people prefer, and which it is often too difficult or costly to provide in large general state hospitals. Such findings indicate that priorities between private donors and public funders are rather different, and that those of the one group would not easily substitute for those of the other. Turning to the US literature, it has been concluded that there is limited evidence of a general redistributive effect from the nonprofit sector; major giving, for example, is largely dedicated to facilities like universities and large national or regional cultural institutions from which the middle and upper classes are the main direct beneficiaries (Clotfelter, 1992; Reich, 2005). In a society where there is high income inequality, the strong positive links between giving and wealth result in unequal access to the opportunity to give, or to shape the contribution of philanthropy to the public good.

Volunteering and giving

While this paper has a principally monetary focus, it is important to remember that people also give substantially to others in non-monetary ways, through volunteering their time, skills and expertise, through gifts of food, clothes and other items, and even their blood and bodily organs. Research is increasingly exploring whether, and how, different ways of giving might be related behaviours, and share motivational and other characteristics. Economists are interested in whether the giving of money and of time substitute for, complement, or crowd each other out. In a recent study in the UK (Mohan and Bulloch, 2012), it was claimed that a well-off 'civic core' of eight percent of the population is responsible for both 49 percent of volunteering and four percent of the monetary value of giving. Amongst chief executives and chairs of large UK companies, all of whom served as charitable trustees, a mix of attitudes towards whether they should give time, money or both was found (Walker and Pharoah, 2000). One respondent said 'a business leader contributes a unique mixture of skills and money: you can't get away in charities from money' (Walker and Pharoah, 2000: 50). Further investigation is taking place about particular groups' volunteering and giving dispositions (Bekkers, Chapter 7). However, such indications that giving and volunteering are complementary behaviours and largely carried out by the same kinds of people is not borne out in all research. Other studies suggest that they are negatively related and may substitute for each other (Duncan, 1999; Feldman, 2009). Apinunmahakul *et al.* (2009) argue, however, that any apparent substitution disappears for those in paid employment. Whatever the individual's choices about giving and volunteering, a growing body of research indicates that civic behaviours and attitudes constitute a closely-related mesh, of which giving and volunteering are a part. As indicated above, participation in local associations of various kinds appears to lead individuals on to giving and volunteering (Wuthnow, 1991; Kwak, 2004; Eikenberry, 2009). A particularly strong case for the links between different voluntary activities is put by Eckstein (2001), who distinguishes between those which are individually inspired and those which grow from being a member of a group or community. She finds that in the latter '[g]iving, volunteering, and joining are mutually reinforcing' (Eckstein 2001: 830). It is not clear how far giving and volunteering simply co-exist for a number of external reasons, such as the proximity of opportunity, or are derived from the same motivational forces, but some psychologists have explained different helping behaviours in terms of the theory of our identity (Lee *et al.*, 1999). They found that volunteering, giving and making blood donations are all related to identity factors, such as expectations of how we should behave, the models of behaviours provided by our parents, our personal norms, and past behaviour. Different ways of giving, however, were not all influenced in the same way by these identity factors: volunteering of time, 'the most "public" form of donation', appears more strongly influenced by others' expectations than gifts of blood or money. Blood donation is affected more strongly by parents' models than volunteering is, while feelings of moral obligation have a stronger effect on role identity as a blood donor than as a donor of time or money. The extent to which existing activists and volunteers can be motivated to extend their commitment to giving, or vice versa, is at the heart of the relationship-building approaches to fundraising which are widely in vogue today.

Concluding Remarks

This review of the research and thinking on motivation reveals how the impulse to make a philanthropic gift is complex and multifaceted, embedded in personal, spiritual, social and economic contexts of donors' lives and mediated by the way in which gifts are solicited. The importance and interplay of different factors varies for different people, and in different circumstances. Giving can only be fully understood when interpreted as an action within both private and public spheres, within donors' intentions, as well as within their public circumstances. The reasons why giving behaviours appear relatively resilient to change, at least in the short term, are likely to lie in the deep-rooted way in which they are embedded in different private and public contexts.

While this makes motivation and the impulse towards giving a rich and tantalizing subject, it can represent a challenge to those looking for quick, easy or sustained ways to increase giving in our society. It is helpful in this context to draw on Schneewind's (1996) distinction between philanthropy as the expression of a generally humanitarian 'state of mind', and as instrumental activities devoted to specific needs, such as poverty and ill-health, regardless of where the resources come from. The study of patterns of charitable support shows that contribution to the public good is often highly partisan, aimed at reinforcing private passions rather than at meeting publicly-identified needs, and less directly socially instrumental than is recognized in government rhetoric and policy towards its promotion. While the motivation to give is a part of a pluralist and increasingly multi-cultural society, private giving does not in itself create a more pluralistic society in which the full diversity of need is addressed.

This raises the issue of how far individuals' private motivation to give can or should be seen as something which public policymakers can influence. The widespread sending of money back to communities of origin in the developing world by migrants today show how philanthropy arises in contexts of collective responsibility where governmental or other external support is lacking (Schmid and Schaul Bar Nissim, Chapter 10). Today's society in the West, however, is characterized on the one hand by increasingly diverse and fragmented communities, and on the other by increasingly individualist patterns of consumption. Motivating us to give more may only help meet gaps in public welfare if that motivation is strongly aligned with a fresh awareness of need and a renewed sense of social, public and collective responsibility towards the good of all. Current UK government policy implicitly recognizes the inherent public–private tension and aims to influence individual giving motivation and choice through a renewed communitarian emphasis on common public and shared interests. Its approach aims at both cultural and behavioural change (UK Cabinet Office, 2010). In tackling the question of how to motivate people towards specific goals, policy draws heavily on the neo-liberal behavioural economics of Thaler and Sunstein (2009). This defends individual freedom of choice, but at the same time makes the case for private and public institutions to influence choice in ways they see as desirable to themselves or which are, in their view, beneficial to the individual. Achieving a steer can involve 'framing' or manipulating individuals' spending choices in ways which lead them to make the desired decisions. Others involve creating social norms which will influence the motivation to give. The cultural norms approach implicitly recognizes that social and other contexts can have a huge influence on the motivation to give. How social, community-based or other shared senses of values and interests can be built, or developed sufficiently strongly to drive giving motivation towards certain public goods is an area currently under-developed in research, policy or practice; studies of giving remain largely individualistic in their orientation. Because of the uncertainty surrounding the potential of further tax reliefs to incentivize more giving, the UK government is hesitating to introduce further tax reliefs, in particular for the type of life-time giving products very popular in the US, while its recent 'Innovation in Giving' fund focuses rather differently on initiatives which feature the role of exchange in generating giving behaviours. Examples include 'Streetbank', which facilitates giving away time, skills or goods to those living within a mile of the donor's home, and 'Care4Care' which enables people to support the elderly in their own community while building up their own 'care pensions' in return. These are tiny test-beds for motivating giving reciprocity, and have not yet been evaluated. One challenge is that success may be related to the strength of pre-existing neighbourhood networks rather than capacity to forge new links.

A somewhat singular, though innovative, move to direct donor choice towards specific areas of public welfare is taken in a recent report by New Philanthropy Capital (NPC/Barclays Wealth, 2011) which asks if donors should 'be taking a broader, utilitarian view of what can be achieved by charitable donations'. It suggests that, at a time when charities find their income depleted by shifts in public spending and broader financial uncertainty, donors should be less motivated by their hearts and more by their heads. Should potential to make savings in public expenditure be an important motivation alongside, even superseding, other motivations? In reality, this is an approach which aims to move giving further out of the private sphere of voluntary impulse and individual discretionary power within the state. The underlying position is that if donor choice cannot be persuaded to move further into the public sphere, then the donor's discretionary power to give may have to be reduced. This approach interestingly harks back to Halfpenny's (1999) arguments as set out earlier. In implying that donor motivations and choices not based on economic considerations are not rational, it rules out the possibility that motivation can also be influenced through influencing social contexts to encourage people take greater public responsibility for the needs of others. A recent book about major donor motivation written by a leading UK fundraiser places its emphasis on the donor benefit, arguing that 'giving is good for you', and that social inequality is ultimately dysfunctional for society (Nickson, 2013). This society, of course, is one in which the donor's own existing interests – and perhaps those of the fundraiser – are embedded.

In practice, a highly directed type of voluntary giving is more like a form of voluntary public taxation than a private action for public good. The particular example given above could even be considered as leading to a voluntary hypothecated tax, in the sense of the pressure to give towards specific types of causes, a sentiment further reflected in the growing discourse on 'Total Impact' philanthropy (Harrow and Jung, 2015). Growing personal wealth, the burgeoning availability of information and communications through new technology and mass global media have enormously increased people's capacity and opportunity to give, but this is proving a double-edged sword as public and governmental expectations of philanthropy increase alongside this. The study of motivation shows the intricacies of the balance it maintains between private and public spheres. As donors are presented with increasing and ever more difficult demands and choices at every stage of giving, and as governments become increasingly involved in promoting philanthropy, we will need to understand much more about how multiple motivations get articulated and the decision-making process which leads to a gift.

References

Amato, P. R. (1985) 'An Investigation of Planned Helping Behavior', *Journal of Research in Personality*, 19: 232–52.

Andreoni, J. (1990) 'Impure Altruism and Donations to Public Goods: A Theory of Warm-Glow Giving', *The Economic Journal*, Vol. 100, No. 401 (June 1990) pp. 464–77.

Andreoni, J. (2006) 'Philanthropy'. In L.-A. Gerard-Varet, S.-C. Kolm, and J. M. Ythier (eds.), *Handbook of Giving, Reciprocity and Altruism*, pp. 1201–69. North-Holland: Elsevier.

Andreoni, J. and Petrie, R. (2004) 'Public Goods Experiments Without Confidentiality: A Glimpse into Fund-raising', *Journal of Public Economics*, 88: 1605–23.

Andreoni, J., Brown, E., and Rischall, I. (2003) 'Charitable Giving by Married Couples: Who Decides and Why Does It Matter?', *The Journal of Human Resources*, 38 (1), pp. 111–33.

Andreoni, J., Payne, A., Davis Smith, J., and Karp, D. (2011) 'Diversity and Donations: The Effect of Religious and Ethnic Diversity on Charitable Giving'. NBER Working Paper 17618, November 2011.

Apinunmahakul, A., Barham, V., and Devlin, R. A. (2009) 'Charitable Giving, Volunteering, and the Paid Labor Market', *Nonprofit and Voluntary Sector Quarterly*, February 2009, Vol. 38, No. 1, 77–94.

Auten, G., Sieg, H., and Clotfelter, C. (2002) 'Charitable Giving, Income and Taxes: An Analysis of Panel Data', *American Economic Review*, 92(1), 371–82.

Banks, J. and Tanner, S. (1997) 'The State of Donation: Household Gifts to Charity, 1974–96', Institute for Fiscal Studies, London. Available at: www.ifs.org.uk/comms/comm62.pdf [Accessed 10 February 2015]

Batson, C. D., and Shaw, L. L. (1991) 'Evidence for Altruism: Toward a Pluralism of Prosocial Motives', *Psychological Inquiry*, 2: 107–22.

Bekkers, R. (2006) 'Traditional and Health Related Philanthropy: The Role of Resources and Personality', *Social Psychology Quarterly*, 68: 349–66.

Bekkers, R. (2007) 'Measuring Altruistic Behavior in Surveys: The All-or-Nothing Dictator Game', Survey Research Methods 1.

Bekkers, R. and Schuyt, T. N. M. (2005) 'And Who Is Your Neighbor? Explaining the Effect of Religion on Charitable Giving and Volunteering'. Working paper, Department of Philanthropic Studies, Vrije Universiteit Amsterdam.

Bekkers, R. and Wiepking, P. (2007) 'Generosity and Philanthropy: A Literature Review'. Amsterdam: Vrije Universiteit. www.papers.ssrn.com/sol3/papers.cfm?abstract_id=1015507 [Accessed 5 February 2015]

Bekkers, R. and Wilhelm, M. (2008) 'Helping Behavior, Dispositional Empathic Concern, and the Principle of Care.' Working paper, Department of Philanthropic Studies, VU University Amsterdam, the Netherlands.

Burgoyne, C., Young, B., and Walker, C. (2005) 'Deciding to Give to Charity: A Focus Group Study in the Context of the Household Economy', *Journal of Community and Applied Social Psychology*, 15: 383–405. Published online in Wiley InterScience (www.interscience.wiley.com). DOI: 10.1002/casp.832.

Carroll, J., McCarthy, S., and Newmand, C. (2005) 'An Econometric Analysis of Charitable Donations in the Republic of Ireland', *The Economic and Social Review*, Vol. 36, No. 3, Winter, pp. 229–49.

Clain, S. H. and Zech, C. E. (1999) 'A Household Production Analysis of Religious and Charitable Activity', *American Journal of Economics and Sociology*, 58 (4), pp. 923–46.

Clotfelter, C. (1992) *Who Benefits from the Non-Profit Sector?*. University of Chicago Press, Chicago.

Cooper, A. F. (2008) 'Beyond One Image Fits All: Bono and the Complexity of Celebrity Diplomacy', *Global Governance*, 14, 265–72.

Cowley, E., McKenzie, T., Pharoah, C., and Smith, S. (2011) 'The New State of Donation – Three Decades of Household Giving to Charity 1978–2008'. London: Centre for Charitable Giving and Philanthropy, Cass Business School /CMPO, Bristol University. www.cgap.org.uk/uploads/reports/ The new state of donation.pdf [Accessed 2 January 2012].

Davis, S. (1996) 'Philanthropy as a Virtue in Late Antiquity and the Middle Ages'. In J. Schneewind (ed.). *Giving*. Indiana University Press, Indiana, 1–23.

Dawkins, R. (2006) *The Selfish Gene: 30th Anniversary Edition*. Oxford University Press.

Dehne, A., Friedrich, P., Woon Nam, C., and Parsche, R. (2008) 'Taxation of Nonprofit Associations in an International Comparison'. *Nonprofit and Voluntary Sector Quarterly*, April 2008, 37.709.

Driessens, O., Joye, S., and Biltereyst, D. (2012) 'The X-factor of Charity: A Critical Analysis of Celebrities' Involvement in the 2010 Flemish and Dutch Haiti Relief Shows', *Media, Culture and Society*, 34(6), 709–25.

Duncan, B. (1999) 'Modeling Charitable Contributions of Time and Money', *Journal of Public Economics*, 72: 213–42.

Eckstein, S., (2001) 'Community as Gift-Giving: Collectivistic Roots of Volunteerism', *American Sociological Review*, Vol. 66, No. 6, pp. 829–51.

Eikenberry, A. (2009) *Giving Circles, Philanthropy, Voluntary Association and Democracy, Indiana*. University Press. Bloomington.

ESRC/NCVO (2005) *Charitable Giving and Donor Motivation*. ESRC, Swindon.

Farmer, S. M. and Fedor, D. B. (2001) 'Changing the Focus on Volunteering: An Investigation of Volunteers' Multiple Contributions to a Charitable Organization', *Journal of Management*, 27: 191–211.

Feldman, N. E. (2009) 'Time is Money: Choosing Between Charitable Activities', *American Economic Journal: Economic Policy*, 2(1): 103–30.

Ford, J. B and Merchant, A. (2010) 'Nostalgia Drives Donations: The Power of Charitable Appeals Based on Emotions and Intentions', *Journal of Advertising Research*, 50(4), 450–9.

Giving USA. (2014) *Highlights, The Center on Philanthropy at Indiana University*. Indiana University, Purdue University Indianapolis, www.ctphilanthropy.org/sites/default/files/resources/Giving percent20USA percent202014percent20Reportpercent20Highlights.pdf [Accessed 03 June 2015]

Halfpenny, P. (1999) 'Economic and Sociological Theories of Individual Charitable Giving: Complementary or Contradictory?,' *Voluntas*, Vol. 10, No. 3 199, p. 197, 215.

Harrow, J. and Jung, T. (2011) 'Philanthropy is Dead; Long Live Philanthropy?', *Public Management Review*, 13(8): 1048–56.

Harrow, J. and Jung, T. (2015) 'Debate: Thou Shalt Have Impact, Total Impact—Government Involvement in Philanthropic Foundations' Decision-making', *Public Money and Management*, 35(3), p. 176–8.

Havens, J., Schervish, P., and O'Herlihy, M. (2006) 'Charitable Giving: How Much, by Whom, to What, and How?', In W. Powell and R. Steinberg (eds.), *The Non-Profit Sector: A Research Handbook*, 2nd edition. Yale University Press.

Hoge, D. R. and Yang, F. (1994). 'Determinants of Religious Giving in American Denominations: Data from Two Nationwide Surveys', *Review of Religious Research*, 36: 123–48.

Ilchman, W. F., Katz, S., and Queen II, E. L. (1998) *Philanthropy in the World's Traditions*. Bloomington and Indianapolis: Indiana University Press.

Independent Sector (2002) *Faith and Philanthropy: The Connection Between Charitable Behaviour and Giving to Religion*. Washington, DC: Independent Sector.

Jackson, J. M. and Latané, B. (1981) 'Strength and Number of Solicitors and the Urge Toward Altruism', *Personality and Social Psychology Bulletin*, 7: 415–22.

James, R. N. (2008) 'Health, Wealth, and Charitable Estate Planning: A Longitudinal Examination of Testamentary Charitable Giving Plans.' *Nonprofit and Voluntary Sector Quarterly* 38(6): 1026–1043.

James III, R. N. and O'Boyle, M. W. (2014) 'Charitable Estate Planning as Visualized Autobiography.' An fMRI Study of its Neural Correlates, *Nonprofit and Voluntary Sector Quarterly*, 43(2): 355–373.

Jones, A. and Posnett, J. (1991a) 'Charitable Donations by UK Households: Evidence from the Family Expenditure Survey', *Applied Economics*, 23, pp. 343–351.

Jones, A. and Posnett, J. (1991b) 'The Impact of Tax Deductibility on Charitable Giving by Covenant in the UK', *The Economic Journal*, Vol. 101 No. 408 (Sep. 1991) pp. 1117–1129.

Karlan, D. and List, J. (2007) 'Does Price Matter in Charitable Giving? Evidence from a Large-Scale Natural Field Experiment', *The American Economic Review*, Vol. 97, No. 5 (Dec. 2007), pp. 1774–1793.

Kingma, B. (1997) 'Public Good Theories of the Non-profit Sector: Weisbrod Revisited', *Voluntas*, 8:2 (1997), pp. 135–148.

Kwak, N. (2004) 'Connecting, Trusting, and Participating: The Direct and Interactive Effects of Social Associations', *Political Research Quarterly*, Vol. 57, No. 4, pp. 643–52.

LaBarge, M. and Stinson, J. L. (2013) 'The Role of Mental Budgeting in Philanthropic Decision-Making', *Nonprofit and Voluntary Sector Quarterly* Online, July 8.

Lee, L., Piliavin, J. A., and Call, V. R. R. (1999) 'Giving Time, Money, and Blood: Similarities and Differences', *Social Psychology Quarterly*, Vol. 62, No. 3. (Sep. 1999), pp. 276–90.

Levitt, L. and Kornhaber, R. C. (1977) 'Stigma and Compliance. A Re-Examination', *Journal of Social Psychology*, 103: 13–18.

Lincoln, R., Morrissey, C., and Mundey, P. (2008) 'Religious Giving: A Literature Review'. Science of Generosity. Dept. of Sociology, University of Notre Dame.

Lloyd, T. (2004) 'Why Rich People Give'. Philanthropy UK, Association of Charitable Foundations.

McKenzie, T. and Pharoah, C. (2013) 'A Decade of Donations in the UK: Household Gifts to Charity, 2001–11'. Briefing Note 11, Centre for Charitable Giving and Philanthropy, Cass Business School.

Ma, D. and Parish, W. L. (2006) 'Tocquevillian Moments: Charitable Contributions by Chinese Private Entrepreneurs', *Social Forces*, Vol. 85, No. 2.

Mauss, M. (1954) *The Gift*. Cohen and West.

Mohan, J. and Bulloch, S. L. (2012) 'The Idea of a "Civic Core": What are the Overlaps Between Charitable Giving, Volunteering, and Civic Participation in England and Wales?' Third Sector Research Centre.

Mullin, R. (2002) 'The Evolution of Charitable Giving'. In C. Walker, C. Pharoah *et al.* (eds.) (2001), *A lot of Give – Trends in giving for the 21st Century*. Hodder and Stoughton. London.

NCVO/CAF. UK Giving Editions 2005–2011. NCVO. London.

Nickson, J. (2013) *Giving is Good for You*. Biteback Publishing. London

NPC/Barclays Wealth (2011) 'Early Interventions: An Economic Approach to Charitable Giving'.

Ostrower, F. (1997) *Why the Wealthy Give. The Culture of Elite Philanthropy*. Princeton University Press. New Jersey.

Parliamentary Select Committee on International Development (2012). *Thirteenth Report – Private Foundations*. London. House of Commons. www.publications.parliament.uk/pa/cm201012/cmselect/cmintdev/1557/155702.htm [Accessed 20 December 2012].

Payton, R. L. (1996) 'Introduction'. In J. Schneewind (ed.), *Giving*. Indiana University Press. Indiana, ix.

Pharoah, C. (2011a) *Family Foundation Giving 2011*. CGAP. Cass Business School. (Also 2008, 2009 and 2010 editions.

Pharoah, C. (2011b) *Charity Market Monitor 2011*. CaritasData. London. (Also Charity Market Monitor 2008, 2009, 2010, and Charity Trends 1996 to 2006).

Pharoah, C. (2011c) 'Private Giving and Philanthropy – Their Place in the Big Society'. *People, Place & Policy* Online, 5/2, pp. 65–75.

Polonsky, M. J., Shelley L., and Voola, R. (2002) 'An Examination of Helping Behavior – Some Evidence from Australia', *Journal of Nonprofit and Public Sector Marketing*, 10: 67–82.

Radley, A. and Kennedy, M. (1992) 'Reflections upon Charitable Giving: A Comparison of Individuals from Business, "Manual" and Professional Backgrounds', *Journal of Community and Applied Social Psychology*, 2: 113–29.

Reece, W. S. (1979). 'Charitable Contributions: New Evidence on Household Behavior', *The American Economic Review*, 69(1), 142–51.

Reed P. B. and Selbee, L. K. (2002) 'Is There a Distinctive Pattern of Values Associated with Giving and Volunteering? The Canadian Case'. The 32nd ARNOVA Conference. Montreal, Canada.

Reich, R. (2005) 'A Failure of Philanthropy: American Charity Short-changes the Poor, and Public Policy is Partly to Blame', *Stanford Social Innovation Review*, Winter 2005. Stanford, 23–33.

Reuter, M., Frenzel, C., Walter, T., Markett, S., and Montag, C. (2010) 'Investigating the Genetic Basis of Altruism: The Role of the COMT Val158Met Polymorphism', *Social Cognitive and Affective Neuroscience*, Vol. 6, Issue 5, pp. 662–8.

Salamon, L. M., Anheier, H. K., List, R., Toepler, S., Sokolowski, S.W., and associates. (1999) 'Global Civil Society: Dimensions of the Nonprofit Sector'. The Johns Hopkins Comparative Nonprofit Sector Project. Johns Hopkins University. Baltimore.

Sanghera, B. (2011) 'Charitable Giving, Everyday Morality and a Critique of Bourdieusian Theory'. Working Paper. Centre for Charitable Giving and Philanthropy. (forthcoming).

Sargeant, A. (1999) 'Charitable Giving: Towards a Model of Donor Behaviour', *Journal of Marketing Management*, 1999, 15, 215–238.

Schervish, P. G. and Havens, J. J. (1997) 'Social Participation and Charitable Giving: A Multivariate Analysis', *Voluntas: International Journal of Voluntary and Nonprofit Organizations*, 8(3), pp. 235–60.

Schlegelmilch B. B., Diamantopoulos, A., Love, A. (1997) 'Characteristics Affecting Charitable Donations: Empirical Evidence from Britain', *Journal of Marketing Practice: Applied Marketing Science*, 3: 14–28.

Schneewind, J. (1996) 'Philosophical Ideas of Charity: Some Historical Reflections'. In J. Schneewind (ed.), *Giving*, pp. 54–75. Indiana University Press. Indiana.

Schuyt, T. N. M., Smit, J., Bekkers, R. (2004) *Constructing a Philanthropy-scale: Social Responsibility and Philanthropy*. 33d, Arnova Conference. Los Angeles.

Schwartz, S., (2003) 'Mapping and Interpreting Cultural Differences Around the World'. In H. Vinken, *et al.*, *Comparing Cultures, Dimensions of Culture in a Comparative Perspective*. Leiden, The Netherlands. Brill.

Smeaton, D., Marsh, A., Rajkumar, R., and Thomas, A. (2004) 'Individuals' Donations to Charities and their Use of Tax Relief'. Report carried out by BMRB Social Research for HMInland Revenue (UK).

Smith, S. and Scharf, K. (2010) 'The Price Elasticity of Charitable Giving: Does the Form of Tax Relief Matter?'. Working Paper No. 10/247. The Centre for Market and Public Organisation.

Sprecher, S. and Fehr, B. (2005) 'Compassionate Love for Close Others and Humanity', *Journal of Social and Personal Relationships*, 2005, 22, 629. Sage.

Statistics Canada (2010) '2010 Canada Survey of Giving, Volunteering and Participating'.

Stone, D. (2010) 'Private Philanthropy or Policy Transfer? The Transnational Norms of the Open Society Institute', *Policy and Politics*, 38(2), 269–87.

Thaler, R and Sunstein, C. (2009) *Nudge*. London. Penguin Books

Todd, S. J., and Lawson, R.W. (1999) 'Towards a Better Understanding of the Financial Donor: An Examination of Donor Behavior in Terms of Value Structure and Demographics', *International Journal of Nonprofit and Voluntary Sector Marketing*, 4(3), 235–44.

UK Cabinet Office, HM Government (2011) 'Giving White Paper'. Crown 2011 http://www.cabinetoffice.gov.uk/resource-library/giving-white-paper [Accessed 3 June 2015].

United Way (2015) 'About United Way Worldwide', http://www.unitedway.org/pages/about-united-way-worldwide/ [Accessed 3 June 2015].

Vesterlund, L. (2006) 'Why Do People Give?'. In W. E. Powell and R. Steinberg (eds.), *The Nonprofit Sector: A Research Handbook*, pp. 568–90. Yale University Press.

Vriens, M., van der Scheer, H. R., Hoekstra, J. C., and Bult, J. R. (1998) 'Conjoint Experiments for Direct Mail Response Optimization', *European Journal of Marketing*, 32: 323–39.

Walker, C. and Pharoah, C. (2000) 'Making Time for Charity'. Charities Aid Foundation. West Malling. Kent. UK.

Walker, C. and Pharoah, C. (2002) *A lot of Give – Trends in giving for the 21st Century*. Hodder and Stoughton. London.

Wilhelm, M. O., Rooney, P. M., and Tempel, E. R. (2007) 'Changes in Religious Giving Reflect Changes in Involvement: Age and Cohort Effects in Religious Giving, Secular Giving, and Attendance', *Journal for the Scientific Study of Religion*, 46: 217–32.

Wolpert, J. (1988) 'The Geography of Generosity: Metropolitan Disparities in Donations and Support for Amenities', *Annals of the Association of American Geographers*, Vol. 78, No. 4 (Dec., 1988), pp. 665–79.

Wunderink, S. R. (2002) 'Individual Financial Donations to Charities in The Netherlands: Why, How and How Much?', *Journal of Nonprofit and Public Sector Marketing*, 10(2), 21–39

Wuthnow, R. (1991) *Acts of Compassion: Caring for Others and Helping Ourselves*. Princeton. Princeton University Press.

Wuthnow, R. (1999) 'Mobilizing Civic Engagement: The Changing Impact of Religious Involvement'. In Theda Skocpol and Morris Fiorina (eds.), *Civic Engagement in American Democracy Brookings Institution*. Washington, DC.

Yen, S.T. (2002) 'An Econometric Analysis of Household Donations in the USA', *Applied Economics Letters*, 9, pp. 837–41.

Yörük, B. K. (2010) 'Charitable Giving by Married Couples Revisited', *The Journal of Human Resources*, 45(2), pp. 497–516.

Zaleski, P. A. and Zech, C. E. (1992) 'Determinants of Contributions to Religious Organizations. Free Riding and Other Factors', *American Journal of Economics and Sociology*, 51(4), 459–72.

5

Women and philanthropy

Debra J. Mesch and Andrea Pactor

With demographic factors widely considered as being strongly related to giving, women's philanthropy has been significantly shaped by their changing economic position and social roles. Looking at data from the US, for example, the proportion of women participating in the labour force has steadily increased, from 40 percent in the 1970s, to around 60 percent at present (Bureau of Labor Statistics, 2014). While women's earnings continue to be lower than men's, over the last 25 years, the gender pay gap has decreased from 40 percent to 20 percent (Bureau of Labor Statistics, 2011), the numbers of wives earning more than their husbands has grown to a total of 26 percent (Fry and Cohn, 2010), and the proportion of working women with a college degree has almost tripled (Bureau of Labor Statistics, 2011). Similar trends can be identified globally. Of the world's 2.9 billion workers, 1.2 billion are women, representing a worldwide increase of about 200 million women employed in the past 10 years (International Labour Organization, 2007, 2014), a growing number of women are gaining access to education (International Labour Organization, 2008), and women's share of professional and managerial jobs is, albeit slowly, increasing (International Labour Organization, 2008).

Combined with an emerging research base, these demographic changes point to the importance of getting a better understanding of women's philanthropy. Not only is women's philanthropy a key area of growth and transformation, but it has the potential to change the face of philanthropy. This is especially true at a global level: 'men are more active philanthropists in developed countries, but in emerging countries, women take the lead' (Barclays Wealth, 2010: 2).

Notwithstanding the substantial literature on giving that exists across multiple disciplines (Pharoah, Chapter 4), knowledge on gender differences in philanthropy has only recently seen increased scholarly attention. It is an area in need of further, more detailed, exploration: the more we understand any variance, the better informed we can be in meeting today's challenges and preparing for tomorrow's opportunities. To this end, our chapter provides an overview of the literature on women's philanthropic behaviours. While such behaviours include the giving of time, talent and treasure, we focus especially on the giving of money to charity and focus on three overarching themes: *Women as Givers*, provides an overview of gender differences as to how and why men and women give; *Mobilizing Women's Giving*, highlights the institutional and grassroots efforts aimed at strengthening women's philanthropy; and *Women as Leaders*, reflects on women as philanthropists and leaders in philanthropic institutions. We conclude with directions for future research and highlight the challenges facing the leaders and practitioners of our nonprofit institutions as how to best incorporate and translate these insights into sound practice.

Women as givers

Motivations

Across different disciplines, a substantial literature exists that points to gender differences in altruism, prosocial, empathy, and other motives for helping. For the most part, this finds women to be more selfless, prosocial, nurturing, empathetic, and/or generous than men (Hoffman, 1977; Eisenberg and Lennon, 1983; Eagly and Crowley, 1986; Piliavin and Charng, 1990; Erdle, et al., 1992; Eckel and Grossman, 1998; Andreoni and Vesterlund, 2001; Skoe, et al., 2002; Kottasz, 2004; Jolliffe and Farrington, 2005; Cox and Deck, 2006; Einolf, 2011; Mesch et al., 2011). This is partly ascribed to four overarching issues. First of all, there are differences in gender roles and in the socializing of women as the caregivers of their families (Gilligan, 1982). Second, whereas men might give due to social roles, such as status and social expectations (Eagly and Steffen, 1984; Skoe et al., 2002; Croson et al., 2009), women might view philanthropy as a way to show their caring and to express their moral beliefs (Newman, 1995). Third, the experience of emotions differs between men and women (Harshman and Paivio, 1987). Finally, compared to the more competitive nature of men, women tend to be more egalitarian and likely to engage in reciprocal behaviour (Croson and Gneezy, 2009).

Given that there is a strong and positive relationship between these categories and philanthropy (Bennett, 2003; Wilhelm and Bekkers, 2010; Bekkers and Wiepking, 2011; Mesch et al., 2011), it is useful to examine how such differences translate into the motivations for giving. Even after controlling for empathic concern and principle of care measures, Mesch et al. (2011) highlight significant differences in motives by gender, as well as differences in the likelihood of giving and amount given: men gave approximately 12 percent less on average than women and were significantly less likely to give to charity than women in the full regression model. This resonates with Simmons and Emanuele's (2007: 547,546) findings that, on average, women donate more of both money and time, and that 'altruism is a major contributing factor' where 'society places more expectations on women to be altruistic and to act in an altruistic manner'. Similarly, Wymer (2011: 840) points to significant gender differences in motives for giving and volunteering: women were more likely to donate or volunteer for an organization that helps people in need, while men scored higher on motives that assumed some level of risk-taking and danger, such as rescuing others.

Similar gender differences in motivations for giving can be identified when focusing on high net worth (HNW) individuals. This is illustrated by the following findings from a recent study by the Center on Philanthropy (2011). High net worth women are more motivated than their male counterparts to give when they believe their gift will make a difference (81.7 percent vs. 70.9 percent), when they know the organization is efficient (80.5 percent vs. 69.2 percent), and to give back to the community (78.2 percent vs. 63.3 percent). Women are more likely than men to give because they volunteer at the organization (65.7 percent vs. 49.8 percent) and because they wish to set an example for young people (43.6 percent vs. 25.1 percent). Men were more likely than women to support the same organization annually (67.9 percent vs. 59.5 percent).

Although much of this work is US based, there is evidence of cross-national gender differences in motivations for philanthropy. According to the World Values Survey (2006), data indicate that globally a larger number of women than men believe that service to others is very important; women, more than men, are likely to state that it is very important to provide basic needs; women are more prone to believe that the poor are poor because of unfairness rather than laziness; and women, rather than men, are inclined to argue that the government is not doing enough to fight poverty. This is further supported by Schwartz and Rubel's (2005) assessment of gender differences in values across 19 countries, using the 2002–2003 European Social Survey. It reveals that men attribute more importance than women to self-enhancement values, such as power and achievement, which encourage pursuit of one's own interests; women rate benevolence and universalism values higher, those which emphasize concern for the welfare of others. As Wiepking and Einolf's (2011) analysis of data from the Gallup World View Survey and the World Database of Happiness shows, such differences appear to translate to gender differences in charitable giving as a potential result of variations in: empathy, the degree of religious commitment, income, education, and connection to social networks within different countries. Accordingly, women are more likely to give in some countries because they are more empathic and religious than men; men are more likely to give in other countries because they are more able to give – due to income and wealth – and are more frequently asked (Wiepking and Einolf, 2011).

Differences in giving behaviours

By and large, significant gender differences in the ways in which men and women give are highlighted in the research literature. Several studies find that while females are more likely to give, males might give higher amounts (Weyant, 1984; Belfield and Beney, 2000; Andreoni *et al.*, 2003; Bekkers, 2004; Kottasz, 2004; Einolf, 2006; Lyons and Nivison-Smith, 2006; Mesch *et al.*, 2006; Piper and Schnepf, 2008). Andreoni and Vesterlund's (2001: 1) seminal study demonstrates differences in the 'demand curves for altruism', where men are more responsive to the price of giving. They conclude that men are more generous when it is cheap to give; women are more generous when it is more expensive to give. That is, men are more likely to be either perfectly selfish or perfectly selfless, whereas women tend to be 'egalitarians' who prefer to share evenly, an insight that seems to be supported by tests on giving behaviour outside laboratory settings (Andreoni *et al.*, 2003). Cox and Deck (2006), however, argue that women's generosity is more income elastic: women base their decision of whether to be generous on the costs associated with the decision. That is, women, unlike men, are more likely to be generous when the stakes are lower, and are more responsive to variations in the cost of giving than men.

When looking at charity choices, much of the empirical research indicates that men and women exhibit notable differences. Women tend to give to organizations that have had an impact on them, or someone they know personally (Parsons, 2004; Burgoyne *et al.*, 2005); they are more likely to spread the amounts they give across a wide range of charities (Andreoni, Brown and Rischall, 2003; Brown, 2006; Piper and Schnepf, 2008; Yörük, 2010). Furthermore, women appear to be more keen to give to educational causes (Einolf, 2006; Rooney *et al.*, 2007; Piper and Schnepf, 2008), human services, children, and health-related charities (Midlarsky and Hannah, 1989; Marx, 2000; Einolf, 2006; Bekkers, 2007b; Piper and Schnepf, 2008; Wymer, 2011), the environment (Israel, 2007), overseas causes (Micklewright and Schnepf, 2009), animal welfare (Piper and Schnepf, 2008), and cultural heritage (Bertacchini *et al.*, 2011).

Men, on the other hand, seem to have a tendency to strategically concentrate their giving among a few charities; they often display a preference for giving to sports and recreational groups (Andreoni *et al.*, 2003; Micklewright and Schnepf, 2009), or to causes in which they receive social returns (Kottasz, 2004). However, some insights might be context dependent. For example, Agypt *et al.* (2012) analyze employee giving at a public university. Notwithstanding scholarship's consistent findings that women give more than men, Agypt *et al.*'s (2012) findings suggest that neither sex, nor age, are predictors of giving behaviour in workplace giving campaigns. They note the possible influence on their result of not being able to directly measure marital status – for example, dual career couples may alternate years in which they support workplace giving – and, as another perspective, cite Schlegelmilch *et al.* (1997), where men are more impulsive givers and are more likely to give than women when other people observe their giving.

In terms of religious giving, findings are mixed. Kamas *et al.* (2008) argue that women give more in anonymous giving across all religious denominations, and that women with a high income give significantly more than high-income men. Some research indicates that while men give larger amounts to religion (Brown and Ferris, 2007; Einolf, 2011), women give more to secular causes and for helping those in need (Regnerus *et al.*, 1998; Brown and Ferris, 2007). Other studies, however, find that females are more likely to give to religion (Newman, 1995; Yen, 2002; Piper and Schnepf, 2008). More specifically, Piper and Schnepf (2008: 114) point out that while married men and women show the same level of support for religious organizations, among single people, women are nearly twice as likely as men to give to them; even after controlling for different characteristics – age, income, living alone, region, education, and proxies for wealth – this gender difference remains significant. Again, data analysis from the 2013 Canadian General Social Survey on Giving, Volunteering and Participating reports that, in 2013, women and men gave about the same average annual amount to religious organizations, about $220 a year. However, since women were more likely to make a donation, they contributed 53 percent of the total donations made to religious organizations (Turcotte, 2015).

A recent study, conducted at the Women's Philanthropy Institute at the Center on Philanthropy at Indiana University, highlights significant differences in philanthropic giving between single-headed male and female households: across income levels; by marital status; and across charitable subsectors – as to the likelihood of giving as well as the dollar amount given – controlling for other factors that affect giving (Mesch, 2010). Piper and Schnepf (2008), examining the probability of giving and the amount given by men and women across 15 charities in Great Britain, find the percentage of female donors to be significantly higher than that of male donors for almost all causes. Using the Center on Philanthropy Panel Study of Income Dynamics, the *Women Give 2010* report highlights that women are as, or even more, likely to give across all charitable subsectors (Mesch, 2010). A somewhat different perspective is proposed by Eckel and Grossman (2003). Their research indicates that men and women exhibit a high degree of similarity in their charity choice, but that women are more generous than men in six of their ten cases. In general, this research finds that female-headed households are more likely to give, and give more, to charity than male-headed households across all charitable subsectors and income levels. Other research supports these findings as well (Mesch, *et al.*, 2006; Simmons and Emanuele, 2007; Rooney *et al.* 2005, 2007).

Using a series of field experiments, List (2004) examines the effect of age and gender on giving. It finds that mature men and women give more than their younger counterparts, the lowest rates coming from young men. He concludes, 'charitable giving profiles appear to have different temporal aspects across gender, with men's rates of giving and gift size showing much larger increases over time than women's' (List, 2004: 140). A longitudinal study using the Center on Philanthropy Panel Study focused on gender differences by older American households and finds that Baby Boomer and older women are more likely to give and to give more than their male counterparts. These findings are consistent for the entire sample, as well as those households in the top 25 percent of permanent income (Center on Philanthropy, 2012).

Gender effects on household decisions to give

Although there is some work on how charitable giving is managed within a household and how these decisions are made (Burgoyne *et al.*, 2005), little research has examined the role of gender in reaching these decisions. Because men's and women's preferences and motives for giving are different, research has begun to examine the question as to who in the household is the primary decision maker in giving to charity. The findings indicate that the attributes or the characteristics of the other spouse matters. Focusing only on individual respondents, without considering the dynamic that is going on within the household in making charitable giving decisions, may leave out important information about giving. What is the extent to which giving may be a joint family activity and how may this influence both whether, and how much, to give to a particular cause?

Andreoni *et al.*'s (2003) study examining intra-household decision-making finds evidence that bargaining, predominantly favouring husbands, characterizes how household charitable decisions are made. When decisions were made jointly, husbands had more influence over their wives in deciding on charitable giving. However, they also find that education and income are the primary determinants of control over charitable resources: being the primary earner strengthens one's bargaining power in marriage, as does the husband's education relative to the wife's. When the woman is the decision maker, however, she is significantly more likely to give to education than her husband or a jointly deciding couple. In line with this work, Rooney *et al.* (2007) also finds that women decision makers were more likely to have a positive effect on both the likelihood and amount of giving to education. Furthermore, when females were the main decision makers, results indicate a positive effect on secular giving, but no effect on religious giving, holding other factors constant.

Replicating the Andreoni *et al.* study using data from the 2003 wave of the Panel Study of Income Dynamics (PSID), Yörük (2010), however, comes to the conclusion that jointly deciding households' charitable giving looks more like what the wives would have chosen, and that jointly-deciding households give more than one would predict from the behaviour of households with a sole decision maker. Specifically, he finds that bargaining increases household giving by about seven percent on average. This is mirrored in the work of Wiepking and Bekkers (2010). Using data from the Netherlands, they argue that separate deciding households give significantly less on average than all other couples, when the effect of couples' tastes for giving is considered in the model. However, the statistical significance disappears after controlling for other factors that may affect charitable giving, such as income, education, or home ownership. Their study further supports that, among jointly deciding families, couples with opposing tastes for giving give less than those with similar tastes. However, female deciding households are more generous than separate and joint deciding households in the case of total donations. In the case of donations over €50, male deciding households no longer donated higher amounts compared to female deciding households after traditional gender role characteristics are held constant. Further support for the influence of women in decision-making about giving comes from Kamas *et al.*'s (2008) laboratory study. Using dictator experiments across mixed-sex pairings, men adjusted their giving upward due to their more generous female partners: 'increasing women's participation in traditionally male spheres of decision-making may result in more altruistic economic behavior' (Kamas *et al.*, 2008: 23).

Mobilizing women's giving

Women have always been involved in philanthropy, giving generously of their time, talent, and treasure to improve their community. Today, there are a kaleidoscope of opportunities for women to be involved in philanthropy. These include organized efforts such as women's funds, giving circles, and networks within nonprofit organizations and on college campuses. The myriad ways for women to be engaged in philanthropy expands exponentially the number of women across generations who seek the niche best suited to them to put their values into action.

In the US, the establishment of the Ms. Foundation for Women in 1972 signaled the emergence of the contemporary women's philanthropy movement. Since then, more than 160 women's funds have been founded across the globe: from Mama Cash, the oldest international women's fund, established in the Netherlands in 1983, to Rosa – the UK's fund for women and girls, launched in 2008. Today, women's funds can be found in over 30 emerging and developed countries, and across all continents (Women's Funding Network, 2015a). With more than $535 million in total assets across the Women's Funding Network, the membership organisations make annual grant allocations of over $70 million in areas affecting women and girls (Women's Funding Network, 2015b). This model of women's engagement in philanthropy has provided leadership opportunities at the staff and volunteer level for thousands of women.

Giving circles took root in the US in the 1990s. They are defined as a form of philanthropy where groups of individuals

> pool their resources and then decide together where these resources should be distributed. They also include social, educational, and engagement aspects that seem to engage participants in their communities and increase their understanding of philanthropy and community issues.
>
> *(Eikenberry et al., 2009: 8)*

This model of engagement can range from extremely informal settings such as four or five women seated around a kitchen table deciding how to allocate their 'coupon money' to extremely sophisticated, structured and formal programs such as the Women Donors Network or Rachel's Network. Within this context, Impact 100 groups are an example of giving circles in which 100 female donors contribute $1,000 to raise major funds ($100,000 or greater) for the greatest impact on the community in which they live. From the initial group created in 2001, there are now more than a dozen Impact 100 groups in the US (Impact 100, 2015).

In the early 2000s, two national nonprofit organizations, recognizing the potential of this untapped donor segment, created specific initiatives to engage women more deeply in their mission. The American Red Cross' Tiffany Circle Society of Leaders began as a pilot program in 2007. Since then, it has grown to more than 800 female members across the US and has expanded globally with members in Canada, the UK, France and Australia and plans to open Tiffany Circles in seven more countries (Red Cross, 2015). With the giving level starting at $10,000 annually, the group has raised more than $40 million since its inception. United Way Worldwide responded to grassroots organizing efforts by women in local chapters and created a national umbrella, the Women's Leadership Council. Representing 50,000 women, this raised $132 million in 2010. Another initiative, Women Moving Millions, changed the way people think about women and giving by growing million dollar gifts from women. So far, over $500 million have been pledged by 231 donors to areas that advance women and girls across the globe (Women Moving Millions, 2015).

Each of these models in this brief summary reflects the power of the network, one of the key features of the contemporary women's philanthropy landscape. Several research studies attest to the power of purposeful networks to women. Eikenberry *et al.* (2009), in her research on giving circles, suggests this power arises from the building up of internal bonding and trust among members. The 2011 Study of High Net Worth Women's Philanthropy finds the network positively affects women's philanthropic attitudes and behaviours. In particular, high net worth women who participate in a network are more motivated than counterparts who did not participate in a network to give back to the community (87 percent vs. 71.1 percent) and are more motivated to give when they volunteer at an organization (73.1 percent vs. 59.6 percent). Additionally, more than half of networked women report a great deal of confidence in the ability of individuals and nonprofit organizations to solve societal and global problems (Center on Philanthropy, 2011). A study of Lions Clubs across 14 countries shows the power of women in influencing charitable giving (Kou *et al.*, 2012). Findings indicate that belonging to a club where at least half of the members are female, and where there is an increase in the percent growth in female membership in the respondent's country, are associated with both a greater likelihood of donating, as well as giving more to this international service club. These results are robust to specifications that control for country fixed effects. This research reveals the positive impact that the substantial presence of female members within a club or a country has on members' charitable giving.

Women as leaders in philanthropy

Examples of individual women as leaders in philanthropy are found throughout modern history. Generally wealthy, these women are self-made millionaires, entertainers, celebrities, business women, women who inherited their fortune, or royalty. From business perspectives, contemporary entrepreneurial philanthropy provides such a leadership platform, whether in terms of women as 'social entrepreneurs' (Oppedisano, 2004), or more generally emphasizing the active involvement of entrepreneurs in the search for opportunities to address economic and social inequalities (Gordon *et al.*, Chapter 21). This is illustrated in the vignettes on female philanthropreneurs Zita Cobb and Rohini Nilekani in this volume. Other examples include: Shakira, a Columbian-born, internationally-renowned singer-songwriter, who exemplifies a new generation of philanthropic celebrities; Canadian Margot Franssen, founder of The Body Shop Canada, who has used her corporate platform to advocate for causes for women and girls; Queen Rania of Jordan, who has used social media with great success to advocate for better education for Jordanians; and, in China, actress and model Zhang Ziyi, who contributed one million yuan for the Sichuan earthquake relief in 2008.

Although the stories of individual female philanthropists are inspiring, women have yet to achieve significant prominence as leaders of major philanthropic organizations worldwide. In fact, the other two sectors, government and business, have not only tracked women's progress as leaders, but have also seen an increase in the percentage of women represented at the highest levels of leadership. Two examples are the work of the Inter-Parliamentary Union and Catalyst.

The Inter-Parliamentary Union (ND) has tracked the percentage of women in parliament worldwide since 1997. In September 2012, the world average for female representation in both houses of parliament was 20.2 percent, a 39 percent increase from ten years earlier. In the corporate sector, women have made significant gains in leadership roles. Catalyst has focused on examining the expanding opportunities for women in business for fifty years. In terms of women's impact on philanthropy, a 2011 report on gender and corporate social responsibility found that companies with gender-inclusive leadership teams contributed, on average, more charitable funds. Even after controlling for key factors that might influence total donations, the presence of women leaders in Fortune 500 companies still has a significant, positive effect: more women leaders seem to be correlated with higher levels of philanthropy. By keeping gender issues prominent, gender-inclusive leadership likely also affects the quality of CSR initiatives' (Soares *et al.*, 2011). What difference do women make? Marie Wilson (2007: 9), former President of the Ms. Foundation and founder of The White House Project, writes:

> Women tend to include diverse viewpoints in decision making, have a broader conception of public policy, and offer new solutions. Females … define women's issues more broadly than most of their male colleagues, and they put these issues at the top of the legislative agenda – bills dealing with children, education, and healthcare, for instance.

Although the evidence from the political and corporate sectors indicates that diversity and inclusivity generate stronger results, the philanthropic community does not have a systematic methodology to track women's progress in reaching the top leadership level. Women Count: Charity Leaders 2012 (Jarboe, 2012), a recent initiative in the UK, aims to index female participation as trustees, chairs, and the most senior executives at the UK's largest charities. It draws attention to the gender imbalance at the top philanthropic leadership levels. This is not to say that there are no examples of women who have served as chief executives at a number of the top foundations and nonprofits in the US. For example, Susan Berresford served as CEO of the Ford Foundation, the second largest foundation in the US, from 1996–2007; Judith Rodin, formerly president of the University of Pennsylvania, became CEO of the Rockefeller Foundation in 2005; Melinda Gates is one of three board members of the Gates Foundation; and Jennifer Buffett, married to Warren Buffett's son Peter, is Co-founder and President of the NoVo Foundation with assets of $2 billion USD. However, these still remain exceptions. As such, the last few years have seen growing on increasing diversity in philanthropic leadership. Within the US, the Council on Foundations launched an initiative in 2009, Career Pathways to Philanthropic Leadership, to address approaching leadership transitions due to the retirement of many Baby Boomer leaders, to improve leadership in the field, and to encourage more inclusive practices in recruiting talent. A quantitative study at that time found that 48.7 percent of new foundation executive appointees were women. The study also found more diversity by race and ethnicity for the women appointees than for the male appointees. The largest percentage of female CEOs were appointed to corporate foundations (57.1 percent), family foundations (55.6 percent), and community foundations (53.2 percent) (Council on Foundations, 2009).

Conclusions and directions for future research

Women have always been philanthropic but their stories and actions have not always been included in the historical narrative. There is an extensive literature from education and history that provides an historical perspective of female philanthropists of colour (Walton, 2005; Robertson, 2007). The empirical research should incorporate these perspectives and disciplines. What has changed through this contemporary women's philanthropy movement is that more women across the globe and at all income levels are vocal, visible, active, and telling the story daily of their philanthropic involvement around the world. Benefiting from demographic changes and expanding roles in society, as well as increased access to education and income, two key predictors of philanthropy, women are often the household charitable decision makers and generous donors. Moreover, women have created innovative new models of engagement such as women's funds and brought new life to the notion of collective action through giving circles. They have formed an array of networks that often reach across the globe, strengthen levels of trust, deepen involvement with charities, and result in increased giving.

Given these changes in demographics around the world, and the changing role of women in philanthropy, further research is needed to better understand the role of gender in philanthropy.

Women, indeed, are different from their male counterparts in terms of motivations for giving, patterns of giving, and likelihood and amount of giving. In fact, most of the empirical research reviewed in this chapter comprises studies that have been conducted within the last ten years. As research builds a stronger foundation for this field, it will contribute substantially to a future in which philanthropy is more gender balanced. Below, we provide several areas for future research that will facilitate and explain the impact of women's expanding role in philanthropy.

We know very little about how and where males and females learn to be philanthropic. Who are the role models for philanthropy and what are the characteristics of these role models? What prompts men and women to participate or engage in philanthropy? Extant research provides some evidence of a positive relationship of giving and volunteering between children and their parents (Janoski *et al.*, 1998; Mustillo *et al.*, 2004; Bekkers, 2007a, 2011; Wilhelm *et al.*, 2008). Little research, however, has examined this issue by gender. In a recent study, Wilhelm *et al.* (2011) established the importance of role models and conversations about philanthropy in socializing children and adolescents in charitable giving and volunteering. Regarding gender, they found role-model associations for girls were stronger than for boys, but conversations about giving were more highly associated for boys. This is an exciting new area of research and will help to explain the patterns of giving that we find in the results reported in this chapter. Further research needs to address the underlying reasons for the gender differences, as well as the gendered pathways leading to prosocial behaviour that result in gender differences in philanthropic behaviour found in the current research literature.

Although the field has moved beyond using gender as a control variable in philanthropic giving, there is a paucity of research that examines the intersection of gender and other factors such as race/ethnicity, religion, culture, and stage in life as factors in giving and volunteering. How do these factors affect giving by gender and across cultures? Are there differences in giving across race and ethnicity? How does giving among women change through the generations? In particular what are the differences in how Baby Boomer and older women give from those in Generation Y and younger? Although the religion subsector has received the largest slice of individual giving for over 50 years (Giving USA Foundation, 2011), scant research has explored the role of gender in this area. Are there differences in the way men and women give to philanthropy according to religious denominations? A recently released report by the Pew Research Center (2015) found that one in five adults have no religious affiliation, and young adults today are much more likely to be unaffiliated than previous generations were at a similar stage in their lives. Is the gap that has been found in the past between men and women for religious motives in giving narrowing across the cohorts as religion becomes less important? Are these findings consistent across countries?

We have much to learn about how charitable giving decisions within a household are made. What is the impact of involving other family members in these decisions? Are there differences across race, culture, and nations in the way decisions are made and how gender influences these decisions across cultures? We need a much better understanding of not only *who* is in charge of making philanthropic decisions, but also whether or not this will allow us to estimate how much will be given and where it will go. Knowing who makes the decision to give and how decisions to give are reached within a household provides important information in understanding the influence of gender in giving. What are the factors that influence men's and women's giving within a household and how does this affect giving decisions? Previous research indicates that whoever has the most education has the most power in bargaining; having more education than one's spouse significantly increases the likelihood of being the primary charitable giving decision maker. This research also indicates that there has been a much stronger role for the wife in charitable decision-making over time, especially compared to data from 20 years ago.

As women are gaining in education across the globe, this area of research can provide fruitful information for fundraisers and nonprofit organizational leaders to better understand how to target, solicit, and cultivate different donors.

Additionally, other research indicates that the proportion of females is significantly linked to the amount of influence women hold on corporate boards (Wang and Coffey, 1992; Campbell and Mínguez-Vera, 2008; Bear et al., 2010; Soares et al., 2011; Ahern and Dittmar, 2012). Marquis and Lee (2013), finding that the increased presence of women senior managers and directors leads firms to make greater philanthropic contributions, suggest that particular interest for future research is the effect of gender at CEO level, as this position is so central to corporate philanthropy and corporate strategy in general. More research is also needed to better understand how the growing representation of women in nonprofit organizations, particularly those in developing countries, impacts civil society.

Despite the overwhelming evidence that women today have the capacity for, and participate actively in, philanthropy, a predisposition to a male-centered and male-dominated climate is still evident in the fundraising community and nonprofit sector.

Gender does matter in philanthropy. Women and men differ in their motivations for giving. They exhibit different giving patterns. What works for men may not work for women. New fundraising strategies which include both spouses from the beginning of the conversation and also include single women acknowledge the evolving dynamics of who is a philanthropist and who is philanthropic. As the twenty-first century unfolds, women worldwide will continue to push the limits, explore the possibilities, and bring new perspectives and ideas to enrich and energize their communities for the common good. Fundraisers, practitioners, and nonprofit professionals who embrace the new normal of a more balanced gender approach to philanthropy will find a willing, loyal, and generous group of donors among the women in their database.

References

Agypt, B., Christensen, R. K., and Nesbit, R. (2012) 'A Tale of Two Charitable Campaigns Longitudinal Analysis of Employee Giving at a Public University', *Nonprofit and Voluntary Sector Quarterly*, 41(5), 802–825.

Ahern, K. R. and Dittmar, A. K. (2012) 'The Changing of the Boards: The Impact on Firm Valuation of Mandated Female Board Representation', *The Quarterly Journal of Economics*, 127(1): 137–97.

Andreoni, J. and Vesterlund L. (2001) 'Which is the Fair Sex? Gender Differences in Altruism', *The Quarterly Journal of Economics*, 116(1): 293–312.

Andreoni, J., Brown, E., and Rischall, I. (2003) 'Charitable Giving by Married Couples: Who Decides and Why Does it Matter?', *The Journal of Human Resources*, 38(1): 111–33.

Barclays Wealth (2010) 'Global Giving: The Culture of Philanthropy'. A White Paper in Co-operation with Ledbury Research.

Bear, S. Rahman, N., and Post, C. (2010) 'The Impact of Board Diversity and Gender Composition on Corporate Social Responsibility and Firm Reputation', *Journal of Business Ethics*, 97(2): 207–21.

Bekkers, R. (2004) 'Giving and Volunteering in the Netherlands: Sociological and Psychological Perspectives'. Ph.D. Dissertation, Department of Sociology, Utrecht University, Utrecht, the Netherlands.

——. (2007a) 'Intergenerational Transmission of Volunteering', *Acta Sociologica*, 50(2): 99–114.

——. (2007b) 'Measuring Altruistic Behavior in Surveys: The All-or-Nothing Dictator Game', *Survey Research Methods*, 1(3): 39–144.

——. (2011) 'Charity Begins at Home: How Socialization Experiences Influence Giving and Volunteering', Unpublished manuscript. Amsterdam: VU Amsterdam.

Bekkers R. and Wiepking, P. (2011) 'A Literature Review of Empirical Studies of Philanthropy: Eight Mechanisms that Drive Charitable Giving', *Nonprofit and Voluntary Sector Quarterly*, 40(5): 924–73.

Belfield, C. R. and Beney, A. P. (2000) 'What Determines Alumni Generosity? Evidence for the UK', *Education Economics*, 8: 65–80.

Bennett, R. (2003) 'Factors Underlying the Inclination to Donate to Particular Types of Charity', *International Journal of Nonprofit and Voluntary Sector Marketing*, 8: 12–29.

Bertacchini, E., Santagata, W., and Signorello, G. (2011) 'Individual Giving to Support Cultural Heritage', *International Journal of Arts Management*, 13(3):41–55.

Brown, E. (2006) '"Married Couples" Charitable Giving: Who and Why'. In *The Transformative Power of Women's Philanthropy*, (M.A. Taylor & S. Shaw-Hardy eds.), Wiley Periodicals Inc.: San Francisco: CA, 69–80.

Brown, E. and Ferris, J. M. (2007) 'Social Capital and Philanthropy: An Analysis of the Impact of Social Capital on Individual Giving and Volunteering', *Nonprofit and Voluntary Sector Quarterly*, 36: 85–99.

Bureau of Labor Statistics (2011) 'Women at Work'. Online. Available <www.bls.gov/spotlight/2011/women/> [Accessed June 6, 2015].

—— (2014) 'Women in the Labor Force: A Databook'. www.bls.gov/opub/reports/cps/women-in-the-labor-force-a-databook-2014.pdf [Accessed June 6, 2015].

Burgoyne, C. B., Young, B., and Walker, C. M. (2005) 'Deciding to Give to Charity: A Focus Group Study in the Context of the Household Economy', *Journal of Community & Applied Social Psychology*, 15(5): 383–405.

Campbell, K. and Mínguez-Vera, A. (2008) 'Gender Diversity in the Boardroom and Firm Financial Performance', *Journal of Business Ethics*, 83(3): 435–51.

Center on Philanthropy at Indiana University (2011) '2011 Study of High Net Worth Women's Philanthropy and the Impact of Women's Giving Networks'. Unpublished manuscript.

——. (2012) 'Women Give 2012', Unpublished manuscript.

Council on Foundations. (2009) *Career Pathways to Philanthropic Leadership 2009 Baseline Report*. Arlington, VA: Council on Foundations. Online. Available www.cof.org/sites/default/files/documents/files/careerpathwaysconvo.pdf [Accessed November 19, 2012].

Cox, J. C. and Deck C. A. (2006) 'When are Women More Generous than Men?' *Economic Inquiry*, 44(4): 587–98.

Croson, R. and Gneezy, U. (2009) 'Gender Differences in Preferences', *Journal of Economic Literature*, 47(2): 448–74.

Croson, R., Handy, F., and Shang, J. (2009) 'Gendered Giving: The Influence of Social Norms on the Donation Behavior of Men and Women', *International Journal of Nonprofit and Voluntary Sector Marketing*, 15(2): 199–213.

Eagly, A. H. and Steffen, V. J. (1984) 'Gender Stereotypes Stem from the Distribution of Women and Men into Social Roles', *Journal of Personality and Social Psychology* 46(4): 735–54.

Eagly, A. H. and Crowley, M. (1986) 'Gender and Helping Behavior: A Meta-Analytic Review of the Social Psychology Literature', *Psychological Bulletin* 100(3): 283–308.

Eckel, C. and Grossman, P. J. (1998) 'Are Women Less Selfish than Men?: Evidence from Dictator Experiments', *Economic Journal*, 108: 726–35.

——. (2003) 'Rebate versus Matching: Does How we Subsidize Charitable Contributions Matter?', *Journal of Public Economics*, 87: 681–701.

Eikenberry, A., Bearman, J., Han, H., Brown, M., and Jensen, C. (2009) *The Impact of Giving Together: Giving Circles' Influence on Members' Philanthropic and Civic Behaviors, Knowledge and Attitudes*. Forum of Regional Associations of Grantmakers; The Center on Philanthropy at Indiana University; The University of Nebraska at Omaha.

Einolf, C. J. (2006) 'The Roots of Altruism: A Gender and Life Course Perspective' Retrieved from ProQuest Digital Dissertations. (AAT 3235030).

——. (2011) 'Gender Differences in the Correlates of Volunteering and Charitable Giving', *Nonprofit and Voluntary Sector Quarterly*, 40: 1092–1112.

Eisenberg, N. and Lennon, R. (1983) 'Sex Differences in Empathy and Related Capacities', *Psychological Bulletin*, 94: 100–131.

Erdle, S., Sansom, M., Cole, M. R., and Heapy, N. (1992) 'Sex Differences in Personality Correlates of Helping Behavior', *Personality & Individual Differences*, 13: 931–6.

Fry, R. and Cohn, D. (2010) *New Economics of Marriage: The Rise of Wives*. Pew Research Center: Washington D.C. Online. Available www.pewresearch.org/pubs/1466/economics-marriage-rise-of-wives> [accessed March 20, 2011].

Gilligan, C. (1982) *In a Different Voice: Psychological Theory and Women's Development*. Harvard University Press: Cambridge, MA.

Giving USA Foundation (2011) *Giving USA 2011: The Annual Report on Philanthropy for the Year 2010*. Online. Available www.givingusareports.org.

Harshman, R. A. and Paivio, A. (1987) '"Paradoxical" Sex Differences in Self-Reported Imagery', *Canadian Journal of Psychology* 41(3): 287–302.

Hoffman, M. K. (1977) 'Sex Differences in Empathy and Related Behaviors', *Psychological Bulletin*, 84(4): 712–22.

Impact 100 (2015) *The Impact 100 Story*. Online. Available www.impact100.org/about-us/ (accessed June 6, 2015).

International Labour Organization (2007) *Global Employment Trends for Women Brief 2007*. Geneva, Switzerland: Author. Online. Available www.ilo.org/wcmsp5/groups/public/---ed_emp/---emp_elm/---trends/documents/publication/wcms_114287.pdf [Accessed June 6, 2015].

——. (2008) *Global Employment Trends for Women 2008*. Geneva, Switzerland: Author. Online. Available www.ilo.org/wcmsp5/groups/public/---dgreports/---dcomm/documents/publication/wcms_091225.pdf [Accessed June, 6, 2015].

——. (2014) *Global Employment Trends 2014. Risk of a jobless recovery?* Online. Available www.ilo.org/wcmsp5/groups/public/---dgreports/---dcomm/---publ/documents/publication/wcms_233953.pdf [Accessed June 6, 2015].

Inter-Parliamentary Union (ND) *Women in National Parliaments*. Online. Available www.ipu.org/wmn-e/world.htm [Accessed November 19, 2012].

Israel, D. K. (2007) 'Charitable Donations: Evidence of Demand for Environmental Protection?', *International Advances in Economic Research*, 13: 171–82.

Janoski, T., Musick, M., and Wilson, J. (1998) 'Being Volunteered? The Impact of Social Participation and Pro-Social Attitudes on Volunteering', *Sociological Forum*, 13(3): 495–519.

Jarboe, Norma (2012) *Women Count: Charity Leaders 2012*. Online. Available www.women-count.org/Women-Count-Report-2012.pdf [Accessed June 6, 2015].

Jolliffe, D. and Farrington, D. P. (2005) 'Development and Validation of the Basic Empathy Scale', *Journal of Adolescence*, 29(4): 589–611.

Kamas, L., Preston, A., and Baum, S. (2008) 'Altruism in Individual and Joint-Giving Decisions: What's Gender Got to do With it?', *Feminist Economics*, 14: 23–50.

Kou, X., Hayat, A., Mesch, D., and Osili, U. (2012) 'The Global Dynamics of Gender and Philanthropy: A Study of Charitable Giving by Lions Clubs International Members'. Unpublished manuscript. Center on Philanthropy.

Kottasz, R. (2004) 'Differences in the Donor Behavior Characteristics of Young Affluent Males and Females: Empirical Evidence from Britain', *Voluntas*, 15: 181–203.

List, J. A. (2004) 'Young, Selfish, and Male: Field Evidence of Social Preferences', *Economic Journal*, 114: 121–49.

Lyons, M. and Nivison-Smith, I. (2006) 'Religion and Giving in Australia', *Australian Journal of Social Issues*, 41: 419–36.

Marquis, C. and Lee, M. (2013) 'Who is Governing Whom? Executives, Governance, and the Structure of Generosity in Large US Firms', *Strategic Management Journal*, 34(4), 483–97.

Marx, J. D. (2000) 'Women and Human Services Giving', *Social Work*, 45: 27–38.

Mesch, D. J. (2010) Center on Philanthropy: Indianapolis, IN. www.philanthropy.iupui.edu/files/file/women_give_2010_report.pdf [Accessed June 6, 2015].

Mesch, D. J., Rooney, P. M., Steinberg, K. W., and Denton, B. (2006) 'The Effects of Race, Gender, and Marital Status on Giving and Volunteering in Indiana', *Nonprofit and Voluntary Sector Quarterly*, 35: 565–87.

Mesch, D. J., Brown, M. S., Moore, Z., and Hayat, A. H. (2011) 'Gender Differences in Charitable Giving', *International Journal of Nonprofit and Voluntary Sector Marketing*, 16 (4): 291–7.

Micklewright, J. and Schnepf, S. V. (2009) 'Who Gives Charitable Donations for Overseas Development?' *Journal of Social Policy*, 38: 317–41.

Midlarsky, E. and Hannah, M. E. (1989) 'The Generous Elderly: Naturalistic Studies of Donations Across the Life Span', *Psychology and Ageing*, 4: 346–51.

Mustillo, S., Wilson, J., and Lynch, S. M. (2004) 'Legacy Volunteering: A Test of Two Theories of Intergenerational Transmission', *Journal of Marriage and Family*, 66(2): 530–41.

Newman, R. H. (1995) 'Perception of Factors Relating to Gender Differences in Philanthropy'. Unpublished doctoral dissertation. Retrieved from ProQuest Digital Dissertations. (AAT 9532669).

Oppedisano, J. (2004). 'Giving Back: Women's Entrepreneurial Philanthropy', *Women in Management Review*, 19(3), 174–7.

Parsons, P. H. (2004) 'Women's Philanthropy: Motivations for Giving'. Unpublished doctoral dissertation. Retrieved from ProQuest Doctoral Dissertations. (AAT 3155889).

Pew Research Center (2015) *America's Changing Religious Landscape.* Online. Available www.pewforum. org/2015/05/12/chapter-4-the-shifting-religious-identity-of-demographic-groups/ (accessed June 6, 2015).

Piliavin, J. A. and Charng, H. (1990) 'Altruism: A Review of Recent Theory and Research', *Annual Review of Sociology*, 16: 27–65.

Piper, G. and Schnepf, S. V. (2008) 'Gender Differences in Charitable Giving in Great Britain', *Voluntas: International Journal of Voluntary and Nonprofit Organizations*, 19(2): 103–24.

Red Cross (2015) *The Tiffany Circle Story.* Online. Available www.redcross.org.uk/Donate-Now/Make-a-major-donation/Tiffany-Circle/History-of-the-Tiffany-Circle (accessed June 6, 2015).

Regnerus, M. D., Smith, C., and Sikkink, D. (1998) 'Who Gives to the Poor? The Influence of Religious Tradition and Political Location on the Personal Generosity of Americans Toward the Poor', *Journal for the Scientific Study of Religion*, 37: 481–93.

Robertson, N. M. (2007) *Christian Sisterhood, Race Relations, and the YMCA, 1906–1946.* University of Illinois Press: Champaign-Urbana, IL.

Rooney, P. M., Mesch, D. J., Chin, W., and Steinberg, K. S. (2005) 'The Effects of Race, Gender, and Survey Methodologies on Giving in the US', *Economics Letters*, 86: 173–80.

Rooney, P., Brown, E., and Mesch, D. (2007) 'Who Decides in Giving to Education? A Study of Charitable Giving by Married Couples', *International Journal of Educational Advancement*, 7(3): 229–42.

Schlegelmilch, B. B., Love, B. A., and Diamantopoulos, A. (1997) 'Responses to Different Charity Appeals: The Impact of Donor Characteristics on the Amount of Donation', *European Journal of Marketing*, 31(8): 548–60.

Schwartz, S. and Rubel, T. (2005) 'Sex Differences in Value Priorities: Cross-Cultural and Multimethod Studies', *Journal of Personality and Social Psychology*, 89(6): 1010–1028.

Simmons, W. O. and Emanuele, R. (2007) 'Male-Female Giving Differentials: Are Women More Altruistic?' *Journal of Economic Studies* 34(6): 534–50.

Skoe, E. E. A., Cumberland, A., Eisenberf, N., Hansen, K., and Perry, J. (2002) 'The Influences of Sex and Gender-Role Identity on Moral Cognition and Prosocial Personality Traits', *Sex Roles: A Journal of Research*, 46(9–10): 295–309.

Soares, R., Marquis, C., and Lee, M. (2011) *Gender and Corporate Social Responsibility: It's a Matter of Sustainability.* Catalyst. Online. Available www.catalyst.org/file/522/gender_and_corporate_social_responsibility_final.pdf [Accessed May 4, 2014]

Turcotte, M. (2015) *Volunteering and charitable giving in Canada, Spotlight on Canadians: Results from the General Social Survey, Statistics Canada.* Online. Available www.statcan.gc.ca/pub/89-652-x/89-652-x2015001-eng.pdf

Walton, A. (2005) *Women and Philanthropy in Education.* IU Press: Bloomington, IN.

Wang, J. and Coffey, B. S. (1992) 'Board Composition and Corporate Philanthropy', *Journal of Business Ethics*, 11(10): 771–78.

Weyant, J. M. (1984) 'Applying Social Psychology to Induce Charitable Donations', *Journal of Applied Social Psychology*, 14: 441–7.

Wiepking, P. and Bekkers, R. (2010) 'Does Who Decides Really Matter? Causes and Consequences of Personal Financial Management in the Case of Larger and Structural Charitable Donations', *Voluntas*, 21: 240–63.

Wiepking, P. and Einolf, C. (2011, March) 'Cross-National Gender Differences in Giving: An International Perspective'. Paper presented at the 22nd Annual Symposium of the Center on Philanthropy at Indiana University, Chicago, IL.

Wilhelm, M. O. and Bekkers, R. (2010) 'Helping Behavior, Dispositional Empathic Concern, and Principle of Care', *Social Psychology Quarterly* 73(1): 11–32.

Wilhelm, M. O., Brown, E., Rooney, P. M., and Steinberg, R. (2008) 'The Intergenerational Transmission of Generosity', *Journal of Public Economics*, 92(10–11): 2146–2156.

Wilhelm, M. O., Estell, D. B., and Purdue, N. G. (2011) 'Role-Modeling and Conversations about Giving in the Socialization of Adolescent Charitable Giving and Volunteering'. Unpublished manuscript.

Wilson, M. (2007) *Closing the Leadership Gap: Add Women, Change Everything.* Penguin Books: New York, NY.

Women Moving Millions (2015) Online. Available <www.womenmovingmillions.org/ [Accessed April 18, 2012].

Women's Funding Network (2015a) *A Growing Network, A Movement for Change.* Online. Available www.womensfundingnetwork.org/about/ [Accessed June 6, 2015].

Women's Funding Network (2015b) *Membership.* Online. Available. www.womensfundingnetwork.org/membership/ [Accessed June 6, 2015].

World Values Survey (2006) *European and World Values Surveys: Four-Wave Integrated Data file*, 1981–2004, v.20060423. Tilburg, Netherlands: European Values Study Group and World.

Wymer, W. (2011) 'The Implications of Sex Differences on Volunteer Preferences', *Voluntas*, 22: 831–51.

Yen, S. T. (2002) 'An Econometric Analysis of Household Donations in the USA', *Applied Economics Letters*, 9: 837–41.

Yörük, B. K. (2010) 'Charitable Giving by Married Couples Revisited', *The Journal of Human Resources*, 45: 497–516.

6

Charity communications
Shaping donor perceptions and giving

Sally Hibbert

In 1952, Gerhard Wiebe asked the question 'Why can't you sell brotherhood like you can sell soap?' Since then, the charity sector has developed high levels of expertise in marketing and fundraising communications. Backed by other elements of the charity's strategy, these now play an important role in triggering, and shaping, the donation decisions of millions of people who, each year, give time, money and other forms of in kind support to an array of causes. Donors learn about charities and the causes that they support via communications from a variety of sources, and charities cannot directly influence all forms of communication about their organization or cause. However, it is vital that, where they have a degree of control, they develop communication strategies that effectively serve to trigger giving and are conducive to sustainable donor support.

Developing appeals that resonate with donors requires considerable skill and creativity. Poorly conceived campaigns that lack credibility or are perceived to manipulate, pressure or badger potential donors can engender resistance and resentment rather than encourage donors to join the charity in working for a particular cause; repeat errors in this area can severely tarnish a charity's reputation. Hence, research that demonstrates and illuminates how fundraising communications influence philanthropy is vital to support fundraisers tasked with managing donor communications and engagement. Given considerable innovations in fundraising, the need for such insights has increased over the last few years. New ways in which individuals can support good causes continue to emerge with developments in technology, media and in the context of changing relations between charities, government, business, communities and individual donors.

This chapter reviews current understanding of the ways in which fundraising communications shape donor behaviour and examines the communication challenges that charities face in the twenty-first century. It examines elements of fundraising communications that influence donor perceptions and their inclination to give, and considers the challenges that face fundraisers operating in contemporary communications environments.

Fundraising communications

The majority of donations to charity are made in response to solicitations (Bekkers, 2005; Bryant *et al.*, 2003). Over the years, a reasonable body of research has emerged that informs our understanding of how to shape donor perceptions and trigger giving. A variety of features have been found to influence donor perceptions and behaviour, which can be grouped under three generic themes, namely, the source and content of the message and the nature of the request for help (Bendapudi *et al.*, 1996) which are used to structure this review of the extant literature. One-way forms of communication remain prominent in fundraising but new technologies that afford opportunities for charity-donor interactions, donor-to-donor interactions and, indeed, communications between various stakeholder groups demand that charities also build understanding of how dialogical communications will shape the meaning of philanthropy and donation behaviour going forward. Hence, towards the end of the chapter, attention turns to some of the new challenges facing fundraisers and the emergent research that provides insights into fundraising in the new communications landscape.

The source of fundraising messages

When individuals interpret communications, they are heavily influenced by the credibility of the source. As fundraising messages emanate from charities, individuals' perceptions of their brand image – the embodiment of a charity's character – is a key determinant of donation decisions (Bennett and Gabriel, 2003; Michel and Rieunier, 2011).

Charity brand image

A recognized and trustworthy brand is extremely powerful for charities. When donors give to charity, they are essentially 'buying' an intangible service and, as the service provider, the charity is a focal point in their decision-making (Venables *et al.*, 2005). In many Western countries, the charity marketplace is crowded; the decision of which charity to give to is potentially very complex. So, people frequently donate to a well-known charity, using their knowledge of the charity brand as a short cut to a good, or at least satisfactory, donation decision. Michel and Rieunier (2011) illustrate this with data on donations to the Asian tsunami, which show that the amount collected by the various humanitarian aid charities closely matched rates of spontaneous charity recognition amongst the general public.

For many donors, charities provide a means by which they can help others and support causes when it is not viable for them to be directly and actively involved in helping. There is a set of core attributes – 'efficient', 'effective' and 'accountable' – that people associate with the charity sector as a whole (Sargeant *et al.*, 2008) and that are highly influential in their decisions to donate (Michel and Rieunier, 2011). In addition, personality traits related to trustworthiness such as 'honest', 'reputable' and 'reliable' are widely linked to charity brands in people's minds (Venables *et al.*, 2005; Sargeant *et al.*, 2008). Trust is essential to promote charitable giving and charities are sorely aware that trust in the whole sector is damaged by bad practices in just a small minority of charities (Webb *et al.*, 2000). Accordingly, there have been sector-wide initiatives to assure donors of charities' integrity by establishing standards for best practice and increasing transparency. Other traits that are widely applied to charities are those that reflect the nurturing roles that charities often assume, such as 'caring' and 'compassionate' (Venables *et al.*, 2005). Marketing scholars have suggested that because people tend to associate these generic traits with all charities, it does not make sense for charities to concentrate on these features as they craft their brand image (Sargeant and Hudson, 2008). Nonetheless, perceptions that charities are well managed and trustworthy are vitally important in shaping attitudes that predispose people to give; transparent reporting of the charity's operations through annual reports, reviews, accounts and websites is essential to enable donors to assess the charity's performance in terms of core attributes if they so wish. Such information is also available from regulators and independent enterprises, such as Intelligent Giving and Guidestar. Further, the last few years have seen a burgeoning interest amongst charitable organizations in measuring and reporting on impact, as donors become increasingly concerned to learn how their donated resources have made a difference (Hebb with MacKinnon, Chapter 29; Schnurbein, Chapter 30).

The more abstract dimensions of brands – brand values, personality, heritage – afford better opportunities to create a unique brand image. A study by Sargeant *et al.* (2008) identified four types of attributes, linked either with causes or organizations, on which a differentiated brand image can be based: 'emotional stimulation traits', including traits such as exciting, fun, heroic, innovative, inspiring and modern; 'service traits', being approachable, compassionate, dedicated; 'voice traits', being ambitious, authoritative, bold; and 'tradition traits', being traditional. This is by no means a comprehensive list of characteristics that can be promoted to differentiate a charity's brand image but it highlights the types of traits that help to distinguish charities in donors' minds and enables them to identify charities that work for their preferred causes in ways that they advocate. For instance, the ethos of The Big Issue homeless charity is 'a hand up, not a hand out', which appeals to donors who recognize the importance of empowering people who have become homeless rather than simply putting a roof over their heads (Hibbert *et al.*, 2005).

In addition to creating a distinctive brand, charities also need to consider the appeal of their brand image to different donor segments. There is very little published research on this issue, but a study by Bennett (2003) investigated donor preferences for charities with different organizational values. Based on a content analysis of the websites and promotional literature of the UK's top 50 charities (in terms of income), he produced a list of common organizational values espoused by charities. These include: changing society as we know it, making people independent and self-sufficient, looking after every aspect of the beneficiary's life, being innovative and creative and empowering the people the charity is trying to help. The analysis of donor preferences revealed that individuals' personal values are important determinants of the organizational values that they favour. For instance, people who value achievement favour charities with ambitions to 'change society as we know it' and individuals who value hedonism favour 'empowering the people the charity is trying to help' as an organizational value. Hence, psychographic information on the charity's supporters and engagement with them is vital to be able to cultivate a charity brand identity that is congruent with donors' self-image.

The content of fundraising messages

It is important for fundraising messages to come from a credible source, but the persuasiveness of the message is also dependent on its content. Five aspects of message content have been found to influence donor responses to solicitations: the need for help, the representation of beneficiaries, beneficiary-donor similarity, labeling and social comparison (Bendapudi *et al.*, 1996). An overview of research on each of these issues is set out below.

The need for help

Becoming aware that someone is threatened by or actually suffering undesirable consequences is an important trigger for philanthropy (Guy and Patton, 1989). Charities' fundraising communications are not the only source from which people learn that others are in need; channels such as media and word of mouth are influential too, but fundraising communications have an important role to play in raising awareness of causes. Research carried out over several decades has established that perception of need increases the likelihood of people behaving altruistically in general and, more specifically, of contributing to fundraising appeals (Berkowitz, 1968; Bickman and

Kamzan, 1973; Sinha and Jain, 1986; Cheung and Chan, 2000; Lee and Farrell, 2003). However, individuals' interpretations of the circumstance surrounding the need for help moderate their responses. In particular, they consider whether beneficiaries are responsible for their situation, the severity and urgency of the need and the potential consequences for the beneficiaries and for themselves as helpers (Guy and Patton, 1989). Individuals are more inclined to help when they believe that the beneficiaries' circumstances are beyond their control (Piliavin *et al.*, 1975) than when they believe they are due to the beneficiaries' own dispositions and behaviour (Campbell *et al.*, 2001). Emergency disaster appeals often attract widespread support because those affected are blameless, the need is intense, urgent and there are dramatic consequences if help is not given. Not surprisingly, awareness of a need for help increases when the potential beneficiaries of a charitable organization are known to an individual (Burgoyne *et al.*, 2005, Wiepking, 2006; Bekkers and Meijer, 2008) or when their own experiences relate to the cause (Bennett, 2003).

Although donors develop predispositions to support certain causes, they tend to want to help in specific ways. An important development by charities has been the move to afford donors choice about how they help by asking them which scheme (e.g., habitat conservation, educational programs) they would like to support or, at a more specific level, which type of animal they would like to sponsor. Packaging needs into 'products' also help to communicate that donors' help will be effective. This is an important consideration when individuals are making donation decisions. When fundraising messages represent the need as a grand problem (e.g. 'millions of children die every year as a result of drinking contaminated water') potential donors are likely to feel that their help will be inconsequential, whereas a narrower conception of the need and specification of a way of helping (e.g. 'by purchasing one water filter you can protect Joe's family for five years') enables donors to envisage the impact of their support.

Representation of beneficiaries

A key feature of fundraising appeals that influences donor responses concerns the portrayal of beneficiaries by charities. In particular, research interest has centred on whether appeals should represent beneficiaries' negative circumstances or the positive outcomes that can be achieved through the charity's work. Traditionally, negative portrayals of beneficiaries' circumstances were widely used by charities, but, over the years, there was growing opposition to this practice because it contributed to the stigmatization and disadvantage of beneficiaries. For instance, by representing people with disabilities as dependent and helpless, charities were counteracting broader movements to build equality and change attitudes towards diversity. Consequently, recent years have witnessed a shift towards more positively framed communications by many charities. For example, the UK charity Scope states 'Our vision is a world where disabled people have the same opportunities to fulfil their life ambitions as everyone else'. Some charities have even changed their name to better reflect the charity's mission. Negative portrayals of beneficiaries' circumstances have not disappeared, but there is now a balance between negatively and positively framed appeals. An audit of charity advertisements that appeared in the British newspaper *The Guardian* in 2007 (Ridge, 2008) revealed that 53 percent of advertisements presented a positive aspect and 47 percent presented a negative one, and a negative perspective is more widely adopted for certain types of appeals such as social welfare and international aid.

A number of studies have examined the question of how effective are positive or negative appeals in soliciting donations, but the findings are somewhat mixed. Several studies that have compared positive and negative appeals have found no difference in their capacity to solicit donations (Feldman and Feldman, 1985; Brolley and Anderson, 1986; Adler *et al.*, 1991). However, Eayrs and Ellis (1990) found that responses to a door-to-door appeal were lower when a negative rather than positive appeal was used, while recent research by Fisher *et al.* (2008) found negative appeals to be more effective than positive appeals in a fundraising campaign by a television station. A study by Small and Verrochi (2009) revealed that donors were more responsive to advertisements featuring beneficiaries with sad rather than happy or neutral facial expressions. However, there may be important moderating influences on these relationships that, as yet, are ill understood. For instance, Chang and Lee (2009) illustrated that temporal framing (i.e. the time scale linked with the need and consequences) has an impact on whether positive or negative appeal are more effective. Fisher *et al.* (2008) note that progress in understanding the effects of emotional fundraising appeals has been hindered by inadequate theoretical development and call for new scholarship to develop robust conceptual foundations for research into these issues.

In addition to research that compares generic positive and negative appeals, a number of studies have examined the effectiveness of appeals that arouse specific types of emotions. Guilt appeals have received greatest attention and the evidence suggests that the arousal of guilt does promote giving (Basil *et al.*, 2006, 2008; Hibbert *et al.*, 2007). There is some debate about the intensity of emotions that should be aroused to maximize effects. Some scholars suggest that the arousal of moderate levels of guilt is most effective in generating desired responses (Coulter and Pinto, 1995; Yinon *et al.*, 1976), but other studies have found no evidence that audiences are resistant to guilt-intensive communications (Bennett, 1998), and this debate rumbles on. Curiously, despite the increasing use of positive emotional appeals, very little research has been undertaken to investigate the effects on giving of specific positive emotions such as pride and elevation (Hibbert and Chuah, 2009). Another outstanding area of inquiry concerns ways in which individual differences moderate the arousal of emotions in audiences and their cognitive and behavioural responses. Psychological features – such as perceived locus of control, self-blame, inherent guilt and self-esteem – affect individuals' responses to guilt appeals (Ghingold, 1981; Bennett, 1998), and theoretical work around moral emotions suggests that individuals' values and self-identity are likely to influence how they respond to specific positive and negative emotional appeals. More research is, however, needed to build an adequate knowledge based to inform charities' use of emotional appeals. This is a research direction that may be given further impetus from UK media reports that some charity requests, in their framing and volume, are becoming too demanding, even intimidating for some would-be donors (Hussein and Barrow, 2015), raising the question of fundraising's regulation (Breen, Chapter 14).

Literature concerned with beneficiary portrayals has also investigated whether gender and physical appearance influence the responses of prospective donors. This is a very limited area of inquiry, but evidence suggests that the presentation of female rather than male beneficiaries leads to greater donor compliance (Feinman, 1978) and that physically attractive subjects are perceived to be more worthy of help (Latane and Nida, 1981).

Beneficiary/donor similarity

As discussed above, a primary motive for philanthropy is that individuals experience personal distress when they are aware of a need. The intensity of their distress is greater when the person in need is similar in some way to the prospective benefactor (Piliavin *et al.*, 1981; Margolis, 1982). The similarity may relate to physical characteristics or to more intangible factors such as ethnicity, culture and personal values. For instance, an experimental study by Collaizi *et al.* (1984) found that people were more willing to help others who were of the same sex as themselves. Research suggests that the influence of beneficiary donor similarity on giving is moderated by personal characteristics. For example, Mitchell and Byrne (1973) found that the tendency to support beneficiaries similar to oneself is greater amongst authoritarian personality types than those who are more egalitarian and have greater tolerance for people from 'out-groups' (i.e. social groups of which they are not a member/who are dissimilar to them). Scholarship on discriminatory helping practices also suggests that features of the helping situation are likely to play a moderating role (Saucier et al., 2005).

Social labeling

Alongside persuasion tactics, fundraisers make use of labeling to encourage giving. Labeling theory proposes that individuals act in ways that are consistent with the social labels and behaviours that others attribute to them. A primary means by which labeling influences behaviour is via its potential to manipulate and affirm aspects of self-identity (Burger and Caldwell, 2003). Early research by Kraut (1973) applied this principle to charitable giving and found that people labeled as 'charitable' gave more and those labeled as 'uncharitable' gave less than control groups in the study. Subsequent research has provided support for his findings and generated further evidence that attaching labels such as 'generous' and 'philanthropic' to individuals augments their motivation to help, results in more helping behaviour (Swinyard and Ray, 1977; Wechasara et al., 1987) and improves attitudes towards charities requesting support (Moore et al., 1985). Labeling is suggested to have a greater influence on people for whom giving is not central to their self-identity, because their motivation is more dependent on external factors. In such cases, labeling tends to be more effective when it comes from credible sources, such as established, high profile charities while committed philanthropists, motivated by their internal moral self, are more accepting of labeling from less prominent charities (Bendapudi et al., 1996). But labeling is not inconsequential for established donors. Indeed, research into donor loyalty suggests that labeling techniques are an important aspect of relationship building and that charities' application of words such as 'kind', 'helpful' and 'generous' to its supporters is an important aspect of feedback (Sargeant et al., 2001; Sargeant and Woodliffe, 2007). This body of research suggests that when ad hoc and relational fundraising communications incorporate elements that refer to donors, rather than focusing entirely on beneficiaries, it is advantageous to make use of labeling to create feelings of pride and motivate a positive response from donors.

Social comparison

There is widespread acknowledgement that social influences are important in shaping philanthropy. Research shows that people who are well integrated into social institutions such as social clubs, religious organizations and schools are more prone to give than those who are not (Radley and Kennedy, 1995). More broadly, when individuals recognize that giving is normative, their propensity to donate increases (Martin and Randal, 2005). The practice of announcing how much has been donated to a current campaign or a telethon is an example of the application of this principle in that individuals are moved to respond and make a donation themselves when they see that thousands of other people have deemed it the 'right thing to do'. People are similarly influenced when they learn that aspirational reference groups support a cause, an effect harnessed by the 2012 Give Blood campaign in the UK that features sports stars and claims 'Celebrities back campaign to boost blood stocks for 2012'. Informing people how much others have given also influences the amount that they donate, such that they increase their contribution if they learn that others have given more and decrease it if they learn that others have given less (Shang and Croson, 2006; Croson and Shang, 2008). The normative influence is magnified when people are also given information about the consequences of helping (LaTour and

Manrai, 1989), as people find it more difficult to argue against helping when the benefits for the beneficiary are clearly articulated. Other research suggests that people are more likely to help when rewards for helping – praise, thanks, social and material benefits – come via a social group of which an individual is, or aspires to be, a member (Fisher and Ackerman, 1998). One way in which charities have sought to leverage social and self-presentation influences is by enabling 'conspicuous compassion' (Grace and Griffin, 2006, 2009; West, 2004), providing wrist bands and empathy ribbons for supporters who make a donation.

The nature of the request

The way in which charities approach donors can make a considerable difference to the success of a fundraising campaign and can also enhance or damage perceptions of the charity. The nature of the request for help is an important element of the communication process that influences donation decisions, and research has found that prospective donors are influenced by the method of solicitation and how much they are asked to give.

The method of solicitation

People give to charity through cash donations, direct debits, credit and debit cards or cheques and payroll giving, and in response to solicitations through mail, telephone, TV and radio, canvassing in the street or door-to-door, workplace schemes, collections at places of worship, events, sponsorship, raffles and in memoriam. Other donations come through legacies, payment of fees, purchases and when people approach a charitable organization unprompted. In recent years, with changes in technology, people have been presented with new opportunities to give through mobile phones, at ATMs and card payment systems at till points and online, while developments in corporate social responsibility have increased opportunities for individuals to contribute through partnerships between charities and businesses. The amount of income generated through each of these methods is not a reflection of their popularity. For example, the value of donations collected at places of worship is very high compared to the proportion of people who give in this way. Information such as level of income and longevity of donor relationships needs to be used to make decisions about investment in different fundraising mechanisms. In addition, charities need to track new trends and invest for the future. For instance, recent research suggests that giving through new technologies lags behind usage for other purposes. In 2011, the NCVO reported that while two-thirds of consumers shop online, only seven percent had made a donation online (NCVO, 2011). Charity income coming from online donations is growing year on year and charities are responding by developing communications to support giving in this way (e.g. websites, Twitter, Facebook), but further investment is needed if they are to seize the opportunity of connecting with donors through new channels.

Some of the methods indicated above (e.g. direct mail, telephone, door-to-door/in-street canvassing, workplace schemes, sponsorship, legacies) have attracted considerable research interest and discrete bodies of literature have emerged that focus on understanding the influence on giving via these specific methods. In addition, the more general questions of which forms of solicitation are more successful, and why, have attracted academic attention over several decades. Early research found personal forms of solicitation to be more successful than impersonal or telephone requests in terms of rates of compliance (Long, 1976; Brockner et al., 1984) and the amount donated (Thornton et al., 1991). In part, these effects relate to social influences and the conspicuousness of the donation. Indeed, research suggests that the effects of face-to-face solicitations are even stronger when made by people who are familiar, of close social distance or similar to the prospective donor (Bekkers and Wiepking, 2007; Meer, 2010). Responses to different forms of solicitation are also shaped by beliefs about philanthropy. Research carried out in the UK has illustrated that there is opposition to methods that transgress people's beliefs that philanthropy should be an act of free will and a nonprofit activity. Hence, donors disapprove of forms of solicitation that are perceived to pressure donors or to be intrusive (e.g. telephone calls), as well as methods that involve for-profit enterprises (e.g. external agencies contracted to undertake door-to-door collections) (Hibbert and Horne, 1997; Sargeant and Jay, 2004; Sargeant and Hudson, 2008). Going forward, there is considerable scope to extend research in this area and, in particular, to examine the implications of recent changes in the communications landscape for charitable solicitations. With a growing number of stories about the power of social media for fundraising (Bernholz, Chapter 28), more rigorous research is needed to examine ways in which these new social media tools can be deployed to increase the effectiveness of requests for funds and develop theoretical frameworks to explain their effects.

Scholars who have examined the effects of past experience with a charitable organization on subsequent donations have affirmed that once a donor has been successfully recruited by a charity, it is more likely that he or she will give again to that charity (Kaehler and Sargeant, 1998). Trust is central to ongoing support and the development of trust between charitable organizations' and their donors is clearly linked to donor loyalty (Sargeant and Lee, 2004). Research by Sargeant (2001) and Burnett (2002) has concluded that the perceived quality of the charitable organizations' service to beneficiaries, the perceived impact of previous donations and the extent to which the donors feel they exert control over their relationship with the charity all significantly affect the likelihood of retaining a committed and loyal donor base. Hence, for repeat donations, it is not simply the method of solicitation that is important but the broader management of the relationship with donors. There is little research into the effectiveness of solicitation methods for repeat or committed donors, but insights from the donor relationships literature suggest that it is important that the solicitation of repeat donations affords donor choice and control, with careful attention to donor preferences and giving histories.

The size and timing of the request

A key question for charities concerns the amount that they should ask donors to give. It has long been agreed that asking for a specific sum is a better strategy than not proposing an amount to donate (Brockner et al., 1984; Fraser et al., 1988). This approach has been widely adopted by charities for solicitations through a variety of channels and it is common practice to give options about the size of the donation by suggesting amounts. However, research has provided less clear guidance on how much to ask for. An early study by Schwarzwald et al. (1983) compared requests for low, medium and high amounts and nonspecified amounts and did not find any differences in donors' responses. Weyant and Smith (1987) found that a request for a small amount increased compliance rates and did not affect the average size of donations, whereas a request for a large contribution negatively impacted compliance rates and average donations were unaffected. In contrast, research by Doob and McLaughlin (1989) found that asking for large amounts had no effect on compliance rates but it did increase average donations. The difference between these studies was partly explained by the research context, and Doob and McLaughlin suggested that requests for large amounts are more likely to be successful when the charity has an existing relationship with the donors. Further, they stressed that when charities request large amounts they should ensure that it is within an acceptable range for the target group. Surveys have similarly found that donors place a high level of importance on charities 'asking for appropriate sums' (Sargeant and Jay, 2004). Recent research has pursued this issue and emphasises that past donation behaviour (Desmet and Feinberg, 2003) and donation reference price are important factors that moderate people's responses to requests for specific amounts (Verhaert and van den Poel, 2011). It may be more fruitful, then, for charities to adapt the amount requested to the target group or even to individual donors if they have data on giving histories.

In addition, a number of studies have examined how legitimizing small donations affects compliance (Cialdini and Schroeder, 1976). Evidence suggests that legitimizing small donations with phrases such as 'every little helps' increases compliance with face-to-face donation requests (Reingen, 1978; Weyant, 1984; Reeves et al., 1987; Fraser et al., 1988), although this does not necessarily hold true in the case of previous donors (Doob and McLaughlin, 1989) and it is not as effective for impersonal forms of fundraising (Brockner et al., 1984; Reeves et al., 1987; Weyant and Smith, 1987; DeJong and Oopik, 1992) when donors' decisions are less time pressured and social influence processes are weaker. Dolinski et al. (2005) demonstrated that meaningful social interactions amplify the effectiveness of legitimizing paltry contributions. This study revealed that a monologue directed at donors prior to asking for a contribution increased compliance rates, but the effects were even greater when donors were engaged in a dialogue prior to a request accompanied by the statement 'every little helps'. These findings are of particular significance in relation to some new mechanisms for giving (e.g. rounding up) that promote regular, small gifts but new research is required to understand how to maximize compliance (e.g. role of sales staff, use of avatars, framing of messages) when solicitations are technology mediated.

The timing of donations has received very little attention, yet this is a key issue for donors and some are scared off when the only option is to commit to regular donations through mechanisms such as direct debits. In most fundraising contexts, charities do offer donors choice regarding the timing of gifts, for example, through monthly direct debits and annual subscriptions. New technologies are extending this further; for instance, fundraising via monthly SMS (short message service) messages is increasingly moving donors from one-time gifts to regular monthly commitments, made with ease. However, there is a need for rigorous studies to examine how different approaches to timing influence response levels, amounts and rates of donor attrition.

Looking to the future

The communications issues addressed above have long been of concern to charity fundraisers who face the tough job of developing high quality requests for funds and fostering donor loyalty in an ever more crowded marketplace. It is important that the sector continues to build knowledge about how to ask for support and shares practice-based learning and experience. At the same time, changes in the contemporary communications landscape are creating pressures on fundraisers to shift more attention towards e-philanthropy (Bernholz, Chapter 28). Rapid technological developments in recent years have meant that the internet, social networking and technology-mediated service delivery have become increasingly prominent aspects of lifestyle. These technologies are increasingly establishing themselves as essential tools of fundraising. Charities are using websites, social networking and collaborations with industry partners to enable giving through mechanisms such as ATMs, rounding up and online shopping platforms. Further, collaborative ventures continue to experiment with new giving formats (e.g. Open Fundraising developed a regular SMS donation package by which donors could confirm or skip a monthly donation by responding to a text, Aldridge, 2010). Elements of our existing knowledge about asking for donations will be relevant to solicitation through these new mechanisms. For instance, labeling and social comparison might feature in a text message in the same way as they do in a radio advertisement. But there is still much for charities to learn to enable them to harness this diverse range of new mechanisms, which are vital for engaging the next generation of donors.

Research on these relatively new ways of connecting with donors is starting to emerge, although most early studies have focused on charities' adoption of new mechanisms and technologies (Goatman and Lewis, 2007; Waters *et al.*, 2009) and few studies (Bennett, 2009) examine prospective donors' experiences of communications from or with charities through channels such as websites, texts, emails, social network sites or rounding up schemes. One very important change that has accompanied the innovations in communication technologies is the shift from one-way communications (from charities to donors) towards a dialogue between charities, donors and, in some instances, other stakeholders. The opportunity for donors to be more active players has implications for both the nature and the purpose of communications with donors (Prahalad and Ramaswamy, 2000); whereas one-way communications typically convey information and emotive content intended to persuade and encourage compliance with a request for help, a dialogue with donors aims to promote broader engagement recognizing their potential to support the charity through monetary contributions but also by volunteering and supporting advocacy and campaigning activities. Technology now enables charities to have a conversation with individuals and groups of donors as a starting point for sharing a broad set of resources – ideas, skills, knowledge, information, time, votes – that support the charity, its beneficiaries and satisfy the motives of their supporters. There is a burgeoning body of literature that examines how people are engaging with new forms of technology – investigating phenomena such as e-WOM (word of mouth e.g. blogs, online bulletin boards, chat rooms, newsgroups, consumer reviews) (Hennig-Thurau *et al.*, 2004) and online communities (Kozinets *et al.*, 2010) – that can be drawn upon by charities to develop communications strategies and skills geared to the new environment, but the sector also needs a programme of research and forums for sharing experience and learning to understand how these phenomena translate to philanthropic contexts.

Concluding comments

The fundraising landscape is changing and the coming decades will undoubtedly witness the introduction of many new mechanisms for fundraising. Yet solicitations are likely to remain a vital means of triggering donations and finding the best ways to ask will continue to challenge fundraisers. Research that informs fundraising communications has attracted steady interest, from a variety of disciplines, over several decades. Together this body of literature has provided insights into key features of fundraising communications that influence donors. However, in many areas, the evidence is sparse or dated and there is a need for a more rigorous programme of research, grounded in theory, to generate a sound and contemporary evidence base to enable charities to continue to improve the quality of their requests for support and adapt them to the current environment. Given that research in this area emanates from several disciplines, there is potential to deliver a rich understanding of the factors that shape responses to charitable solicitations, but dialogue across disciplines is needed to deliver the benefits and avoid the creation of a disjointed body of knowledge. As the changing mechanisms for donating to charity raise new questions about solicitation, one would also hope to see new knowledge coming from disciplines that have not previously contributed to the research in this area.

References

Adler, A. B., Wright, B. A., and Ulicny, G. R. (1991) 'Fundraising Portrayals of People with Disabilities: Donations and Attitudes', *Rehabilitation Psychology*, 36(4): 231.

Aldridge, N. (2010) 'The Big Society On-line: Harnessing Technology for Social Change', London: Cabinet Office.

American Express (2007) *American Express Charitable Giving Survey*, Indiana University.

Basil, D. Z., Ridgeway, N. M., and Basil, M. D. (2006) 'Guilt Appeals: The Mediating Effect of Responsibility', *Psychology and Marketing*, 23: 1035–54.
——. (2008) 'Guilt and Giving: A Process Model of Empathy and Efficacy', *Psychology and Marketing*, 25(1): 1–23.
Bekkers, R. (2005) 'Charity Begins at Home: How Socialization Experiences Influence Giving and Volunteering', 34th Annual ARNOVA Conference, Washington DC.
Bekkers, R. and Wiepking, P. (2007) 'A Literature Review of Empirical Studies of Philanthropy: Eight Mechanisms That Drive Charitable Giving', *Nonprofit and Voluntary Sector Quarterly*, 40(5): 924–73.
Bekkers, R. and Meijer, M-M. (2008) 'Straight From the Heart', in M. Goldner and S. Chambre (eds.), *Patients, Consumers and Civil Society: US and International Perspectives. Advances in Medical Sociology*, Bingley, UK: Emerald Group Publishing, 10.
Bendapudi, N., Singh, S. N., and Bendapudi, V. (1996) 'Enhancing Helping Behaviour: An Integrative Framework for Promotion Planning', *Journal of Marketing*, 60(3): 33–49.
Bennett, R (1998) 'Shame, Guilt and Responses to Nonprofit and Public Sector Ads', *International Journal of Advertising*, 17: 483–99.
Bennett, R. (2003) 'Factors Underlying the Inclination to Donate to Particular Types of Charity', *International Journal of Nonprofit and Voluntary Sector Marketing*, 8: 12–29.
——. (2009) 'Impulsive Donation Decisions During On-line Browsing of Charity Websites', *Journal of Consumer Behaviour*, 8: 116–34.
Bennett, R. and Gabriel, H. (2003) 'Image and Reputational Characteristics of UK Charitable Organisations: An Empirical Study', *Corporate Reputation Review*, 6(3): 276–89.
Berkowitz, L. (1968) 'Responsibility, Reciprocity and Social Distance in Help-Giving: An Experimental Investigation of English Social Class Differences', *Journal of Experimental Social Psychology*, 4: 46–63.
Bickman, L. and Kamzan, M. (1973) 'The Effect of Race and Need on Helping Behaviour', *Journal of Social Psychology*, 89(1): 73–7.
Brockner, J., Guzzi, J. K., Levine, E., and Shaplen, K. (1984) 'Organisational Fundraising: Further Evidence on the Effects of Legitimising Small Donations', *Journal of Consumer Research*, 11(June): 611–14.
Brolley, D. Y. and Anderson, S. C. (1986) 'Advertising and Attitudes', *Rehabilitation Digest*, 17: 15–17.
Bryant, W. K., Slaughter, H. J., Kang, H., and Tax, A. (2003) 'Participation in Philanthropic Activities: Donating Money and Time', *Journal of Consumer Policy*, 26: 43–73.
Burger, J. and Caldwell, D. (2003) 'The Effects of Monetary Incentives and Labeling on the Foot-in-the-Door Effect: Evidence for a Self-Perception Process', *Basic and Applied Social Psychology*, 25(3): 235–41.
Burgoyne, C. B., Young, B., and Walker, C. M. (2005) 'Deciding to Give to Charity: A Focus Group Study in the Context of the Household Economy', *Journal of Community and Applied Social Psychology*, 15: 383–405.
Burnett, K. (2002) *Relationship Fundraising*, Jossey Bass: San Francisco.
Campbell, D., Carr, S. C., and Maclachlan, M. (2001) 'Attributing "Third World Poverty" in Australia and Malawi: A Case of Donor Bias?', *Journal of Applied Social Psychology*, 31(2): 409–30.
Chang, C-T. and Lee, Y-K. (2009) 'Framing Charity Advertising: Influences of Message Framing, Image Valence, and Temporal Framing on a Charitable Appeal', *Journal of Applied Social Psychology*, 39(12): 2910–2935.
Cheung, C. K. and Chan, C. M. (2000) 'Social-cognitive Factors of Donating Money to Charity, with Special Attention to an International Relief Organisation', *Evaluation and Program Planning*, 23: 241–53.
Cialdini, R. B. and Schroeder, D. (1976) 'Increasing Compliance by Legitimizing Paltry Contributions: When Even a Penny Helps,' *Journal of Personality and Social Psychology*, 34: 599–604.
Collaizzi, A., Williams, K. J., and Kayson, W. A. (1984) 'When Will People Help? The Effects of Gender, Urgency and Location on Altruism', *Psychological Reports*, 55: 139–42.
Coulter, R. H. and Pinto, B. M. (1995) 'Guilt Appeal in Advertising: What are Their Effects?', *Journal of Applied Psychology*, 80: 697–705.
Croson, R. and Shang, R. (2008) 'The Impact of Downward Social Information on Contribution Decisions', *Journal of Experimental Economics*, 11(February): 221–33.
DeJong, W. and Oopik, A. J. (1992) 'Effect of Legitimizing Small Contributions and Labelling Potential Donors as "Helpers" on Responses to a Direct Mail Solicitation for Charity', *Psychological Reports*, 71: 923–8.
Desmet, P. and Feinberg, F. M. (2003) 'Ask and Ye Shall Receive: The Effects of the Appeals Scale on Consumers' Donation Behaviour', *Journal of Economic Psychology*, 24: 349–76.

Dolinski, D., Grzyb, T., Olejnik, J., Prusakowski, S., and Urban, K. (2005) 'Let's Dialogue About Penny: Effectiveness of Dialogue Involvement and Legitimizing Paltry Contribution Techniques', *Journal of Applied Social Psychology*, 35(6): 1150–1170.

Doob, A. N. and McLaughlin, D. S. (1989) 'Ask and You Shall be Given: Request Size and Donations to a Good Cause', *Journal of Applied Social Psychology*, 19(12): 1049–1056.

Eayrs, C. B. and Ellis, N. (1990) 'Charity Advertising. For or Against People With A Mental Handicap?' *British Journal of Psychology*, 29: 349–60.

Feinman, S. (1978) 'When Does Sex Affect Altruistic Behaviour?', *Psychological Reports*, 43: 1218.

Feldman, D. and Feldman, B. (1985) 'The Effect of A Telethon on Attitudes Toward Disabled People and Financial Contributions', *Journal of Rehabilitation*, 51: 42–5.

Fisher, R. J. and Ackerman, D. (1998) 'The Effects of Recognition and Group Need on Volunteerism: A Social Norm Perspective', *Journal of Consumer Research*, 25(3)(December): 262–79.

Fisher, R. J., Vendenbosch, M., and Kersid, A. (2008) 'An Empathy-Helping Perspective on Consumers' Responses to Fund-Raising Appeals', *Journal of Consumer Research*, 35(3): 519–31.

Fraser, C., Hite, R. E., and Sauer, P. L. (1988) 'Increasing Contributions in Solicitation Campaigns: The Use of Large and Small Anchorpoints', *Journal of Consumer Research*, 15: 284–7.

Ghingold, M. (1981) 'Guilt Arousing Marketing Communications: An Unexplored Variable', in K. B. Monroe (ed.) *Advances in Consumer Research*, Ann Arbor: Association for Consumer Research, 8: 442–8.

Goatman, A. K. and Lewis, B. R. (2007) 'Charity E-volution? An Evaluation of the Attitudes of UK Charities Towards Website Adoption and Use', *International Journal of Nonprofit and Voluntary Sector Marketing*, 12(1): 33–46.

Grace, D. and Griffin, D. (2006) 'Exploring Conspicuousness in the Context of Donation Behaviour', *International Journal of Nonprofit and Voluntary Sector Marketing*, 11(2): 147–54.

——. (2009) 'Conspicuous Donation Behaviour: Scale Development and Validation', *Journal of Consumer Behaviour*, 8(1): 14–25.

Guy, B. S. and Patton, W. E. (1989) 'The Marketing of Altruistic Causes: Understanding Why People Help', *Journal of Consumer Marketing*, Vol. 6(1)(Winter): 19–30.

Hennig-Thurau, T., Gwinner K. P., Walsh G., and Gremler D. D. (2004) 'Electronic Word-of-Mouth Via Consumer-Opinion Platforms: What Motivates Consumers to Articulate Themselves on the Internet?' *Journal of Interactive Marketing*, 18(1): 38–52.

Hibbert, S. A. and Horne, S. (1997) 'Donation Dilemmas: A Consumer Behaviour Perspective', *International Journal of Nonprofit and Voluntary Sector Marketing*, 2(3): 261–74.

Hibbert, S. A. and Chuah, S-H. (2009) 'Appealing to Moral Emotions: Examining Donor Responses to Fundraising Ads Through a Dictator Game Experiment', NCVO/VSSN Conference, University of Warwick.

Hibbert, S. A., Hogg, G., and Quinn, T. (2005) 'Social Entrepreneurship: Understanding Consumer Motives for Buying the Big Issue', *Journal of Consumer Behaviour*, 4(3): 159–72.

Hibbert, S. A., Smith, A., Davies, A., and Ireland, F. (2007) 'Guilt Appeals: Persuasion Knowledge and Charitable Giving', *Psychology and Marketing*, 24(8): 723–42.

Hussein, A. and Barrow, B. (2015) 'Charities Accused of Bullying their Donors', *The Sunday Times*, 24 May.

Kaehler, J. and Sargeant, A. (1998) 'Returns on Fund-raising Expenditures in the Voluntary Sector', Working Paper 98/06, University of Exeter.

Kozinets, R. V., De Valck, K., Woknicki, A. C., and Wilner, S. J. S. (2010) 'Networked Narratives: Understanding Word-of-mouth Marketing in On-line Communities', *Journal of Marketing*, 74(2): 71–89.

Kraut, R. E. (1973) 'Effects of Social Labeling on Giving to Charity', *Journal of Experimental Social Psychology*, 9: 551–62.

Latane, B. and Nida, S. (1981) 'Ten Years of Research on Group Size and Helping', *Psychological Bulletin*, 89(2): 308–24.

LaTour, S. A. and Manrai, A. K. (1989) 'Interactive Impact of Informational and Normative Influence on Donations', *Journal of Marketing Research*, 26: 327–35.

Lee, B. A. and Farrell, C. R. (2003) 'Buddy, Can You Spare a Dime? Homelessness, Panhandling, and the Public', *Urban Affairs Review*, 38: 299–24.

Long, S. H. (1976) 'Social Pressure and Contributions to Health Charities', *Public Choice*, 28: 55–66.

Margolis, H. (1982) *Selfishness, Altruism, and Rationality*, Cambridge University Press: Cambridge.

Martin. R and Randal, J. (2005) 'Voluntary Contributions to a Public Good: A Natural Field Experiment', Working paper, School of Economics and Finance, Victoria University of Wellington, New Zealand.

Meer, J. (2010) *Brother Can You Spare a Dime? Peer Pressure in Charitable Solicitation*, Unpublished PhD, Texas A&M University.

Michel, G. and Rieunier, S. (2011) 'Nonprofit Brand Image and Typicality Influences on Charitable Giving', *Journal of Business Research*, doi:10.1016/j.jbusres.2011.04.002.

Mitchell, H. E. and Byrne, D. (1973) 'The Defendant's Dilemma: Effects of Jurors' Attitudes and Authoritarianism on Judicial Decisions', *Journal of Personality and Social Psychology*, 25(1): 123–9.

Moore, E. M., Bearden, W. O., Teel, and J. E. (1985) 'Use of Labeling and Assertions of Dependency in Appeals for Consumer Support', *Journal of Consumer Research* 12(1): 90.

National Council for Voluntary Organisations (2011) *UK Giving 2011*, NCVO/CAF: London.

Piliavin, I. M., Piliavin, J. M, and Rodin, J. (1975) 'Costs of Diffusion and the Stigmatised Victim', *Journal of Personality and Social Psychology*, 32: 429–38.

Piliavin, I. M., Dovido, S. L., Gaeitner, S. L., and Clark, R. D. (1981) *Emergency Intervention*, New York: Academic Press.

Prahalad, C. K. and Ramaswamy, V. (2000) 'Co-opting Customer Competence', *Harvard Business Review*, 78(January): 79–90.

Radley, A. and Kennedy, M. (1995) 'Charitable Giving by Individuals: A Study of Attitudes and Practice', *Human Relations*, 48(6): 685–709.

Reeves, R. A., Macolini, R. M., and Martin, R. C. (1987) 'Legitimising Paltry Contributions: On The Spot Versus Mail-in Requests', *Journal of Applied Social Psychology*, 17: 731–8.

Reingen, P. H. (1978) 'On Inducing Compliance With Requests', *Journal of Consumer Research*, 5: 96–102.

Ridge, K. (2008) *What are Charities Doing? A Content Analysis of Charity Print Media*, Unpublished Masters Dissertation, University of Nottingham, Nottingham, UK.

Sargeant, A. (2001) 'Relationship Fundraising: How to Keep Donors Loyal', *Nonprofit Management and Leadership*, 12(2): 177–92.

Sargeant, A. and Jay, E. (2004) 'Reasons for Lapse: The Case of Face-to-face Donors', *International Journal of Nonprofit and Voluntary Sector Marketing*, 9(2): 171–82.

Sargeant, A. and Lee, S. (2004) 'Trust and Relationship Commitment in the United Kingdom Voluntary Sector: Determinants of Donor Behaviour', *Psychology and Marketing*, 21(8): 613–35.

Sargeant, A. and Woodliffe, L. (2007) 'Gift Giving: An Interdisciplinary Review', *International Journal of Nonprofit and Voluntary Sector Marketing*, 12: 257–307.

Sargeant, A. and Hudson, J. (2008) 'Donor Retention: An Exploratory Study of Door-to-door Recruits', *International Journal of Nonprofit and Voluntary Sector Marketing*, 13(1): 89–101.

Sargeant, A., West, D. C., and Ford, J. B. (2001) 'The Role of Perceptions in Predicting Donor Value', *Journal of Marketing Management*, 17: 407–28.

Sargeant, A., Ford, J., and Hudson, J. (2008) 'Charity Brand Personality: The Relationship with Giving Behaviour' *Service Industries Journal*, 28(5): 615–32.

Saucier, D. A., Miller, C. T., and Doucet, N. (2005) 'Differences in Helping Whites and Blacks: A Meta-Analysis', *Personality and Social Psychology Review*, 9(1): 2–16.

Schwartzwald, J., Bizman, A., and Raz, M. (1983) 'The Foot-in-the-Door Paradigm: Effects of Second Request Size on Donation Probability and Donor Generosity', *Personality and Social Psychology Bulletin*, 9 (September): 443–50.

Shang, J. and Croson, R. (2006) "The Impact of Social Comparisons on Nonprofit Fund Raising", in R.M. Isaac and D.D. Davis (eds.) *Experiments Investigating Fundraising and Charitable Contributors (Research in Experimental Economics, Volume 11)*, Emerald Group Publishing, 143–56.

Sinha, A. K. and Jain, A. (1986) 'The Effect of Some Benefactor and Beneficiary Characteristics on Helping Behavior', *Journal of Social Psychology*, 126(3): 361–8.

Small, D. A. and Verrochi, N. M. (2009) 'The Face of Need: Facial Emotion Expression on Charity Advertisements', *Journal of Marketing Research*, 46(6): 777–87.

Swinyard, W. R. and Ray, M. L. (1977) 'Advertising – Selling Interactions: An Attribution Theory Experiment', *Journal of Marketing Research*, 14 (Winter): 22–32.

Thornton, B., Kirchner, G., and Jacobs, J. (1991) 'Influence of a Photograph on a Charitable Appeal: A Picture May Be Worth a Thousand Words When It Has to Speak for Itself', *Journal of Applied Social Psychology*, 21: 433–45.

Venables, B. T., Rose, G. M., Bush, V. D., and Gilbert, F. W. (2005) 'The Role of Brand Personality in Charitable Giving: An Assessment and Validation', *Journal of the Academy of Marketing Science*, 33(3): 295–312.

Verhaert, G. A. and van den Poel, D. (2011) 'Improving Campaign Success Rate by Tailoring Donation Requests along the Donor Lifecycle', *Journal of Interactive Marketing*, 25(1): 51–63.

Waters, R. D., Burnett, E. Lamm, A., and Lucas, J. (2009) 'Engaging Stakeholders through Social Networking: How Nonprofit Organizations are Using Facebook', *Public Relations Review*, 35: 102–6.

Webb, D. J., Green, C. L., and Brashear, T. G. (2000) 'Development and Validation of Scales to Measure Attitudes Influencing Monetary Donations to Charitable Organisations', *Journal of the Academy of Marketing Science*, 28(2): 299–309.

Wechasara, G., Motes, W. H., Boya, U. O. (1987) 'Examining the Effects of Positive Social Labeling, Time, and Request Sizes on Compliance in a Multistage Marketing Survey Context', *Journal of the Academy of Marketing Science*, 15(4): 15–21.

West, P. (2004) *Conspicuous Compassion: Why Sometimes it Really is Cruel to be Kind*, Civitas Institute for the Study of Civil Society: London.

Weyant, J. M. (1984) 'Applying Social Psychology to Induce Charitable Donations', *Journal of Applied Social Psychology*, 14: 441–7.

Weyant, J. M. and Smith, S. L. (1987) 'Getting More by Asking for Less: The Effects of Request Size on Donations of Charity', *Journal Of Applied Social Psychology*, 17: 392–400.

Wiepking, P. (2006) 'Birds of a Feather Flock Together. Why People Donate to Specific Charitable Organizations', presented at the 35th Annual ARNOVA Conference, Chicago.

Yinon, Y. L., Bizman, A., Cohen, S., and Segev, A. (1976) 'Effects of guilt arousing communication in volunteering for the civil guard', *Bulletin of the Psychonomic Society*, 7: 493–4.

Part III

The geographies and scales of philanthropy

Vignette: The Geographies and Scales of Philanthropy

Philanthropy in India

Emily Jansons and Femida Handy

Philanthropy in India is simultaneously age-old and new, easy and difficult. On the one hand deep-rooted cultural customs and religious beliefs have defined India's philanthropic traditions, and continue to do so. Historically, much of India's wealth has come from the land or other traditional forms of capital. As part of this, wealthy families, except a few notable exceptions, such as the Tatas, often emphasized religious giving rather than charitable philanthropy. On the other hand, India, over the past few decades, has seen a generation of new skills-based professionals from more diverse backgrounds gain wealth in new sectors. These are usually linked to the global economy, such as information technology. This has created both the wealth and the conditions for a novel kind of Indian philanthropy that reflects various global models. These new philanthropists have greater interest in pursuing systemic change, using markets, and incorporating their experience from business and abroad. In this vignette, we give two examples to illustrate these emerging trends in Indian philanthropy. The first focuses on the Indian philanthropist Rohini Nilekani; the second on the Dasra foundation.

Philanthropist Rohini Nilekani

Roots

Rohini Nilekani, born in an upper-middle class family in Mumbai, was a social activist and prospective journalist when she met her husband, Nandan Nilekani, at a quiz contest at the Indian Institute of Technology, Madras. In 1981, Nandan co-founded Infosys, now India's second largest IT services company. As part of the company's growth process, Nandan had to work on site with clients in the US for several years. During that period, Nilekani remained socially engaged; she volunteered in organizations such as Women for Peace in Chicago and continued with journalistic assignments. Reflecting on the period, she recalls having an 'exhilarating time' while volunteering – even in tasks such as licking stamps and putting them on envelopes as part of Harold Washington's campaign for Mayor of Chicago – while also gaining immensely from the public library system. Eventually, Nilekani's 1.41 percent stake in Infosys made her wealthy, but her deep roots in social activism enabled her to see an excellent opportunity for investing money strategically towards philanthropic use. To this end, she has been actively engaged in a spectrum of activities.

Alongside having donated over \$40 million to various organizations, dealing with issues related to education, microfinance, healthcare, the environment, access to clean water, sanitation services and good governance, Nilekani has served on several expert advisory and audit committees for the government and on the boards of numerous nonprofits. These include the Ashoka Trust for Research in Ecology and the Environment (ATREE) and Sanghamithra Rural Financial Services, where she funded its first microcredit programme for the urban poor. She is also the author of Uncommon Ground, which evolved from a television programme to a popular book featuring rare dialogues between social and corporate leaders – and she has authored the thriller-novel *Stillborn*.

Arghyam and Pratham books

A former chairperson of the Akshara Foundation in Bangalore, a foundation working towards having 'Every Child in School and Learning Well', Nilekani's largest contribution has been to two foundations where she currently acts as chair, Arghyam and Pratham Books. Arghyam is a public charitable foundation that Nilekani founded in 2001. It aims to promote equity and sustainability in water access. Finding no existing entity focused on water issues that was capable of absorbing the amount of funds she wanted to donate, she established Arghyam as a holding structure for the funds and a platform for giving. With India's vast size and diversity, many organizations struggle to scale up to meet the country's immense needs and create an impact. Nilekani realized that success was dependent on building partnerships with the government, NGOs, and various other institutions. Arghyam supports sustainability and impact by awarding grants to grassroots organizations, promoting new models and undertaking participatory action research and advocacy. One example is Arghyam's India Water Portal, an initiative encouraged by the National Knowledge Commission that has become one of the foremost sources in India for knowledge building and information sharing on matters such as water, sanitation, agriculture, climate change and biodiversity.

Pratham Books, established in 2004, is a nonprofit publisher with a goal of democratizing the joy of reading and access to books in India, so that every child can be empowered in a society that places a premium on textual knowledge, but where one in three school children is unable to read fluently. Pratham Books has published over 11 million books with 225 titles in 12 languages, printed over ten million story cards – sheets of laminated paper folded to make a story and priced as low as INR 2.5 (\$.04 US) to make them accessible to poor rural customers – and reached a readership of over 50 million, targeting marginalized groups. The initiative addresses challenges particular to India, a widely diverse and poor country where costs need to be kept low. In a nation with 22 officially recognized languages and, by some estimates, more than 780 spoken languages[1], and where good professional translators are expensive and difficult to find, Pratham Books has developed an innovative approach. It uses Creative Commons licensing that allows anyone to use, tweak, rewrite and translate their books. Furthermore, most of their books are freely available online and are distributed as audiobooks and iPad apps. Additionally, its 'library-in-a-classroom' program provides activity kits, tracking sheets and books for schools that cannot afford the cost of a full library.

Reflections

Nilekani's philanthropy permits reflection upon Indian tendencies of founder intervention in organizational activities. Many early-generation American foundations, such as the Rockefeller, Ford, Carnegie and Mellon, separated their activities from the family and relied on professional managers. In India, however, philanthropists and their families often tend to operate around caste, traditions and community lines, and are highly involved in the strategy, implementation and monitoring of foundation activities. Nilekani is unique in that, as a means of pursuing her passion for systemic change and the empowerment of people, she is highly involved in the strategy, relationship building and professionalization of organizations, but takes a 'hands-off' approach once she finds the right individuals and creates the right institutions. With Arghyam, for example, the recipients of grants are trusted to spend money responsibly.

Nilekani's approach to philanthropy also demonstrates flexibility as priorities change and a willingness to simultaneously undertake philanthropy in multiple areas of interest. It helps that she is not directly involved in creating the wealth that funds her philanthropy; thus, she has greater independence than business leaders who can be seen as leveraging their philanthropic activities to improve their company's image as being socially responsible. With private money, she feels free to support organizations and individuals that may seemingly be at cross-purposes with each other, for example, supporting left-leaning media alongside groups that believe markets will solve societal solutions. Her philanthropic activities are distinctly her own – she does not allow herself to be defined as the wife of a billionaire who does charitable work on behalf of the family. Within India's cultural context that values anonymous gifting with detachment from the outcome, Nilekani's willingness to undertake structured and public philanthropy indicates a new approach to the public-private divide of Indian philanthropy.

Strategic funder Dasra

The Dasra foundation demonstrates the importance of knowledge and information to catalyzing social change, and the need to build comfort levels and trust as a fundamental step in allowing the vast amounts of philanthropic wealth in India to be effectively put to use. Mumbai-based, Dasra was founded in 1999 by Deval Sanghavi and Neera Nundy, both former investment bankers in New York. It is among India's leading strategic philanthropic organizations. Dasra believes that 'if philanthropists and social entrepreneurs are equipped with the knowledge, funding opportunities and people to make their work more strategic, then the social sector in India will be transformed dramatically'.

Sanghavi and Nundy took the lessons and approaches they learned from investment banking, including the focus on management as an enabler for organizations to grow and become more profitable, and applied them to the nonprofit sector. The challenge has been to seek out high-quality organizations and entrepreneurs in India, invest in improving their management and help them scale their models. Dasra's success lies in its ability to work with both philanthropists and social entrepreneurs and bring together knowledge, funding and people. To this end, Dasra shares knowledge through research reports and training, helps social entrepreneurs network and build skills by hosting the annual Indian Philanthropy Forum and leverages the Dasra Giving Circles to generate funding. Over the last fifteen years, Dasra has strengthened and aided the growth of more than 900 nonprofits and social businesses, engaged with over 600 philanthropists globally, published 28 research reports and given over $37 million US to 'social impact' organizations.

Dasra's annual Indian Philanthropy Forum (IPF) brings together a wide range of individuals, including philanthropists, corporate CEOs, social sector leaders and heads of foundations and think tanks. Together, they discuss social sector reform in India, strategies for effective funding, lobbying for relevant regulatory changes, possible viable solutions to address India's challenges and skills that can be employed to mentor social sector leaders. The IPF plays a critical role in developing the donor base in India, dispelling myths about the social sector, and serving as a platform for learning and sharing experiences about philanthropy.

Dasra Giving Circles are collaborative efforts, each comprising ten members who pool their individual funding of INR 1 million (about $16,200 US) annually for a period of three years, and collectively decide on the one nonprofit to receive the INR 30 million (about $485,000 US) grant disbursement. Dasra also provides the selected organization up to 300 days of hands-on assistance. This process mitigates the common pitfall of everyone wanting to fund the 'perfect' organization already deemed trustworthy and with strong management. The reality is that few such organizations currently exist in India. Many are held back by a lack of clear strategies, weak organizational structures, inadequate systems and processes and shortage of skilled staff. Therefore, rather than simply fund an imperfect NGO, Dasra works to directly address these challenges and build up NGOs through managerial assistance and hands-on support. The hope is that with stronger organizations, improved evaluation practices and impact measurement will follow. All of these steps enable Dasra to engage in-depth conversations with organizations and high net worth (HNW) donors, who then increasingly trust Dasra and are willing to contribute larger amounts of capital.

Dasra's emphasis on research helps spur more strategic, informed and direct funding, leading to investment in good organizations and encouraging donors to consider less conventional areas of need. As a donor in India, it can be daunting to choose an area of philanthropic focus, simply because the country's needs are so great in arguably every sector. Nonetheless, most private philanthropy in India goes to education, healthcare and livelihoods. Dasra's research reports range from use of sport for development, to preservation of indigenous values in educational modernity, to women's empowerment. In October 2012, Dasra published a research report, entitled 'Squatting Rights', on access to toilets and sanitation in urban areas, with the plan to launch a Giving Circle around the theme. While initially worried that there would be limited enthusiasm to donate to 'a topic commonly held to be unpalatable at best', fitting into common stereotypes of Indian philanthropists as shying away from 'dirty' topics, they were pleasantly surprised by the interest and enthusiasm (Patel 2013). Dasra shows that Indian philanthropists need to be steered into new sectors, and that organizations like Dasra play an important role in addressing this need.

The lessons that can be gathered from Dasra reflect some broader trends in Indian philanthropy. First, HNW individuals are starting to acknowledge the value and effectiveness of funding existing organizations rather than establishing their own foundations, even though ultra-HNW philanthropists are likely to continue setting up their own operational foundations. Second, business practices are being embraced and transferred to the philanthropic sector. Dasra does this through its research and Giving Circles, highlighting to donors which organizations are poised for scale and close to the 'tipping point' of success, then mobilizing HNW donors to invest in them. Last, in India, finding sufficient funds is not the main issue; rather, the challenge is that currently most funds are given ineffectively. A shift in the mindset and processes of fund flow is necessary for organizations to receive the support needed to make an impact.

Conclusions

Rohini Nilekani and Dasra are two progressive examples of Indian philanthropy, indicative of the direction Indian philanthropy is heading. In a globalizing world, lessons in philanthropy cross borders. Nilekani and Dasra founders Sanghavi and Nundy are no exceptions – both have spent significant amounts of time in the USA, which in some part influences their approaches to philanthropy in India. Nonetheless, their philanthropy also mirrors national and regional tendencies, adapting to local needs and circumstances. Furthermore, their tendencies to collaborate and support the growth of community-level organizations are a more sustainable model than creating operational foundations, which has been the traditional pattern in India. As India's wealth continues to increase, and more funds from both individuals and companies pours into the philanthropic sector alongside traditional approaches to giving, there will inevitably be a growing movement of strategic, impactful, innovative and diverse approaches catalyzing social change in India.

Note

1 The People's Linguistic Survey of India has counted over 780 languages and estimate there are another 100 additional languages (www.peopleslinguisticsurvey.org/default.aspx). The 2001 Census of India lists a total of 122 languages and 234 mother tongues with over 10,000 speakers. (www.censusindia.gov.in/Census_Data_2001/Census_Data_Online/Language/data_on_language.aspx)

Reference

Patel, A. (2013) 'Philanthropy Must Be Prepared to Talk Dirty,' *Alliance*, May 6, www.alliancemagazine.org/blog/philanthropy-must-be-prepared-to-talk-dirty/ [Accessed 05 June 2015].

7

Regional differences in philanthropy

René Bekkers

The practices and traditions of philanthropy vary strongly across the globe. From one place to another, such differences do not only relate to the size and nature of philanthropy, but also to the methods people use to give. Furthermore, regional differences do not only occur between countries. At a smaller geographic scale, contrasts can be found between states (Putnam, 2000; Bielefeld *et al.*, 2005), provinces, regions and departments (CERPHI, 2010), municipalities (Bekkers and Veldhuizen, 2008), neighbourhoods and zip codes. Focusing predominantly on the contribution of money to nonprofit organizations, this chapter explores these regional differences. Alongside helping us to develop a better understanding of philanthropy, knowledge of any differences in giving also has practical relevance: it informs fundraising practices (Schneider, 1996). Nonprofit organizations, for example, use, often quite small scale, geographic criteria to segment their donor database and to select target groups of potential donors for fundraising campaigns (Sargeant *et al.*, 2010: 160).

Regional differences in philanthropy in Europe

The majority of studies on regional differences seek to understand country differences in philanthropy, and a lot of these focus on variations between European countries. Here, three datasets are of special importance: the Eurobarometer survey (EB) from 2004 on civic engagement, a series of opinion polls commissioned by the European Commission; the Gallup World Poll (GWP), an omnibus survey on a broad variety of topics; and the European Social Survey (ESS), a biennial general household survey. The picture that emerges from these datasets is provided in Figure 7.1. This presents country differences regarding the likelihood of donating to nonprofit organizations across these three datasets. Only those countries that were covered in all of the datasets are included in this figure and the countries are ordered by the average proportion of respondents reporting donations in the three datasets.

As can be seen, the EB data show that the proportion of the population reporting donations to at least one out of 14 categories of nonprofit organizations varies from 20 percent in Spain to almost 80 percent in the Netherlands. The GWP data indicates that the proportion of the population reporting donations to charity in the course of a calendar year varies from 79 percent in the UK to 7 percent in Greece (CAF, 2011). Finally, the ESS, from 2002, also shows

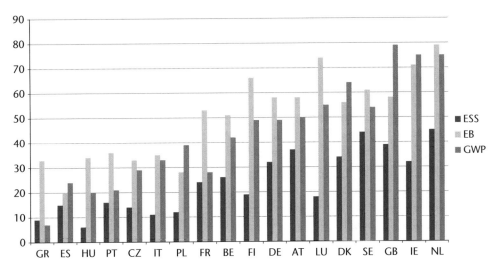

Figure 7.1   Likelihood (%) of donating to nonprofit organizations reported in the European Social Survey 2002 (ESS), the Eurobarometer 2004 (EB), and the Gallup World Poll (GWP)

considerable differences between countries in Europe. The country differences are spread over different ranges in the three datasets. In the ESS, the scores vary from 6 percent in Hungary to 45 percent in the Netherlands; in the EB, the scores vary from 20 percent in Spain to 79 percent in the Netherlands; and in the GWP, they vary from 7 percent in Greece to 79 percent in the UK.

As these numbers demonstrate, the proportion of the population reporting engagement in philanthropy varies considerably for specific countries between the three datasets. The figures for Finland are 65 percent in the Eurobarometer but only 50 percent in the Gallup World Poll. The figures for the UK show an opposite difference: a higher percentage (79 percent) in the Gallup data than in the Eurobarometer (58 percent). In the ESS, only 19 percent of the respondents in Finland reported donations, and 39 percent of the respondents in the UK.

The discrepancies between these proportions vividly illustrate that in research on philanthropy 'methodology is destiny' (Rooney *et al.*, 2001, 2004): the different sampling strategies, data collection modes and questions used to measure philanthropy can yield very different estimates for specific countries. While the proportions are markedly different for some countries, the correlations between the proportions from the three datasets are, however, fairly strong: the EB-ESS correlation is .74; the ESS-Gallup correlation is .81 and the EB-Gallup correlation is .80. The fact that these correlations are so high underscores that there are reliable cross-country differences in philanthropy.

How can the differences between countries in Europe in the engagement in philanthropy be explained? What are the commonalities between countries with high proportions of donors in the various datasets, and what are the commonalities between countries with low proportions? One commonality of more philanthropic countries seems to be a geographic location in the richer northwestern part of Europe, opposed to the more southern location and lower gross domestic product (GDP) of less philanthropic countries. Furthermore, when looking outside Europe, we see high proportions of the population engaging in philanthropy in countries with a higher GDP, like Australia and the US (CAF, 2012). In other respects, however, the highest proportions of donors are found in a quite heterogeneous collection of countries. Both densely populated countries, like the Netherlands, and sparsely populated countries, like Sweden, have high proportions of donors. While a predominantly Catholic religious tradition is a commonality of the low ranking countries, we also see high proportions of donors in two Catholic countries (Ireland, Luxemburg), amidst predominantly Protestant countries (Denmark, Sweden) and secular countries (the Netherlands). Additionally, there is a mix of both large (Great Britain, Sweden), as well as small countries (the Netherlands, Luxemburg) at the top, and we also find large (Spain), as well as small countries (Czech Republic) at the lower end of the distribution.

A warning on the analysis of regional differences

While for fundraising purposes it may be enough to know which zip codes yield the highest levels of giving, for scholars, any regional differences pose an interesting, yet notoriously difficult, research problem with both theoretical and empirical challenges. From a theoretical point of view, regional differences can be explained by a plethora of different theories and hypotheses. These theories, and a review of the empirical evidence surrounding them, are at the heart of this chapter. The methodological concerns involved in testing hypotheses on regional differences pervade the literature and discussing them is beyond the space available. However, it does seem just to issue a general warning.

One of the most pressing problems is the ecological fallacy that arises from correlating macro-level characteristics with each other (Snijders and Bosker, 1999). Analyses that report correlations between characteristics of regions suggest that contextual, i.e. 'ecological', effects are at work. In fact, however, compositional effects are often driving regional differences. In most cases, differences in the composition of the population are generating regional differences; not so much the nature of the region. Without adequate data, and statistical models to analyze them, the results of comparative studies can be highly misleading. In the 1990s, hierarchical, or 'multilevel', regression models were popularized as a statistical tool for the analysis of context influences (Snijders and Bosker, 1999 for a useful introduction). Multilevel models can be used to test whether regional differences are due to compositional or contextual influences.

The typical finding in multilevel analyses is that contextual influences are fairly small, usually explaining only 5 to 10 percent of the variance. This means that the strong correlations that are often found between regional characteristics are primarily due to the composition of the population. An example is the correlation of .77 between voter turnout and the proportion of blood donors in municipalities in the Netherlands (Bekkers and Veldhuizen, 2008). A subsequent multilevel analysis (Veldhuizen and Bekkers, 2011), however, showed that only 6.5 percent of the variance in blood donation at the individual level is due to the characteristics of the municipality: 93.5 percent of the variance was due to composition effects. Voter turnout was one of the significant municipality characteristics, but it explained only 0.03 percent of the variance. Another example is the .58 correlation between GDP and the proportion of the population reporting engagement in philanthropy (CAF, 2010). In a multilevel model, Gesthuizen, Van der Meer and Scheepers (2008b) found the correlation between GDP and engagement in philanthropy at the individual level to be only .005. These two examples should remind us that aggregate correlations are likely to be substantially higher than the contextual influence. The implication for research on regional differences is that explanations of regional differences should take the composition of the population into account.

Two types of explanations of regional differences

Explanations for regional differences originate in different disciplines. Mirroring the wider, cross-cutting nature, of philanthropy, these include cross-cultural psychology, political science, economics, history, sociology, and geography. Each of these its own theories and perspectives. In this sense, the explanation of regional differences is similar to the explanation of differences at the individual level (Adloff, Chapter 3; Pharoah, Chapter 4; Mesch and Pactor, Chapter 5): a comprehensive understanding of regional differences requires a multidisciplinary approach.

Across these different disciplines, explanations of philanthropic activity can be grouped into two types (Bekkers and Wiepking, 2011a): explanations that focus on the characteristics of donors (and nondonors), and explanations that focus on the characteristics of situations in which people donate (or do not donate). At the individual level, the first type of explanation answers the question 'Who gives?'; the second type answers the question 'When do people give?'. At the country level, the first type of explanation implies that philanthropy is flourishing in some countries simply because these countries are populated by more philanthropic citizens. This type of explanation figures prominently in cross-national comparative research. However, the composition of the population is hard to influence by policymakers and fundraising professionals. In contrast, the second type of question focuses on situations that are amenable to change and influence. Hence, it is this type of question that should occupy policymakers, fundraising professionals and other professionals and stakeholders in the nonprofit sector.

Mechanisms that explain country differences in philanthropy

A comprehensive review of the empirical literature on philanthropy by individuals and households by Bekkers and Wiepking (2011a) groups the characteristics of situations into eight mechanisms that drive charitable giving: (1) awareness of need; (2) solicitation; (3) costs and benefits; (4) altruism; (5) reputation; (6) psychological benefits; (7) values; (8) efficacy. Translating these mechanisms from the individual level to a higher level of aggregation, individuals are expected to give more when they live in regions in which they (1) are more strongly aware of the needs for contributions; (2) are more actively solicited for contributions; (3) face lower material costs and reap more benefits from contributing; (4) are more strongly concerned with the welfare of recipients; (5) obtain more social rewards or avoid larger punishments for contributing; (6) feel better about their contribution or avoid feeling bad about not contributing; (7) more strongly recognize their contribution as a way to create a world that is consistent with their ideal world view; (8) experience their contribution to be more effective. The remainder of this chapter is a discussion of these mechanisms. For each mechanism, the hypothesis is presented, followed by a discussion of the empirical evidence in research on regional differences.

Awareness of need

The awareness of need mechanism implies that knowing about the existence of a need for contributions is a necessary condition for philanthropy. It is not a sufficient condition, however. The empirical literature on philanthropy shows that many factors are moderating the effect of need on giving (Bekkers and Wiepking, 2011a). The road from objective need to donations is difficult, twisting and turning between the hills of the media landscape and the mountains of denial of responsibility. Potential donors get information about objective needs through various information channels: from nonprofit communications (Hibbert, Chapter 6) to news media. The news media infrastructure, especially, affects the information available to individuals. As part of that, news media preferences of consumers determine the selection of information that reaches them, with potential donors interpreting this information in a way that fits their worldview and that suits their psychological needs. Research in social psychology shows that people have refined ways of legitimizing inaction when faced with opportunities to give. These individual level processes, however, do not seem to be much different between regions.

A general hypothesis is that freedom of press and a higher level of activity of news media increases the availability of information on social needs. A more specific hypothesis is that individuals in countries with a stronger international orientation, have a higher awareness of needs among distant recipients, and the amount contributed to international relief and development organizations is larger. Individuals living in countries with a stronger focus on local issues will be less likely to know about natural disasters, famine, war and disease overseas and will therefore be less likely to engage in international philanthropy. The assumption that individuals in countries with a stronger international orientation are less parochial and more prosocial towards anonymous strangers in other countries receives support in an experiment (Buchan *et al.*, 2008) and in an advanced analysis of data on willingness to help immigrants from the European Values Study (Koster, 2007). The specific hypothesis about engagement in international philanthropy has not been tested extensively. A comparison of donations to international relief and development in the US and the Netherlands provides support for the hypothesis. The US media are more strongly focused on domestic and local issues than the Dutch media (Janssen *et al.*, 2008). Correspondingly, international giving accounts for a much smaller portion of total giving in the US than in the Netherlands. Further comparisons of additional countries are required to test this hypothesis.

At a smaller scale, awareness of local needs may translate into higher giving to address these needs. For instance, one would expect higher levels of giving to local organizations in regions with higher proportions of unemployed and homeless people. To date, only one national study has tested such predictions. Borgonovi (2006) found that the percentage of the population in poverty in US counties is not related to either religious or secular giving, controlling for individual level covariates. This finding shows that 'voluntary resources are manifestly not funneled to those most in "need", nor are organizations agglomerated in the most needy areas of the metropolitan region', as Wolch and Geiger (1983: 1078) concluded in an early study of voluntarism in the Los Angeles metropolitan area. More recently, Britto *et al.* (2011) analyzed data from 20 counties in the greater Metro Atlanta Area, finding that engagement in philanthropy actually decreased with an index of community problems composed of the percentage below poverty, the crime rate, and the median income of the respondent's county. This finding shows that the capacity to engage in philanthropy is an important factor in responsiveness to need. As community problems increase, the resources to engage in philanthropy to fight these problems decrease.

Solicitation

Many forms of philanthropy occur in response to solicitations for contributions. Without solicitations, people are unlikely to engage in philanthropy spontaneously. However, it is difficult to estimate the causal effect of solicitation at the individual level using cross-sectional survey data. As targeting donors is selective, and often based on past donation behaviour, solicitations are endogenous (Lim, 2010; Paik & Navarre-Jackson, 2011). Experiments show that many people actively avoid situations in which they are likely to be asked to donate money (Pancer *et al.*, 1979; DellaVigna *et al.*, 2012). Participants in these experiments who do receive solicitations are more likely to donate. This does not mean, however, that an exogenous increase in the number of solicitations will lead to higher levels of giving. In fact, two large scale studies among donors of health charities in the Netherlands, one field experiment and an analysis of registered contributions, even find that donors receiving an additional solicitation decrease the level of giving, at least in the short run (Van Diepen *et al.*, 2009a, 2009b).

No studies to date have tested the hypothesis that individuals residing in places that are targeted more heavily for fundraising campaigns are more likely to donate. One study has tested whether the presence of a higher number of active nonprofit organizations in a region makes individuals in that region more likely to contribute. Controlling for numerous other factors, Bielefeld *et al.* (2005) find no relationship between the number of active nonprofit organizations in an area and the volume or likelihood of engagement in philanthropy; Rotolo and Wilson (2012) do find a positive relationship between the number of nonprofit organizations in a state and the likelihood of secular volunteering at the individual level, but not with religious volunteering.

Costs

Access to financial resources lowers the costs of engagement in philanthropy (Wilson and Musick, 1997; Bryant *et al.*, 2003). At the individual level, a higher level of education, household income, income from wealth, and a stronger sense of financial security are associated with higher levels of philanthropy (Bekkers and Wiepking, 2011b; Wiepking and Bekkers, 2012). Mohan *et al.* (2004) document the importance of resources in regional differences in blood donation. Gesthuizen *et al.* (2008b) analyze data on charitable giving of money from the EB in a multilevel model; they find that donations are lower in countries with more highly educated citizens, taking individual level education into account.

Citizens in countries with a more stable economy can be expected to feel more financially secure and to donate more as a result. The level of financial security is likely to be lower in countries with higher levels of income inequality, especially among lower educated citizens. Higher GDP, national wealth, and lower levels of income inequality are likely to be associated with higher levels of philanthropy, in part through a higher sense of financial security. The World Giving Index (CAF, 2010) shows a positive association between the proportion of the population in a country reporting donations to charity and GDP. This analysis, however, did not take individual level characteristics into account. Data from the Eurobarometer show a negative relationship between income inequality and donations, controlling for many individual level characteristics of households (Gesthuizen *et al.*, 2008a). A study of donations in Indonesia also shows a negative relationship between income inequality and giving (Okten and Osili, 2004). A sophisticated analysis of data from the US, however, shows no relationship between income inequality at the county level and household giving (Borgonovi, 2006). The same paper also shows a surprisingly negative relationship between mean county income and secular household giving. A previous analysis at the aggregate level of giving in metropolitan areas in the US does reveal a positive relationship between median income and amounts donated (Wolpert, 1988). A historical geography of almshouses in the UK shows a positive relationship between accumulated wealth of regions and the number of almshouses (Bryson *et al.* 2002). Olson and Caddell (1994) find that individuals contribute less to their congregation when the average income of fellow congregation members increases. This is most likely the result of 'free riding': a lower perceived need for contributions.

People in different countries experience different levels of fiscal incentives for charitable giving (Dehne *et al.*, 2008), affecting the monetary costs of financial donations. One testable hypothesis in this area is that countries which offer a deduction for donations have higher levels of philanthropy. Another one is that persons with more financial resources will be more likely to engage in philanthropy in countries which allow charitable deductions in the income tax. Individual tax benefits for giving resulting from these fiscal incentives are larger for people with more financial resources (Simmons and Emanuele, 2004). It should be noted, however, that the establishment of such laws depends on the attitudes and political preferences of citizens.

Estimates of the cross-national or regional effects of tax laws should therefore take political values (discussed below) into account. Without such controls, it is difficult to avoid finding support for a crowding in hypothesis. Long (2000) also warns for omitted variable bias, but does not examine political values.

Benefits

The benefits expected to be received upon a donation increase the likelihood of giving to a nonprofit organization. If the organization provides collective goods to its members, such as in the case of a church, a trade union or a sports club, members of smaller groups contributing to collective goods enjoy more benefits from their contributions (Olson, 1965). Support for the hypothesis that selective benefits increase giving is provided by the finding that giving is higher in congregations in which the size of the church budget per person is higher (Peifer, 2010).

The more general hypothesis is that philanthropy decreases with group size. This hypothesis could also be explained as a result of 'free riding': the larger the number of potential other contributors, the lower each individual contribution is required to be in order to produce the desired level of the collective good. In addition, the 'bystander effect' also leads to the hypothesis that group size is negatively related to philanthropy (Darley and Latané, 1968). In larger groups, the feeling of responsibility for collective well-being is spread over more thinly over a larger number of people. At a higher level of aggregation, research on experimental games across different cultures shows strong regional differences in monetary offers to anonymous others in an ultimatum game (Henrich et al., 2005). The experiments show that stronger market integration is positively related to offers in ultimatum games. This finding can also be explained as an investment with uncertain revenue. Individuals who are used to economic interdependence upon strangers tend to have a higher level of trust that their investment will be rewarded.

Altruism: The crowding out hypothesis

The altruism mechanism implies that individuals engage in philanthropy in order to help recipients (Adloff, Chapter 3). Economists have tested the implications of theoretical models of giving including altruistic motives by testing the 'crowding out hypothesis'. Assuming that individuals are motivated to give, at least partly, because they care about the well-being of recipients, they should lower their own contributions when others increase their contributions. Vice versa, donors should increase their contributions when others decrease theirs. At the regional level, individuals should lower their contributions to nonprofit organizations as the amounts contributed by other individuals, corporations, institutional donors, or government increase.

Research testing the crowding out hypothesis in philanthropy has focused mainly on the relationship between the level of government funding and private contributions to nonprofit organizations within a specific country, yielding mixed results (Bekkers and Wiepking, 2011a: 936, 949-951). Some studies find no significant relationship between government funding and private giving (Brooks, 1999); some do find that government funding crowds out private giving – though the crowd out is usually less than 'perfect' (Payne, 1998; Brooks, 2003a); still others find crowding in: the level of government funding is positively related to the level of private giving (Khanna et al., 1995; Khanna and Sandler, 2000; Brooks, 2003b). One study of donations to American theatres found that government funding from the federal, state, and local level affected donations differently (Borgonovi, 2006). A study of religious giving (Peifer, 2010) found that contributions were lower in congregations with higher levels of alternative funding from investments or fees.

Because most of the evidence cited above comes from data about one single region, it is not necessarily bearing on the cross-national relationship. The relevant question is whether the level of private giving to nonprofit organizations is lower in regions that provide higher levels of government funding for these organizations. Many studies on volunteering have tested such a crowding out hypothesis. Most find no crowding out (Salamon and Sokolowski, 2001; Ruiter and De Graaf, 2006; Van Oorschot and Arts, 2005; Van Oorschot, Arts and Gelissen, 2006), except for two recent studies who find, albeit weak, crowding out (Stadelmann-Steffen, 2011; Hackl, Halla, and Pruckner, 2012). In respect to charitable giving, however, research has been limited. One study in the context of public broadcasting contributions (Kropf and Knack, 2003) finds some support for 'crowding in'. It is not clear though whether government subsidies increase private giving or vice versa, or both. Another study on donations to a variety of non-profit organizations in Europe based on EB data finds no relationship between social security expenditure of countries and engagement in philanthropy at the individual level (Gesthuizen *et al.*, 2008b). A recent study (Sokolowski, 2013) reports a positive correlation between government payments to nonprofit organizations and aggregate levels of private giving, but fails to take individual level correlates into account.

Reputation

Individuals living in regions in which philanthropy is valued positively will be able to obtain positive social rewards for making donations as a form of action in line with the norm. In the literature on volunteering, it has been argued that the presence of religious groups creates a positive social norm with respect to volunteering (Ruiter and De Graaf, 2006). This argument can be generalized to all forms of prosocial behaviour, including kindness to strangers (such as in the parable of the Good Samaritan; Wuthnow, 1991) and organized philanthropy. The level of compliance with the norm depends on the level of cohesion within the group: the higher the level of cohesion, the higher the level of compliance (Bekkers and Schuyt, 2008). This hypothesis has been labeled the 'community explanation' for the differences in levels of philanthropy between religious groups (Wuthnow, 1991; Bekkers and Schuyt, 2008).

From this perspective, it is not merely an individual's religiosity that encourages philanthropy, but also the religious context in which individuals decide on donations. A testable hypothesis is that regions with a higher level of religiosity have higher levels of philanthropy, net of individual level religiosity. Gitell and Tebaldi (2006) find that average the charitable contribution per tax filer in US states decreases with the proportion of the population that is Catholic, and increases with the proportion that is protestant or has another religion. A similar finding is reported for 453 municipalities in the Netherlands (Bekkers and Veldhuizen, 2008). It should be noted, however, that these studies did not include religious affiliation at the individual level. A study on charitable donations in 23 European countries shows that not only individual religious values affect donations, but also the religious context in which people live (Wiepking *et al.*, 2014). In her article on differences in giving and volunteering across US counties, Borgonovi (2006) finds that religious giving and volunteering increased with the county level of devoutness, controlling for individual levels of religiosity. In addition, religious giving is lower in counties dominated by Catholics. County level religious heterogeneity is associated with a lower likelihood of religious volunteering. In an analysis of country level data (n=15), Sivesind and Selle (2009) report that the negative association between public welfare spending and donations is weaker in religious heterogeneous countries.

Several other findings can be viewed as support for the influence of reputation. Assuming that communities in less densely populated areas are more close-knit, one would expect negative relationships between population density and engagement in philanthropy. Indeed, lower population density has been associated with acts of helpfulness shown by local residents to strangers in field experiments (Levine *et al.*, 1994; Levine *et al.*, 2008). Borgonovi (2006) find religious household giving to be higher in less densely populated counties. While these findings are surprising from an economies of scale hypothesis (Booth *et al.*, 1989), they fit the 'community explanation' of giving and volunteering.

The behaviour of others can be taken as a proxy or cue for the social norm that individuals need to comply with in order to maintain a positive reputation. Indeed, survey studies suggest that people adapt their giving to what others in their environment are giving (Olson and Caddell, 1994; Wu *et al.*, 2004; Carman 2006). It is important to note, however, that positive 'peer effects' may also be the result of psychological benefits. For example, one might feel good about conforming to internalized social norms and bad, or guilty, when departing from the norm. Additionally, 'peer effects', as observed in surveys in the form of a (partial) correlation between contributions of individuals in the same environment, may be the result of either correlations among omitted variables, or of self-selection of individuals with similar gift levels in the same environment, or of both (An, 2011). In a survey study on social influences in workplace giving, Carman (2006) finds that charitable giving is especially influenced by behaviour of co-workers in the same salary quartile. Bekkers (2012) analyzes a large sample of tax payers in the Netherlands and finds that individuals living in municipalities with a higher proportion of citizens donating more than 1 percent of income are more likely to do so themselves.

Assuming that the reputational damage of not engaging in philanthropy is bigger in those regions with higher levels of prosocial behaviour, one would expect to find higher levels of philanthropy in such regions. Kropf and Knack (2003) show that contributions to public broadcasting are higher in areas with stronger civic norms, measured by an index of census response rates, voter turnout, and belief in the honesty of others. In their early study on United Way contributions, Booth *et al.* (1989) find voter turnout to be positively correlated to the amount raised. In a study of donations to secular charities, Bekkers and Veldhuizen (2008) find a very strong correlation between voter turnout and the amount donated per household in municipalities in the Netherlands.

Values

Values are crucial for engagement in philanthropy. At the individual level, religious, political, and altruistic values can explain differences in charitable giving (Bekkers and Wiepking, 2011b). As these values are more dominant in a region, they can be expected to create a culture in which giving is viewed as more positive and desirable.

Altruistic values

Engagement in philanthropy may be motivated by altruistic concerns for recipients. Such concerns may be internalized into a stable disposition, which we call altruistic values. Several studies have found positive relationships between altruistic values and engagement in philanthropy at the individual level. It is likely that cultural differences in value systems are associated with differences in philanthropy. To study cultural differences in value systems, several models of values have been advocated in cross-cultural psychology (Schwartz, 1992; Hofstede, 2001). One testable hypothesis based on Hofstede's system is that individuals in collectivist cultures are more likely to engage in informal helping family members and friends, but are less likely to help strangers. One study testing this hypothesis (Kemmelmeier *et al.*, 2006) found that more individualistic states in the US had higher rates of donors to causes that represent individualist values – self-actualization, personal growth and development, and individual achievement. This study, however, did not include individual level controls. From Schwartz's theory, benevolence and universalism would be expected to be associated with engagement in philanthropy (Plagnol and Huppert, 2010). To date, however, no study has tested this hypothesis.

Religious values

Religious involvement is one of the strongest correlates of charitable behaviour by households and individuals (Bekkers and Wiepking, 2011b). The stronger people's religious involvement, the more actively they follow their group's (positive) norms on altruistic behavior (Wuthnow, 1991; Bekkers and Schuyt, 2008). As explained above, individuals in more religious regions may be more active in philanthropy due to higher levels of solicitations and reputational benefits. A third perspective on the relationship between religion and philanthropy is that religion is an institution that instils prosocial values in individuals (Einolf, 2011). From this perspective, it is not merely being asked more often or the social pressure to be a good citizen that explains the relationship between religiosity and philanthropy, but also the endorsement of religious values that inspires people to engage in philanthropy.

Political values

Political values are also important factors in philanthropy, though the relationship at the individual level is complicated because of conflicting influences of cultural conservatism and prosocial value orientation (Malka *et al.*, 2011). In a book primarily about the US, Brooks (2006) argues that the extent to which people believe in state-induced income redistribution is negatively related to philanthropy. In Europe, however, persons with a left wing political orientation are found to be more active participants in voluntary associations (Van Oorschot *et al.*, 2006). A study on philanthropy in the Netherlands found that persons with a left-wing political orientation are more likely to give to charitable organizations (Bekkers and Wiepking, 2006). Hughes and Luksetich (1999) find that total private contributions to art museums are higher in states with a higher proportion of the population voting Republican in presidential elections. In contrast, Bielefeld *et al.* (2005) find no support for a link between political colour of a state and individual giving. Positive relationships between democratic history and donations are found in two studies (Gesthuizen *et al.*, 2008a, b).

Political values are embodied in institutions and visions of the role of the state in the provision of welfare (Salamon and Anheier, 1998). In the literature on civic engagement, several studies have examined whether volunteering rates differ between types of welfare states (Van Oorschot *et al.*, 2006). Based on the work of Esping-Andersen (1990), nation states with different work and social welfare policies are expected to have different volunteer rates. The usefulness of the typology in comparative research has been contested, as the level of welfare effort seems to be the driving influence behind the differences between types (Scheepers *et al.*, 2002). Salamon and Anheier (1998) present four ideal types of regimes by crossing government social welfare spending (low vs high) with the size of the nonprofit sector (small vs large), hypothesizing that the level and nature of volunteering varies between these types. Comparisons of means suggest support for these hypotheses (Salamon and Sokolowski, 2001) but they are not formal statistical tests. The low numbers of countries in some of the types would make such tests fairly meaningless.

Efficacy

Countries differ in their legal systems and their treatment of nonprofit organizations (Salamon, 1997; Dehne *et al.*, 2008). These differences may translate into differences in philanthropy. One important pathway is through charitable deductions, which lower the costs of giving (see above). In addition, legal systems influence philanthropy through regulation of the activities of nonprofit organizations, including fundraising practices. The regulation of fundraising and the level of transparency of charitable organizations are likely to affect the level of charitable confidence among the general public (Bekkers, 2003). The level and nature of regulation differs strongly between countries (Breen, Chapter 14). Ortmann and Svítková (2006) formulated a theoretical model of regulation and predicted that certification increases the quality of services provided by charitable organizations, as well as private donations. One would expect that regions with more strict requirements for registration, transparency and accountability of charitable organizations – such as the US, UK and the Netherlands – would experience fewer cases of fraud, abuse of donations and the misleading of potential and actual donors (Bekkers, 2003). As a result, one would expect public support for charitable organizations in these regions to be higher. In a comparison of US states, however, Irvin (2005) discovers no difference in amounts donated between states with loose and stricter nonprofit regulation. In a cross-sectional analysis, however, it may be that regions with higher levels of fraud and abuse are found to have imposed more strict regulation to reduce these problems. Also donors may suspect that irregularities are more frequent in countries with more strict regulations. Another problem in the identification of effects of regulation is that more regulation causes more bureaucracy, which may decrease actual or perceived efficacy, as well as private donations (Charity Commission, 2005).

Investigating donations to 'activist organizations' – humanitarian and environmental, peace, and animal organizations – Evers and Gesthuizen (2011) find that the national level of trust is positively related to engagement in philanthropy in a regression analysis including individual level trust as well. This finding is consistent with the explanation that citizens in high trust countries have more confidence in fundraising nonprofit organizations and are therefore more likely to engage in philanthropy. Unfortunately, however, confidence in nonprofit organizations was not measured in this study.

Conclusion

There seem to be strong regional differences in philanthropy. A higher GDP, a northwestern location in Europe and a less Catholic cultural background seem to be characteristics that countries with higher levels of engagement in philanthropy have in common. One should be careful to make such generalizations because different datasets yield very different estimates of the proportion of the population engaging in philanthropy in specific countries. Also, it should be noted that data on amounts donated in different countries are not yet available for comparative research. In an ongoing research project (Wiepking and Handy, 2015), existing datasets are compiled. Given the differences in the research methodology used in different datasets, however, it will be extremely difficult to estimate the magnitude and origins of the differences in philanthropy.

Progress in research on regional differences in philanthropy is hampered by a lack of high quality data. The collection of high quality data on philanthropy that allow for a cross-national comparative study should be placed at the top of the priority list of scholars in this field. When such data become available, researchers should use adequate statistical models to test for the origins of regional differences. Such hierarchical or multi-level models should include both individual, as well as country level predictors. The current practice in many studies suggests regional differences to be due to context effects, but fails to take account of composition effects. Do citizens give less in Catholic countries because a Catholic tradition discourages giving or because Catholics give less, regardless of where they live? Do citizens in higher GDP countries give more because of the more favourable macro-economic situation in their countries or because these citizens have higher incomes and are more likely to have wealth in assets? In addition to GDP and religious tradition, there are likely to be other regional characteristics that are correlated with philanthropy, such as a democratic history, welfare state regimes and openness of the economy. Given the current state of research, it is too early to jump to conclusions about the existence and origins of regional differences.

In the absence of high quality data, I have discussed some of the hypotheses that can be constructed to explain regional differences in philanthropy. When high quality data become available, these hypotheses should be tested using appropriate statistical models.

Notes

A previous version of this paper has been presented at the 41st Arnova Conference, November 15, 2012, in Indianapolis and at the 6th ERNOP conference, July 11, 2013, in Riga. I thank the editors of the volume, John Wilson and Pamala Wiepking for helpful remarks. The current chapter is a revision of part 1 of the conference paper.

References

An, W. (2011). 'Models and Methods to Identify Peer Effects, in J. Scott and P. J. Carrington (eds), *The Sage Handbook of Social Network Analysis* (pp. 514–32). London: Sage Publications.

Bekkers, R. (2003). 'Trust, Accreditation, and Philanthropy in the Netherlands'. *Nonprofit and Voluntary Sector Quarterly*, 32(4): 596–615.

Bekkers, R. (2012). 'Limits of Social Influence on Giving: Who is Affected When and Why?'. Paper presented at 'Social Influences and Charitable Giving' 24th February 2012, Royal Over-Seas League, London.

Bekkers, R., and Wiepking, P. (2006). 'To Give or Not to Give … That is the Question'. *Nonprofit and Voluntary Sector Quarterly*, 35(3): 533–540.

Bekkers, R. and Schuyt, T. N. M. (2008). 'And Who is Your Neighbor? Explaining the Effect of Religion on Charitable Giving and Volunteering'. *Review of Religious Research*, 50(1): 74–96.

Bekkers, R. and Veldhuizen, I. (2008). 'Geographical Differences in Blood Donation and Philanthropy in the Netherlands: What Role for Social Capital?'. *Journal of Economic and Social Geography*, 99(4): 483–96.

Bekkers, R. and Wiepking, P. (2011a). 'A Literature Review of Empirical Studies of Philanthropy: Eight Mechanisms that Drive Charitable Giving'. *Nonprofit and Voluntary Sector Quarterly*, 40(5): 924–73.

Bekkers, R. and Wiepking, P. (2011b). 'Who Gives? A Literature Review of Predictors of Charitable Giving. Part One: Religion, Education, Age, and Socialisation'. *Voluntary Sector Review*, 2(3): 337–65.

Bielefeld, W., Rooney, P., and Steinberg, K. (2005). 'How Do Need, Capacity, Geography, and Politics Influence Giving?', in A. C. Brooks (ed.), *Gifts of money in Americas communities* (pp. 127–58). Lanham, MD: Rowman & Littlefield.

Booth, A., Higgins, D., and Cornelius, R. (1989). 'Community Influences on Funds Raised by Human Service Volunteers'. *Nonprofit and Voluntary Sector Quarterly*, 18(1), 81–92.

Borgonovi, F. (2006). 'Do Public Grants to American Theatres Crowd-out Private Donations?'. *Public Choice*, 126 (3–4): 429–451.

Britto, S., Van Slyke, D. M., and Francis, T. I. (2011). 'The Role of Fear of Crime in Donating and Volunteering: A Gendered Analysis'. *Criminal Justice Review*, 36(4): 414–34.

Brooks, A. C. (1999). 'Do Public Subsidies Leverage Private Philanthropy for the Arts? Empirical Evidence on Symphony Orchestras'. *Nonprofit and Voluntary Sector Quarterly*, 28(1), 32–45.

Brooks, A. C. (2003a). 'Do Government Subsidies to Nonprofits Crowd Out Donations or Donors?'. *Public Finance Review*, 31, 166–79.

Brooks, A. C. (2003b). 'Taxes, Subsidies, and Listeners Like You: Public Policy and Contributions to Public Radio'. *Public Administration Review*, 63, 554–61.

Brooks, A. C. (2006). *Who Really Cares. The Surprising Truth about Compassionate Conservatism*. New York: Basic Books.

Bryant, W. K., Jeon-Slaughter, H., Kang, H., and Tax, A. (2003). 'Participating in Philanthropic Activities: Donating Money and Time'. *Journal of Consumer Policy*, 26(1):43–73.

Bryson, J. R., McGuiness, M., and Ford, R. G. (2002). 'Chasing a Loose and Baggy Monster: Almshouses and the Geography of Charity'. *Area*, 34(1): 48–58.

Buchan, N. R., Grimalda, G., Wilson, R., Brewer, M., Fatas, E., and Foddy, M. (2008). 'Globalization and Human Cooperation'. *PNAS*, 106(11): 4138–42.

CAF (2010). *The World Giving Index 2010*. West Malling: CAF.

CAF (2011). *World Giving Index 2011: A Global View of Giving Trends*. West Malling: CAF.

CAF (2012). *World Giving Index 2012: A Global View of Giving Trends*. West Malling: CAF.

Carman, K. G. (2006). 'Social Influences and the Private Provision of Public Goods: Evidence from Charitable Contributions in the Workplace'. Discussion Paper, Stanford Institute for Economic Policy Research, Stanford University

CERPHI (2010). *Le don d'argent des ménages aux associations et aux foundations: Étude des dons realisés par les Français en 2008, enregistrés dans les declarations de revenus 2009*. Paris: CERPHI.

Charity Commission (2005). 'Report of Findings of a Survey of Public Trust and Confidence in Charities'. Opinion Leader Research.

Darley, J. M., & Latané, B. (1968). 'Bystander Intervention in Emergencies: Diffusion of Responsibility'. *Journal of Personality and Social Psychology*, 8(4): 377–83.

Dehne, A., Friedrich, P., Nam, C. W., and Parsche, R. (2008). 'Taxation of Nonprofit Associations in an International Comparison'. *Nonprofit and Voluntary Sector Quarterly*, 37(4): 709–29.

DellaVigna, S., List, J. A., and Malmender, U. (2012). 'Testing for Altruism and Social Pressure in Charitable Giving'. *Quarterly Journal of Economics*, 127 (1): 1–56.

Einolf, C. J. (2011). 'The Link Between Religion and Helping Others: The Role of Values, Ideas, and Language'. *Sociology of Religion*, 72(4), 435–55.

Esping-Andersen, G. (1990). *The Three Worlds of Welfare Capitalism*. Oxford: Polity Press.

Evers, A. and Gesthuizen, M. (2011). 'The Impact of Generalized and Institutional Trust on Donating to Activist, Leisure, and Interest Organizations: Individual and Contextual Effects'. *International Journal of Nonprofit and Voluntary Sector Marketing*, 16(4): 381–92.

Gesthuizen, M., Van der Meer, T., and Scheepers, P. (2008a). 'Ethnic Diversity and Social Capital in Europe: Tests of Putnams Thesis in European Countries'. *Scandinavian Political Studies*, 32(2): 121–42.

Gesthuizen, M., Van der Meer, T., and Scheepers, P. (2008b). 'Education and Dimensions of Social Capital: Do Educational Effects Differ Due to Educational Expansion and Social Security Expenditure?'. *European Sociological Review*, 24(5): 617–32.

Gittell, R., and Tebaldi, E. (2006). 'Charitable Giving: Factors Influencing Giving in the U.S. States'. *Nonprofit and Voluntary Sector Quarterly*, 35, 721–36.

Hackl, F., Halla, M., and Pruckner, G. J. (2012). 'Volunteering and the State'. *Public Choice*, 151: 465–95.

Henrich, J., Boyd, R., Bowles, S., Camerer, C., Fehr, E., Gintis, H., McElreath, R., Alvard, M., Barr, A., Ensminger, J., Henrich, N. S., Hill, K., Gil-White, F., Gurven, M., Marlowe, F. W., Patton, J. Q., and Tracer, D. (2005). 'Economic Man in Cross-cultural Perspective: Behavioral Experiments in 15 Small-scale Societies'. *Behavioral and Brain Sciences*, 28, 795–815.

Hofstede, G. (2001). *Cultures Consequences: Comparing Values, Behaviors, Institutions, and Organizations Across Nations*. Thousand Oaks: Sage.

Hughes, P. N. and Luksetich, W. A. (1999). 'The Relationship among Funding Sources for Art and History Museums'. *Nonprofit Management and Leadership*, 10: 21–37

Irvin, R. (2005). 'State Regulation of Nonprofit Organizations: Accountability Regardless of Outcome'. *Nonprofit and Voluntary Sector Quarterly*, 34(2): 161–78.

Janssen, S., Kuipers, G., and Verboord, M. (2008). 'Cultural Globalization and Arts Journalism: The International Orientation of Arts and Culture Coverage in Dutch, French, German, and U.S. Newspapers, 1955 to 2005'. *American Sociological Review*, 73: 719–40.

Kemmelmeier, M., Jambor, E. A., and Letner, J. (2006). 'Individualism and Good Works: Cultural Variation in Giving and Volunteering Across the United States'. *Journal of Cross-Cultural Psychology*, 37(3): 327–44.

Khanna, J. and Sandler, T. (2000). 'Partners in Giving: The Crowding-in Effects of UK Government Grants'. *European Economic Review*, 44: 1543–56.

Khanna, J., Posnett, J., and Sandler, T. (1995). 'Charity Donations in the UK: New Evidence Based on Panel Data'. *Journal of Public Economics*, 56: 257–72.

Koster, F. (2007). 'Globalization, Social Structure, and the Willingness to Help Others: A Multilevel Analysis Across 26 Countries'. *European Sociological Review*, 23(4): 537–51.

Kropf, M., and Knack, S. (2003). 'Viewers Like You: Community Norms and Contributions to Public Broadcasting'. *Political Research Quarterly*, 56, 187–97.

Levine, R. V., Martinez, T. S., Brase, G., and Sorenson, K. (1994). 'Helping in 36 U.S. Cities'. *Journal of Personality & Social Psychology*, 67, 69–82.

Levine, R. V., Reysen, S., and Ganz, E. (2008). 'The Kindness of Strangers Revisited: A Comparison of 24 US Cities'. *Social Indicators Research*, 85: 461–81.

Lim, C. (2010). 'Mobilizing on the Margin: How Does Interpersonal Recruitment Affect Citizen Participation in Politics?'. *Social Science Research*, 39: 341–55.

Long, J. E. (2000). 'Omitted-variable Bias When Using State Tax Rates to Estimate the Tax Price Effect on Itemized Deductions', *Public Finance Review*, 28(2): 120–33.

Malka, A., Soto, C. J., Cohen, A. B., and Miller, D. T. (2011). 'Religiosity and Social Welfare: Competing Influences of Cultural Conservatism and Prosocial Value Orientation'. *Journal of Personality*, 79(4): 1–30.

Mohan, J., Barnard, S., Jones, K., and Twigg, L. (2004). 'Social Capital, Place and Health: Creating, Validating and Applying Small-area Indicators in the Modelling of Health Outcomes'. London: NHS Health Development Agency.

Okten, C. and Osili, U. O. (2004). 'Contributions in Heterogeneous Communities: Evidence from Indonesia'. *Journal of Population Economics*, 17(4), 603–626.

Olson, Jr., M. (1965) *The Logic of Collective Action: Public Groups and the Theory of Groups*. Harvard University Press: Cambridge, MA.

Olson, D. V. A. and Caddell, D. (1994). 'Generous Congregations, Generous Givers: Congregational Contexts that Stimulate Individual Giving'. *Review of Religious Research*, 36, 168–180.

Ortmann, A. and Svítková, K. (2006). 'Certification as a Viable Quality Assurance Mechanism: Theory and Suggestive Evidence'. CERGE-EI Working Paper 228. Center for Economic Research and Graduate Education, Academy of Sciences of the Czech Republic Economics Institute.

Paik, A. and Navarre-Jackson, L. (2011). 'Social Networks, Recruitment, and Volunteering: Are Social Capital Effects Conditional on Recruitment?'. *Nonprofit and Voluntary Sector Quarterly*, 40: 476–96.

Pancer, S. M., McMullen, L. M., Kabatoff, R. A., Johnson, K. G., and Pond, C. A. (1979). 'Conflict and Avoidance in the Helping Situation'. *Journal of Personality and Social Psychology*, 37: 1406–11.

Payne, A. A. (1998). 'Does the Government Crowd-out Private Donations? New Evidence from a Sample of Non-profit Firms'. *Journal of Public Economics*, 69:323–45.

Peifer, J. L. (2010). 'The Economics and Sociology of Religious Giving: Instrumental Rationality or Communal Bonding?'. *Social Forces*, 88(4): 1569–94.

Plagnol, A. C. and Huppert, F. A. (2010). 'Happy to Help? Exploring the Factors Associated with Variations in Rates of Volunteering Across Europe'. *Social Indicators Research*, 97: 157–76.

Putnam, R. D. (2000). *Bowling Alone: The Collapse and Revival of American Community*. New York: Simon & Schuster.

Rooney, P. M., Steinberg, K. S., and Schervish, P. G. (2001). 'A Methodological Comparison of Giving Surveys: Indiana as a Test Case'. *Nonprofit and Voluntary Sector Quarterly*, 30(3): 551–68.

Rooney, P. M., Steinberg, K. S., and Schervish, P. G. (2004). 'Methodology Is Destiny: The Effect of Survey Prompts on Reported Levels of Giving and Volunteering'. *Nonprofit and Voluntary Sector Quarterly*, 33(4): 628–54.

Rotolo, T. and Wilson, J. (2012). 'State-Level Differences in Volunteerism in the United States: Research Based on Demographic, Institutional, and Cultural Macrolevel Theories'. *Nonprofit and Voluntary Sector Quarterly*, 41(3): 452–73.

Ruiter, S. and De Graaf, N. D. (2006). 'National Context, Religiosity, and Volunteering: Results from 53 Countries'. *American Sociological Review*, 71(2): 191–210.

Salamon, L. M. (1997). *The International Guide to Nonprofit Law*. John Wiley & Sons.

Salamon, L. M., and Anheier, H. K. (1998). 'Social Origins of Civil Society: Explaining the Nonprofit Sector Cross-Nationally'. *Voluntas*, 9(3): 213–48.

Salamon, L. M. and Sokolowski, W. (2001). 'Volunteering in Cross-National Perspective: Evidence from 24 Countries'. Working Papers of the Johns Hopkins Comparative Nonprofit Sector Project, no. 40. Baltimore: The Johns Hopkins Center for Civil Society Studies. www.ccss.jhu.edu/wp-content/uploads/downloads/2011/09/CNP_WP40_2001.pdf [Accessed 9 October 2015].

Sargeant, A., Shang, J., and Associates (2010). *Fundraising Principles and Practice*. San Francisco: Jossey-Bass.

Scheepers, P., Te Grotenhuis, M., and Gelissen, J. (2002). 'Welfare States and Dimensions of Social Capital: Cross-national Comparisons of Social Contacts in European Countries'. *European Societies*, 4(2): 185–207.

Schneider, J. C. (1996). 'Philanthropic styles in the United States: Toward a theory of regional differences'. *Nonprofit and Voluntary Sector Quarterly*, 25(2), 190–210.

Schwartz, S. H. (1992). 'Universals in the Content and Structure of Values: Theoretical Advances and Empirical Tests in 20 Countries'. *Advances in Experimental Social Psychology*, 25: 1–64.

Simmons, W. O. and Emanuele, R. (2004). 'Does Government Spending Crowd Out Donations of Time and Money?'. *Public Finance Review*, 32, 498–511.

Sivesind, K. H. and Selle, P. (2009). 'Does Public Spending Crowd Out Nonprofit Welfare?', in B. Enjolras and K. H. Sivesind (eds.), *Civil Society in Comparative Perspective* (pp. 105–134). Bingley: Emerald.

Snijders, T. and Bosker, R. (1999). *Multilevel Analysis*. London: Sage.

Sokolowski, S. W. (2013). 'Effects of Government Support of Nonprofit Institutions on Aggregate Private Philanthropy: Evidence from 40 Countries'. *Voluntas*, 24: 359–81.

Stadelmann-Steffen, I. (2011). 'Social Volunteering in Welfare States: Where Crowding Out Should Occur'. *Political Studies*, 59: 135–55.

Van Diepen, M., Donkers, B., and Franses, P. H. (2009a). 'Dynamic and Competitive Effects of Direct Mailings: A Charitable Giving Approach'. *Journal of Marketing Research*, 46: 120–33.

Van Diepen, M., Donkers, B., and Franses, P. H. (2009b). 'Does Irritation Induced by Charitable Direct Mailings Reduce Donations?'. *International Journal of Research in Marketing*, 26: 180–8.

Van Oorschot, W. and Arts, W. (2005). 'The Social Capital of European Welfare States: The Crowding Out Hypothesis Revisited'. *Journal of European Social Policy*, 15(1): 5–26.

Van Oorschot, W., Arts, W., and Gelissen, J. (2006). 'Social Capital in Europe: Measurement and Social and Regional Distribution of a Multifaceted Phenomenon'. *Acta Sociologica*, 49: 149–67.

Veldhuizen, I. and Bekkers, R. (2011). 'Social Capital and Blood Donation in the Netherlands'. Paper presented at the 40th Arnova Conference, Toronto, November 18, 2011.

Wiepking, P., Bekkers, R. H., and Osili, U. O. (2014). 'Examining the Association of Religious Context with Giving to Non-profit Organizations'. *European Sociological Review*, 30(5):640–54.

Wiepking, P. and Handy, F. (eds.). *The Palgrave Handbook of Global Philanthropy*. Hampshire, UK: Palgrave MacMillan.

Wilson, J. and Musick, M. (1997). 'Who Cares? Toward an Integrated Theory of Volunteer Work'. *American Sociological Review*, 62, 694–713.

Wolch, J. and Geiger, R. (1983). 'The Urban Dimension of Voluntary Resources: An Exploratory Analysis'. *Environment and Planning*, A 15, 1067–1082.

Wolpert, J. (1988). 'The Geography of Generosity: Metropolitan Disparities in Donations and Support for Amenities'. *Annals of the Association of American Geographers*, 78(4): 665–79.

Wu, S.-Y., Huang, J.-T., and Kao, A.-P. (2004). 'An Analysis of the Peer Effects in Charitable Giving: The Case of Taiwan'. *Journal of Family and Economic Issues*, 25(4): 483–505.

Wuthnow, R. (1991). *Acts of Compassion: Caring for Others and Helping Ourselves*. Princeton, NJ: Princeton University Press.

8

Philanthropy at the community level

Supporting community empowerment

Michael D. Layton

The word philanthropy usually conjures up images of a wealthy individual dedicating some part, sometimes a very significant part, of a great fortune to a noble cause. More often than not, the philanthropic practices of such individuals seem to draw inspiration from a perspective articulated by Andrew Carnegie more than one hundred years ago, of the millionaire as a trustee of the poor, 'administering it for the community far better than it could or would have done for itself' (Carnegie, 1901: 18). From this perspective, it is precisely the rich and powerful who are in a position to be philanthropic, tackling social problems more ably than communities by using the same skills and talents that allowed them to amass their fortunes to tackle social problems 'far better' than the community itself could. Bishop and Green (2008: 13) go so far as to call today's philanthrocapitalists 'Carnegie's children', and claim that giving them a copy of Carnegie's *Gospel of Wealth* could help them along.

The concept of community philanthropy turns this thinking on its head. It embraces the idea that those embedded in the community, and thereby closest to its problems, are in a unique position to address shared challenges. The assumption is that they can do this 'far better' than external millionaire donors. The European Foundation Centre (EFC, 2004) offers a comprehensive definition of the concept:

> Community philanthropy is the act of individual citizens and local institutions contributing money or goods, along with their time and skills, to promote the well-being of local people and the improvement of the community in which they live and/or work.

The EFC also distinguishes between the 'informal and spontaneous' and the 'formal and organized' ways in which this phenomenon occurs. The former is illustrated by collections during natural disasters, the latter by citizens giving contributions to local organisations. These organisations can then use these resources for initiatives improving the local community's quality of life on a long-term or permanent basis (European Foundation Centre, 2004). It is important to emphasize that the concept includes contributing time and skills, as well as money, and that there is an explicit goal of building and empowering community leadership.

This chapter focuses on the more informal and spontaneous expressions of community philanthropy. It leaves the discussion of the more formal and organized expression of community philanthropy – community foundations – to Chapter 19. The goal of this contribution is to explore the forms of philanthropy at the community level that tend to spring up in the developing world or in more marginalized communities of the developed world, and which often do not find more formal, institutionalized expressions. To borrow a metaphor from Smith (2000: 12), this might be considered part of the 'dark matter' of the philanthropic universe, as a very significant phenomenon that is often overlooked by traditional scholars (Chen, 2010).

At first blush, community philanthropy is a very appealing concept in terms of community self-help: neighbours helping one another are the embodiment of empowerment. It fits nicely with our democratic sensibilities. The key idea is that each person can contribute and that this collective action could offer a firmer, more balanced basis for the funding of social causes. Here is a deeper issue underlying the difference between what one might call Carnegie-style philanthropy and community philanthropy. As Robert Reich has argued, philanthropy has at best an 'uneasy', if not a 'rocky', relationship with equality (Reich, 2006). The philanthropy of the wealthy is precisely a function of the accumulation of great fortunes and hence inequality. In his contemporary review of *Gospel of Wealth*, the Methodist Bishop Hugh Price Hughes characterized the proliferation of millionaires as 'an anti-Christian phenomenon, a social monstrosity, and a grave political peril'. He asserted, 'millionaires at one end of the scale involved paupers at the other end, and even so excellent a man as Mr. Carnegie is too dear at that price' (quoted in Nasaw, 2007: 352).

Could community philanthropy, then, represent a more democratic alternative to the philanthropy of the few? While the practice might assuage our democratic sensibilities, the serious challenge for community philanthropy is whether this practice can address the deep issues of social injustice and marginalization that plague the poorest of communities. If the community is not, say, Medina, Washington where the Gates' mansion is located, how can it mobilize resources to overcome the worst aspects of poverty given that the defining characteristic of an impoverished community is precisely its lack of resources? This is a key point of Jeffrey Sachs' (2005) thinking on the problem of development: the necessity to import capital from wealthy to poor nations. Conversely, if philanthropies outside the community offer their assistance, might this intervention undermine the indigenous processes of mutual support and solidarity?

This chapter first explores diverse practices of community philanthropy. The goal is to capture some of the variety without pretending to offer an exhaustive account of the phenomenon. This exploration teases out some of the key common underlying elements, and leads to a discussion of its main challenge: gauging the impact of community philanthropy. I argue that the main focus of this impact is the empowerment of those who give, rather than a change in the situation of the recipient. Documenting and quantifying the impact of community philanthropy is a key open challenge for practitioners and for researchers.

It is important to note that much of the material published on the issue of community philanthropy is generated through projects supported by funders interested in promoting community philanthropy, especially its more formal expression in community foundations. Studies by Knight (2012), Wilkinson-Maposa and colleagues (2005), Bearman (2007), the European Foundation centre (2004) and the 2006 articles in *Alliance* magazine (Kingman and Edwards; Mirciu; Yamsuan) were either commissioned by funders, or written by practitioners. While this is not to disparage the quality of the research, it is important to note that there are few strictly scholarly studies of the field. This fact creates an important opportunity for future research, especially in terms of the impact of community philanthropy.

Diverse practices of community philanthropy

There are perhaps as many expressions of philanthropy at the community level as there are civilizations and ages in human history. While taking into account the fact that the word 'philanthropy' has developed specific Western connotations and understandings, it is safe to say that the expression of philanthropy is a near universal aspect of human behaviour across cultures and across time, frequently linked to religion (Ilchman *et al.*, 1998; Berry, 1999; Mottiar and Ngcoya, Chapter 9). The goal of this section is not to present an exhaustive review but a sample of the diversity of the practices of community philanthropy, to be followed by a discussion of its most essential aspects.

In the US, formal campaigns to promote community philanthropy were initiated by the US Sanitary Commission, a private relief agency established by Congress in 1861 to assist those wounded in the Civil War (Zunz, 2011: 44-45). At the turn of the twentieth century, there emerged in the US a new expression of the philanthropic impulse – what Zunz (2011: 44) terms 'mass philanthropy' or 'people's philanthropy' – which gave philanthropy 'even more of a central place in modern American life' than the dedication of fortunes to social causes by Carnegie and Rockefeller. Zunz argues that this novel effort combined the invention of mass campaigns with the creation of a new culture of giving, tapping what one reformer termed 'large subterranean pools of benevolence' (quoted in Zunz, 2011: 45). The most successful and novel US campaign at the time was the sale of Christmas seals to support the fight against tuberculosis. In essence, this involved the selling of additional stamps or 'seals' at post offices. Rather than having a postage value, the proceeds from selling these seals went to care and research surrounding tuberculosis. Imported from Copenhagen, where the idea had been pioneered in 1904, a national US programme was set up in 1908 that was initially jointly run by the National Association for the Study and Prevention of Tuberculosis (NASPT) and the American National Red Cross. The success of this effort, as well as a multiplicity of local fundraising efforts, led to the community chest movement. According to Zunz (2011), the leaders of these efforts wanted to circumvent the wealthy, as well as local ethnic groups and instead draw upon a notion of 'metropolitan community'. The most intense effort was to come during relief efforts linked to World War I, and helped to 'reinforce the perception that giving was part of being American' (Zunz, 2011: 56). A key feature of the growth of these two key manifestations of mass philanthropy – the community chest and also the March of Dimes during the administration of Franklin Delano Roosevelt (Helfand *et al.*, 2001) – was the active engagement and support of the federal government and high profile philanthropists and fundraisers. In a sense, this involvement underlined the tension between community philanthropy and its *ethos* of community empowerment on the one hand, and mass philanthropy on the other.

More recently in the US, researchers have detected nostalgia for more direct involvement in giving. Beginning in the early twenty-first century, the creation of 'giving circles' became an important movement which also spread to Canada. Eikenberry (2006) and other academics have identified this as a manifestation of the beginning of a 'new era' in American philanthropy. They argue that,

> this "new philanthropy" is unique in that it is more engaged, guided by individual donors with an emphasis on collaboration; hands-on, unconventional modes of giving and volunteering; and a focus on small organizations and grassroots, entrepreneurial problem solving.
>
> *(Eikenberry, 2006: 517)*

The organizational form that embodies this new philanthropy is the giving circle. A group consisting of anywhere between five and 500 individuals comes together to pool their resources – both time and money – and identify worthy projects in their community (Bearman, 2007: 1). Their activities take place in living rooms, rather than foundation boardrooms, and often entail significant volunteer labour and engagement as well.

According to a recent survey, these entities have appeared in 44 US states, plus the District of Columbia, as well as Canada, with at least 400 giving circles in which 8,000 individuals participate, although firm numbers are hard to come by due to their grassroots nature (Eikenberry, 2006: 520; Bearman, 2007: 6-9). This tendency seems to bring the practice of community philanthropy full circle in the US, with initial expressions of the human philanthropic impulse occurring at the community level, then finding a more institutionalized expression in community foundations, and, with giving circles, seeing this tendency come back to its roots. Participants in giving circles bring a certain sense of ambivalence to the question of evaluation. As Bearman (2007: 18) reports: 'assessing impact is hard without asking for additional reporting from grantee organizations – something most giving circles hesitate to do'. The capacity of giving circles to 'build community' is seen as one of their most important contributions or impacts.

While giving circles are a recent innovation in North America, other nations are also experimenting with distinctive forms of community philanthropy. In the Philippines today, there is a practice similar to the community chest movement in the US but on an even smaller scale. *Pondo ng Pinoy (PnP)*, which can be translated as the Filipinos' fund, uses a strategy called 'gathering crumbs' to promote poverty alleviation. The idea is that people donate 25 centavos, less than a US penny, in numerous collection bottles placed throughout the country. While critics liken such giving, compared to the scale of the problem, as 'shovelling snow with a spoon', the project's founder, now retired Manila Archbishop Gaudencio Rosales, 'sees filling up a bottle with 25 centavos coins not as fundraising but as what he calls "developmental evangelization" – … it is the aim of *Pondo ng Pinoy* to have individuals realize that they can develop themselves and, in the process, help others develop' (Yamsuan, 2006: 33). Since its founding in 2004, the practice of giving the equivalent of a penny a day has rapidly spread from a single village to a national effort. The founder chafed at the idea that the program should be transformed into a 'corporate-style' system of 'promotion, collection, disbursement, and evaluation', and argued that its nature was to be 'a programme for the poor that changes not just the receiver but also the giver so that the cycle of love is never broken' (Yamsuan, 2006: 33). This criterion of success defies easy assessment. One concrete measure is the amount raised. During the annual campaign that ended in June 2012, the effort raised nearly one million USD, a ten percent decline from the previous year's total (Macairan, 2012). This decline was attributed to the retirement of the founder, and might indicate that this is a more hierarchical and leadership-centred effort than an expression of community philanthropy.

In Romania, another expression of community philanthropy takes a distinct approach, emphasizing the role and responsibility of educated elites in community betterment. In the 1970s, boys and girls from rural villages who showed promise received state-sponsored scholarships to attend a university. These *fiii satului* (or village children) went on to have successful careers in urban centres. With the fall of communism and the return of land to its original owners, 'many *fiii satului* groups became more active in village life' (Mirciu, 2006: 47). A study of this phenomenon found that this philanthropy was largely top-down, however, with *fiii satului* supporting local capital improvements or festivals celebrating local customs, and that few projects were 'developmental – let alone transformational – in character' (2006: 47). This weakness in the nature of the projects supported reflects the motivation of the donors, which is related to enhancing their image and status: 'It is more about the need of the giver to be seen than about producing real change in the community' (Mirciu, 2006: 47).

A similar effort can be found in the African Women's Development Fund (AWDF) in that it supports women's organizations in Africa who 'are seeking ways in which to engage the high net worth and middle class African women who have thus far been rendered largely invisible in the global discourse on finance and resourcing for gender equality' (Mukasa, 2011). Their efforts to mobilize resources based on the community of sisterhood include workplace giving, creation of social enterprises, building endowments and donations to feminist organizations and initiatives. But in this case there is an explicit goal of encouraging the empowerment of women via strong organizations:

> Organising that builds strong social movements of women and institutions who are able to define their own agenda and develop appropriate responses that encompass the breadth and depth of women's realities on the continent, and that holds the state and other duty bearers accountable for their commitments to women's rights. *This approach suggests a shift from regarding our constituencies as beneficiaries to working with them as active and autonomous citizens.*
>
> *(Mukasa, 2011, emphasis added)*

This effort identifies the provision of financial support through community philanthropy as part of a strategy of empowering women to participate more fully in the process of development so that empowerment becomes a key criterion of success. The measure of success applies to the involvement of donors in philanthropy and of recipient organizations. In its report on grantmaking for 2012, the AWDF related that it awarded over $2 million to nearly 200 organizations from 32 African countries, across the following categories: Women's Human Rights (34 percent), Economic Empowerment and Livelihoods (21 percent), Governance, Peace and Security (14 percent), Reproductive Health and Rights (six percent), and Arts, Culture and Sports (five percent) (African Women's Development Fund, 2013). The report provides no further analysis or reflection upon the impact of that support, beyond the notion that involving women in philanthropy is in itself empowering.

But the potential of community philanthropy for community empowerment is not always realized. In a field study of philanthropy in China during the 1990s, Shue (1998) describes the phenomenon of establishing local foundations and charity drives to galvanize private support to assist the 'deserving poor' via entities that technically are established as *minjian* (popular) organizations but are primarily staffed by state agencies (Shue, 1998: 340). In an interview, a functionary from the Civil Affairs Bureau in Hangzhou explained that they engaged in this corporate sleight of hand because 'under Chinese conditions, it is necessary for the State to take the lead' (Shue, 1998: 341). Another Civil Affairs official in Qingdao put it more bluntly, 'the intention is to use the force of the State to mobilize the forces in society'. Shue insightfully observes that while fundraising was important, officials placed equal or greater emphasis upon 'using these charity campaigns to raise the tone of social life, to "raise the quality of the people" … a phrase one hears everywhere in China today, to set a good example, and to promote social stability' (Shue, 1998: 342). More recently, Shue (2011) has turned her attention to a new phenomenon in China, the 'charity supermarket'. This is an attempt to adapt a variation of the Good Will Store model of facilitating donations and the sale of low-cost goods for resale to the needy. Rather than relying on local donations of used goods, the stores tend to rely upon government budget allocations and goods from state agencies. Although academic evaluations of these stores have found much to criticize in their operation, Shue (2011: 761) remains optimistic that the stores 'could serve to focus and raise people's sense of solidarity, mutual aid, and humane compassion'. Her goal in recounting this development is to demonstrate 'how tough and elusive actually attaining an authentic "mutual empowerment" of state and society in the Chinese context still remains' (Shue, 2011: 753). With the state exercising such a strong influence, it is difficult to envision how empowerment can occur, but the emphasis upon the moral impact of giving upon the giver is noteworthy.

In both indigenous North American communities and the Indian subcontinent, the expression of a philanthropic impulse is difficult to disentangle from ongoing social relations and the understanding of what it is to live in a community. According to Grim, 'Native American' philanthropy entailed being generous and helping others, ideas woven into the fabric of community life as part of the one's integration of the whole and thus deeply grounded upon the 'inherent cosmological values of particular (indigenous) peoples'. Thus, 'philanthropy is not separated out from the socioeconomic lifeway of the people' but is a seamless aspect of community life (Grim, 1998: 49). Anderson (1998: 75) notes that in India, particularly regarding the Hindu traditional teachings of giving of gifts, such action is often seen as an obligation and is undertaken in pursuit of merit, with the roles and obligations of the giver and receiver heavily defined by context: 'The transactional quality in the Hindu comprehension of the gift demands analysis of motives of self-interest as well as an analysis of community'. In both cases, the act of giving is an integral part of community life, and it is not subject to an evaluation of its impact beyond maintaining community bonds.

Another tradition of community self-help emphasizes a universal contribution of labour – rather than goods or cash donations – for community betterment. In Mexico, *Tequio* or *faena* is

> the unpaid work of indigenous people, which is done for the benefit of the community, as decided upon by the community or by its formal authorities, and the failure to perform such work may result in the imposition of certain social or legal sanctions.
>
> *(Saldaña, 2006: 2, author's translation; Bonfil Batalla, 1996: 31)*

These sanctions might include fines or even incarceration, and such a tradition can be viewed as a form of taxation or involuntary servitude. In fact, the Indigenous and Tribal Peoples Convention, (Convention 169), of the International Labour Organization (ILO), recognizes this problem. Article 8 states, 'These peoples shall have the right to retain their own customs and institutions, where these are not incompatible with fundamental rights defined by the national legal system and with internationally recognised human rights;' while Article 11 states, 'the exaction from members of the peoples concerned of compulsory personal services in any form, whether paid or unpaid, shall be prohibited and punishable by law, except in cases prescribed by law for all citizens' (International Labour Organization, quoted in Saldaña 2006: 6). The inclusion of an explicit regulation of unpaid labour in an official ILO document speaks to the importance and widespread nature of this practice. The question arises here as to whether, due to its mandatory nature, this can be viewed as a philanthropic contribution despite being unpaid labour for community improvement that in turn generates social capital.

Community mobilization is also a central feature of *harambee*, a uniquely Kenyan tradition as the word even appears on the national coat of arms. It is from Swahili, translated literally as working together or pulling together, and has come to mean a collection for a community project – seemingly an ideal form of community philanthropy (Chepkwony and Gemelli, 2009). Its practice has evolved in a rather ironic manner over the course of the twentieth century, from its first meaning of collective efforts to clear land or harvest crops; to its second, a more formal and participative development effort, where government and project beneficiaries would each contribute; until today, when *harambee* is a very public and publicized charitable collection that largely aims to put on display politicians' generosity in an effort to influence votes. In short, it has been bastardized from a bottom-up development practice to a top-down form of electoral corruption (Chepkwony and Gemelli, 2009). Transparency International Kenya undertook a study of the practice and found that politicians, from the President on down, take a prominent role in organizing and donating to *harambees* and that the amounts collected spike upwards during election years (Ndii and Waiguru, 2001). The report calls for greater transparency in terms of both who is donating and use of funds. This unfortunate evolution of *harambee* vitiates its potential for community empowerment.

Perhaps the greatest contribution to systematic thinking about community philanthropy, theoretically sound and empirically grounded, comes from the co-authors of *The Poor Philanthropist*. As part of the Building Community Philanthropy (BCP) Project, this research was conducted in four countries in Southern Africa: Mozambique, Namibia, South Africa and Zimbabwe. As in many parts of the global south, the term 'philanthropy' does not have the same meaning that it does in the north (see the discussion of the concept of *ubuntu* by Mottiar and Ngcoya, Chapter 9). Horizontal philanthropy or 'philanthropy *of* community' (PoC) which is associated with the networks of mutual self-help and solidarity is distinguished from vertical philanthropy or 'philanthropy *for* community' (PfC) which refers to transfers from rich to poor as reflected in development assistance and charity (Wilkinson-Maposa *et al.*, 2005: 4). PoC embodies a moral philosophy of *collective* self, offering a networked and reputation-mediated system of mutual assistance that affords self-respect and mutual survival. This phenomenon is an integral part of life in the communities studied:

> Help between poor people is widespread, deeply embedded, morally grounded and operates as a vital element for both survival and progress. Rather than random or disorganised, horizontal philanthropy is part and parcel of the social fabric. It follows proven, unwritten, acculturated rules with associated sanctions for non-compliance.
>
> *(Wilkinson-Maposa et al., 2005: x)*

Rather than arising from abundance, this form of PoC arises from a sense of interdependence and potential vulnerability to the vicissitudes of life. As one study participant observed, 'someone who doesn't help you is someone with everything' (Wilkinson-Maposa *et al.*, 2005: 74). While in Carnegie's vision, it is precisely those 'with everything' who are in a position to be philanthropic, in this formulation, the same position from which traditional philanthropy arises essentially precludes participation in philanthropy of community.

The idea that philanthropy of community can go beyond sharing the basics of survival to promoting development is then debated by the same authors. Although their fieldwork shows that most helping behaviour is aimed at resolving issues of basic survival, they find a potential for this form of community philanthropy to enhance the recipient's life chances. Wilkinson-Maposa and colleagues (2005: 115, emphasis added) identify this as an opportunity for research: 'a much clearer picture of the extent to which "help" provides for movement in developmental directions, and how this can be achieved, *is a critical area for further exploration*'. Another critical issue open to question is the relationship between PfC and PoC. The tension resides in whether outside efforts at promoting development can effectively complement more indigenous work to the same end, or if outside support crowds out or drowns out more local traditional relationships of mutual self-help. We will return to this issue later in the chapter. A meeting convened by TrustAfrica has raised the biggest issue for this and all forms of philanthropy of community. As the resulting report states:

> Giving amongst people with little "keeps the lid on poverty" just as much as it speaks to a deeply rooted culture of mutual aid and reciprocity. A key theme in the East Africa philanthropy convening was if and how African philanthropy could more effectively grapple with structural and systemic issues of poverty and injustice.
>
> *(TrustAfrica and the WINGS Global Fund for Community Foundations, 2008: 2)*

In other words, can community philanthropy in the poorest contexts do more than just help people get by; rather can it provide the means for community empowerment and for social justice?

From this brief review of activities that have been called community philanthropy, it is obvious that the term is applied to a wide range of phenomena. Returning to the definition offered by the European Foundation Centre (2004), however, each example complies with the chief characteristic, that is, contributing money, goods, time or skills to enhance the well-being of local people and improvement of their community.

Is community philanthropy really 'philanthropy'?

In describing systems of mutual aid and material support among poor communities, are we talking about 'philanthropy,' or something else? In a provocative essay Kingman and Edwards (2006: 44) make the argument that allowing the term 'community philanthropy' to expand too much undermines a distinctive universe of behaviour, such as 'features of mutual aid and solidarity systems … institutions and cultural norms based on shared values, shared commitment to a cause, or simply membership. Are we afraid of this language?' Their response is worth quoting at length:

> We believe that the dominance of neo-liberal economic orthodoxy, and with it the culture of individualism, is now so deeply embedded that the language of mutual aid and solidarity, even of "cooperation" in its institutional sense, has been effectively banished. … A natural response to articulating forms of giving that do not fit the dominant definition of philanthropy is thus to widen the definition. But this temptation should be resisted, as should any attempt to promote "community philanthropy" that might risk weakening solidarity mechanisms.
>
> *(Kingman and Edwards, 2006: 44)*

In short, they fear that this expansion of the definition of philanthropy encroaches on territory that is best characterized as mutual aid and cooperative societies, and that this is much more fertile territory for development efforts. Kingman and Edwards (2006: 43) then go on to define philanthropy 'as giving outside of one's family' and community philanthropy as 'catalysing and raising resources from a community on behalf of a community' and observe that it exhibits 'a significant element of selflessness'. They further argue that one of the key advantages of these systems of mutual aid is that they promote processes of community engagement that can effectively defend and advance the rights of disadvantaged communities – processes that are more self-sustaining and less reliant upon outside resources.

What Kingman and Edwards seem to be talking about is a form of community organizing that aims at generating social capital. Putnam (2000: 116-117) explains that while it is important to distinguish social capital ('doing with') from philanthropy ('doing good for other people'), he also observes that 'social networks provide the channels through which we recruit one another for good deeds, and social networks foster the norms of reciprocity that encourage attention to others' welfare'. His conclusion is that formal and informal giving and volunteering are all strongly predicted by social capital, but that the two should remain distinct concepts

Is philanthropy selfless, as Kingman and Edwards contend? If we return to Andrew Carnegie, his claim was that philanthropy by the wealthy could bring about peace on earth, concluding that philanthropy would solve the problem of the rich and poor in a manner such that, 'the laws of accumulation will be left free; the laws of distribution free. Individualism will continue, but the millionaire will be but a trustee for the poor' (Carnegie, 1901: 18). That seems to be not exactly selfless, coming from one of the world's greatest capitalists. So, perhaps community philanthropy and more traditional philanthropy are not so far apart after all: they both seem to reaffirm existing social relations.

In a study of precolonial Africa, Feierman (1998: 4) offers a rebuke to those who over-estimate the possibilities of reciprocity, 'the world never existed where reciprocity was a constant and reliable safety net'. He then offers a succinct description of the social context in which mutual aid took place:

> Sub-Saharan Africa, in the centuries before colonial conquest, was a region where voluntary giving was, in a majority of cases, grounded in reciprocity, and yet where inequalities existed, where kindly help was as double-edged as it is in the philanthropic West – *a peculiar combination of caring and dominance.*
>
> *(Feierman, 1998: 4; emphasis added)*

In this case, the practice of community philanthropy is more akin to traditional Western philanthropy, but in an uncomplimentary way. The author de-mythologizes and de-romanticizes the practice of mutual aid and reciprocity as an uncomplicated cardinal virtue among the poor and places it in the context of complex and hierarchical social relations, at the same time 'helping the weak and preserving privilege' (Feierman, 1998: 7). At least at first blush this is consistent with what Carnegie had in mind.

Conclusion: The impact of community philanthropy

This chapter began with the claim that community philanthropy had an advantage over more traditional or Carnegie-style philanthropy, that those embedded in the community and closest to its problems are in a unique position to address shared challenges; that they can do 'far better' for themselves than a traditional philanthropist ever could. Yet, the survey of community philanthropy has provided mixed evidence regarding its impact.

In general, the impact of philanthropy is two-fold, affecting both the recipient and the giver. On his definitive work on philanthropy, Frumkin (2006: 18) identifies two key functions of philanthropy, a public function, which has four goals (change, innovation, redistribution, and pluralism), as well as a 'private, consumptive, and expressive function of philanthropy [which] is directed at meeting the psychic and social needs of donors'. He goes on to elaborate the benefits of philanthropy for the philanthropist and how these benefits are an integral element of its rationale:

> Philanthropy exposes donors to new ways of seeing the world and brings givers into contact with people whom they otherwise would never meet. It also allows givers to translate passions and commitments into action and worldly deeds, a process that can be profoundly satisfying. In this sense, it is impossible to talk about the functions or purposes of philanthropy without recognizing that it has an important impact on the giver that must be considered part of the core rationale for philanthropy.
>
> *(Frumkin, 2006: 19)*

In stating that philanthropy 'brings givers into contact with people whom they otherwise would never meet', Frumkin implies that he is not discussing philanthropy of community as it is normally considered and practised. Yet advocates of community philanthropy would endorse the notion that its practice 'allows givers to translate passions and commitments into action and worldly deeds', but largely within their own communities.

While the warm glow experienced by Bill and Melinda Gates by giving away billions of dollars is usually viewed as secondary to the impact of their philanthropy upon the eradication of disease in Africa, the sense of empowerment experienced by giving circles in the US or the bonds of community nurtured by horizontal philanthropy in South Africa are a critical aspect of community philanthropy. What community philanthropy does is reaffirm the connectedness of individuals within the context of a geographic or self-defined form of community. Per the discussion above, in the developing world, these relationships might reinforce traditional, hierarchical relationships, but in developed nations they are often more horizontal in nature and reaffirm democratic values, in contrast to the elite-driven nature of traditional or Carnegie style philanthropy.

In an earlier discussion of this 'supply side' of philanthropy, Schervish and Havens (2001: 225) admonish that the public function of philanthropy cannot be ignored, and that 'one of the key questions for reflection is whether your philanthropy will fulfil the needs of others'. At least one leading researcher in the field of giving circles is not sure that this reflection is paramount. As Eikenberry (2008) observes, the public and the private aspects of at least one form of community philanthropy are in tension. While there is a growing chorus of voices who stress the need for greater philanthropic involvement in light of government cut-backs:

> The trends in the new philanthropy seem to be headed in the opposite direction, or at least there is strong competition for philanthropy to focus on enabling donors to participate in the community in their own way and for their own benefit instead of to allocate funding where it is most needed.
>
> *(Eikenberry, 2008: 150)*

Thus the key question remains open, is the empowerment of donors enough to justify the claim that informal community philanthropy empowers communities and represents an advance in terms of social justice?

Although nearly all the examples of community philanthropy discussed claim that donors are empowered, this claim is largely an assertion made without systematic evidence. In the case of *PnP* in the Philippines, its promoter remains optimistic about how those who give a few cents are empowered, but this assertion is untested. In the case of the *fiii satului* in Romania, their empowerment seems to come about with little or no accounting for true community needs. In the case of China, government officials are attempting to promote community involvement and empowerment, but the transition to community engagement has been elusive and power largely remains in the hands of the bureaucracy.

Whether community philanthropy has an enduring impact upon recipients is largely overlooked. While Bearman's (2007) evaluation of giving circles takes up the issue, its recognition of their reticence to seek additional grantee reporting is already noted above, partly arising from the perception that the limited financial resources that they offer should not come with too many strings. For example, one case study in Durham, North Carolina of the promotion of giving circles among African American males documented donations of about $55,000 to 20 organizations over six years, nearly $10,000 a year or almost $3,000 per organization (Community Investment Network, 2011: 22). The very title of the report, 'The Impacts of Giving Together: Giving Circles as a Civic Engagement Strategy', explains that the main influence this form of community philanthropy is upon donors. The sponsor of the report, the Community Investment Network, is a national network of giving circles that 'inspires, connects and strengthens African Americans and communities of color to leverage their collective resources and create the change THEY wish to see' (Community Investment Network, 2011). Thus community empowerment and social justice are at the core of this philanthropic endeavour.

When the goal of community empowerment is realized with the aim of social justice, the full potential of community philanthropy is made evident. When this occurs another advantage of community philanthropy emerges, which is its sustainability. As the authors of *The Poor Philanthropist II* state:

> The fundamental tenet is that sustainable impact and enduring change does not lie in the provision of resources. Rather, it rests in people's lives being changed by themselves and not by others. … External development agencies may command material resources – including money – as well as vast reservoirs of knowledge and experience. But, in the final analysis, the poor have the power to sustain a development intervention and its impact (or not).
>
> *(Wilkinson-Maposa and Fowler, 2009, p. xi)*

Wilkinson-Maposa and Fowler (2009) contend that the community philanthropy's greatest impact could be achieved by combining, in a mutually reinforcing manner, more traditional and community forms of philanthropy or, in their terms, horizontal and vertical philanthropy. In this ideal scenario, it would seem that participants in community philanthropy can do 'far better' for themselves than a millionaire, or billionaire, ever could. Research has yet to establish the circumstances under which this ideal scenario can be realized.

References

African Women's Development Fund. (2013) *AWDF's Grant Making in 2012*. www.awdf.org/wp-content/uploads/2009/08/Thematic-Areas-Matrix-Updated.pdf [accessed 15 May 2015].

Anderson, L. (1998) 'Contextualizing philanthropy in South Asia: A textual analysis of Sanskrit sources.' In W. F. Ilchman, S. N. Katz and E. L. Queen II (eds.). *Philanthropy in the world's traditions*. Bloomington, IL: Indiana University Press, 57–78.

Bearman, J. E. (2007) *More giving together: The growth and impact of giving circles and shared giving*, Forum of Regional Associations of Grantmakers. www.givingforum.org/sites/default/files/resources/More%20Giving%20Together%20%20The%20Growth%20and%20Impact%20of%20Giving%20Circles%20and%20Shared%20Giving.PDF [accessed 15 May 2015].

Berry, M. L. (1999) 'Native-American philanthropy: Expanding social participation and self-determination.' In *Cultures of caring: Philanthropy in diverse American communities*. Washington, DC: Council on Foundations, 29–106. www.pnwlibrary.wdfiles.com/local--files/tribal-philanthropy/NativeAmerPhil.pdf [accessed 29 March 2012].

Bishop, M. and Green, M. (2008) *Philanthrocapitalism: How the rich can save the world*. New York: Bloomsbury Press.

Bonfil Batalla, G. (1996) *México profundo: Reclaiming a civilization*. Austin, TX: University of Texas Press.

Carnegie, A. (1901) The Gospel of wealth and other timely essays. The Century Co, New York.

Chen, K. K. (2010) Book Review: Angela M. Eikenberry 'Giving circles: Philanthropy, voluntary association, and democracy,' *Nonprofit and Voluntary Sector Quarterly* 39(5): 958–60.

Chepkwony, K. C. and G. Gemelli. (2009) Harambee movement in Kenya: Its roots in civil society and contribution to socio-economic development. *Giving: Thematic Issues on Philanthropy and Social Innovation*, Issue on community philanthropy: An evolutionary framework, (1): 17–26.

Community Investment Network. (2011) *The impacts of giving together: Giving circles as a civic engagement strategy*. www.givingforum.org/sites/default/files/resources/The%20Impact%20of%20Giving%20Together.PDF [accessed 10 May 2015].

Eikenberry, A. M. (2006) 'Giving circles: Growing grassroots philanthropy,' *Nonprofit and Voluntary Sector Quarterly*, 35(3): 517–32.

——. (2008) 'Fundraising in the new philanthropy environment: The benefits and challenges of working with giving circles,' *Nonprofit Management and Leadership*, 19(2): 141–52.

European Foundation Centre – Community Philanthropy Initiative. (2004) *Community Philanthropy Watch: Europe 2004*, European Foundation Centre. www.issuelab.org/resource/community_philanthropy_watch_europe_2004 [accessed 13 February 2012].

Feierman, S. (1998) 'Reciprocity and assistance in precolonial Africa.' In W. F. Ilchman, S. N. Katz and E. L. Queen II (eds.). *Philanthropy in the world's traditions.* Bloomington, IL: Indiana University Press, 3–24.

Frumkin, P. (2006) *Strategic giving: The art and science of philanthropy.* Chicago: University of Chicago Press.

Grim, J. A. (1998) 'A comparative study in Native American philanthropy.' In W. F. Ilchman, S. N. Katz and E. L. Queen II (eds.). *Philanthropy in the world's traditions.* Bloomington, IL: Indiana University Press, 25–53.

Helfand, W. H., Lazarus, J., and Theerman, P. (2001). "" … So That Others May Walk": The March of Dimes.' *American Journal of Public Health,* 91(8), 1190.

Ilchman, W. F., Katz, S. N. and Queen II, E. L. (1998) 'Introduction.' In W. F. Ilchman, S. N. Katz and E. L. Queen II (eds.). *Philanthropy in the world's traditions.* Bloomington, IL: Indiana University Press, ix–xv.

Kingman A. and Edwards J. (2006) 'Who's afraid of mutual aid?.' *Alliance Magazine,* 11(1): 43–5.

Knight, B. (2012) *The value of community philanthropy: The results of a consultation.* Aga Khan Foundation and Charles Stewart Mott Foundation. www.mott.org/files/pubs/thevalueofcommunityphilanthropy. pdf [accessed 19 April 2012].

Macairan, E. (2012) Pondo ng Pinoy collection drops by P5 million, *The Philippine Star,* September 2. www. philstar.com/metro/2012/09/02/844485/pondo-ng-pinoy-collection-drops-p5-million [accessed 8 February 2013].

Mirciu, R. (2006) '*Fiii satului* giving in Romania – Scaling up for local development.' *Alliance Magazine,* 11(1): 47.

Mukasa, S. (2011) The importance of funding our own movements – African women and philanthropy, *African Women's Development Fund* in *News from AWDF.* www.awdf.org/the-importance-of-funding-our-own-movements-african-women-and-philanthropy/ [Accessed 9 October 2015].

Nasaw, D. (2007) *Andrew Carnegie.* New York: Penguin.

Ndii, D. and Waiguru, A. (2001) *Harambee: Pooling together or pulling apart?* Nairobi: Transparency International Kenya.

Putnam, R. D. (2000) *Bowling alone: The collapse and revival of American community.* New York, NY: Simon and Schuster.

Reich, R. (2006) 'Philanthropy and its uneasy relation to equality.' In W. Damon and S. Verducci (eds.). *Taking philanthropy seriously: Beyond noble intentions to responsible giving.* Indiana: Indiana University Press, 33–49.

Sachs, J. (2005) *The end of poverty: Economic possibilities for our time.* New York: Penguin.

Saldaña, R. (2006) *El tequio o faena ¿Practica legal o ilegal?* Centro de Investigación y Estudios Superiores en Antropología Social, V Congreso de la Red Latinoamericana de Antropología Jurídica; Oaxtepec, Morelos, Mexico, 16–20 October 2006. www.ciesas.edu.mx/proyectos/relaju/documentos/Saldana_ Jesus.pdf [accessed 14 February 2012].

Schervish, P. G. and Havens, J. J. (2001) 'The new physics of philanthropy: The supply-side vectors of charitable giving. Part 2: The spiritual side of the supply side.' *CASE International Journal of Educational Advancement,* 2(3): 221–41.

Shue, V. (1998) 'State power and the philanthropic impulse in China Today.' In W. F. Ilchman, S. N. Katz and E. L. Queen II (eds.). *Philanthropy in the world's traditions.* Bloomington, IL: Indiana University Press, 332–54.

——. (2011) 'The political economy of compassion: China's "charity supermarket" saga.' *Journal of Contemporary China;* 20(72): 751–772.

Smith, D. D. (2000) *Grassroots associations.* Thousand Oaks, California: Sage Publications.

TrustAfrica and the WINGS Global Fund for Community Foundations. (2008) *Discussion paper: Philanthropy of Africa.* TrustAfrica. www.trustafrica.org/en/publications-trust/workshops-and-convenings?download =295:discussion-paper-philanthropy-of-africa&start=40 [accessed 9 October 2015].

Wilkinson-Maposa, S. and Fowler, A. (2009) *The poor philanthropist II: New approaches to sustainable development.* Southern Africa–United States Centre for Leadership and Public Values at the Graduate School of Business, University of Cape Town. http://clpv.sanford.duke.edu/documents/Poor_ Philanthropist%20II_webres.pdf [accessed 3 March 2013].

Wilkinson-Maposa, S. Fowler, A., Oliver-Evans C. and Mulenga, C. F. N. (2005) *The poor philanthropist: How and why the poor help each other.* The Southern Africa-United States Centre for Leadership and Public Values at the Graduate School of Business, University of Cape Town. http://clpv.sanford.duke.edu/ documents/Poor_philanthropist_screen.pdf [Accessed 4 March 4 2013].

Yamsuan, P. (2006) 'Pondo ng Pinoy – A new way of life.' *Alliance Magazine,* 11(1): 33.

Zunz, O. (2011) *Philanthropy in America: A history.* Princeton. New Jersey: Princeton University Press.

9

Indigenous philanthropy

Challenging Western preconceptions

Shauna Mottiar and Mvuselelo Ngcoya

'*African philanthropy is actually at the centre of the universal meaning or even practice of world traditions of philanthropy*'

Moyo, 2011:2

Indigenous philanthropic practices in South Africa challenge a number of the, often normative, assumptions implicit in popular philanthropy literatures: that philanthropy flows from the better resourced to the lesser resourced and that philanthropy is invariably motivated by generosity or altruism (Habib *et al.*, 2008). Widespread, and rooted within the philosophy of *ubuntu*, indigenous South African philanthropy envisages an actualization of one's humanity through the act of giving in which the giver and recipient are mutual bearers of humanity. The *ubuntu* worldview stresses the importance of community, solidarity, caring, and sharing; it suggests a profound dynamic process of interdependence and emphasizes that true human potential can only be realized in partnership with others. In this way, interactions are judged by how well they promote the mutual reinforcement of both 'the self' and 'the other' in a community. The resulting forms of philanthropy are thereby more horizontal than vertical in nature. Based on reciprocity and cooperation, they cast givers as equal in standing to recipients. Furthermore, the departure point for these indigenous philanthropic practices is abundance, as opposed to scarcity, and the underlying motivations are complex. As studies of African philanthropy more generally indicate, philanthropy, or what, for ease of translation, is often termed 'giving' or 'indigenous philanthropy' is 'deeply embedded, morally grounded and operates as a vital element for both survival and progress' (Wilkinson-Maposa *et al.*, 2004: x). Some of these African conceptions of philanthropy therefore assume different forms to the dominant professional perspective of philanthropy.

Our main charge against mainstream philanthropy perspectives is that it precludes indigenous and pre-existing understandings of philanthropy. The main purpose of this chapter is to refute the hyperbolic assertion that philanthropy is a predominantly Western idea. To this end, we outline and reflect on alternative conceptualizations of philanthropy and discuss their relevance for developing a more holistic understanding of philanthropy. To begin, we trace the contours and characteristics of philanthropy among indigenous African communities, particularly in KwaZulu-Natal, South Africa. Thereafter, we examine motivations of these philanthropic activities and discuss the *ubuntu* philosophy, the cornerstone of indigenous understandings of philanthropy among the people we interviewed in KwaZulu-Natal. To conclude, we consider some of the implications of our argument for philanthropic studies in general.

Indigenous forms of philanthropy in South Africa

Disentangling the 'indigenous archive' of philanthropy is a very complicated task in that indigenous philanthropic practices are often symbiotically related to ideas that have become more dominant. In fact, philanthropic activities inspired by indigenous perspectives, such as *ubuntu*, share certain traits with conventional understandings of philanthropy. They are voluntary activities, usually initiated by social agents, communities, individuals, and groupings outside of what we would consider the state and, in addition to individual benefit, they have a social or widespread concern at their core.

Therefore, we are not arguing, nor can we demonstrate, that all indigenous philanthropic practices are inherently positive or that dominant Western forms of philanthropy are irredeemably negative. Our argument is less ambitious but still provocative as it brings to the fore what should be a truism: there are multiple domains and types of philanthropy with differing logics and ethical considerations. The universal processes of institutional philanthropy have been emphasized at the expense of other philanthropic logics. Moreover, philanthropy was never written on a blank slate in the African context; indigenous conceptions of philanthropy are not simply knee-jerk derivatives of their more professional cousin.

This is demonstrated by a survey of giving trends in South Africa. It reflects that giving in South Africa is an act as common in poor and marginalized communities as it is in better endowed communities across the urban and rural divide (Seleoane, 2008: 121). Furthermore, patterns of giving move beyond individual to collective giving and may follow a conscious decision or may occur spontaneously and organically. Examples of such forms of philanthropy include women within a community purchasing vegetables or washing materials and sharing them with their neighbours (Seleoane, 2008). These items are a necessity for household cooking and cleaning, but when women cannot afford them all, they purchase what they can afford and share. Similarly, a young person within a community will purchase a newspaper and share it with other youngsters for the purposes of job hunting. There is no specific roster for the purchase of this paper, whoever has money will buy the paper and everyone will, in commune, peruse job adverts. Other examples include the way people in a community will assist newcomers to build a homestead or a shack. Likewise, newcomers or neighbours will be given access to water and electricity without the expectation of payment. In the case of bereavement, philanthropy would take the form of an entire community rallying around the affected family to make donations towards the burial and helping with funeral preparations. These forms of philanthropy have been described as 'part and parcel of the social fabric' of many African communities (Wilkinson-Maposa *et al.*, 2004: x).

Notwithstanding the definitional debates surrounding the meaning of 'philanthropy' highlighted by the editors in the introductory chapter, it seems that these indigenous forms of philanthropy approximate the original Greek perspective of philanthropy as 'love for humankind' far more than dominant institutional forms of philanthropy. Indeed, in the classic parable frequently used as a call to philanthropy, the Good Samaritan, a member of an excluded ethnic minority helps a traveler who has been brutalized by thieves. It is intriguing, that this most quintessential of philanthropic acts might not pass muster in some of the current standards of philanthropy. It does not fit the bill of institutional philanthropy on at least three fronts: it is horizontal in that this is the case of philanthropy between social equals, wretched as they seemingly were; there is no formal philanthropic organization involved, no reports and evaluations written; and the exchange is not immediately material. These telling characteristics distinguish indigenous conceptions of philanthropy from its professional counterpart.

First of all, within the context of African indigenous philanthropy, the idea of the well-endowed almoner distributing charity to impecunious actors is put under severe assault. Symmetry obtains. While the actors in giving and receiving are often friends and neighbours, they also include local associations and formal civil society associations. Help or giving amongst members of a community is particularly strong in rural settings (Ngcoya and Mottiar, 2011), where it is common for one household to provide another with food, candles or clothing. It is also common practice to assist neighbours to build or refurbish their homesteads and maintain their crops. Help or giving in urban settings (Ngcoya and Mottiar, 2011) often takes the form of survivalist community based organizations or *stokvels* (saving clubs). Survivalist organizations usually provide critical services related to health, for example, or comprise charitable feeding schemes of a more vertical nature. *Stokvels* are essentially credit unions, where a group of people enter into an agreement to contribute a fixed amount of money at regular periods. The pooled money may then be drawn by participating members, either in rotation or at a time of need (Lukhele, 1990 cited by Ngcoya, 2009: 27). Examples of *stokvels* include cooking cooperatives where a group of people would pool resources to buy groceries, cook meals and share in order that there is enough food to feed their families. The practicality of a cooking cooperative is that even if a family has no income for the month, it would still be provided with food during the period by virtue of it being a member of the *stokvel*. *Stokvels* for sewing cooperatives and burial arrangements are also common. The practice of horizontal philanthropy, therefore, casts givers and recipients as equal in the philanthropic act. The implications of this are that recipients are not debased or humiliated by giving or helping nor is there a reinforcement of hierarchy established between the giver and the recipient.

Second, horizontal philanthropy is embodied in both material and nonmaterial forms, it covers the entire spectrum of philanthropy as the use of 'treasure, time and talent'. 'Giving' can include exchanges of money, food, clothing, candles and other household items, while 'helping' would include the expending of one's time, labour or skills. Nonmaterial forms of philanthropy are particularly important. An emphasis on money or financial giving devalues the human inspiration underlying African indigenous philanthropy and nonmaterial forms help to fulfil the underlying philosophy of giving: 'if you have, you must give no matter how little' (Wilkinson-Maposa *et al.*, 2004: xi). Nonmaterial giving ensures that both givers and recipients remain active philanthropists; it is also of central importance within development discourses as people coming together to build homes, grow food etc., ensure community collaborations survive and move beyond poverty.

Third, indigenous conceptions of philanthropy in South Africa are based on principles of reciprocity and cooperation grounded in unwritten, but widely understood, behaviours of giving. When there are material exchanges, the giver does not necessarily expect the goods to be paid for or returned. The expectation is one of reciprocal behaviour in the future, where the giver becomes the recipient. In cases where money is given, reciprocity would include the 'giving back' in alternative ways, such as sharing livestock or milk and eggs from owned livestock. Philanthropy is perceived as 'sharing' and results in an intricate system of maintaining the well-being of communities.

As recent South African research studies highlight, however, such notions of horizontal philanthropy are changing (Ngcoya and Mottiar, 2011). In rural settings, this has been linked to changes in the way dwellers sustain livelihoods – less by growing their own food and more from having to trade informally. Food is, therefore, in shorter supply and attained at higher (financial) cost. The extension of the state grant to pensioners, many of whom head households, and for child support also transforms giving patterns: everyone is now being understood to be provided for, eradicating the need for systems of sharing and giving. In other words, responsibility for community members is seen to have shifted from the community to the state which, before the advent of democracy in South Africa, catered only for a white minority. In urban settings, lack of social cohesion contributes to the decline of intricate sharing and giving systems. This lack of cohesion is related, for example, to tension between formal township residents and informal, shack dwelling, township residents. The tension is often based on competition over access to housing and water, as well as electricity services. Indigenous practices of philanthropy are eroded when people 'expect rather than give' (Ngcoya and Mottiar, 2011: 8). They are also affected when bonds between community members become strained.

Finally, unlike their professional counterparts, indigenous practices of philanthropy are not always structured according to formal and/or organizational lines. The traditional prominence of such boundaries in mainstream philanthropy thinking is illustrated by the approach taken by the editor and contributors to *Giving: Western Ideas of Philanthropy* (Schneewind, 1996). In the introductory chapter, the professional aspects of philanthropy are emphasized, focusing on the activities of formal institutions, where clear demarcations between givers and recipients can be established; philanthropy, then, is seen as a niche that can offer training in fundraising and grantmaking (Payton, 1996: xii). Similarly, notwithstanding his favourable view of indigenous philanthropy, the bias towards institutionalization is evident in Axelrad's (2011) study of philanthropy in the developing world. Because most indigenous philanthropy flows through individual and community capillaries of trust and compassion, he argues there is no evidence 'that such informal practices will be institutionalized in the long term' (Axelrad, 2011:151). As a result, his study is preoccupied with philanthropic initiatives of the new elites in the developing world. He argues that the burgeoning trend of elite driven indigenous philanthropy has expanded the 'diversity of actors involved in the delivery of public services, funding activities from public health projects to social justice campaigns' (Axelrad, 2011:145-6). We think they need not necessarily be formalized in order to count as philanthropy. The problem with standard features of organized philanthropy is that they unwittingly contribute to the view of Africans as passive objects of charity. As we further illustrate in the following section, many South Africans are involved in philanthropic acts and activities to transform their lives outside the purview of institutional philanthropy.

Motivations for indigenous philanthropy in South Africa

Studies of horizontal philanthropy in Southern Africa and South Africa reveal that the underlying motivation for giving and helping is need (Wilkinson-Maposa *et al.*, 2004; Murenha and Chili, 2011). A more complex understanding of need prevails, however, in that givers are often in the same position of need as their recipients, but it is through the philanthropic act or system that this need is held off. Philanthropy is practiced by those who themselves know what it is to lack, and perhaps still lack, and for this reason they give – empathy rather than sympathy is therefore invoked. Philanthropic practice is further motivated by an element of survival, especially where there is a lack of local service delivery and socially progressive economic policy (Habib, 2005). Interestingly enough, many givers and recipients, such as *stokvel* participants do not harbour expectations of state help; they consider themselves to be independent, self-sufficient and empowered. Underlying need and survival, motivations for the practice of horizontal philanthropy include 'love', 'friendship', 'good neighbourliness' or a 'sense of community'. These infer altruism, but are still grounded in indigenous social norms.

Such social norms are well reflected in the Zulu traditions of *ukwenana, ukusisa* and *ilimo*. *Ukwenana* is a cultural form of exchange which does not adhere to accumulation of interest. The recipient will accept intending to return that which was accepted, or reciprocate in kind; the giver will engage in the action knowing that there may not, in fact, be reciprocation. In *ukusisa*, givers who have more or are 'wealthy' will give part of their wealth, such as cattle, to those who have less or are 'poor'. Following the same example, the cattle will eventually be returned, but the offspring of the cattle will become the property of the recipient. *Ukusisa*, or any exchange for that matter, succeeds in repelling total want and a war of all against all because it creates bonds between people. The exchange of the 'thing' is significant because the 'thing' embodies persons. The exchange of goods and services is inseparable from the persons exchanging them. This process of building the wealth of individual families or community members means that the causes of lacking are addressed as opposed to their symptoms. This is in keeping with basic distinctions that have been made between charity and philanthropy (Shaw, 2002; Faber and McCarthy, 2005; Anheier and Leat, 2006). In *ilimo*, the recipients will initiate the giving action by providing food and drink, and inviting givers to help plough or harvest their lands with the, albeit unstated understanding that the action will be reciprocated. This form of sharing labour skills and capacity has an element of sustainability in that, although noncontracted, labour will be available across the parts of the community network. This practice also ensures that although givers play an important role, recipients remain at the centre of the philanthropic action. These are important considerations given that normative critiques of (vertical) philanthropy have centred on challenges of both sustainability and legitimacy of philanthropic endeavours (Frumkin, 2006).

Taken together then, although generosity and altruism have significant bearings, the motivations underlying horizontal philanthropy are more complex than that; they are closely linked to entrenched social practices and moral obligation emanating from a shared identity based on the concept of a common humanity: 'my humanity is tainted if your humanity is not recognized and assisted when in need' (Wilkinson-Maposa *et al.*, 2004: xi). This idea of a common humanity is entrenched in the African philosophy of *ubuntu*.

Ubuntu

The worldview of *ubuntu*

Since the end of apartheid, *ubuntu* has become one of most important keywords in South Africa (Ngcoya, 2009). While difficult to translate into English, it is generally understood to mean: I am because we are (*umuntu umuntu ngabantu*) or, a person is a person through others. This worldview is predicated on a profound sense of interdependence. It emphasizes that our true human potential can only be realized in partnership with others. The philosophy of *ubuntu* shares traits with other indigenous philosophies underpinning philanthropic action. One such example is the Indian *swadhyaya*, a process of self-study and self-development which argues that 'one is impoverished without the other' (Giri, 2011: 20). *Ubuntu* rejects the idea of a rugged sovereign individual as insanity. Accordingly, it advocates respect, autonomy, relatedness, reciprocity and hospitality, and connectedness as the ethical pillars of a just and sustainable society. As the philosopher Mogobe Ramose (2001:1) argues, the morphological structure of the word *ubuntu* consists of the prefix *ubu*, indicating a general state of being, and the stem *ntu*, meaning person, or the nodal point at which being assumes concrete form, such that *ubu* and *ntu* are mutually founding; they are two aspects of being, an indivisible wholeness. Magobo More (2004:149) puts it well when he says in the *ubuntu* perspective,

> Moral practices are founded exclusively on consideration and enhancement of human well-being; a preoccupation with "human". It enjoins that what is morally good is what brings dignity, respect, contentment, and prosperity to others, self and the community at large.

The individual is an abbreviation of a community, and a community the amplification and self-actualization of the individual. In other words, while individual autonomy is encouraged, it is simply the other side of relatedness; to wit, the sinews of autonomy are located in a community (Ngcoya and Mottiar, 2011).

The philosophy of *ubuntu* is ever present in many communities throughout Africa. Although *ubuntu* is a Nguni word – Nguni languages being those spoken throughout southern Africa and include Ndebele, Swati, Xhosa and Zulu – it is a pan-African concept, expressed in numerous African languages with multiple phonological variations: it is *umundu* in Kikuyi (Kenya), *bumuntu* in KiSukuma and KiHaya (Tanzania), *vumuntu* in shiTsonga and shiTswa (Mozambique), and *gimuntu* in the kiKongo and giKwese languages of the Democratic Republic of Congo (Ngcoya, 2009: 4). This variance is also reflected in the proverbs, idioms, and aphorisms of numerous African languages (Ngcoya, 2009: 6):

- Sesotho (Lesotho and South Africa): *A botho ba gago bo nne botho seshabeng* – let your welfare be the welfare of the nation (Mokgoro, 1997);
- IsiZulu (South Africa): *Umuntu umuntu ngabantu* – a person is a person through (or by means of other people);
- Xitsonga (Mozambique and South Africa): *Rintiho rinwe a rinusi hove* – one finger cannot pick up a grain;
- Setswana (Botswana and South Africa): *Moeng goroga re je ka wena* – come guest, we feast through you; and
- Chichewa (Malawi): *Mwana wa nzako ndi wako yemwe* – someone's child is your child, and *Ali awiri ndi anthu ali ekha chinyama* – those that are more than one are people and s/he who is alone is an animal (Tambulasi and Kayuni, 2005: 149).

Although *ubuntu* has found wide, and varied, use in post-apartheid South Africa, it is an ancient philosophy and tradition. Notwithstanding the apartheid system's attempt to denigrate things indigenous, *ubuntu* remained entrenched during successive apartheid governments, albeit at the family and community level. Indeed, the people we interviewed took it for granted that *ubuntu* is a quintessential part of Zulu philosophy and practice. Moreover, *ubuntu* featured in the writing and thinking of influential activists during the struggle against apartheid. As Ngcoya (2009: 116-117) points out, Bantu Biko's writing on the philosophy of Black Consciousness is replete with references to *ubuntu*. For example, during his 1976 trial, he offered what he called African communalism as an alternative to capitalism because 'we are African socialists or we believe in sharing .... [M]y relationship with my property is not so highly individualistic that it seeks to destroy others. I use it to build others' (Biko 1979: 64). This political view is consonant with philanthropic characteristics of *ubuntu*.

Ubuntu's relevance for understanding philanthropy

Two of *ubuntu*'s defining and related attributes are relevant for a more encompassing perspective of philanthropy: an acceptance of the human being, and the anchoring in plenitude rather than scarcity.

First, from an *ubuntu* perspective, philanthropy is more than a mere exchange of goods or services. It suggests the recreation of humanity or 'the whole-hearted identification of the self with the other' (Shutte, 2001: 52). Put differently, there are no distant strangers. There are no 'free gifts' and no aliens as Alain Testart (1998) would have us convinced. For him, when a passerby offers money to a beggar in a city, that is an exchange between distant strangers. Such an exchange creates no expectation of any kind of reciprocation by either party and the transaction suggests no interdependence between the two. An *ubuntu* view of this transaction does not see the two parties as aliens. The very act of giving or receiving is, a priori, reciprocal in that humanity is being constructed; it is a process of mutual recognition. Thus, giving and receiving are more than material exchanges of goods or services. Philanthropy is not merely a patrician or matrician concern for the good of the poor. The giver actualizes his or her humanity by the act of giving. Both giver and recipient are mutual bearers of humanity. As the Zulu people put it: *ukupha ukuzibekela*: giving is investing in oneself. The conventional vertical lines of philanthropy are therefore breached. It seems Ralph Waldo Emerson had something similar in mind when he declared,

> The only gift is a portion of thyself. Thou must bleed for me. Therefore the poet brings his poem; the shepherd, his lamb; the farmer, corn; the miner, a gem; the sailor, coral and shells; the painter, his picture; the girl, a handkerchief of her own sewing.
>
> *(Emerson and Eliot, 1909: 230)*

In other words, giving is neither the privilege nor the burden of the rich, all people can give.

Second, while conventional understandings of philanthropy are based on a theory of scarcity, *ubuntu* views of the same are grounded in plenitude. In light of assumptions that human interactions are driven by calculating, self-interested, individuals, philanthropy is seen as the exceptional opposite. In this conventional ideological framework, philanthropy is distinguished from obligatory exchanges and pure gifts that have no hallmarks of self-interest. Notwithstanding the many accents of capitalism, to neoclassical economic thinkers, the attraction of capitalist modes of production and exchange is that capitalism generates maximum returns from presupposed preliminary conditions of scarcity. Abundance, of supply or demand, is a fundamental problem. This is central to Lionel Robbins' (1945: 16) oft-quoted definition of economics as the scientific study of 'human behaviour as a relationship between ends and scarce means which have alternative uses'. Even the most affluent capitalist economies operate on the principle of severe scarcity. It is the fundamental determinant of value and the fuel for modern capitalism (Kincaid, 1983: 407). Conventional views of giving mirror, and are informed by, this view. Philanthropy is seen as a necessity in light of the scarcity of resources; scarcity is an inescapable constraint and ineluctable fact of political and socioeconomic life.

From an *ubuntu* perspective, however, this notion of scarcity is at best contrived or artificial. There is nothing inherently natural about the scarcity of time or resources; it is our creation – the bankruptcy of our morality and our understanding of our relationships with ourselves, others, and the environment. Furthermore, rectifying the problem of scarcity is not a matter of scientific-technological mastery of the environment as dominant economic theories will have us believe. There is always enough for everyone to share and everyone has a share of everything. As the Zulu proverbs go: *izingane zandawonye zihlephulelana inhloko yentethe* – children who belong together will share even a grasshopper's head, and *akudlulwa ngendlu yakhiwa*– one does not simply walk by when a house is being built. In the *ubuntu* perspective, giving then does not create society through an immediate give-and-take approach. These transactions are long term investments; rewards may be immediate or deferred; personal and impersonal; and interested and disinterested.

The indigenous challenge to philanthropy

What are the implications of our argument? In other words, does *ubuntu* have application more broadly? On one hand, the answer has to be an unequivocal no. *Ubuntu*, like all knowledges, is anchored in institutional, cultural, and social moorings and, therefore, relevant to particular people and specific settings and times. Yet, at the same time, the answer is in the affirmative. Instead of drawing clear lines around the domains of philanthropy, this approach highlights the importance of multiple domains and different logics in philanthropy. We are not asserting that *ubuntu*-inspired philanthropy is superior to other forms of philanthropy, especially Western understandings thereof. In the particular context of South Africa, the *ubuntu* form of philanthropy thrives alongside other more globally familiar types of philanthropy. By highlighting its continued relevance, we are contributing to the efforts of thinkers on philanthropy which show that there are many more shapes and forms of philanthropy than the dominant view has led us to believe.

Studies of Latin American philanthropic practices reveal diverse mechanisms for mutual aid and collective assistance practised among those who sought to survive economic poverty and preserve their cultural traditions in the face of political or ethnic persecution (Sanborn, 2005: 7). For example, the *ayllu* (or *wachu* in Peru) has been revitalized by indigenous societies in Bolivia and Ecuador. *Ayllu* is an ancient concept of community based on territorial federation, characterized by rotating leadership, extensive consultation, with the goals of communal consensus and an equitable distribution of resources (Korovkin, 2001: 38). Béjar (1997: 379) shows that there are thousands of what he calls peasant and native communities in Peru, involved in 'communal work, and in use and free disposition of land, as well as in economic and administrative operation'. These autonomous organizations have substituted or complemented the state's role in the building and maintenance of mainly communication, irrigation channels and schools.

In contemporary Japanese Buddhist thought, mercy (*maitracittata*) is the basic concept of charity and it has two roots: *maitrya* (true brotherly love or pure parental love) and *kurana* (affection or kindness) (Hayashi, 1991: 119 cited by Lohmann, 1995: 148). Similarly, in rural Indonesia practices of *gotong royong*, forms of mutual aid are an integral part of living, where it is believed that man does not exist alone but only as part of the community, social environment and natural, spiritual universe. This practice is underpinned by socially accepted norms of maintaining good relations among humans based on the principle of equality (Quebral and Terol, 2002). These types of knowledge and practices have often been ignored or subjugated. Without recognition by academics, government, professional philanthropy, society, and others, they will remain so. This point was highlighted at an assembly of the African Grantmakers Network in 2010, where it was argued that the impact of grantmaking and philanthropic practice in Africa is reduced by its failure to take into account traditional forms of giving. Synthesising best philanthropic practices in Africa was promoted as a potentially powerful force to address poverty (Malombe, 2010: 6).

It should be emphasized, however, that indigenous philanthropy is not always informal and horizontal. There are various contemporary examples of indigenous philanthropic initiatives that have developed formalized structures. For example, the International Funders for Indigenous Peoples (IFIP) is the only affinity group in the US solely dedicated to international philanthropy (IFIP, 2015). Through education, conferences and publications, IFIP seeks to bridge the cultural gulfs between grantmakers and indigenous communities. That way, the organization encourages innovative investment strategies in indigenous and philanthropic worlds. The Circle on Philanthropy and Aboriginal Peoples in Canada (CPAPC) does the same in Canada. A network of foundations, nongovernmental organisations and individuals, it is committed to promoting philanthropy (giving, sharing and social investing) to empower indigenous peoples of Canada to build stronger, healthier communities (CPAPC, 2009: 5). It notes that while every indigenous culture has an embedded rich history of giving and sharing, there is a vast chasm between modern philanthropy and indigenous peoples. However, while the organization recognizes that indigenous communities are not 'charity cases', nor philanthropy a strange concept in indigenous cultures, it focuses on formal institutions and philanthropic structures that promote interventions among indigenous societies (CPAPC, 2009: 40). A good example is the work of the National Aboriginal Achievement Foundation (NAAF), a philanthropic organization run by indigenous peoples themselves 'dedicated to raising funds to deliver programs that provide the tools necessary for Aboriginal peoples, especially youth, to achieve their potential' (CPAPC, 2009: 40).

We cite these examples to highlight the varied experiments in indigenous philanthropy and to emphasize the global breadth of the revival of indigenous philanthropic initiatives. Furthermore, it is important to stress that we are not of the view that indigenous perspectives of philanthropy are beyond critique; quite the opposite. They should be interrogated and expanded upon. Indeed, as we have pointed out elsewhere, the idea of giving or sharing for the 'good of the community' is too easily exploited (see Ngcoya and Mottiar, 2011).

The consequences of neoliberal economic policies, for example, especially privatization, is that while profit is individualized, risk is collectivized and indigenous philanthropic perspectives are most useful in this regard. In the South African context, *ubuntu* has been marshaled by government to promote home-based care for HIV/AIDS patients. Lund (2010: 505) argues that this community care has led to task shifting whereby tasks that were previously reserved for skilful and thus expensive workers, such as qualified nurses, are delegated to community workers with lower skills to take the burden of care. In the context of limited resources and a burdened health services system, the state saves money by delegating its functions to communities, thus abrogating its social responsibilities.

Conclusion

These political and ethical dilemmas notwithstanding, the broadening of philanthropy's conceptualization is a matter of urgency. There are numerous reasons why indigenous philanthropy deserves attention. First, as Axelrad (2011: 151) points out, such contributions 'sustain essential social work and strengthen civil society in the developing world'. Second, this is not just a concern with philanthropy in the developing world. Examining indigenous philanthropic activities might further contribute to identifying alternative philanthropic activities within the West. For example, in a survey of African American philanthropy from slavery to the present, the historian Adrienne Lash Jones (2004) provides a strong account of mutual support and demonstrates how this tradition has been inferiorized as 'self-help', and not philanthropy which is deemed superior. The race and class connotations of such distinctions are all too apparent when understandings of philanthropy contribute to the elision of the contribution of blacks in philanthropic studies. So, by retrieving the plurivocal expressions of philanthropy, we might be able to rescue 'other' conceptions of philanthropy within the modern world. In short, this is no exercise in relativism or provincialism but an attempt to emphasize that indigenous philanthropic approaches have received scant attention in philanthropic studies. This has come at a great cost for non-Western peoples and limited our understanding of philanthropy in the West itself.

We have demonstrated the benefit of interrogating *ubuntu* inspired forms of philanthropy in South Africa. Our investigation challenges various normative assumptions implicit in philanthropy literature, key among which is that philanthropic acts flow from the top (well resourced) to the bottom (poor). Thus horizontal philanthropy among indigenous communities tends to be more circular than unidirectional. The flattening of the structures of giving in indigenous philanthropy has other implications. Instead of simple altruism and generosity, we found many actors were influenced by a desire for the actualization of one's own humanity. Here, the act of giving was seen as a coproduction of selves in which the giver and recipient are mutual bearers of humanity. The complexity of indigenous philanthropy disrupts the familiar conceptions of philanthropy in the literature. If we are to cultivate a more global understanding of philanthropy, we have to explore those paths and take unfamiliar routes through unfamiliar terrain.

Notes

We are grateful to Kabo Botlhole for assistance with some of the translations.

References

Anheier, H. K. and Leat, D. (2006) *Creative philanthropy: Toward a new philanthropy for the twenty first century*. Los Angeles: University of California.

Axelrad, E. (2011) '(Re)Vitalizing Philanthropy: The Emergence of Indigenous Philanthropy and its Implications for Civil Society throughout the Developing World', *Ethics and Economics*, 8(1): 143–53.

Béjar, H. (1997) 'Non-governmental organisations and philanthropy: The Peruvian case', *Voluntas: International Journal of Voluntary and Nonprofit Organizations*, 8(4): 371–85.

Biko, S. B. (1979) *Black Consciousness in South Africa*. Edited by Millard Arnold. Toronto: Random House.

Circle on Philanthropy and Aboriginal Peoples in Canada (CPAPC) (2009) A report by Aboriginal Philanthropy in Canada: A Foundation for Understanding. Online. Available www.philanthropyandab-originalpeoples.files.wordpress.com/2011/01/aboriginalphilanthropyincanada.pdf [Accessed 15 October 2012].

Emerson, R. W. and Eliot, C. W. (1909) *Essays and English traits*. Volume 5 Harvard Classics. New York: P. F. Collier & Son.

Faber, D. R. and McCarthy, D. (eds) (2005) *Foundations for social change: Critical perspectives on philanthropy and popular movements*. New York: Rowman & Littlefield.

Frumkin, P. (2006) *Strategic giving: The art and science of philanthropy*. Chicago: University of Chicago Press.

Giri, A. K. (2011) 'Self development and social transformations? The vision and practice of the self-study mobilization of swadhyaya', *Man in India, Special Issue: Religion, Philanthropy and Development*, 91(9): 19–37.

Habib, A. (2005) 'State-civil society relations in post-apartheid South Africa', *Social Research*, 72(3): 671–92.

Habib, A., Maharaj, B. and Nyar, A. (2008) 'Giving, development and poverty alleviation', in A. Habib and B. Maharaj (eds) *Giving and solidarity: Resource flows for poverty alleviation and development in South Africa*. Cape Town: HSRC Press.

IFIP (2015) International Funders for Indigenous Peoples, www.internationalfunders.org/ [Accessed 8 October 2015].

Jones, A. L. (2004) 'Philanthropy in the African American experience', in More, M. 'Philosophy in South Africa under and after apartheid', in *A Companion to African Philosophy*. Wiredu (ed). Malden, MA: Blackwell, 149–60.

Kincaid, J. (1983) 'Of time, body, and scarcity: Policy options and theoretic considerations.' *International Political Science Review*, 4(3): 401–16.

Korovkin, T. (2001) 'Reinventing the communal tradition: Indigenous peoples, civil society, and democratization in Andean Ecuador', *Latin American Research Review*, 36 (3): 37–67.

Lohmann, R. (1995) 'Buddhist commons and the question of a third sector in Asia', *Voluntas*, 6(2): 140–58.

Lund, F. (2010) 'Hierarchies of care work in South Africa: Nurses, social workers and home-based care workers', *International Labour Review*, 149(4): 495–509.

Malombe, J. (2010) 'A summary report of the first Pan African Assembly of the African Grantmakers Network'. November 3rd–5th, 2010: African Grantmakers Network.

Mokgoro, Y. (1997) '*Ubuntu* and the Law in South Africa', Paper presented at the First Colloquium on the Constitution and the Law, Potchefstroom, South Africa, 31 October 1997.

More, M. P. (2004). 'Philosophy in South Africa under and after apartheid', in K. Wiredu (ed). *A Companion to African Philosophy* (pp. 149–160). Oxford: Blackwell.

Moyo, B. (2011) 'The future of philanthropy and development in the pursuit of human wellbeing', The Bellagio Initiative: Transformative Innovations in African Philanthropy Paper. Dakar.

Murenha, A. and Chili, S. (2011) 'How and why poor people help each other: A perspective from the Maphumulo rural community in KwaZulu-Natal,' Young Researchers Philanthropy Initiative II, Centre for Civil Society, University of KwaZulu-Natal, Durban.

Ngcoya, M. (2009) '*Ubuntu*: Globalization, accommodation and contestation in South Africa', PhD Dissertation, American University, Washington D.C.

Ngcoya, M. and Mottiar, S. (2011) 'Understanding horizontal philanthropy in KwaZulu-Natal South Africa', Paper presented at IRSP Conference, Dublin, Ireland, April 2011.

Payton, R. L. (1996) 'Introduction', in J. B. Schneewind, (ed). *Giving: Western ideas of philanthropy*. Bloomington: Indiana University Press.

Quebral, M. and Terol, N. (2002) *An introduction to Asian philanthropy and NGOs, Asia-Pacific Philanthropy Consortium, investing in ourselves: Giving and fund raising in Asia*. Manila: Asian Development Bank.

Ramose, M. B. (2001) 'An African perspective on justice and race, polylog', *Forum for Intercultural Philosophy*, 3, Social Justice: Voices from the South.

Robbins, L. (1945) *An essay on the nature and significance of economic science*. London: Macmillan and Co. Limited.

Sanborn, C. (2005) 'Philanthropy in Latin America: Historical traditions and current trends', in C. Sanborn and F. Portocarrero (eds). *Philanthropy and social change in Latin America*. Cambridge, Massachusetts: Harvard University Press.

Schneewind, J. (ed). (1996) *Giving: Western ideas of philanthropy*. Bloomington: Indiana University Press.

Seleoane, M. (2008) 'Resource flows in poor communities: A reflection on four case studies', in A. Habib, and B. Maharaj (eds). *Giving and solidarity: Resource flows for poverty alleviation and development in South Africa*. Cape Town: HSRC Press.

Shaw, A. (2002) *Social justice philanthropy: An overview*. New York: The Synergos Institute.

Shutte, A. (2001) *Ubuntu an ethic for a New South Africa*. Pietermaritzburg: Cluster Publications.

Tambulasi R. and Kayuni, H. (2005) 'Can African Feet Divorce Western Shoes? The Case of *Ubuntu* and Democratic Good Governance in Malawi', *Nordic Journal of African Studies*, 14(2): 147–69.

Testart, A. (1998) 'Uncertainties of the "Obligation to Reciprocate": A critique of Mauss', in N. J. Allen and W. James (eds). *Marcel Mauss: A centenary tribute*. New York: Berghahn Books.

Wilkinson-Maposa, S., Fowler, A., Oliver-Evans, C. and Mulenga, C. F. N. (2004) 'The poor philanthropist: How and why the poor help each other', Research Report, University of Cape Town, Graduate School of Business, South Africa.

10

The globalization of philanthropy
Trends and channels of giving

Hillel Schmid and Hanna Shaul Bar Nissim

The past three decades have witnessed growth in the scope and volume of global giving, as well as in the impact of private philanthropists on global issues. The emergence of private philanthropists alongside foundations and diaspora communities as key actors in the arena of international giving means we need to develop a better understanding of the phenomenon of transboundary philanthropy. This chapter provides insights into the essence of global giving and analyzes various aspects of international philanthropy.

'Transboundary' philanthropy includes the transfer of money, in kind services, and volunteer time across borders, both by individuals and institutions who support human and environmental causes outside of their countries of residence (Anheier and Themudo, 2004; Metcalf-Little, 2010). The three main channels of transboundary philanthropy are: institutional giving by foundations; global philanthropic activity by corporations; and individual contributions by philanthropists and among diaspora communities of immigrants. In 2010, the total monetary transboundary transfers by foundations, corporations and individuals were estimated at $575 billion US – three times more than the amount of Official Development Assistance (ODA) (Hudson Institute, 2012). Between 1998 and 2008, total international philanthropy, including all three sources, almost doubled (Grimm *et al.*, 2009; Hudson Institute, 2009; World Bank, 2013). Eighty percent of the economic engagement of donors in global issues is done by channels of private financial flows (Hudson Institute, 2013). Given a lack of information, however, it is difficult to accurately assess the total or country-specific value of monetary transboundary transfers. Most international donations originate in the US; in 2010, they were reported to be $38 billion (Millennium Development Goal Task Force, 2011). A recent report revealed that in 2013, China, India, Brazil, and South Africa alone account for a disproportionate $103 billion in private philanthropic flows compared to $577 billion from the 23 developed donor countries (Hudson Institute, 2013). The amounts vary considerably across other countries. For example, in France, transboundary contributions to developing countries were $1 billion in 2008; in Italy, about half this amount ($583.1 million), but still much more than the total contributions from the Italian government to ODA, which were about $162 million (Hudson Institute, 2011; 2012). In Japan, private philanthropy to International Development causes amounted to $5.51 billion, while the Government's transfers to ODA amounted to 467 million. These official, but partial, data indicate that in every country, the amount of individual and institutional philanthropy was greater than the amount of corporate philanthropy – and together, both sources of support were greater than the amount of government assistance to developing countries (Hudson Institute, 2013).

We first present theoretical approaches that explain the impetus for international giving, then consider the differing patterns of contributions and engagement by various sets of philanthropic actors, reflect on the dilemmas they face, and conclude with suggestions for future research.

A theoretical framework

The underlying rationales for cross-border philanthropy can be assessed using three main-stream theoretical approaches: social exchange; identification; and the identifiable victim effect theory.

According to social exchange theory (Emerson, 1962; Blau, 1964), international philanthropists seek to expand the scope of their international business initiatives, as well as to influence governments in order to gain benefits for their philanthropic investment. The motives of these philanthropists are also expressed in their desire to gain international recognition and prestige through their contributions, highlight the social value of their contributions, and position themselves as leaders or as influential forces in the international arena. Thus, exchange relations are developed between global philanthropists and the countries that need their contributions.

The second theoretical approach, identification theory, assumes that the basis for philanthropic activity is empathic identification with the needs of others and subordination of self-interests to the interests of others (Schervish and Havens, 1995; Schervish et al., 2001; Schervish, 2005). According to this theory, transboundary giving by individual immigrants and immigrant communities derives from a sense of identification with the residents of their countries of origin. In so doing, they show empathy with marginal, low socioeconomic status (SES) populations in their countries of origin who need assistance for social, health, economic, and cultural development.

The third approach is the 'identifiable victim effect' theory. This explains the tendency of diaspora philanthropists to contribute to family members who remain in their country of origin. The theory highlights two major aspects that encourage philanthropic giving – identifiable victims and identifiable nationality. According to this theory, willingness to help people with whom one has no real connection increases when information is available about a specific victim who needs assistance so that the victim can be identified and distinguished from others whom one knows nothing about (Kogut and Ritov, 2005). This theory is most appropriate for examining transboundary philanthropy in which individuals and communities of immigrants contribute to individuals and families in their countries of origin because they have identified the beneficiaries as relatives who need their assistance and financial support. The philanthropists have a personal connection with these beneficiaries, who are perceived as 'victims' and are considered worthy of financial and in kind support.

These three theoretical approaches provide complementary aspects of a framework for analyzing the processes and trends described in this chapter. The exchange between donors and recipient individuals or communities is based on some sort of exchange or 'give-and-take' relations. The philanthropists identify individual victims or communities and donate personally out of a sense of empathy with the 'victims'. In so doing, the donors gain intrinsic and extrinsic rewards, prestige or recognition for their contributions, and they position themselves in the arena of influential national and international philanthropists. Although it may seem that this kind of philanthropy is driven by altruistic motives and by identification with others, it is also driven by pragmatic and personal interests.

Driving and restraining forces

The international philanthropy movement is gaining momentum. It has grown and expanded, despite a certain decline following the economic and financial crisis in 2008–2009. There has been an increase in the number of individual philanthropists, philanthropic foundations, and corporate philanthropists, as well as an increase in the scope of transfers from diaspora communities, community foundations and internet transfers. In addition, there has been an increase in donations of emergency aid following natural disasters such as the tsunami, earthquakes, armed conflicts, and other events that led to global mobilization of philanthropic capital for humanitarian purposes. What factors are driving the increase in transborder giving, and what are the primary barriers obstructing and restraining its development?

The globalization process: Globalization encouraged economic and industrial development, which has generated wealth and prosperity among certain groups in Western societies. This has been accompanied by the growth of poverty and domestic violence in developed and developing countries, as well as by the proliferation of epidemics, damage to the environment, humanitarian disasters and exposure of certain countries to external threats and internal armed conflicts (Benjamin and Quigley, 2010). The impetus for providing financial support to countries and societies also derives from the complex, bureaucratic mechanisms of international organizations, such as the United Nations, the World Bank, and the International Monetary Fund, and by the inability of those organizations to cope with global poverty, mass migration of refugees and domestic conflicts (Petersen and McClure, 2011).

Technological advancement and electronic communication: Today, the internet provides cheap and immediate access to information about international needs. This development has led to the growth of online philanthropy aimed at providing international assistance, relief, and development (Clark and Themudo, 2003; Micklewright and Wright, 2005). Online giving has become a preferred mode of transboundary giving: it overcomes the physical obstacles and barriers of distance, cuts bureaucratic red tape, reduces the costs of contributions and aims to establish direct contact between donors and beneficiaries. Through this mode of giving, philanthropists have more control over the allocation of contributions for initiatives within and between countries, as well as across different sectors (Desai and Kharas, 2010; Metcalf-Little, 2010). Furthermore, the rapid progress of information systems and electronic communication technology has facilitated transboundary partnerships by reducing the costs of communication and coordination between philanthropic institutions.

Fiscal policy: Tax laws and regulations affect the scope of international contributions by reflecting governmental legitimization for the role of philanthropy, but can also place barriers in the path of donors. Notwithstanding wider questions about the relationship between tax incentives and philanthropy (Pharoah, Chapter 4), a generous taxation policy that provides incentives for charitable giving, including to foreign organizations, might promote international philanthropy. However, many countries have a stringent taxation framework that deters donors from making international contributions. In the case of cross-boundary philanthropy, it is possible to prohibit or severely limit tax deductions for direct contributions to foreign organizations. For example, in the US (which is by no means an outlier), private donors to foreign organizations are deductible only if made to those approved by the tax agency; alternatively, tax deductible support for international work has to be made through a US tax exempt organization with operations abroad or through a tax exempt organization established in the US as a 'friend of' a foreign charity (Paine, 2005; Johnson, 2011). In Europe, private and institutional donors encounter statutory and tax obstacles and are even discriminated against because of a clear preference for domestic organizations (Anheier and Daly, 2006; Vahlpahl, 2009; Hohati, 2010);

legislation that would enable charities to be treated evenly across all member states has been proposed, but not yet enacted.

Over-regulation: In many countries, local and transboundary philanthropic activity is governed by a combination of regulations, laws and tax policies that were originally intended for the private and public sectors but not for the new wave of philanthropic giving. The attempt to regulate philanthropic activity has created an administrative and bureaucratic burden, where multiple authorities deal with licensing, oversight of activities and financial auditing (Johnson, 2011). Extensive regulation affects the impetus for international philanthropy, particularly its contribution to innovation and newness (Heydemann and Kinsey, 2010). Following the September 11th attacks in 2001, the tightening of regulation over international donations affected donors' willingness to engage in international philanthropy. In the US, about 60 percent of the foundations reported that post-September 11th regulations increased their reluctance to contribute directly to other countries (Foundation Center, 2008).

Political (in)stability and corruption: Political stability, or lack thereof, in countries that receive donations from abroad can affect the motivation to give and the scope and frequency of international contributions. Studies have revealed that international donors tend to contribute to countries with a stable political, economic, and social situation; they refrain from contributing to least developing countries (LDCs) that lack political stability. Chervalier and Zimet (2006) found that most institutional contributions, up to 60 percent of all grants, have been made to emerging economies, notably China, South Africa, Brazil, Mexico and India. These findings have been corroborated by Marten and Witte (2008), who revealed that 45 percent of grants from US foundations are allocated to emerging economies which show more political and economic stability than LDCs.

Donors' confidence that their capital will reach the beneficiaries in its entirety is undermined when transboundary philanthropic capital is known, or perceived, to be susceptible to corruption in the beneficiary organizations or beneficiary governments (Desai and Kharas, 2010). Loss of confidence arises from financial corruption, particularly in government and non-governmental organization (NGO) bureaucracies and online platforms, as well as from moral corruption among senior officials who look after their own interests (Maxwell *et al.*, 2008).

While international philanthropy is being driven as part of the overall pattern of globalization, a number of these factors are also applying the brakes – to what extent, we do not really know. What is evident is that different agents of transborder philanthropy have different goals and patterns of contributions.

The goals of global giving

International giving has numerous goals and objectives which respond to the different needs at various levels – individuals, communities, societies and countries. At the individual level, international philanthropy aims primarily to eradicate poverty and hunger, enhance individuals' education, reduce child mortality and improve the health and well-being of individuals (Petersen and McClure, 2011). At the level of societies and countries, global philanthropy aims to achieve broader goals. First, international philanthropists work toward disseminating the values of democracy and laying the foundations for a better civil society throughout the world, encouraging minorities and disenfranchised populations to be more active in the political arena (Anheier and Daly, 2004; Benjamin and Quigley, 2010). During the transitions of the 1990s, for instance, American foundations donated about $75 million a year for the promotion of democracy, economic reforms and social services in Eastern Europe and Africa (Török, 2005). Second, domestic conflicts and assisting the poorest developing countries with basic services, such as health and education, have been an important focus. Following the September 11th attacks, foundations were also encouraged to do much more, to assist longer term reform that would avert the issues that were factors perpetuating this sort of terrorism (Bach, 2002). Third, global crises – emergency situations such as natural disasters, economic crises and situations of political unrest – generate an immediate increase in the availability of international philanthropic capital (Kapucu, Chapter 11). In 2010, there was an increase of about 15.3 percent in American donations to international causes following the destruction incurred by the earthquake in Haiti (Giving USA, 2011). This rise was hindered with a decline of 6.7 percent in 2013 (total of almost $US 15 million). This change is attributable partially to lower overall corporate support for charities in 2013, and the fact that some donors are choosing to give directly to overseas organizations working in that arena (Giving USA, 2014). Moreover, the total contributions of the 23 largest corporations following the 2004 tsunami in Southeast Asia and Hurricane Katrina and the Kashmir earthquake in 2005 totaled $US 263 million (Muller and Whiteman, 2009).

International philanthropists – who are they?

The characteristics of philanthropists who contribute to international causes have been identified in a number of studies. These include mega donors, donors who choose international rather than domestic causes for giving, those who give nationally and internationally, and those who send remittances and gifts to their home communities. The level of education of donors is an important factor (Ribar and Wilhelm, 1995) as it affects the motivation and readiness of donors to contribute to organizations that provide international assistance (Schmid and Rudich-Cohen, 2012; Bekkers, Chapter 7). A study conducted among households in the US (Okten and Osili, 2007) supports these findings, and adds a gender dimension: women and individuals with higher education tend to contribute more to international causes than do men and people with relatively low levels of education. Ribar and Wilhelm (1995) also find that per capita income, regulation laws, and taxation policies influence individual philanthropists' willingness to give. Occupation also matters. Yoshioka (2008) reveals that affluent Americans who made their fortunes in hightech entrepreneurship, science, communications, and medicine showed a high tendency to engage in international philanthropy. This tendency is also affected by household size (Okten and Osili, 2007), which may be associated with more recent immigrant families. In a study of Canadian philanthropists, Rajan et al. (2009) find that most of the donors who contributed to international causes were not born in Canada; they were religious people with high levels of income and education, and they exhibited high social and political involvement.

Affiliation with an ethnic group and racial loyalty encourages contributions to causes that benefit that group (Luttmer, 2001). Cheung and Chan (2000) report that older individuals who had traveled around the world were motivated to contribute to international causes out of a sense of empathy with the individuals and societies to which they had been exposed. The presence of immigrants in the donor's community also provides an incentive for contributions to the immigrants' country of origin. Consistent with this argument, Okten and Osili (2007) highlight that the larger the number of immigrants in a given community, the greater their tendency to contribute to international causes, and the immigrants' country of origin affects the regions and types of causes to which people contribute.

In addition, international philanthropy, particularly through online platforms such as Kiva and GlobalGiving, is influenced by the type of the programs or project presented for funding (Desai and Kharas, 2010), suggesting the value of helping entrepreneurs seeking microfinance develop good project ideas. The importance of donor confidence in the recipient organization is supported by a study conducted in Hong Kong (Cheung and Chan, 2000). This concludes that international giving is associated with: the donor's awareness of the international cause; past experience with donations to a specific cause and moral commitment to it; and perceived effectiveness of how contributions are used.

Recent years have witnessed the emergence of a distinctive segment of international philanthropists: the new generation of philanthropists who acquired wealth in business, electronics, high tech, and start-up ventures. The *Forbes* report of world billionaires recently informed that there are 1,826 billionaires, with an average net worth of $US 3.86 billion and a total net worth of $US 7.05 trillion. Some 46 of these billionaires are under the age of 40. Moreover, from this list, a striking number of 1,191 are self-made billionaires (*Forbes*, 2015). These new philanthropists do not limit themselves to contributions within their countries of residence. Rather, they believe it is necessary to remedy injustice throughout the world, and have become major actors in the arena of global philanthropy (Schervish, 2008). These donors, who have also been referred to as 'entrepreneurial' philanthropists, have the financial capital, expertise and knowledge needed to identify sustainable solutions to global problems. Their connections and reputation assist them in getting to the root of complex social problems, and promote economic and social development on a global scale (Gordon *et al.*, Chapter 21). These mega donors also tend to emphasize, often quite vocally and visibility, their philanthropic activity in the international media and in business fora (Fleishman, 2007; Bishop and Green, 2008).

Foundation grantmaking

Philanthropic institutions play an integral role in the redistribution of wealth throughout the world (Okten and Osili, 2007). They serve as local agents that promote global social change (Benjamin and Quigley, 2010), encourage social entrepreneurship and support non-governmental organizations (Moran, 2009; Heydemann and Kinsey, 2010); their capital helps them finance the UN Millennium development goals (Bach, 2002; Micklewright and Wright, 2005) and enables them to contribute towards improving the quality of life for impoverished, deprived and disadvantaged populations. The intervention of private mega donors and foundations that channel their contributions to developing countries to some extent reflects the process of privatization in foreign aid in recent decades, and highlights the important role of transboundary philanthropic activities in offsetting the deficits in foreign aid. In particular, international philanthropy plays an essential role in countries where official development assistance does not even reach the threshold of 0.7 percent of the Gross National Product established by the Organisation for Economic Co-operation and Development (OECD) (Edwards, 2009; Rajan *et al.*, 2009; Davis and Dadush, 2010).

The very large foundations are major players in global philanthropy. According to the European Foundation Centre (Marten and Witte, 2008), half of the foundations in the European Union engaged in activities in foreign countries, and about one-fourth of them operated in 126 countries. In the US, contributions to overseas countries by foundation amounted to $US 4.3 billion in 2010 from 1,300 foundations, a decrease of 24.1 percent from 2008 (Foundation Center, 2012). The amount granted by some of these large foundations and their mega donors is significant. For example, in 2010 the Bill and Melinda Gates Foundation granted over $1.6 billion for the promotion of global health, and in 2012, the net worth of the Foundation was around $3.7 billion. By comparison, the budget of the World Health Organization was $5 billion in 2009, and the funds were raised by 193 member countries. Other examples of international mega donors include: the Ford Foundation, which allocated $198 million for strengthening democracy in different parts of the world and for encouraging transparency in global financial systems; the William and Flora Hewlett Foundation, which granted about $106 million for environmental quality, development and governance throughout the world in 2010; and the Open Society Foundation, which was founded by George Soros and contributed $100 million to the Human Rights Watch Organization in 2010 (Marten and Witte, 2008; Grimm *et al.*, 2009; Benjamin and Quigley, 2010; The Million Dollar List, 2010; Foundation Center, 2012; Shaw *et al.*, 2013). Foundations often channel their contributions via domestic intermediary nonprofit organizations, which are the main providers of social services in most developing countries, thereby building organizations' capacity as well as serving beneficiaries. They are also beginning to collaborate among themselves to some degree so as to achieve 'collective impact' (Kania and Kramer, 2011) in addressing complex problems. Over the last decade, a variety of partnerships among philanthropic institutions, such as the Global Fund to Fight AIDS, 'Europe and the World', and the Global Alliance for Vaccines and Immunization (GAVI), have emerged that aim to overcome international barriers and obstacles for giving and achieve economies of scale (Casas and Fiennes, 2007).

Global corporate giving

Globalization, liberalization and privatization of social and governmental services have led multinational corporations to broaden their activities and increase their influence throughout the world. These corporations have provided employment opportunities and created new jobs in various countries, where they have also become involved in the political arena. International corporate giving has been modest, however, at least in relation to international private giving. In the US, corporate contributions account for five percent of all charitable giving in 2013, about $17.9 billion (Giving USA, 2014); corporate support for international causes was about 19 percent of total US international philanthropy (Hudson Institute, 2012) and is estimated between $US 1.4 and $4.4 billion (Global Impact, 2013). Expectations and practices of social responsibility of corporations are intensifying as they exhibit leadership, responsibility and accountability through diverse philanthropic enterprises, as well as among different institutes and interest groups (Fortanier and van Tulder, 2009; Grimm *et al.*, 2009; Jamali, 2010; Ho *et al.*, 2012). Following the demand for transparency in corporate social and communal circles, various methods have been developed for corporations to exhibit their social responsibility. Corporations have begun reporting about their impact on global development in areas such as the war on poverty; they highlight this impact through quantitative measures, such as reports about the creation of new jobs and expansion of employment opportunities, and many are promoting standards of fair trade (Fortanier and van Tulder, 2009). The motives for corporate giving are strategic and derive from the company's business plan, as well as from the merits achieved by the philanthropic initiatives (Moran and Branigan, Chapter 24). The contributions made by these companies reflect their areas of expertise and availability of resources, and help them improve the company's reputation, broaden their business opportunities and facilitate recruitment of skilled, educated and competent workers (Grimm *et al.*, 2009).

Notably, the strategies for corporate giving vary nationally and internationally, across different societies and regions. Corporate policies can be set according to the standards of the corporation's country of origin and implemented universally, or they can be adapted to the standards of the country in which the corporation operates (Husted and Allen, 2006). McDonald's program for the promotion of health among children and their families, for instance, is implemented in the same way throughout the world. In contrast, the ABBOTT Pharmaceutical Corporation contributes to a variety of causes, including AIDS prevention, responsible advertizing and accessibility of clean drinking water and sanitation, in accordance with the policies of the countries in which it operates (Merz *et al.*, 2010). Many of these programs have both a community and a company benefit. The Anglo–American Mining company offers programs to combat AIDS and HIV in Africa, which also promote the health of the company's own staff members; Coca–Cola finances water purification and the production of drinking water amounting annually to $US 28 million, which also facilitates the manufacture of its own product in countries that have a water shortage; and Pfizer Pharmaceuticals mobilized staff members who specialize in the field of health, disease control and environmentalism to participate in rehabilitation efforts following the tsunami in Southeast Asia (Kasper and Fulton, 2006; Muller and Whiteman, 2009; Foundation Center, 2011; Global Impact, 2013).

Diaspora philanthropy

Globalization has led to the opening of national borders and to the free movement of goods, people and services. With an estimated 215 million people, that is three percent of the world's population, living in diaspora communities outside of their countries of origin (Werbner, 2004; World Bank, 2013), diaspora philanthropy has been growing rapidly since the beginning of the twenty-first century (Metcalf–Little, 2010). Sheffer (2002) defines diasporas as ethnic minority groups of migrant origins residing and acting in host countries but maintaining strong sentimental and material links with their countries of origin – their homelands. Werbner (2002) adds that diasporas are multinational networks of individuals who are linked by cultural, religious and social traditions and a sense of mutual responsibility across national, imperial and political borders. Members of the community feel a sense of connection and commitment to their country of origin and are even involved in its struggles and achievements (Vertovec, 2003; Brinkerhoff, 2012;). Their connections across borders encourage and enable financial resources to be channeled from immigrant donors in the host countries to individuals and communities in their country of origin, entirely bypassing governments (Newland *et al.*, 2010). Civil society organizations, religious institutions and diaspora foundations – such as the Ayala Foundation USA, which raises donations from the Filipino diaspora – in the host country are important means of making transfers, with financial institutions and online platforms competing for a share of this growth market.

Diaspora philanthropy has several characteristics and goals (Orozco, 2006; Sidel, 2004, 2007, 2008): it supports social development and the establishment of nonprofit organizations, and the civil society; provides education opportunities and transfer of advanced knowledge; and builds community capacities. Contributions to the country of origin also enable immigrants to express their identity, particularly when they are marginalized in the host country. Many immigrants have a hybrid identity, characterized by dual identification with their country of residence and their homeland (Lavie and Swedenburg, 1996). They attempt to preserve their cultural identity, gain social reinforcement, and maintain their sense of national pride by belonging to a group and by supporting or participating in programs that have a political or economic impact on their homeland. Werbner (2002) argues that diaspora philanthropy emerges out of a process which involves *material* considerations, including activities that express the immigrants' support for and identification with their country of origin, but because immigrants are 'invisible' (or 'transparent'), they also aim to reinforce their *symbolic* status as loyal citizens of their homeland. This process includes material and cultural cross-border contributions such as political lobbying and fundraising. These motives drive immigrants to join various diaspora organizations and engage in philanthropic giving. In addition, giving to the country of origin can derive from a desire for social status, recognition, political influence, reputation and material resources (Nielsen and Riddle, 2009; Brinkerhoff, 2011). Other driving, and sometimes restraining, forces that affect immigrants giving relate to the feeling that they need to give back to their homeland, as well as their sense of moral obligation and their desire to assist the weaker elements of their community of origin.

In some countries, the share of diaspora giving is much larger than the share of local philanthropy. Thus, for example, the state of Israel is considered to be the largest importer of philanthropic contributions from overseas. For many years, donations from abroad amounted to 75 percent of philanthropic contributions to Israel (Schmid, 2011). This situation has been changed slightly in recent years, and diaspora philanthropy comprises 62 percent of all philanthropic contributions to Israel (Schmid, 2011).

Diaspora philanthropists use a variety of channels and means for contributions (Orozco, 2006; Aysa-Lastra, 2007; Johnson, 2007; Sidel, 2007; Metcalf-Little, 2010; Newland et al., 2010). Two of the most common means are individual remittances, which are directly transferred to relatives and friends in the country of origin, and collective remittances, which aggregate the money of immigrants in order to increase their influence back home. In 2013, the estimated remittances of immigrants totaled $US 536 billion (World Bank, 2013), most of which are transferred to developing countries and constitute a substantial share of their Gross Domestic Product (GDP). Besides cash remittances, this channel of assistance is measured in terms of hours of volunteer work that immigrants contribute in their countries of origin. For example, the value of volunteer time in 2009 was equivalent to $US 3 billion, and most of the assistance was directed to relief and development efforts (Hudson Institute, 2011). As for the impact of remittances, studies reveal contradictory findings. With regard to legitimization, it has been argued that the beneficiary countries attempt to provide leverage for remittances as a national financial resource rather than considering them as personal transfers between families and communities (Brinkerhoff, 2011).

In addition to financial contributions and volunteerism, in kind donations of professional and technological know-how and commercial and political connections can be transferred directly to the beneficiaries in the country of origin. However, it is difficult to assess their scope and distribution. Examples of such initiatives include: contributions from the Indian diaspora between 1991 and 2000, estimated to be equivalent to $US 835 million, and contributions worth millions of dollars from the Vietnamese diaspora in the US following the floods in Vietnam in 1999 (Sidel, 2007). Finally, various programs bring second- and third-generation diaspora youth to their countries of origin and expose them to the local values, culture, and tradition (Newland et al., 2010). These programs include Birthright, which is financed by Jewish philanthropists in the US and aims to foster Jewish identity and reduce assimilation among Jewish youth, as well as to strengthen ties with Israel among diaspora Jewry.

It is important to note that the selection of means and channels of contribution by immigrants is related to a growing sense of compassion toward individuals, and a decline in empathy and sensitivity toward larger organizations and governments, which are considered bureaucratic, corrupt, inefficient and ineffective. A recent example is the tax imposed by The Martelly Administration on funds remitted by Haitian immigrants to their relatives back home, amounting to more than $1 billion a year (Pearson, 2011). The trend toward giving to individuals has been intensifying in many diasporas which have lost their confidence in state institutions, as well as in some large, professional and commercialized nonprofit organizations whose social and civic ideology has been replaced by a business orientation that ensures their survival in changing, competitive and turbulent environments (Johnson et al., 2004).

The impact of diaspora contributions on the country of origin has been examined extensively in the literature. Most studies have found that contributions made by immigrants, especially in Israel, China, India, Ireland and Mexico, serve as a catalyst for integrating their country of origin into the international economy (Freinkman, 2000; Kuznetsov, 2006). In their countries of origin, the immigrants are perceived as agents of change and development who initiate a variety of civic and philanthropic activities, who are an important source of foreign investments and who can be instrumental in improving political and economic relations with Western countries (Orozco, 2006; Portes *et al.*, 2007). The country of origin can place obstacles through political measures or fiscal legislation however that deter diaspora donors from giving to their homeland. Such laws are perceived as anti-democratic and undermine the relationships between the immigrants and their countries of origin. For example, as a result of the proposed legislation in Israel to impose a high tax on foreign donations, and in the anti-democratic atmosphere that has been created by such legislation, Jewish donors in the US have reservations about contributing to organizations in Israel.

In sum, donations from diaspora communities are reflected in transfers of treasure, time and talent. Transfers of treasure benefit populations in distress or for social and rehabilitative programs; those of time provide hands-on volunteers, and those of talent provide technological, scientific, economic, medical and other knowledge and networks. The most prominent mode of contribution is transfer of money, which comprises a substantial component of the GDP in some of the beneficiary countries. Nonetheless, the extent to which different forms and modes of monetary contributions have had a meaningful impact on the beneficiaries is unclear, owing to the lack of human, physical and technological infrastructures in the home countries that can provide leverage for monetary contributions and intellectual property. Moreover, in some countries, there is no clear policy governing cross-border contributions.

Dilemmas for transboundary giving

The global political climate affects the extent of engagement among international philanthropists. Over the past decade, philanthropists have become involved in domestic and international affairs, and the ethical boundaries of their activity have been blurred. As a result, attempts have been made to implement national and international regulation of cross-border philanthropic capital. Control over international contributions has tightened, in both developing and Western countries, and rules have been established to more closely monitor international giving (Owens, 2005; Paine, 2005; Sidel, Chapter 16). Regulation has increased considerably since September 11, 2001, when cases of international contributions that were used to finance acts of international terror were brought to light (Smith *et al.*, Chapter 17). For example, the Global Relief Foundation raised funds for Al Qaeda and the Holy Land Foundation for Relief and Development was exposed as an organization that raises funds for Hamas (Paine, 2005). The development of regulation aimed at preventing the transfer of funds to organizations that provide clandestine backing for terror organizations has generated a public debate regarding the role of international philanthropy, the involvement of international donors in political issues and the establishment of global norms for cross-border philanthropic activity.

Transparency is essential for the credibility of giving; it provides public and official legitimacy for philanthropic activity. It ensures that activities will not be clandestine and reduces the risk of corruption and embezzlement. Lack of transparency affects public confidence in philanthropic and intermediary third-sector organizations and casts doubt on the motives of international philanthropists. A lack of confidence intensifies when there is distrust of the public sector in general, and governmental agencies in particular (Johnson, 2011). Moreover, the absence of criteria for transparency set by governmental institutions has a negative impact on cooperation in international philanthropy, whereas when donors are required to adhere to transparency standards, they tend to engage in innovative activity, seek to form partnerships and make a difference in the societies that they support (Edwards, 2009; Metcalf-Little, 2010).

In recent years, there have been increasing demands on civil society organizations to report on the use of philanthropic funds that are transferred to them, and on the impact of those funds. Foundations, mega donors, and the public at large, demand that beneficiary organizations submit reports on the use of donations, as well as on their organizational effectiveness and on the implementation of measures of success (Carman, 2009). However, international philanthropy is not subject to the same extent of exposure or public scrutiny as domestic nonprofits and philanthropy. Spero (2010) argues that international donors need to adopt norms of conduct that include adherence to the domestic laws and policies of the beneficiary country, collaboration with local authorities and mobilization of local support for the philanthropic activity.

Transboundary philanthropy has the potential to widen social and economic inequality in the world. The ability of wealthy private philanthropists and corporations to contribute to some regions rather than others creates gaps between countries and societies. In addition, affluent and stable diaspora communities are able to give back more to their countries of origin than poor diaspora communities that are still struggling to establish their status and citizenship in the host country. In this global process, there are no checks and balances, nor are there any mechanisms to ensure equity and equality in capital allocations. In such cases, philanthropic activity not only fails to solve problems, but it can even create conflicts between affluent and poor, marginalized populations. The power of these philanthropists vis-à-vis the organizations that receive contributions is also a risk factor. The situation in which wealthy philanthropists deal with nonprofit organizations that are desperate for funding creates a structural imbalance in the relationships between the donors and beneficiaries. This often places the philanthropists in a position of moral dogmatism, where they impose their views on their surroundings; their behaviour is paternalistic or maternalistic and they disregard real needs and professional expertise (Reich, 2006).

The legitimacy accorded to philanthropic activity depends on the consent of governmental and public agencies, private agencies and the public at large. Legitimacy is obtained through governmental recognition as reflected in government policies, as well as in taxation policies, regulation and administrative bylaws. The sources of public legitimization for philanthropic activity in public domains are not always clear, nor is it clear whether such legitimization derives mainly from the philanthropists' economic resources. These issues have remained unresolved, and there are still questions to be dealt with both at the national and international levels. In many countries, the entry of international philanthropic capital can upset the existing political and social situation. Despite the important contribution of international philanthropic capital to the economy and society of the beneficiary countries, it also brings in 'noise' and interference in areas where different interest groups compete for these resources.

Concluding thoughts

Transboundary philanthropy is multifaceted. It is driven by various motives, including altruistic, ideological, personal and utilitarian considerations. Altruistic motives include a sense of social consciousness among wealthy individuals who feel they need to contribute to improving the welfare of excluded, marginalized and low-SES populations. These considerations have led to the emergence of donors who make generous contributions for combating poverty, hunger, disease and illiteracy, as well as for creating employment opportunities throughout the world. Besides these billionaires and mega billionaires, there are individual immigrants and immigrant communities who identify with the status of their relatives and community members from their country of origin. They donate money and in kind contributions of time and knowledge for the benefit of family members abroad who deal with daily stressors of life. Undoubtedly, however, these actors (including billionaires, foundations, corporations and individuals of modest means) have vested interests and seek to gain personal and organizational rewards and benefits, positioning themselves as influential personalities in the beneficiary communities or countries and in the global arena. Beyond the altruistic-universal dimension of philanthropic giving, then, there is a utilitarian, pragmatic dimension of local and international philanthropy at the individual and national levels.

As shown in this chapter, transboundary contributions comprise a large share of the GDP in many developed countries. Nonetheless, there is still a lack of information about the impact of international contributions in the beneficiary countries, societies and communities. Initially, the microfinance movement and efforts to encourage the development of small businesses in disadvantaged communities abroad were received enthusiastically. However, this enthusiasm has waned in light of the limited success in rehabilitating and advancing disadvantaged populations that seek to develop small businesses. In the same vein, the extent to which these donations in fact promote technological, physical and health infrastructures or social and educational programs in developing countries is unclear. Undoubtedly, personal remittances improve the economic situation of individuals who receive such assistance. For example, there is no question that the $US 32 billion transferred by 22 million Mexican immigrants to their country of origin improved the economic situation of individual recipients (MPI, 2014). Nonetheless, it is not clear whether this money and other financial support has led to changes at the level of the local and central government that can generate a systemwide improvement in the situation of disadvantaged citizens. Moreover, the scope of transboundary philanthropic capital raises questions as to its impact on changes and trends of ODA that Western countries distribute in developing countries.

The philanthropists who transfer capital across borders regularly encounter complex bureaucratic red tape and corruption, and it is apparent that politicians abroad have used some of the funds for their own personal benefit. This has weakened the motivation of donors to make contributions. In addition, there are no clear policies for international philanthropy and for the transfer of capital from developed to developing countries. Nor are there sufficient tax incentives, and the cost of international transfers is high due to conflicting, bureaucratic rules and multiple intermediaries who benefit from the transfers. All of this not only discourages wealthy philanthropists from contributing to foreign countries and to the organizations in those countries, but detracts from the donors' confidence in those countries. Hence, it is essential for countries that receive transboundary donations to develop efficient and effective systems characterized by transparency and accountability to overcome governmental corruption, promote policies that encourage transboundary philanthropy and set taxation policies that will provide incentives for international contributions. If this happens, we can expect that the flow of transboundary philanthropy will grow. This, in turn, can benefit individuals, societies and countries that face existential problems and that have slim prospects for economic, social and technological progress if they do not receive appropriate resources.

The interventions of the different global individuals, corporations and foundations are a major area for learning and investigating. More data need to be gathered about the streaming of the capital between the countries and the real impact they create in the beneficiary countries and societies. More attention should be paid to research on the factors that can encourage global giving and remove obstacles that discourage world philanthropy to be involved in certain societies. We should also know more about the relationships that develop between the philanthropists and the governments in the different countries in order to improve communication and cooperation among philanthropists, corporations, civil society organizations and the government. More alliances and partnerships are required in order to promote synergy and achieve a real change in societies that desperately need resources for their survival and development. Unfortunately, these issues have not been examined systematically, and there is a need to invest efforts in further research.

References

Anheier, H. K. and Daly, S. (2004) 'Introduction: The future of global philanthropy.' In M. Kaldor, H. K. Anheier, and M. Glasius (eds.) *Global civil society yearbook 2004/2005*. London: Sage, 1–27.

——. (eds.) (2006) *Politics of foundations: A comparative analysis*. London: Routledge.

Anheier, H. K. and Themoudo. N. (2004) 'The internationalization of the nonprofit sector.' In R. D. Herman and Associates (eds.). *The Jossey-Bass handbook of nonprofit leadership and management*, 2nd edition. San-Francisco: Jossey-Bass, 102–27.

Aysa-Lastra, M. (2007) 'Diaspora philanthropy: The Colombian experience.' In P. D. Johnson (ed.). *Diaspora philanthropy: New roles and emerging models*. Boston: The Philanthropic Initiative, Inc. and The Global Equity Initiative, Harvard University.

Bach, R. L. (2002) 'New priorities for philanthropy,' *Ethics and International Affairs*, 16(2): 20–6.

Benjamin, L. M. and Quigley, K. F. F. (2010) 'For the world's sake: US foundations and international grant making, 1990-2002.' In H. K. Anheier and D. C. Hammack (eds.). *American Foundations*. Washington, DC: Brookings Institution Press, 237–61.

Bishop, M. and Green, M. (2008) *How the rich can save the world: philanthro-capitalism*. New York: Bloomsbury Press.

Blau, P. M. (1964). *Exchange and power in social life*. New York: Wiley.

Brinkerhoff, J. M. (2011) 'David and Goliath: Diaspora organizations as partners in the development industry,' *Public Administration and Development*, 31: 37–49.

——. (2012) 'Creating an enabling environment for diasporas: Participation in homeland development,' *International Migration*, 50(1): 75–95.

Carman, J. G. (2009) 'Nonprofits, funders, and evaluation: Accountability in action,' *The American Review of Public Administration*, 39: 374–90.

Casas, L. and Fiennes, C. (2007) *Going global: A review of international development funding by UK trusts and foundations*. London: New Philanthropy Capital.

Chervalier, B. and Zimet, J. (2006) *American philanthropic foundations: Emerging actors of globalization and pillars of the transatlantic dialog*. Washington, DC: The German Marshall Fund on the United States.

Cheung, C. K. and Chan, C. M. (2000) 'Social-cognitive factors of donating money to charity, with special attention to an international relief organization,' *Evaluation and Program Planning*, 23(2): 241–53.

Clark, J. and Themudo, N. (2003) 'The age of protest: Internet based "dot causes" and the "anti-globalization" movement.' In J. Clark (ed.). *Globalizing civic engagement*. London: Earthscan, 109–26.

Davis, K. E. and Dadush, S. (2010) 'The privatization of development assistance: Symposium overview,' *NYU Journal of International Law and Politics*, 42(4): 1079–89.

Desai, R. M. and Kharas, H. (2010) 'Democratizing foreign aid: Online philanthropy and international development assistance,' *Journal of International Law and Politics*, (42)4: 1111–42.

Edwards, M. (2009) 'Why "philanthrocapitalism" is not the answer: Private initiatives and international development.' In M. Kremer, P. van Lieshout, and R. Went (eds.). *Doing good or doing better: Development policies in a globalized world*. Amsterdam: Amsterdam University Press, 237–54.

Emerson. R. M. (1962) 'Power-dependence relations,' *American Sociological Review*, 27: 31–41.

Fleishman, J. (2007) *The foundation: A great American secret: How private wealth is changing the world*. New York: Public Affairs, Perseus Book Group.

Forbes. (2015) 'The World's Billionaires,' *Forbes*. www.forbes.com/billionaires/ [Accessed 28 May 2015].

Fortanier, F. N. and van Tulder, R. J. M. (2009) *Corporate societal responsibility 2009: Building blocks, employee perspectives*. Rotterdam: Krauthammer International.

Foundation Center. (2008) *International grantmaking IV: An update on U.S. foundation trends*. New York: Foundation Center.

——. (2011) *Foundation giving trends*. www.foundationcenter.org/gainknowledge/research/nationaltrends.html [Accessed 1 October 2011].

——. (2012) *International grantmaking IV: An update on U.S. foundation trends*. New York: Foundation Center.

Freinkman, L. (2000) *Role of the diasporas in transition economies: Lessons from Armenia*. Washington, DC: Armenian International Policy Research Group.

Giving USA. (2011) *The annual report on philanthropy for the year 2010*. Indianapolis, IN: The Center on Philanthropy at Indiana University.

Giving USA. (2012) *The annual report on philanthropy for the year 2011*. Indianapolis, IN: The Center on Philanthropy at Indiana University.

Global Impact. (2013) 'Assessment of U.S giving to international causes'. www.charity.org/about-us [Accessed 29 May 2015].

Grimm, S., Humphrey, J., Lundsgaarde, E. and John de Souza, S. (2009) 'European development cooperation to 2020: Challenges by new actors in international development,' European Development Co-operation 2020 Working Paper No.4, Seventh Framework Program. www.edc2020.eu/fileadmin/Textdateien/EDC2020_WP4_Webversion.pdf [Accessed 15 September 2011].

Heydemann, S. and Kinsey, R. (2010) 'The state and international philanthropy: The contribution of American foundations 1919–1991.' In H. K. Anheier and D. C. Hammack (eds.). *American foundations: Roles and contributions.* Washington DC: The Brookings Institution, 205–36.

Ho, N. F., Wang, H. M. D. and Vitell, S. J. (2012) 'A global analysis of corporate social performance: The effects of cultural and geographic environments,' *Journal of Business Ethics*, 107(4): 423–33.

Hohati, P. (2010) 'Why national governments should support the European Foundation Statute,' *Effect: Exploring the intersection of foundations in Europe*, 4(1): 20–1.

Hudson Institute. (2009) *The index of global philanthropy and remittances.* Washington, DC: Center for Global Prosperity. www.hudson.org/content/researchattachments/attachment/979/index_of_global_philanthropy_and_remittances_2009.pdf [Accessed 9 October 2015].

——. (2011) *The index of global philanthropy and remittances.* Washington, DC: Center for Global Prosperity. Online. www.hudson.org/content/researchattachments/attachment/977/2011_index_of_global_philanthropy_and_remittances_downloadable_version.pdf [Accessed 9 October 2015].

——. (2012) *The index of global philanthropy and remittances.* Washington, DC: Center for Global Prosperity. www.hudson.org/index.cfm?fuseaction=publication_details&id=8841 [Accessed 1 September 2012].

——. (2013) *The index of global philanthropy and remittances.* Washington, DC: Center for Global Prosperity. www.hudson.org/content/researchattachments/attachment/1229/2013_indexof_global_philanthropyand_remittances.pdf [Accessed 14 May 2015].

Husted, B. and Allen, D. (2006) 'Corporate social responsibility in the multinational enterprise: Strategic and institutional approaches,' *Journal of International Business Studies*, 37(6): 838–49.

Jamali, D. (2010) 'The CSR of MNC subsidiaries in developing countries: Global, local, substantive or diluted?,' *Journal of Business Ethics*, 93: 181–200.

Johnson, P. D. (2007) *Diaspora philanthropy: Influences, initiatives and issues.* Boston: TPI. www.tpi.org/sites/files/pdf/diaspora_philanthropy_final.pdf [Accessed 9 October 2015].

——. (2011) *Global institutional philanthropy: A preliminary status report.* Boston: WINGS and TPI. www.tpi.org/sites/files/pdf/global_institutional_philanthropy_a_preliminary_status_report_-_part_one.pdf [Accessed 9 October 2015].

Johnson, P., Johnson, S. and Kingman, A. (2004) *Promoting philanthropy: Global challenges and approaches.* Guterslohs, Germany: The Bertelsmann Foundation.

Kania, J. and Kramer, M. (2011) 'Collective impact,' *Stanford Social Innovation Review*, 9(1): 36–41.

Kasper, G. and Fulton, K. (2006) *The future of corporate philanthropy: A framework for understanding your options*, Monitor Institute. www.monitorinstitute.com/downloads/TMIFuture_Corporate%20Philanthropy.pdf [Accessed 1 September 1 2011].

Kogut, T. and Ritov, I. (2005) 'The identified victim effect: An identified group or just a single individual?,' *Journal of Behavioral Decision Making*, 18: 157–67.

Kuznetsov, Y. (2006) *Diaspora networks and the international migration of skills: How countries can draw on their talent abroad.* Washington, DC: The World Bank.

Lavie, S. and Swedenburg, T. (1996) 'Introduction.' In S. Lavie and T. Swedenburg (eds.) *Displacement, diaspora, and geographies of identity.* Durham, NC: Duke University Press, 1–25.

Luttmer, E. F. (2001) 'Group loyalty and the taste for redistribution,' *Journal of Political Economy*, 109(3), 500–28.

Marten, R. and Witte, J. M. (2008) 'Transforming development? The role of philanthropic foundations in international development cooperation,' Global Public Policy Research Paper no.10. Berlin: Global Public Policy Institute.

Maxwell, D., Bailey, S., Harvey, P., Walker, P., Sharbatke-Church, C. and Savage, K. (2008) *Preventing corruption in humanitarian assistance.* Transparency International, Berlin. www.humanitarianoutcomes.org/sites/default/files/pdf/Preventingcorruptioninhumanitarianassistance.pdf [Accessed 9 October 2015].

Merz, A. M., Peloza, J. and Chen, Q. (2010) 'Standardization or localization? Executing corporate philanthropy in international firms,' *International Journal of Nonprofit and Voluntary Sector Marketing*, 15(3): 233–52.

Metcalf-Little, H. (2010) 'The privatization of assistance in international development,' *Journal of International Law and Politics*, 42(4): 1091–1111.

Micklewright, J. and Wright, A. (2005) 'Private donations for international development.' In A.B. Atkinson (ed.) *New sources of development finance*. Oxford, England: Oxford University Press, 132–55.

Millennium Development Goal Task Force. (2011) *The global partnership for development: Time to deliver*. London: United Nations. www.un.org/millenniumgoals/2011_Gap_Report/11-38394%20(E)%20MDG%20Gap%20Report%202011_WEB%20NEW.pdf [Accessed 20 September 2012].

Moran, M. (2009) 'New foundations, the new philanthropy and sectoral 'blending' in international development cooperation.' Paper presented at the Australian Political Studies Association Conference, Macquarie University, Sydney, 28–30 September, 2009.

Muller, A. and Whiteman, G. (2009) 'Exploring the geography of corporate philanthropic disaster response: A study of Fortune Global 500 firms,' *Journal of Business Ethics*, 84: 589–603.

Newland, K., Terrazas, A. and Munster, R. (2010) *Diaspora philanthropy: Private giving and public policy*. Washington, DC: USAID, Migration Policy Institute.

Nielsen, T. M. and Riddle, L. A. (2009) 'Investing in peace: The motivational dynamics of diaspora investment in post-conflict economies,' *Journal of Business Ethics*, 89: 435–48.

Okten, C. and Okonkwo-Osili, U. (2007) *Preferences for international redistribution*. Indianapolis, IN: Department of Economics, Indiana University – Purdue University at Indianapolis.

Orozco, M. (2006) 'Diasporas, philanthropy and hometown associations: The Central American experience.' Paper presented for Global Equity Initiative Conference, Harvard University March 22, 2006.

Owens, M. S. (2005) 'Legal framework of international philanthropy: The potential for change *Pace Law Review*, Paper 30. http://digitalcommons.pace.edu/cgi/viewcontent.cgi?article=1170&context=plr [Accessed 9 October 2015].

Paine, R. (2005) 'The tax treatment of international philanthropy and public policy,' *Akron Law Review*, (19): 1–24.

Pearson, E. (2011) 'Haiti's new tax on money sent to relatives sparks outrage in Brooklyn community,' *Daily News*. www.nydailynews.com/new-york/haiti-new-tax-money-relatives-sparks-outrage-brooklyn-community-article-1.156354 [Accessed 9 October 2015].

Petersen, A. C. and McClure, G. (2011) 'Trends in global philanthropy among U.S. foundations: A brief review of data and issues,' *The Foundation Review*, 2(4): 88–100. www.researchgate.net/publication/233693850_Trends_in_Global_Philanthropy_Among_U.S._Foundations_A_Brief_Review_of_Data_and_Issues [Accessed 9 October 2015].

Portes, A., Escobar, C. and Walton-Radford, A. (2007) 'Immigrant transnational organizations and development: a comparative study,' *International Migration Review*, 41(1): 242–81.

Rajan, S. S., Pink, G. H. and Dow, W. H. (2009) 'Sociodemographic and personality characteristics of Canadian donors contributing to international charity,' *Nonprofit and Voluntary Sector Quarterly*, 38(3): 413–40.

Reich, R. (2006) 'Philanthropy and its Uneasy Relation to Equality.' In W. Damon and S. Verducci (eds.) *Taking philanthropy seriously: Beyond noble intentions to responsible giving*. Bloomington, IN: Indiana University Press, 33–49.

Ribar, D. C. and Wilhelm, M. O. (1995). Charitable contributions to international relief and development, *National Tax Journal*, 48(2): 229–44.

Schervish, P. G. (2005). 'Major donors. Major motives: The people and purposes behind major gifts,' *New Directions for Philanthropy and Fundraising*, 47: 59–87.

——. (2008) 'Why the wealthy give: Factors which mobilize philanthropy among high net-worth individuals.' In A. Sargeant and W. Wymer (eds.) *The Routledge companion to nonprofit marketing*. London: Routledge. 173–90.

Schervish, P. G. and Havens, J. J. (1995) 'Do poor people pay more? Is the U-shaped curve correct?,' *Nonprofit and Voluntary Sector Quarterly*, 24(1): 79–90.

Schervish, P. G., Havens, J. J. and O'Herlihy, M. H. (2001) 'Agent-animated wealth and philanthropy: The dynamics of accumulation and allocation among high-tech donors,' Social Welfare Research Institute Boston College. Online. https://dlib.bc.edu/islandora/object/bc-ir:104109/datastream/PDF/view [Accessed 9 October 2015].

Schmid, H. (2011) *Characteristics of the Israeli philanthropy in the 21st century: Motives and barriers for giving and future developments*. Jerusalem: The Hebrew University of Jerusalem, The Center for the Study of Philanthropy in Israel.

Schmid, H. and Rudich-Cohen, A. (2012) 'Elite philanthropy in Israel,' *Society*, 49: 175–181.

Shaw, E., Gordon, J., Harvey, C. and Maclean, M. (2013) 'Exploring contemporary entrepreneurial philanthropy,' *International Small Business Journal*, 31(5): 580–99.

Sheffer, G. (2002) 'A nation and its diaspora: A re-examination of Israeli-Jewish diaspora relations,' *Diaspora: A Journal of Transnational Studies,* 11(3): 1044–2057.

Sidel, M. (2004) 'Diaspora philanthropy for India: A perspective from the United States.' In: P. Geithner, P. Johnson and L. Chen (eds.). *Diaspora philanthropy and equitable development in China and India.* Cambridge, MA: Global Equity Initiative, Harvard University Press, 215–257.

——. (2007) 'Vietnamese-American diaspora philanthropy to Vietnam.' Paper prepared for the The Philanthropic Initiative and The Global Equity Initiative. Boston, MA: www.tpi.org/sites/files/pdf/vietnam_diaspora_philanthropy_final.pdf [Accessed 9 January 2011].

——. (2008) 'A decade of research and practice of diaspora philanthropy in the Asia Pacific region: The state of the field.' University of Iowa Legal Studies Research Paper No. 08-09.

Spero, J. (2010) *The global role of US Foundations.* New York: The Foundation Center.

The Million Dollar List (2010), Indiana University Lilly Family School of Philanthropy, Indianapolis, IN.

Török, M. (2005) 'Gaining trust is a must: Hungarian NGOs and private giving.' In K. E. Koncz (ed.). *NGO sustainability in Central Europe.* Budapest: Open Society Institute, 173–94.

Vahlpahl, T. (2009) '(Still) unknown land? The international dimension of foundation in Europe,' *Trust & Trustees,* 15(5): 289–95. www.transcomm.ox.ac.uk/working%20papers/WPTC-02-02%20Vertovec.pdf [Accessed 10 September 2011].

Vertovec, S. (2003) 'Migrant transnationalism and modes of transformation.' Paper presented at the International Migration Review conference on Conceptual and Methodological Developments in the Study of International Migration, Princeton: Princeton University.

Werbner, P. (2002) 'The place which is diaspora: Citizenship, religion and gender in the making of chaordic transnationalism,' *Journal of Ethnic and Migration Studies,* 28(1): 119–33.

——. (2004) 'Theorizing complex diasporas: Purity and hybridity in the South Asian public sphere in Western Europe,' *Journal of Ethnic and Migration Studies,* 30(5): 895–911.

World Bank. (2013) *Migration and Remittances Factbook,* 2nd edition. Washington, DC: Author.

Yoshioka, T. (2008) *An analysis of million dollar gifts, January 2000 – September 2007.* Center on Philanthropy at Indiana University. https://scholarworks.iupui.edu/bitstream/handle/1805/5651/2008ccsfellowship report.pdf?sequence=1&isAllowed=y [Accessed 9 October 2015].

11

The role of philanthropy in disaster relief

Naim Kapucu

Disasters are times when people tend to act with sympathy for victims and appear more responsive to calls for donations. In particular, major disasters stimulate philanthropic behaviour. However, motivations and behavioural patterns for individuals and organizations vary significantly (Martin *et al.*, 2006). Individuals might approach disasters with empathy, but not necessarily with knowledge of how and what to donate. Corporations, on the other hand, may have quite mixed motives and may or may not have applicable expertise. Some establish deep, long lasting relationships with disaster relief agencies; many others make ad hoc contributions that may end up congesting the system since they are not organized properly (Zhang *et al.*, 2009).

Philanthropic behaviour varies from one disaster to another and not all disasters receive the same amount of attention. For instance, total donations raised in the US for the Haitian earthquake were about $US 900 million, while only $US 25 million were raised for the 2010 Pakistan floods (Neely, 2010; Niazi and Khan, 2011). In response to the 2004 Southeast Asia earthquake and ensuing tsunami, the United Nations raised about $US 2.5 billion from institutional and individual donors, which accounts for almost half of the total money raised for the disaster relief efforts (Thomas and Fritz, 2006: 114). Companies that had developed long-term relationships with relief organizations and other non-governmental organizations (NGOs) participated effectively in a coordinated response. For example, Coca-Cola used its production facilities and supply chain to provide drinking water to disaster victims in the region. On the other hand, many other unsolicited donations coming from individuals and corporations were stuck at airports due to a lack of coordination and previously established relationships (Thomas and Fritz, 2006).

Why do some events attract massive support while others are virtually ignored? How and why is giving during disasters different than normal situational giving? The impact of the media and the nature of disasters are influential to a donor's decisions about how much and when to donate, but there are several other factors that are influential in philanthropic actions. The argument presented in this chapter is that giving and other support for humanitarian aid in the event of major crises can shape patterns of giving in strange ways. This chapter considers individual and organizational responses in contemporary disaster contexts with a view to understanding motivations, challenges and emerging trends. It assesses current research on philanthropy during disasters and highlights some of the broader issues of philanthropy, not only a narrow focus on disaster management.

Motives and management of giving in disasters and humanitarian crises

Philanthropy in response to disasters and humanitarian crises is not a new phenomenon. Having roots in the early stages of charity operations, donations to humanitarian efforts and disaster response emerged out of a need for charitable efforts with assistance, including donations of time, cash, food, clothing and other material items made both domestically and internationally (Curti, 1988; Ribar and Wilhelm, 2002; Singer, 2008; Brewis, 2010). A review of the literature on philanthropy, both in times of disaster relief and in humanitarian efforts, identifies two categories of giving: philanthropy in immediate response to disasters, and philanthropy for humanitarian assistance, aid and development, including the longer term recovery following disasters. The first is a reflection of giving in response to a specific event (O'Neill, 2002; Singer, 2008): 'in emergencies, it involves setting up feeding stations, providing medical facilities, delivering food, building shelters, and protecting the rights of vulnerable populations' (Barnett and Weiss, 2011: 17). The second type covers all aspects of humanitarian development, often complex sets of issues that require long term horizons for their solutions. Charitable giving for humanitarian aid is more strategic and planned than are one-time, often spontaneous donations in response to sudden disasters. Most of the funding for humanitarian assistance is channeled through aid organizations that have agendas for giving and development which are not restrictive to responding to disasters and that operate as a 'global network of organizations' (Smillie and Minear, 2004: 11). With limited space, this chapter focuses on the first type – short and medium term philanthropic responses to sudden disasters.

Motivations for philanthropy in response to disasters

Currently, disasters receive a lot of attention, both from the charitable sector and from individual donors. Christie *et al.* (2007) convey that this may be because a disaster is something that can be remedied with a relatively faster return to normalcy than other situations, such as HIV or long-term drought. Disasters create their own 'cultures and subcultures' in relation to donations (Alexander, 2006: 8), and it is important to understand the motives behind giving behaviours at these times. While much research on propensity to donate concentrates on donor characteristics, it has shown how the situational characteristics of recipients, i.e. country contexts and disaster specificities, matter (Andorfer and Otto, 2013). During such events, people tend to extend themselves outside of their daily norm and reach out to affected communities in many different ways. This behaviour can also account for the unstructured patterns of giving in response to disasters; people responsively give in certain events but also suffer from donor fatigue in times of multiple or concurrent disasters, producing irregular patterns of giving (Alexander, 2006). Donations to a single event can often overshadow the efforts of other significant disaster events leading sometimes to an 'overabundance' of funding in one area, and little to nothing in another. Marjanovic *et al.* (2012) examine whether trait variables, such as empathy and perceived human responsibility, predict and interact to predict people's helping natural disaster victims. Here, judgement of human responsibility predicted helping when participants were familiar with the target disaster, but did not predict helping when the disaster was unfamiliar.

The reasons associated with giving in times of disasters are argued by Douty (1972) to be aspects of cooperative economic behaviour. Individuals who have been impacted by a disaster, and have prepared themselves, will become more charitable as a way of assisting others. Those outside of the disaster zone will feel compassion for those 'less well-off materially' (Douty, 1972: 582) and give until they see some benefit from their efforts. This perspective asserts that following a disaster, individuals feel there is an 'obligation' to help others, specifically those in their circle that would help them. This can be considered a form of 'insurance benefits' shared by individuals of a social clique. Not taking part in these activities can result in the individual being excluded from benefits next time they require help. Like individuals, private firms also feel obligated to help and utilize disasters as an opportunity to create goodwill within the community. In contrast to this notion that anticipation of direct benefits is the most influential motivator of charitable giving, Amos (1972) finds they are the least likely motivator.

Another reason for donating in disasters is the strong personal connections of individuals and familiarity of the situation. Donating within one's community, or as a result of wanting to return what was once familiar back to normal, may also shed light on why some disasters attract more attention and funding. Several studies have focused on the feelings associated with charitable giving in times of disasters, allowing us to compare different responses to different events. Jeong (2010: 327) examines the support provided during the 2010 Haiti earthquake and finds that feelings of sympathy were 'positively associated with support through personal donation'. Focusing on the role that 'controllability' played on a donor's choice to donate in response to this disaster, Jeong (2010) argues that feelings of sympathy and pity were not affected by whether the event could have been controlled in any way, supporting the role strong emotions play in donating. When donors hear about, or are presented with images of, a disaster, they experience powerful feelings of mental discord that leads them to donate in hopes of 'restoring their mental balance' (Waters, 2008). As Alexander (2006: 8) notes, a sense of urgency compels giving, and 'publicity, or the lack of it, can turn donations to a relief appeal on and off like a tap', creating an overabundant supply of aid to the area that is the most visible. Relief organizations tend to present the community affected through graphic images and video, along with fundraising appeals to encourage charitable giving (Waters, 2008). Atkinson et al. (2012), examining 25 years of changing trends in UK individuals' overseas giving to charities, include considerations of the role of globalization in that giving's growth, for example, where direct experiences of global conditions through increased travel, may mean that people are more responsive to disaster appeal requests.

As with other types of philanthropy (Pharoah, Chapter 4; Bekkers, Chapter 7) income, socialization and practice of a faith are significant factors in giving to disasters. Steinberg and Rooney (2005) found that household income was also an important determinant of donations after the September 11th attacks. As for contributing volunteer hours, they found that those who attended church regularly or had previous volunteer experience 'donated significantly more hours' than those who were not churchgoers or lacked previous experience (Steinberg and Rooney, 2005:122).

As examined in the next section, the 'supply chain' is also important – the availability and actions of nonprofits to organize fundraising and conduct relief efforts. In the decade from 1995 to 2005, individual donations to nationally based nonprofit organizations whose focus is on international issues grew faster than any other of cluster of nonprofits, as analyzed by the Congressional Research Service (Newland et al., 2010). Despite the number of nonprofits working internationally, however, individuals who live outside of disaster zones generally donate smaller portions of their overall assets to disaster relief than to other charitable causes (Douty, 1972; Clinton, 2007).

The philanthropy supply chain in disaster relief

The management of relief efforts and philanthropic giving to support them, as well as assistance in longer term recovery and development, is almost never in the hands of a single organization. It can be better understood as a network, or a 'supply chain', of many different types of organizations and governments.

NGOs play a major role. This is due to the large 'capacity' they bring (e.g. Red Cross or the Red Crescent Society), differing specializations, fundraising expertise, coordination capacities (e.g. United Nations agencies) and ability of local nonprofits to work at the community level. The level of public trust placed with NGOs in addressing humanitarian assistance is high: Smillie and Minear (2004) find that more credibility is placed with NGOs than governments, enabling some of them to provide more aid than a government is capable of delivering. Governments as donors play key roles in a disaster environment. Research shows that donor counties provide more aid to those disaster-stricken areas in which special, trade or political interests can be fostered (Raschky and Schwindt, 2012). This type of favouritism allows donor countries to further secure their ties to the country of interest, in turn allocating more aid to one area over another. The problems associated with this type of funding, and with the influence of donor countries, over the process greatly affect humanitarian operations and can limit the scope of work conducted, as well as the speed of fund allocation (Christopher and Tatham, 2011). As a result, many donors prefer to use intermediaries, such as NGOs and international agencies, as their source of funding relief operations.

Media plays a major role in international relief efforts. With most donor funding coming from the more well off countries, the media is the major source for relaying catastrophic images, while the literature on media and disasters is itself widely seen as an emerging and interdisciplinary area of research (Joye, 2014). Some of the media's power, as Aguirre (2001: 157) demonstrates, comes from its role 'in defining a crisis and influencing state and multilateral political powers', though the media must be careful in properly portraying the disaster environment. Internationally, however, this job is not easily accomplished: dangerous political environments and lack of a complete understanding of the situation can mislead donors regarding the severity and logistics of the relief operation (Aguirre, 2001). These misunderstandings can then lead to mistrust as donors, completely unaware of the political environment, assume that their assistance is not properly allocated to victims as a result of mismanagement by charitable organizations. Equally, however, it may be argued that in humanitarian aid organizations, the logistics of disaster relief has long been perceived as 'a back office function' aimed at supporting key 'programmes and frontline activities' (Schulz, 2009: 3). This underestimation of the logistics function is beginning to change, amongst academics, donors and practitioners.

Often in underdeveloped disaster stricken countries, accountability measures are either purposely hindered or no longer working; as a result, the sense of donation effectiveness is lower, creating possible discontent for donors (Rashky and Schwindt, 2012). More straightforwardly, where governments lead or encourage emergency management coordination groups, participating NGOs may well not demonstrate upward accountability. This was identified by Cooper (2015: 2) in her analysis of the National Disaster Management Network in the Caribbean (Harrow, Chapter 31). Competing news cycles also make a difference as Brown and Wong (2009) argue with news coverage of the O.J. Simpson trial and donations for the 1994 Rwandan genocide: as media coverage for the trial increased, donations for Rwanda decreased.

Legislative incentives and assistance

Appropriate public policy and tax incentives help to induce an environment of charitable giving. Such legislative assistance is provided in three ways: through tax credits/deductions for donors; determining which organizations qualify to receive tax credits and deductions; and government forgiveness of debt.

Tax incentives have long been a vehicle to spur philanthropic donations because in many countries, charitable donations to qualified organizations reduce the income taxes paid by individual donors. Donations such as those that assist to 'ease the burden on government provided services' are often looked upon favourably by government and incur tax benefits (Newland et al., 2010: 20). The extent to which individuals benefit depends on the size of their donations and income levels: the larger the donation and the higher the income of the donor, the greater the relative benefit. On the other hand, tax incentives for small donations appear to provide less of a benefit to the donor, and indeed, many donors do not bother claiming them (Phillips and Smith, Chapter 13; Carmichael, Chapter 15), leading to the assumption that tax benefits do not necessarily increase giving that is on a smaller scale. In many disasters, governments will, for a period, match the contributions by individuals and corporations, creating an added incentive for donations of any amount.

Tax incentives for charitable organizations, specifically those providing relief operations, aid in quicker allocation of resources and funding. In the US, for example, federal exemptions allow charitable organizations to use much of their funding for service provision rather than tax payments, though there are service parameters that organizations must fit when taking advantage of the exempt tax status. Generally, assistance must fall into three restricted categories to be eligible: aid to individuals; aid to businesses; and aid to a charitable class, that is, individuals in need (Kennedy et al., 2002). Legislative assistance may take the form of approval of status for additional charities to engage in relief work, as occurred after the September 11th attacks when the Internal Revenue Service (IRS) took measures to quickly speed up the 'process for organizations to apply for exempt status', enabling greater charitable response to the event (Kennedy et al., 2002: 1). In times of disasters, legislative actions can also be overlooked or suspended for a limited time and cause. Again, in the case of the September 11th attacks, Congress implemented a 'special statutory rule' that allowed 'charitable organizations to disburse aid to victims … and their families without the charity making a specific assessment of need' (Kennedy et al., 2002: 94). This enabled nonprofits to provide resources to individuals in a timelier manner with less financial burden and bureaucratic processes to deal with.

The third type of legislative assistance is in the form of government forgiveness of debt. An example of this is the relief-financing conference that took place after the 2004 Indian Ocean tsunami when finance ministers of seven countries 'agreed to support the suspension of debt payments for affected countries' (Butcher, 2005: 206).

The role of nonprofit organizations

The nonprofit sector has a large role in disaster response and humanitarian relief (Kapucu, 2006), with the networks provided by well-established nonprofits assisting in ways that governments are not able to do so. Steuerle (2002: 1) goes further in arguing that the charitable sector is 'more flexible and innovative than the government sector, responding to crises quickly and encountering fewer administrative hurdles'. In particular, nonprofits succeed as a result of the collaborative efforts and partnerships needed in response to disasters. They also play a large role in advocacy, for instance, advocating for the rights of victims and ensuring that special needs are met, and in longer term policy development for reconstruction. These actions enable some NGOs to become very visible in the field of disaster relief, establishing trust not only with the victims and donors but also potential relief partners.

Kapucu (2007: 559) stresses the importance of establishing trust in times of disaster as there are 'no clear policy or guidelines available to the participant organizations and individuals'. Particularly in uncertain times, individual and corporate donors gravitate towards those they trust in fulfilling their philanthropic efforts. Barrow and Jennings (2001: 16) highlight that the reasons individuals are more apt to donate to visible NGOs rather than governments include: 'poor performance of official donor programs in reaching the poor' in the 1960s and 1970s leading to a lack of confidence in governments; nonprofits' popularity and visibility in the education and health fields, giving them legitimacy; their 'effectiveness and flexibility in dealing with emergencies and relief'; and perceptions of corruption by governments in under developed nations. These trust factors may shed light on why some areas or disasters receive more attention than others.

In an environment rich in love and duty for one's neighbour, faith-based organizations have become an inherent partner in humanitarian and disaster relief. Overall, 35 percent of all donations from US tax-deductible funding sources are received by faith-based organizations, whereas nine percent is allocated to human services and eight percent to general public benefit agencies (Newland *et al.*, 2010). In disaster situations, faith-based organizations at the local and national level are taking on more of a role in assistance. Locally, churches are often able to respond quickly to an event prior to national or federal assistance (Bin and Edwards, 2009), due to their close proximity to disaster-inflicted regions, pre-established visibility within a community, 'extensive infrastructure at the grass-roots level', and various hierarchies of coordination and administration' (Wuthnow, 1990: 11). They also create an environment where members of the community may find themselves inclined to participate in philanthropic behaviours because of the social capital they generate and the environment encouraging of participation they provide. Faith-based organizations also partner with other nonprofit and public organizations in delivering services. In a study by Bin and Edwards (2009: 606), social capital gained through church attendance was positively associated with local business philanthropy in disaster stricken areas. It concluded that managers who engaged in the community through religious activities were 'more likely to learn about specific needs and more likely to be approached to provide assistance' than others.

There are limitations, however, because of sensitivity issues surrounding participation of these types of organizations. Faith-based entities must not only consider the situation of their own congregations but be sensitive to that of others receiving and delivering disaster assistance. Looking at the role of Muslim faith-based organizations, De Cordier (2009) makes three suggestions which can be applicable to many religious settings and situations in which services need to be integrated. First, faith-based organizations must consider the role religion plays in the affected communities and the commonality that may or may not occur with other local faith-based organizations. Second, there is a need for formal and informal networks of individuals to implement the resources. Third, consideration of the perceptions that are held by all recipients and understanding the sensitivity surrounding faith-based interactions is needed. Looking past the limitations that may be imposed, faith-based organizations of varying denominations are now seen as a critical aspect of local responses and social capital during disasters, and their members appear to be highly active in philanthropic behaviour.

The role of corporations

The involvement of corporations in humanitarian relief has increased significantly in recent years, and there has been a movement to call on the 'private sector for leadership, solutions and resources' (Berman and Klepper, 1993: 9). There are various reasons, including positive image and staff motivation, that for-profits choose to become involved in disaster and humanitarian relief. The 2004 earthquake in Southeast Asia brought about record donations from the private sector and provided a new opportunity to examine the motives behind such actions (Thomas and Fritz, 2006). In a study regarding corporate philanthropic disaster response in China, Zhang and colleagues (2009) find that privately owned corporations provided more funding than government agencies in response to a 2008 earthquake. Indeed, corporate giving can be looked at as a new addition to charitable giving when compared to past decades. The old norm, as Douty (1972: 588) stated, is that 'firms that do not have a major commercial interest in the survival of the stricken area are not, in general, important post-disaster donors'. In today's climate, this is far from the truth. The interruption of daily business transactions and overall economic impact, as well as a broader definition of their 'best' interests, encourages a wide range of corporations to get involved (Thomas and Fritz, 2006).

Another reason for participation from the corporate sector is the pressure to be socially responsible to both customers and staff (Thomas and Fritz, 2006). These pressures, as well as the need to create goodwill within the community, encourage their participation in humanitarian and disaster relief. Zhang *et al.* (2009: 60) view corporate donations as a type of 'investment in the community and society', building new or stronger connections between the firm and local citizens, with the added advantage that such ties may create a sense of belonging for the staff and the clients served. Thomas and Fritz (2006: 116) observe that company involvement in disaster philanthropy has been 'associated with increased employee satisfaction, recruitment, and reten-tion', and employees are now calling on their companies to participate in humanitarian relief (Berman and Klepper, 1993). This is not restricted by any means to contributions of money. Not often considered so, but a form of assistance nevertheless, able minds are an important type of gift-in-kind during a disaster, which may come from universities or large global companies with access to a wealth of knowledge or business expertise beneficial to recovery operations (Thomas and Fritz, 2006).

The benefits of corporate contributions, however, do not outweigh the hardships such assis-tance can create when the need is not properly considered. During the 2004 earthquake in Southeast Asia, there was no guidance provided to corporations regarding what resources were required for disaster relief. As a result, some donations never made it the intended source (Thomas and Fritz, 2006). The issues affecting delivery of charitable goods from corporations occur mainly due to a lack of pre-coordinated relationships that would enable easier donation processes. Hindrances also include corporate image or previous contracted obligations restrict-ing interactions (Thomas and Fritz, 2006). Because of this dilemma, some humanitarian and disaster agencies are not able to, or do not want to, accept corporate donations. The next section discusses various cases to highlight some new and important aspects of how various actors are involved; how philanthropy in the context of disaster relief is becoming innovative and diverse.

Cases on philanthropy in disaster relief

It is apparent that philanthropy in the event of catastrophic disasters is commonplace, though the scale and form may vary depending on the disaster or donor. Taking a closer look into the events that shaped charitable efforts in the September 11th attacks, the earthquake in Haiti in 2010, the Van earthquake in Turkey 2010, and the 2011 earthquake and subsequent tsunami in Japan, this section highlights common factors and emerging trends of philanthropic efforts in mobilizing the resources needed to respond to, and recover from, these crippling disasters. The cases, albeit from predominantly US-centric perspectives, identify some common themes, notably: the out-pouring of support; the creation of organizations to organize and distribute funds; the role of celebrities in attracting massive donations, and the changing role of social media.

September 11, 2001, terrorist attacks in New York City

The attacks on the World Trade Center devastated American citizens, especially those living in proximity to 'ground zero'. A total of 2,650 lives were reported to be lost with effects to New

York City's economy estimated between $US 63 billion and $US 125 billion (Cuccaro *et al.*, 2002). The philanthropic response to the September 11th terrorist attacks was overwhelming: a total of 1,607 organizations, with 1,196 of those being identified as philanthropic organizations (Kapucu, 2007), were quickly engaged. Within hours after the disaster, donations began pouring in. Nonprofits were confronted with the challenge of how to efficiently disperse these funds. This was particularly apparent for the American Red Cross which, within 12 hours after the attack, had collected more than $1 million (Cuccaro *et al.*, 2002: 13). More than $57 million was raised in the first week following the disaster on just six websites, and total contributions from all donors would rise to between $1.5 and $2 billion (Cuccaro *et al.*, 2002: 12). Searching for a way to assist, the nation was able to mobilize one of the fastest growing charitable responses of all time, leaving researchers asking why people gave in such numbers and amounts.

Steinberg and Rooney (2005) find that the reasons for giving in response to September 11th are consistent with the general reasons for philanthropy, although their study lacks questions that gauge personal feelings associated with the attack. Considering whether demographics played a role in the increased level of giving after the 9/11 attacks, the study discovers no significant relationship, noting that giving of one's time or money in general increased in response to this event. Highlighted in this research is the fact that there is very little previous literature available regarding individual financial donations during disasters.

In order to meet the needs of those affected by this disaster, funding to victims needed to be expedited as quickly as possible. As Kapucu (2007: 553) notes, 'in extreme disasters standard procedures cannot be followed and they require dynamic systems to adapt to unanticipated and rapidly changing conditions'. Partnerships were the solutions to this problem. The most notable is the creation of the September 11 Fund which was formed by the president of the New York Community Trust and executives of the United Way of New York City just hours after the event (Cuccaro *et al.*, 2002). It received a total of $506 million, of which $336 million was used for 'cash assistance and services, recovery efforts at the three attack sites, and support to rebuild communities devastated' and $170 million for counseling, employment assistance, and a variety of related needs (Kapucu, 2007: 556). In an interview, the president of the New York City Trust stated that funding came from 'more than two million individuals as well as "hundreds" of institutional and corporate donors and "foreign corporations and charities"' (Cuccaro, 2002: 113). Addressing not only the immediate needs of survivors, this fund was also successful in creating a long-term recovery plan as a way of securing a healthy future for those affected. A different initiative, the Victims Compensation Fund, was created and funded by the US government for those who lost loved ones in the attacks. Set up as a tort litigation and life insurance substitute (Cuccaro, 2002), this fund was created to protect airlines from the mass litigation lawsuits – and their potential demise that would follow – and to provide efficient compensation to the families of those who lost their lives (Melber, 2003). Individual family members were given the responsibility of self-applying to this fund, in turn foregoing the right to any litigation against the airlines once a financial agreement was reached; each case was assessed on an individual basis, contributing to the fairness of fund allocation. On average, participants received $1 million per loss, with the possibility of larger benefits depending on many factors (Melber, 2003).

While charitable organizations were busy mobilizing efforts to assist victims, celebrities were taking various initiatives in funding relief efforts. Five major tribute concerts were held after the terrorist attacks, raising an estimated $190 million (Oldenburg, 2001). The two most notable were the October 20th Concert for New York City, which contributed about $30 million (Wiederhorn, 2001), and the America: A Tribute to Heroes concert/telethon, which, by featuring 'four dozen of the biggest stars in show business', raised $150 million in just two hours (Oldenburg, 2001).

Two important lessons were learned from the massive outpouring of public support for the victims of 9/11, the first to feature online giving in any significant way. The first was the need for coordination and partnership among nonprofits: the response system broke down but was quickly rebuilt through collective efforts. The second relates to the issue of what nonprofits should do when philanthropic contributions for disaster relief exceed immediate needs while appropriately honouring donor intent. As Katz notes (2003: 331), 'charities engaged in 9/11 relief received more donations than they could pass onto victims without enriching them, as opposed to simply relieving their suffering'. Could the charities use the funds for future needs? This dilemma was experienced most acutely by the American Red Cross, but also by other funds that provided financial support to relatively small sets of victims and first responders.

Earthquake in Haiti in 2010

On January 12, 2010, at 4:53 pm, a magnitude 7.0 earthquake shattered the island of Haiti with an epicenter just ten miles outside of the major city of Port-au-Prince (Fox News, 2010). It is estimated that three million people, approximately one-third of the overall population, were affected by the earthquake (Margesson and Taft-Morales, 2010) with an estimated 220,000 lives lost. A global philanthropic response was quickly mobilized with over $US 3 billion donated privately, topped up by $6 billion in government official aid (Ramachandran and Walz, 2012). The US Congress approved immediate tax deductions for charitable cash contributions for the relief of earthquake victims (Sherlock, 2010). Within three weeks, Americans had donated more than $600 million. At that time, it 'was the largest outpouring of American support to any foreign natural disaster' (Goldstein, 2010). The American corporate community began securing funds totaling $122 million coming from 300 businesses through the Business Civic Leadership Center associated with the US Chamber of Commerce (Banjo and Kalita, 2010). This involvement is interesting since there is not a large opportunity base for American corporations that serve Haiti as customers. Some of the largest donation totals went to faith-based organizations, many of which had a long history of working in Haiti: Catholic Relief Services raised $136 million, World Vision $41 million, and the United Methodist Committee on Relief $14.5 million (Adelman, 2011).

Donations through text messaging became widely popular in response to the Haiti earthquake, illustrated by 6.5 million people using text-to-donate outlets who contributed a total of $50 million through this source alone. Previously, mobile fundraising had raised no more than $1 million for any single event (Rogers, 2010: NP). With an average contribution of $10, it is remarkable that nearly 20 percent of all donations received by the American Red Cross in the first week after the earthquake were made through text messaging (Sherlock, 2010). In total, $275 million was raised through text messaging in that first week, making Haiti the 'tipping point' for spurring future text messaging philanthropy (Rogers, 2010: NP).

Celebrities also played a significant role in securing donations for the citizens of devastated Haiti. The most successful of these efforts was the Hope for Haiti telethon. This was aired globally and collected $66 million (Adelman, 2011). As with many other telethons, celebrities not only performed but answered the phones to accept donations. In addition, celebrities were also drawn to personally donate large sums. Stars, such as Sandra Bullock and Leonardo Dicaprio each gave $1 million (Adelman, 2011), and Haitian-born US-based rapper, and later presidential candidate, Wyclef Jean, raised $9.1 million through his Yele Haiti Foundation (Newland et al., 2010). The National Football League in association with Haitian American players committed to raising $2.5 million for relief efforts (NFL, ND). In addition to entertainment and sports celebrities, a unique partnership was formed at the request of President Barack Obama; former presidents Bill Clinton and George W. Bush united forces to create the Clinton Bush Haiti Fund. With the goal of not only rebuilding Haiti but encouraging a strong and stable economic sector, this nonprofit raised $54.4 million, supporting microfinance, job training and the development of small businesses, until it closed at the end of 2012 (CBF, 2012).

The case of Haiti illustrates the speed and global reach of philanthropic responses to disasters with the entry of mobile fundraising on a massive scale and the participation of celebrities. Five years after the disaster, with NGOs still operating many human services, questions are being raised about transparency and accountability and the long-term impact of the billions donated for relief and reconstruction (Ramachandran and Walz, 2012).

Van earthquake in Turkey in 2011

The October 2011 earthquake in Van, a major province in the eastern part of Turkey (USGS, 2012), has been the stage for various philanthropic actions: from both the domestic and international community and from newly established civil society organizations that played a significant role in delivering assistance to the victims (Heinrich, 2007). The earthquake left 605 people dead and many others injured. In the first few hours after the disasters, individuals organized through social media for disaster relief. Individual actions mostly concentrated on volunteer participation in search and rescue, providing clothing, food donations and housing for earthquake survivors. Within a few hours after the quake, two journalists initiated a movement on Twitter with the hashtag EvimEvindirVan, which literally means 'my home is your home Van', encouraging their followers to offer accommodations for the thousands of people who were displaced by the disaster. More than 17,000 people responded to this call and joined this movement (Letsch and Walker, 2011). The Twitter plea also encouraged corporations to take action, for example, prompting cell phone carriers to provide free calls and text messages to those located in the disaster stricken area.

Additional philanthropic action occurred under the coordination of the government, charity foundations and disaster relief organizations, and conventional media. Local and central governments coordinated aid coming from individuals and channeled them to the disaster areas alongside governmental aid; foundations and disaster relief organizations organized significant philanthropic campaigns for disaster victims. For instance, the Kimse Yok Mu charity (KYM) mobilized its disaster relief teams in more than ten cities. This enabled them to provide 120 truckloads of relief goods to the area and the assistance of more than 500 KYM volunteers. Aid collected from donors was organized and packaged in the organization's logistics centre and distributed to victims in a well-coordinated effort (KYM, 2012a). Through KYM, countries such as Indonesia and Pakistan provided cash donations to victims in Van (KYM, 2011, 2012b). Overall, KYM's aid campaigns exceeded those led by the Turkish government. Several television channels organized special telethons; the first TV channel to host this kind of show, working in cooperation with KYM and having celebrities participate, raised 65M Turkish Liras, approximately $US 35.9 million, in one night (Today's Zaman, 2011a). Other TV channels organized similar telethons, generating in total an equivalent amount (Today's Zaman, 2011b). Major corporations contributed to the campaign with cash contributions and other kinds of donations, such as the building company FiYapi's donation of construction materials for new housing for the victims. Philanthropic actions continued in Van for the recovery stage with the Turkish Philanthropy Fund (TPF) playing a major role in raising funds and grantmaking to nonprofits for reconstruction, rehabilitation and rebuilding phases (TPF, 2012).

Response to the Van earthquake demonstrates the similarity of approaches in engaging philanthropic action, including the involvement of entertainment media and celebrities. What is distinctive about the Van response is that, in a Twitter era, social media is being used not just to channel funding to nonprofit disaster relief organizations, but to mobilize collective action directly (Bernholz, Chapter 28). Still, foundations and organizations are essential to coordinating and managing volunteers on the actual ground.

Japanese earthquake and tsunami in 2011

The damage caused in March 2011 by the Great East Japan Earthquake and Tsunami (GEJET), a 'massive 9.0 underwater earthquake occurred 70 km off the eastern coast of Japan' (Cervone and Manka, 2011) followed by a tsunami and mass fires is the country's most destructive disaster, worse than the 1995 Kobe earthquake. The death toll was almost 16,000 with another 4,000 people missing (Nohara, 2011). Due to lessons learned from past disasters, Japan had taken action to strengthen disaster response; while much of the damage from the Kobe earthquake was a result of vulnerabilities caused by poor infrastructure and development (Tanaka, 2012), this was not the case in 2011. The most heavily damaged areas (Fukushima, Miyagi and Iwate) were affected as a result of their geography, which consists of deep peninsulas and bays allowing for increased water levels and lengthened waves heights (Nohara, 2011).

What is now turning out to be common practice, text messaging encouraged individual giving with the option of $10 or $5 donations via mobile devices made available through companies such as mGive Foundation or Mobile Giving Foundation, both of which are nonprofits charities that manage and assist in mobile fundraising. To further promote mobile donations of cash assistance, over 12 nonprofits, ranging from the Red Cross and Salvation Army to faith-based organizations such as the Convoy of Hope and Save the Children, participated in mobile fundraising. Mobile phone companies, such as Sprint Nextel, Verizon Wireless and AT&T, also assisted by suspending text messaging fees for customers donating for the cause and also provided free communication from the US to Japan for their subscribers (Woyke, 2011). Overall, the Center on Philanthropy at Indiana University reports that $4 million of the $163 million donated by US charities was a direct response from mobile giving, of which the American Red Cross was the largest beneficiary (McQueen, 2011).

A new aspect of social media, the world of virtual gaming, found a niche in disaster philanthropy in Japan. With a platform that is one of the largest social media tools available, Zynga, the company that produces many of Facebook's games, released certain goods or special items that could be purchased within its game and shared on donors' personal profiles as support. These items cost $5 each with proceeds, as well as any commission gained from Facebook (Lieu, 2011), benefiting Direct Relief International (DRI). This not only created a new outlet for donation funding but also increased the visibility of DRI at the same time as it provided moral and financial support to Japanese victims. Shaw and Takeuchi (2012: 116) observe that 'individuals who are not affected by the disaster use social media to get information on the disaster to understand the disaster, donate money or goods, and in some cases offer moral support or informational support', and this seems to be the case when taking advantage of virtual game donations. Overall, contributions via gaming raised about $US 605,000 for humanitarian and relief efforts (Lieu, 2011).

As with other millennial disasters, the Japanese earthquake and subsequent events brought about the involvement of celebrities. Instead of specifically donating large sums of funding, with the exception of Sandra Bullock who donated $1 million to the American Red Cross, most donated portions or all of sales of certain items: Charlie Sheen gave $1 of each tour show tickets sold; Lady Gaga designed and sold support wrist bracelets raising a total of $250,000 in 48 hours; and rapper Snoop Dog designed a t-shirt with proceeds going to benefit Japanese earthquake victims (Green et al., 2011).

One aspect of philanthropy that occurred in response to the Japanese disaster, but not common in the other cases, was funding for research. Given that the earthquake eventually led to meltdowns in nuclear facilities, a unique opportunity, and need, for research was presented. The normal processes to generate grant funding would be far too time-consuming, and decisions to support this cause had to be made quickly due to the nature of the research (Gose, 2011). In response, the Gordon and Betty Moore Foundation provided a $4 million grant, with an approval turnaround time of just 15 days, to examine the levels of radiation in the waters of the Pacific Ocean. This is an interesting aspect of philanthropy. It provides a possible new outlet for donor funding as governments are likely consumed by response operations initially with little attention being paid to possible research (Tanaka, 2012).

In general, the scope and scale of philanthropy in response to the Japanese earthquake has been slightly less when compared to other major disasters. Although this has been approached in the literature, it has not been fully explained. Six days after the GEJET $49 million was raised for its victims. This is a small amount compared to the response for the 2010 earthquake in Haiti that raised $296 million, or the 2004 Southeast Indian Ocean tsunami that raised a reported $250 million in the first week (Oren and Cathy, 2011). Reflecting on the reasons for this, Patrick Rooney highlights donors' perception of need by the stricken area: the fact that Japan may be seen as wealthier as and more self-sufficient than other disaster-inflicted countries may have damped international giving (Oren and Cathy, 2011). Other possibilities are that people understand that the destruction of such a large scale tsunami and nuclear meltdown will require long term funding, leading individuals to become paralyzed by the wait-and-see aspect of response; the resilient nature of the Japanese people may also have led donors to take a step back from funding (Oren and Cathy, 2011).

Conclusion

It is obvious from the literature that there are multiple reasons why individuals give in response to disasters and the need for humanitarian assistance. These reasons include feelings of sympathy, an urge to contribute, and the need to return to normalcy, as well as religious and social values. Another spectrum of large scale philanthropy during times of disaster emanates from corporations is generated on the basis of creating good will within the community, satisfying employee and client wishes and as a way of promoting a positive organizational image. Recognizing need, organizations and individuals are moved to act quickly with cash and in kind donations. Despite longer term relief and reconstruction needs, donations to humanitarian crises tend to diminish on average six months after the initial event, suggesting that philanthropy in response to disasters is distinct from most charitable actions pursued by citizens.

As is the case with other areas of philanthropy research, the current research on disaster philanthropy is sporadic and covers a wide array of topics. As a way to better assess disaster-responsive philanthropy, this chapter identified key fundraising efforts that have utilized modern techniques such as social media and even touched on the new opportunity of donating through virtual gaming sites. Given that the average gamer is 37 years old, with 29 percent over the age of 50 and women representing a significant portion of players (ESA, 2011), gaming may be an important new avenue that is yet to be fully tapped in philanthropy as disaster response. Both domestic and superstar celebrities play very visible roles in this form of philanthropy, although the value of their involvement is debated. While philanthropy can mobilize significant private resources for disaster response, it is no substitute for governments who retain a unique and essential position in disaster responsiveness. Future research on the patterns of individual donations, as well as the role that social media plays in disaster philanthropy may further assist in understanding the motives and effectiveness of giving in times of disasters.

Notes

I would like to thank Rebecca Dodson, Sana Khosa, and Dr. Fatih Demiroz for their assistance in this research. I would also like to acknowledge those who assisted in providing information and additional sources for this article: Dr. Rajib Shaw, Dr. Abdul Akeem Sadiq, Dr. Sitki Corbacioglu and Aya Okada.

References

ABC News. (2001) '60 Million watch America: A tribute to heroes,' 21 September. www.abcnews.go.com/Entertainment/story?id=102309&page=1 [Accessed 26 June 2012].

Adelman, C. (2011) 'Haiti: Testing the limits of government aid and philanthropy,' *Brown Journal of World Affairs*, 17(2): 89–97.

Aguirre, M. (2001) 'The media and the humanitarian spectacle,' in Humanitarian Studies Unit (ed.). *Reflections on humanitarian action: Principles, ethics and contradictions*. Pluto Press: Sterling, VA.

Alexander, D. (2006) 'Globalization of disaster: Trends, problems and dilemmas,' *Journal of International Affairs*, 59(2): 1–22.

Amos, O. (1972) 'Empirical analysis of motives underlying individual contributions to charity,' *Atlantic Economic Journal*, 10(4): 45–52.

Andorfer, V. A. and Otto, G. (2013) 'Do contexts matter for willingness to donate to natural disaster relief? An application of the factorial survey.' *Nonprofit and Voluntary Sector Quarterly*, 42(4), 657–88.

Atkinson, A. B., Backus, P. G., Micklewright, J., Pharoah, C., and Schnepf, S. V. (2012) 'Charitable giving for overseas development: UK trends over a quarter century.' *Journal of the Royal Statistical Society: Series A (Statistics in Society)*, 175(1), 167–190.

Banjo, S and Kalita, M. (2010) 'Once robust charity sector hit with mergers, closings,' *The Wall Street Journal*, February 2. www.wsj.com/articles/SB10001424052748704586504574654404227641232 [Accessed 26 June 2012].

Barnett, M and Weiss, T. (2011) *Humanitarianism contested: Where angels fear to tread*, Routledge, New York, NY.

Barrow, O. and Jennings, M. (eds.) (2001) *The charitable impulse: NGOs and development in East and North-East Africa*. Oxford: James Currey.

Berman, M. and Klepper, A. (1993) *Corporate disaster relief*. Ottawa, ON: The Conference Board.

Bin, O. and Edwards, B. (2009) 'Social capital and business giving to charity following a natural disaster: An empirical assessment,' *Journal of Socio-Economics*, 38(4): 601–7.

Brewis, G. (2010) '"Fill full the mouth of famine": Voluntary action in famine relief in India 1896–1901.' *Modern Asian Studies*, 44(04), 887–918.

Brown, P. and Wong, P. (2009) 'Does the type of news coverage influence donations to disaster relief? Evidence from the 2008 cyclone in Myanmar,' *Social Science Research Network*, www.dx.doi.org/10.2139/ssrn.1489909 [Accessed 30 June 2012].

Butcher, J. (2005) 'Financing the relief effort,' *Lancet*, 365(9455): 206.

Cervone, G and Manca, G. (2011) 'Damage assessment of the 2011 Japanese Tsunami using high-resolution satellite data,' *Cartographica*, 46(3): 200–3.

Christie, T., Asrat, G. A., Jiwani, B., Maddix, T. and Montaner, J. S. G. (2007) 'Exploring disparities between global HIV-AIDS funding and recent tsunami relief efforts: An ethical analysis.' *Developing World Bioethics*, 7(1): 1–7.

Christopher, M. and Tatham, P. (2011) *Humanitarian logistics: Meeting the challenge of preparing for and responding to disasters*. Philadelphia, PA: Kogan Page.

Clinton Bush Foundation (2010) *Clinton Bush Haiti Fund*. www.clintonbushhaitifund.org/programs/ [Accessed 15 May 2015].

Clinton, W. (2007) *Giving: How each of us can change the world*. New York, NY: Alfred A. Knopp.

Cooper, T. (2015) 'Empirical research on inter-organizational relations within a national disaster management network in the Caribbean.' *Public Organization Review*, 15(1), 1–16.

Cuccaro, E., Kinsella, K., Loe, C., Nauffts, M. and Schoff, R. (2002) *September 11 perspectives from the field of philanthropy*. New York, NY: The Foundation Center.

Curti, M. (1988) *American philanthropy abroad*. New Brunswick, NY: Rutgers University Press.

De Cordier, B. (2009) 'Faith-based aid, globalization and the humanitarian frontline: An analysis of western-based Muslim aid organizations,' *Disasters*, 33(4): 608–28.

Douty, C. (1972) Disasters and charity: some aspects of cooperative economic behaviour, *The American Economic Review*, 62(4): 580–590.

Entertainment Software Association. (2011) 'Sales, demographic and usage data: Essential facts about the computer and video game industry.' www.isfe.eu/sites/isfe.eu/files/attachments/esa_ef_2011.pdf [Accessed 30 June 2012].

Fox News. (2010) 'Fast facts: Haiti earthquake,' 13 January. www.foxnews.com/world/2010/01/13/fast-facts-haiti-earthquake/ [Accessed 27 June 2012].

Goldstein, D. (2010) 'Will we abandon Haiti?' *The Daily Beast*, 3 February. www.thedailybeast.com/articles/2010/02/03/where-america-gives-its-money [Accessed 15 June 2012].

Gose, B. (2011) 'A foundation's fast action after Japan's disaster,' *Chronicle of Philanthropy*, 23(15): 12.

Green, M., Greer, C., Hallett, K., Levy, D. S., Nahas, A., Triggs, C. and Leonard, E. (2011) 'Star power,' *People*, 75(15): 28.

Heinrich, F. F. (ed.). (2007) *Civicus: Global survey of the state of civil society*. Bloomfield, CT: Kumarian Press.

Jeong, S. (2010) 'Public support for Haitian earthquake victims: Role of attributions and emotions,' *Public Relations Review*, 36(4): 325–28.

Joye, S. (2014) 'Media and disasters: Demarcating an emerging and interdisciplinary area of research.' *Sociology Compass*, 8(8), 993–1003.

Kapucu, N. (2006) 'Public-nonprofit partnerships for collective action in dynamic contexts,' *Public Administration: An International Quarterly*, 84(1): 205–20.

Kapucu, N. (2007) 'Nonprofit response to catastrophic disasters,' *Disaster Prevention and Management*, 16(4): 551–61.

Katz, R. A. (2003) 'A pig in a python: How the charitable response to September 11 overwhelmed the law of disaster relief,' *Indiana Law Review*, 36(25): 252–333.

Kennedy, M., Capassakis, E. and Wagman, R. (2002) *Guide to charitable giving*. Hoboken, NJ: John Wiley & Sons.

Kimse Yok Mu (KYM) (2011) 'Indonesia didn't forget to show it's loyalty towards Van.' www.hizmetmovement.blogspot.co.uk/2011/11/indonesia-didnt-forget-to-show-its.html [Accessed 26 June 2012].

———. (2012) 'Pakistan Loyalty; 100 thousand dollars donated to Van.' www.hizmetmovement.blogspot.co.uk/2012/02/pakistani-loyalty-100-thousand-dollars.html [Accessed 26 June 26 2012].

Letsch, C. and Walker, P. (2011) 'Turkey earthquake: Twitter plea for help gets 17,000 responses,' *The Guardian*, 24 October. www.guardian.co.uk/world/2011/oct/24/turkey-earthquake-twitter-plea-help?intcmp=239 [Accessed June 26 2012].

Lieu, D. (2011) 'Aid group raises money with online-game tie-in,' *Chronicle Of Philanthropy*, 23(17): 12.

McQueen, M. P. (2011) 'Japan scams spread,' *The Wall Street Journal*, 2 April. www.online.wsj.com/article/SB10001424052748704530204576232534235321802.html?KEYWORDS=Center+on+Philanthropy [Accessed 27 June 2012].

Margesson, R. and Taft-Morales, M. (2010) 'Haiti earthquake: Crisis and response,' *Congressional Research Reports for the People*. www.fas.org/sgp/crs/row/R41023.pdf [Accessed 15 May 2015].

Marjanovic, Z., Struthers, C. W. and Greenglass, E. R. (2012) 'Who helps natural-disaster victims? Assessment of trait and situational predictors,' *Analyses of Social Issues and Public Policy*, 12(1), 245–67.

Martin, S., Forbes, F., Weiss, P., Poole, A. and Karim, S. (2006) *Philanthropic grant-making for disaster management: Trend analysis and recommended improvements*. Washington, DC: Institute for the Study of International Migration, Georgetown University.

Melber, J. (2003) 'An act of discretion: Rebutting Cantor Fitzgerald's critique of the victim compensation fund,' *New York University Law Review*, 78(2): 749–81.

National Football League (NFL) (ND) 'NFL pledges $2.5m to aid Haiti earthquake relief efforts,' *The National Football League*. www.nfl.com/news/story?id=09000d5d815bff52 [Accessed 28 June 2012].

Neely, B. (2010) Why we've given less to Pakistan's flood victims, *National Public Radio*, 2 September, www.npr.org/templates/story/story.php?storyId=129605789 [Accessed March 28 2012].

Newland, K., Terrazaras, A. and Munster, R. (2010) *Diaspora philanthropy: Private giving and public policy*. Washington, DC: Migration Policy Institute.

Niazi, J. and Khan, I. (2011) 'Comparative analysis of emergency response operations: Haiti earthquake in January 2010 and Pakistan's flood in 2010,' Unpublished Thesis, Monterey, California, Naval Postgraduate School.

Nohara, M. (2011) 'Impact of the great east Japan earthquake and tsunami on health, medical care and public health systems in Iwate Prefecture, Japan, 2011,' *Western Pacific Surveillance and Response Journal*, 2(4).

Oldenburg, A. (2001) 'Celebs have helped raise $200M in past 3 months,' *USA Today*, 18 December. www.usatoday.com/life/2001-12-18-charities.htm [Accessed 26 June 2012].

O'Neill, M. (2002) *Nonprofit nation: A new look at the third America*. San Francisco, CA: Jossey-Bass.

Oren, D. and Cathy, G. (2011) 'No donor rush to aid Japan,' *USA Today*, 17 March. www.usatoday30. usatoday.com/printedition/news/20110317/1ajapangiving17_cv.art.htm [Accessed 27 June 2012].

Ramachandran, V. and Walz, J. (2012) *Haiti: Where has all the money gone?* Washington, DC: Center on Global Development.

Raschky, P. A. and Schwindt, M. (2012) 'On the channel and type of aid: The case of international disaster assistance,' *European Journal of Political Economy*, 28(1): 119–31.

Ribar, D. and Wilhelm, M. (2002) 'Altruistic and joy-of-giving motivations in charitable behaviour,' *Journal of Political Economy*, 110(2): 425–57.

Rogers, K. (2010) 'Haiti donations,' *The Nonprofit Times*, 1 April. www.thenonprofittimes.com/article/detail/haiti-donations-2519 [Accessed 26 June 2012].

Schulz, S. F. (2009) *Disaster relief logistics: Benefits of and impediments to cooperation between humanitarian organizations*. Berne: Haupt Verlag AG.

Shaw, R. and Takeuchi, Y. (2012) *East Japan earthquake and tsunami evacuation, communication, education and volunteerism*. Kyoto: Research Publishing, Kyoto University, Japan.

Sherlock, M. F. (2010) 'Charitable contributions for Haiti's earthquake victims,' *Congressional Research Reports for the People*. www.fas.org/sgp/crs/misc/R41036.pdf [Accessed 26 June 2012].

Singer, A. (2008) *Charity in Islamic societies*. Cambridge, UK: Cambridge University Press.

Smillie, I. and Minear, L. (2004) *The charity of nations: Humanitarian action in a calculating world*. Bloomfield, CT: Kumarian Press.

Steinberg, K. and Rooney, P. (2005) 'America gives: a survey of Americans' generosity after September 11,' *Nonprofit and Voluntary Sector Quarterly*, 34(1): 110–35.

Steuerle, E. (2002) 'Managing charitable giving in the wake of disaster,' *Urban Institute*, 12. www.urban.org/url.cfm?ID=310471 [Accessed 26 June 2012].

Tanaka, Y. (2012) 'Disaster policy and education changes over 15 years in Japan,' *Journal of Comparative Policy Analysis: Research and Practice*, 14(3): 245–53.

Thomas, A. and Fritz, L. (2006) 'Disaster Relief, Inc.,' *Harvard Business Review*, (11): 111–22.

Today's Zaman (2011a) 'STV, Kimse Yok Mu raise TL 65 million for quake victims,' 26 October, Online. www.todayszaman.com/newsDetail_getNewsById.action?newsId=261003> [Accessed 26 June 2012].

——. (2011b) 'TV stations raise TL 129 million for earthquake victims,' 27 October. www.todayszaman.com/news-261124-tv-stations-raise-tl-129-million-for-earthquake-victims.html [Accessed 26 June 2012].

Turkish Philanthropy Fund (TFP) (2012) Van Earthquake Relief Fund Update. www.tpfund.org/2012/01/van-earthquake-relief-fund-update-3/ [Accessed 9 October 2015].

United States Geological Survey (2012) 'Magnitude 7.1 - Eastern Turkey.' www.earthquake.usgs.gov/earthquakes/eqinthenews/2011/usb0006bqc/#summary [Accessed 26 June 2012].

Waters, R. (2008) Examining the role of cognitive dissonance in crisis fundraising, *Public Relations Review*, 35: 139–43.

Wiederhorn, J. (2001) 'Concert for New York City raises over $30 million: Money raised for Robin Hood relief fund to aid September 11 victims' families.' www.mtv.com/news/1450484/concert-for-new-york-city-raises-over-30-million/ [Accessed 27 June 2012].

Woyke, E. (2011) 'How to donate money by cell phone to Japan quake victims,' *Forbes.com*, Vol. 19.

Wuthnow, R. (1990) *Faith and philanthropy in America: exploring the role of religion in America's voluntary sector*, Jossey-Bass Inc. Publishers, San Francisco, CA.

Zhang, R., Rezaee, Z. and Zhu, J. (2009) 'Corporate philanthropic disaster response and ownership type: Evidence from Chinese firms' response to the Sichuan earthquake,' *Journal of Business Ethics*, 91: 51–63.

Part IV

The intersections of philanthropy and public policy

Vignette: The intersections of philanthropy and public policy

Muddy waters

Difficulties in the relationship between philanthropy, the private and the public sectors

Diana Leat

The delicate and complex nature of the boundaries between philanthropy and the public and private sectors frequently becomes apparent when the 'normal' order is upset, when a crisis occurs or a disaster happens. Such instances also throw into sharp relief the difficult and different ways in which relationships across these areas are negotiated. This is prominently illustrated in the case of the natural disaster that hit Queensland in late December 2010 and early January 2011. At the time, significant flooding occurred; three-quarters of the state were declared as a disaster zone. Perspectives on, and approaches to, helping the victims did however differ markedly across different stakeholder groups, as is evident from the post-disaster timeline of activities. This vignette demonstrates the extent and intricacies of these differences, drawing on cited media reporting and public documents.

Coming to the rescue

To help those affected by the Queensland flooding, the State Premier, Anna Bligh, quickly set up a disaster relief appeal: The Premier's Flood Relief Appeal. Launched on 29th December 2010, the Appeal was described as a Trust Fund to assist those who suffered loss due to the disaster. It stated that '[a]ll money raised by the fund will be directed to address the greatest need'. To this end, the Queensland government made an initial donation of $11 million; by 19th January 2011, the Appeal had raised over $100 million with substantial donations from businesses, the Commonwealth and several state and foreign governments. A Distribution Committee was announced, chaired by Dr. David Hamill AM, Chairman of the Australian Red Cross Blood Service and a former Queensland state Treasurer. Alongside this Fund, charities were making their own fundraising appeals. These included the Salvation Army and St Vincent de Paul, and in mid-January, supermarket chain Woolworths Australia announced that it would match donations, dollar for dollar, made to the Salvation Army Flood Appeal through Woolworths stores.

195

On January twentieth, three weeks after the creation of the Premier's Appeal, the distribution committee announced the release of the first round of appeal funds. Targeting people 'most affected by this disaster' and 'who will find it hard to recover from the impact of the floods without financial assistance', payments of $2,000 per adult and $1,000 per child were to be made (Media release qld.gov.au twentieth January 2011). Dr. Hamill said that the hope was that first payments on straight forward applications would be made within ten days of receipt of the application.

On the same day as Hamill's announcement, Prime Minister Julia Gillard flagged the possibility of a one-off federal government 'levy' to pay for flood damage in Queensland and other parts of the country. The Leader of the Opposition, Tony Abbott, immediately opposed a levy as an 'unnecessary tax' by a government engaged in 'indulgent spending' (www.theage.com.au/business/pmflags-oneoff-floods-tax-20110120). The possibility of a tax sparked what was to become an increasingly heated debate about responsibility, charity and government. The following comment was fairly typical of one strand. Having pointed out that people chose to buy houses on a flood plain, one member of the public said: 'I am sorry that they have lost everything, however, they should not expect others to pay for it all .... We donate and donate, and pay tax and pay tax …'.

Disagreement and disjointment across and within the sectors

Relations between the insurance industry and the federal government became increasingly fraught. The Insurance Council of Australia had agreed that home owners and businesses would not have automatic flood cover for flood damage in Brisbane and nearby Ipswich; customers in other parts of the state would have cover where damage was a result of storm water rather than flooding, the latter not being automatically covered by most insurers. The Queensland Treasurer warned the companies that they could face a competing government insurance scheme if they failed to insert a standardized flood clause into all policies and if flood cover was not offered to all policy holders. Unsurprisingly, the insurance industry was opposed to any such government scheme.

By the end of January 2011, cracks in the relations between sectors were beginning to widen. For example, on 24th January 2011, the Community Council of Australia (CCA) issued a statement protesting that community organizations could not understand why they were ineligible to receive recovery grants that were available to other organizations, such as small businesses and primary producers (CCA media release 24/1/11).

Then the insurance industry started its own, internal, squabbles. On 25th January the CEO of RACQ, a large 105-year-old mutual with 1.2 million members, announced the launch of a $20 million dollar assistance package for victims of the Queensland floods. The $20 million would be allocated between the Premier's Disaster Relief Appeal ($2 million), a new RACQ charitable foundation to support communities rebuilding across the State and other charitable purposes ($8 million), plus $10 million for 'compassionate financial assistance to those RACQ Insurance house and contents customers who were victims of the floods'. The package was to be funded from RACQ's reserves, and by waiving the payment of a dividend from the insurance company. RACQ's decision was explained as follows: 'RACQ cannot pay claims where there is no insurance cover. Without reinsurance and premiums to cover flood, the company is simply unable to fund the payment of claims where the customer has not taken the option of flood cover. However, RACQ is a proud Queensland citizen and wants to be as compassionate as possible without compromising the ongoing viability of the club and its insurance company for the benefit of all its members'.

The new charitable foundation was not to support individuals. Rather, it was 'to support the recovery of community facilities across the State affected by the flood disaster as well as other charitable purposes'.

On 27th January, three major insurance companies announced that they would consider claims individually, but make payments according to policies. Allianz said that its home policies 'clearly indicate' that river flooding was not covered; '[i]t would be unfair to other policyholders if their premiums were used, or had to be increased, to pay a claim that was not covered under a policy and towards which no premium contribution had been made'. RACQ Insurance CEO Bradley Heath commented that the issue of moral hazard – whether ex gratia payments encourage people not to take special flood insurance – was always a risk (*Courier Mail* 27th January 2011 Special payouts 'unfair to others').

Then on 30th January, the Commonwealth Bank Group announced a $57 million package for flood affected customers. For CommInsure home insurance customers who were not covered under their policy for river flooding, there would be $50 million to provide financial assistance as a gesture of 'compassion'. Of this, $5 million was set aside for community groups.

Opposition to Prime Minister Gillard's proposed levy was now growing. Who should pay it? Who should be exempt? If you had donated or volunteered, should you pay again? If you were a flood victim, should you pay? Then, stories started to emerge 'that people who were previously working hard to raise money for the floods have now decided there is no point, because the Government is going to tax them anyway'. It was claimed that Gillard's flood tax was 'undermining our community … crowding out civil society' (www.menzieshouse.com.au/?p=3705).

Meanwhile the Premier's Appeal continued to raise money – $220 million by 24th February 2011 – but the distribution committee was encountering problems. At this stage, the committee had distributed $12 million to around 5,000 residents. Now it was reported that the committee was being slowed down by ineligible or fraudulent claims – an estimated 10,000 such claims out of a total of 18,000. 'The number of claims would appear to be significantly above the number of properties we know to be affected by the floods or the cyclone' (*Brisbane Times*, 23rd February 2011).

The following day, 25th February, *The Courier Mail* weighed in. Pointing out that the Premier had 'very personally associated herself with the fund-raising efforts' the paper called for equal close personal attention to the distribution of the funds. Hamill, the chair of the distribution committee, was 'well qualified to oversee the proper accounting of large amounts of money' but 'this is far more than an accounting exercise', it is a matter of 'extreme urgency' and they 'simply cannot afford to wait until some extended, but no doubt thorough, bureaucratic process is completed'. The article went on to note that 'only three Queensland public servants are working full time on the appeal'. The job requires 'empathy, compassion and plain-speak', 'not always apparent in the make up of those who become treasurers. Now is not the time for thinking of reasons why money cannot be distributed …'. Of course 'it is complex and due process needs to be followed, but red tape cannot take precedence over common sense and compassion. Unfortunately that appears to be the case' (Bligh needs to act quickly on fund delivery *The Courier Mail* 25/02/2011). David Hammill commented that the volume of applications – 1,000 per day in the last two weeks – was making the job 'challenging'.

That night, Premier Bligh announced that a 'large team' of public servants, said to be over 100, from the Communities Department would now be deployed to help fast track cash payments within 72 hours of claim approval. Dissatisfied with the speed of the distribution, Bligh had asked her department to discuss new arrangements with Centrelink, the Australian Government Department of Human Services' payment and service provider.

On 4th March 2011, *The Australian* newspaper reported that Prime Minister Gillard had agreed to rewrite the terms of the Commonwealth's 30-year-old natural disaster relief and recovery arrangements. The amount of funding given to states after a catastrophe would now be contingent on their insurance arrangements. This was the condition of Senator Xenophon's crucial vote, needed to get the $1.8 billion flood levy passed. Queensland Deputy Premier Paul Lucas said this would come as 'a major kick in the guts to the taxpayers and ratepayers of Queensland, and a major win to overseas insurance companies (www.theaustralian.com.au/news).

By the end of May, the Premier's Appeal was clearly still struggling to distribute the money raised. It was announced that the charity St Vincent de Paul would distribute $10 million from the Premier's Disaster Relief Appeal. Premier Bligh said that the move meant that people who may not meet the eligibility criteria for Appeal funds, or who are waiting on insurance pay outs, can apply to St Vincent de Paul. She continued: 'St Vincent de Paul is an experienced community based organisation with a well-established internal accountability structure and a strong network of over 8,000 trained volunteers across the State. These are the people on the ground in our flood and cyclone affected communities working to help people rebuild their lives' (Queensland Government, Media Statement, Wednesday 25th May 2011).

'St Vincent de Paul will have flexibility regarding the amount allocated per household and its purpose' the Premier said, 'Today's decision recognises that devastation is not uniform. It doesn't follow criteria and it can affect families and individuals in ways that no guidelines, no matter how generous, can always capture' (Queensland Government, Media Statement, Wednesday 25th May 2011).

Reflections

The state government had a clear political imperative to address both the widespread need, and widespread public demand, for action. These appear to be the perfect conditions for taxation. However, for the state government there were already issues about taxation and public spending. Perhaps equally important was that if the state government started to tax it would be treading on insurance industry toes, possibly alienating those who had paid insurance and potentially encouraging more insurance 'free-riding' in the future.

Creation of a 'charitable' fund may have appeared to offer a solution. In other words, the State government used a nonprofit form, i.e. a voluntary donation scheme, as way of: raising revenue/providing services; channeling/corralling good will without taxing; without encroaching on the principle of insurance as in the private market domain, i.e. maintaining flood cover as a matter for the market.

So, one interpretation is that the State government used the mechanisms of third party government to reconcile the need and desire for public services without apparently either increasing revenue raising or state apparatus, and at the same time, maintaining insurance as a private market matter. Arguably, one problem was that the State government did not increase the state apparatus, but still tried to maintain control and identification, whereas third party government involves a degree of letting go and farming out. So, the State government attempted to run a huge and complicated 'benefit' system without increasing apparatus and, initially, without farming out. This appears to have had two consequences: lack of administrative capacity led to crucial delays in distribution which were probably compounded by an assumption that distribution would be conducted according to standards and processes of public sector provision; using public sector rules and processes – standards, fairness, procedure etc. – predictably led to unfavourable comparisons with the 'flexibility' and speed of voluntary sector responses.

Meanwhile, parts of the insurance industry used a nonprofit form – the grantmaking foundation – to reconcile demonstrating compassion and good corporate citizenship and, at the same time, preventing the movement of flood relief from a private to a collective good, i.e. a charitable foundation was used as a way of demonstrating compassion and maintaining individual responsibility to insure, and avoiding likelihood of free riding in the future.

In some respects, the Federal government was the only major player that behaved entirely true to sector. The Federal government did what government does – meets needs/provides collective goods (infrastructure) by taxing (and, in this case, by also maintaining the responsibility of states to insure). The problem was that this collided with the public perception that giving and tax are alternatives not complements.

Further research is required to establish how key players within the nexus of philanthropy and the private and public sectors in especially challenging times perceive what they are doing. On what do they really base their strategies? What are the considerations and assumptions, especially concerning proactivity or reactivity, organizational collaboration, or independence? To what extent are their actions strategic, problematically emergent, or simply a matter of muddling through?

12

The evolving state relationship

Implications of 'big societies' and shrinking states

John Healy and Gemma Donnelly-Cox

The perceived role of the state, the state's responsibility to provide services for its citizens, and the governance of service provision are all undergoing major transformations (Ball, 2008; Chapman *et al.*, 2010; Kendall, 2010; Daly, 2011). Within this context, policy initiatives that expect philanthropy to fill any voids left by the withdrawal of the state need to understand philanthropy and how it has historically related to the state. Yet, in the current development of 'big society, small state' policies being implemented around the globe, philanthropy is allocated a major role with little attention paid to, and understanding of, its underlying nature (Edwards, 2010; Sievers, 2010; Groves and Lowe-Petraske, 2011; Pharoah, 2012).

This chapter examines the various factors that influence how public policy towards philanthropy is shaped. We examine how philanthropy is viewed from different public policy perspectives by exploring the philosophical positions that underpin them. We also discuss some of the main institutional logics prevalent in modern philanthropy, and consider how the state is viewed within the various movements within the field of philanthropy. We argue that the policy of the state towards philanthropy has been, and will continue to be, strongly influenced by prevailing political belief systems within and across countries, and the actions, and reactions, of philanthropists towards the state will be influenced by their belief systems about how best to realize the social changes they seek. This then enables us to put in perspective recent attempts to chart new directions in the relationship between the state and philanthropy, most notably the 'Big Society' concept (Ishkanian and Szreter, 2012), and to gauge the likely reaction of philanthropists and foundations to reductions in public funding of programs as the state retreats in the light of fiscal and sovereign debt crises. We find that 'big society' proposals lack synchronicity with the prevailing beliefs and practices within philanthropy and argue that public policymakers need to better understand how actors within organized philanthropy perceive their roles in relation to the state.

Political economy theories of the relationship between the state and philanthropy

How the private giving of money and the activities of government relate to each other are explained by a range of theories. These are underpinned by differing beliefs and assumptions about the appropriate role of government and private property in society, and have profound implications for how society views philanthropy. Four primary theories of this relationship highlight the different aspects of harmony, interdependence, tension and conflict that exist in this relationship.

Public goods theory

The public goods theory of charitable contributions assumes that those who donate to non-profit activity are dissatisfied with the level of provision of a public good and that they wish to see more of it provided. Becker (1974) uses a model of a donor whose utility is a function of personal consumption and the extent of some charitable activity. These two goods are assumed to be normal goods and the donor/consumer maximizes his or her utility subject to a budget constraint. This theory also depends on Nash conjectures: that everyone takes everyone else's contributions as given when deciding how much to donate. If donor X donates money for a service from a nonprofit, this will reduce substantially the amount that donor Y will subsequently donate (Sugden, 1982). Weisbrod (1975) claims that differences in preferences jointly determine the relative share of services provided by government and the nonprofit sector. The public goods theory predicts that government spending on social programs will crowd out contributions to charitable activity. From a public goods theory perspective, philanthropy is a legitimate expression of societal contribution that may be lost if the state overextends its reach. However, Clotfelter (1985) found no empirical evidence in the US of significant crowding out between charitable giving as a whole and state expenditure on public goods. Looking at the relationship from a different angle, Steinberg (1997) has observed that new studies generally concur with the consensus that donations will replace only a small fraction of governmental cutbacks.

Andreoni (1989, 1990) argues for incorporating the psychic reward from the act of giving itself as a partial explanation as to why people give. It is argued that this captures the fact that an individual's own gift has characteristics that are independent of its properties as a public good. He refers to this as the 'warm-glow' effect of giving and claims that people who donate, in part to see others better off through a public good and in part to make themselves feel better, are 'impurely altruistic'. Andreoni (1990) claims that this model explains why individuals do not necessarily reduce their philanthropy when state spending on social programs increases. The theory assumes that private individuals voluntarily finance public goods through philanthropy and the relationship is primarily a harmonious one in which individuals and the state share, at least in part, a common objective of addressing social goals. An optimum outcome is freely reached where even so-called 'impure altruism' increases the level of public goods provided.

Within this framework, it is assumed that the state provides public goods up to a point that satisfies the preferences of citizens. Private donations then supplement this to provide those public goods that are under provided by the state, as judged by individuals who have the preference and capacity to contribute. Importantly, donor preferences and private wealth play a determining role in the provision of these additional services. The public good is often theorized as a 'market failure' that requires intervention by government. It is assumed that a state is needed to gather tax and provide services to avoid free riding by those who wish to see a certain level of social provision, but who might avoid paying for them without the power of the state to compel them to do so. This is what Frumkin (2006) refers to as 'complementary' donations. The additional public goods that are provided by these philanthropists are often accorded tax relief as recognition that this expenditure is in the public interest and not normal consumption on the part of the donor.

Democratic theory

This perspective emphasizes the role that giving of private wealth has in sustaining democracy. The power of the state needs a counterbalance and a civil space for citizens to organize: this is financed by private giving. It is often reflected in the referencing of the nonprofit sector as the 'independent' sector. In the 1830s, Alexis de Tocqueville famously described privately financed voluntary organizations as central to the American ideal of democracy. Fleishman (2009: 205) makes the case that the 'unfettered freedom' from the market and voters enjoyed by philanthropic foundations empowers 'them to add to the richness and complexity of America's polyarchy'. According to Payton and Moody (2008: 155), 'it is not possible for a democracy to thrive without a healthy philanthropic sector'. Within this theory, the power of private wealth is benign, counterbalancing the power of the state and the power of corporations by funding the voluntary association of citizens. The state is an institution that needs to be kept in check by the actions of private citizens.

Within civil democratic conceptions of this relationship, the appropriate role for the state is to serve the needs of the citizen, while the primary role of philanthropy is to ensure that this relationship is not rebalanced toward the state. The state has a latent power to usurp the supremacy of the citizen in the pecking order, and one role of philanthropy is to ensure a harmonious positive relationship exists.

Realist theory

Within realist theory, society is seen as conflictual with different interest groups vying for influence to achieve desired social outcomes. Wealth influences the policymaking process, and individuals and organizations use their available power to affect their desired outcomes. Private property rights are accorded higher status than political equality rights and, therefore, a realist approach is adopted. Debates over contentious political issues are decided in part by access to capital which influences the ability to shape the political discourse. For charities campaigning for the abolition of the death penalty in the US or civil liberties in the UK, for example, tapping into wealthy donors is crucial. The state adopts various approaches to limit the direct influence of philanthropic activity on the political process by curtailing the advocacy activities of donors and recipients (Troyer and Varley, 2009).

Theoretical underpinnings for this status quo are provided by Hayek (1944) and Friedman and Frieds (1962). They argue that, while private property might impinge upon democracy, private property rights must be accorded higher status. Any attempt to significantly redistribute wealth by the state – no matter how well intentioned – would lead over time to totalitarian governments (Hayek, 1944). That said, a realist theory of the relationship of the state and philanthropy recognizes the imperfection of the status quo. Society is seen as more conflictual than in the participatory democracy approach: philanthropists 'choose sides' on the socially contentious issues of the day and pursue social objectives rather than support the free association of citizenry. For instance, social justice philanthropists seek to address underlying causes of perceived injustice, while conservative philanthropists seek to limit the role of government, promote individual liberties, and advocate for socially conservative causes.

Critical theory

From a critical theory viewpoint, philanthropy is not a selfless gift of private resources for public benefit. Instead, at best, it is an attempt to ameliorate the symptoms of an unequal distribution of resources; at worst, it is an attempt by those wielding the power of private property to socially engineer society in the shape of their own interests and values. Relinquishment of wealth itself may thus be viewed as a declaration of power (Hanson, 2014). According to Bulmer (1999) since at least 1910, the activities of philanthropists and foundations have been subject to harsh criticism as institutions which seek to further the interests of powerful elites or privileged classes. The role for the state is to redistribute wealth and equalize power, and to render philanthropy obsolete by adopting a prominent role in the provision of social goods and the organization of society. Accumulation of private wealth is seen as unjust; any effort to voluntarily redistribute a portion of this wealth for public benefit is seen as a cynical effort to paper over the fundamental class schisms within society. In this view of the relationship, the role of the state is, and should be, paramount: it directs the provision of public services.

From a public policy perspective, these different views highlight that the relationship between the giving of private resources for charitable purposes and the role of the state in facilitating and regulating this activity is complex, dependent on wider understandings of the role of private property and civil society. In the next section, we provide some illustrative examples of these dynamics.

How different political cultures interpret the role of philanthropy

Do differing views and assumptions about the appropriate role of government and private property in society have implications for how philanthropy is construed? Will what the state believes about philanthropy impact its role within society and, specifically, its ability to address social concerns (Smyllie et al., 2011)? Given that, after many decades of increased social spending, there is now an international trend for the state to review welfare provisions, the current fiscal and policy context offers an opportunity to explore the impact of differing societal views of philanthropy. As part of the rolling back of the welfare state, there is a tendency internationally to 'let philanthropy back in'. What it is let back in to do will to some degree reflect the prevailing ideologies and political philosophies that are guiding state thinking at the time (Jennings, 2011; Deas, 2013).

From the 1980s up until quite recent times, social spending by governments as a percentage of gross domestic product (GDP) has increased significantly. According to the Organisation for Economic Co-operation and Development's (OECD) Social Expenditure Database, gross public social expenditure grew on average across the OECD from 16 percent of GDP in 1980 to 19 percent in 2007 (OECD, 2012). Currently, however, social spending as a percentage of GDP has started to trend downwards across many OECD countries in response to fiscal and debt crises. There are intense debates about the appropriate boundaries between private and public funding on social programs (Anheier and Daly, 2008; Ball, 2008; Daly, 2011), and these debates underpin many issues within contemporary public policy discourses (Kavanagh, 1990; Micklethwait and Wooldridge, 2004). The role of the state and its responsibilities to its citizens has again become a central topic of debate (Ishkanian and Szreter, 2012; OECD, 2012). For example, in the final days of the 2012 US presidential election, framed as it was by the damage from an east coast hurricane that required massive levels of public expenditure and publically coordinated disaster response, the different orientations of the two main candidates to the role of 'big government' became a matter of intense debate (Editorial, 2012).

The relationships between the public and private realms have at times been turbulent, with the state seeking to exert control over private giving (Anheier and Toepler, 1999). At such times, political cultures and ideologies have influenced public policy towards philanthropy and institutional logics have influenced the practice of philanthropy. In the US, there have been a number of seminal moments when Congress has questioned the legitimacy of the field of organized philanthropy and investigated philanthropic practice (Karl and Katz, 1999; Smith, 2009). In February 2012, the European Commission published a proposal for a European Foundation Statute (European Commission, 2012). Its development has been strongly supported by the European Foundation Centre in recognition of the increased internationalization of European giving and the need to accord foundations legitimacy (Borms, 2005). In China, more than a decade before the emergence of Big Society in the UK, there was experimentation with a 'big society, small state formula' (Brødsgaard and Strand, 1998; Béja, 2006: 69). How do these positions relate to underlying views and assumptions about the role of philanthropy?

Public goods theory would lead us to expect that when there is big government, philanthropy will be crowded out. The corollary is that if the state rolls back, then philanthropy will increase. It is assumed that philanthropy is complementary to state provision, and there is interdependence between philanthropy and state. These assumptions seem to be central to the big society view of philanthropy that has been articulated in the UK (Jennings, 2011; Norman, 2011), and they underpin the state response to the challenges of funding large scale welfare provision. In the context of the welfare state, albeit with a hiatus during the more conservative years of the 1980s, philanthropy has for generations been understood, within the UK, as a 'niche activity' (Harrow and Jung, 2011: 1048) that is subordinate, supplementary and perhaps sometimes complementary to the state.

In contrast, democratic theory assumes that philanthropy buffers civil society from the market and from voters. One of the roles of philanthropy is to keep the power of the state and market in check. Unsurprisingly, this view of philanthropy as being at the heart of democratic societies fits most easily with the political frame of the US with its emphasis on checks and balances, but is also accepted, albeit to a lesser extent, in the UK. In mainland Europe, the role of philanthropy in the support of civil society historically has not been as prevalent. In Belgium, Germany and the Netherlands, the state funds civil society to deliver services, and in the Mediterranean countries such as Italy, Spain and Greece, direct provision by the state is more common and there are debates about the appropriate level of political control of foundations (Borms, 2005). This was also the main rationale for international foundations providing significant support for civil society organizations in the emerging democracies of Central and Eastern Europe in the 1990s.

Within societies where the assumptions that underpin the realist political perspective predominate, the state does not view influence of philanthropy as benign. Debates over contentious political issues are decided, at least in part, by access to capital which influences the ability to shape the political discourse, and philanthropy enables those who oppose the position of the state to lobby. Thus, a realist philosophical perspective guides states to careful examination of the objects of philanthropy and regulation of its scope and direction.

Finally, we would expect that in societies in which the assumptions that underpin a critical perspective predominate, there would be denial of a role for philanthropy in the public sphere, with philanthropy viewed as usurping the legitimate role of the state. Here, the role of the state would be regarded as paramount in directing public service provision. It is, therefore, interesting to note that the notion of 'small government, big society' appears to have emerged in China in the 1990s as part of a program of planned administrative reform. Brødsgaard and strand (1998) provide a fascinating account of the development of the policy framework and its implications for Chinese civil society. What are the implications of the 'big society, small state' formula for China? Official discourse is speaking of a significant transformation in Chinese society, a shift from the state as the only legitimate provider of the public good (Wang et al., 2011) to a system of 'corporate socialism' under which the provision of social service may be transferrable to charitable providers and NGOs (ChinaToday, 2010). But as of yet, the state is the organ for defining the public good and how it can be served. The emerging regulatory apparatus for supporting philanthropic giving is cumbersome and unwieldy (Sidel, Chapter 16).

Perceptions of the role of the state in different movements of philanthropy

The institutional logics prevalent within philanthropy strongly influence how philanthropists and foundations viewed their own roles. These logics and beliefs have changed significantly as the role of state has expanded. The central argument of this section is that the political understanding of the legitimate relationship between philanthropy and the state – and the worldview of philanthropists about their own roles and competencies – have to be aligned for voluntary collaborations between philanthropy and the state to be successful and sustainable. Four movements within philanthropy have had significant impacts on how philanthropists view the state.

Palliative views

Philanthropy, in its early forms, was strongly influenced by religious and humanitarian ideals. The charitable activity that was financially supported was seen as being morally beneficial to the donor and, in a Christian tradition, as following in the example of Christ who sought to alleviate suffering. This gave rise to a large increase in the number and scale of organizations addressing the immediate needs of the poor in the second half of the nineteenth century in the US (Hall, 2001). The Victorian model of philanthropy in the UK emphasized the duty of the donor. The role of the state was minimal and charities provided palliative support for social problems. While the philanthropy of the Victorian era was 'unimaginative and superficial' in its diagnosis of social problems, it was enlightened in terms of who was accorded sympathy. This had an impact on concepts of citizenship. 'Philanthropists brought drunkards, lunatics, orphans, prostitutes, tramps, and sweeps into the sphere of public concern' (Harrison, 1966: 362). The role of the state had not yet expanded to the provision of social programs, and philanthropy was the primary and legitimate driver of these services, with its main purpose being the temporary alleviation of suffering.

Philanthropy's palliative tradition of treating the symptoms of social problems has continued among those organizations which seek solely to deliver services, and those philanthropists who fund these services and who see advocacy or efforts to change the status quo as inappropriate charitable activities. This type of philanthropy often has a religious or moral motivation. It is therefore related not only to improving the lot of those who benefit from the services provided, but also to fulfilling the moral responsibilities of the donor. Assuming that the beneficiaries of the services are considered 'deserving' by society, this type of philanthropy could be considered an act of providing a public good and thus a substitute for government provision. On this basis, it would be claimed to benefit from a facilitative fiscal and legal environment designed to encourage such philanthropy.

Scientific approaches

The rise of modernity in social thinking introduced a significant new strand into philanthropic thought. Many of the 'new' philanthropists, like Carnegie and Rockefeller, had benefitted from the rationalist, business methods and the industrialization of society had been enabled by scientific progress (Karl and Katz, 1999). They were actively hostile to concepts of palliative philanthropy or traditional charity which they perceived as doing more harm than good. According to Carnegie (1889: 4),

> one of the serious obstacles to the improvement of our race is indiscriminate charity. It were better for mankind that the millions of the rich were thrown into the sea than so spent as to encourage the slothful, the drunken, the unworthy. Of every thousand dollars spent in so-called charity to-day, it is probable that nine hundred and fifty dollars is unwisely spent—so spent, indeed, as to produce the very evils which it hopes to mitigate or cure'.

For philanthropists such as Rockefeller and Carnegie their philanthropy was motivated in part by a desire to improve society, using the same concepts of scientific progress as they saw driving their business success, and they felt strongly that their resources should be targeted at underlying or root causes (Karl and Katz, 1999). Over time, they established foundations with paid staff and assembled boards whose members were seen as enlightened and esteemed members of the community. They initially focused heavily on universities and medical research. Increasingly, with the rise of Keynesianism in macroeconomics and the role of political science informing international affairs, the role of philanthropy moved into supporting initiatives designed at informing the practices of government (Smith, 2009; Jung and Harrow, 2016). With the rise of the New Deal in the US, and the welfare state in Europe, the role of organized philanthropy shifted increasingly towards informing the social sphere.

The most recent incarnation of this strand of 'scientific' thinking within philanthropy has been the application of techniques from management science into formally organized philanthropy. There has also been a rise of business thinking and strategic planning within the public sector that has facilitated collaborations on specific areas of common interest. The role of philanthropy within this partnership with the state is often more focused on the research and development aspects or the early stage design and launching phases. This shared 'instrumental' approach, to use Frumkin's (2005: 22) phrase, to achieving social objectives has facilitated programs of collaboration between the state and philanthropy on common areas of interest; examples include the White House Office on Social Innovation and collaboration between the Bill and Melinda Gates Foundation and overseas aid provision by governments with the partnerships being specified in terms of deliverables. Within this approach to philanthropy has been a desire to better the practice of the provision of social programs, rather than to replace government in the delivery of these social programs. Rather than these initiatives seeing each other's spending as substitutes, the programs are designed as collaborations that speak to the funding competencies of both states and philanthropy. The value added of philanthropy is to invest in innovative approaches through technical development, research, capacity building, demonstration projects and evaluation.

Social values

Influencing public discourse and intentionally affecting what is considered legitimate is one of the most profound ways to shape the activities of the state and social objectives it pursues. While the social context of all philanthropy and the values of the donor have a significant impact on the causes that are supported, starting in the late 1960s, more explicit efforts were made by organized philanthropy to influence the role of the state in society. Up to that point, large foundations such as Ford and Rockefeller had predominantly focused on informing social progress and did not perceive themselves as ideological; rather, they saw themselves as part of neutral movement attempting to advance the welfare of society (Smith, 2009). Conservative foundations in the US, such as the John M. Olin Foundation and the Lynde and Harry Bradley Foundation, began to finance a conservative countermovement to push back against what was perceived as the bankrolling of social sciences in ways that facilitated an expanded role for the state in public life (Micklethwait and Wooldridge, 2004; Smith, 2009). Institutions, such as the American Enterprise Institute, the Heritage Foundation, and the Cato Institute, all provided the intellectual underpinnings for making the case that the state's involvement in aspects of American life is illegitimate, and they also influenced thinking in countries like the UK. With different outcomes in mind, social justice foundations have funded public interest litigation and advocacy within the legal limits to achieve improved social provision by government, especially for minorities and underprivileged groups (Smith, 2009). Both sides of these debates are accommodated within a realist understanding of the limits of the state and the imperfections of democracy. The organizations on each side go beyond simply presenting their analyses, and advocate for a particular point of view underpinned by an explicit values set. The state regulates the debate by putting limits on what role foundations can play in terms of lobbying, but leaves significant scope for private wealth to influence public opinion and policy (Troyer and Varley, 2009). Underpinning much of the ideological advocacy that organized philanthropy has funded, have been differing views of the legitimate role of the state in society, whether held by the individual philanthropists or by foundation staff directing the funding.

Donor engagement

Within the movement of venture philanthropy, there is a high premium placed on individual ingenuity and private sector approaches to address social problems. Bureaucracies, such as large nonprofits or governments, need to be held to account for delivering on specified performance targets. There is often a latent hostility to the concept of separate public, private and nonprofit sectors per se, and a core belief is that an enhanced role for the private sector can make organizational life generally operate more dynamically and efficiently. One of the defining features of 'venture' philanthropy is to help nonprofits build more effective organizations, requiring that specific targets be set for them and be monitored carefully by the funder. While there is sometimes a desire to innovate and influence government funded services, often the state bureaucracy is regarded as inefficient and part of an outmoded way of delivering services. Although venture philanthropy is often presented as a new distinct movement, it actually draws on the logics of earlier philanthropists such as Carnegie and Rockefeller who exhorted philanthropists to get personally involved in their philanthropy and to deploy their business skills. What is different about the venture philanthropy movement is the degree of personal involvement of the donors, including sometimes taking positions on grantees boards, and the extent to which they seek to grow service delivery by nonprofits as opposed to influencing existing large government bureaucracies.

Although a minority of foundations actively subscribe to the venture model, there has been a marked increase in the general level of engagement by donors and foundations with the organizations they support so that the impact of the venture movement has been felt outside of the network of donors and foundations that are its converts and proponents. Foundations, such as the Bill and Melinda Gates Foundation and the Packard Foundation, describe themselves as highly engaged, and many of the large international foundations have been influenced by a desire for more specific results, both in terms of programs and grantee organizational development. From a public policy perspective, the greater the degree of specificity associated with donor objectives and the greater the level of agency of those involved in philanthropy, the less scope there is to incentivize those givers to move into areas where they are not currently active.

In sum, the institutional logics that have guided the various movements within philanthropy have generated different kinds of debates about philanthropy's relationship with the state. With the institutionalization of the scientific approach to philanthropy and more recently the popularity of a high-engagement model, it is unlikely that these funders would be interested in substituting for public funding if the state withdraws from areas of public provision of services. These funders are more likely to be interested in a complementary relationship with the state, focusing instead on innovation rather than replacing service provision so as to palliatively alleviate suffering of those in need. The more active engagement by donors, and the rise of the 'Giving While Living' movement, means that the values and preferences of the donors will be increasingly to the fore in terms of the design and implementation of programs. For public policymakers interested in collaborating with philanthropy there are increased incentives and opportunities to collaborate with philanthropists. It would be unwise, though, to assume that philanthropists see their role as the palliative provision of public goods. Rather, philanthropy as a field of practice increasingly perceives its legitimate role as increasing efficiency in public and charitable provision through a competency in developing and testing innovative ways to address social problems.

Conclusion

In assessing the evolving state-philanthropy relationship, we have positioned the current concern with 'big societies' and shrinking states as the latest – but unlikely to be last – phase in this interplay. Current trends in philanthropy can reduce the relevance of the state to philanthropy and can mould philanthropic vehicles that do not act as replacements for state social investment. While philanthropy can be complementary to state spending on social programs, it does not serve well as a substitute. In the context of the changing, shrinking role of the state, it does not follow that citizen philanthropists will step into the financial gap to support the services that the state wants them to support. Thus, a central assumption of the 'big societies' thesis is not well supported by philanthropic theory or practice.

Nonetheless, we conclude that the evolving relationship is one that raises several important issues regarding the role of philanthropy in public policy, the responsibilities of the state to its citizens and the ways in which these can be fulfilled, and the myriad of expectations that are held for philanthropy. We conclude by raising these as a series of questions, and we position a number of relationship options that might emerge.

From a public policy view, what is the role of philanthropy? Views within society on the legitimacy of philanthropy range from seeing it as a legitimate agent for providing social goods to one that needs to be heavily regulated to achieve public policy ends. These views change over time. As states seek to harness the resources of private givers, their arguments increasingly draw on prevailing norms. Thus, in China we see an articulation of philanthropy as an appropriate element of a developing market economy, albeit within a tightly proscribed state framework. In England, the articulation of a 'big society' response to a rolled back state is presented as calling for a new philanthropic response that resonates with core philanthropic values. Here, however, and reflecting Cunningham's argument (Chapter 2), colourful critiques question whether there really is anything new in the 'new philanthropy' (Breeze et al., 2011). Elizabeth Macadam's (1934) prior characterization during the 1930s in the UK of 'the new philanthropy' as the partnership between public and private resources, with its 'combining' of government and voluntary action, suggests not. Again, questions remain concerning whether the 'big society' is anything more than 'a post-modern version of Victorian do-gooding – charity and philanthropy dressed up in "crowd-sourced" clothing' (Talbot, 2011: 11).

Public policy perspectives on the role of philanthropy thus both set the agenda for the relationship and are contested by stakeholders. What are the implications in the context of shrinking states seeking big societies? So far, we cannot point to consistent evidence that a shrinking state leads to growing philanthropy, no more so than others have been able to demonstrate that increased social spending by the state crowds out philanthropy. As Steinberg (1997) commented more than a decade ago, it is quite likely that philanthropy would cover only a small percentage of government cutbacks. Public policy needs to accommodate the possibility that there could be an outcome of a small state *and* a small philanthropic sector.

To what extent do public policy expectations of philanthropy match up with philanthropy's own expectations? We conclude that in terms of organized philanthropy, it is increasingly looking to solve specific problems identified through its own analysis. The scientific approach to philanthropy has increased in influence so that strategic planning is commonplace; as can be seen throughout this *Companion*, it ranges from major foundations to small giving circles. Although we can identify examples of partnership between philanthropy and public policy and illustrate cases of mutual influence, we cannot present a picture of an accord between public policy's expectation of philanthropy and philanthropic agency (Thümler, 2011; Almog-Bar and Zychlinski, 2012; Jung *et al.* 2014). In terms of philanthropy's expectations of how its agency will relate to state policy, two distinct views are evident. On one hand, organized philanthropy seeks to influence the state so that when the interventions it funds prove to be of value, they will be presented for 'mainstreaming' by the state. In this regard, philanthropy sees its role as supporting social invention, but does not conceive for itself a long term role in the ongoing funding of the resulting social innovation. It does not see itself as a substitute for public provision of social service. On the other hand, philanthropy sees itself as an independent and long term agent in identifying and supporting the provision of social goods, but again does not see itself as a substitute for public provision of them.

When we consider the internationalization of philanthropy, moving away from the context of a specific state or group of states, we find that the philanthropist is out of the sphere of the state and away from localism arguments. From the internationalist perspective, the concept of the accountability of philanthropy to a local community, in which it is substituting for state provision or answering to states at all, does not arise.

We therefore conclude that public policy expectations of philanthropy do not concur with philanthropy's expectations of itself. One implication of a policy emphasis on 'big societies' in co-evolution with the shrinking state may be increasing gaps in social provision with a growing chasm between the state and philanthropic provision.

There is of course a middle ground and actors who will populate that space. For example, recent research in China points to the legitimacy that accrues to corporations that give to accepted causes, as measured in terms of stock market performance (Su and He, 2010; Wang *et al.*, 2011). Indeed, in the UK, Breeze (2011) has noted that public regard, and reward, for philanthropic engagement has a long history. Other commentators have noted that if the state really wishes to inculcate philanthropic giving, it must incentivize donors rather than 'hector' them to give (Pharoah, 2010). Currently, it is fair to conclude that while the state may see philanthropy as being the domain of what it can't, won't or shouldn't do (Karl and Katz, 1999), this view is not generally held by philanthropy.

What are the state's obligations to its citizens and what role, if any, does philanthropy play in this? This may now seem to be *the* obvious question. Within a democratic society, the framework within which philanthropy will play a role is developed around the relationship between the state and its citizens. Philanthropy may support the provision of services to citizens, and it may seek to influence the state's decision-making processes for determining how services are provided.

It may advocate in order to influence the discourse on what the role of the state is. None of these roles, however, match what appears to be an implicit assumption within the 'big society' framework: that philanthropy can somehow meet those needs of citizens that are understood as needs that the state is obligated to address. In the current phase of negotiation of the state-philanthropic relationship, it would appear that its development would be well served by an articulation of the distinction between democracy and private property, and the development of democratic governance mechanisms to assure that solutions acceptable to citizens may be developed (2010). Otherwise, 'big societies' may find themselves in scenarios where the controllers of wealth value animal rights and the majority of the citizens value healthcare and education for their children – and the mechanisms for creating real public value are absent.

Sievers (2010) has argued that a fundamental task for philanthropy is to evaluate the democratic process, examining whether it provides a framework within which philanthropy can effectively negotiate its own role. Big societies require clarity on the roles and responsibilities of the state to its citizens, frameworks for delivering public goods (from wherever they are created), and mechanisms for assessing public value creation. Whatever the assumptions about big societies facilitating shrinking states, philanthropy's role is dependent upon a functioning democratic process. Policy issues that require consideration may include regulation (Breen, Chapter 14), fiscal incentives (Carmichael, Chapter 15), and the role of public policy in promoting philanthropy and affecting what is deemed civic behaviour (Cotterill et al., 2012).

We have structured our discussion of 'big societies' and shrinking states within the framework of theories of state orientations to philanthropy and philanthropic perspectives on the state, and in these discussions we have indicated that there is a spectrum of possible positions on state-philanthropy relations. Views on roles of philanthropy and the state, and the boundaries between them, reflect positioning within these spectrums. We have observed that the current concern with big societies marks just one stage in the development of philanthropic-state relations. For now, it would appear that within the biggest 'big society', the role of the state, remains paramount.

Notes

We wish to acknowledge, with thanks, Ida Lunde Jørgensen, Department of Business and Politics, Copenhagen Business School, for her comments on an early draft of this chapter.

References

Almog-Bar, M. and Zychlinski, E. (2012) 'A facade of collaboration. Relationships between philanthropic foundations and the government in social policymaking in Israel,' *Public Management Review*, 14, 6, pp.795–814.

Andreoni, J. (1989) 'Giving with impure altruism: Applications to charity and Ricardian equivalence,' *Journal of Political Economy*, 97(6): 1447–58.

Andreoni, J. (1990) 'Impure altruism and donations to public goods: A theory of warm-glow giving,' *The Economic Journal*, 100(401): 464–77.

Anheier, H. K. and Toepler, S. (1999) *Private funds, public purpose: Philanthropic foundations in international perspective*. New York, NY: Kluwer Academic/Plenum Publishers.

Anheier, H. K. and Daly Y. S. (2008) *The politics of foundations: A comparative analysis*. Abingdon, OX: Taylor and Francis.

Ball, S. J. (2008) 'New philanthropy, new networks and new governance in education,' *Political Studies*, 56(4): 747–65.

Becker, G. S. (1974) 'A theory of social interactions,' *Journal of Political Economy*, 82(6): 1063–93.

Béja, J.-P. (2006) 'The changing aspects of civil society in China,' *Social Research*, 73(1): 53–74.

Borms, L. T. (2005) *Foundations: Creating impact in a globalised world*. Chichester: John Wiley & Sons.

Breeze, B. (2011) 'Is there a "new philanthropy"?,' In C. Rochester, G. Campbell Gosling, A. Penn and M. Zimmeck (eds.). *Understanding the roots of voluntary action: Historical perspectives on current social policy*. Brighton: Sussex Academic Press.

Breeze, B., Gouwenberg, B., Schuyt, T. and Wilkinson, I. (2011) 'What role for public policy in promoting philanthropy?,' *Public Management Review*, 13(8): 1179–1195.

Brødsgaard, K. E. and Strand, D. (1998) *Reconstructing twentieth century China: State control, civil society, and national identity*. Oxford: Oxford University Press.

Bulmer, M. (1999) 'The history of foundations in the United Kingdom and the United States: Philanthropic foundations in industrial society.' In H. K. Anheier and S. Toepler (eds.). *Private funds and public purpose: Philanthropic foundations in international perspective*. New York: Kluwer Academic/Plenum Publishers.

Carnegie, A. (1889) 'The gospel of wealth,' *The North American Review*, 148(June): 653–64.

Chapman, T., Brown, J., Ford, C. and Baxter, B. (2010) 'Trouble with champions: Local public sector-third sector partnerships and the future prospects for collaborative governance in the UK,' *Policy Studies*, 31(6): 613–30.

China Today. (2010) 'Adventures in 'Big Charity,' *China Today*, 59: 68–70.

Clotfelter, C. T. (1985) *Federal tax policy and charitable giving*. Chicago: University of Chicago Press.

Cotterill, S., Moseley, A., and Richardson, L. (2012) 'Can nudging create the Big Society? Experiments in civic behaviour and implications for the voluntary and public sectors,' *Voluntary Sector Review*, 3(2), 265–74.

Daly, S. (2011) 'Philanthropy, the Big Society and emerging philanthropic relationships in the UK,' *Public Management Review*, 13(8): 1077–1094.

Deas, I. (2013) 'Towards post-political consensus in urban policy? Localism and the emerging agenda for regeneration under the Cameron government,' *Planning Practice and Research*, 28(1): 65–82.

Editorial. (2012) 'A big storm requires big government.' *New York Times*, 30 October: A26.

Edwards, M. (2010) *Small change: Why business won't save the world*. San Francisco: Berrett-Koehler Publishers.

European Commission. (2012) *Proposal for a council regulation on the statute for a European foundation*. Brussels: European Commission. www.ec.europa.eu/internal_market/company/docs/eufoundation/proposal_en.pdf [Accessed 15 February 2015].

Fleishman, J. L. (2009) *The foundation: A great American secret, how private wealth is changing the world*. New York, NY: Public Affairs.

Friedman, M. and Friedman, R. D. (1962) *Capitalism and freedom*. Chicago, IL: University of Chicago Press.

Frumkin, P. (2005) *On being nonprofit: A conceptual and policy primer*. Cambridge, MA: Harvard University Press.

——. (2006) *Strategic giving: The art and science of philanthropy*. Chicago: University of Chicago Press.

Groves, C. and Lowe-Petraske, A. (2011) 'Giving to the full,' *Lawyer*, 25: 38–38.

Hall, P. D. (2001) *Inventing the nonprofit sector and other essays on philanthropy, voluntarism, and nonprofit organizations*. Baltimore, MD: Johns Hopkins University Press.

Hanson, J. H. (2014) 'The anthropology of giving: Toward a cultural logic of charity,' *Journal of Cultural Economy*, published online 23 September.

Harrison, B. (1966) 'Philanthropy and the Victorians,' *Victorian Studies*, 9(4): 353–74.

Harrow, J. and Jung, T. (2011) 'Philanthropy is dead; Long live philanthropy?,' *Public Management Review*, 13(8): 1047–56.

Hayek, F. A. V. (1944) *The road to serfdom*. London: George Routledge and Sons Ltd.

Ishkanian, A. and Szreter, S. (2012) *The Big Society debate: A new agenga for social welfare?* Cheltenham: Edward Elgar Publishing.

Jennings, J. (2011) 'Tocqueville and the Big Society,' *The Political Quarterly*, 82(Supplement): 68–81.

Jung, T. and Harrow, J. (2016) 'Philanthropy: Knowledge, practice and blind hope.' in K. Orr, R. Bain, B. Hacking, S. Nutley and S. Russell (eds.), *Knowledge and practice in business and organisations*, Routledge: London.

Jung, T., Kaufmann, J. and Harrow J. (2014) 'When funders do direct advocacy: An exploration of the United Kingdom's Corston Independent Funders' Coalition,' *Nonprofit and Voluntary Sector Quarterly*, 43, 36, pp.36–56.

Karl, B. D. and Katz, S. N. (1999) 'American private philanthropic foundation and the public sphere 1890-1930.' In E. C. Lagemann (ed.) *Foundations: New scholarship, new possibilities*. Bloomington and Indianapolis, IN: Indiana University Press.

Kavanagh, D. (1990) *Thatcherism and British politics: The end of consensus?* Oxford: Oxford University Press.

Kendall, J. (2010) 'Bringing ideology back in: The erosion of political innocence in English third sector policy,' *Journal of Political Ideologies*, 15(3): 241–58.

Macadam, E. (1934) *The New Philanthropy: A study of the relations between the statutory and voluntary social services*. London: George Allen and Unwin.

Micklethwait, J. and Wooldridge, A. (2004) *The right nation: Conservative power in America*. New York: Penguin Press.

Norman, J. (2011) 'The intellectual origins of the 'Big Society',' *Total Politics*, 18 February. www.totalpolitics. com/articles/45293/the-intellectual-origins-of-the-and39big-societyand39.thtml [Accessed 10 May 2015].

OECD. (2012) *Social Expenditure Database*. Paris: OECD. www.oecd.org/social/expenditure.htm [Accessed 28 January 2012].

Payton, R. L. and Moody, M. P. (2008) *Understanding philanthropy: Its meaning and mission*. Bloomington, IN: Indiana University Press.

Pharoah, C. (2010) 'Hectoring the wealthy won't inspire a culture of philanthropy,' *Third Sector*, 3 August. www.thirdsector.co.uk/cathy-pharoah-hectoring-wealthy-wont-inspire-culture-philanthropy/ fundraising/article/1019832 [Accessed 29 January 2012].

——. (2012) 'Funding and the Big Society.' In A. Ishkanian and S. Szreter (eds.). *The Big Society debate: A new agenda for social welfare?* Cheltenham: Edward Elgar Publishing.

Sievers, B. R. (2010) 'Philanthropy's role in liberal democracy,' *The Journal of Speculative Philosophy*, 24(4): 380–98.

Smith, J. A. (2009) 'Private foundations and public policymaking: A historical perspective.' In J. M. Ferris (ed.). *Foundations and public policy: Leveraging philanthropic dollars, knowledge, and networks for greater impact*. New York, NY: The Foundation Centre.

Smyllie, S., Scaife, W. and McDonald, K. (2011) 'That's what governments do,' *Public Management Review*, 13(8): 1139–1154.

Steinberg, R. (1997) 'Overall evaluation of economic theories,' *Voluntas*, 8(2): 179–204.

Su, J. and He, J. (2010) 'Does giving lead to getting? Evidence from Chinese private enterprises,' *Journal of Business Ethics*, 93(1): 73–90.

Sugden, R. (1982) 'On the economics of philanthropy,' *The Economic Journal*, 92(June): 341–50.

Talbot, C. (2011) 'One year on: The five states we're in,' *Public Finance*, 20 April, 10–11. www.publicfinance. co.uk/2011/04/one-year-on-the-five-states-we-are-in-by-colin-talbot [Accessed 10 May 2015].

Thümler, E. (2011) 'Foundations, schools and the state: School improvement partnerships in Germany and the United States as legitimacy-generating arrangements,' *Public Management Review*, 13(8): 1095–1116.

Troyer, T. A. and Varley, D. (2009) 'Private foundations and public policymaking: Latitude under federal Law.' In J. M. Ferris (ed.). *Foundations and public policy: Leveraging philanthropic dollars, knowledge, and networks for greater impact*. New York, NY: The Foundation Center.

Wang, L., Graddy, E. and Morgan, D. (2011) 'The development of community-based foundations in East Asia,' *Public Management Review*, 13(8): 1155–78.

Weisbrod, B. A. (1975) 'Toward a theory of the voluntary sector in a three sector economy.' In E. S. Phelps (ed.). *Altruism, Morality and Economic Theory*. New York: Russell Sage Foundation.

13

Public policy for philanthropy

Catching the wave or creating a backwater?

Susan D. Phillips and Steven Rathgeb Smith

Philanthropy and the third sector are both undergoing significant changes, although seemingly taking different, perhaps contradictory directions. While the third sector continues to grow and diversify in terms of missions and revenues, philanthropy is becoming more concentrated with a smaller number of donors providing a larger proportion of giving and volunteering (CAF, 2012: 4). Many foundations and major donors, propelled by the movement to achieve greater impact, are concentrating their support on fewer causes and organizations, and in seeking financial, as well as social returns are turning to 'social investment' rather than traditional giving (Martin, 2011; Salamon 2014; Thümler, Chapter 23). Under pressures of austerity and philosophies of smaller states, governments are looking to private resources as substitutes for public spending (Milbourne 2014), yet the distribution of philanthropy remains highly skewed and poorly aligned with public policy goals. Philanthropy is increasingly transborder – whether through the massive international granting of Gates and other mega foundations, or the micro acts of purchasing goats on Kiva for impoverished families in developing countries. Yet, most third sector organizations remain localized, and many governments are reluctant to facilitate more transborder giving outside of humanitarian aid (Sidel, Chapter 16).

Is public policy 'catching the wave' – responsive and adaptive to evolving pressures facing philanthropy and the third sector – to produce an enabling, accountable environment for both to thrive? Or, does policy for philanthropy increasingly resemble a backwater, either as policy drift because governments fail to update their approaches to reflect changing circumstances, or as active resistance to emerging trends? This chapter assesses the direction of public policy for philanthropy, providing a high level assessment of international trends for the 'Anglo-Saxon' cluster (Salamon *et al.*, 2003).

Policy for philanthropy is often equated narrowly with the goal of promoting charitable giving through tax incentives. Although tax concessions are a major component, we take a broader view of the goals and instruments of philanthropy policy, especially focusing on financial contributions by individuals. The chapter begins by articulating these goals and aligning them, conceptually, with potential policy tools. The chapter then considers the nature of the 'problem' that philanthropy policy needs to address, and provides an assessment of international trends across the US, England, Canada, and Australia. To this end, it draws on a wide range of official government policy documents, sector briefs and media reports. The analysis shows a mix of policy drift and experimentation which is resulting in a growing divergence in policy responses across countries, stark contrasts in public discourses related to tax incentives and, overall, a pattern in which policy is failing to grapple with the evolving globalization of philanthropy and the capacity of third sectors for affecting social change.

Goals and instruments of philanthropy policy

Public policy for philanthropy has both a supply (or production) and demand (or consumption) side (Frumkin, 2006). This is outlined in Table 13.1. The dominant policy goal has long been oriented to the supply side, specifically to maintaining, and increasing, the amount of philanthropy that is available to charities and nonprofits to achieve public purposes. On the basis of reliable data across 12 countries, the picture that emerges is that, on average, philanthropy from all sources constitutes about 23 percent of total revenues for nonprofits (Salamon *et al.*, 2012: 5), although this varies by country and across types of organizations. Gifts and bequests from individuals account for more than 80 percent of philanthropy (Anheier, 2014; Giving USA, 2014). Tax rebates, which lower the cost of giving thereby encouraging larger amounts to be contributed, have been the primary means of incentivizing philanthropy. These rebates may be structured as deductions, such as in the US or Australia, or as credits, as in the Canadian case, and may be accompanied by matching government subsidiaries provided directly to the recipient

Table 13.1 Goals and instruments of philanthropy policy

Policy Goals	Operational Goals	Primary Instruments
Supply-side Goals		
Generate private resources for public purposes, that in aggregates are at least stable if not expanding over time	• Encourage private giving • Balance costs of incentives against tax expenditures; protect the integrity of the tax system • Control (or promote) cross-border giving • Prevent abuse and fraud by givers	• Tax incentives • Regulation • Regulation/information/ transparency
Promote a culture and awareness of philanthropy	• Create a broad and expanding base of giving and volunteering • Cultivate public dialogue and deepen understanding about the benefits and value of philanthropy	• Tax incentives; education, moral suasion • Collaboration; program spending
Demand-side Goals		
Influence the distribution of philanthropy	• Use philanthropy to complement, or substitute, for public spending • Assist donors in making 'good' choices	• Legislation/regulation of legal definition of 'charity;' differential tax incentives • Information/transparency; education
Promote effective use of philanthropy and its accountability	• Ensure contributions are spent on philanthropic purposes; prevent abuse and fraud by recipients • Create capable organizations and third sector • Promote continuous improvement and innovation	• Information/transparency; regulation of activities of charities; • Self-regulation; spending • Collaboration; evaluation; spending

charities, an approach illustrated by Gift Aid in the UK. Deductions tend to benefit those in higher income brackets to a higher degree, while the effects of credits are more equalized across income brackets. This difference in design influences concerns about the regressive nature of charitable tax benefits in the US in a way that is not comparable in the UK or Canada. For eligible organizations, the privilege of providing a tax benefit is normally accompanied by various regulations including a requirement for registration with the tax agency or independent 'charity' commission accompanied by annual reporting and limits on certain activities, particularly advocacy and business.

Supply side goals pertain not only to the amount of resources raised but the breadth of participation across the population. Philanthropy has been shown to have positive effects on givers' happiness, psychological and physical well-being (Aknin *et al.*, 2013; Helliwell *et al.*, 2015; Post, 2007) and on creating social capital and promoting citizenship (Putnam, 2000; Warren, 2011). Tax incentives alone do not ensure a culture of philanthropy, in part because tax filers need to have sufficient incomes for tax rebates to make a difference and the gifts need to be large enough to bother claiming. Indeed, only about 30 percent of those who report donating make a tax claim (Department of Finance Canada, 2015). Information campaigns about the benefits of philanthropy or facilitating the ease of giving (for example, through ATMs) are additional means of engaging large numbers of citizens, if in individually small acts. Some, but surprisingly few, governments have integrated support for philanthropy into their overarching political philosophies: in the UK, for instance, New Labour's 'Third Way' embraced 'active citizenship' that gave rise to a variety of programs, third sector partnerships and government machinery, while the Conservatives' 'Big Society' promoted volunteering and catalyzing local philanthropy, albeit with fewer institutional supports (Alcock, 2015).

The consumption side of policy addresses how philanthropic resources are distributed, and whether they are used effectively to produce societal benefits. As Frumkin (2006: 33) observes, 'one of the deepest and most intriguing questions about philanthropy is whether donors will be led through a new invisible hand to a set of philanthropic decisions and arrangements that truly benefit the public'. Should giving to a soup kitchen be valued and treated in the same way as giving to the symphony? The question of whether government should attempt to influence the private choices of philanthropy is vigorously debated (Reich, 2005), and is underpinned by more fundamental issues of whether philanthropy is, or should be, a substitute for government spending (Parachin, 2014) and whether government or philanthropy is the more effective means of allocation (Brooks, 2001). In promoting a movement for 'effective altruism', in which reason and evidence of results guide philanthropic choices, Singer (2015) makes a case for a directive approach on the basis that some causes *are* more worthy than others. Across the Anglo-Saxon countries, however, public policy has strongly favoured donor choice and the benefits of pluralism (Frumkin 2006: 36). Governments establish the range of these purposes, though, and thus control the field of organizations eligible to issue tax receipts. In common law countries, the basis for such determination has been the 1601 Statute of Charitable Uses, later categorized by the 1891 Pemsel case into four heads: advancement of religion, relief of poverty, advancement of education and other purposes beneficial to communities as defined by law. As discussed later, all, except Canada, have moved to expand or modernize the traditional common law categories.

Policy also seeks to encourage effective use of philanthropy, whether in a narrow sense of ensuring recipient organizations actually spend donations on 'charitable' purposes and are accountable for their use, or in a more expansive sense that these uses have positive societal value. The former has entailed mandatory reporting and regulation of advocacy and business activities as ancillary to charitable service, although these limits vary considerably across countries (Carmichael, Chapter 15). The bigger aspiration of directing philanthropic resources to uses that have the greatest impact is much more difficult; it relies on the availability of evidence of impact and the actual use of such evidence in decision-making by potential donors. Moreover, government encouragement of philanthropic institutions towards resource allocation with 'high impact' can be seen as reflecting governments' own 'short termism', with potentially critical implications for philanthropy's governance (Harrow and Jung, 2015). Provision of information on effectiveness has then been left primarily to charities and nonprofits, foundations and other institutional funders, and independent third party 'watchdogs' which often provide their own rating criteria. Donors do not have a strong record on being well informed, however, as only about two-thirds indicate they conduct any research about the organizations to which they give (Ottenhoff and Ulrich, 2010). There is some indication this is beginning to change, particularly among Millennials, women and High Net Worth (HNW) donors with a business background who are very likely to conduct due diligence and often volunteer with the organizations they are considering before making financial commitments (Mesch and Pactor, Chapter 5; Gordon *et al.*, Chapter 21)

In theory, then, philanthropy policy has a varied toolkit from which it can draw to address both supply and demand side goals. In assessing how well different goals are being met by contemporary policy, we need to consider the nature of the policy 'problem', if indeed philanthropy has a policy problem at all.

Does philanthropy have a policy 'problem'?

In aggregate, philanthropy would seem robust. Internationally, individual giving is recovering from the hit it took in the 2008 financial crises (NCVO/CAF, 2012; McLeod 2012), although it is estimated to take until 2018 before a return to its 2007 level (Blum and Hall, 2013). The rebound has been greatest at the very high end, with the number of gifts over $80 million (in the US) growing by 172 percent in 2014 over the previous year (McCambridge, 2015). More than 125 of the world's billionaires have committed to dedicating the majority of their wealth to philanthropy through the Giving Pledge initiated by Warren Buffet and Bill and Melinda Gates. The Boomer generation, those born between 1945 and 1964, have continued the commitment to philanthropy of their 'civic generation' parents (Putnam, 2000). The expectation that the substantial wealth acquired by the Boomers will be passed to their children, and some portion to charity, over the next few decades – a transfer estimated for the US alone to be $58 trillion – has been dubbed a new 'golden age' for philanthropy (Havens and Schervish, 2014: 27). Already, the Boomer grandchildren, the Millennials, have defied the stereotypes of their generation with high rates of giving, albeit still in modest amounts due to limited means, and they closely link their giving to volunteering and activism (Achieve, 2014). It remains to be determined however, if the predictions of increased giving materialize.

With such impressive aggregate numbers, as well as positive generational patterns, is there a policy 'problem' to be solved? Or, should we conclude that all is well: philanthropy policy should simply continue along its current path? Our case is that evolving trends in philanthropy are presenting new challenges that public policies are not yet addressing effectively, and in some cases that have not yet appeared on policy agendas.

The first issue is that aggregate philanthropy, both giving and volunteering, is becoming more reliant upon affluent and older people. The overall percentage that households donate – an average of three percent of their income in the US, about 0.4 percent in the UK – has remained unchanged for decades (Cowley *et al.*, 2011: 3). Low and middle income households give a higher percentage of their income than do the affluent (Cowley *et al.*, 2011: 3; Daniels and Narayanswamy, 2014), and this percentage has increased slightly in recent years while that of the affluent has decreased (Daniels, 2014a). The aggregate level of philanthropy remains strong in spite of a declining base and stagnant household rates because the size of gifts has grown, particularly among a small subset of the very wealthy. In the extreme case of the US, the wealthiest one percent of households, those earning over $380,000 per year, provide a third of donations (Zinsmeister, 2013). In Australia, seven percent of the population account for almost 60 percent (McCleod, 2012: 6), and in Canada ten percent carry 66 percent of giving (Turcotte, 2015: 3). This group of contributors is older than in the past. In the UK, those over 65 carry 35 percent of all giving as compared to 25 percent in 1978 (Cowley *et al.*, 2011: 3), and in the US, the Boomers are responsible for 43 percent of all individual giving.

Given the dependence of philanthropy on a core of older, affluent donors, one policy challenge is to maintain and expand their level of contributions to ensure a continuing, stable source of revenue for the nonprofit sector and the public purposes it serves. When the gifts are substantial, the importance of getting a tax benefit increases, although the motivation of making a difference is still paramount (US Trust, 2014). The financial tradeoff of expanded benefits is the cost of the associated tax expenditures, but research points to positive returns in stimulating giving (Bakija and Heim, 2011; Department of Finance, 2015; Rosenberg *et al.*, 2014). The related challenge is to broaden participation across the population. This will require more than tax breaks. Some considerations for policy 'reform', however, have tended to shift from radical to more limited options for change (Pharoah, 2010). The already high rates of engagement by the Millennials may contribute to the expansion of participation across their life and earning stages, assuming this is easily facilitated by technology given their strong preferences for giving online (Bernholz, 2015).

A second issue is that philanthropy is becoming increasingly transborder. In developed countries, mega-foundations are working to enhance global health or alleviate poverty among the world's poorest; a cadre of globally-oriented, mainly young, donors seek to affect systemic change; millions provide micro-loans to those in developing countries through online platforms such as Kiva; and people support disaster relief wherever it is needed. The changing geography of wealth across the income spectrum is also affecting the flows of philanthropy. Worldwide, the number of super wealthy households, those with assets of more than $100 million, is rising (Kharas, 2010; CAF, 2013), the greatest growth coming from Asia. Expanding rapidly, the portion of the world's middle class residing in the Global South is predicted to constitute 80 percent by 2030 (UNDP, 2013: 14). Although individual amounts may be small, the collective transfer of remittances among diaspora communities is already larger than governments' Official Development Assistance (Schmid and Shaul Bar Nissim, Chapter 10), adding the challenge for governments to incorporate remittance-giving within tax relief systems (Pharoah and Mackenzie, 2013). While giving is more transnational, policies for philanthropy have been remarkably place-bound, focused on supporting domestic organizations by in-country donors. Yet, with increasingly large, potentially footloose pools of individual and corporate capital seeking to support social innovation, the relative (dis)incentives afforded by the regulatory and policy regimes of different jurisdictions may influence where they give or invest.

A third challenge relates to the intertwined issues of the distribution, impact and transparency of philanthropy (Harrow, Chapter 31). Simply put: who benefits, to what extent, and how do we know? In theory, philanthropy is argued to be inherently redistributive, transferring from those with resources to those in need and affecting systemic change, and pluralistic, supporting diverse causes that governments would not. Its practice, however, has been widely criticized for failing to be redistributive or pluralistic (Reich, 2005). As shown in Table 13.2, the current pattern is that the primary destination, particularly among households with incomes under $100,000, is religion. This attracts a third of all donations in the US, 35 percent in Australia and

Table 13.2 Distribution of giving by individuals

Cause	Percentage of Total Donations Directed to: (by Individuals)			
	USA	UK	Canada	Australia
Religion	31	17	37	35
Education/Schools	16	4	14	8
Human Services	12	19	28	16
Health, inc. Medical Research/Hospitals	10	33	15	13
Arts & Culture	5	1	1	2
International	4	10	1	12
Environment & Animal Welfare	3	7	3	5
Sports & Recreation	N/A	3	2	6
Public Benefit to Society (e.g. Advocacy)	7	N/A	1	N/A
Foundations	11	N/A	N/A	N/A

Sources: Giving USA, 2014; NCVO/CAF, 2012; Department of Finance Canada, 2015; Turcotte, 2015; McCleod, 2012

37 percent in Canada, even though Australia and Canada are generally seen to be a less religious countries than the US. HNW donors favour their own foundations and Donor Advised Funds (DAFs), as well as higher education, medical research and cultural institutions, with the large gifts usually made 'close to home' in terms of both locale and institutions that have been part of their lives (McCambridge, 2015). The tax system continues to favour donor choice, underpinned by the legacy of a legal view of charity that is wholly inadequate in guiding the fiscal treatment of nonprofits in ways that benefit societal welfare (Frumkin, 2006; Carmichael, 2011; Parachin 2014). The combination of the rising inequality of wealth, the growing influence of the very wealthy on philanthropy and the observation that the rich give to rich institutions (McCambridge, 2015) is creating a scenario in which the redistributive and democratic benefits of philanthropy are being seriously questioned, and in the US is producing a divided discourse about tax deductions.

The mantra of philanthropy has become a desire for social innovation and impact. Although the rhetoric of impact may be inflated beyond its actual influence on individual decision-making, HNW donors say that by far their major hesitation is that their gift will not be used well (BMO *et al.*, 2015). The ability to achieve innovation and impact requires capable organizations that have an evidence-based understanding of the issues and can intervene at multiple points of what is likely a long, complex chain of causes. Often, this entails not only providing services to ameliorate the symptoms of problems in the short term, but advocating for policy changes to address root causes – that is, taking approaches akin to the 'scientific' philanthropy of the early twentieth century and its twenty-first century cousin, 'strategic' philanthropy. A misalignment of such aspirations and current philanthropy policy occurs in two ways, however. The legal framework was built on the concept of 'charity' which, for example, supports relief, but not prevention of poverty as a charitable purpose and does not view advocacy as a charitable activity. While the eligible purposes of charity have been extended across most of the Anglo-Saxon cluster, the limitations on advocacy vary considerably, often constraining the kinds of organizations that can be funded and ways in which they can pursue impact. In addition, the extent to which governments see a role in building the capacity of nonprofits varies greatly, but in recent years, public spending and programs supporting capacity-building have decreased across the board.

Transparency has acquired new saliency due to the affordances of technology and expectations of donors (Phillips, 2013; Tyler, 2013). As a condition of being recognized as an official 'charity,' 'public benefit organization' or 501(c)(3) registration with the tax agency or charity commission and annual reporting is required[1]. Because this reporting was designed primarily to detect abuse and ensure that these organizations are actually spending their revenues on charitable purposes, it has been dominated by the collection of financial information: it is not particularly useful for donors in assessing programs and impacts. In addition, reporting is replete with errors and ease of public accessibility is variable (Blumberg, 2012a; Charity Commission, 2015). In the absence of meaningful results-oriented reporting, the public has gravitated to the simple – and fundamentally misleading – measure of 'overhead' ratios (administrative and fundraising costs to revenues) as a proxy for organizational effectiveness. Not only are overhead ratios imprecise, but the means of keeping them low is under investment in organizational infrastructure that would enhance performance (Sargeant et al., 2008; Pallotta, 2012).

The growing popularity of Donor Advised Funds (DAFs), particularly those held by commercial institutions, is accentuating concerns over transparency of philanthropy's distribution. As the fastest growing destination for contributions by HNW donors in the US and expanding rapidly elsewhere (McLeod, 2012; Giving USA, 2014), DAFs collectively hold $US 45 billion, more than the world's largest foundation, the Bill and Melinda Gates Foundation (NPT, 2014). They serve as convenient and flexible personal giving vehicles, particularly for people whose levels of contributions are substantial, but not large enough to warrant creation of a private foundation. The concerns relate to the extent to which DAFs disperse their assets in a timely manner, and whether there is adequate transparency about where the contributions go, given that donations from commercial funds are generally made anonymously. Debate is sharpest in the US where there is no mandated minimum percentage of assets that must be distributed annually, leading to criticism that DAFs are 'where charity goes to wait' (Neyfakh, 2013) and calling for mandatory pay-out rates (Madoff, 2011)[2]. Transparency issues extend to foundations as they constitute large pools of assets under private control and do not have a strong history of voluntary transparency. For example, only ten percent of US foundations had a web presence in 2013, only about a third of those with assets over $100 million (Camarena, 2013).

A final consideration is the misfit that occurs when philanthropy meets social finance and a new set of hybrid organizations (Smith, Chapter 20; Skelcher and Smith, 2014). Philanthropy policy was built on assumptions that the only legal forms are charities, trusts or foundations and that the funding vehicle is a gift. However, social investment uses a variety of instruments that offer financial, as well as social returns (Salamon, 2014; Thümler, Chapter 23) and a hybrid set of entities, labeled as the 'fourth' sector (Sebati, 2009), combines features of nonprofit, for-profit and public organizations.

In sum, the evolving trends in philanthropy are presenting new challenges. They point to the need to increase support by HNW individuals, who are more responsive to tax incentives, and encourage a broader range of donors who are indifferent to them. While increased transborder philanthropy creates a potential to attract in-flows of capital, it may also extend external influences over the domestic sector (Schmid and Shaul Bar Nissim, Chapter 10), produce increased out-flows, and make oversight of philanthropy for possible fraudulent or terrorist activities more difficult. Because philanthropy has favoured pluralism and donor choice, the resulting distribution is skewed and insulated from other public policy goals. Transparency has become an independent force in regulation as big open online data has enabled the creation of multiple third party agents capable of acting in semi-regulatory roles. The entrance of new hybrid kinds of actors and new tools for social investment has left a regulatory system designed for charities with significant gaps, and with the need for an expanded toolkit. In the next section, we examine recent developments across the four Anglo-Saxon countries in policies related to both the demand and supply sides of philanthropy.

Policy directions: Converging, drifting, diverging

Until recently, philanthropy policy has been strongly path dependent, continuing in well carved channels and generally resistant to change. In part, the institutional implications of reliance on tax measures and their associated regulations have been responsible for this path dependence. From an institutional perspective, taxation is controlled by powerful and compliance-oriented government departments, the finance/treasury and tax agencies, which have little need to build organizational alliances within government or cross-sectoral collaborations. As a result, philanthropy policy has tended to have little 'bandwidth' of interest within government and has not widely engaged with external constituencies. Recent developments in philanthropy policy are taking different directions, converging in some aspects, but also demonstrating considerable divergence in spite of shared trends in giving and third sectors. In addition, there is a growing dissonance between policies supporting the supply side of philanthropy and governments' relationships with third sectors.

Policy for philanthropy's supply side

As a general policy framework, the case countries are committed to supporting and expanding philanthropy through tax incentives, although a discourse linked to income inequality is giving rise to an American exceptionalism. In terms of increasing charitable tax incentives, Canada has been out in front with significant expansion beginning in the late 1990s and continuing to the present. This development is partly the result of advocacy by the sector, but is also supported by government's interest in compensating for a shrinking welfare state. In 2013, a first time donor 'super credit' was introduced, designed to expand the donor base with limited cost in tax expenditures (Parachin, 2013). Furthermore, exemptions from capital gains taxes on donations of private securities and real estate that mainly benefit HNW donors were announced in 2015. Similarly in the UK, expanding charitable giving was a central plank of the Coalition's Big Society vision; following recommendations of a 2011 White Paper (HM Government, 2011), giving has been made easier through ATMs and other means, with some reform for small charities of the complex system of gift aid. In Australia, the focus has been on making the system for granting charitable tax benefits less cumbersome and more equitable. However, the current government has not yet responded to the 2013 report of a working group charged with identifying revenue-neutral options (Cavena, 2014). When the UK government and a Canadian province proposed caps on charitable tax incentives, these found little resonance with the public and were quickly retracted (Morris, 2014; Graveland, 2015). In the US, a more divisive public discourse exists that connects the disproportionate benefits of tax deductions for those in higher income brackets to concerns over income inequality. For the seventh time, President Barack Obama's 2015 budget called for a cap on charitable deductions for individuals with incomes over $200,000 and couples earning more than $250,000 based on the dual rationales of deficit cutting and promoting greater fairness in the tax system (Daniels, 2014b). Notwithstanding that the sector has produced extensive data on the negative implications for giving, and successfully fended off previous attempts to cap the deduction, a tight fiscal situation and legislative gridlock makes the future generosity of the tax benefit uncertain.

The policy responses to more internationalized philanthropy are also divergent, displaying both increased openness and greater protectionism. The US has, within limits, operated at the more open end of a continuum of facilitating cross-border giving. Following a series of court rulings that set out a principle of nondiscrimination of tax benefits for similar charities across member states, the European Union is moving in a more open direction, although progress is currently stalled (von Hippel, 2014). At the same time, many countries have imposed a variety of restrictions on cross-border philanthropy in recent years, including caps on inflows and outflows, limiting the activities (notably advocacy) that can be done with foreign funding and imposing burdensome reporting (Rutzen, 2015; Sidel, Chapter 16). Such measures are mainly associated with less than democratic regimes, but Australia and Canada have also taken steps that are restrictive of transborder funding. Australia recently reinstated an 'in Australia' provision that reflects a particularly restrictive approach intended 'simply to prohibit income-tax-exempt cross-border activity for all, but the most incidental of transactions' (McGregor-Lowdnes et al., 2015: NP). This requires that tax exempt organizations operate principally (more than 50 percent) in the country for 'the benefit of the Australian community' (with some exemptions). While the Canadian tax agency used to provide a, somewhat arbitrary, pre-approved list of foreign charities that qualify for tax credits in the same manner as domestic ones, in 2014 it began requiring foreign charities to apply for such status and limiting it to those involved in 'disaster relief, humanitarian aid or "activities in the national interest"' (Gray, 2014). In addition, more extensive reporting rules on receipt of foreign funding were introduced after the government expressed annoyance at environmental groups advocating against energy development using some funding from US foundations. Given that foreign funding accounts for less than 0.5 percent of the revenues of Canadian charities (Blumberg, 2012b), widespread perceptions are that the motivation is to control domestic advocacy by organizations that the governing party does not like.

The indecisiveness of policy stances toward transborder flows reflects an abiding aspect of philanthropy policy: it was created as, and continues to be, domestically oriented. It developed without any sense of regulatory competition – that other jurisdictions might outbid the domestic regime in attracting capital with more favourable incentives or more innovative third sectors. With changing geographies of wealth, particularly the hyper-wealthy emerging from Asia and the rise of the middle class in the Global South, nonprofits are looking internationally in their fundraising and investments. The desirability, and feasibility, of continuing to protect domestic philanthropy versus opening to globalized giving and investment are poorly understood, and often overshadowed by domestic partisan politics.

Policy for philanthropy's demand side

The ability of philanthropy to deliver societal benefit depends on the kinds of causes and organizations it supports, strong organizations capable of putting it to good use, and demonstration of its benefit. Anglo-Saxon countries have been less inclined than others to use differential tax incentives to direct giving to particular kinds of causes (with exceptions in some US states), favouring the principle of donor choice and treating all eligible charities in a uniform, undifferentiated manner across eligible cause purposes (Carmichael, 2013)[3]. Where differentiation does occur, it is in the degree of restrictiveness in determining the eligibility of particular types of organizations able to issue tax receipts and the restrictions on their political and business activities. While still rooted in the common law definition of charity, England and Australia have modernized and expanded it with a 'public benefit' test in charity legislation, and the US articulates tax exempt purposes in its tax code. Only Canada lacks a statutory basis, ostensibly due to constitutional limits on federal jurisdiction, and its interpretation of both charitable purposes and allowable activities are the most constrained. Indeed, in 2014, the tax agency required the Canadian affiliate of the international Oxfam confederation to change its mission statement as a result of its determination that a goal of preventing poverty is not charitable, only relieving poverty is acceptable (Beeby, 2014).

Third sectors and their ability to affect and demonstrate impact are being significantly reshaped through: expansion of transparency; accommodation of the growing hybridization of the sector; and tensions in government-third sector relationships.

The provision of more accessible information about philanthropy's recipient organizations is a common development and an improvement on reporting requirements. With the creation of the Australian Charities and Not-for-Profits Commission in 2012, all of the Anglo-Saxon countries, extending to New Zealand, Ireland, Scotland and Northern Ireland, have registration and mandatory annual reporting of charities, greatly enhancing basic transparency[4]. The ease of public accessibility of these reports varies considerably: the most accessible as open data is Canada, where the tax agency is also working with academics to revamp content to make reporting more donor (and research) relevant. In the US third parties, such as Charity Navigator and Guidestar, have dominated access to information and assumed important roles in rating effectiveness, whereas they have had limited presence in the other countries. A movement for more meaningful information, particularly about impact, is also occurring. Among regulators, the Charity Commission of England and Wales has led the way with a 2011 requirement that the trustees' reports which are appended to the mandatory annual filings by charities include a description of how their activities provide a public benefit (Morgan and Fletcher, 2013). Although compliance has been spotty, particularly among small charities as they become accustomed to providing this kind of information, the new standard is beginning to gain traction (Morgan and Fletcher, 2013). Third parties are taking impact reporting even further: for example, Charity Navigator has begun using a 'results logic' employing criteria of whether nonprofits have a theory of change and publish program evaluations. The US watchdogs are also collaborating to lead 'The Overhead Myth' campaign intended to put an end to the domination of overhead ratios as a primary means of assessing the effectiveness of nonprofits, notwithstanding that they made extensive use of this ratio in the past. A variety of sector-driven and independent online platforms are providing user-friendly, outcome-oriented information, some of them influenced by the notion of effective altruism (Matthews, 2015) and some aligned with efforts of the sector to enhance self-regulation. Such transparency should, in theory, better enable donors to conduct due diligence, not just of financials, but of the effectiveness of programs, although it is still unclear if most donors are interested in this type of outcome information.

Governments share an interest in accommodating hybridization of the sector and supporting social investment, although rhetoric has tended to outpace policy. A variety of new corporate forms have been created, such as the community interest company (CIC) in the UK and the low-profit limited liability corporation (L3C) and B Corp in the US, which have been emulated by several Canadian provinces and are under review in Australia. These forms are intended to better facilitate the work of hybrid organizations that have a social mission achieved through a business-like model, and allow foundations and other funders to more easily flow grants and program-related investments through them. Adoption of these new forms has been slower than anticipated, raising questions about the need for a separate regulator, akin to England's CIC 'light touch' regulator, or other measures to promote investor confidence and greater take-up by foundations for program-related investing (Pearse and Hopkins, 2013). New pools of public and private capital, such as the UK's Big Society Capital, have been created to grow and diversify social investment markets; its US counterpart, the Social Innovation Fund, provides matching funds to intermediary grantmakers to support nonprofits that create economic opportunities and are willing to be evaluated on their results. Both funds champion social impact bonds,

bonds that combine governmental 'pay by results' approaches with private sector investment and risk sharing (Clifford and Jung, 2016), which have also been adopted as official policy by the government of New South Wales (NSW, 2015). In 2014, the UK introduced the world's first tax relief for social investment aimed at encouraging support for social enterprises (including CICs) and social finance, including investment in social impact bonds. To what extent these social investment incentives will, at maturity, divert contributions from traditional philanthropic giving or whether they are different 'markets' that will operate in parallel is uncertain. In its early stages, social investing has been demonstrated to rely upon philanthropy as a catalyst (Koh *et al.*, 2012) and to ready the third (and fourth) sectors for the opportunities to scale up. Public policy is also critically important as stressed by the report of the Social Impact Investment Task Force (2014), chaired by the UK presidency of the G8: it issued a call to governments to build, participate in and steward these markets through: tax and other incentives; access to capital and procurement practices; creation of appropriate legal forms; removing regulatory barriers that inhibit innovation and entrepreneurial risk-taking; building capacity of social sector organizations to participate; and giving foundations the freedom and encouraging them to invest in impact investments. As participating countries in the task force formulate their policy responses, significant developments might occur, although the potential market for social impact bonds and other related initiatives may be smaller than initially anticipated, especially since many nonprofits have relatively small market niches.

In another important respect, however, governments have been inattentive to their relationships with third sectors and poor at listening to or learning from them as consumers and intermediaries of philanthropy (Healy and Donnelly-Cox, Chapter 12; Phillips and Smith, 2014). For example, the plan by the Abbott government to disband the Australian charity commission after only a year – in the face of the sector's fight to keep it – revealed a lack of understanding about the sector or a determination to put other interests before it. The funding cuts to the Charity Commission of England and Wales badly injured its legitimacy (NCVO, 2015), and the long running debate in the US over a cap on the tax deduction, and the polarized politics that surround it, has opened fissures in the government–sector relationship. Further, serious cuts to the budget of the Internal Revenue Service have greatly hampered its ability to effectively oversee the nonprofit sector or mount new initiatives designed to promote transparency. In Canada, the ability to engage in advocacy has been a particular sore point (Phillips, 2013) with government imposing more stringent reporting and the tax agency undertaking increased auditing of environmental and other charities that have taken controversial policy stances, raising concerns about political interference in the regulatory process. Concerns over repercussions of advocacy activities have created a chill elsewhere so that many nonprofits self-limit their voices (Pekkanen and Smith, 2014). The problem this creates for philanthropy is that it shuts down one avenue for achieving impact – which on some of society's wicked issues may be the most effective means of affecting change.

Conclusion: Wave or backwater?

The expectations of what philanthropy can achieve are high. With predictions of a new golden age created by the intergenerational transfer of wealth and the rise of the middle class in the Global South, these expectations are rising – perhaps unrealistically so: '[g]overnments' enchantment with philanthropy seems set to prefer idealism to realism' (Harrow and Jung, 2011: 1055). Public policy for philanthropy has overwhelmingly focused on ensuring a good supply of private resources, no matter how they are distributed or used for public good. But, this measure does not address the challenges ahead: to broaden participation, facilitate full engagement of the

Millennials who are mixing their giving and activism in different ways than their parents, and promote greater transparency for purposes of due diligence and personal learning. Although the dominance of religion as the primary destination for philanthropy may decline as younger, less devout generations enter their prime giving years, there are few signs that public policy will attempt to reengineer overall patterns of distribution. Transborder giving will undoubtedly increase, and governments need to assess their stance toward it, knowing that supportive policies will entail both inflows and outflows.

What is likely to significantly reshape the sources and destinations of private resources used for public benefit is social and impact investing. If expectations of demonstrated impact begin to actually influence giving decisions and as impact investing creates a global market in which impact is in effect a traded commodity, the types of projects and organizations that are supported may look very different than they do at present. Governments have a vital role in not only incentivizing and capitalizing these markets, but in building the capacity of civil society organizations to participate as the agents generating impact. Investment in the capacity of organizations to be effective agents for philanthropy has been shrinking over the past decade, however, and needs to be more firmly bolted on to a social impact agenda.

Public policy alone will not enable philanthropy to remain consistently out in front of the waves of change, and a variety of self-regulation and capacity building initiatives emanating from the third sector are also evident. In many respects, however, philanthropy policy has been allowed to drift or has been overshadowed by the current interest in its associate, social investment. This drift mixed with the incursion of domestic partisan politics is leading to more strained relationships between governments and the nonprofit sectors that are so central to the capacity of philanthropy to be sustainable and impactful.

Notes

1 In Australia, recognition as a charity and registration with its charity commission does not automatically confer tax receipting status, which has to be granted separately by the tax agency. As a result, religious organizations per se (which are regarded as charitable purposes under common law) may not be eligible to issue tax receipts although most have established a variety of funds and trusts that are so entitled.
2 The counter argument to a mandated distribution rate is that DAFs (particularly those held by community foundations) are already paying out at higher rates than private foundations (Council on Foundations 2009: 2), although the data are contested. In Canada, DAFs are subject to the same distribution rate as private foundations. The UK does not require minimum distribution amounts from foundations or DAFs, and the merits of introducing them are debated (Pharoah and Harrow, 2010). In Australia, Private Ancillary Funds (as DAFs are known) are reported to be distributing about eight percent of assets annually, above the minimum five percent required (McLeod, 2012).
3 Note that differentiation does occur between charities and political parties, the latter generally receiving a greater tax incentive.
4 The future of Australia's commission is precarious, however: after only a year, the Abbott government announced it would dissolve the commission as part of its reducing 'red tape' agenda in spite of strong opposition from the sector, but in 2015 the Commission won a reprieve.

References

Achieve. (2014) *2014 Millennial impact report: Millennial usability testing*. Indianapolis, IN: Achieve Inc.
Aknin. L. B., Barrington-Leigh, C. P., Dunn, E. W., Helliwell, J. F., Burns, J., Biswas-Diener, R., Kemeza, I., Nyende, P., Ashton-James, C. E., and Norton, M. I. (2013) 'Prosocial spending and well-being: Cross-cultural evidence for a psychological universal,' *Journal of Personality and Social Psychology*, 104(4): 635–52.
Alcock, P. (2015) 'After the Big Society: Changing state and third sector relations in the UK.' Paper presented to the International Research Society for Public Management (IRSPM), Birmingham, UK: March.

Anheier, H. K. (2014) *Nonprofit organizations: Theory, management, policy*, 2nd ed. London: Routledge.

Bakija, J. and Heim, B. T. (2011) 'How does charitable giving respond to incentive and income? New estimates form panel data,' *National Tax Journal*, 64(2): 615–50.

Bank of America. (2012) *The 2012 Bank of America study of high net worth philanthropy*. Boston, MA and Indianapolis, IN: Bank of America and Indiana University.

Beeby, D. (2014) 'Canada Revenue Agency says "preventing poverty" not allowed as goal for charity,' *Globe and Mail*, 24 July. www.theglobeandmail.com/news/politics/canada-revenue-agency-says-preventing-poverty-not-allowed-as-goal-for-charity/article19763321/ [Accessed 15 January 2015].

Bernholz, L. (2015) *Philanthropy and social economy: Blueprint 2015*, New York, NY: Foundation Center.

Blum, D. and Hall, H. (2013) 'Donations barely rose last year as individuals held back,' *Chronicle of Philanthropy*, 17 June. www.philanthropy.com/article/Fundraisings-Recovery-Could/154701 [Accessed 12 March 2015].

Blumberg, M. (2012a) 'How accurate are the T3010 charity returns when it comes to political activities?.' 8 April. www.canadiancharitylaw.ca/blog/how_accurate_are_the_t3010_registered_charity_information_returns [Accessed 8 January 2014].

Blumberg, M. (2012b) 'Total revenue received from all sources outside Canada by Canadian Charities in 2010.' 16 January. www.globalphilanthropy.ca/images/uploads/Total_revenue_received_from_all_sources_outside_Canada_by_Canadian_Charities_in_2010.pdf [Accessed 9 January, 2014].

BMO Harris Private Banking, Canadian Association of Gift Planners, GIV3 and Philanthropic Foundations of Canada. (2015) 'The philanthropic conversation: Understanding philanthropic advisors' approaches and high net worth individuals' perspectives.' Toronto, ON: GIV3.

Brooks, N. (2001) 'The tax credit for charitable contributions: Giving credit where none is due.' In J. Phillips, B. Chapman and D. Stevens (eds.), *Between state and market*. Montreal, QC: McGill-Queen's University Press, 457–84.

Camarena, J. (2013). 'Meet the new Glasspockets website.' *Philanthropy News Digest*. www.pndblog.typepad.com/pndblog/2013/12/meet-the-new-glasspockets-web-site-.html [Accessed 24 March 2014].

Carmichael, C. M. (2011) 'Charity misplaced: The formation in common law of a deficient fiscal concept,' *Charity Law and Practice Review*, 13(2): 27–49.

Carmichael, C. M. (2013) 'Doing good better? The differential subsidization of charitable contributions,' *Policy and Society*, 29(3): 201–17.

Cavena, L. (2014) 'NFP tax concession report revealed, *pro-bono*.' 25 February. www.probonoaustralia.com.au/news/2014/02/exclusive-nfp-tax-concession-report-revealed [Accessed 14 January 2015].

Charities Aid Foundation (CAF). (2012) *Mind the gap: The growing generational divide in charitable giving – a research paper*. London: CAF.

Charities Aid Foundation (CAF). (2013) *Future world giving: Unlocking the potential of global philanthropy*. London: CAF.

Charity Commission. (2015) *The quality of charity accounts*. London: Charity Commission.

Clifford, J. and Jung, T. (2016) 'Social Impact Bonds: exploring and understanding an emerging funding approach.' In O. Lehner (ed.), *The Routledge Handbook of Social and Sustainable Finance*. Routledge: London

Council on Foundations (2009) *Donor Advised Funds provide the majority of grant funds awarded by communiy foundations*. New York, NY: Council on Foundations.

Cowley, E., McKenzie, T., Pharoah, C. and Smith, S. (2011) *The new state of donation: Three decades of household giving to charity 1978-2008*, London: Centre for Charitable Giving and Philanthropy, Cass Business School City University London and CMPO, University of Bristol.

Daniels, A. (2014a) 'As wealthy give smaller share of income to charity, middle class digs deeper,' *Chronicle of Philanthropy*, 5 October. www.philanthropy.com/article/As-Wealthy-Give-Smaller-Share/152481 [Accessed 10 January 2015].

Daniels, A. (2014b) 'Obama 2015 budget would cap charitable deduction at 28% for wealthy,' *Chronicle of Philanthropy*, 4 March. www.philanthropy.com/article/Obama-2015-Budget-Would-Cap/145099/ [Accessed 10 January 2015].

Daniels, A. and Narayanswamy, A. (2014) 'The income-inequality divide hits generosity,' *Chronicle of Philanthropy*, 5 October. www.philanthropy.com/article/The-Income-Inequality-Divide/152551 [Accessed 12 February 2015].

Department of Finance Canada. (2015) *Tax expenditures and evaluations*. Ottawa, ON: Department of Finance Canada.

Dunn, E., Aknin, L. and Norton, M. (2008) 'Spending money on others promotes happiness,' *Science*, 319: 1687–88.

Frumkin, P. (2006) *Strategic giving: The art and science of philanthropy*. Chicago, IL: Chicago University Press.

Giving USA. (2014) 'The Annual Report on Philanthropy for the Year 2013,' Indianapolis: Giving USA Foundation and Indiana University Lilly Family School of Family.

Graveland, B. (2015) 'Prentice reverses stance on charity tax credit, calls reduction plan "wrong,"' *Globe and Mail*, 21 April. www.theglobeandmail.com/news/alberta/prentice-reverses-stance-on-charity-tax-credit-calls-reduction-plan-wrong/article24053684/ [Accessed 25 April 2015].

Gray. J. (2014) 'Canada Revenue Agency delists foreign charities,' *Globe and Mail*, 18 August. www.theglobeandmail.com/report-on-business/industry-news/the-law-page/canada-revenue-agency-delists-foreign-charities/article20104693/ [Accessed 15 February 2015].

Harrow, J. and Jung, T. (2011) 'Philanthropy is dead; Long live philanthropy?' *Public Management Review*, 13(8): 1048–56.

Harrow, J. and Jung, T. (2015) 'Debate: Thou shalt have impact, total impact – government involvement in philanthropic foundations' decision-making,' *Public Money and Management*, 35(3), 176–8.

Havens, J. J. and Schervish, P. G. (2014) 'A golden age of philanthropy still beckons: National wealth transfer and potential for philanthropy,' *Technical Report*. Boston, MA, Boston College, Center on Wealth and Philanthropy.

Helliwell, J. F., Huang, H. and Wang, S. (2015) 'The geography of world happiness.' In J. F. Helliwell, R. Layard and J. Sachs (eds.). *World happiness report 2015*. New York: Sustainable Development Solutions Network.

HM Government. (2011) 'Giving White Paper'. London: Her Majesty's Stationery Office.

Kharas H. (2010) 'The emerging middle class in developing countries,' Working paper no. 285, Paric: OECD Development Centre.

Koh, H., Karamchandani, A. and Katz, R. (2012) *From blueprint to scale: The case for philanthropy in impact investing*. Cambridge, MA: Monitor Group with the Acumen Fund.

McCambridge, R. (2015) 'Do the fruits of philanthropy now fall closer than ever to the tree?,' *Nonprofit Quarterly*, 25 March. Available at: www.nonprofitquarterly.org/philanthropy/25838-do-the-fruits-of-philanthropy-now-fall-closer-than-ever-to-the-tree.html [Accessed 2 April 2015].

McGregor-Lowndes, M., Tarr, J-A. and Silver, N. (2015) 'The Fisc and the frontier: Approaches to cross-border charity in Australia and the UK, The Philanthropist,' 18 May. www.thephilanthropist.ca/2015/05/the-fisc-and-the-frontier-approaches-to-cross-border-charity-in-australia-and-the-uk/ [Accessed 2 April 2015].

McLeod, J. (2012) *Australian gving trends - signs of recovery from the gloom*. Sydney: JBWere Wealth Management.

Madoff, R. D. (2011) 'It's time to reform donor advised funds.' *Tax Notes*, 133: 1265–71.

Martin, M. (2011) 'Four revolutions in global philanthropy,' Impact Economy Working Papers Vol. 1, Geneva: Impact Economy.

Matthews, D. (2015) 'You have $8 billion. You want to do as much good as possible. What do you do?,' *Vox*, 24 April. Available at: www.vox.com/2015/4/24/8457895/givewell-open-philanthropy-charity [Accessed 26 April 2015].

Milbourne, L. (2014) *Voluntary sector in transition: Hard times or new opportunities?* Bristol: Policy Press at the University of Bristol.

Morgan, G. G. and Fletcher, N. J. (2013) 'Mandatory public benefit reporting as a basis for charity accountability: Findings from England and Wales.' *Voluntas*, 24(3): 805–30.

Morris D. (2014) 'Recent developments in charity taxation in the UK: The law gives and the law takes away.' In A. O'Connell and M. Stewart (eds.), *Not-for-profit law: Theoretical and comparative perspectives*. Cambridge: Cambridge University Press.

National Philanthropic Trust (NPT). (2014) *2014 Donor Advised Fund report*. Jenkintown, PA: National Philanthropic Trust.

NCVO. (2015) *Charity Commission independence, NCVO discussion paper*. London: National Council of Voluntary Organisations.

NCVO/CAF. (2012) *UK Giving 2012*. London: National Council of Voluntary Organisations and Charities Aid Foundation.

New South Wales Government. (2015) *Social investment policy*. Sydney, NSW: Office of Social Impact Investment.

Neyfakh, L. (2013) 'Donor advised funds: Where charity goes to wait.' *Boston Globe*, 1 December. Available at: www.bostonglobe.com/ideas/2013/12/01/donor-advised-funds-where-charity-goes-wait/tYa8P5trm6av9BnXPhyQTM/story.html [Accessed 1 March 2015].

Ottenhoff, B. and Ulrich, G. (2010) *Money for good.* San Francisco: Hope Consulting.

Pallotta, D. (2012) *Charity case: How the nonprofit community can stand up for itself and really change the world.* San Francisco, CA: Jossey-Bass.

Parachin, A. (2013) 'Reflections on the first-time donor credit: The link between donation incentives and the regulation of legal charity,' *Canadian Tax Journal,* 61(4): 1109–22.

Parachin, A. (2014) 'The role of fiscal considerations in the judicial interpretation of charity.' In M. Harding, A. O'Connell and M. Stewart (eds.), *Not-for-profit law: Theoretical and comparative perspectives.* New York: Cambridge University Press.

Pearse, J. A. II and Hopkins, J. P. (2013) 'Regulation of L3Cs for social entrepreneurship: A prerequisite to increased utilization,' *Nebraska Law Review,* 92(2): 259–88.

Pekkanen, R. J. and Smith, S. R. (2014) 'Nonprofit advocacy in Seattle and Washington, DC.' In R. J. Pekkanen, S. R. Smith and Y. Tsujinaka (eds.), *Nonprofits and advocacy: Engaging community and government in an era of retrenchment.* Baltimore, MD: Johns Hopkins University Press, 50–60.

Pharoah, C. (2010) 'Challenges for tax policy towards individual charitable giving: The experience of recent attempts to "reform' the UK Gift Aid scheme,' *Voluntary Sector Review* 1(2): 259–67.

Pharoah, C. and Harrow, J. (2010) 'Payout with an English accent: Exploring the case for a foundation "distributon quota' in the UK.' Paper presented to the ARNOVA annual conference, Alexandria, VA.

Pharoah, C. and Mackenzie, T. (2013) 'Giving back to communities of residence and origin. An analysis of remittances and charitable donations in the UK.' London: Centre for Charitable Giving and Philanthropy, Cass Business School, City University, London.

Phillips, S. D. (2013) 'Shining light on charities or looking in the wrong place? Transparency and co-regulation in Canada,' *Voluntas,* 24(3): 881–905.

Phillips, S. D. and Smith, S. R. (2014) 'A dawn of policy convergence? Third sector policy and regulatory change among the "Anglo-Saxon" cluster,' *Public Management Review,* 16(8):1141–63.

Post, S. G. (2007) *Altruism and health: Perspectives from empirical research.* New York, NY: Oxford University Press.

Putnam, R. D. (2000) *Bowling alone: The collapse and revival of american community.* New York, NY: Simon & Schuster.

Reich, R. (2005) 'A Failure of philanthropy: American charity shortchanges the poor, and public policy is partly to blame,' *Stanford Social Innovation Review,* Winter: 24–33.

Rosenberg, J., Steurele, C. E., Steele, E. and Eng, A. (2014) *Preliminary estimates of the impact of the Camp Tax Reform Plan on charitable giving.* Washington, DC: Urban Institute and Brookings Institution.

Rutzen, D. (2015) 'Aid barriers and the rise of philanthropic protectionism,' *International Journal of Not-for-Profit Law,* 17(1): 5–44.

Salamon, L. M. (2014) *Leverage for good: An introduction to the new frontiers of philanthropy and social investment.* New York, NY: Oxford University Press.

Salamon, L. M., Wojciech Sokolowski, S. and List, R. (2003) *Global civil society: An overview.* Baltimore: Johns Hopkins Center for Civil Society Studies.

Salamon, L. M., Wojciech Sokolowski, S. and Haddock, M. (2012) 'Measuring civil society and volunteering: New findings from implementation of the UN Nonprofit Handbook.' Paper presented to the International Society for Third Sector Research, Siena, Italy.

Sargeant, A., Jay, E. and Lee, S. (2008) 'The true cost of fundraising: Should donors care?,' *Journal of Direct, Data and Digital Marketing Practice,* 9: 340–53.

Sebati, H. with the Fourth Sector Network Concept Working Group. (2009) *The emerging Fourth Sector.* Washington, DC: Aspen Institute.

Singer, P. (2015) *The most good you can do: How effective altruism is changing ideas about living ethically.* New Haven, CO: Yale University Press.

Skelcher, C. and Smith, S. R. (2014) 'Theorizing hybridity: Institutional logics, complex organizations, and actor identities – the case of nonprofits,' *Public Administration,* Online July.

Social Impact Investment Task Force. (2014) *Impact Investment: The invisible heart of markets.* London: UK Presidency of the G8.

Turcotte, M. (2015) *Volunteering and charitable giving in Canada.* Ottawa, ON: Statistics Canada.

Tyler, J. (2013) *Transparency in Philanthropy: An analysis of accountability, fallacy and volunteerism.* New York, NY: Philanthropy Roundtable.

United Nations Development Programme. (UNDP). (2013) 'The rise of the South: Human progress in diverse world,' *Human Development Report 2013.* New York, NY: UNDP.

US Trust and Lilly Family School of Philanthropy. (2014) *The 2014 US Trust Study of high net worth philanthropy*. Boston, MA and Indianapolis, IN: US Trust and Lilly Family School of Philanthropy, Indiana University.

Von Hippel, T. (2014) *Taxation of cross-border philanthropy in Europe after Persche and Stauffer : From landlock to free movement?* Brussels: European Foundation Centre.

Warren, M. E. (2011) 'Civil society and the deepening of democracy.' In M. Edwards (ed.), *The Oxford Handbook of Civil Society*. Oxford: Oxford University Press.

Zinsmeister, K. (2013) 'Donation: Which Americans give most to charity?,' *Philanthropy Magazine*, Summer. Available at: www.philanthropyroundtable.org/topic/donor_intent/donation [Accessed 26 February 2015].

14

Minding the pennies

Global trends in the regulation of charitable fundraising

Oonagh B. Breen

This chapter explores current global trends in fundraising regulation. The perennial issue of effective fundraising regulation has thwarted many policymakers the world over. Indeed, what constitutes effective regulation is a contested issue. Overly prescriptive regulation dates quickly and becomes moribund as technology changes the manner in which funds are raised and the problems associated with these ventures. Enabling regulations, on the other hand, that require agency input for effective oversight, can be hostages to fortune being either dependent upon the good offices of an agent, such as a local authority, police, or tax authority, whose primary concern may be far removed from charity regulation per se, or purely self-regulatory and thereby lacking the necessary teeth of enforcement and sanction. The growing ability of organizations to fundraise across state/country borders, prompted in part by donor migration and the ease with which remote e-donations may now be made, has brought to the fore technical legal issues relating to registration requirements, jurisdiction to regulate non-state fundraisers, particularly when the donations in question are unsolicited, and the burden of conflicting regulatory requirements that apply when an organization seeks to run a nationwide fundraising campaign, not to mention newly emerging concerns prompted by the nature of electronic fundraising.

The emergence of hybrid regulation, also referred to as 'co-regulation', which seeks to combine the operational benefits of local nonstatutory enforcement with the deterrent force of potential statutory intervention should grassroots oversight fail, provides an interesting twist on the traditional options of statutory versus nonstatutory regulation. Recent attempts to develop uniform standards and regulatory requirements across associations of fundraising organizations, and from the perspective of independent fundraising regulatory bodies, in conjunction with moves at state level to develop uniform registration requirements in some jurisdictions also merit further exploration.

This chapter begins by setting out a theoretical framework for the regulation of fundraising before turning to a consideration of recent global trends in the context of both statutory and nonstatutory initiatives. To this end, particular consideration is given to the growing resort to cross-jurisdictional fundraising and emerging regulatory and facilitative innovations to support such activity. Attention is also paid to new, and emerging, forms of electronic fundraising and the question as to whether it is too soon to regulate this form of giving is explored. Finally, the chapter examines the place of charitable fundraising within the broader regulatory framework, and how connections with other regulators influence the oversight of fundraising before assessing the potential for greater global convergence in fundraising regulatory trends.

Theoretical framework

To date, much has been written on the theory of effective fundraising regulation, and research has produced diverse results. Academics and practitioners are divided on issues of donor interest in fundraising costs (Steinberg, 1986; Sargeant, Jay and Lee, 2008), the value and appropriateness of spending ratios (Steinberg, 1991; Tinkelmann, 1999; Flack, 2004) and the extent to which information asymmetries relating to program, fundraising and overhead costs do, or should, affect the behaviour of the giving public (Greenlee and Brown, 1999; Berman and Davidson, 2003; Bowman, 2006; Jacobs and Marudas, 2007). The existence of such diversity inevitably influences the regulatory models available. Thus, in attempting to provide a useful lens through which to examine these various regimes, it is helpful, in light of these identified differences, to acknowledge the effect of the following variables on the regulatory model in question: the 'evil' which the regime seeks to address; the intended target audience of the regulation; and the choice of regulator entrusted with the task of enforcement, along with the timing of such regulation.

In designing any regulatory regime, the first concern must be the nature of the evil the regime seeks to redress. With fundraising regulation, the most oft cited objective is the protection of the public and preservation of public confidence in charities. The likely evils at issue would, therefore, include the prevention of fraud, either through deceptive fundraising practices or embezzlement of money raised for charity. Falling short of fraud, another worthy objective of a regulatory regime may be to ensure the charity's effective management of funds raised. A third and common rationale for fundraising regulation is the desire to empower donors so that they make informed decisions when donating to charities. The regulatory mechanism used will vary according to the 'evil' in question (Breen, 2009). If the goal of the regime is to empower donors in their giving, the form of regulation chosen may focus on the quality and volume of information conveyed to donors, both before and at the time of solicitation. If, on the other hand, the goal is to ensure effective management of funds raised, the regulatory emphasis may focus more on the interrogation of the financial accounts filed by the charity. When the concern is to ensure that only legitimate charities have access to the public's largesse, the most appropriate regulatory tool may take the form of vetting or licensing process to filter those allowed access to the donating public.

As to timing, there are generally three opportunities to give effect to these objectives during the life cycle of a fundraising campaign, namely, the pre-solicitation period when it is possible to impose licensing requirements regulating access to the public; the period during solicitation itself when the charity 'ask' is made; and finally, the post-solicitation period when organizations can be made accountable for the money raised and how it is subsequently expended (Breen, 2009).

Knowing which problem is at issue may require policymakers to have a good understanding of the intended charity target audience. The composition of the charity sector and its need for a particular type of regulation will vary over jurisdictions depending upon the state of development of the sector. In examining the charity sector, one could break down this target audience into four sections: the well-intentioned, well-informed charities (which have a tendency to be large charities that enjoy good support staff and tend to be to the fore in terms of regulatory compliance); well-intentioned, ill-informed charities (these bodies often comprise mid-size and emergent charities that have few paid staff and voluntary boards that play a hands-on role in their day-to-day management, resulting in well-intentioned, but time-poor charities); ill-intentioned, ill-informed charities (representing those organizations that are often unaware of their regulatory responsibilities and are not proactive in compliance matters, thus needing constant prompting and supervision); and finally, the ill-intentioned, well-informed charities (those bodies that subvert the charity form for their own gain, by playing fast and loose with the regulatory requirements – one might think of certain noncharitable clothes collectors in this category) (Breen, 2012).

Analysing the composition of the charity audience in this manner can enable regulators to align likely evils that may exist in the sector with the most appropriate regulatory form for redressing them, recognizing that sometimes the audience may be composed of a mix of these categories. It is in this regard that the choice of regulator becomes all the more pressing. Traditionally, three regulatory enforcers present themselves – the state, normally in the guise of a charity regulator, a tax authority, a local authority or a company regulator; charities themselves, whether in the form of pure self-regulation or peer regulation; and the donating public, in the context of the onus being placed upon the public to identify and report charitable misdeeds. Research shows that it is difficult for any one of these interested parties to successfully enforce fundraising regulation single-handedly (Dale, 2007; Breen, 2009): a triumvirate approach involving all stakeholders in enforcement may prove to be more effective (Breen, 2009: 125).

In practice, the particular state body chosen to oversee fundraising can influence the regulatory approach adopted. Yet, the nature of this effect has to be studied on an individual country basis as experience shows that even when similar regulators are used, this does not necessarily lead to consistency in approach or outcomes. Thus, Canada, the US and Ireland (until 2014) use tax authorities to regulate charities. Whereas the Canada Revenue Agency (CRA) has adopted an operational interest approach, issuing guidance on fundraising practice (CRA, 2009) and imposing intermediate sanctions for breach of these rules, the US Internal Revenue Service (IRS, 2010) has recently become more interested in extracting information on funds raised and spent at the reporting stage. To this end, its recently revised tax return for charities, Form 990, now requires greater disclosure and breakdown on fundraising expenses. In complete contrast, the Revenue Commissioners play no similar role in Ireland, neither issuing guidance on fundraising practices nor collecting fundraising information on an annual basis.

Similarly, in jurisdictions in which a charity regulator plays an active role, the attention given to fundraising regulation varies. Thus, the Charity Commission for England and Wales has issued core guidance on fundraising to charities and entered into a memorandum of understanding with the independent fundraising regulator, the Fundraising Standards Board (Charity Commission, 2007; 2011). Part 3 of the *English Charities Act 2006* makes the Commission the lead regulator of public charitable collections, although the relevant provisions have yet to be commenced, and are absent from the recent *Charities Act 2011*, which consolidates existing charity legislation. Lord Hodgson's review found that implementing Part 3 of the 2006 Act was unaffordable and also may not be effective (Cabinet Office, 2012a: 99), thus forcing the Cabinet Office and other stakeholder to rethink this model. One might suspect that a similar explanation lies behind the New Zealand experience, where the New Zealand Charities Board,[1] despite its statutory powers to investigate 'serious wrongdoing' which includes 'unlawful or a corrupt use of the funds or resources of the entity; or an act, omission, or course of conduct that constitutes a serious risk to the public interest in the orderly and appropriate conduct of the affairs of the entity',[2] does not provide any published guidance to registered charities on fundraising practices.

Trends in global regulation

Over the past decade, there has been a general global shift away from purely prescriptive legislative initiatives that seek to regulate all matters relating to charitable solicitation in favour of a mixed system, comprising a legislative framework (often focusing on licensing issues) coupled with a nonstatutory scheme that seeks to oversee the operational issues associated with fundraising regulation.

Statutory initiatives

Notwithstanding the growing popularity of co-regulation and sector certification models, new statutory regimes are still emerging. In 2011, the US State of Oregon debated new fundraising legislation that would have introduced administrative cost ratios for charities. Under Senate Bill 40, the state attorney general would have been empowered to declare that donations to charitable organizations that did not expend at least 30 percent annually on program services (averaged over a three-year period) would no longer be tax deductible, and the charities would have to notify potential donors of that status, or face fines. The Bill, passed by an overwhelming majority in the Oregon Senate in April 2011, never made it out of the House Committee on Revenue (Oregonian, 2011; Row, 2011), but Oregon's Attorney General remains committed to alerting the public to excessive administrative expenditure by charities (Oregon State Department of Justice, 2012). Disaster relief has also focused legislative attention on the management of charitable funds raised for natural disasters, and examples of new statutory regulations introduced to better police money raised in these circumstances can be found in Tennessee.[3]

Notwithstanding this emergence of new statutory regulations, many jurisdictions are moving away from pure command and control regimes towards 'soft' law. Thus, in 2009, the Hong Kong Independent Commission against Corruption (ICAC) launched best practice guidelines to provide assistance to Hong Kong charities on good governance and internal control in the context of fundraising activities. The guidelines, which have government support, cover proper budgeting, good record keeping, regular auditing of accounts, capping administrative expenses, safekeeping donations and publicizing audited accounts of fundraising activities (Independent Commission Against Corruption, 2009). Despite the impressive name of the underwriting institution the guidelines remain voluntary.

Another example is Canada's Fundraising Guidance, which replaces the CRA's previous charity disbursement quota rules.[4] The new 'rules', introduced in 2009, clarify what constitutes prohibited fundraising activity, as well as distinguishing (allowable) expenditure on charitable activity from fundraising expenditure (which is then evaluated by CRA for evidence of excessiveness) (CRA, 2009). According to the CRA, fundraising expenditures include all costs related to any activity that includes a solicitation of support, or that is undertaken as part of the planning and preparation for future solicitations of support.

Expenditures can be allocated as charitable activities, and not fundraising, if substantially all (90 percent) of the purpose was other than fundraising or if a charity can answer 'no' to each of a four part test, namely: was the main objective of the activity fundraising; did the activity include ongoing or repeated requests, emotive requests, gift incentives, donor premiums, or other fundraising merchandise; was the audience selected because of their ability to give; and was commission-based remuneration or compensation tied to the number or amount of donations? The proportion of revenue spent on fundraising activity is then judged on a ratio basis with ratios under 35 percent unlikely to generate questions, ratios over 35 percent calling for more detailed assessment of expenditure and ratios over 70 percent raising CRA concerns and requiring an acceptable explanation (CRA, 2009). Viewing the fundraising guidance as soft law, Phillips (2012) points out that to date, no charity has had its charitable status revoked solely on the grounds of excessive fundraising expenditure.

Mixed statutory initiatives

Mixed regimes consisting of both statutory elements (relating to licensing requirements) and nonstatutory elements involving sector codes of practice (increasingly related to the operational elements of solicitation) are becoming more common in many jurisdictions. A growing trend has been the provision in legislation of a ministerial reserve power to introduce statutory regulation of fundraising if nonstatutory efforts fail to achieve this task.[5] Such statutory powers to regulate are then held in abeyance on the condition that the nonprofit sector establishes and oversees the appropriate standards of fundraising conduct that result in an environment respectful of donors and ultimate beneficiaries and assurance of fundraising methods that are both honest and open. Thus, the UK, through the Institute of Fundraising (IoF) and the Fundraising Standards Board (FRSB), and Ireland, through Irish Charities Tax Research Group in partnership with the Department of Justice, are currently trying hybrid fundraising regulatory schemes (Breen, 2009; 2012). Only the UK, however, has laid down benchmarks for measuring whether such regulation is successful (Home Office, 2005). Lord Hodgson's review of the *Charities Act 2006* provided the first formal opportunity to examine the operation of the FRSB and its achievements to date (Cabinet Office, 2012a, Chapter 8) and his recommendations concerning the need to rationalize further the confusing regulatory landscape in the UK have been broadly accepted by the government (Cabinet Office, 2012b).

Nonstatutory initiatives

Aside from the hybrid systems of regulation, a number of purely ethical or self-regulatory regimes also exist. Ratified by national fundraising organizations in 30 countries,[6] the International Statement of Ethical Principles in Fundraising (AFP, 2006) consists of five universal principles (honesty, respect, integrity, empathy and transparency) and six standards of practice which address fundraisers' responsibility to donors, their relationship with stakeholders, their responsibility for communications, reporting, payments and compensation and their compliance to national laws. First mooted by the US Association of Fundraising Professionals (AFP) at the first International Fundraising Summit in 2003, the Statement has no legal force and no sanctioning mechanism. According to its proponents, however, the existence of this universally recognized set of standards for the fundraising sector has begun to inform practice. Reports from the sixth international fundraising summit, held in London in 2010, revealed that the Fundraising Institute of Australia (FIA) had used the Statement as the guiding document during its comprehensive review of its own codes of practice and that the Statement was also influencing reform in Poland and the Ukraine (Paulette, 2010).

Whereas the International Statement of Ethical Principles and the related international fundraising summits bring together the various national organizations of fundraising professionals, the International Committee of Fundraising Organizations (ICFO) comprises the association of national fundraising monitoring agencies. Established in 1958 and based in the Netherlands, with full member representation from 12 countries (ICFO, 2010), ICFO's aim is to help to harmonize accreditation procedures and standards, and to provide an international forum for discussion and debate on accreditation issues. To this end, ICFO developed a set of International Standards (2003) for good governance and management for international nongovernmental, or nonprofit, private organizations that directly, or indirectly through subsidiary bodies, raise funds from the public for charitable or public benefit purposes.

ICFO's prescribed standards relate to five areas: membership and responsibilities of the governing body; fulfilment of public benefit goals; fiscal control, management and reporting;

fundraising practices; and provision of public information. In particular, ICFO expects fundraising public benefit organizations 'to present their accounts of income and expenditure in a common format to enable appropriate thresholds to be set for categories of expenditure and for meaningful inter-organizational comparisons to be made'. This move towards uniformity in accountancy presentation across a wide variety of member countries, if achieved, would be significant progress. The ability of ICFO members to bring this change about, however, is dependent upon the practical strength of these monitoring organizations in their home countries. Of the twelve countries with full member representation (Austria, Canada, France, Germany, Italy, The Netherlands, Norway, Spain, Sweden, Switzerland, Taiwan and the USA) some purport to monitor only organizations within a specific sector (as is the case with the Canadian Council of Christian Charities and the US Evangelical Council for Financial Accountability) while others make no reference at all to their oversight role for national fundraising (as is the case with the Austrian Österreichische Forschungsstiftung für Entwicklungshilfe [ÖFSE]). Interestingly, there is no full member from the UK (such as the FRSB) with only 'supporting' member presence in the form of the Charities Aid Foundation (CAF) and the consumer association Which.

A third take on a nonstatutory regulatory initiative, this time led entirely by the sector itself, is the ambitious project undertaken by Imagine Canada in its Standards Program (Imagine Canada, 2011a). Initially conceived as an ethical code relating to fundraising only (Imagine Canada, 2011b), admission of new applicants to the Ethical Code Program was suspended in December 2011 and in December 2013, the Ethical Code Program was formally merged with the new Standards Program. This program offers a Canada-wide set of shared standards for charities and nonprofits designed to strengthen their capacity in five core areas: governance; financial accountability; fundraising; staff management; and volunteer involvement. Participation is voluntary in a process that entails peer-reviewed accreditation, with ongoing monitoring based on complaints and selected annual audits, enabling those accredited organizations to display a trustmark that publicly demonstrates their successful adherence to the new standards. It remains to be seen how this structural change in self-regulation will impact on fundraising regulation in Canada. Of the 89 new Standards, all of which must be addressed, 20 relate directly to fundraising, mirroring the existing Ethical Code fundraising principles. Previously, 363 charities had signed up to the Ethical Code Program (Imagine Canada, 2010), a far cry from the hoped for 15,000 adherents (Phillips, 2012); in the first two years of the new program, 150 organizations have been successfully accredited (Imagine Canada, 2015). As Phillips acknowledges (2012), the Standards Program is unlikely ever to get buy-in from the bulk of sector, comprising small independent nonprofits. Yet, one would have to critically question the ability of, or indeed appetite for, the majority of Canadian charities to seek accreditation across all 89 standards, if so few in the past managed to sign up for just the 20 fundraising standards.

Cross-border regulation projects: US, Australia and Europe

When donors give to charities outside their home state or country, the resulting donation may raise regulatory issues for the recipient charity, particularly if tax benefits accrue to either the donor or charity as a result of the donation. If the charity may be viewed as having solicited the donation, this may also raise registration issues for the charity in the donor's jurisdiction. The regulatory complexities that such cross-border donations create have resulted in some innovative 'solutions' in various parts of the world.

In the US, the Multi-State Filer project (2010), a joint venture initiated in 1998 between the National Association of State Charity Officials (NASCO) and the National Association of Attorneys General (NAAG), was set up to provide charities that fundraised nationally or in multiple states with a user-friendly alternative to registering individually in each cooperating state. The project developed a 'uniform registration statement' (URS) that is now accepted in 36 states and the District of Columbia, whereas 13 other states will accept the URS upon the filing of supplemental documentation. (National Association of State Charity Officials and National Association of Attorneys General, 2010)[7] It should be noted however, that the URS covers registration issues only and not subsequent reporting requirements, which still require individual attention on a state-by-state basis (Usry, 2008). Nave (2004: 235) has made a strong argument for greater US federal involvement in the streamlining of concurrent regulatory burdens on national fundraising charities through greater reliance on the constitutional Commerce clause and its role in preventing state regulation that 'unduly burdens interstate commerce and thereby imped[es] free private trade in the national marketplace'. Given the acknowledged reluctance of US courts to favour challenges under the dormant commerce clause and charities' natural averseness to litigation (Nave, 2004: 243), it remains to be seen whether this negative approach will result in real change to the law in the short to medium term.

An interesting approach to the issue of cross-border regulation of fundraising activities is the legislative solution that has been under consideration in Australia. In 2010, the Council of Australian Governments (COAG) proposed reforms to develop a nationally consistent approach to fundraising regulation and the adoption of a standard chart of accounts where possible (COAG, 2010). COAG tasked a NFP Reform Working Group (NRWG) to review, develop and recommend fundraising regulatory reform options (COAG, 2012). This call for reform came at a time when Australia was seeking to streamline charity regulation with the introduction of a new national charity commission.[8] In its scoping study for a national regulator (Treasury, 2011), the Treasury noted the high regulatory burden borne by Australian nonprofits as a result of inconsistent fundraising regulation and legislation across the states, territories and the Commonwealth. The study also acknowledged the difficulties of divorcing fundraising regulatory reform from broader nonprofit regulatory reforms, recommending that the Government review and coordinate issues common to both the Not-for-Profit Regulator (which could conceivably play a role in the oversight of fundraising regulation) and the COAG consideration of fundraising reform. To that end, the Australian Government published its Fundraising Discussion Paper in February 2012 (Australian Government, 2012), proposing a national framework for charitable fundraising regulation that would apply to all charities registered with the Australian Charities and Not-for-profits Commission (ACNC). Charities raising more than $50,000 would be required to register with the ACNC, as would all charities that fundraise over the internet. The proposed framework would require charities to meet minimum information disclosure requirements at the time donations are solicited, as well as broader reporting and record-keeping requirements. The intent was that charities would be subject only to the national fundraising regulatory framework, thereby avoiding duplication by State and Territory government regulation. Although efforts by the states to advance fundraising legislation harmonization (Office for the Not-for-Profit Sector, 2012) at times seemed promising, progress has stalled, and so far no significant reform of antiquated fundraising laws has been accomplished (McGregor-Lowndes, 2015). In addition, the current government had vowed to abolish the charity commission as part of reducing red tape agenda, although these plans appear presently to be on hold.

Against the backdrop of COAG's top down regulatory reform process, another initiative worthy of consideration is the Australian Centre for Philanthropy and Nonprofit Studies' (ACPNS) independent Nonprofit Model Law Project. The ACPNS project aims to develop streamlined and seamless regulation of nonprofit organizations in Australia through a bottom–up approach, with nonprofits playing a more proactive role in the design of their regulatory environment than typically is possible in a government-led process. ACPNS specifically identifies fundraising as a priority area for attention. To this end, it has facilitated discussion of the key challenges for fundraising regulatory reform amongst key sector and government stakeholders and sought to advance evidence-based policy proposals. In April 2011, ACPNS held a fundraising regulation conference that invited international speakers to join in a symposium with leading Australian policymakers and charities, thereby enabling a broadening of the national debate on regulatory tools. The Nonprofit Model Law Project has a projected duration of five to ten years, which compares favourably with other comparative model law projects, and in stage three of the project is currently producing draft model laws and regulatory instruments.

A particularly European response to taxation problems raised by cross-border giving in Europe has been the Transnational Giving Europe project. It is still common in the EU for some member states to discriminate between domestic charities and resident 'foreign' European charities when it comes to tax relief and exemptions. Although such discrimination has been held to violate the free movement of capital between EU member states,[9] change comes slowly. In this interim period, the TGE foundations based in 17 European countries facilitate tax-efficient cross-border giving by acting as initial domestic recipients of a donor's bounty. Upon receipt the national TGE foundation transfers the gift to the intended foreign recipient while simultaneously providing the donor with the associated national tax reliefs that may flow from the gift. The TGE project thus enables fundraising organizations to ensure income tax deductible gifts for their foreign donors and facilitates the holding of tax efficient fundraising campaigns in other TGE countries. Figures released by TGE in 2015 demonstrate the growing trend towards global giving with more than 5,000 donors using TGE to transfer €12m in 2014, a growth of 37 percent, compared to 2013 when 8.7 M € was channelled (TGE, 2015).

New and emerging areas of concern – is it too soon to regulate?

As the nature of fundraising changes, so too does the type of regulation required. Internet solicitation is not a new phenomenon and the cross-border regulatory issues that it raises are well appreciated, if not yet satisfactorily resolved. Early attempts in the US through the development of the Charleston Principles in 2001 and their subsequent revision (NASCO, 2001) have made some headway in this area, providing nonbinding guidance intended as a resource to help individual states develop their own regulatory approach to the internet. The Charleston Principles focus on the requirement of active charity websites to register with states in order to raise money online. Yet, the past decade has seen such radical changes in the nature of electronic fundraising with new and innovative uses of social media and mobile technology (Bernholz, Chapter 28) that guidelines focusing solely on a charity's website as the gateway for e-fundraising fail now to capture the immense breadth of virtual mechanisms for raising funds, many of which do not begin with (and may not even include) the actual charity in whose name the funds are solicited.

Social networks, like Facebook and Twitter, enable individuals to solicit money from friends and relatives in support of charities much more easily than in the past whereas websites such as Mycharity.ie or Justgive.org raise money on behalf of many different charities, the latter not necessarily having any control over the money raised in their names. For charity regulators, the biggest concerns with such e-endeavours is how best to protect donors from fraud. The very process of internet solicitation by its nature makes it more difficult for the donor to verify the identity of the fundraiser or to interrogate that fundraiser in a direct fashion. Given that donors receive nothing in return for their donations, there is no obvious safety check to ensure that online donations are received by those intended and used for the purposes for which they have been donated. This information asymmetry problem is not a new one in the world of nonprofit law (Hansmann, 1980), but the tendencies for large-scale fraud are more prevalent when the internet, as opposed to face-to-face solicitation, is the chosen medium. The law tends to lag behind practice in this area, particularly given the fast rate of innovation. Certain regulatory policy issues also remain to be worked out even when fraud is not a concern. If, for instance, a website collects donations on behalf of a charity, how long should that website be able to hold on to such proceeds before it is required to release the funds to the charity in question? Where a website charges fees for collecting donations on behalf of a charity, what requirements should govern disclosure of this information to potential donors?

Issues may also arise around the use of what may be described as a 'digital poorbox', a facility whereby an online shopper is given the option when checking out to add a charity donation to the total purchase. Some online sellers will work directly with a particular charity or charities to develop this option. An example of this direct partnership model is the G–Team approach of Groupon, a website that uses collective buying power to secure discounted goods and services for clients. The G–Team model enables charitable donations to be made to a particular campaign through all its deal pages on a given day (Groupon, 2011). An alternative to the direct partnership model involves a business partnering with an intermediary organization that processes all charitable donations and ensures they reach their intended charity, thus allowing benefit to be spread amongst a broader group of charities. An example of the intermediary facilitation model is eBay's partnership with Mission Fish in the UK (eBay, 2011), whereby Mission Fish certifies the eligible nonprofit recipients, collects the donations from eBay users and passes them on to the recipient nonprofits, as well as managing the tax benefits of giving through eBay. 'Round the pound' schemes, whereby shoppers have the option when paying by credit card to round up their bills to the next pound with the balance going to a designated charity, present similar regulatory challenges (Pennies Foundation, 2010; Give Change Make Change, 2011). The issue in all cases remains the same for the regulator: how should such online donations be monitored to ensure the money goes to its intended recipient in a timely fashion?

Other forms of e-giving continue to emerge regularly. Charitable donations via SMS on mobile phones are a particular growth area. In its Giving White Paper, the English Cabinet Office (2011: 17) noted that over 89 percent of 16–65 year olds own a mobile phone in the UK, accounting for 34 million people. In the past, small charities did not avail of text donation options due to prohibitive set up costs. Following a government challenge to make giving via mobile phone easier, Vodafone UK and Just Giving collaborated to create 'Just Text Giving', launched in May 2011, which enables all charities regardless of size to set up a free service to avail of mobile phone giving, whereby all proceeds raised go directly to the charity. With the growth in availability of this method of giving, however, will come new challenges. If overused, the receipt of numerous text messages all seeking solicitations may amount to a nuisance with the recipient donor having little ability to separate the legitimate appeals from the scam artists. What safeguards should be put in place to enable a donor verify that the text sender is a registered charity or an authorized agent working on its behalf?

A further area still under development is automated teller machine (ATM) giving. ATM giving itself is not new. ATM donations in Colombia started in 1998 and an average of 100,000 donations a month are made there, with the average donation value equaling a dollar (Pickard, 2010). In 2002, HSBC Mexico launched an initiative that enabled customers to make ATM and online donations to various regional social organizations and causes working to help children. By 2008, HSBC reported that customers had contributed over US $8.7 million to a wide range of educational, community-based and health services, providing an innovative link between customers, the community and the financial sector (HSBC, 2009: 17). HSBC rolled out a similar initiative in the UK in 2005 but with less success (CAF, 2011). Undeterred, the UK's ATM operators' consortium, LINK, in response to calls by the government, announced in 2011 that it would put in place a system, whereby customers of its 100 million ATM machines would be able to choose to donate to charities chosen by the individual ATM operator (Cabinet Office, 2011). To date, rollout of this scheme has been piecemeal. In October 2012, an independent panel chaired by NCVO Chief Executive Sir Stuart Etherington selected 30 charities from an applicant field of over 550 charities to benefit from ATM giving. The selection panel divided the UK into five regions (Scotland, Wales, Northern Ireland, Northern England and Southern England) and allocated each region six different charities to benefit from the scheme (Weakley, 2012). At the end of 2012, only an estimated 9,000 of a total 65,000 ATMs were able to facilitate donations and some bank cards were not enabled to give (Ribeiro, 2012). From a regulatory perspective, challenges will lie in building this new form of giving into the existing tax efficient Gift Aid scheme. On a cross-border note, Ulster Bank, which operates in both Northern Ireland and the Republic of Ireland, became the first bank in Ireland to provide its customers with the option of making ATM charity donations in 2012. Ulster Bank customers can donate between €1 and €250 in a single transaction to any of eight pre-selected Irish charity recipients (Ulster Bank, 2012). Since choice over recipient charities does not lie with the donor in either jurisdiction and no indication of the rate of likely turnover of recipient names is provided, some charities may find it difficult to break into this new medium.

Given the vast array of fundraising technological options, regulators face an uphill task in providing guidance to charities and advice to donors. To date, the UK's IoF (2006) and Australia's FIA (2011) have issued Codes of Practice on Fundraising by electronic means. In November 2012, the IoF consolidated its 28 codes of practice on fundraising into one single code of practice. The new 20-chapter code is supplemented by 27 guidance notes (IoF, 2012). Chapter 9, therein, now deals with digital media ranging from e-donations and online trading, social media interaction and website content. Those charities that have relations with online providers still need to consult the Guidance Note for Charities Working with Business. Whereas the 2006 Code comprised a checklist of questions for charities, the chapter on digital media is now presented as a series of 'ought' or 'must' statements. The regulatory concerns remain the same: Has a solicitation occurred? Are benefits to fundraisers transparent, authorized and reasonable? Has a charity received its promised dues within a reasonable time period? In the absence of a reform of outdated primary legislation to take account of modern fundraising practices (an absence common in many jurisdictions), organizations such as the IoF and FIA are forced to operate in a regulatory vacuum in their attempts to provide comprehensive and clear guidance to charities and fundraisers in the field of e-fundraising.

Place of fundraising regulation within broader regulatory framework

As discussed earlier in this chapter, there are three moments in time at which regulation of fundraising typically occurs – pre-solicitation, during solicitation and post-solicitation. Yet these moments often find the intersection of other regulatory concerns that may either impinge upon the fundraising policy brief, or duplicate the regulatory burden. Thus, for a public authority or police force tasked with licensing public collections, often the predominant agency concern is one of maintaining public order and avoiding public nuisance by limiting the number of collectors active within a particular locality at any given time. There may be some attention to the legitimacy of the collecting organization, but this generally tends to involve verification that the organization is not subversive in its aims.

Operationally, the regulation of the actual act of solicitation largely falls under the remit of existing sector fundraising regulatory codes although it may depend on media type chosen. Where the solicitation is made on radio or television, the broadcasting standards board and its codes of operation can affect the content and delivery of the message, as happened recently with the UK banning of the One Foundation's television advert for relief of poverty (Digital Spy, 2011).

Post-solicitation regulation will raise a number of non-fundraising regulatory concerns. Apart from any requirement for charities to report directly to funders on the success of fundraising campaigns, regulatory requirements for financial reporting are becoming more developed, requiring charities to account for fundraising income raised, associated costs (whether specifically fundraising costs or more general overhead costs) of raising that income and how then that income is treated in the accounts of the charity. These requirements may arise through the completion of a tax return (as in the US Form 990 (IRS, 2011)), through compliance with a set of standards relating to the preparation of financial accounts (such as the UK's Charities Statement of Recommended Practice (ASB, 2005)) or through additional averments made in relation to fundraising practice in the context of annual accounts and annual reports (as in Ireland under public compliance procedures for fundraising code signatories (ICTR, 2011)).

Data protection issues will also arise in the context of fundraising regulation. Databases of donor contact details, preferred methods of giving, history and patterns of giving and eligibility of donations for gift aid comprise vital information for any charity. Issues will arise over the use made by the charity of such information, the manner in which such information is stored and the circumstances in which it is retained and, quite crucially, the identity of those with access to this information and the circumstances in which it may be shared with third parties.

Equally, certain donations will be eligible to avail of tax incentives introduced to encourage tax-efficient giving. These schemes vary in detail, but most result in either the charity reclaiming all/some of the tax originally paid by the individual on the donated sum or allowing a corporation to donate at a lower cost through the use of tax deductions. Safeguards to ensure that charitable receipts affording such tax relief are issued only in respect of legitimate charitable donations introduce an additional sphere of financial audit and oversight in the prevention of fraud, as is particularly evident in Canada, where in recent times the Canadian Revenue Agency has cracked down on tax shelter schemes and revoked charitable status of charities found to have issued tax receipts for values exceeding charitable donations received (Blumberg, 2011).

The essential point is that since the oversight of fundraising does not take place in a regulatory vacuum, in focusing on fundraising issues, policymakers cannot shut their eyes to the broader regulatory picture and how all of these other areas impinge on fundraising. Rather, the regulation of fundraising is intrinsically related to other larger regulatory issues ranging from data protection, financial reporting standards, taxation issues and broader public nuisance, trade practices and advertising standards issues. Successful resolution of fundraising 'problems' thus requires macro policy solutions or at the very least cooperation from other regulatory agencies.

Conclusion

This chapter set out to review the current global trends in fundraising regulation. In undertaking this journey, we uncovered numerous examples of recent regulatory reform as many different stakeholders struggle to develop effective and efficient fundraising regulatory regimes. Thus, there is much evidence of state intervention and statutory regulation and the emergence of soft law guidance (although the exact degree of its 'soft' nature has yet to be tested fully), alongside regimes that make fundraising professionals or independent fundraising standards bodies (with or without the input of charities themselves) the creators of fundraising codes and the primary enforcement bodies for those charities willing to sign up to such oversight of their fundraising activity. Regulatory reform in the area of fundraising regulation is thus a hot topic in many jurisdictions at present.

With regards to possible convergence in regulatory practice, there is certainly evidence that generic problems are being experienced in many countries. Concerns exist over the lack of regulatory consistency demonstrated by state or regional regulators and federal regulators, making it difficult for charities in these jurisdictions to fundraise on a national basis. Multiple accountabilities to various public agencies has not lessened the fundraising compliance burden for charities or necessarily provided better oversight for the public at large. Promised plans to centralize the oversight function for fundraising, for instance in the UK, have yet to be brought into force[10]. While the last player to the regulatory reform table, Australia, appeared to be headed toward elimination of competing state standards and creation of a central authority charged with fundraising oversight on a national basis, progress is stalled and the future of its charity commission uncertain.

The continuously developing area of internet and mobile fundraising is set to be a moving target for regulatory purposes in the coming decade and will force policymakers and regulators to review standards constantly and amend them accordingly as fundraising activities and practices continue to evolve. And yet, the old adage, '*plus ça change, plus c'est la même chose*' remains particularly pertinent in the field of fundraising regulation. Notwithstanding the technological changes that have transformed the practices of solicitation, the underlying questions that inform our regulatory efforts appear to remain constant: has the donor received trustworthy information that allows him/her to donate in confidence that the money will go to a legitimate charity and be used by that body for its charitable purposes? Are there safeguards in place to protect both the giving public and charities themselves from unscrupulous tricksters? How should we regulate the middleman in charitable solicitation whether that middleman is a third party fundraiser or commercial partner, and whether it is physically present or a virtual presence only? Can safeguards be employed in a manner that is strategic in aim and proactive in effect such that onerous duties are not imposed on compliant entities while the ne'er do wells avoid proactive scrutiny? Challenges, indeed, abound with no easy answers to hand, making the area of fundraising regulation an area to watch in the decade ahead.

Notes

1 The New Zealand Charities Commission was abolished by s.9 of the *Charities Amendment Act (No 2) 2012* and replaced by a Charities Board run from within the New Zealand Ministry of Social Development and the Department of Internal Affairs.

2 *New Zealand Charities Act, 2005*, s. 4(1) and s.10(i), reprint as at July 1, 2012, taking account of changes made by *Charities Amendment Act (No 2) 2012*.

3 State of Tennessee, *Public Chapter No. 232*, signed into law May 20, 2011.

4 The CRA disbursement quota rule required that the amount a charity spent each year on charitable activities—including gifts to qualified donees—be at least the sum of: 80 percent of the previous year's tax-receipted donations, plus other amounts relating to enduring property and transfers between charities (charitable expenditure rule); and 3.5 percent of all assets not currently used in charitable activities or administration if these assets exceed a threshold of $25,000 (capital accumulation rule). This rule was repealed in the 2010 Federal Budget.

5 Such a statutory reserve power exists in the English *Charities Act, 2006*, s. 69; in the Irish *Charities Act, 2009*, s. 97; in the *Charities Act (Northern Ireland) 2008*, s. 158; and in the *Charities and Trustee Investment (Scotland) Act 2005*, s.90.

6 Currently national fundraising organizations in the following countries have ratified the International Statement: Argentina, Hong Kong, Singapore, Australia, Indonesia, South Africa, Belgium, Italy, Spain, Canada, Kenya, Sweden, Finland, South Korea, Switzerland, France, Netherlands, Ukraine, Germany, New Zealand, the United Kingdom, Hungary, Poland, and the United States.

7 Thus, the URS is not accepted in just three states, Florida, Oklahoma and Colorado.

8 *Australian Charities and Not-for-profits Commission Act 2012* and *Australian Charities and Not-for-profits Commission (Consequential and Transitional) Act 2012*. See further www.acnc.gov.au/ [Accessed 15 January 2013].

9 Case C-386/04 *Centro di Musicologia Walter Stauffer v. Finanzamt Munchen fur Korperschaften* [2006] ECR I-8203, which prohibits a Member State from discriminating against an EEA-established charity on the grounds that its principal place of business is in another EEA member state; see also Case C-318/07 Hein *Persche v. Finanzamt Lüdenscheid* [2009] E.C.R. I-359.

10 The British Cabinet accepted in full the recommendations of the Etherington (2015) Review of Fundraising in October 2015, including the proposals to replace the Fundraising Standards Board with a new Fundraising Regulator to be funded by charities themselves and to transfer the code of Fundraising Practice from the Institution of Fundraising to the new regulator.

References

Accounting Standards Board. (2005) *Accounting and reporting by charities: Statement of recommended practice. (SORP).* www.charitycommission.gov.uk/Library/guidance/sorp05textcolour.pdf [Accessed 21 October 2011].

Association of Fundraising Professionals (AFP). (2006) *International statement for ethical principles in fundraising.* www.afpnet.org/Ethics/IntlArticleDetail.cfm?ItemNumber=3681 [Accessed 4 November 2011].

Australian Government. (2012) *Charitable fundraising regulation reform: Discussion Paper and draft regulation impact statement.* www.treasury.gov.au/documents/2297/PDF/Charitable_fundraising_discussion_paper.pdf [Accessed 17 February 2012].

Berman, G. and Davidson, S. (2003) 'Do donors care? Some Australian evidence,' *Voluntas*, 14(4): 421–9.

Blumberg, M. (2011) *CRA Revokes Choson Kallah Fund of Toronto as tax shelter donation arrangement.* www.globalphilanthropy.ca/blog/cra_revokes_choson_kallah_fund_of_toronto [Accessed 3 February 2012].

Bowman, W. (2006) 'Should donors care about overhead costs? Do they care?,' *Nonprofit and Voluntary Sector Quarterly*, 35(2): 288–310.

Breen, O. (2009) 'Regulating charitable solicitation practices – The search for a hybrid solution,' *Financial Accountability and Management*, 25(1): 115–43.

Breen, O. (2012) 'The perks and perils of non-statutory fundraising regulatory regimes: An Anglo-Irish perspective,' *Voluntas*, 23(3): 763–90.

Cabinet Office. (2011) *Giving White Paper* (Cmnd. 8084) London: HMSO.

——. (2012a) *Trusted and independent: Giving charity back to charities. Review of the Charities Act 2006.* www.gov.uk/government/uploads/system/uploads/attachment_data/file/79275/Charities-Act-Review-2006-report-Hodgson.pdf [Accessed 14 January 2013].

——. (2012b) *Interim charities review response from the Minister for civil society*, Mr. Nick Hurd, December 2012. www.gov.uk/government/uploads/system/uploads/attachment_data/file/79277/Charities-Act-Review-2006-response-Nick-Hurd.pdf [Accessed 14 January 2013].

Canada Revenue Agency (CRA). (2009) *Guidance: Fundraising by registered charities—CPS 028*, Canada Revenue Agency, Ottawa. www.cra-arc.gc.ca/chrts-gvng/chrts/plcy/cgd/fndrsng-eng.html [Accessed 13 May 2015].

Charity Commission for England and Wales and Fundraising Standards Board. (2007) *Memorandum of understanding between the Charity Commission and the Fundraising Standards Board.* London: CCEW and FSB.

Charity Commission for England and Wales. (2011) *Charities and fundraising*, CC 20. London: Charities Commission.

Charities Aid Foundation (CAF). (2011) *Charities Aid Foundation response to the Cabinet Office's Giving Green Paper.* London: CAF.

Council of Australian Governments (COAG). (2010) *COAG Communiqué*, April 19–20. www.coag.gov.au/sites/default/files/2010-20-04.pdf [Accessed 14 January 2013].

——. (2012) *Terms of reference – COAG NFP Reform Working Group.* www.treasury.gov.au/PublicationsAndMedia/Publications/2012/COAG-NFP-reform/TOR [Accessed January 14, 2013].

Dale, H. (2007) 'Study on models of self-regulation in the nonprofit sector.' In Panel on the Nonprofit Sector. *Principles for good governance and ethical practice: A guide for charities and foundations – Reference edition.* Washington DC: Independent Sector, 75–129. www.independentsector.org/principles_reference_redirect [Accessed October 21, 2011].

Digital Spy. (2011) *U2 Bono's Charity Advert banned.* www.digitalspy.ie/media/news/a344535/u2-bonos-charity-advert-banned.html [Accessed 21 October 2011].

eBay. (2011) *eBay for charity: Frequently asked questions.* www.pages.ebay.co.uk/ebayforcharity/help.html [Accessed October 21, 2011].

Flack, T. (2004) 'The mandatory disclosure of cost of fundraising ratios: Does it achieve the regulators' purposes?' *CPNS Working Paper,* No. CPNS26. Brisbane, QLD: Queensland University of Technology.

Fundraising Institute of Australia. (2011) *Standard of electronic fundraising practice.* Chatswood, NSW. www.fia.org.au/data/documents/Resources/Principles__Standards/Standard_of_Electronic_Fundraising_Practice_2011.pdf [Accessed September 20, 2012].

Give Change Make Change. (2011) *Information for retailers.* www.givechangemakechange.com/ [Accessed October 21, 2011].

Greenlee, J. S. and Brown K. L. (1999) 'The impact of accounting information on contributions to charitable organizations,' *Research in Accounting Regulation,* 13: 111–25.

Groupon. (2011) *Supporting causes and causing a scene.* www.groupon.com/g-team [Accessed October 21, 2011].

Hansmann, H. (1980) 'The role of nonprofit enterprise,' *Yale Law Journal,* 89: 835–901.

Home Office, Charities Unit. (2005) *Principles for assessing the success of self-regulation of fundraising'.* A consultation paper. London: Home Office.

HSBC. (2009) *Community Investment at HSBC.*

Imagine Canada. (2010) *Progress report 2010: Ethical Code Program.* www.imaginecanada.ca/files/www/en/ethicalcode/ethical_code_2010_progress_report_en_09142011.pdf [Accessed January 13, 2012].

——. (2011a) *Standards for Canada's charities and nonprofits 2011 pilot standards.* www.imaginecanada.ca/files/www/en/standards/standards_imagine_canada_dec2011.pdf [Accessed January 13, 2012].

——. (2011b) *Ethical Code Handbook 2007, revised edition 2011.* www.imaginecanada.ca/files/www/en/ethicalcode/ec_handbook_2011_en.pdf [Accessed January 13, 2012].

——. (2015) *Standards Program reaches 150 milestone as 25 more charities accredited.* www.imaginecanada.ca/who-we-are/whats-new/news/standards-program-reaches-150-milestone-25-more-charities-accredited [Accessed May 27, 2015].

Independent Commission Against Corruption Hong Kong. (2009) *Management of charities and fundraising activities: Best practice check list.* Hong Kong: Corruption Prevention Department. www.icac.org.hk/filemanager/en/Content_1031/fund_raising.pdf [Accessed May 25, 2015].

——. (2011) *Form 990.* www.irs.gov/pub/irs-pdf/f990.pdf [Accessed October 21, 2011].

Institute of Fundraising. (n.d.) *Charities working with business code of practice.* London: IoF. www.institute-of-fundraising.org.uk/library/charities-working-with-business/iof-code-of-fundraising-practice-charities-working-with-business.pdf [Accessed February 3, 2012].

——. (2006) *Fundraising through electronic media code of fundraising practice.* London: IoF. www.institute-of-fundraising.org.uk/library/fundraising-through-electronic-media/2iof-code-of-fundraising-practice-fundraising-through-electronic-media.pdf [Accessed February 3, 2012].

——. (2012) *Code of Fundraising Practice.* London: IoF. www.institute-of-fundraising.org.uk/guidance/code-of-fundraising-practice/ [Accessed 15 January 2013].

Internal Revenue Service. (2010) *Instructions for Schedule G (Form 990 or 990-EZ) supplemental information regarding fundraising or gaming activities.* www.irs.gov/pub/irs-pdf/i990sg.pdf [Accessed November 25, 2011].

International Committee of Fundraising Organizations (ICFO). (2003) *International Standards Online.* Zurich: ICFO. www.oneworldtrust.org/csoproject/images/documents/INTL19.pdf [Accessed November 4, 2011].

——. (2010) *Annual Report 2010.* Zurich: ICFO.

Irish Charities Tax Reform Group (ICTR). (2011) *Compliance checklist.* www.ictr.ie/files/Compliance%20Checklist.pdf [Accessed October 21, 2011].

Jacobs, F. and Marudas N. (2007) *The impact of fundraising inefficiency on donations to nonprofit organizations, proceedings of the American Society of Business and Behavioural Sciences* (February) www.google.ie/url?sa=t&rct=j&q=the%20impact%20of%20fundraising%20inefficiency%20on%20donations%20to%20nonprofit%20organizations%22&source=web&cd=4&sqi=2&ved=0CD4QFjAD&url=http%3A%2F%2Fpure.ltu.se%2Fportal%2Ffiles%2F1275604%2FJacobs-F-2007&ei=1Se0ToqFA87t-gaKiIWFBg&usg=AFQjCNGmQN6wU8C4XiXYoEK0J-QcUngxFw&cad=rja [Accessed November 4, 2011].

McGregor-Lowndes, M. (2015) *The regulatory riddle of putting the wind beneath the wings of fundraisers.* Syd Herron Oration, Fundraising Institute of Australia. Brisbane, QLD, February 19.

National Association of State Charity Officials (NASCO). (2001) *The Charleston Principles: Guidelines on charitable solicitations using the internet.* www.nasconet.org/wp-content/uploads/2011/05/Charleston-Principles-Final.pdf [Accessed October 21, 2011].

National Association of State Charity Officials and National Association of Attorneys General. (2010) *Multi-State Filer Project*. www.multistatefiling.org/index.html [Accessed October 21, 2011].

Nave, C. (2004) 'Charitable state registration and the dormant Commerce Clause,' *William Mitchell Law Review*, 31(1): 227–43.

Office for the Not-for-Profit Sector. (2012) *Submission to the Senate Standing Commission on Community Affairs on the inquiry into the Australian Charities and Not-for-Profits Commission Bill 2012*, Canberra: Office for the Not-for-Profit Sector.

Oregon State Department of Justice. (2012) *Attorney General Rosenblum announces Oregon's 20 worst charities for 2012*, December 13, 2012. www.doj.state.or.us/releases/Pages/2012/rel121312.aspx [Accessed January 14, 2013].

Oregonian. (2011) *2011 Session: Senate Bill 40*. www.gov.oregonlive.com/bill/2011/SB40/ [Accessed February 10, 2012].

Paulette's Point of View. (2010) *International fundraising summit*. www.paulettespov.blogspot.com/2010/07/international-fundraising-summit.html [Accessed November 4, 2011].

Pennies Foundation. (2010) *Pennies – The electronic charity box*. www.pennies.org.uk/ [Accessed October 21, 2011].

Phillips, S. D. (2012) 'Canadian leapfrog: From regulating charitable fundraising to co-regulating good governance,' *Voluntas*, 23(3): 808–29.

Pickard, J. (2010) 'Charity donations invited at cash machines,' *Financial Times*, 29 December 2010. www.ft.com/cms/s/0/0f48e3c8-12c1-11e0-b4c8-00144feabdc0.html#axzz1dRWFgpjV [Accessed November 11, 2011].

Ribeiro, C. (2012) 'ATM giving rollout has been "piecemeal", says bank machine,' *Civil Society*, 22 November 2012. www.civilsociety.co.uk/fundraising/news/content/13865/atm_giving_roll-out_has_been_piecemeal_says_bank_machine [Accessed November 27, 2012].

Row, D. K. (2011) 'Senate Bill 40, which proposed to punish underperforming charities, dies in Oregon Legislature,' *The Oregonian*, 6 July. www.oregonlive.com/pacific-northwestnews/index.ssf/2011/07/senate_bill_40_which_proposed_to_punish_underperforming_charities_dies_in_oregon_legislature.html [Accessed February 10, 2012].

Sargeant, A., Jay E. and Lee S. (2008) 'The true cost of fundraising: Should donors care?,' *Journal of Direct, Data and Digital Marketing Practice*, 9(4): 340–53.

Steinberg, R. (1986) 'Should donors care about fundraising?.' In S. Rose-Ackerman (ed.) *The economics of nonprofit institutions—Studies in structure and policy*. New York: Oxford University Press.

——. (1991) 'The Economics of Fundraising.' In D. F. Burlingame and L. J. Hulse (eds.) *Taking fund raising seriously: Advancing the profession and practice of raising money*. San Francisco, California: Jossey-Bass, 239–56.

Tinkelmann, D. (1999) 'Factors affecting the relation between donations to not-for-profit organizations and an efficiency ratio,' *Research in Government and Nonprofit Accounting*, 10: 135.

Transnational Giving Europe. (2015) www.transnationalgiving.eu/tge/details.aspx?id=219950&LangType=1033 [Accessed June 2, 2015].

Treasury, Government of Australia. (2011) *Final report: Scoping study for a national not-for-profit regulator*. http://archive.treasury.gov.au/documents/2054/PDF/20110706%20-%20Final%20Report%20-%20Scoping%20Study.pdf [Accessed January 20, 2012].

Ulster Bank. (2012) *Ulster Bank opens ATM network to charitable giving scheme*. 18 October 2012. www.group.ulsterbank.com/media/press-releases/republic-of-ireland/2012/18-10-12.ashx [Accessed November 27, 2012].

Usry, J. (2008) 'Charitable solicitation regulation for the nonprofit sector: Paving the regulatory landscape for future success,' *Policy Perspectives*. Salt Lake City: Center for Public Policy and Administration, University of Utah. www.imakenews.com/cppa/e_article001162331.cfm?x=b6Gdd3k,b30DNQvw,w [Accessed October 21, 2011].

Weakley, K. (2012) '30 charities to benefit from ATM giving scheme revealed,' *Civil Society*. www.civilsociety.co.uk/fundraising/news/content/13582/30_charities_to_benefit_from_atm_giving_scheme_revealed [Accessed November 27, 2012].

15

The fiscal treatment of philanthropy from a comparative perspective

Calum M. Carmichael

Since antiquity, private persons have voluntarily contributed their resources in order to provide certain goods and services, either to their societies as a whole, or to particular groups with whom they have no immediate or personal ties; for as long, governments, recognizing how such voluntarism could undercut or support their own objectives, have sought either to discourage the donors, or to encourage and guide them. Through various means, governments seek to influence not only the amount and form of the contributions, but also their deployment – the organizations that receive them, the goods and services that are to be provided, and the groups that are to benefit (Carmichael, 2009, 2011). In wielding this influence, they have attempted to strike a balance between protecting options and employing compulsion so as to preserve, but also enlist and direct the underlying voluntarism.

With the development of tax systems capable of distinguishing donors, the donee organizations, and the contributions themselves, governments acquired additional tools with which to wield this influence. These fiscal tools now include subsidies for contributions, as well as tax reductions for donee organizations. The subsidies lower the outlay that donors must make in order to provide organizations with a given quantity of funds, doing so by offering either the donee a matching grant, or the donors a deduction from income otherwise taxed, or a credit against taxes otherwise paid. The tax reductions could involve exempting from taxation the organizations' income on investments or business activity, or they could involve lowering or eliminating the goods and services (GST) or value added tax (VAT) that the organizations collect on their outputs. By awarding such fiscal privileges, governments fund the donee organizations indirectly by forgoing tax revenues – as opposed to either funding them directly through grants or contracts, or funding government agencies that provide similar goods and services to similar groups.

This chapter performs two tasks: it categorizes the theoretical rationales for governments awarding fiscal privileges to certain types of nonprofit organizations; and it reviews the actual practices by which eight national governments both identify these eligible organizations, and award three types of privileges. It does so in recognition of the enduring importance, heightened in an era of ongoing fiscal consolidation, of questions that deal with why, and how, any privileges should be awarded. The chapter does not answer these questions. Rather, it compares existing rationales and practices in the hope of assisting researchers and practitioners to become more aware of contending outlooks and approaches, and hence better able to situate and perhaps reappraise their own. Most of the theoretical rationales for why fiscal privileges should be awarded have been developed over the past 40 years by American tax scholars – subsequent to the introduction of many of the privileges that now exist, and unrelated to many of the countries in which they now operate. The eight national governments that have been selected to illustrate how the privileges are being awarded are Australia, Canada, Germany, India, Japan, Sweden, Turkey, and the US. This sample includes Asia, Europe and North America. It also combines both common and civil law traditions, represents the four 'nonprofit regime types' proposed by Salamon and Anheier (1998), and demonstrates the diversity of contemporary practices.

Rationales for fiscal privileges

Various theoretical rationales have been offered to justify the existence and design of fiscal privileges which apply to certain nonprofit organizations. Here, they are categorized according to whether their arguments are based on procedural, deontological, or consequentialist grounds.

Exercising democracy

The first category assumes that it is the role of governments to allocate their indirect funding in response to the demonstrated preferences of donors. This would enable governments both to facilitate a form of direct democracy and avoid the need of determining independently the appropriateness or effects of their fiscal choices. With respect to exempting an organization's income from taxation, Hall and Colombo (1991) recommend that governments provide this privilege only to organizations for which contributions make up a sizable proportion, say, one-third of gross revenues. Eligibility would thus be determined by the relative 'deservedness' of organizations as demonstrated by donors, rather than by the 'ad hoc normative judgments' or 'intensely empirical inquiries' of governments (Hall and Colombo, 1991: 1388). With respect to subsidizing contributions, Levmore (1998) endorses this privilege as a means by which governments can tie their indirect funding to the philanthropic 'ballots' cast by donors. Schizer (2009) and Benshalom (2009) make the same endorsement, but add, respectively, that subsidies might encourage wealthy donors to monitor donee performance and that higher subsidies for poorer donors might temper the plutocratic implications of treating contributions as votes.

Ensuring Fairness

The second category of rationales assumes that governments' role is to provide donors or donees with fair or due treatment. In some instances, the notion of due treatment is based on assertions that either the motive of donors or the stature of donees is sacrosanct. In other instances, the notion is based on assertions that the income or transactions in question are unattributable or unmeasurable, and hence not suited to taxation. With respect to donor motive, Atkinson (1990: 635) describes the action of donors and the provision of goods and services by donees as being 'altruistic', and hence 'inherently desirable and prima facie worthy of encouragement through tax exemption'. With respect to donee stature, Brody (1998: 586-87) justifies extending fiscal privileges to charitable organizations on the basis of governments perceiving them as a 'parallel sovereign' deserving independence and containment: paraphrasing Matthew 22:21, 'charities go untaxed because Caesar should not tax God (or the modern secular equivalent)'. With respect to income being unattributable, Bittker and Rahdert (1976) point to conceptual and practical difficulties in calculating the net income and appropriate tax rate for nonprofit organizations. On the basis of 'established principles of income taxation', they argue that such organizations are 'not suitable targets' (Bittker and Rahdert, 2006: 357, 304). Rushton (2007) also supports exempting from taxation the net income of nonprofit organizations, not because the income is difficult to calculate, but because it, unlike the retained earnings of corporations, is not owned by private shareholders. In regard to transactions being unattributable, Andrews (1972) and Buckles (2005) start with a 'Haig-Simons' definition of taxable income which comprises consumption plus accumulated wealth. By their account, contributions lie outside that definition because they do not divert scarce resources to the exclusive use of the donor. Thus they should be deducted from the donor's taxable income, and thereby subsidized. Aujean et al. (1999: 146) and Ebrill et al. (2001: 90-93) refer to the conceptual and practical difficulties of taxing transactions for which no explicit consideration or return payment can be identified. Such difficulties may be associated with the types of outputs that nonprofit organizations provide either at no charge or at fees below market value, and therefore warrant lowering or eliminating a GST or VAT.

Increasing welfare

The third category of rationales assumes that the role of governments is to correct so-called 'market failures', that is, transactions for which the participating sellers and buyers do not perceive or experience the full social costs and benefits involved. Because of this, the sellers and buyers might choose types and levels of transactions that either leave in some avoidable social costs, or leave out some potential social benefits. Governments can reduce the ensuing losses in social welfare by judiciously taxing or subsidizing the transactions or their participants.

As regards exempting an organization's income from taxation, Weisbrod (1975) describes a political system in which the government responds to the preferences of the median voter, and an economy in which collective goods can be provided alternatively by the government using taxes, corporations using profits, or nonprofit organizations using contributions and government funding. In this system, the government could improve the well-being of the median voter by providing fiscal privileges to nonprofit organizations, particularly if citizens differ greatly in their tastes for such goods. Alternatively, Hansmann (1981) describes a situation in which nonprofits' 'nondistribution constraint' (discussed in the next section) not only reduces the supply of their products by blocking the organizations from capital markets, but also increases the demand for their products by making the organizations more trustworthy. In this circumstance, the government could alleviate the ensuing excess demand by exempting the organizations from income tax. Drawing upon Weisbrod and Hansmann, Steinberg (1991: 362) argues that nonprofit organizations satisfy 'diverse demands for public goods', 'innovate and experiment' in the type, delivery and management of services, and hence provide a 'benchmark' and a 'competitive check on governments'. Because of these sector-wide benefits, he proposes that the burden of proof falls on those who would remove or reduce the fiscal privileges awarded those organizations.

In respect to subsidizing contributions, the public finance field in economics has given considerable attention to situations in which donors' incentives overlook the social benefits that would be generated if they were to increase or reallocate their contributions. These situations could exist whether donors' incentives were based either on: the portions of the goods and services they receive (Hochman and Rodgers, 1977); the approbation or 'warm glow' they garner (Andreoni, 1990); or the impact they envisage (Duncan, 2004). Subsidies could lead donors to increase and reallocate their contributions in ways that would raise both their own well-being and social welfare more generally – *if* those subsidies reduced the private costs of donation by amounts that approximated the social benefits that donors would otherwise overlook. Higher subsidies would typically be warranted in situations where contributions are price sensitive (i.e. elastic as opposed to inelastic), where government grants would reduce (i.e. crowd out) rather than increase (i.e. crowd in) contributions, where governments place priority on the goods and services and the populations receiving them, and where nonprofit organizations are more effective or efficient than government agencies (Feldstein, 1980; Roberts, 1987). The optimal subsidy rates would have no relation to the income tax rate faced by donors, and thus should be conferred by a credit, not a deduction (Saez, 2004). What is more, they are unlikely to be uniform across the various activities performed by nonprofit organizations (Carmichael, 2012b).

Finally, in regards to eliminating a GST or VAT, Ebrill *et al.* (2001: 69-78, 93-94) argue that certain outputs that are often provided by nonprofit organizations (e.g. basic food, health, education) generate social benefits beyond the ones received by the immediate consumers. These social benefits would be lost if consumption taxes reduced demand. For governments that place priority on the well-being of the poor, the losses to social welfare would be even greater if the poor spend proportionately more on these outputs than the rich. Ebrill and colleagues (2001) caution, however, that its implications for social welfare are not clear. For one thing, in order to pursue distribution goals, most governments have access to better fiscal tools than reducing consumption taxes. For another, GST or VAT relief for nonprofit organizations might introduce market distortions, not simply correct them.

Overview

These three theoretical rationales for awarding fiscal privileges are normative in the sense that they prescribe what governments should do, rather than describe or predict what governments could or would do. In surveys of the fiscal treatment of nonprofit organizations, such rationales often appear in blended forms (Clotfelter, 2012). Here, however, they are categorized and distinguished according to their assumptions about the *desired* role of governments: whether that is to respond to the priorities of donors (procedural), or to treat donors or donees fairly (deontological), or to correct market failures (consequentialist). So categorized, the rationales can be further distinguished according to their implications about the locus of fiscal authority, the information requirements of governments, and certain attributes of the ideal set of privileges. For example, the first category of rationales, 'exercising democracy', would vest fiscal authority with the donors – the natural or legal persons with the resources and incentives to contribute – making them the arbiters of which nonprofit organizations or subsectors are the most deserving of indirect government funding. The information requirements of governments are thus relatively low, centring on the revenue sources of those organizations and subsectors. The ideal set of privileges, however conferred, would tend to be uniform across the organizations or subsectors that have been identified on the basis of received contributions. The second category, 'ensuring fairness', would vest the authority with governments, making them the arbiters of who is entitled to what. The information requirements are again relatively low, involving the definition and identification of the transactions, forms of income, or organizations that are deemed inviolable. The ideal set of privileges would be conferred through immunity from taxation, whether this applies to the eligible contributions of donors, or to the income and outputs of the eligible organizations. The third category, 'increasing welfare', would also place the authority with governments, making them the arbiters of which groups in society are the most needy, what goods and services are the most needed, and which fiscal tools would allow those groups to receive those services with the least amount of tax revenue either spent or forgone. Thus, the information requirements are relatively high. And the ideal set of privileges, however conferred, would tend to be graduated: greater for those nonprofit organizations or subsectors that provide the most needed goods and services to the most needy groups, or that do so most efficiently and effectively (Carmichael, 2012a: 397-99). For this category, the information requirements include not only the effects of any privileges on the contributions that nonprofit organizations receive and the revenues that they retain, but also the consequences of those effects upon social welfare. By focusing on those effects, the third category of rationales is the one most closely tied to the insights and limitations of empirical work. Such insights include measurements of how contributions have been or might be affected by increases in subsidies or direct funding. Their limitations include the ambiguity that comes from those measurements varying across either the estimation techniques employed, the contending influences controlled for, or the dataset, time period, and jurisdiction selected (Bakija and Heim, 2011: 615-19; Bekkers and Wiepking, 2011: 932-33, 948-49).

Awarding fiscal privileges

By awarding a variety of fiscal privileges, governments can influence the contributions and overall funding that nonprofit organizations receive, the revenues they retain and the kind and amount of goods and services they deliver. In order to wield this influence, regardless of the rationale, governments must decide both the reach and the range of their fiscal tools. That is to say, governments must decide not only the particular nonprofit organizations or subsectors that are eligible, but also the combination of privileges that are awarded. In this section, these decisions are illustrated with reference to the practices circa 2013 by which eight national governments (Australia, Canada, Germany, India, Japan, Sweden, Turkey and US) award three types of privileges (exemption from income tax, elimination of output tax, and subsidization of cash contributions). As described in the next section, the practices differ considerably.

The reach of fiscal privileges

The source, type and adjudicator of the criteria that are used to identify the nonprofit organizations or subsectors eligible to receive fiscal privileges are summarized in Table 15.1. In terms of source, all governments specify in legislation certain criteria required for organizations to hold what is variously referred to as 'public benefit', 'charitable', 'public-interest', 'tax-privileged' or 'tax-exemption' status. This area of lawmaking has been active in recent years. For example, in 2008, both Japan and Turkey introduced legislation to revise the terms of this status for associations. In 2013, Australia enacted charities' legislation which provides a statutory (and expanded) definition of charity (ACNC, ND) and amendments to India's Finance Act in 2009 added preservation of the environment to its list of charitable purposes (ICNL, 2015). All of the governments except Turkey specify in legislation what Hansmann (1980: 838) referred to as the 'nondistribution constraint'. In order to be eligible, the organizations may earn a profit or show net earnings; however, those earnings may only be used to finance the goods and services that the organization has been approved to provide, and may not be distributed to the private benefit of any persons exercising control, such as members, directors or donors. Germany is an exception as its General Fiscal Law [1976] allows a foundation to use up to one-third of its income for the donor and the donor's near relatives, without losing its tax-privileged status. Three of the governments – Germany, India, and Turkey – include what Hansmann (1980: 838) referred to as 'reasonable compensation' which specifies that nonprofits may not exceed market norms in remunerating persons for their labour, capital, and materials.

Table 15.1 Fiscal definition of philanthropy

	Australia	Canada	Germany	India	Japan	Sweden	Turkey	US
Source	Common law; legislation[i]	Common law; legislation[ii]	Legislation[iii]	Common law; legislation[iv]	Legislation[v]	Legislation[vi]	Legislation[vii]	Common law; legislation[viii]
Criteria	Purpose; activity; type of organization; organization	Purpose; activity	Purpose; activity	Purpose; activity; population; organization	Purpose; type of organization	Purpose; type of organization; organization	Purpose; activity; type of organization	Purpose; activity
Adjudicator	Courts; Australian Charities and Not-for-profits Commission; Australian Taxation Office	Courts; Canada Revenue Agency	State tax agencies	Courts; tax commissioners	Public Interest Corporation Commission; Ministry of Finance; National Tax Administration	Swedish Tax Agency; seven county governments	Council of Ministers; Ministry of Finance; other relevant ministries	Courts; Internal Revenue Service

Notes: Australia's Extension of Charitable Purposes Act [2004] extends the common-law meaning of charity to include child care, affordable rental housing, self-help groups, and closed or contemplative religious orders. The Australian Charities and Not-for-profits Commission (ACNC), established in December 2012, determines charitable status, and the Charities Act 2013, which took effect in January 2014, introduced a more comprehensive statutory definition of charity. The Australian Tax Office endorses organizations for certain fiscal privileges, accepting the ACNC determination. Under the new statutory definition, political activities that support a political party or candidate for office remain 'disqualifying'; however, political activities that attempt to change public opinion, a law, or government policy related to charitable purposes are not (Australian Government, the Treasury [2011b]).

[ii]The Canadian Income Tax Act [1985] identifies three types of registered charities: organizations that carry on activities that serve charitable purposes as defined in common law; public and private foundations that do not carry on those activities but fund other registered 'qualified donees'. Qualified donees comprise not only charities, but also designated nonprofit organizations (e.g. national amateur athletic associations, low-cost housing corporations, the United Nations). Charities can lose their registration by explicitly supporting a political party or candidate for office, or by using more than ten percent of their resources (20 percent for smaller charities) to advocate changing a law or policy of any government (Canada Revenue Agency, 2003a). New reporting requirements and compliance oversight of political activities were introduced in 2012 (Department of Finance, 2012: 205). Charitable private foundations can lose their registration if they carry on any business activity, although some accommodation was made in the 2015 budget to allow investment in limited partnerships. Charitable organizations and public foundations can lose their registration if they carry on business activity other than what is 'related' (i.e. either run by volunteers, or linked but subservient to their charitable purpose) (Canada Revenue Agency, 2003b). Short of losing their registration, the charities may be liable to a penalty of five percent of their gross revenues from business activity that is not related.

[iii]In Germany, the General Fiscal Law [1976] outlines the conditions for fiscal privileges. These include the organizations (e.g. associations, foundations, limited-liability corporations) operating for 'tax-privileged' purposes. The purposes are either of public benefit, charitable (supporting individuals of low income who are dependent 'on account of their physical, mental, or emotional state', or church-related). These organizations must not use funds to support political parties or candidates for office, although organizations do not jeopardize their status by occasionally engaging in public debate or attempting to influence public opinion on laws or policies related to their tax-privileged purposes.

iv Existing legislation in India defines charitable purpose to include: relief of poor, education, medical relief, preservation of environment and monuments or places of historic interest and the 'advancement of any other object of general public utility'. This omits 'advancement of religion': a religious organization or fund can only be charitable if it operates exclusively for the benefit of the under-privileged members of the religious community. The 2015 Finance Bill added yoga as a special category of charitable purpose. It also slightly relaxes but maintains restrictions on business activities of organizations involved in the 'advancement of general public utility:' business activities must be undertaken in the course of carrying out these charitable purposes and revenues must not exceed 20 percent of total receipts. Organizations operating under the other divisions of legal charity can freely engage in 'incidental' business activity conducted in the course of carrying out a charitable activity. Charitable organizations may engage either in basic political education or 'incidental' political activity that involves lobbying and advocacy on matters that advance 'general public utility' or are otherwise related to their charitable purpose. It is understood, however, that such activity cannot be their focus, and cannot support a political party or candidate for office.

v To be eligible for fiscal privileges in Japan, nonprofit organizations must implement activities that advance the public interest. Separate laws tied to the Civil Code [1897] enable the Ministry of Finance to certify 'special public interest corporations' that perform certain of these activities (e.g. establishing private schools or hospitals and medical clinics; providing religious services). Alternatively: the Specified Nonprofit Activities Promotion Law [1998] enables the Economic Planning Agency to certify 'specified nonprofit activities corporations' implementing activities among the 17 listed in the Schedule to the Law. The Association and Foundation Law [2008] and the Law on Recognizing Organizations as Public Interest [2008] enable the Public Interest Corporation Commission to certify 'public interest incorporated associations and foundations' implementing activities among the 23 listed in the latter law. These two lists of activities overlap but are distinct. Only 'public interest incorporated associations' and foundations are automatically eligible for fiscal privileges. All other organizations must apply for them – either to the Ministry of Finance or to the National Tax Administration – and meet separate requirements. In general, the organizations may carry on business activity, although the Law on Recognizing Organizations as Public Interest [2008] requires more than half of the profits be used for their public interest activity. In general, the organizations are able to engage in political activity (e.g. supporting political parties and candidates for office; or attempting to change public opinion, a law, or government policy) that is a means of advancing their public interest activities. The Specified Nonprofit Activities Promotion Law [1998] stipulates that 'promoting, supporting, or opposing a political principle' or 'recommending, supporting, or opposing a candidate, a person holding a public office, or a political party' are not in themselves public interest activities.

vi Sweden's Income Tax Act [1999] outlines the conditions for fiscal privileges. In some instances, these are by category of organization (e.g. health care facilities and private schools) or by specific organizations (e.g. Swedish Committee for UNICEF). In some instances, these include purposes that differ by organization type; for example, there are six qualifying purposes for foundations (caring of children, funding of education, relief of people in need, promotion of scientific research, promotion of Nordic cooperation, strengthening defence). Other 'public' purposes for associations (religious, charitable, social, political, sporting, artistic, and cultural) are also included.

vii In Turkey, the Council of Ministers grants public benefit status to associations and tax-exemption status to foundations on the basis of existing activities that not only fall under certain purpose areas, but also extend beyond a group or region, and reduce the service undertakings of the state: see Foundations Law No. 5253 [2004] Article 27 and Associations Law No. 4962 [2008]. The purpose areas are defined for foundations (health, social aid, education, scientific research and development, culture, environmental protection and forestation), but not for associations. The Council of Ministers acts upon the proposal of the Ministry of Finance and the Ministry of Interior for associations, that in turn take into account the opinions of not only the ministries with activities in the same areas, but also either the Department of Associations or the Directorate General of Foundations.

viii The US Internal Revenue Code [1986] §501(c)(3) exempts from income tax 'corporations, and any community chest, fund, or foundation, organized and operated exclusively for religious, charitable, scientific, testing for public safety, literary, or educational purposes, or to foster national or international amateur sports competition ..., or for the prevention of cruelty to children or animals'. The same list of purposes, less 'testing for public safety', appears in §170(c)(2) to identify the 'public charities' eligible to receive deductible 'charitable contributions'. Both sections limit the political activity of these organizations: they cannot participate in any campaign for elective or appointive public office; churches and foundations cannot make lobbying expenditures to influence legislation; the others cannot regularly make lobbying expenditures above 30 percent of their 'exempt purpose expenditures'.

All eight governments require the organizations to focus their activities on purposes officially recognized as being of 'public benefit', or words to that effect. Only Canada does not provide a statutory reference for such purposes, relying instead on the courts' interpretation of the common law meaning of charity (which identifies four main categories or 'heads' – relief of poverty, advancement of education, advancement of religion, and other purposes beneficial to the community). Other common law countries have itemized in legislation certain purposes deemed 'beneficial to the community': the US since 1894; India since 1961; and Australia since 2004 (Carmichael 2012a: 404-07).

For Canada, Germany, India and the US, the purposes that qualify as eligible for tax benefits are generally the same across organizational types, and these purposes are linked to a common set of privileges. For the other governments, the purposes differ. In Australia, for example, a narrow set of purposes (relief of poverty, sickness, distress, and the like) distinguishes 'public benevolent institutions' from the broader, overlapping categories of 'charities' and 'deductible gift recipients'. In Japan, the 17 activities listed for 'specified nonprofit activities corporations' are only partially represented in the 23 activities listed for 'public interest incorporated associations and foundations'. In Sweden, the qualifying purposes listed for foundations are fewer than the public purposes for associations. Whereas the purpose areas for foundations holding tax exemption status in Turkey are listed in jurisdiction, those for associations holding public benefit status are not.

For most of the governments, certain degrees of political or business activity make organizations ineligible for fiscal privileges; however, the thresholds differ. In terms of political activity, Sweden is the least restrictive: political purposes are among the public purposes for associations, although not for foundations. In India and Turkey, there are no legislated prohibitions or limits. Turkey's Law 5253 [2004] omits the article of the previous statute that forbid associations from 'engaging in any form of political activity', and does not specify new limits; it is understood, however, that anything beyond incidental activity would not be condoned. In Japan, political activity is acceptable if it is a means of furthering an organization's public interest purposes, and does not become a focus or end in itself. In Australia and Germany, supporting or opposing a political party or candidate for office is not permitted, but advocacy or lobbying to change a law or government policy is acceptable if it remains a means, not an end in itself. In Canada and the US, supporting or opposing a party or candidate is not permitted; however, advocacy or lobbying is acceptable (apart from churches and foundation in the US) if the expenditures remain below specified limits. Canada has recently introduced efforts to 'enhance' reporting on these activities and the regulation of charities' compliance in this regard (Blumberg, 2013).

The thresholds also differ for business activity. In Turkey, such activity is permitted, but the income is taxed. In Australia and Japan, it is permitted and at least a portion of the income that is used for the organization's public benefit purposes is exempt from taxation. In Germany, Sweden (for associations) and the US, it is also permitted; the income is exempt, however, only if the activity itself is, respectively, 'dedicated', 'naturally connected' or 'related' to the organization's purposes. In Canada and India, business activity is not permitted unless it is, respectively, 'related' or 'incidental' to those purposes, in which case the income is exempt. For India, if the purposes fall under the residuary division of 'any other object of general public utility', then the restriction is tighter: any business activity with annual gross receipts in excess of one million rupees is not permitted.

In all of the countries, administrative and ultimately judicial or political authorities determine whether or not the purposes and activities of an organization warrant public benefit status. The administrative authorities are variously situated in tax agencies, line departments, or independent commissions – their location conceivably tilting their priorities toward either protecting the tax base, accommodating political pressures, or expanding the sector and its activities. Australia moved the administrative functions from a tax agency to a commission in late 2012; Canada, Germany, India, Sweden and the US position them in tax agencies; Turkey, in a line department; and Japan, in all three, depending on the type of nonprofit organization. The role of political authorities is uniquely explicit in Turkey: the Council of Ministers decides whether to grant tax exemption or public benefit status, taking into account not only the organization's purposes, but also the extent to which its ongoing activities reduce the service undertakings of the state. The role of the courts has been traditionally important in common law jurisdictions. The High Court of Australia, for example, recently decided that political objects are compatible with charitable purposes if they are pursued by advocacy or lobbying to change a law or government policy (*Aid/Watch Incorporated v Commissioner of Taxation* [2010] HCA 42).

The range of fiscal privileges

The significance of public benefit status, or its counterparts, rests primarily on the fiscal privileges that accompany it. These privileges are summarized in Table 15.2, taking into account whether or not they are awarded *exclusively* to the organizations holding the status, *comprehensively* across those organizations, and *uniformly* across those organizations that have been awarded the privileges.

Among the eight governments, Turkey alone does not exempt public benefit associations or tax-exempt foundations from income tax. Most of the others do not award the exemption exclusively to the organizations holding public benefit status. Instead, they award it either to nonprofit organizations generally (e.g. Australia, Canada, Germany, US) or to other nonprofit organizations identified in legislation (e.g. India, Sweden). Across public benefit organizations, Japan does not award it comprehensively (e.g. the income of medical corporations is taxed); and Japan and Sweden do not award it uniformly. In Japan, different types of organizations are able to deduct different amounts – from 20 to 100 percent – of the business income used for their public interest purposes. In Sweden, although both associations and foundations are exempt from taxes on their investment income, only associations are exempt from taxes on their income from real estate or business activity that is 'naturally connected' to their public purposes.

The US does not have a GST or VAT; although India has proposed a national GST, it has yet to introduce one. Among the other six governments that have a GST or VAT, only Canada and Sweden eliminate the tax collected on the outputs of certain organizations holding public benefit status, doing so either by making the outputs taxable, but 'zero-rated' (i.e. the organizations can still claim credits for the tax they pay on inputs purchased to produce the outputs), or by making the outputs untaxed or 'exempt' (i.e. the organizations are treated as 'final consumers of the taxed inputs and cannot claim those credits). The GST relief awarded by Canada is neither exclusive, nor uniform: certain outputs of charitable and some nonprofit organizations are exempt. What is more, these organizations receive a credit – from 50 to 100 percent – of the tax they pay on the inputs used to produce exempt outputs, depending on their area of activity. The VAT relief awarded by Sweden is not comprehensive. Although Swedish foundations collect the tax, associations with public purposes do not: all of their outputs are exempt – in violation of the European Commission's VAT Directive.

Finally, all of the governments except Sweden subsidize the cash contributions made by individuals and corporations to organizations holding public benefit status. In Canada and Japan, the standard subsidy on the contributions from individuals is conferred by nonrefundable income tax credits that are independent of the taxpayer's marginal tax rate. Otherwise, the standard subsidy on contributions from individuals and corporations is conferred by deductions from

Table 15.2 Fiscal application of philanthropy

	Australia	Canada	Germany	India	Japan	Sweden	Turkey	US
Income Tax Exemption	yes[1]	yes[2]	yes[3]	yes[4]	yes[5]	yes[6]	no[7]	yes[8]
Exclusive	no	no	no	no	yes	no	NA	no
Comprehensive	yes	yes	yes	yes	no	yes	NA	yes
Uniform	yes	yes	yes	yes	no	no	NA	yes
VAT/GST Exemption	no[9]	yes[10]	no[11]	NA[12]	no	yes[13]	no	NA
Exclusive	NA	no	NA	–	NA	no	NA	–
Comprehensive	NA	yes	NA	–	NA	no	NA	–
Uniform	NA	no	NA	–	NA	yes	NA	–
Contribution Subsidy for Individuals	yes, deduction[14,15]	yes, credit[16]	yes, deduction[17]	yes, deduction[18]	yes, credit or deduction[19,20]	no	yes, deduction[21]	yes, deduction[22]
Exclusive	no	no	no	no	yes	NA	yes	no
Comprehensive	no	yes	yes	yes	no	NA	yes	yes
Uniform	yes	no	yes	no	yes	NA	yes	yes
Contribution Subsidy for Corporations	yes, deduction[14]	yes, deduction[23]	yes, deduction[24]	yes, deduction[18]	yes, deduction[19,25]	no	yes, deduction[21]	yes, deduction[22]
Exclusive	no	yes	yes	no	yes	NA	yes	no
Comprehensive	no	yes	yes	yes	no	NA	yes	yes
Uniform	yes	yes[26]	yes	no	yes	NA	yes	yes

Notes

[1] The Income Tax Assessment Act [1997] exempts nonprofit organizations generally, except for "nonprofit companies" operated for the joint or common benefit of their members. The exempt organizations include the overlapping classes of charities and "deductible gift recipients", as well as "income tax exempt funds" which provide grants to deductible gift recipients and are endorsed by the Taxation Office. The 2011-12 Budget extends the exemption to profits generated by any "unrelated commercial activities" that are directed to the organizations' "altruistic" purposes.

[2] The Income Tax Act [1985] Paragraph 149.1 (1) exempts nonprofit organizations as well as registered charities and other "qualified donees". An exception: the investment income of nonprofit organizations with the main purpose of providing recreational services to their members is taxable above $2000.

[3] The Corporate Income Tax Law [1999] §5 exempts nonprofit organizations including those operated for "tax-privileged" purposes. For the latter, the General Fiscal Law [1976] Part III §§64, 65 does not exempt income from business activity above €35,000 unless the activity is "dedicated" to the tax-privileged purposes (i.e., necessary for achieving them, and not unnecessarily competing with the business activity of non-privileged organizations).

[4] The Direct Taxes Code [2010] Chapter IV exempts the income associated with the charitable activity of nonprofit organizations, including that derived from any "incidental business" conducted in the course of carrying out that activity. The 7th Schedule lists a broader range of funds and organizations "not liable to income tax". The 6th Schedule Paragraph 22 exempts the income of political parties, except that from business activity.

5 Nonprofit organizations acquire legal personality in part because their main activities are other than the 34 "profit-making activities" identified as taxable by the Corporation Tax Law [1965] Article 5. However, the income of Medical Corporations is not exempt, unless their health care services are tied to academic research, or unless they have been approved by the Ministry of Finance as public welfare hospitals on the basis of receiving fees from the social insurance system. "Public Interest Incorporated Associations and Foundations" may deduct the income from any profit-making activities if it is used for their core public-interest activities; whereas "Special Public Interest Corporations" may deduct 50% of it; and "Specified Nonprofit Activities Corporations" may deduct 20%: Ministry of Finance (FY2008) Tax Reform Main Points.

6 The Income Tax Act [1999:1229] Chapter 7 exempts types of income for certain organizations. The organizations named in §17 (e.g., private licensed gaming companies, the Nobel Foundation) are taxed only on income from real estate. Foundations operating for the qualifying purposes in §4 are exempt from taxes on investment income. Associations operating for the public purposes in §7 are exempt from taxes on income from business activity or real estate that has a "natural connection" to those purposes. By §§5, 9 the exempted income of foundations and associations must be "almost exclusively" dedicated to their qualifying or public purposes.

7 An exception: public-benefit associations and tax-exempt foundations do not pay corporate tax on membership dues, donations, or grants.

8 The Internal Revenue Code §§501-530 identifies the nonprofit organizations exempt from income tax. There are exceptions to the exemption awarded to the "public charities" identified in §501(c)(3): for example, by §§511-513, public charities are taxed on income from unrelated business, apart from that either performed substantially by volunteers or involving the sale of donated goods; by §4911, public charities not prohibited from lobbying by §501(h) pay a 25% excise tax on lobbying expenditures that exceed at least 20% of their tax-exempt purpose expenditures; and by §4940, private foundations pay 2% excise tax on net investment income.

9 An exception: a few outputs are zero-rated only if provided by a charity or deductible gift recipient (e.g., non-commercial sales made at a discount below cost or market value, or accommodation for seniors): A New Tax System - Goods and Services Tax - Act [1999] Chapter 3. The 2011-12 Budget clarifies that any GST concessions do not extend to these organizations' "unrelated commercial activities".

10 The Excise Tax Act [1985] §123(1) Schedule V makes exempt certain outputs supplied by registered charities (e.g., short-term rental accommodation, catering). On their taxable outputs apart from capital and real property, registered charities remit 60% of the GST they collect: Canada Revenue Agency (2008), GST/HST information for charities. Certain outputs are exempt if supplied by either charities or nonprofit organizations (e.g., those sold at direct cost, food and accommodation for needy persons). Charities and "qualifying" nonprofit organizations for which government funding is at least 40% of total revenue receive a rebate of 50% of the GST paid on eligible purchases used to produce exempt outputs. Charities and nonprofit organizations that carry on specific activities receive higher rebates: Excise Tax Act [1985] §259. For the activities of school authorities, public colleges, and universities, the rebate is 67% of the GST paid; for the activities of hospitals and health care service providers, it is 83%; and for the activities of municipalities, it is 100%.

11 An exception: by the Value Added Tax Law [1999] part II §4, outputs of "tax-privileged" organizations engaged in "economic activity" are either subject to the standard VAT rate of 19% if the activity is not "dedicated" to the tax-privileged purposes of the organization, or subject to the reduced rate of 7% if it is.

12 A VAT was introduced in 2005: however, it has not been adopted by all state governments; and those adopting it do not apply uniform rates, and do not provide credits for the VAT paid on inputs from outside their jurisdiction. The Constitution (115th Amendment) Bill [2011] would allow a GST to be introduced and applied uniformly and concurrently by the central and state governments. The proposed GST would replace all existing indirect taxes – including the state-level VAT.

13 The Value Added Tax Act [1994:200] Chapter 4 §2 makes exempt all outputs supplied by associations having a public purpose. In 2008, the European Commission ruled this comprehensive treatment of associations' outputs to be in violation of Article 132 of the VAT Directive that makes exempt only certain "public-interest" outputs. In 2011, the Commission rejected Sweden's offer to maintain its comprehensive treatment for only associations with a turnover below one million kronor.

14 The Income Tax Assessment Act [1997] Division 30 defines "deductible gift recipients" as nonprofit organizations or funds that are eligible to receive tax deductible contributions by: being named specifically; falling under one of the listed categories and being endorsed by the Taxation Office; or having been endorsed as a certain type of charity. Those types include public benefit institutions (i.e., charities organized for the direct relief of poverty, sickness, suffering, distress, misfortune, or disability) and health promotion charities. Charities that advance religion are not deductible gift recipients.

15 Individuals are able to deduct contributions to political parties, up to $1,500.

[16] The Income Tax Act [1985] 118.1 (1) enables individuals to receive a credit for contributions to registered charities and other "qualified donees", up to 75% of their net income. The credit is 15% of contributions up to $200, and 29% thereafter – these rates corresponding to the lowest and highest marginal taxes. For finite periods following certain international disasters, the government has matched the contributions of individuals to organizations engaged in relief (e.g., the December 2004 tsunami in Southeast Asia; the July 2011 declaration of famine in East Africa). Since 2001, the government has also matched individuals' contributions to endowments of approved performing arts organizations. Individuals receive a credit for contributions to political parties calculated as 75% of their contributions up to $400, 50% of additional contributions up to $750, and 33.33% of additional contributions up to $1275.

[17] The Income Tax Law [1997] §10b enables individuals to deduct contributions to organizations operated for "tax-privileged" purposes, up to 20% of their annual income, and up to €1 million divided over 10 years if made to an endowment of such organizations. In addition, §§10(b), 34(g) enable individuals either to deduct or to receive a 50% tax credit on contributions to political parties, up to €1,650.

[18] The Direct Taxes Code [2010] Clause 79 (with reference to the 16th Schedule) enables individuals and corporations to deduct: 50% of their contributions to registered charitable organizations, as well as a range of nonprofit organizations and named funds (e.g., historic buildings of worship for their repair; the National Children's Fund); 100% of contributions to another range (e.g., universities; the Indian Olympic Association); 125% of contributions to universities and research associations if for statistical and social science research; and 175% of contributions to similar institutions if for scientific research and development. Deductible contributions can not exceed 10% of gross income if the allowed deduction is 50%. In addition, Clause 81 enables individuals and corporations to deduct 100% of their contributions to a political party, up to 5% of gross income.

[19] Upon being certified by the Public Interest Corporation Commission, Public Interest Incorporated Associations and Foundations are simultaneously certified as "Special Public Interest Promoting Corporations" by the Ministry of Finance, and thus eligible to receive subsidized contributions (italics added). Other nonprofit organizations only become eligible by separately applying either to the Ministry of Finance for similar certification, or (as for Specified Nonprofit Activities Corporations) to the National Tax Administration to be certified as "Tax Deductible". The requirements differ. Among the "Special Public Interest Corporations", Religious Corporations and Medical Corporations other than public welfare hospitals can not be certified to receive subsidized contributions.

[20] In general, individuals may either deduct contributions in excess of ¥2000 to eligible organizations, or they may receive a tax credit for 50% of those contributions: Ministry of Finance (FY2011) Tax Reform Main Points. The deduction or credit applies to contributions of up to 40% of total income.

[21] Individuals and corporations may deduct contributions, up 5% of their taxable income to public-benefit associations or tax-exempt foundations, or up to 10% if those organizations operate in "development priority" regions. Individuals and corporations may also deduct unlimited contributions to foundations for the "maintenance, repair, restoration, or sustenance" of cultural properties: Law 5735 [2008] Article 77.

[22] The Internal Revenue Code [1986] §170(b)(1), (2) enables individuals and corporations to deduct contributions to not only the public charities identified in §170(c)(2), but also two forms of mutual-benefit organizations: veteran associations and foundations, and cemetery companies owned and operated for members. In general, individuals are able to deduct up to 50% of their adjusted gross income, and corporations up to 10% of their taxable income. The American Jobs Act of 2011 (H. Doc. 112-53) (S. 1549) §401 would limit individuals' deduction to 28%, even if their marginal tax rate was higher.

[23] The Income Tax Act [1985] 110.1(1) enables corporations to deduct up to 75% of their net income contributed to registered charities and other qualified donees.

[24] The Corporate Income Tax Law [1999] §9 enables corporations to deduct contributions to organizations operated for "tax-privileged" purposes, either up to 20% of their annual income, or up to .4% of the sum of revenues, salaries and wages.

[25] In general, corporations may deduct up to 5% of their annual income contributed to eligible organizations.

[26] An exception: since 2001, the government has matched the contributions of corporations to the endowments of approved performing arts organizations.

taxable income. Thus for corporations, contributions are treated similarly to business expenses. There are large differences across jurisdictions in the annual limits to the contributions that can be subsidized. On the high end, Australia applies no cap, and Canada limits the contributions from both individuals and corporations to 75 percent of their net income. In the middle, the US, Japan, and Germany, respectively, limit contributions to 50, 40, and 20 percent of individuals' gross income, and 10, five, and 20 percent of corporations' gross income. On the low end, India and Turkey, respectively, limit the contributions to 10 and five percent of gross income for both individuals and corporations. Practices also differ in terms of coverage. Except in Japan and Turkey, the subsidies are not awarded exclusively to the organizations with public benefit status. For example, Australia, Canada, Germany, and India, also subsidize the donations of individuals to political parties, albeit with different rates; the US also subsidizes donations to certain mutual benefit organizations. Australia and Japan do not award the subsidies comprehensively. For example, in Australia, religious organizations – although charitable – do not fall within the categories of 'deductible gift recipients'. And in Japan, religious corporations and medical corporations – although 'special public interest corporations' – cannot receive subsidized contributions. Canada and India do not award the subsidies uniformly. In Canada, for example, following certain international disasters individuals' contributions to relief organizations generate not only a tax credit for the donors, but also a matching government grant for the donee. And in India, the percentage of a donation that can be deducted depends on the donee organization, ranging from 50 percent for most charities, to 175 percent for university-based scientific research and development.

Overview

National governments adopt different practices in order to define the reach and range of the fiscal privileges that they award nonprofit organizations. Sure enough, there are similarities in the practices of the eight governments considered here. In defining the reach of those privileges, for example, all eight require that the eligible organizations focus on certain purposes deemed to be publicly beneficial, and most require that their profits not be distributed and that their business or political activities not exceed certain thresholds. That said, the purposes and thresholds differ not only across jurisdictions, but also across organizational types within some jurisdictions. In defining the range of privileges, most of the governments exempt income from taxation, and also subsidize individual and corporate contributions. Again, however, such exemption and subsidization differ across jurisdictions and organizational types, and differ in terms of whether the privileges are awarded exclusively, comprehensively, or uniformly to organizations. When reforming the range or reach of fiscal privileges, the governments are certainly aware of practices elsewhere (Australian Government, the Treasury, 2011a: 19-28; 2011b: 25-43). Nevertheless, there is little evidence of any international convergence around a set of common or best practices.

There is also limited evidence on the extent to which or specifically how fiscal privileges affect the amount of support from government or the overall size of the nonprofit sector and significance of philanthropy.

Table 15.3 illustrates this third point by summarizing the labour and revenue resources, albeit circa 2000, of the nonprofit sector in seven of the eight countries considered in this chapter. The first row represents the size of the sector in terms of the percentage of the economically active population working in it. Fiscal privileges alone do not explain the large differences, say, between Canada and the US on the one hand, and India and Japan on the other. The final four rows present the percentage breakdown of the sector's revenues coming from four sources: self-generated income; direct funding from government; individual and corporate contributions;

Table 15.3 Revenue and labour resources of nonprofit sector circa 2000

	Australia	Canada	Germany	India	Japan	Sweden	Turkey	US
Paid and volunteer workforce as percentage of economically active population	6.3	11.1	5.9	1.4	4.2	7.1	–	9.8
Income as percentage of total revenues	51.0	34.9	21.3	35.2	47.8	31.7	–	47.4
Government direct funding as percentage of total revenues	25.4	45.4	42.5	24.9	41.5	14.6	–	25.6
Contributions as percentage of total revenues	5.1	8.4	2.3	8.9	2.4	4.6	–	10.8
Imputed value of volunteer labour as percentage of total revenues	18.5	11.2	33.9	31.0	8.3	49.1	–	16.1

Data sources: Hall *et al.* (2005); Salamon *et al.* (2004). Turkey was not included in these studies

- For India and Sweden data exclude contributions and volunteer labour for religious worship organizations.
- 'Income' includes membership dues, charges paid directly by clients for supplies, and investment income.
- 'Government direct funding' includes grants, contracts, statutory transfers, and third-party payments that come from all branches and levels of government.
- 'Contributions' include individual and corporate donations, and foundation grants.
- The value of volunteer labour is calculated by converting volunteer labour into full-time equivalent jobs, and then multiplying by the average wage in the particular subsector.

and the imputed value of volunteer labour. Fiscal privileges do not include the government support provided through direct funding. Such support is relatively high in Canada, Germany, and Japan; relatively low in Australia, India, Sweden, and the US. What is more, they do not determine the extent of philanthropy and its significance to the sector. Compare Sweden with Germany and the US, recalling that Sweden does not subsidize contributions, whereas both Germany and the US award a deduction. On the basis of contributions, philanthropy is more significant in Sweden than in Germany – in spite of the Swedish data omitting contributions to religious organizations. And on the basis of combined contributions and volunteer labour, philanthropy is more significant in both Sweden and Germany than in the US.

Concluding observations

The awarding of fiscal privileges to certain nonprofit organizations is now an almost universal policy across market economies. And yet the theoretical rationales for awarding them, and the actual practices of doing so, are very different. This chapter describes these differences. It categorizes and compares the rationales, their assumptions and their implications, and it compares the practices by which eight national governments identify eligible organizations and award three types of privileges. The analysis intentionally does not come up with a 'best' rationale or set of best practices. There are several reasons for this. First, endorsing a rationale or set of practices would require a preliminary agreement not only on the desired role of government toward the nonprofit sector, but also on the desired size and role of the nonprofit sector within the society, economy, and polity of which it is a part – issues that exceed the scope of what can be covered here. Second, it would benefit from a comprehensive and conclusive empirical literature on the effects of fiscal privileges – a literature that does not yet exist in a single jurisdiction, let alone multiple ones. And third, the reach, range, and level of fiscal privileges can influence, but not determine the amount of government support, the size of the nonprofit sector, or the extent and significance of philanthropy.

Although this chapter does not endorse a particular rationale or set of practices, it recognizes the importance of questions around why and how any fiscal privileges should be awarded – and the associated need for researchers and practitioners to consider opportunities and strategies for their reform. The questions around why and how are connected. The desired reach and range of fiscal privileges are not self-evident, regardless of whether one justifies the existence of any privileges in terms of observed donor support, supposed fair treatment, or estimated social welfare. Where and with what criteria is the line to be drawn to separate the organizations or subsectors that are eligible for privileges – on whatever terms – from those that are not? What purposes are they to pursue? What groups are they to serve? What political or business activities are to be permitted? How are such criteria to be enforced, and by what institutions? Among the organizations and subsectors deemed eligible, are some more worthy than others? What combinations and levels of privileges are warranted? Should and can those levels be graduated on the basis of relative worthiness? The areas of inquiry are extensive. By framing and describing the different ways in which the questions around why and how have been addressed, it is hoped that the comparative tasks performed here will assist the researchers and practitioners who are seeking answers for particular jurisdictions.

References

Andreoni, J. (1990) Impure altruism and donations to public goods: a theory of warm-glow giving, *The Economic Journal*, 100(401): 464–77.

Andrews, W. D. (1972) Personal deductions in an ideal income tax, *Harvard Law Review*, 86(2): 309–85.

Atkinson, R. (1990) Altruism in nonprofit organizations, *Boston College Law Review*, 31(4): 501–639.

Aujean, M., Jenkins, M., and Poddar, S. (1999) A new approach to public sector bodies, *International VAT Monitor*, 10(4): 144–49.

Australian Charities and Not-for-Profits Commission (ACNC). (No Date) Legal meaning of charity. www.acnc.gov.au/ACNC/Register_my_charity/Who_can_register/Char_def/ACNC/Edu/Edu_Char_def.aspx [Accessed 25 May 2015].

Australian Government, the Treasury. (2011a) *Better targeting of not-for-profit tax concessions: Consultation paper*. Canberra: Commonwealth of Australia.

——. (2011b) *A definition of charity: Consultation paper*. Canberra: Commonwealth of Australia.

Bakija, J. and Heim, B. T. (2011) How does charitable giving respond to incentives and income? New estimates from panel data, *National Tax Journal*, 64(2): 615–50.

Bekkers, R. and Wiepking, P. (2011) A literature review of empirical studies of philanthropy: Eight mechanisms that drive charitable giving, *Nonprofit and Voluntary Sector Quarterly*, 40(5): 924–73.

Benshalom, I. (2009) The dual subsidy theory of charitable deductions, *Indiana Law Journal*, 84(4): 1046–97.

Bittker, B. I. and Rahdert, G. K. (1976) The exemption of nonprofit organizations from federal income taxation, *The Yale Law Journal*, 85(3): 299–358.

Blumberg, M. (2013) *Five good ideas about registered charities and political activities*. Toronto, ON: Maytree. www.maytree.com/fgi/five-good-ideas-about-registered-charities-and-political-activities.html [Accessed 25 May 2015].

Brody, E. (1998) Of sovereignty and subsidy, *The Journal of Corporation Law*, 21(4): 585–629.

Buckles, J. R. (2005) The community income theory of the charitable contributions deduction, *Indiana Law Journal*, (80) 4: 947–86.

Canada Revenue Agency. (2003a) Political activities. Policy statement CPS-022. Ottawa, ON: Canada Revenue Agency. www.cra-arc.gc.ca/chrts-gvng/chrts/plcy/cps/cps-022-eng.html [Accessed 3 June 2015].

——. (2003b) What is a related business? Policy statement CPS-019. Ottawa, ON: Canada Revenue Agency. www.cra-arc.gc.ca/chrts-gvng/chrts/plcy/cps/cps-019-eng.html [Accessed 3 June 2015].

Carmichael, C. M. (2009) Managing munificence: The reform of naval finance in Classical Athens, *Historical Methods*, 42(3): 83–96.

——. (2011) Charity misplaced: The formation in common law of a deficient fiscal concept, *Charity Law and Practice Review*, 13(2): 27–49.

——. (2012a) Dispensing charity: The deficiencies of an all-or-nothing fiscal concept, *Voluntas*, 23(2): 392–414.

——. (2012b) Sweet and not-so-sweet charity: A case for subsidizing contributions to different charities differently, *Public Finance Review*, 40(4): 497–518.

Clotfelter, C. T. (2012) Charitable giving and tax policy in the US. Paper prepared for the CEPR Public Policy Conference on Altruism and Charitable Giving, Paris, 11–12 May.

Department of Finance (Canada). (2012) Jobs, growth and long-term prosperity: Economic Action Plan 2012. Ottawa, ON: Public Works and Government Services Canada. www.budget.gc.ca/2012/plan/pdf/Plan2012-eng.pdf [Accessed 3 June 2015].

Duncan, B. (2004) A theory of impact philanthropy, *Journal of Public Economics*, 88(9–10): 2159–80.

Ebrill, L. P., Keen, M. and Summers, V. P. (2001) *The modern VAT*. Washington, DC: The International Monetary Fund.

Feldstein, M. (1980) A contribution to the theory of tax expenditures: The case of charitable giving. In H. J. Aaron and M. J. Boskin (eds.). *The economics of taxation*. Washington, DC: The Brookings Institution, 99–122.

Hall, M. A. and Colombo, J. D. (1991) The donative theory of the charitable tax exemption, *Ohio State Law Journal*, 52(5): 1379–1476.

Hall, M. H., Barr, C. W., Easwaramoorthy, M., Sokolowski, S. W. and Salamon, L. M. (2005) *Canadian nonprofit and voluntary sector in comparative perspective*. Toronto, ON: Imagine Canada.

Hansmann, H. B. (1980) The role of nonprofit enterprise, *The Yale Law Journal*, 89(5): 835–901.

——. (1981) The rationale for exempting nonprofit organizations from corporate income taxation, *The Yale Law Journal*, 91(1): 54–100.

Hochman, H. M. and Rodgers, J. D. (1977) The optimal tax treatment of charitable contributions, *National Tax Journal*, 30(1): 1–18.

International Center for Not-for-Profit Law (ICNL). (2015) *NGO law monitor – India*. www.icnl.org/research/monitor/india.html [Accessed 25 May 2015].

Levmore, S. (1998) Taxes as ballots, *The University of Chicago Law Review*, 65(2): 387–431.

Roberts, R. D. (1987) Financing public goods, *Journal of Political Economy*, 95(2): 420–37.

Rushton, M. (2007) Why are nonprofits exempt from the corporate income tax? *Nonprofit and Voluntary Sector Quarterly*, 36(4): 662–75.

Saez, E. (2004) The optimal treatment of tax expenditures, *Journal of Public Economics*, 88(12): 2657–84.

Salamon, L. M. and Anheier, H. K. (1998) Social origins of civil society: Explaining the nonprofit sector cross-nationally, *Voluntas*, 9(3): 213–47.

——., Wojciech Sokolowski, S. and Associates. (2004) *Global civil society: Dimensions of the nonprofit sector*, Vol. 2. Bloomfield, CT: Kumarian Press.

Schizer, D. M. (2009) Subsidizing charitable contributions: Incentives, information, and the private pursuit of public goals, *Tax Law Review*, 62(2): 221–68

Steinberg, R. (1991) 'Unfair' competition by nonprofits and tax policy, *National Tax Journal*, 44(3): 351–64.

Weisbrod, B. (1975) Toward a theory of the voluntary non-profit sector in a three-sector economy. In E. S. Phelps (ed.). *Altruism, morality, and economic theory*. New York, NY: Russell Sage, 171–95.

16

Philanthropy in Asia
Evolving public policy

Mark Sidel

Philanthropy in Asia presents a rich tapestry of old and new, of tradition and innovation, at a time of rapid change in the landscape for giving throughout the region and across the broader international community. Within their extraordinary diversity, Asian societies are tapping traditional sources of charitable giving while finding new ways to access the generosity that is present in each society. As Asia is too large and too diverse to cover – even in its philanthropic activities – in any comprehensive way in a single chapter, this chapter focuses on the changing nature of philanthropy in two of the region's largest and most important countries: the People's Republic of China and India. A number of the developments within these contexts symbolize and reflect changes in other parts of the region. The chapter then discusses various challenges for the development and expansion of philanthropy across the region.

Philanthropy policy in the people-rich tapestry of China

As is the case throughout Asia, philanthropy in China presents both traditional and newer elements. It is a common misnomer to view the development of philanthropy and charitable giving in China as emerging only since the end of the Cultural Revolution in 1976 or only as a product of its more recent reform era. As Chinese and western scholars have long pointed out, charitable giving and activity have existed in China for many centuries, and in many different forms, leading to the diversity we see today (Xu, 2014). These traditional forms of charitable giving in China include: giving by citizens to each other within villages and other communities; gifts and donations of labour to temples and other religious clans or community groups; giving or the organization of labour by religious organizations, clans and community groups to poor citizens and community projects such as building schools, temples, clinics or other facilities; and other forms of philanthropy that began long ago, but have only expanded in the past 40 years.

More recently, newer philanthropic institutions and practices have joined this mix, along with a rapid expansion of direct giving and volunteering for NGOs and other civil society organizations. These include the entry of two different types of foundations (*jijinhui*) that were officially recognized in 2004 with the promulgation of new regulations on the activities of foundations: 'public fundraising' foundations (*gongmu jijinhui*) that are generally closer to the government and are allowed to raise funds from the public, and 'non-public fundraising' foundations (*feigongmu jijinhui*), akin to private foundations in other countries, that receive funds largely from major donors and generally are not permitted to raise funds from the public. In addition to these foundations, there are multiple forms of nonprofit organizations (NPOs) in China (ICNL, 2005; Council on Foundations, 2014) that include social organizations (*shehui tuanti*), civil non-enterprise institutions (*minban fei qiye danwei*), and unregistered, local organizations (including small grassroots organizations), among others. Some of these NPOs, such as the Chinese Red Cross, have a special status and exist under their own individual statutes, regulations or other forms of permission.

The foundation sector, which is the focus of this discussion, has grown quickly, particularly in the past decade. In the 1980s, China had only a few dozen foundations, all of which were government-affiliated. As of 2015, there were over 4,400 public and private foundations in China (China Foundation Center, 2015). A number of foreign foundations also work in China, such as the Ford Foundation. Ford pioneered modern foreign grantmaking in China in the early 1980s and established a regional office in Beijing in 1988. Since then, the Ford Foundation has devoted more than $300 million to grantmaking in China (Ford Foundation, ND). It has been joined by the China offices of the Bill and Melinda Gates Foundation, the Asia Foundation, and various other US and international philanthropic organizations.

Foundations in China work in different and diverse ways, but, even at this relatively early stage, some common patterns in the practices of the new philanthropic institutions are evident. Both public fundraising and non-fundraising foundations have been wary of grantmaking to Chinese NGOs and other domestic voluntary sector organizations due to concerns about the quality of services provided, professionalism of staff, financial controls, constraints imposed by local government bodies, and a host of other obstacles to the work of the local nonprofit sector. As a result, and as a consequence of the preferences of their family donors, many of the new Chinese foundations – which dominate the country's recently developed philanthropic sector – have, in effect, become operating foundations (Leat, Chapter 18), focused on running and controlling their own programs. In addition, a significant amount of the new Chinese philanthropy has arisen in response to natural disasters, such as the 2008 Sichuan earthquake and other incidents. This is highly laudable, but at the same time, it is often difficult to translate disaster philanthropy into other forms of giving in non-disaster times (Kapucu, Chapter 11).

A number of policy and regulatory constraints and obstacles are also encountered by the new Chinese philanthropic sector. China's policy and regulation has sought to keep up with, mould, and control, the development of new institutions, as well as the growth in domestic, diaspora, and foreign giving in China (Simon, 2013). In these policy and regulatory decisions, China faces the continuing tension between a framework that facilitates civic participation, giving and philanthropy, and one that controls, constrains and constricts civil society and independent giving. The ways in which this key underlying tension is balanced and resolved will play a decisive role in the development of philanthropy and civil society in China over the next several decades.

Fueled by the Chinese government's dual political aims of encouraging while also constraining and controlling the directions that philanthropy and the broader nonprofit sector will take, the legal, regulatory and fiscal framework for philanthropy has become increasingly complex in recent years. While only a brief outline can be provided within the space of this chapter, the roots of regulation lie in the Chinese Constitution of 1982. Although earlier Chinese constitutions of 1954 (Article 87), 1975 (Article 28), and 1978 also included formal rights to freedom of association, Article 35 of the 1982 Constitution states: 'Citizens of the People's Republic of China (1982) enjoy freedom of speech, of the press, of assembly, of association, of procession and of demonstration'. It is not too bold a statement, however, to say that the official Chinese definition of what a right to freedom of association means is more limited than in many other countries. Nevertheless, the constitutional framework for freedom of association is how China frames its policy and legal efforts in these areas, even though the reality of policy and law does not generally live up to the freedoms promised in the Constitution.

Over the years, this basic constitutional reference has resulted in a number of regulatory efforts. These include highly restrictive provisions on philanthropy and nonprofits in the 1950s, which made it very difficult for foundations and other charitable entities to register and operate, and the gradual introduction of more facilitative documents in the 1980s and 1990s. China's current policy and legal framework for this sector is rooted in several regulatory documents issued in the 1990s, including: the *Regulations on the Registration and Administration of Social Organizations* issued by the State Council in 1998; the *Interim Regulations on the Registration and Administration of Civil Non-enterprise Institutions*, also in 1998; the *Public Welfare Donations Law*, enacted by the Standing Committee of the National People's Congress in 1999; and the *Regulations on the Management of Foundations* issued by the State Council in 2004. There are of course many other policy and legal documents governing the sector, but these are some of the key ones, along with a variety of tax laws and documents that begin the process of outlining tax exemption and deductibility issues. These basic documents, and the more specific implementing documents associated with them, have provided an initial framework for the formation, registration, governance, oversight, tax status, and other key elements of nonprofits.

The fiscal framework for this activity has rapidly become considerably more complex, yet it still mirrors the political policy of encouraging philanthropic and nonprofit activity that the government favours (particularly in service provision), while serving to discourage, control and constrain nonprofit activity that the government does not want to occur. The International Center for Not-for-Profit Law (ICNL) describes the current fiscal framework in this way:

> In practice, donations, state subsidies, and some other forms of income are tax exempt. Contributions to NPOs are deductible from income tax, with limits depending on the type of taxpayer, the type of beneficiary, and the use of the contribution…. Contributions to informal NPOs, however, are [generally] not tax deductible…. NPOs that engage in nursing, medical, educational, cultural, or religious activities or activities in which services are performed by the disabled are exempted from the Business Tax on the sale of services. However, informal NPOs that are registered as businesses are required to pay the Business Tax.
>
> *(Council on Foundations, 2014: NP)*

In the governance of philanthropy, rather than of nonprofits, the available legal documents and the overall framework are somewhat more sparse. There are, as noted, the *Regulations on the Management of Foundations* (2004) and the *Public Welfare Donations Law* (1999), as well as some more detailed implementing documents issued over the years that deal with specific foundation and other philanthropic issues. They govern the basics of the philanthropic sector, at least as envisioned in the early part of the last decade, including the two types of foundations. As ICNL notes,

> Chinese foundations, like social organizations, are regulated by both a registration and administration agency, usually the Ministry of Civil Affairs in Beijing or a provincial, municipal, or local Civil Affairs bureau or office, and by a professional agency such as the relevant government ministry or agency at the national, provincial, municipal, or local level.
>
> *(Council on Foundations, 2014: NP).*

This philanthropic regulatory framework – which is beginning to shift toward single reporting mechanisms in some parts of the country – also incorporate, particularly in the 2004

Foundation Regulations, general principles expressed in regulatory form for the governance of foundations. These cover reporting requirements, audit and the like, and provisions for government oversight. In addition, more specific implementing documents issued over the years on foundation matters include, for example, regulations on their names, information disclosure, annual inspection, and audit guidelines for them. We can find even more specific regulatory documents on particular issues in the philanthropic arena, notably documents on foreign philanthropy and donations of foreign exchange to domestic organizations.

Despite all this regulation making, virtually all observers seem to agree that the current framework for legal regulation, of both the broader nonprofit sector and the philanthropic subset of it, began as incomplete and inadequate; it was made either overly general, or – partly due to the march of time, developments around China, and an increasing tendency to explore different approaches and reforms in this sector – has quickly become dated and obsolete. The obsolescence, however, comes from some positive developments, including the growth of the sector and its increasing roles in Chinese society. At the same time, the regulatory structure and the broader legal framework outside of nonprofits have been unable to fully respond to emerging problems, such as increased instances of fraud or inappropriate practices in the sector. Many observers would also agree on another conclusion: the legal framework for the philanthropic and nonprofit sector has done a considerably better job at facilitating state control of the growth and programmatic directions of the sector than at safeguarding the rights of those who try to form and register organizations or work in them. What has emerged is what some Chinese scholars call 'differentiated management', in which the policy and legal framework enables a wide range of responses by the state to the activities of non-governmental and philanthropic organizations, depending on whether they are pursuing activities, services, policy advocacy, or other work that the state approves of or seeks to discourage.

What are the key issues for policy and regulation in Chinese philanthropy going forward? From multiple conversations, over a number of years, with government officials and nonprofit leaders in China, as well as through an extensive review of press sources which now identify these issues on a frequent and frank basis, a number of problems can be identified that Chinese policymakers and regulators are working to resolve, and will continue to work on under often complex and difficult circumstances. The first is how to move from the highly controlled 'dual management' registration and reporting system for Chinese nonprofits, which requires two different government agencies to agree to formation of an entity, toward a more streamlined system of formation, registration, and reporting for foundations and other nonprofits, an approach that has been pioneered in southern China and elsewhere. A second issue is whether to allow social organizations and other types of charitable organizations to raise funds from the public: a right generally now only available to public fundraising foundations and a few national charitable entities. Accommodating the work of foundations is a third category in need of attention. This encompasses: making more flexible – but in a prudent way – restrictions on investment of assets by foundations and other Chinese nonprofits, including whether a minimum portion of assets (say 90 percent) should be required to be held in safe instruments such as state bonds or bank accounts; whether to require minimum outlays (donations) by foundations for public benefit purposes; how to protect donor rights on restrictions and requirements placed on the use of funds; and how to strengthen foundation and nonprofit information disclosure mechanisms, transparency, and accountability through a combination of government regulation and industry self-regulation. The current dual definition of foundations – public fundraising versus non-public fundraising by which some foundations are permitted to raise funds and others are not – will itself become increasingly problematic. Fourth, tax incentives for nonprofits of various kinds, including foundations, need to be addressed: should they be enhanced through strengthened tax exemption, tax deductibility and other provisions? A related concern is how to regulate the business and investment activities of charitable organizations in general, and whether to differentiate among them in these areas. Finally, with expansion of the sector and increased hybridization that is occurring worldwide, the regulatory framework will need to deal with new forms of charitable and philanthropic organizations and new forms of giving. At present, many giving vehicles such as charitable trusts and the use of stock for charitable giving are largely unregulated by current law, at least in their early years.

In wrestling with these complex questions for the future of the philanthropic and nonprofit sector, China has had to cope with the obsolescence, generality and difficulty of enforcement of that first generation of regulation in this area. One possible resolution, which has been in draft form for many years, reworked many times, and finally introduced into the national legislature in December 2014, is an overall Charity Law (*Cishanfa*) governing the sector. This Charity Law reflects a somewhat more pragmatic approach by government to the philanthropic and nonprofit sector (China Briefing, 2015). It would require all charities to register directly with the government and allow some organizations to register without seeking government partner organizations. The Charity Law may also make it easier for a range of organizations to raise funds and may solidify some of the tax incentives that the finance authorities have grudgingly permitted in recent years. Greater transparency would allay concerns over their operations. Given its drawn out history, it is unclear when the Charity Law will be enacted: debates continue on key issues in the law, including all those discussed here, and rapidly changing circumstances are overtaking the terms of these debates amid growing demands for the Law's promulgation.

Another concern – this from the Party and government – has been the activities of foreign NGOs and foreign funders. In the years leading up to 2015, it became more difficult for Chinese organizations, universities, and other groups to receive foreign funding due to informal or formal government restrictions. In early 2015, a draft Law on the Management of Overseas NGOs emerged, proposed by the Ministry of Public Security, that would bring most issues of foreign funding within the purview of public security (police), require all foreign organizations to register after locating and signing an agreement with a designated Chinese partner organization that would be responsible for its activities in China, and restricting the fields and work that foreign organizations and funders could undertake in China. This proposed new legislation, restricting and further controlling foreign funding, prompted a major backlash from Chinese and foreign organizations alike. At the time of writing, the draft law is under consideration by the National People's Congress. If it is enacted, then its implementation rules and practice will provide a guide to how far foreign NGOs and funders will be limited in their work in China in the years ahead.

Yet another approach to these complex problems of regulation has been to supplement government regulation with various forms of self-regulation and information disclosure generated by the philanthropic sector itself. The Chinese discussion of nonprofit self-regulation has its roots in business self-regulation, with initial principles for nonprofit self-regulation advanced by the nonprofit leader Shang Yusheng and the China NPO Alliance in 2001. On the philanthropic front, the Chinese Private Foundation Forum issued self-regulatory principles for private foundations in 2009, asking the new private foundation community to abide by these (Hui, 2009; Sidel, 2014). Since 2009, discussion of the Private Foundation Forum self-regulatory principles seems to have faded somewhat. But, there remains strong interest in Chinese NPO and philanthropic circles in self-regulation, and discussion of its feasibility and potential forms can be expected to grow in the years ahead.

Organizational disclosure and transparency are closely related to self-regulation and to organizational autonomy, and thus in recent years, we have seen the emergence of several forms of disclosure requirements. For foundations, information disclosure is required and has been strengthened under the *Regulations on the Administration of Foundations* (2004) and through multiple implementing documents issued since then. Information disclosure is now also accomplished through regulatory mandates of the Ministry of Civil Affairs which oversees philanthropic and charity regulation, through the China Charity Disclosure and Information Center (CCDIC), which is a Ministry mandated mechanism, and through an initiative for philanthropic organizations that arises from the philanthropic community, the China Foundation Center.

National level tax legislation dealing with income tax status, tax deductions for charitable donations, and the possibility of an estate tax has also been gradually developing. China has a developing infrastructure that permits tax deductions for charitable donations (up to prescribed levels) and provides tax exemptions for various kinds of charitable organizations. This tax infrastructure will continue to be modified in the years ahead, likely facing considerable conflict between calls from civil society to increase the incentives for giving and misgivings on the part of tax and other officials. This is a complex area, and one that will see continuing change (Council on Foundations, 2014).

Other policy and regulatory documents affect the domestic, diaspora or international philanthropic and nonprofit sectors. Examples of these abound; one recent and important example is Notice 63 issued by the State Administration of Exchange Control that took effect in March 2010. This makes it more difficult for some, especially unregistered, social organizations to receive foreign funding. The draft law on management of overseas NGOs is a further development of these foreign currency restrictions.

In recent years, consistent with national political policy that seeks both to encourage *and* constrain the development of civil society and philanthropy, local policy and regulatory activity on philanthropy has emerged as a key area of development and experimentation. In many provinces and centrally-administered municipalities, legal and policy documents on philanthropy, charitable giving, donations, and foundations have now been issued, and in some cases, are being used to explore new and more flexible approaches to state regulation of the philanthropic sector. Some provinces and municipalities (such as Guangdong, Shenzhen, Shanghai, Jiangsu, and Beijing, among others) have become well-known for their progress in this area, including local experimentation with new forms of administration for the central authorities in Beijing. These are important experiments to watch and learn from, and at times draw upon in remaking national policy.

Local authorities, with approval from Beijing, have at times carefully expanded and made more flexible such areas as: rules on formation, registration and management of social organizations and foundations; local experiments and procedures for 'social contracting' (government contracting with nonprofits to provide social services); local initiatives in transparency and disclosure and local supervision and management of foundations; and experimentation with new rules and policies on local fundraising by local organizations that begin to weaken earlier restrictions on fundraising, among other initiatives. The willingness of central government authorities to allow provincial and subnational implementation and, in some cases, experimentation with new procedures on the registration, management and oversight of foundations, social organizations and other entities is an important set of developments in Chinese philanthropy policymaking. But, it has not yet risen to the level of provincial or other sub-national 'competition' for philanthropic resources in the way that in the past subnational regulation represented for foreign investors interested in arbitraging the differences among local incentives for foreign investment.

In short, the local developments in philanthropy policymaking and regulation represent some local specificity and, at times, local experimentation with approaches that may or may not be scaled up for other provinces or cities or as national promulgation. However, Beijing is carefully watching their progress. As ICNL (2015a: NP) has stated:

> Over the last few years, there have been important local policy experiments in the Chinese nonprofit and philanthropic sector, mostly at the provincial level. These policy experiments are important because they provide the central authorities with policy ideas and experiences that play a role in shaping national-level legislation. They therefore [may] serve as harbingers of changes in national-level legislation.

China continues to pursue a nuanced, if constrained, policy toward the development of civil society and philanthropy. The policy and legal framework encourages the growth and, in some cases, registration of social service organizations and other groups undertaking activities favoured by the state, while discouraging through a range of means the formation of groups and advocacy activities that the state disfavours. This policy of guided development is likely to continue. Organizations will, over time, probably have easier routes to formation, registration, fundraising and other operations, with organizations and foundations that provide state-favoured social services privileged over groups that engage in advocacy, which are often – though not always – a bane of the state. At the same time, the Chinese state will keep a very close watch over the entire philanthropic and nonprofit sector, allowing wide swaths of the sector to expand with increased activities and public fundraising, while keeping an even closer watch and much tighter restrictions on disfavoured advocacy groups, especially those that show any sign of fostering public discontent or that appear to be emerging as broader social movements.

Philanthropy policy in India

India, like many countries of Asia, has an extraordinarily diverse philanthropic and nonprofit sector. More traditional temple and other giving (Agarwal, 2010) mixes with newer forms of online giving, corporate philanthropy, and giving circles. As with many other countries in Asia, the level of giving in India is generous, particularly when multiple forms – money, goods, volunteering and social investing – are combined. India also has an array of philanthropic and nonprofit forms, including societies, trusts, foundations, and other kinds of civil society organizations. Government regulation is carried out through a combination of national regulation, most specifically in areas of taxation and foreign funding, and state-based regulation, which focuses on organizational form, formation, governance, reporting and related issues. Much of Indian philanthropic and nonprofit regulation is adapted from earlier British legislation of the nineteenth century, heavily amended to fit modern Indian realities. But a key feature of that colonial system – the need for regulatory approvals – remains an important and much critiqued part of modern Indian nonprofit regulation. Indeed, it is sometimes called the 'raj' system of nonprofit regulation in modern India.

Constitutional freedom of association forms the backdrop for the wide diversity of philanthropic and nonprofit forms in India. Yet, regulatory constraints and complexity are an important part of the picture as well. Other treatments of Indian philanthropic life (Cantegreil *et al.*, 2013; National Foundation for India, 2013; Handy *et al.*, forthcoming) discuss the constraints and opportunities for Indian civil society in more detail. Here the focus is on several issues that have proven of particular interest, and controversy, in India's philanthropy policy.

Set against a backdrop of complex organizational forms – societies, trusts, nonprofit companies and others – the Indian state seeks, as all governments do, to influence and shape philanthropy and civil society activity toward its desired ends, away from activities that would threaten the state or particular state policies. For example, with enactment of the *Companies Act 2013* India now requires charitable contributions by a range of Indian companies. As the prominent Indian newspaper *The Hindu* (2012) noted, 'India [has] become the first country to mandate corporate social responsibility (CSR) through a statutory provision'. These new CSR requirements require some companies to provide charitable contributions, spending two percent of average annual profits on CSR activities. This new mandated CSR spending applies to companies with a net worth of approximately $US 90 million or more, or turnover of about $180 million or more, or net profits above approximately $900,000. The baseline for calculating CSR required spending will be a company's net profit before tax, averaged over the previous three years. A committee of a company's board, including at least one independent director, must sign off on these required CSR activities. A number of provisions seek to make this required CSR spending easier for companies: for example, companies required to make such contributions may jointly pool them with other companies. In addition, the *Income Tax Act* provides incentives for corporate giving: for instance, 'shared value', in which donations that benefit a company's business, but also benefit social or related goals are permitted. Such required CSR activities and giving may also be performed directly, or through a range of other Indian nonprofits. However, CSR-related giving must be directed toward projects and activities in India, rather than overseas.

What kind of activities will count toward fulfilling the CSR requirements? The list under the legislation is broad, although it does not include a full range of advocacy activities. Available activities and goals include: eradicating extreme hunger and poverty; supporting education; promoting gender equality and empowering women; reducing child mortality and improving maternal health; combating HIV, AIDS, malaria and other diseases; ensuring environmental sustainability; strengthening employment-enhancing vocational skills; supporting social business projects; contributing to the Prime Minister's National Relief Fund or funds for the welfare of the Scheduled Castes and Tribes, minorities or women; and assisting with such other goals and activities as may later be added through legislative or regulatory provisions.

These developments have drawn wide attention in philanthropic and nonprofit communities around India, the region, and well beyond (Bapat, 2013; EY, 2013; Kordant Philanthropy Advisors, 2013). The precise number of companies subject to the required CSR spending and the amount that could be added to nonprofit giving in India each year, however, remains difficult to measure in these early stages. AccountAid (New Delhi), the well-known accounting and financial services organization working with the Indian philanthropic and nonprofit sector and the accounting firm EY (2013) estimates that the new CSR spending requirements may apply to more than 2,500 companies in India and may account for several billion dollars more in social sector spending per year.

Other developments reflect a longstanding Indian concern with certain types of foreign funding to Indian nonprofit organizations. The *Foreign Contributions (Regulation) Act* (*FCRA*), enacted during the Indian Emergency of the mid-1970s, with a range of amendments since, seeks to limit foreign funding for political, advocacy, journalism and other sensitive endeavours in India. It has long been opposed by parts of the Indian philanthropic sector that seek to raise funds abroad, both because of its policy constraints on foreign funding and its cumbersome and difficult licensing procedures. In general terms, the *FCRA* requires organizational or transaction-by-transaction permission for Indian philanthropic and nonprofit organizations to receive foreign funds (including, in many cases, Indian diaspora funds) for many charitable, cultural and other purposes. It is without doubt the most controversial and actively opposed component of the regulation of philanthropy and nonprofits in India. And, the *FCRA* is now serving as a model for restriction of foreign funding to domestic nonprofits and philanthropic organizations in Pakistan and Bangladesh, developments that have aroused the concern of non-profit advocates in each of these countries and throughout the region.

Although earlier amendments tightened the scope and enforcement of the *FCRA*, modifications in 2010 and new rules issued in 2011 expanded its scope of enforcement and its constraints on organizations that seek foreign funding for their work. For example, the *FCRA* is now applicable to individuals and some companies, as well as to NGOs. The Act requires organizational or transactional permission for donations from companies with 50 percent or more foreign equity, thus bringing donations from such well-known entities as Infosys, Cadbury and others within its regulatory scope. The Act also prohibits 'speculative activity' with foreign funds, and, as AccountAid (Agarwal, 2012) has pointed out, this conflicts with the more relaxed *Income Tax Act*'s permission for NGOs to invest in certain vehicles, such as mutual funds, which might be considered 'speculative activity' under the *FCRA*. The Act's broad discretionary grounds for the government (through the Ministry of Home Affairs) to refuse NGO applications to register under the Act in order to receive foreign funding have long been criticized, but show no signs of being moderated (Ministry of Home Affairs, ND). In 2014 and 2015, the Indian Ministry of Home Affairs took additional steps to amend and tighten the *FCRA*, to prune several thousand organizations from the list of those authorized to receive foreign funding, and to tighten funding restrictions on about 15 foreign organizations, including the Ford Foundation.

These restrictions on foreign funding for voluntary, political and other purposes in India have been strengthened over time and have, as noted above, served as a model for other governments' attempts to stifle advocacy activities by constricting the foreign foundation, development aid and other funding that helps to make advocacy possible. In Bangladesh, for example, attempts to strengthen restrictions on foreign funding for NGOs and civil society have included the proposed *Foreign Donations (Voluntary Activities) Regulation Act* which, if adopted, would require government permission for foreign donations to Bangladeshi NGOs and would strengthen other regulatory obstacles to overseas funding for advocacy and development work in Bangladesh. If adopted in its draft form, this Act would be quite sweeping as it would: prohibit individuals and organizations from receiving foreign donations or contributions for the purpose of carrying out any voluntary activity without prior government approval; require all organizations wishing to receive and use foreign donations/contributions to register with Bangladesh's NGO Affairs Bureau; require all organizations seeking to carry out activities with foreign donations to secure advance project approval; and penalize NGOs if the Director General of the NGO Affairs Bureau believes that NGOs are engaged in activities that are 'illegal or harmful for the country' (ICNL, 2015b).

These developments in Bangladesh are reflective of attempts in other parts of Asia to control and channel the nonprofit and voluntary sector. For example, information legislation is increasingly being used to target civil society activists. Bangladesh's 2006 information legislation (Art. 57(1)) states that

> if any person deliberately publishes or transmits or causes to be published or transmitted in the website or in electronic form any material which … causes to deteriorate or creates possibility to deteriorate law and order, prejudice the image of the State or … instigates against any person or organization, then this activity of his will be regarded as an offence.

Such an offence was originally punishable by ten years imprisonment, although in 2012 the penalty was increased to a maximum of 14 years imprisonment, along with heavy fines. In addition, the 2012 amendments to the information and communications legislation allowed arrest under the statute without warrant, and made alleged offences under the statute 'nonbailable', meaning that detainees could be held without the opportunity to post bail. These provisions were used against the Director of the Dhaka-based rights-based NGO, Odikhar, in the late summer of 2013 (ICNL, 2015b).

Moves to restrict foreign funding are also underway in Pakistan, again modeled after the Indian *FCRA* legislation. A draft bill introduced in 2012 targets NGOs, setting high barriers for groups to accept foreign contributions and is applicable to NGOs registered in Pakistan or abroad. The draft *Foreign Contributions Regulations Act* would allow the government to deny a group permission to receive foreign funding if the group is deemed likely to use the funding for 'undesirable purposes', as stated in the very broad language that often characterizes restrictions on civil society organizations in Asia. As in India, NGOs operating in Pakistan would be required to obtain advance governmental permission to receive foreign contributions; that permission would last for only five years before relicensing would be required; and the grounds for government review of such applications would be vague and highly discretionary. The government would be free to ban foreign funding to groups as it 'deems fit', including when it deems such funding might be used for 'undesirable purposes' or might implicate 'the security, strategic, scientific or economic interest of the State', 'the public interest', or 'friendly relations with any foreign state'. The draft legislation would allow the government to cancel a foreign funding license without judicial or other review, and with a three-year bar before reapplication is possible. Government inspection powers under the statute would be exceptionally broad, with no procedural safeguards, no judicial role, and no requirement that advance notice be given. Imprisonment and organizational liability are among the penalties drafted (ICNL, 2015c).

Conclusion: Challenges for the expansion of philanthropy in Asia

Philanthropy and the nonprofit sector in Asia have expanded rapidly in recent years. They face many obstacles and impediments to future development – some as a result of recent growth and some resulting from governmental and political constraints on philanthropic activity. In the coming years, the expansions of philanthropy will face several key challenges.

First, the emergence of new forms of giving will present different types of regulatory issues. As online, crowd sourced, and other forms of charitable giving grow throughout Asia, philanthropic organizations are faced with new competition for giving: citizens increasingly donate online and directly to organizations they wish to support, rather than through philanthropic intermediaries. Governments face the problems of tracking the diversification of giving which outstrips their ability to spot trends and identify security or other problems. Nonprofits are increasingly pressured to find ways of identifying new sources of funding at a time when traditional means of fundraising are being supplanted by new technologies and direct, internet-based appeals.

Government restrictions on foreign funding and on domestic fundraising increasingly conflict with more internationalized, transborder philanthropy. As the discussion of India, Bangladesh and Pakistan indicates, governments in these countries and throughout the region are deeply concerned about the use of foreign funds to support NGO advocacy, political and religious causes, and other activities they may perceive as threatening. Governments' responses in a number of countries around Asia have been to tighten the constraints on overseas giving, with particular emphasis on advocacy. In South Asia, and beyond, civil society organizations have tried to blunt the force of these restrictions, but often with little success. For much of elite philanthropy in these countries, restrictions on foreign funding are considered a world apart and a political issue to be avoided. In India and a few other countries, however, even local philanthropy recognizes that their freedom of movement may soon be affected and that foreign funding plays an important role in promoting participatory and sustainable development, rights-based projects, and other worthy causes. In many Asian countries domestic fundraising also faces tight restrictions (ICNL *et al.*, 2012; UNHR, 2013). Given how civil society is changing, however, these combined obstacles to the sector's development will come under significant stress in the years ahead.

Throughout Asia, tax incentives for charitable giving, and tax exemptions for philanthropic and nonprofit organizations remain relatively small. Some of this is understandable: finance ministries, for example, are inevitably focused on revenue generation rather than on the flowering of a well-funded, diverse, healthy philanthropic sector. But the years ahead will see increased pressure on governments and tax authorities to open the spigot, at least somewhat further, to incentivize both individual and corporate donations for nonprofit activity – a process that is likely to be long and for advocacy by the philanthropic sector, arduous.

In addition to addressing foreign funding and tax incentives, there is a need for more broadly enabling legal frameworks for philanthropy. In a number of Asian countries, the regulatory barriers to formation, registration, permitted activities and operations, investment of assets, restrictions on fundraising, and other key aspects of philanthropic and nonprofit activity remain remarkably high. In the years ahead, pressure will grow on governments to reduce these high barriers to growth of this sector. In many cases, governments will slowly, and in some cases grudgingly, begin to dismantle some of those impediments, but always watching the activities of nonprofits carefully and likely adopting policies that seek to channel philanthropic giving toward social services and away from advocacy.

The need for self-regulation by the philanthropic and nonprofit sectors can also be expected to increase over the next few years. Self-regulatory impulses are already strong in Asia, particularly in the business sector which in a number of countries has developed self-regulatory mechanisms, with governments being willing to devolve some regulatory mandates to these regimes. Self-regulation has been much slower to take hold in philanthropy and nonprofit activity, however. As discussed, China has very initial explorations of self-regulation underway in the philanthropic sector in the form of a kind of code of conduct. India's sector has experimented with multiple forms of self-regulation, with government encouragement, although none have taken hold on a national scale or throughout the various subsectors of the philanthropic and nonprofit arena (Sidel, 2010a). As this sector seeks to avoid stricter government regulation, self-regulation will emerge more strongly as a theme in the years ahead.

In addition, cooperation of philanthropic institutions and nonprofits with the state will expand. As governments privatize social services or undertake other measures intended to make the provision of social services more efficient, a number of countries across Asia have either adopted (e.g. India, Hong Kong) or are experimenting with (e.g. China) a variety of forms of social contracting by which national and local governments contract with nonprofits to provide social services to citizens. Some philanthropic and nonprofit organizations welcome this trend because it represents the broadest opportunity for government funding ever made available in their countries or regions. Others are more wary, seeing social contracting as a form of government co-optation of the nonprofit sector, channeling organizations from advocacy to direct provision of social services. In sum, Asia will be a landscape of considerable change – and contradictions – as policy and regulatory frameworks catch up to an expanding and diversifying philanthropy.

Notes

1 There is of course a wide array of regulatory documents on specific issues and sub-sectors, including on health that are too numerous to list here. See the International Center for Not-for-Profit Law (ICNL) Law Monitor, www.icnl.org/research/monitor/china.html and its United States International Grantmaking (USIG) Country Notes on health policies see (Sidel, 2014).

2 Similar draft legislation and a similar set of debates have been underway in Vietnam for many years on what is called the Law on Associations (*Luat ve Hoi*); see Sidel (2010b).

3 Among the best ways of tracking these regulatory developments are the materials available on the website of the International Center for Not-for-Profit Law (ICNL, www.icnl.org), and its publications, including the U.S. International Grantmaking country reports, *NGO Law Monitor*, and the *International Journal of Not-for-Profit Law*.

References

Agarwal, S. (2010) *Daan and other giving traditions in India: The forgotten pot of gold*. New Delhi: AccountAid India. www.accountaid.net/Books/Daan/Daan%20-%20Aug%2010-%20Adobe%207.pdf [Accessed 15 May 2015].

———. (2012) *AccountAble Handbook - FCRA 2010: Theory and Practice*, 2nd edition. New Delhi: AccountAid. www.accountaid.net/Books/FCRA/FCRA%202010%20Cover%20to%20Cover%20rev%20300413. pdf [Accessed 15 May 2015].

Bapat, S. (2013) Challenges of the 2% CSR Paradigm, *Forbes (India)*, 19 March. www.forbesindia.com/ blog/business-strategy/challenges-of-the-2-csr-paradigm/ [Accessed 15 May 2015].

Cantegreil, M., Chanana, D. and Kattumuri, R. (eds.). (2013) *Revealing Indian philanthropy*. London: Alliance Publishing Trust.

China Briefing. (2015) *New draft of Charity Law submitted to China's National Legislature*. www.china-briefing. com/news/2015/01/16/china-drafts-new-charity-law.html#sthash.FIsL02HM.dpuf [Accessed 15 May 2015].

China Foundation Center. (2015) *Foundation database online*. www.en.foundationcenter.org.cn/online.html [Accessed 30 June 2015]

Council on Foundations. (2014) *China, USIG Country Note*. www.cof.org/content/china [Accessed 10 May 2015].

Ernst & Young (EY). (2013) *Understanding Companies Bill 2012: Analysis of accounting, auditing and corporate governance changes*. www.ey.com/publication/vwluassets/ey_understanding_companies_bill_2012/$file/ ey-understanding-companies-bill-2012.pdf [Accessed 12 May 2015].

Ford Foundation. (ND) *China*. New York, NY: Ford Foundation. www.fordfoundation.org/pdfs/library/ China-brochure-2011.pdf [Accessed 21 May 2015].

Handy, F., Kassam, M. and Janson, E. (forthcoming) *The practice and promise of philanthropy in India*. New Delhi: Sage.

Hui, W. (2009) Changes in the development of private foundations, *China Development Brief*, 43(fall). www.chinadevelopmentbrief.cn/wp-content/uploads/2011/09/Special-Issue-hard-copy-copy.pdf [Accessed 17 May 2015].

International Center for Not-for-Profit Law (ICNL). USIG country Note for China, 2015, www.cof.org.

———. (2015a) *NGO Law Monitor: China*. www.icnl.org/research/monitor/china.html [Accessed 20 May 2015].

———. (2015b) *NGO Law Monitor: Pakistan*. www.icnl.org/research/monitor/pakistan.html [Accessed 20 May 2015].

———. (2015c) *NGO Law Monitor: Bangladesh*. www.icnl.org/research/monitor/bangladesh.htm [Accessed 20 May 2015].

———. (2012), World Movement for Democracy Secretariat and the National Endowment for Democracy. *Defending civil society*, 2nd edition. Washington, DC: World Movement for Democracy. www. defendingcivilsociety.org [Accessed 16 May 2015].

Kordant Philanthropy Advisors. (2013) *The 2% CSR clause: New requirements for companies in India*. www. kordant.com/assets/2-Percent-India-CSR-Report.pdf [Accessed 15 May 2015].

Ministry of Home Affairs, India. (ND) *Frequently Asked Questions on FCRA*. www.mha.gov.in/fcra/intro/ FAQs.pdf [Accessed 15 May 2015].

National Foundation for India. (2013) *Emerging philanthropy in India: Analysis of gaps and recommended interventions*. New Delhi: National Foundation for India. www.nfi.org.in/sites/default/files/nfi_files/ Emerging%20Philanthrophy%20in%20India_NFI.pdf [Accessed 15 May 2015].

People's Republic of China. (1982) *Constitution of the People's Republic of China*. www.english.people.com. cn/constitution/constitution.html [Accessed 5 May 2015].

Sidel, M. (2010a) The promise and limits of collective action for nonprofit self-regulation: Evidence from Asia, *Nonprofit and Voluntary Sector Quarterly*, 39(6): 1039–56.

———. (2010b) Maintaining firm control: Recent developments in nonprofit law and regulation in Vietnam, *International Journal of Not-for-Profit Law*, 12(3): 52–67. www.icnl.org/research/journal/vol12iss3/art_1. htm [Accessed 20 May 2015].

———. (2014) The shifting balance of philanthropic policies and regulations in China. In J. Ryan, L. C. Chen and T. Saich (eds.). *Philanthropy for health in China*. Bloomington, IN: Indiana University Press, 40–56.

Simon, K. (2013) *Civil society in China: The legal framework from ancient times to the "New Reform Era"*. Oxford: Oxford University Press.

The Hindu. (2012) New Companies Bill mandates CSR spending, 19 December. www.thehindu.com/business/companies/new-companies-bill-mandates-csr-spending/article4217872.ece [Accessed 25 May 2015].

United Nations Human Rights (UNHR). (2013) *Report of the Special Rapporteur on the rights to freedom of peaceful assembly and of association*. New York: United Nations General Assembly, 7 August. www.icnl.org/research/library/files/Transnational/specrap.pdf [Accessed 17 May 2015].

Xu, Y. (2014) Toward a healthier philanthropy: Reforming China's philanthropic sector. In J. Ryan, L. C. Chen and T. Saich (eds.). *Philanthropy for health in China*. Bloomington, IN: Indiana University Press, 268–80.

17

The darker side of philanthropy

How self-interest and incompetence can overcome a love of mankind and serve the public interest

David Horton Smith with Sharon Eng and Kelly Albertson

Philanthropy has a 'dark side' or 'darker side', just like any other individual or collective human activity. Smith (2016) argues that the 'angelic' nonprofit sector, including foundations and other charitable organizations, can be a site of deviance, crime, and ethical misconduct. The underlying reason is simple: as well as being able to act from altruism and philanthropic concerns, humans, in any context, organized or informal, often act out of egotism and self-interest. Humans can also create dysfunctions or negative outcomes through ignorance and incompetence as unintended consequences of their actions.

Even though the vast majority of foundations, charities, and other NPOs and their leaders, staff and volunteers are law abiding, moral, and pursue goals that can benefit society, there are significant exceptions. Sometimes this deviance is *un*intentional; sometimes, it is intentional. The darker side of philanthropy refers to ways in which philanthropy, specifically involving foundations and other 'philanthropic' nonprofit organizations (NPOs), can become 'deviant'. The term 'deviant' or 'deviance' refers here to a broad spectrum – of varying degrees of seriousness – of rule breaking: from potentially tolerable, minor, deviance arising from customs or social expectations that lead to unintended harm (dysfunction), through behaviour that violates noncriminal moral norms (misconduct), to acts that are serious crimes (felony).

Approaching the topic from a US perspective and context, this chapter examines three aspects of this darker side. First, the chapter focuses on the potential for dysfunctions, misconduct, and crime through, and by, foundations and philanthropic trusts. The second section discusses such rule breaking in, and by, transnational humanitarian aid and relief NPOs based in the high income nations of the Global North, that are attempting to help people in the low income nations of the Global South. In the third section, we consider the role of charities in financing terrorist groups as potentially being underground, fundamentally, deviant NPOs.

The darker side of foundations and trusts

Foundations and trusts have a special legal classification in most countries (Anheier and Toepler, 1999). The various types of foundations are examined in other chapters of this volume (Leat, Chapter 18; Harrow *et al.*, Chapter 19). Our main concern is with 'private' foundations that make 'philanthropic … grants to individuals or nonprofits or both' (Smith *et al.*, 2006: 90). Most private foundations make grants only to other NPOs, although in the US, and a few other nations, they may make grants to individuals. Characteristically, private foundations have an endowment from which they make their grants. In this regard, private foundations are quite different in their structure and functioning from community foundations and from public foundations which routinely raise funds locally each year, and as grantmakers they also differ from operating foundations which spend the large majority of their disbursements on internal projects.

The fundamental rationale of private foundations – the accumulation and allocation of private wealth for public purposes – remains essentially undisputed in the US, Europe and most other nations (Anheier and Toepler, 1999; Heydemann and Toepler, 2006). The definitive legal approval of the private foundation as a form of tax exempt organization and the provision of tax subsidies for such foundations, beginning in the late nineteenth and early twentieth centuries, remains unchallenged in any significant way (Prewitt 2006a,b; Fleishman, 2007). Furthermore, private foundations are generally seen as integral and exemplary parts of the larger nonprofit sector, which enjoys widespread public participation and high levels of public approval in most nations (Noble and Wixley, 2014). In the US this perception, combined with the size of the foundation subsector, cements the essential legitimacy of private foundations to an extent unheard of in many other countries (Frumkin 2005).

The unique nature of private foundations has been widely noted (Nielsen, 1972; Anheier and Daly, 2007; Arnove and Pinede, 2007). They can be characterized as relatively autonomous and undemocratic entities (similar to business corporations) that are controlled by comparatively small numbers of individuals (mostly donors and self-perpetuating trustees), often with effectively no external stakeholders (unlike business corporations). As such, some commentators have highlighted that foundations constitute a veritable 'wealthy elite who apply tax protected dollars to enact their vision of the public good' (Prewitt, 2006b: 374; Prewitt 2006a; Fleishman 2007; Anheier and Hammack, 2010). Notwithstanding that the majority of foundations do a lot of laudable work, this social and structural situation provides a context ideal for rule breaking deviance in pursuit of self-interest by both original foundation donors and subsequent foundation leaders. This rule breaking can occur in several distinct ways. In many cases potential 'misconduct' is quite legal, though nevertheless unethical and contrary to the purported public interest mission and purposes of foundations as an organizational form.

Foundations as tax shelters

Whatever the philanthropic language and public spirited declarations of a private foundation's charter (or its articles of corporation or mission statement), one motivation by the original donor(s) of assets can be tax relief: substantial assets might be sheltered from inheritance taxes and, for living donors, from current income taxes. Given the amount of private wealth tied up in American foundations, the concern raised over several decades about tax sheltering has been most strongly voiced in the US. In his extensive critique of American charity, Wagner (2000: 97) argues that the donors who created the major US foundations in the period 1900 to 1930 were substantially motivated by tax avoidance or evasion, as they 'found a way to perpetuate their family wealth legally while saving fortunes in taxes'. In addition, donors might create foundations because they seek social power, prestige, and even immortality for their 'generosity' (Wagner, 2000: 108-111). The cosponsor of the 1969 Tax Reform Act, US Congressman Wright Patman, stated in a hearing on the bill that, 'philanthropy – one of mankind's more noble instincts – has been perverted into a vehicle for institutionalized, deliberate evasion of fiscal and moral responsibility to the nation' (Crimm, 2001: 1119). The 1969 Act improved the situation, but foundation misconduct remains a significant problem in the US and elsewhere.

More recently, Langley (1997: A1), a nonprofit consultant, was quoted in the *Wall Street Journal* as saying, 'the majority of these so-called charitable foundations [are] motivated more for avoiding taxes and supporting pet projects than helping society'. Although no quantitative survey data is available to back up these impressions, they are supported by other qualitative research (e.g., Nielsen, 1985; Odendahl, 1990; Marcus, 1992; Ostrower, 1995; Wagner, 2000), and seem credible. Valid quantitative, survey research on rule breaking is very difficult to conduct, however, because it is so easy for respondents to lie or, at least, not be completely candid about motivations.

A study of the timing of such gifts reinforces the case. Yermack (2009) conducted a quantitative analysis of large ($US 1 million plus) charitable stock gifts by the chairpersons or CEOs of public companies in the US to their own private family foundations in the period 2003 to 2005. He notes that such gifts are not subject to insider trading laws, and hence these laws are not widely observed. Yermack (2009: 118) concludes that, 'CEOs make these charitable stock gifts just before sharp drops in their share prices, a pattern that increases the value of their personal income tax deductions arising from the gifts'. Other information indicates support for the perspective that CEOs also tend to backdate the timing of such gifts to maximize tax deductions and make use of insider information on prospective negative information likely to affect stock prices. Yermack further states (2009: 188), 'while seeking to subsidize good works in society, [CEOs] simultaneously follow aggressive tax evasion strategies'. Although such tax avoidance is legal, 'idealists' again object to the motivations and actions involved, viewing them as legally sanctioned misconduct.

This perception that foundations might be created mainly for purposes of tax avoidance, rather than for 'purely' philanthropic purposes, is accentuated when they pay very substantial fees to their trustees for relatively limited work.

Excessive fees

Governments give special tax exemptions to foundations as they are assumed to serve the common good and a public interest. This assumption is questionable when foundations, usually larger ones, provide substantial fees to the members of their boards or senior staff. Excessive fees significantly reduce the funds available to serve the public interest purposes of the foundation. They may also be legal ways of self-dealing, favouring financially the donor(s)' family, descendants and friends or the foundation's executive staff.

Ahn and colleagues (2003) analyzed trustee remuneration for 176 of the largest US private foundations and of a purposive sample of 62 smaller ones. Data were collected from federal (990-PF) tax returns for tax year 1998, and also from telephone interviews in 2001. The findings, while not representative of all foundations, are striking. Some 64 percent of the large foundations and 79 percent of the smaller ones paid fees to their trustees. In total, the full sample of foundations paid over $31 million to individual board members in 1998 (Ahn *et al.*, 2003: 6). The amounts paid were variable and had little relation to the size of foundation endowments. Leaving aside fees for bank trustees (which constitute 31 percent of total fees), of those paying fees that year, the large foundations paid on average a total of $219,000 to their trustees, while the smaller ones paid on average a total of $128,700 (authors' calculations from data reported). Since most boards have a relatively small number of members (about 15), the estimated average annual fees per trustee were about $14,600 in large foundations and $8,600 in smaller ones (computations from reported data, assuming an average of 15 trustees per foundation).

Given the relatively small amounts of time involved for most trustees in most foundations, such disbursements seem excessive, and hence could be considered ethical misconduct. At the upper end of fee amounts, the results were clearly contrary to the philanthropic purposes of foundations. Ahn *et al.* (2003: 7) state that, on an annual basis, 'fourteen of the large foundations paid their trustees more than $100,000 each'. Some 50 percent of the foundations providing fees paid each trustee $25,000 or more annually, as did 63 percent of the smaller fee paying foundations. Among large foundations providing fees, 24 percent paid total trustee fees amounting to two percent or more of all their grants in 1998; for smaller foundations providing fees, 59 percent paid more than five percent of their total grant amounts (authors' computations from data provided). Clearly, from this sample, it seems that when foundations provide trustee fees, as they routinely do, these fees often seem excessive. This situation seems even more like ethical misconduct in the form of nepotism and cronyism when one takes into account that trustees are often family members, descendants, friends, or business contacts of the original donors or their relatives.

Foundation scandals, crimes and fiduciary neglect

So far, our discussion has focused on a few general studies of foundation conduct that is fully within the law. In this section, we touch briefly on one major scandal involving a specific trust that has achieved notoriety and aroused widespread public ire, and consider the extent of foundation misconduct that falls well outside the law. The case of the Kamehameha Schools/Bishop Estate (KSBE) is perhaps the most egregious example of foundation or charitable trust misconduct in American history. This trust, established in 1887, runs a preparatory school in Hawaii that accepts, with very few exceptions, only students of native Hawaiian ancestry (King and Roth, 2006). The KSBE has long been the largest landholder in Hawaii and the largest charitable trust in the US by asset value. Although a trust rather than a private foundation, and functioning more like an operating than a grantmaking entity, the case is nonetheless noteworthy.

As one example of extreme ethical misconduct, trustees of KSBE were each paid an average of $US 900,000 annually from 1994 to 1997 (Frumkin and Andre-Clark, 1999: 425). In addition, the trustees appear to have violated nearly every rule of law regarding fiduciary responsibility over many years (King and Roth, 2006). As a result, the Trust had its Internal Revenue Service (IRS) tax exemption removed retroactively and was liable to pay about $1 billion in back taxes (King and Roth, 2006: 254; Brody, 1999). The head of the IRS Exempt Organizations Division stated, 'the scope and magnitude of abuse were unparalleled' (paraphrased in King and Roth, 2006: 255).

There are many other examples of flagrant misconduct by foundations that could be discussed, but space constrains such detail (Nielsen 1985; Wagner 2000; White 2006). In a quantitative study, Fremont-Smith and Kosaras (2003) examine wrongdoing by officers and directors of many US charities, based on a total national sample of press reports in several key newspapers for the period 1995 to 2002. They focused only on 'instances of alleged wrongdoing by persons who have primary fiduciary responsibility for the charity involved' (2003: 3); wrongdoing by charity employees was excluded, although also frequently reported by the newspapers. Some 152 incidents of civil or criminal wrongdoing were identified over the seven year period. The authors indicate that 35 of these incidents (23 percent) involved foundations. Foundations accounted for about 18 percent of incidents of alleged criminal wrongdoing, but nearly 30 percent of breaches of fiduciary duties (our calculations). For anyone who thinks foundations are somehow free of involvement in crime and misconduct at the highest levels, these results should be sobering. Nearly a quarter of press reports of scandals or wrongdoing involved foundations, even though foundations represent only 10 percent of all charities. Thus among all charities, US foundations seem unusually misconduct prone. However, we must note, as did the authors of the report, that the 152 incidents reported in the mass media involve a *very* tiny fraction of the more than 120,000 private foundations that existed in the US during this period (Urban Institute 2009).

Some of the foundation scandals involved very large amounts of money, however, particularly when Ponzi schemes were used. There was a $570 million loss in one case and a median dollar loss of $130,000 across all criminal incidents (authors' calculation from data provided in Fremont-Smith and Kosaras, 2003: Criminal Activity Table). The foundations involved in top level misconduct were highly varied in their structural types, ranging from grantmaking to operating foundations, and from public to private. Most foundations implicated seemed to be metropolitan or statewide, rather than national in scope, and most seemed to be public foundations (raising money each year from public donations) not private foundations. Thus, as might be expected, national private foundations made the best showing. The label 'foundation' was probably used in some cases when it did not technically apply to these nonprofits which may have been operating 'charities'. Such relatively common but misleading use of the label 'foundation' by nonprofits is legal, and probably occurs in order to secure greater public trust and donations, but this practice can be seen as another kind of NPO deception.

Our analysis has focused on the US, opening the question of whether US foundations are more prone to misconduct and scandal than those elsewhere. Rather than inferring, differences in ethical behaviour or effectiveness of regulation, we note simply the number of foundations in the US, and our lack of access to published evidence of similar rule breaking and dysfunctions by foundations elsewhere. Anecdotal evidence would suggest that there is no fundamental difference, and that rule breaking also exists among foundations in Europe and elsewhere.

Dysfunctions, accountability and regulation

To what extent is government regulation effective in controlling such misconduct, particularly of the criminal kind? In a brief history of foundation rule breaking and regulation by the federal government and state governments in the US, Crimm (2001: 1132) sees the crux of the problem as the tension between the fact that 'private foundations' funding, governance, and management are intimate and private, but the foundations must pursue public benefits'. There have been various federal laws attempting to regulate foundations, but foundation and trust misconduct continues to occur. Crimm (2001: 1180-1196) suggests various improvements in such laws, particularly strengthening the IRS and more education for foundation donors, managers, and trustees/directors. Brody and Tyler (2010), however, seek to debunk the idea that the assets of foundations, as autonomous organizations, are inherently 'public' and should be subject to democratic controls; they argue that governments are using the wrong logic of 'public money' to interfere with the use of foundation and NPO funds in their activities and expenditures.

Orosz (2007) addresses the issues from the perspective of improving foundation management, with a variety of useful suggestions for better management practices. His general point is that foundation leaders (both trustees and executives) need more sophisticated knowledge in order to do foundation work better and more effectively. Intentional misconduct is one thing, but simple ineptitude and ignorance can be even more damaging – and far more pervasive. Orosz (2007: xix) quotes Michael Porter from Harvard Business School: 'foundation scandals tend to be about pay and perks, but the real scandal is about how much money is pissed away on activities that have no impact. Billions are wasted on ineffective philanthropy'. This, too, is foundation deviance in the form of dysfunctions, albeit largely unintentional. Humans in all kinds of organizations and groups tend to be inept frequently. There seem to be no quantitative surveys of this 'grey side' of foundation imperfections and flaws.

Even though the general public does not elect or appoint foundation leaders, many larger foundations have had significant impacts on the foreign policy of their nations. For instance, the Carnegie, Ford, and Rockefeller Foundations have long had such influence in the US, according to Berman (1984). In addition, Arnold (1999), and more recently Brulle (2014) suggest that wealthy foundations have had, and are having, an 'undue influence' on US environmental policy. Nielsen's (1985) book on the 'great foundations' in the US makes similar suggestions about their political influence (Odendahl, 1990; Roelofs, 2003; Prewitt, *et al.*, 2006). For some observers, such undue political influence of the wealthy using publicly supported, i.e. tax exempt, funds is ethical misconduct.

Finally, foundations tend to channel, dampen, and suppress the activist and social change goals of advocacy NPOs by mainly supporting non-change oriented NPOs (Roelofs, 2003). Many NPOs soften or eliminate their social change goals in order to obtain grants from private foundations. This is not surprising since private foundations, with a few exceptions, mainly seek the *status quo* oriented visions of their very wealthy and conservative founders and donors and their descendants or friends (Nielsen, 1985; Odendahl, 1990; Arnove and Pinede, 2007).

The darker side of transnational humanitarian aid and relief NGOs

One major form of philanthropy in the world for at least the past century has been the attempts of NPOs (often referred to as 'NGOs') in wealthier nations to provide relief and humanitarian aid to people in poorer nations who have suffered famine, epidemics, geographical displacement, civil and guerrilla wars, invasions by neighbouring nations, and other calamities (Kapucu, Chapter 11). Sometimes floods, tsunamis, earthquakes, and other natural disasters have caused these humanitarian emergencies, but most have had sociopolitical roots, not roots in geophysical events.

According to Karlan and Appel (2011: 5), more than $US 2.3 trillion in humanitarian aid, relief, and development assistance has flowed from the Global North to the Global South, especially to Africa, Latin America, and Asia, over the past 50 years. Although development assistance has been the larger concern in recent decades, Humanitarian Aid and Relief (HAR) continues to be very important in terms of philanthropy directed to the Global South, and the number of HAR NGOs has grown greatly in the past two decades (Barnett, 2011: 3). Although there are many aspects of the darker side of HAR NGOs as a multinational form of philanthropy, we consider only a few aspects here, drawing on extensive research by many authors.

Following fads, chasing funding, and serving donors

Transnational HAR NGOs all have had positive, compassionate *official* values and goals in their mission statements. They all focus on helping poor, hungry, ill, homeless, and otherwise needy and vulnerable people in developing nations with their immediate survival problems. Unfortunately, the *de facto* or *unofficial* goals and values of many such NGOs have long been their own survival and growth as organizations. Terry (2002: 233) argues that 'a logic of institutional preservation dominates much of the organizational responses and behavior of aid agencies with respect to other actors within the aid regime'. In addition, Maren (1997: 278) notes, 'the first priority of an NGO, like any bureaucracy, is its own survival'. The technical term for this situation is 'goal displacement', in which organizational preservation and enhancement over time replace ostensible, altruistic, official goals of an organization (Smith *et al.*, 2006: 98). This occurs with many NPOs, especially large, paid staff NPOs, not just HAR NGOs.

Because HAR NGOs generally raise their philanthropic funding from the general public in nations of the Global North, they are eager to preserve their 'good will' or general positive image among the publics of such nations and be seem to do things that their donors favour. Keen (2008: 127) identifies the fundamental problem as 'organizational health (and individual careers) may sometimes be better served by satisfying donors and host governments than by satisfying ostensible beneficiaries'. Tvedt (1998: 229) goes further in stating that HAR NGOs mainly seek to satisfy their donors in the Global North, not their intended recipients in the Global South. Sometimes donors in the Global North are national governments, which often use HAR NGOs to advance geopolitical aims, not really to help the neediest people of the Global South (Terry 2002; Keen, 2008).

A related challenge is that HAR NGO relief and aid projects are often planned only in the Global North at NGO headquarters, involving little or no consultation with intended recipients. Riddell (2007: 369) observes that relief fails because of 'insufficient consultation with recipients'. There is a long tradition of charities in the Global North providing philanthropic aid to the poor and needy in their own nations without consulting them about their own view of their 'needs' (Wagner 2000; Cunningham, Chapter 2). Consequently, some critics have argued that HAR NGOs are in the business of creating delusions, which can be seen as dysfunctional. De Waal (1997: 221) suggests that the greatest harm done by such NGOs is that 'Western governments and the donating publics are deluded into believing the fairy tale that their aid can solve profound political problems, when it cannot'. Polman (2010: 173) concludes similarly, that 'humanitarian crises are almost always political crises or crises for which only a political solution exists'. De Waal (1997: 221) further notes, 'most significantly, local people ("recipients" or "beneficiaries") are deluded into believing that salvation can come from other than their own actions'.

An arresting statistic is that in 2004, less than 25 percent of overseas development assistance was given to the poorest countries (Polman, 2010: 161). In 2005, over half of total humanitarian aid funds went to Sudan (Keen, 2008: 134), neglecting less popular aid emergencies elsewhere. The challenge, Polman argues (2010: 176), is that 'transnational aid moves to the next big crisis'. As Keen (2008: 134) notes, 'a concern with organizational growth can encourage a concentration of NGO efforts on high profile crises and even on those parts of crises and affected areas that are easily accessible to the media'. There is no 'master plan' regarding how HAR NGOs should best deal with the full set of global humanitarian crises at any time, nor how to prioritize any future crises. This constitutes serious dysfunction for the entire set of such NGOs.

At any given moment in history, there are thus 'donor darlings' – popular crises, and corresponding NGOs, to which people give substantial money – and 'donor orphans' – unpopular or less visible crises and their corresponding NGOs that are overlooked (Polman, 2010: 158; Kapucu, Chapter 11). Of course, donors are free to ignore any crisis anywhere, irrespective of its severity and extent: 'Aid is a lottery' (Polman, 2010: 158). Keen (2008: 134) observes that 'donors have fads and fashions, and local and international NGOs may be quick to learn and adapt'. To cope with changing perceived humanitarian and relief needs, NGOs shift their stated emphases and the words they use in seeking donations as 'marketing' changes, often without any real changes in their programs. Being a favoured NGO can be problematic, however; as Tvedt (1998: 215) argues, 'easily available funds may be a "source of distraction" and may create "opportunistic" NGOs'. Given that humanitarian aid and relief is a lottery, rather than a rational, comprehensive, global system, potential recipient NGOs and governments may also be engaged in 'marketing' to ensure they distinguish their needs from those of others. Insofar as Global South national governments are involved in the aid and relief process, government corruption and other flaws may substantially reduce aid flow and effectiveness (Maren, 1997; Spector, 2005; Collier, 2007; Riddell, 2007; Moyo, 2009). This is especially true for the 'bottom billion' population of the poorest nations which are not developing, but rather 'are falling behind, and often falling apart' (Collier, 2007: 3).

Structural and operational deficiencies

A variety of operational weaknesses of HAR NGOs contribute to aid that is too slow and of poor quality. These various dysfunctional practices include: too many agencies and inexperienced staff; high staff turnover; short term contracts for projects; weak coordination within and across agencies; falsification of local need assessments; over focus on resources and on a few high profile emergencies; and general inability to learn from experiences (Keen, 2008: 136; also Riddell, 2007: 369). Particularly troublesome is the lack of adequate impact evaluation of projects. A thoughtful study group of experts focusing on HAR NGOs concluded, 'the humanitarian system still lacks a systematic and regular means of assessing its overall performance' (Polman, 2010: 176). Keen (2008: 130) notes that such aid is only evaluated superficially by counting the movement of goods (food, clothing, medicine, etc.) because these movements are visible and relatively easy to measure and report. But there is insufficient attention to real, longer-term outcomes, and to the livelihoods of recipients or intended recipients. The usual 'bean counting' approach of HAR NGOs grossly misrepresents actual impact by over estimating it. For instance, Catholic Relief Services has focused on the number of recipients, not on the impact of its food aid, and some HAR NGOs are essentially money raising organizations that mainly benefit their staff, with little funding reaching needy recipients, according to Maren (1997: 8, 151).

There are many serious, recent critiques of all aspects of HAR NGO operations and practices (de Waal, 1997; Maren, 1997; Tvedt, 1998; Rieff, 2002; Terry, 2002; Kennedy, 2004; Easterly, 2006; Riddell, 2007; Barnett and Weiss, 2008; Keen, 2008; Moyo, 2009; Holmén, 2010; Polman 2010), but none of these has had much effect on actual NGO activities. De Waal (1997: xvi) remarks that HAR NGOs 'have an extraordinary capacity to absorb criticism, not reform [themselves], and yet emerge strengthened'. HAR NGOs need to submit 'to genuinely rigorous forms of local accountability to recipients' and to demonstrate transparency'. The result, as Kennedy (2004: xviii; xx) observes, is that HAR NGOs often 'promise more than can be delivered – and come to believe our own promises,' creating self-delusion and a gap 'between good impulses and [recipients'] bad experiences'.

More than an inadequate evaluation and a gap in expectations is the concern that HAR NGOs are not transparent about, or they actively ignore, their failures. Because these NGOs raise funds mainly from the general public in Global North nations, they have a deep and persistent self-interest in hiding their inefficiencies, ineffectiveness, and other flaws, failures, and dysfunctions. Terry (2002: 231-232) writes that their reliance on donations from the general public

> discourages open discussion among the organizations about the failures or negative consequences of humanitarian actions. ... Aid organizations depend on an image of "doing good" for their support and are reluctant to jeopardize this image by airing concerns that aid may or may not serve the purpose for which it was intended'.

This is the simple logic of NGO self-preservation.

In sum: A half century of dysfunctions in HAR

HAR NGOs from the Global North do some good for some people and nations in the Global South, but long-term success stories seem limited when objective, comprehensive success criteria are applied. Research by many experts seems to suggest that the overall situation might resemble a massive, multitrillion dollar 'scam' perpetrated over the past half century by Global North and South governments, multinational intergovernmental agencies like the United Nations (UN) and

World Bank, businesses based in the Global North, and more recently by Global North transnational NGOs (Hancock, 1992; Maren, 1997; Tvedt, 1998; Terry, 2002; Kennedy, 2004; Michael, 2004; Easterly, 2006; Collier, 2007; Keen, 2008; Holmén, 2010; Polman, 2010). All of this has happened with purported good intentions. Objectively, one has to wonder just how deep, altruistic, and committed such good intentions really are, given the persistent and widespread failures of government, intergovernmental, and NGO aid, relief, and development programs and projects in the Global South. There are many elements of power, prestige, deception, and corruption involved throughout both the global aid/relief and global development systems (Hancock, 1992; Tvedt, 2010), which work to the advantage of Global North governments, businesses, and NGOs (Hancock, 1992; Riddell, 2007).

Many experts (Riddell, 2007), including multinational organizations such as the OECD (2009), have made suggestions for improvements in transnational aid, relief, and development assistance. However, nothing much has changed. Some experts have suggested that the entire 'philanthropic helping' model is deeply flawed as a way to assist the Global South: it creates or maintains perpetual economic dependency rather than long-term economic independence and growth (Moyo, 2009). Perhaps the time has come to challenge the general 'philanthropic imperialism' identified by de Waal (1997: 214), which assumes that the general philanthropy model of helping others in need works, and recognize it rarely helps in all situations.

A focus on the darker side of philanthropy points to the need to delve more deeply into the motivations of philanthropy, including transnational NGO philanthropy. As Rieff (2002: 334) notes, however, 'the tragedy of humanitarianism [and, we add, philanthropy more generally] may be that for all its failings and all the limitations of its viewpoint, it represents what is decent in an indecent world'.

Terrorist financing by philanthropy

Bell's assertion that there is 'terrorist abuse of nonprofits and charities' (2007: 450) brings us to the 'darkest' question in this chapter: philanthropy and charitable giving as a component in financing terrorist organizations. The latter is understood as 'the act of knowingly providing something of value to persons and groups engaged in terrorist activities' (Weber, 2008), with 'terrorism' being 'the calculated use of violence or threat of violence, to attain goals that are political, religious or ideological in nature by an illegitimate and unestablished power against a legitimate and established state … done through intimidation, coercion or by instilling fear' (Napoleoni, 2005: 256). There is widespread agreement that closing, or even diminishing, of terrorist financing would reduce terrorist groups' activities and impact (Greenberg et al., 2002; Biersteker and Eckert, 2008).

Weber (2008) emphasizes that historically, the development of philanthropic institutions has been a powerful tool in challenging states. He goes on to note that organizations such as criminal or hate groups, e.g. mafia-kind organizations and religious fundamentalist groups, have set up systems that, rather than being complementary to any official welfare regimes, openly try to fill the gap of those states that are 'weak' or which have 'failed', and, which, for various reasons, are unable to provide basic social services (Weber, 2008: 2). Within this context, contemporary abuse of charities by terrorist groups may occur with, or without, the knowledge of the donors, officers, and management of these organizations, knowingly or unknowingly acting as cover for terrorist financing (Bell, 2007). Philanthropic funding for terrorist activities may therefore be intentional, whereby recipient charities are established as 'fronts' whose purpose is to channel money into those activities, whose donors understand its purpose, or unintentional, whereby, often through complex networks of connected charities, donations make their way to funding terrorism without the donors' knowledge or intent.

Paradoxically, it is philanthropy's and NGOs' legitimacy, both in doing good and doing so voluntarily, that make them targets for terrorist groups' close attention. This paradox is further extended in the exploitation of faithfulness. Conway (2006: 283), for example, highlights that charities are also popular with Islamic terrorist organizations 'probably because of the injunction that observant Muslims make regular charitable donations'. So far, knowledge on the amounts of money involved in financing terrorism, and the ways in which funds are spread, is limited (Giraldo and Trinkunas, 2007: 31). What research does, however, show is the immensity of terrorist financing. Cassara and Jorisch (2010: 142), for example, state that, in the case of Al Qaeda, an estimated $US 30 million per year over many years was received, totaling $US 300 to $500 million until 9/11/2001. Research further indicates that there are a variety of types of sources of financing of terrorism; the extent, and relative dependence, of terrorist financing on charitable and quasi-charitable funds, warrants further exploration. Notably in relation to those of Islamic charities implicated in terrorist financing, the area that has seen the greatest scrutiny in recent years, Ehrenfeld (2003: 2, 73) lists a spectrum of major sources. Alongside charitable organizations, these include wealthy individuals, but also international organizations such as the UN and the European Union. In the context of counterterrorism's international scrutiny of charities in, and restricting money flows to, Saudi Arabian charities, Altermann (2007: 75) comments that 'because it remains unclear how much of a conduit charities ever were for terrorist financing, it is even less clear how much restricting formal channels for charitable giving helps stem the flow of cash to terrorist groups'.

The link between charities and armed organizations is not new. From an Islamic perspectives for example, Napoleoni (2005: 251), translating jihad as 'striving in the cause of God', reports that Islamic charities actively engaged the anti-Soviet jihad, and, once that war was over, 'many continued to support Muslims fighting similar wars in other countries such as Bosnia and Chechnya' (Napoleoni, 2005: 173; Wittig, 2011). Casting the web wider, Benthall (2007: 2), considering the association of Islamic charities with transnational mujahideen, points out that 'on a smaller, bilateral scale, an analogy could be made with Noraid, or Irish Northern Aid, the New York-based charity that since 1969 has raised funds in the US for Republican – that is to say Catholic – charities but that was regularly accused of spending some of the funds on weapons until the Irish Republican Army accepted the peace process in 1996'.

Further complexity is presented where funds from terrorist sources also reach charities. Thus, Giraldo and Trinkunas (2007: 24-25) add that terrorist financing also comes from Islamic terrorist groups through fees and donations associated with cultural events, regular contributions from diaspora communities, and special fundraising events, such as dinners for diaspora donors and other sympathizers (Napoleoni, 2005: 171-172). This 'commingling of illicit with licit funds' is advantageous, according to Maras (2013: 103) because of the subsequent difficulties of linking financiers with terrorist acts. In the argument that charities have special advantages for terrorist financing, Giraldo and Trinkunas (2007: 25) emphasise that, as in the legitimate charity sphere, 'it is very difficult to confirm or control the ultimate recipient of a charitable donation'. Given public trust in charities and charities' access to substantial funds, their 'presence' can serve as 'an excellent means of both radicalizing constituents and moving money (Cassara and Jorisch, 2010: 138).

It is in this context of trust that perspectives on both the dynamics, and scale, of the terrorism-charity nexus are developed. For example, Cassara and Jorisch (2010: 138) report the US Central Intelligence Agency as estimating that 'one-third of Muslim charities support terrorist groups or employ individuals who are suspected of having terrorist connections'. Other commentators, however, regard commercial and business association linkages as far more critical – in the sense of being more lucrative – than links to charities, recognizing that some terrorist groups tend to abuse both charities and businesses in their local spheres of operations (Biersteker and Eckert, 2008).

In yet further layers of interaction, many terrorist groups have established their own international networks of 'charities' to provide financing (Ehrenfeld, 2003, 21). In this sense, terrorism groups will have their own 'customer base' of donors and patrons from which they have to raise money through 'selling' their mission, changing mission or specific targets, and activities to suit those customers, not their recipients (Biersteker and Eckert, 2008: 32). Such groups may also undertake charitable acts, whether directly or through affiliates. Ly (2007: 178), for example, emphasizes the importance of this route for gaining the support of local populations, citing research concerning the 1989 Algerian earthquake where aid to victims was provided more efficiently through unofficial channels than via government. Such an example strongly encapsulates Flanigan's (2006: 641) examination of charity being used as a tool by groups of terrorists and political insurgents to shepherd communities along a 'support continuum' towards growing consent with, and participation in, acts of aggression. Finally, it has also been argued that charities as financing vehicles are especially attractive in those jurisdictions where they are subject to limited or no oversight, i.e. registration, record-keeping, and monitoring (Giraldo and Trinkunas, 2007: 25).

There are ongoing major well-funded, national government and intergovernmental efforts to diminish and control terrorism in recent decades, where the financing of terrorism is a major focus (Lindsey and Williams, 2013). In a quieter way, charity regulators are also attempting to follow the money, also with decidedly mixed success given the variety of ways in which charities and philanthropy can be involved, and the complexities of international networks. Meanwhile, this 'dark side of philanthropy' casts an immense shadow over civil society: unwitting donors are defrauded, or cease or lessen their giving, while wholly philanthropic actions can be deterred or erased from areas of urgent need, arguably to terrorism's advantage.

While Howell *et al.* (2008: 82) assert that civil society's space for action and flourishing is threatened by increasing global concerns with security and counterterrorist measures, civil society itself is also endangered by terrorism. This is illustrated by advocacy nonprofits and NGOs becoming particular targets for terrorist action. Murdie and Stapley (2014: 79) theorize that the nonviolent advocacy activities of some nonprofits and NGOs, especially in relation to governments' human rights practices, can shape the perspectives and manners 'of potential terrorist group supporters in ways not liked by terrorist organisations'. The shadow from this very 'dark side' continues to draw us into paradox. From Berman's (2009) examination of radical religious groups involved with terrorism, it is striking that these groups demonstrate characteristics of staying power that we also associate with worthy philanthropic action that involves sacrifice and mutual aid.

Conclusion

Rule breaking, deviance and dysfunctions are present as the darker side of philanthropy worldwide. Most philanthropy in most countries may be beneficial, but some pockets of it, around the globe, manifest ethical misconduct, dysfunctions, and even crime. Donors and philanthropies in the Global North are often more concerned with 'the symbolism of helping that appeals to many people rather than any actual accomplishment' (Wagner 2000: 113). Some foundations and other charities focus more on the process of their giving than the actual, long term impacts and outcomes of their philanthropy. Philanthropy then is more of a kindly gesture based on altruistic intent than demonstrable helping of the intended recipients, especially when such recipients are needy and poor. Similarly, a number of philanthropic organizations seem to be more concerned with their donors and their own survival or enhancement than with genuinely helping the recipients they claim as their primary mission. The monitoring, regulation, and accountability of philanthropic organizations are inadequate on a global scale.

In this chapter, we have only scratched the surface of the darker side of philanthropy (Smith 2016; Eng et al., 2016) and there are wider debates to be had about the nature of 'public benefit' and 'general welfare': these are relative to one's worldview, religion, ideology, and personal experiences. However, we have shown that various kinds of rule breaking and dysfunctions across many societies can be huge in dollar terms and in their negative impact on intended recipients, as well as legitimate philanthropic action. Putting self-interest above the public interest is pervasive, and may be seen as normal for humans, as for other animals. Altruism and the philanthropic impulse and spirit exist as a secondary motivation for most people, but they very much need to be nurtured carefully if they are to have a broad and positive impact on human society. Philanthropy, in all forms everywhere, needs to be more transparent, monitored, and accountable, as does so much of the rest of human activity.

References

Ahn, C., Eisenberg, P. and Khamvongsa, C. (2003) Foundation trustee fees: Use and abuse. Unpublished report. Washington, DC: The Center for Public and Nonprofit Leadership, Georgetown Public Policy Institute, Georgetown University.

Altermann, J. (2007) Saudi charities and support for terror. In J. Alterman and K. Von Hippel (Eds.). *Understanding Islamic Charities*, Significant Issues Series, 29, 7, The Center for Strategic and International Studies, Washington DC., 64–78.

Anheier, H. K. and Toepler, S. (1999) Philanthropic foundations: An international perspective. In H. K. Anheier and S. Toepler (Eds.). *Philanthropic foundations in international perspective*. New York, NY: Kluwer Academic/Plenum Publishers.

Anheier, H. and Daly, S. (Eds.). (2007) *The politics of foundations: A comparative analysis*. London: Routledge.

Anheier, H. and Hammack, D. C. (Eds.). (2010) *American foundations: Roles and contributions*. Washington, DC: The Brookings Institution Press.

Arnold, R. (1999) *Undue influence: Wealthy foundations, grant-drive environmental groups, and zealous bureaucrats that control your future*. Bellevue, WA: Free Enterprise Press.

Arnove, R. and Pinede. N. (2007) Revisiting the 'Big Three' foundations, *Critical Sociology*, 33(3): 389–425.

Barnett, M. (2011) *Empire of humanity: A history of humanitarianism*. Ithaca, NY: Cornell University Press.

Barnett, M. and Weiss, T. G. (Eds.). (2008) *Humanitarianism in question: Politics, power, ethics*. Ithaca, NY: Cornell University Press.

Bell, J. L. (2007) Terrorist abuse of non-profit and charities: A proactive approach to preventing terrorist financing, *Kansas Journal of Law and Public Policy*, 17, 450–76.

Benthall, J. (2007) Islamic charities, faith-based organisations and the international aid system. In J. Alterman and K. Von Hippel (Eds.). *Understanding Islamic Charities*, Significant Issues Series, 29, 7, The Center for Strategic and International Studies, Washington DC., 1–14.

Berman, E. H. (1984) *The influence of the Carnegie, Ford, and Rockefeller foundations on American Foreign Policy: The ideology of philanthropy*. Albany, NY: SUNY University Press.

Berman, E. (2009) Radical, religious and violent: The new economics of terrorism, Massachusetts: Massachusetts Institute of Technology.

Biersteker, T. J. and Eckert, S. E. (2008) *Countering the financing of terrorism*. New York, NY: Routledge.

Brody, E. (1999) A taxing time for the Bishop Estate: What is the IRS role in charity governance?, *University of Hawaii Law Review*, 537: 543–45.

——. and Tyler, J. (2010) Respecting foundation and charity autonomy: How public is private philanthropy? *Chicago-Kent Law Review*, 85(2): 571–617.

Brulle, R. J. (2014) Institutionalizing delay: Foundation funding and the creation of U.S. climate change counter-movement organizations, *Climatic Change*, 122(4): 681–94.

Cassara, J. and Jorisch, A. (2010) *On the trail of terror finance*. Washington, DC: Red Cell Intelligence Group.

Collier, P. (2007) *The bottom billion: Why the poorest countries are failing and what can be done about it*. New York, NY: Oxford University Press.

Conway, M. (2006). Terrorism and the Internet: new media–new threat? *Parliamentary Affairs*, 59(2), 283–98.

Crimm, N. J. (2001) A case study of a private foundation's governance and self-interested fiduciaries calls for further regulation, *Emory Law Journal*, 50: 1093–1196.

de Waal, A. (1997) *Famine crimes: Politics and the disaster relief industry in Africa*. Oxford, UK and Bloomington, IN: African Rights and the International African Institute (James Currey and Indiana University Press).

Easterly, W. (2006) *The white man's burden: Why the West's efforts to aid the rest have done so much ill and so little good*. New York, NY: Penguin Books.

Ehrenfeld, R. (2003) *Funding evil: How Terrorism is financed and how to stop it*. Boulder, CO: Taylor Trade Publishing.

Eng, S., Smith, D. H., Brilliant, E. and Faulkner, L. (2016) Misconduct in conventional associations and fundamentally deviant associations chapter 53. In D. H. Smith, R. A. Stebbins and J. Grotz (Eds.). *The Palgrave research handbook of volunteering, civic participation, and nonprofit associations*. Basingstoke, UK: Palgrave Macmillan.

Flanigan, S. T. (2006). Charity as resistance: Connections between charity, contentious politics, and terror, *Studies in Conflict and Terrorism*, 29(7), 641–55.

Fleishman, J. L. (2007) *The foundation: A great American secret*. New York, NY: Public Affairs.

Fremont-Smith, M. R. and Kosaras, A. (2003) Wrongdoing by officers and directors of charities: A survey of press reports 1995-2002, Working Paper No. 20. Cambridge, MA: Hauser Center for Nonprofit Organizations, Harvard University.

Frumkin, P. (2005) *On being nonprofit*. Cambridge, MA: Harvard University Press.

Frumkin, P. and Andre-Clark, A. (1999) Nonprofit compensation and the market, *University of Hawaii Law Review*, 21: 425–485.

Giraldo, J. K. and Trinkunas, H. A. (2007) *Terrorism financing and state responses*. Stanford, CA: Stanford University Press.

Greenberg, M., Wechsler, W. and Wolosky, L. (2002) *Terrorist financing*. New York, NY: Council on Foreign Relations.

Hancock, G. (1992) *Lords of poverty: The power, prestige, and corruption of the international aid business*. New York, NY: Atlantic Monthly Press.

Heydemann, S. and Toepler, S. (2006) Foundations and the challenge of legitimacy in comparative perspective. In K. Prewitt, M. Doogan, S. Heydemann and S. Toepler (Eds.). *The legitimacy of philanthropic foundations: United States and European perspectives*. New York: Russell Sage Foundation.

Holmén, H. (2010) *Snakes in paradise: NGOs and the aid industry in Africa*. Sterling, VA: Kumarian Press.

Howell, J., Ishkanian, A., Obadare, E., Seckinelgin, H., and Glasius, M. (2008) The backlash against civil society in the wake of the Long War on Terror, *Development in Practice*, 18(1), 82–93.

Kaplan, D. and Appel, J. (2011) *More than good intentions: How a new economics is helping to solve global poverty*. New York, NY: Penguin Group.

Keen, D. (2008) *Complex emergencies*. Cambridge, UK: Polity Press.

Kennedy, D. (2004) *The dark sides of virtue: Reassessing international humanitarianism*. Princeton, NJ: Princeton University Press.

King, S. P. and Roth, R. W. (2006) *Broken trust: Greed, mismanagement and political manipulation at America's largest charitable trust*. Honolulu, HI: University of Hawaii Press.

Langley, M. (1997) Tax break prompts millionaires' mad dash to create foundations, *The Wall Street Journal*, January 27.

Lindsey, S. C., and Williams, M. J. (2013) State-sponsored social control of illegitimate social movements: Strategies used to financially damage Radical Islamic, terrorist-labeled organizations, *Studies in Conflict and Terrorism*, 36(6), 460–76.

Ly, P-E (2007) The charitable activities of terrorist organizations, *Public Choice*, 131(1–2), 177–95.

Maras, M-H (2013) "Charities" entry in *The CRC Terrorism Reader*, Boca Raton, FL: Taylor and Francis Group.

Marcus, C. (1992) *Lives in trust: The fortunes of dynastic families in late twentieth century America*. Boulder, CO: Westview.

Maren, M. (1997) *The road to hell: The ravaging effects of foreign aid and international charity*. New York, NY: The Free Press.

Michael, S. (2004) *Undermining development: The absence of power among local NGOs in Africa*. Oxford, UK and Bloomington, IN: James Currey and Indiana University Press.

Moyo, D. (2009) *Dead aid: Why aid is not working and how there is a better way for Africa*. New York, NY: Farrar, Straus and Giroux.

Murdie, A., and Stapley, C. S. (2014) Why target the 'good guys'? The determinants of terrorism against NGOs. *International Interactions*, 40(1), 79–102.

Napoleoni, L. (2005) *Terror incorporated: Tracing the dollars behind the terror networks.* New York, NY: Seven Stories Press.

Nielsen, W. A. (1985) *The golden donors: A new anatomy of the great foundations.* New York, NY: Dutton Adult.

Noble, J. and Wixley, S. (2014) *Mind the gap: What the public thinks about charities.* London, NPC.

Odendahl, T. (1990) *Charity begins at home: Generosity and self-interest among the philanthropic elite.* New York, NY: Basic Books.

OECD. (2009) *Better aid effectiveness: A progress report on implementing the Paris Declaration.* Paris, OECD.

Orosz, J. J. (2007) *Effective foundation management.* Lanham, MD: AltaMira Press, Rowman & Littlefield.

Ostrower, F. (1995) *Why the wealthy give: The culture of elite philanthropy.* Princeton, NJ: Princeton University Press.

Polman, L. (2010) *The crisis caravan: What's wrong with humanitarian aid?* New York, NY: Metropolitan Books.

Prewitt, K. (2006a) American foundations: What justifies their unique privileges and powers. In K. Prewitt, M. Doogan, S. Heydemann and S. Toepler (Eds.). *The legitimacy of philanthropic foundations: United States and European perspectives.* New York: Russell Sage Foundation.

——. (2006b) Foundations. In W. W. Powell and R. Steinberg (Eds.). *The nonprofit sector: A research handbook,* 2nd ed. New Haven, CT: Yale University Press.

——., Doogan, M., Heydemann, S. and Toepler, S. (Eds.). (2006) *The legitimacy of philanthropic foundations: United States and European perspectives.* New York: Russell Sage Foundation.

Riddell, R. C. (2007) *Does foreign aid really work?* Oxford, UK: Oxford University Press.

Rieff, D. (2002) *A bed for the night: Humanitarianism in crisis.* New York, NY: Simon & Schuster.

Roelofs, J. (2003) *Foundations and public policy: The mask of pluralism.* Albany, NY: State University of New York Press.

Smith, D. H. (2016) *The "Dark Energy" of the Nonprofit Sector: Noxious, Dissenting, and Eccentric Types of Deviant Voluntary Associations, their Impacts, and How They Work.* Bradenton, FL: David Horton Smith International.

Smith, D. H., Stebbins, R. A. and Dover, M. A. (2006) *A dictionary of nonprofit terms and concepts.* Bloomington, IN: Indiana University Press.

Spector, B. I. (2005) *Fighting corruption in developing countries.* Bloomfield, CT: Kumarian Press.

Terry, F. (2002) *Condemned to repeat?: The paradox of humanitarian action.* Ithaca, NY: Cornell University Press.

Tvedt, T. (1998) *Angels of mercy or development diplomats? NGOs and foreign aid.* Trenton, NJ: Africa World Press.

Urban Institute. (2009) Number of nonprofit organizations in the United States, 1999-2009. National Center for Charitable Statistics. www.nccsdataweb.urban.org/PubApps/profile1.php?state=US [Accessed 20 January 2013].

Wagner, D. (2000) *What's love got to do with it ? A critical look at American Charity.* New York, NY: New Press.

Weber, P.C. (2008) Terrorism and philanthropy. Counter terrorism financing regimes, International Civil Society, and Religious fundamentalism, International Society for Third Sector Research, Conference Working Papers, Volume VI, Barcelona, Spain, 1-36. www.istr.org/?WP_Barcelona

White, D. (2006) *Charity on trial.* Fort Lee, NJ: Barricade Books.

Wittig, T. (2011) *Understanding terrorist finance.* New York, NY: Palgrave Macmillan.

Yermack, D. (2009) Deductio *ad absurdum*: CEOs donating their own stock to their own family foundations, *Journal of Financial Economics,* 94(1): 107–23.

Part V

The institutions and expressions of philanthropy

Vignette: The Institutions and Expressions of Philanthropy

Philanthropy as boundary spanning

Reaching in and out for a Qatar-based charity

Aisha Faleh Al-Thani

Reach Out to Asia (ROTA) is a Qatar-based education and development charity. It engages in transnational philanthropy in regions where external philanthropic attention has been relatively limited and where negotiating philanthropic legitimacy can be challenging. Celebrating its first full decade of work in 2015, ROTA is a beyond-borders initiative that has also found itself strongly engaged in youth community service at home. Operating as a fundraising charity and working with a variety of partners, ROTA's mission is 'to ensure that people affected by crises across Asia and around the world have continuous access to relevant and high-quality primary and secondary school education'. With the onset of the Arab Spring in late 2010 and early 2011, ROTA's geographic funding reach experienced re-interpreted flexibility; its work has also been constrained by difficult and deteriorating security settings – in precisely the areas where its vision of access for youth to education and training is most critical. Its success has depended on an ability to navigate these difficult spaces and connect its work and profile beyond borders with its engagement at home. To this end, ROTA's strategy has been to integrate 'in-reach' with its 'out-reach' purposes, and it does so in two main ways. First, it advances its educational vision and programs in the context of particular humanitarian need and donors and recipients, while not itself offering immediate humanitarian relief. Second, it helps develop capacity while retaining sole hold of the concept of youth service within its home community of Qatar.

Reaching in: Community service in Qatar

As an international development charity, ROTA's home presence provides both continuity with, and contrasts to, its international identity and role. Qatar's emphasis on spurring its national education development and its 'National Vision 2030' of a knowledge-based economy gave impetus to ROTA's founding in 2005. It also motivated the location of ROTA within an overarching organizational parent, the Qatar Foundation. This is a private NGO founded a decade earlier to develop Qatari educational potential, both nationally and internationally, through progressive education, research and community welfare (Khodr, 2011). Given that 60 percent of Qatar's expatriate community is of Asian origin, ROTA, from its beginning, added insights into the educational needs and cultural norms of Asian peoples.

As much enabling as expressive, ROTA's strategy, which is part of its longer-term donor plan, has always allowed for local and youth engagement to raise awareness of education and development. This has propelled ROTA towards a significant community development role, particularly through its schools-based volunteer programme of Youth Service Clubs that encourage community service learning (Kandil, 2004). By giving voice to youth concerns, including a regional youth media initiative, and providing youth with hands-on opportunities for civic service, ROTA's success has meant it cannot coordinate enough volunteering activities for all schools and students across Qatar. Instead, it has presented plans for working with Qatar's Supreme Education Council to develop a nationwide school-volunteering national curriculum and a toolkit for use by other organizations.

Sustaining this 'reaching in' position with young education-based volunteers is demanding for ROTA, particularly for donor relations and cultivation: as donors' expectations rise that there are ever expanding opportunities at home, it becomes even more critical to channel philanthropic interest to its international work. Nevertheless, the bulk of ROTA's budget goes to its international objectives and, whilst Qatari community development efforts are steadily expanding, they still remain within ROTA's international mission. For ROTA's board, staff and volunteers, being motivated to be able to simultaneously look outwards and look inwards is a skill in its own right.

Reaching out: A strategic balance

Qatar's increasing geo-political influence (Kamrava, 2011), and helpful brokerage role in peace and stability issues – for example, its mediation efforts in Lebanon, Sudan, Yemen and Palestine – helps sustain motivations to support ROTA from a national-international perspective. ROTA's board, donor, and managerial focus, all require constant attention to the latest geopolitical developments. For its ability to do so, enabling it to provide assistance in conflict related areas, ROTA is seen as an 'exemplar organisation' (Barakat and Zyck, 2010: 36) among NGOs in the Gulf Co-operation Council states.

Operationally, ROTA, like other Middle East philanthropic initiatives, works in what Murphy (2009) describes as the shifting spaces of governments and business. This necessitates continual review and assessment of why, where, how and with whom ROTA works, organizations which are almost always encapsulated in demanding locations, commitments and time scales. This is illustrated by ROTA's work in Pakistan's Swat district: in 2012, three years after the Government Girls High School Chamtalai was destroyed by militants, ROTA and Save The Children inaugurated a new school for 230 female pupils as part of a major educational and community development programme. Similarly attuned to regional developments, with the onset of the Arab Spring, ROTA initiated a new 'reach out to Arabia' campaign.

Now working across ten counties in Asia and the Arab Region, a distinctive feature for ROTA is its pronounced emphasis on service, irrespective of religion or ideology, and its commitment to support people, regardless of race, gender or religion. This neutrality is key to ROTA's reputation within, and beyond, the Middle East, and in both Muslim and non-Muslim philanthropy contexts. Its project strengths – supporting educational development through enhancing skills development, integrating environmental and educational concerns, using sport as an educational tool, and revitalizing language – all gain from a broad, secular stance, and further support ROTA's emphasis on local community ownership.

As part of this, it is important for ROTA to maintain its legitimacy, demonstrating that its choices of projects and locations are based on, and perceived as based on, priority need rather than religion or co-religious concerns: addressing natural disasters, overcoming the impact of wars, and helping the world's poorest nations, as identified by the World Bank. This becomes very clear when ROTA's own credentials are challenged. For example, in November 2013, ROTA's assessment team sought, after initial desk reviews, to travel to Myanmar to examine the conditions impacting children and young people's access to quality education. ROTA focused on Rakhine state. This is characterized by weak infrastructure, high population density, low-income communities, and a variety of ethnic and religious groups. While most Myanmar populations are vulnerable, the Rohingya, an ethnic Muslim population, faced especially severe conditions (*New York Times*, 2013). After delays in finding a facilitating NGO host, eventually selecting the Qatar Red Crescent, which itself operates under Myanmar Red Cross auspices, ROTA was unable to undertake its field visit components due to an inability to gain security clearance, and has subsequently placed its proposed project on hold. Put bluntly, it appears that ROTA was (mis) perceived as a Muslim charity, helping Muslims in a religious conflict zone, thus compromising its legitimacy as a neutral player.

The need for flexibility, when working in poor, crisis-facing countries, and the reality of projects on hold, or quickly scaled down, or scaled up, are all an operating fact of life for ROTA's managers and field staff; an area where quality communication with donors is vital. With a strategy that does not provide direct funding to immediate relief or extracting people to safety, but emphasises information gathering through field assessments of the best possible education efforts in difficult circumstances, a 'patient impatience' is required by the board, donors and field staff. With Arab Spring developments, in areas such as Yemen, Egypt and Syria, some ROTA donors expected immediate action to support education, but soon recognized the value of a more calculated – and educated – response once initial conditions were understood. Programs were discontinued in Syria in 2012 with no re-entry plans until the situation had settled; while in Jordan, projects were responding to the schooling pressures of over 500,000 child refugees, with 55 schools coping with double shifts of students. In Lebanon, where one million plus refuges could not be easily integrated into public schools, facing both space and language difficulties, ROTA worked at building low-cost schools and at launching a sports education programme.

Suspension or withdrawal of programs produces its own frustrations, loss of human capital and capacity building in the medium and longer terms, alongside the immediate necessities of safeguarding of staff, children and young people through risk assessment and child protection. Motivating board, donors, staff and volunteers by maintaining ROTA's sense of progression and action orientation when projects are on hold is critical to keeping up its impetus and its impact (Harrow, 2013). For example, after projects were suspended in Syria and Egypt, ROTA is now taking different directions. In Yemen, a partnership with CARE and Silatech, a prominent Qatar social initiative for youth employment and entrepreneurship in the Arab world, has been launched to create viable alternatives to formal employment for youth. Similarly, scaling up of educational objectives is central for ROTA programs. This is especially notable where school attendance in Asia is seen as unaffordable or linked to gender and conflict issues: parental poverty then becomes the core challenge. In a Nepal programme, for example, mothers of participating children are supported through creating mothers' groups, and organizing collective savings and income generating activities, such as vegetable or poultry farming. The ability to scale has clear implications for ROTA's staffing capacity, making it essential that local project staff pass on their developing experience and knowledge to HQ staff, as well as providing career opportunities within projects and offering favourable employment conditions overall.

Moving forward: Mobilizing women

Education is not solely a 'women's issue', but its role in community development and potential for change through philanthropy is often spearheaded by, as well as focused on, women.

As a ROTA Board member from the very beginning, my own motivation to join the board and contribute as a philanthropist has been twofold. First, I recognize the potential of education to change lives and 'make differences' and to do so over the longer term, supported by sound information, itself a vital component of education. Second, I have great faith in ROTA's chairperson, particularly her commitment, which is articulated in the long-term, but not low key, message that 'ROTA aims to ensure that education is not interrupted in times of crisis, by providing access to safe learning areas and quality education' (ROTA, 2006).

Women's impact on philanthropy in Qatar and the region has already been extraordinary, and there appears more to come as women's wealth and influence grows: the real surge in women's philanthropy is not yet realized. Hence ROTA is now aiming at engaging more women by shifting its approaches to address women's interests and leadership styles, and attract wealthy and powerful women. For these women, the comment from the 12-year-old Nepalese pupil to her ROTA project visitors, '… it enables me to hope that my life will get better and thus I'll never forget you', is likely to be only the starting point of their philanthropic action.

Notes

'Reach Out to Asia' was conceived by Qatar's (then) Heir Apparent, His Highness Sheikh Tamim bin Hamad Al Thani in 2005, and guided subsequently by ROTA's Chairperson, Her Excellency Sheikha Al Mayassa bint Hamad Al Thani and its board. The Reach Out to Asia website is www.reachouttoasia.org/.

Grateful thanks are expressed to ROTA's Executive Director, Essa Al Mannai, ROTA's Programme Coordinator, Rania Musleh, ROTA's Monitoring and Evaluation Specialist, Abdallah Al Abdallah, and Qatar Academy pupil, Tammam Al-Ghraoui, for their willingness to be interviewed.

References

Barakat, S. and Zyck, S. A. (2010) Gulf State Assistance to Conflict-Affected Environments, Research Paper No.10, Kuwait Programme on Development, Governance and Globalisation in the Gulf States, London School of Economics, London.

Harrow, J. (2013) Impetus or Impact? Implications for Emerging Philanthropy, Academy of Philanthropy and World Congress of Muslim Philanthropists Seminar, The Torch, Doha, Qatar, 5 March.

Kamrava, M. (2011) Mediation and Qatari Foreign Policy, *Middle East Journal*, 65, 4, 539–56.

Kandil, A. (2004) Civic Service in the Arab Region, *Nonprofit and Voluntary Sector Quarterly*, 33, 4, Supplement, 395–505

Khodr, H. (2011) The Dynamics of International Education in Qatar: Exploring the Policy Drivers behind the Development of Education City, *Journal of Emerging Trends in Research and Policy Studies*, 2, 6, 514–25.

Murphy, S. (2009) Business and Philanthropy Partnerships for Human Capital Development in the Middle East, Corporate Social Responsibility Initiative, Harvard Kennedy School, Working Paper 52.

New York Times (2013) Editorial, Ethnic Violence in Myanmar, December 11.

Reach Out to Asia Annual Report (2006) From Her Excellency Sheikha Al Mayassa bint Hamad Al Thani.

18

Private and family foundations

Diana Leat

Philanthropic foundations are undergoing a global renaissance. At the beginning of the twenty-first century, it was estimated that three-quarters of the wealthiest Americans had their own foundation (Forbes, 2000). Since then, the idea has attracted evermore interest; over the last two decades, foundations, as the formal organized form of philanthropy, have seen unprecedented global growth (Anheier and Leat, 2013). Our understanding of foundations as an organizational form, however, remains limited. Alternatively described as 'giraffes', strange and improbable organizational creates, (Nielsen, 1972: 3), or as 'Pandora's Boxes', organizations whose mythic properties and outward appeal need to be handled with care (Jung and Harrow, 2015: 50), foundations are currently one of the most unrestricted organizational forms (Anheier and Daly, 2007). As such, this chapter provides an overview of what constitutes a philanthropic foundation, and why individuals and families create foundations. Thereafter, it explores the different ways in which foundations work and the opportunities and challenges they present. Throughout this chapter, the focus is on 'private' and 'family' foundations. These are widely perceived as the sectors' 'rich relations' (Weissert and Knott, 1995); their 'poor cousins' (Hodgson and Knight, 2010), the community foundations are discussed later on in this volume (Harrow *et al.*, Chapter 19).

What is a philanthropic foundation?

Legal definitions of foundations vary between countries. In some countries, such as the UK, there is no legal distinction between charities in general and foundations (Dunn, 2014). In other countries, such as the US, private foundations are legally distinct from other nonprofit 501(c)(3) organizations. Within Europe, there is a mass of complex legal and terminological differences and distinctions, sometimes within one country (Prele, 2014); to complicate matters further, some organizations that call themselves 'foundations' are in fact no different from the general run of charities.

Foundations are generally seen as differing from ad hoc gifts in that they have a relatively permanent identity and purpose and an organizational structure. Prewitt (2006: 355) takes a slightly different, and by his own admission American-centric, approach:

> A key feature of a foundation is a permanent endowment, not committed to a particular institution or activity, that provides a grantmaking capacity reaching across multiple purposes

and into the indefinite future. A permanent endowment attached to a broad, permissive mission is a defining characteristic of present-day foundations. According to Prewitt, this gives foundations considerable latitude to respond to changing conditions and distinguishes them from other types of gift: it is the endowment that differentiates the foundation from the bulk of non profit organizations "that survive through membership dues, fees for services, government contracts, or product marketing".

(Prewitt, 2006: 355)

Foundations come in a diversity of different types, ages, and sizes. Endowed foundations – those which own a body of assets/corpus, on the income from which they meet their needs – are, in a sense, the 'purest' form of foundation in Prewitt's terms. In relation to Anheier's (2001) perspective, these are the foundations with the most autonomy; they are the most self-governing, the most independent. Fully endowed foundations do not have to please anyone, except regulators, in order to survive, and vary radically in size and level of activity. They may derive their original corpus from an individual or family, a company, or a one-off appeal.

'Private' 'family' foundations

So where do 'private' 'family' foundations fit in all this? Perhaps the first point to note is that the term 'private', as applied to foundations, is largely a US convention. It arises in part from the legal distinction in the US between foundations that do not fundraise/accept public donations and those that do. In the UK, parts of Europe, and some other countries, that legal distinction does not apply. Here, the term 'private' is not only less used but, for reasons discussed below, is also contested. The regulations concerning governance of foundations, and the definitions and distinctions between types, vary significantly from country to country in ways that make any generalization perilous.

When we look at research on 'private' or 'family' foundations, we find a rather loose application of definitions. The terms 'private' and 'family' tend to be used together or interchangeably in somewhat vague ways. For example, Schramm (2006, 2007: 371-2) writes:

The private foundation differs in character from other institutions in that it possesses no constituents, no shareholders, and only a slim connection to the market through its invested endowment. It is in the fortunate position … of "having all assets and no liabilities". … It is perhaps best described as an "out-market" institution'.

Similarly, Pharoah (2011: 13-4) defines family foundations as:

'independently governed institutions, with large private assets, often in the form of permanent endowments, which they use to promote public benefit. They are private, funded principally by the personal gift of a family business or family member(s), often with the donor or family members having a position on their governing board. Their main, but not sole, activity is making grants to charities, individuals and other public benefit institutions for which they provide independent support'.

(see also National Center on Family Philanthropy, www.ncfp.org)

So there are various issues here. First, the terms 'private' and family' are confused. In some cases 'private' seems to mean 'family'; in other cases, 'private' seems to mean fully endowed and is used to distinguish an endowed foundation from a community/fundraising foundation or a corporate foundation dependent on company handouts. Second, the notion of foundations as 'private' is both redundant and contested. It is redundant, insofar as all fully endowed foundations are 'private' in the sense that they are resource independent and self-governing (Anheier, 2001). To call endowed foundations private could be seen as about as informative as using the term 'private family' – 'private' does not add anything. Describing endowed foundations as 'private' is also increasingly contested in those countries in which philanthropic gifts and institutions enjoy (public) tax subsidies. In this case, so the argument goes, foundations may be formed with private money but, once created, they are publicly subsidized bodies which, for that reason and because they enjoy the subsidy on the basis of a commitment to public benefit, *have* an obligation to be publicly transparent, if not accountable (Harrow, Chapter 31).

Proponents of the 'private foundation' terminology might argue, however, that such usage serves to distinguish a particular type of foundation from other institutions calling themselves 'foundations', such as the United Way in North America and other organizations that have to raise money from the public or are funded/part controlled by a company or by government. The term 'private' then becomes a short hand for fully endowed, non-fund-seeking and independent of 'external/other' control. The Council on Foundations (2015) makes a further distinction. It differentiates between 'private foundations' and 'private independent foundations'. The former

> make grants based on charitable endowments. The endowment funds come from one or a small handful of sources – an individual, a family or a corporation. Because of their endowments, they are focused primarily on grantmaking and generally do not raise funds or seek public financial support the way public charities (like community foundations) must'; the latter 'are distinct from private family or corporate foundations in that an independent foundation is not governed by the benefactor, the benefactor's family or a corporation [such as the Wallace Foundation in the US, and the Joseph Rowntree Foundation in the UK]. Of the largest private foundations in the United States, most are independent foundations, although they may have begun as family foundations'.
>
> *(Council on Foundations, 2015)*

So here 'family foundations' are a subset of 'private foundations'. But again, the label may be misleading. In some cases, and at some times, it signals that the foundation has been created with the wealth of a single family and is solely or largely controlled by family members. Over time, however, the degree of family control may be reduced either through natural attrition (e.g. later generations lacking interest, time, or commitment) or by deliberate choice (e.g. a decision to seek advice outside the family). Thus, what starts as a family foundation may become a foundation with a few nonfamily advisers, and then a foundation governed by a majority of nonfamily members. Conversely, a foundation established following the death of the donor may be governed by friends rather than family on the board, but may nevertheless behave very much like a family (e.g. frequently referring to 'what x would have wanted' etc.).

It is tempting to suggest that those who cling to the adjective 'private' do so in order to reassert the privacy of that foundation – whatever the arguments for accountability. Terminology and categorization, in other words, may have important political meanings.

Size of and trends in the 'family' foundations sector

One reason definitions matter is that they affect analyses of the size of the 'private' or 'family' foundation sector, and of trends in size over time. If we include within the category of 'private' or 'family' foundations all foundations that have ever had family/donor involvement on the board, but may no longer be family governed, then clearly the size of the sector is far larger than if we include only those foundations still solely, or substantially, governed by family members. The size of the past/existing sector then affects estimates of relative, current growth.

The Council on Foundations, using the distinctions noted above, estimates that most foundations in the US are independent, as distinct from family or other controlled. By contrast, Esposito and Foote (2003: 8) use a relatively inclusive definition of a family foundation as

> a private foundation founded and funded by a donor or donors, in which family members – however they may define family members – play a role in governance. Trustees (by which we also mean directors of corporate-form foundations) often include nonfamily trustees, but family representation on the board is usually designed to pass into the hands of succeeding generations of that family'.

Using this relatively broad definition, they state that in the US they estimate that more than two-thirds of all private foundations 'have family involvement at some level' (i.e. 35,000 to 40,000 of a total of 60,000 foundations).

According to Pharoah (2010), there are around 38,000 family foundations in the US. About one-third of those have been created after 2000. Unfortunately, there are no figures for the total number of family foundations in the UK, only estimates. These indicate that there might be around 10,000 general foundations in total (Pharoah, 2010: 24). A dynamic, changing landscape for UK family foundations is reported by Pharoah et al. (2014: 4,1), as new entrants appear, notably from entrepreneurs in all business sectors; with UK family foundations generally estimated to contribute nearly three-fifths of all foundation giving by value, i.e. 59 percent. In wider Europe, again there are no figures. Furthermore, data are more difficult to obtain because there are fewer mandatory reporting requirements. It is, however, possible that numbers in Europe might be smaller. The reason for that is that '[s]ocial democratic traditions have led to a stronger political emphasis on public redistribution of wealth, and some distrust of institutions such as private foundations' (Pharoah, 2010: 28; Anheier and Daly, 2007). Data for Germany suggests that giving by the largest 100 family foundations was €725 for 2008. In Italy, 90 family foundations gave around €90 million, and the Association of Swiss Grantmaking Foundations estimates that there are 11,000 grantmaking foundations in Switzerland, not distinguished by type, giving an estimated CHF 2 billion per annum (Pharoah, 2010: 29). The 100 largest family foundations in the US and the UK had assets in 2008/09 of $87.3 billion and £25.3 billion respectively; they gave away $8.2 billion and £1.4 billion annually (Pharoah, 2010: 27–28). As Pharoah notes (2010), and as is true of the wider foundation world, assets and giving are heavily skewed with a very small number of foundations accounting for a large proportion of assets and spending. For example, in the US, the Bill and Melinda Gates Foundation accounts for over one-third of the giving of the 100 largest family foundations. I shall return to the issue of why definitions matter in the conclusion. In the following sections, I focus less on precise definitions, worrying less about family and nonfamily, concentrating instead on endowed independent foundations. For the moment, I use 'family' to mean not corporate, not fundraising, not government inspired.

Why create a foundation?

The question of why donors create foundations has at least two elements. First, there is a question about why give away private funds for public good. Second, there is a question about choice of the foundation form as a vehicle for giving. Motivations for giving are discussed in other parts of this *Companion* (Pharoah, Chapter 4; Bekkers, Chapter 7). Here, it is simply worth reflecting on the question of whether foundations created by individuals/families are likely to display some motivations or clusters of motivations more often than types of individual givers. One aspect, highlighted by Rossetto (2014), might be the effects of parental bereavement on philanthropic foundation development. Listening to family foundation creators talk about their giving, however, one frequently hears motives that have as much to do with internal family dynamics as with the urge for salvation, to do good, etc. (Ostrower, 1997; Pharoah, 2011), as well as with the 'philanthropic journey', often referred to by entrepreneurs (MacLean *et al.*, 2015; Gordon *et al.*, Chapter 21). Choice of the foundation form as a vehicle for family giving is also an interesting issue. A foundation may, of course, be only one of several ways in which a family/individual gives, but that makes the issue even more interesting: why are some gifts/areas of giving channeled through a foundation and others given personally, or individually?

In many countries, tax efficiency is a poor explanation of choice of the foundation form in that giving through a foundation is no more tax efficient than any other donation to charity/public benefit. Indeed, in the US, it may be more efficient to set up a donor advised fund within a community foundation than a standalone, private foundation. One of the attractions of the foundation form may be its relatively tangible, enduring form. While individual gifts may earn you a plaque on a wall or a building, a foundation has something closer to the solidity of an edifice. It is also worth observing that family foundations do tend to bear a family name, although there are some notable exceptions to this rule. Paradoxically, naming rights to, say, a building would generally require a much larger gift than the cost of setting up a small foundation. Nevertheless, family foundations do not necessarily attract the support of members of their own family. It is not uncommon to find two or three Jones Foundations, founded separately by brothers, cousins, sons and daughters, etc. This tells us something about the attractions of a foundation in terms of control and making one's own mark. A gift, by contrast, involves handing over/letting go, that is, if it truly is a gift rather than some sort of purchase of service.

Moreover, a further factor in choosing the foundation form may be that it allows for choice, diversity and change over time. The foundation creator can, as for example the UK's Joseph Rowntree did, state a broad direction for the foundation but then gives his/her future trustees more or less leeway to respond to changing needs and strategies. Gifts, by contrast, are only as flexible as the recipient.

The case sometimes advanced by foundations themselves is that the longevity of a foundation allows for learning and change as the work proceeds. The assumption here is that, whereas a gift, once given, cannot be taken back, a foundation can change its mind about its grant recipients and areas of work as it experiments and develops experience over the years.

The foundation form clearly then has a number of advantages but establishing a charitable foundation, alongside with charitable giving more widely, also entails some constraints. Again these are discussed in more detail in other chapters (Breen, Chapter 14; Harrow, Chapter 31), but one example worth noting here is that of Paul Omidyar who, in effect, turned his foundation into a 'network' because the foundation form did not provide the freedom to work across sectors in the ways Omidyar (2011) saw as being necessary to achieve the desired goals.

Roles of family foundations

Philanthropic foundations have traditionally seen their key role in terms of 'innovation', 'pump-priming' 'taking risks' and so on. They have presented themselves as 'start up engines' whose energy is then taken on, and developed, by others (Leat, 1992; Smith, 1999), and as agents of change and institutional entrepreneurs (Quinn *et al.* 2014). Yet, when we look at what foundations actually do, it often seems less than innovative (Arnove and Pinede, 2007; Thümler, 2011). There are various ways of classifying foundation roles. Very broadly, what links foundations at any one time and over the years is an emphasis on 'innovation' in the pursuit of public benefit. What divides them is *how* and *at what level* innovation is sought.

Anheier and Leat (2006) suggest that, as products of their age, foundations tend to take on roles that reflect the thinking of the time in which they were created. Thus, it is possible to trace a very loose trajectory from foundations as providers of charitable services in the nineteenth century, to foundations as seekers of (scientifically) discovered causes of problems in the early twentieth century on to, more recently, foundations as purveyors of sound management and venture capital. But, of course, these are only very broad trends; at any time there will be foundations 'from another age'. Leat (1992) distinguishes between foundations who see their role as 'gift givers', giving generally small, one-off, grants with very little emphasis on accountability or results, and those who consider themselves as 'investors', giving grantees what they asked for and giving more, or less, later if the investment appeared to be generating a 'pay-off' and result. Finally, there are the 'collaborative entrepreneurs' who see their role as identifying needs or gaps, and then working with grantees to develop new initiatives. In recent years, there has been a growing emphasis on distinguishing foundations in terms of their commitment to social change and social justice, i.e. as opposed to foundations that, in effect, fund amelioration of the effects of the status quo/charity. Prewitt (2006) suggests yet another classification in terms of change strategies. He distinguishes between foundations that pursue change through: creating new knowledge; applying knowledge; policy analysis; policy advocacy; social movements and empowerment; and social service delivery.

We know very little about how family foundations perceive their roles. It seems likely that they display very much the same diversity in adopted roles as other foundations, and also likely that their role perceptions may change over time with experience and with new generations. Writing about the UK in 2010, Pharoah (2010: 42) suggests,

> family foundations work in both responsive mode, meeting the need on the ground identified by those seeking support, and by trying to develop more radical solutions in more strategic and innovative modes of working. They fund on both large and small canvasses, often choosing the scale at which they support carefully, and being explicit about their targets. They work at the heart of society as well as its edges, with the powerful as well as the disenfranchised'.

It is interesting to speculate on the extent to which individuals/families that have by definition been financially successful choose to make their philanthropy in their own image. So, for example, do people who have made their money in financial services industries see the role of their foundation as one of venture capital provider? Do subsequent generations remake the foundation in their own images? Or do they stay true to their parents' thinking? If the foundation is created with inherited wealth does this make it more or less likely that the foundation will reflect its source?

Moving down to the level of *what* family foundations fund, again relatively little is known, other than that family foundations appear to display the same diversity as other foundations.

Insofar as foundations tend to work in the 'spaces' left by market and government, consideration of roles inevitably raises the issue of how foundations relate to government. Before looking at foundations' relationships with government, the following section considers *how* foundations work.

How foundations work: Grantmaking versus operating

Having decided to set aside private money for public benefit in the form of an endowment, there are then questions about ways of working. In the US, and some other parts of the Anglophone world, foundations tend to be seen, almost by definition, as fund-distributing rather than operating entities. If, however, we focus on the asset holding part of the definition, then it is clear that, in theory, a foundation has two options: the option of operating their own programs to achieve the foundation's goals or giving grants to other organizations to carry out work which will achieve the foundation's goals. Many foundations do indeed operate their own programs rather than giving grants to others; this is especially true in wider Europe where one, among many, important examples is the Bertelsmann Foundation in Germany. Nevertheless, operating foundations tend to be overlooked in discussions of foundations that focus on grantmaking.

One consequence of identifying foundations with grantmaking is that we do not stop to ask why the grantmaking model developed; whether it is always the most efficient and effective approach for foundations. Another effect is that because operating foundations tend to be excluded from statistics on grantmaking foundations and 'lost' in overall data on charities in general, we know little about them (Toepler, 1999).

In many respects, the emergence and growth of grantmaking foundations was both an accident of history, and a solution to some of the practical issues faced by the emerging group of large foundations (Leat, 2006). For the major early twentieth century US foundations, such as Carnegie and Rockefeller, grantmaking was neither the chosen nor ideal option. Often, such as in the cases of Carnegie and Rockefeller, foundations started out as operating foundations, running other organizations: the Rockefeller Institute, the Carnegie Institution, the Rockefeller Sanitary Commission, and the Carnegie Endowment for International Peace (Jonas, 1989).

Two important advantages of an operating approach are control and the ability to support what might be unconventional, irrespective of grant applications. Such an approach, however, takes time to set up – premises, staffing and so on. Grantmaking may be used as a stopgap. In essence, this was broadly what happened in the case of the Rockefeller Foundation in the early years of the twentieth century. However, both Frederick Gates and Abraham Flexner, key advisors to the Rockefeller Board, were against the grantmaking plan. Gates described the grantmaking program as an 'utterly futile … system of scattered subventions; and Flexner saw it as demeaning keeping 'the recipients on their knees, holding out their hats from year to year' (quoted in Jonas, 1989: 37). The Carnegie Institution, too, conducted a similar experiment with grantmaking as a stopgap and again dropped it in favour of strong effective direction from a central office. Jonas argues that in both cases the problems were:

- Lack of precedent and process – the absence of precedents for grants to independent researchers
- The problem of choice/moral hazard – lack of clarity as to how rational choices could be made among different applications, and the associated dangers of patronage, or perceived patronage
- Control and accountability – uncertainty as to how to ensure that funds were spent on the intended purposes.

Grantmaking thus partly developed as a result of increasing pressure to support others, compounded by the war in Europe (Leat, 2013) and partly because the creation of more operating centres, or the expansion of existing ones, could only be achieved by moving researchers away from universities. With a precedent thus set by major US foundations, and the resulting image that grantmaking was how foundations worked, subsequent foundations in other Anglophone countries adopted the grantmaking approach. As a result, the grantmaking perspective has now widely established itself as the perceived only, or best, model for foundations; the fact that it was only reluctantly developed in the US as a largely pragmatic response to specific politico-historical circumstances is often forgotten. Interestingly, in mainland Europe, the grantmaking focus did not take hold in the same way, and there a stronger tradition of operating foundations has been maintained.

Today, in the US and some other countries, including Australia, there are tax and legal advantages in adopting an operating rather than a grantmaking approach but the effects, if any, of these advantages on donor/board choice are little explored, not least because, as noted above, operating foundations are little studied as significant entities distinct from the mass of fundraising nonprofits (on issues of definition and regulation in the US see Toepler, 1999).

Rationales for grantmaking and operating

Grantmaking clearly has some disadvantages, not least in terms of loss of control over the use and oversight of monies; this, for example, is the reason why the Bertelsmann Foundation chooses to be an operating foundation. But grantmaking also has some advantages. Table 18.1 below sets out some pros and cons of each approach.

Although grantmaking and operating are frequently written about as alternatives in practice, many modern foundations make grants and operate their own programs as and when they choose (most often when there is no external organization well-equipped for the work in question) (Toepler, 1999).

Table 18.1 Operating and grantmaking foundation characteristics: Advantages and disadvantages

Operating Foundations	Grantmaking Foundations
Lack of flexibility (staff choices constrain)	Flexible programs and priorities
Opportunity for strong focus	Risk of a lack of focus
Limited spread of actions	Scope for wide spread of supporting actions
No or little distribution	Support to a range of organizations and activities
'All eggs in one basket'	'Hedging bets'
Selection of recipients, and associated difficulties not a problem	Problems of rational choice and moral hazard in selection for support
Free to 'create' demand but may be restricted by supply	Restricted by availability of projects, agents, demand and supply
Issues of autocratic image	Issues of democratic and responsive image
No transaction costs	High transaction costs
High overhead	Low apparent overhead
High control/direct line management	Lack of control for granted funds/management at a distance
Clear ownership of project results and outcomes	Unclear ownership of project results and outcomes
Scope for follow through	Lack of follow through after grant ceases
Knowledge retained	Loss of knowledge
Direct association with failure and controversy	Distanced from failure and from controversy

Source: Developed from Leat, (2007a :116)

Relationships with government

Insofar as governments take on different responsibilities in different states (and over time), foundations' roles will also differ. This is one of the factors that divides foundations across countries. What foundations in modern democracies have in common, however, is their anomalous, and yet generally uncontested, position. However, as Brilliant (2000) highlights, there are important exceptions, such as France, and, at various times, the US.

Ylvisaker, writing about family foundations, argues that foundations 'provide private persons a freewheeling opportunity to be publicly influential' (Ylvisaker, 1990: 331). To observe that private wealth is influential is hardly news, but for the most part, there are presumed to be controls on wealthy peoples' ability to buy influence. What is interesting about private wealth in this context is that when it is transformed into a foundation the ability to 'buy' influence changes colour and tone:

> Society has offered families what is in effect a permit to engage independently in matters otherwise thought to be the public's business. Philanthropy becomes a legitimate and ennobling process, elevating the accident of kinship into the loftier realm of civic participation and responsibility.
>
> *(Ylvisaker, 1990: 332)*

Similarly, Nielsen (1987) remarked that foundations are the 'strangest beasts in the jungle of American democracy' (Prewitt, 2001, 2006; Anheier and Leat, 2006). The question that then arises is why democratic societies allow, indeed venerate, such private power?

One explanation for the existence of foundations, and their relationship with government, is in terms of government failure (Healy and Donnelly-Cox, Chapter 12). In other words, the role of foundations is to do those things that government finds difficult to do because of lack of popular support, because it is a niche need, etc. (Prewitt, 2006; Schramm, 2006, 2007). According to this view, foundations do the things that government does not, and avoid doing the things that government does. Foundations provide additionality.

As a broad generalization, and with a few exceptions, foundations and governments generally got along fairly well in the last half of the twentieth century, each staying out of the other's way (Karl and Karl, 1999). Foundations provided services that governments did not provide, and in some cases successfully encouraged government to take up such services. Foundations innovated, experimented and 'primed the pump', government paid the longer-term tab. But then, towards the end of the last century, things began to change.

In a number of countries in Europe and in the US (Anheier and Daley, 2006), there was growing concern about public expenditure and perceived limits to government effectiveness. This was coupled with the increase of the neoliberal ideas of New Public Management and the perception that civil society was an instrument/vehicle for government policy and provision. As governments tightened their belts, foundations found that the 'spaces' in which they worked had been enlarged and changed in other ways. Nonprofit organizations, and others, looked to foundations to fill the gaps left by governments, and increasingly foundations found themselves cast in the role of sustainers rather than innovators.

From the viewpoint of governments, private foundations bring benefits, but they also entail costs. On the plus side, foundations may 'fill gaps', fund provision for minority needs, fly kites, take risks, and experiment in ways that governments might find difficult (Abramson and Spann, 1998). On the cost side, foundations may use their money to influence issues and areas of provision; they may start things that governments then find it difficult to refuse to continue (Roelofs, 2005; Anheier and Daly, 2006). Furthermore, if foundations enjoy tax privileges, as they do in many countries, these cost governments money in tax foregone. While most tax incentives are directed at relatively specific goals chosen by government, philanthropic tax incentives are usually as broad as charity law (Breen, Chapter 14; Carmichael, Chapter 15). Governments have no way of knowing whether their lost revenue will encourage giving to dogs or drug rehabilitation, opera or orphans, or whether they permit philanthropic flexibility, and kite flying.

If foundations turn away from funding service provision and back to the old US model of larger foundations as policy shapers and think tanks, governments may come to view their encouragement of foundations in a different light (on foundations as policy thinkers and shapers; see, for example, Ylvisaker, 1987; Smith, 1999 and 2002; Anheier and Leat, 2006; Karl and Karl, 1999; Anheier and Hammack, 2010). An important question that remains, however, is whether foundation autonomy is compatible with democratic accountability? (Prewitt, 2006: 375). The problem, of course, is that the more governments curb the independence and freedom of private philanthropy, the less that wealthy people may be prepared to become involved. Furthermore, it might be argued that by making foundations more democratically accountable, all that is achieved is another body with all of the constraints – and weaknesses – of government, but without its money. On the other hand, it could be argued that governments have little to fear from foundations. First, as various authors have pointed out, foundations tend to err on the side of caution and the establishment (Nielsen, 1987; Dowie, 2001; Roelofs, 2005; Arnove and Pinede, 2007). Second, foundations may be relatively unthreatening; they are actually not that powerful. They are reliant on grantseekers to do the work and foundations have a tendency to hedge their bets, to 'swim downstream' rather than fight the current, to act as supporters of trends rather than innovators (Heydemann and Kinsey, 2010: 210; Prewitt, 2006). Others might, however, point to the supposed influence of the neo-Conservative foundations in the US, widely credited with having shaped the economic policy of the late twentieth century (Covington, 2005). While some, such as Roelofs (2005) may suggest that the neo-Conservative foundations were, in a sense, merely organizing and amplifying the voice of the Republican Party and much of business, it may be that we look for foundation influence in grants and programs rather than in more subtle places and processes. As Heydemann and Kinsey (2010: 235-6) also note:

> Large swaths of the institutional landscape that we now take for granted in addressing international concerns in the sciences, in higher education, and in public policy are the product of international foundation support.... Their contribution, moreover, was as much a result of the broader liberal and cosmopolitan worldview they helped to construct through their grant making as it was the product of any particular grant or program.... If foundation roles and power have often been exaggerated along lines both critical and laudatory, they can, in their role as midwives of the postwar global order, rightly lay claim to a prominent role in the making of the twentieth century'.

Issues of regulation and accountability

As noted above, all private foundations present governments with challenges of regulation and accountability. Family foundations are likely to raise, formally or informally, some particularly tricky issues of regulation in that the foundation's interests will need to be clearly distinguished from those of the family members governing the foundation. Because of the potential for confusion, federal law in the US, for example, imposes certain restrictions on private foundations that do not apply to public foundations. Regulations forbid self-dealing in private foundations, i.e. most business and financial transactions between a private foundation and 'disqualified persons' made up of a broad category of 'insiders' including donors, trustees and managers.

Governance, staffing and costs

Again, issues of governance, staffing and overhead costs arise in all types of foundation, but in family foundations, these issues may be particularly complex. Family foundations are widely regarded as 'high risk and high reward' (Ylvisaker, 1990). The rewards include the satisfactions of 'doing good', the social kudos, and the increased intergenerational family cohesion. But the risks are also potentially high. Unlike an often hierarchical, if not patriarchal, bottomline driven family business, a family foundation has a single corpus, collective decision-making (in theory at least) and no clear cut measures for deciding the 'best' priorities and strategies. Add to that mix, the existing hierarchy of family relationships and the fact that the most senior family member is also likely to be the donor (in the first generation), and you have a potentially toxic brew. In subsequent generations there may be the additional problem of too many, or too few, family members to involve, as well as the tricky issue of whether to involve wives/husbands, and then how to deal with ex-wives and -husbands. It is perhaps not surprising that, as Ylvisaker (1990: 335) notes, family foundations tend, over time, to include outsiders in debate if not on the board: 'In the presence of respected "guests at the dinner table", for example, internal family dissension tends to soften and disappear, and the level of discussion and debate is elevated'. Interestingly, Esposito and Foote (2003) state that 'myth and reality about family foundations diverge', suggesting that the populist picture of a family foundation as a group of wealthy people, forever disagreeing, managing haphazardly, and amateurish in grantmaking, is incorrect. By contrast, Gersick *et al.* (2004) point out that while family businesses tend to draw family members into a common cause, family foundations may drive families apart; family conflicts played out in the foundation may be most apparent at the time of succession.

Stages and succession

Family foundations, like most private foundations, tend to start as an off shoot/formalization of the founder's philanthropy. They are usually run solely as a family matter, with various members of the family playing a part, and only later, if at all, employing paid 'outside' staff. Gersick *et al.* (2004) suggest that there are three types of or stages in family foundations: Controlling Trustee Foundations, Collaborative Family Foundations and Family-Governed Staff-Managed Foundations. Whereas the transition from the first to the second stage is inevitable, the second, they argue, is an organizational choice. Interestingly, Gersick *et al.* (2004) attribute success in family foundations to two key factors: a focused mission relevant to each new generation, and the presence of a strong nonfamily mediator.

Challenges ahead?

Predicting challenges ahead is always a hazardous business. For family foundations, some challenges – such as succession – are inevitable, and, it might also be argued that sooner or later the transition from an all-family, to a mostly-family, to a minority-family, to a family-in-name-only organization is also highly likely. Beyond those 'inevitable' challenges peculiar to family foundations, it seems likely that they will face similar challenges to those likely to be faced by other foundations.

Changing roles and methods

With public expenditure cuts further underlining the paucity of foundation resources, it is possible that foundations will turn increasingly to new roles and new methods. Perhaps, influenced by awareness of the success of the neo-Conservative foundations in the US, foundations may begin to emphasize their roles as change makers rather than service providers. They are likely to adopt different approaches to achieving change – some looking to market models and venture philanthropy, and others appealing to social justice and systemic/political change. The current trend among some foundations to talk less about their money and more about their other resources, including reputation, convening power, independence, knowledge, etc., may spread more widely (Nittoli, 2003; Bales and Gilliam, 2004; Brousseau, 2004; Buteau, 2006; de Borms, 2005; Fulton *et al.*, 2005; Anheier and Leat, 2006; Schramm, 2006, 2007).

Changes in the map?

Alongside the above, foundations may think more carefully about how to get to change and where power lies. This, in turn, may lead to greater interest in business as a means of solving problems and as a locus of power. Foundations may increasingly adopt a systems rather than a sectoral perspective, working across the corporate, statutory and voluntary sectors (Heifetz *et al.*, 2004; Ferris, 2009; Kramer, 2009; Leat, 2006; MacKinnon and Gibson, 2010).

Perpetuity and spend down

As in the wider foundation world, family foundations may be challenged to think more about lifespans, challenging perpetuity as the default setting and considering spend out. A decision to spend out, 'voluntary euthanasia', is unlikely to be an easy decision for any foundation: for family foundations, it may be particularly difficult. If the decision to spend out is made by the original donor, i.e. 'giving while living', that is one thing; a decision to 'kill off' the family foundation by a later generation is presumably quite another, involving complex moral and emotional issues (Toepler, 2004; Billiteri, 2007; Thelin and Trollinger, 2009; ACF, 2010).

Effectiveness and measurement

As illustrated by the UK Cabinet Office's recent interest in foundations having 'Total Impact' (Harrow and Jung, 2015), it seems very unlikely that the pressure for demonstrable 'effectiveness' and measurement will go away. This, in turn, will generate a set of further issues, including: metrics and methods; distinguishing contribution and attribution; innovation, risks and mistakes; and perhaps a debate about the costs and unintended consequences of the demand for results (Leat, 2006).

It is possible that foundations will face an additional challenge. If measurement reveals that foundations are really not very effective, questions may arise about their cost – would the tax subsidy to foundations not be better spent by government? If measurement reveals that foundations are highly effective, will questions arise about the power of unelected people/organizations to shape policy and practice (Ilchman and Burlingame, 1999)?

Greater control/changing practices?

There may be another effect of the emphasis on effectiveness. Grantmaking foundations are very heavily dependent on the quality of their grantees, and various trends suggest that interest in operating rather than grantmaking may be increasing. As already noted, the largest foundation in Germany, and one of the largest in Europe – the Bertelsmann Foundation – has very deliberately chosen to be an operating foundation. Observation of the European foundation field more generally suggests that grantmaking foundations are increasingly operating some projects and functions themselves rather than contracting them out to grantees. It could also be argued that even if foundations do not explicitly operate their own projects, they may increasingly implicitly do so. As grantmaking becomes more professionalized and more concerned with effectiveness, the level of control exercised by the foundations may be such that the grantmaking/operating distinction is eroded, and the benefits of grantmaking called into question.

Money, mission and investment

It seems unlikely that there will be any diminution in the slowly growing movement to consider what foundations do with their assets – the 95 percent, or more, that is not spent each year (Emerson 2002, 2003). Whether moves to align how the money is earned (invested) and how it is spent/given will actually morph into demands for foundations to become active shareholders, or alternatively to pursue selected disinvestment, is anyone's guess. Given the events of recent years, perhaps foundations will take greater responsibility for the practices of the companies in which they invest – but the tensions are obvious.

Taken together, family foundations raise a host of little-explored research questions. Potential questions that warrant further examination could include: Why do some families seem to 'breed' foundations? Is there anything different about family foundations in terms of spending patterns and decisions? What are the issues of succession in family foundations? How, when and why do family only foundations decide to broaden their governance beyond family members? How is the process handled and what effects does it have? Are their rationales and issues in that process any different from those of nonfamily foundations? Are the newer family foundations different from the older ones, now and at the same age? With the growing prominence of foundations in public and policy discourses, it seems important that a stronger research agenda on foundations is developed.

References

Abramson, A. and Spann, J. (1998) *Foundations: Exploring Their Unique Roles and Impacts in Society*, Washington DC: Aspen Institute.

ACF (2010) *Spending out: Learning Lessons from Time-Limited Grantmaking*, London: ACF. www.acf.org.uk/uploadedFiles/Publications_and_resources

Anheier, H. K. (2001) 'Foundations in Europe: a Comparative Perspective', in A. Schluter, V. Then and P. Walkenhorst (eds), *Foundations in Europe Society, Management and Law*, Bertelsmann Foundation, London: Directory of Social Change.

Anheier, H. K. and Leat, D. (2006) *Creative Philanthropy*, New York and London: Routledge.

Anheier, H. K. and Daly, S. (eds) (2006) *The Politics of Foundations: Comparative Perspectives from Europe and Beyond*, London and New York: Routledge.

Anheier, H. and Daly, S. (eds) (2007) *The Politics of Foundations: A Comparative Analysis*, London: Routledge.

Anheier, H. K. and Hammack, D. C. (eds) (2010) *American Foundations Roles and Contributions*, Washington D.C.: The Brookings Institution.

Anheier, H. K. and Leat, D. (2013) Philanthropic Foundations: What Rationales?. *Social Research*, 80(2), 449–72.

Arnove, R. and Pinede, N. (2007) Revisiting the 'Big Three' Foundations. *Critical Sociology*, 33, pp. 389–425.

Bales, S. N. and Gilliam, F. D. (2004) *Communications for Social Good*, foundationcenter.org/gainknowledge/practicematters/.

Billiteri, T. J. (2007) *Money, Mission and the Payout Rule: In Search of a Strategic Approach to Foundation Spending*, Washington: Aspen Institute.

Brilliant, E. (2000) *Private Charity and Public Inquiry: A History of the Filer and Peterson Commissions*, Bloomington: Indiana University Press.

Brousseau, R.T. (2004) *Experienced Grantmakers at Work: When Creativity Comes into Play*, foundationcenter. org/gainknowledge/practicematters/

Buteau, E. (2006) *More than Money: Making a Difference with Assistance Beyond the Grant*, www. effectivephilanthropy.org.

Council on Foundations (2015) *Foundation Basics*, www.cof.org/content/foundation-basics, [Accessed 25 September 2015].

Covington, S. (2005) 'Moving Public Policy to the Right: The Strategic Philanthropy of Conservative Foundations', in D. R. Faber and D. McCarthy (eds), *Foundations for Social Change*, Lanham: Rowman and Littlefield Publishers Inc.

De Borms, L. T. (2005) *Creating Impact in a Globalised World*, London: Wiley.

—— (2005) *Foundations: Creating Impact in a Globalised World*. London: Wiley.

Dowie, M. (2001) *American Foundations: An Investigative History*, Cambridge, MA: MIT Press.

Dunn, A. (2014) 'Regulation Absent: The Chimera of Charitable Foundation Law in England and Wales', in C. Prele (ed), *Developments in Foundation Law in Europe*, Springer: Netherlands, 51–69.

Emerson, J. (2002) 'Horse Manure and Grantmaking', *Foundation News and Commentary*, May/June.

—— (2003) 'Where Money Meets Mission: Breaking Down the Firewall Between Foundation Investing and Programming', *Stanford Social Innovation Review*, Summer 1(2).

Esposito, V. E. and Foote, J. (2003) 'Family Philanthropy in Twenty-First Century America', in F. Ellsworth and J. Lumarda (eds), *From Grantmaker to Leader: Emerging Strategies for Twenty-first Century Foundations*, New Jersey: John Wiley and Sons.

Ferris, J. M. (2009) *Foundation Strategy for Social Impact: A System Change Perspective*, Center on Philanthropy and Public Policy, University of Southern California, Research Paper 30 May 2009.

Forbes Rich List (2000) www.forbes.com/billionaires/list [Accessed 24 September 2015].

Fulton, K. *et al.* (2005) *The Seeds of Change in Philanthropy*, www.futureofphilanthropy.org/files/finalreport.pdf.

Gersick, K. E. with Stone, D., Grady, K., Desjardins, M., and Mason, H. (2004) *Generations of Giving: Leadership and Continuity in Family Foundations*, Lexington Books.

Harrow, J. and Jung, T. (2015) 'Debate: Thou Shalt Have Impact, Total Impact – Government Involvement in Philanthropic Foundations' Decision-making', *Public Money and Management*, May, 176–178.

Heifetz, R. A. *et al.* (2004) 'Leading Boldly', *Stanford Social Innovation review*, Winter, www.ssireview.org/pdf/2004WI_feature_heifetz.pdf.

Heydemann, S. with Kinsey, R. (2010) 'The State and International Philanthropy: The Contribution of American Foundations, 1919-1991', in H. K. Anheier and D. C. Hammack (eds), *American Foundations Roles and Contributions*, Washington D.C.: The Brookings Institution.

Hodgson, J. and Knight, B. (2010) *More than the Poor Cousin? The Emergence of Community Foundations as a New Development Paradigm*. The Global Fund for Community Foundations, www.issuelab.org/resource/more_than_the_poor_cousin_the_emergence_of_community_foundations_as_a_new_development_paradigm.

Ilchman, W. F. and Burlingame, D. F. (1999) 'Accountability in a Changing Philanthropic Environment', in C.T. Clotfelter and T. Ehrlich (eds), *Philanthropy and the Nonprofit Sector in a Changing America*, Indiana: Indiana University Press.

Jonas, G. (1989) *The Circuit Riders: Rockefeller Money and the Rise of Modern Science*, New York: W.W. Norton and Co.

Jung, T and Harrow, J. (2015) 'New Development: Philanthropy in Networked Governance – Treading with Care', *Public Money and Management*, 35(1): 47–51.

Karl, B. D. and Karl, A. W. (1999) 'Foundations and the Government: A Tale of Conflict and Consensus', in C.T. Clotfelter and T. Ehrlich (eds), *Philanthropy and the Nonprofit Sector in a Changing America*, Bloomington: Indiana University Press.

Kramer, M. R. (2009) 'Catalytic Philanthropy', *Stanford Social Innovation Review*, Fall.

Leat, D. (1992) *Trusts in Transition*, York: Joseph Rowntree Foundation.

Leat, D. (2006) 'Grantmaking Foundations and Performance Measures: Playing Pool?,' *Public Policy and Administration*, 21(3), 25–7.

Leat, D. (2013) *Private Battles: A Foundation at War*, European Foundation Centre, London: Alliance Publishing Trust.

Maclean, M., Harvey, C., Gordon, J., and Shaw, E. (2015) 'Identity, Storytelling and the Philanthropic Journey', *Human Relations*, published online before print, April 28.

MacKinnon, A. and Gibson, C. (2010) *Working with Government*, New York: Grantcraft.

Nielsen, W. A. (1972) *The Big Foundations*. New York: Columbia University Press.

Nielsen, W. A. (1987) *The Golden Donors: A New Anatomy of the Great Foundations*, New York: Truman Talley Books, E. P. Dutton.

Nittoli, J. (2003) *Acts of Commission – Lessons from an Informal Study*, foundationcenter.org/gainknowledge/practicematters/.

Omidyar, P. (2011) 'EBay's Founder on Innovating the Business Model of Social Change', *Harvard Business Review*, 89(9), 41–44.

Ostrower, F. (1997) *Why the Wealthy Give*, Princeton University Press, New Jersey.

Pharoah, C. with Keidan, C. (2010) *Family Foundation Giving Trends 2010*, London: Cass Business School.

—— (2011) *Family Foundation Giving Trends 2011*, London: Cass Business School.

Pharoah, C., Goddard, K. and Jenkins, R. (2014) *Family Foundation Giving Trends, 2014 Report*, London, Cass Business School, Centre for Charitable Giving and Philanthropy and Association of Charitable Foundations.

Prele, C. (2014) (ed) *Developments in Foundation Law in Europe*, Springer: Netherlands.

Prewitt, K. (2001) 'The Foundation Mission: Purpose, Practice, Public Pressures', in A. Schluter, V. Then, and P. Walkenhorst (eds), *Foundations in Europe. Society Management and Law*, London: Directory of Social Change.

—— (2006) 'Foundations', in W. W. Powell and R. Steinberg (eds) *The Nonprofit Sector: A Research Handbook*, 2nd Edition, New Haven, CT and London: Yale University Press.

Quinn, R., Tompkins-Stange, M., and Meyerson, D. (2014) 'Beyond Grantmaking Philanthropic Foundations as Agents of Change and Institutional Entrepreneurs', *Nonprofit and Voluntary Sector Quarterly*, 43(6), 950–68.

Roelofs, J. (2005) 'Liberal Foundations: Impediments or Support for Social Change?', in D. R. Faber and D. McCarthy (eds), *Foundations for Social Change*, Lanham: Rowman and Littlefield Publishers Inc.

Rossetto, K. R. (2014) 'Creating Philanthropic Foundations to Deal with Grief: Case Studies of Bereaved Parents', *Death Studies*, 38(8), 531–7.

Schramm, C. (2006–7) 'Law Outside the Market: The Social Utility of the Private Foundation', *Harvard Journal of Law and Public Policy*, 30: 356–415.

Smith, J. A. (1999) 'The Evolving Role of American Foundations', in C. T. Clotfelter and T. Ehrlich (eds), *Philanthropy and the Nonprofit Sector in a Changing America*, Indiana: Indiana University Press.

Smith, J. A. (2002) *Foundations and Public Policymaking: A Historical Perspective*, Center on Philanthropy and Public Policy, University of Southern California, Research Paper 11 May 2002.

Thelin, J. R. and Trollinger, R. W. (2009) *Time is of the Essence: Foundations and the Policies of Limited Life and Endowment Spend-Down*, Washington D.C.: The Aspen Institute.

Thümler, E. (2011) 'Foundations, Schools and the State. School Improvement Partnerships in Germany and the United States as Legitimacy-generating Arrangements', *Public Management Review*, 13, 8, pp. 1095–1116.

Toepler, S. (1999) 'Operating in a Grantmaking World: Reassessing the Role of Operating Foundations', in H. K. Anheier and S. Toepler (eds), *Private Funds and Public Purpose, Philanthropic Foundations in International Perspectives*, New York: Plenum Publishers.

Toepler, S. (2004) 'Ending Payout as We Know It: A Conceptual and Comparative Perspective on the Payout Requirement for Foundations', *Nonprofit and Voluntary Sector Quarterly*, 33:729.

Weissert, C. S. and Knott, J. H. (1995) 'Foundations' Impact on Policy Making: Results from a Pilot Study', *Health Affairs*, 14(4), 275–86.

Ylvisaker, P. (1987) 'Foundation and Nonprofit Organizations', in W. W. Powell (ed), *The Nonprofit Sector: A Research Handbook*, 1st edition, New Haven, CT: Yale University Press.

Ylvisaker, P. N. (1990). 'Family Foundations: High Risk, High Reward', *Family Business Review*, 3(4), 331–5.

19

Community foundations

Agility in the duality of foundation and community

Jenny Harrow, Tobias Jung and Susan D. Phillips

Differentiated from either individual giving or endowed private foundations, the community foundation presence in organized philanthropy offers a distinctive opportunity to see philanthropy in the round: from the perspectives of multiple donors, 'community' and recipients. Although the definition of a community foundation is evolving as new adaptations emerge, the original model refers to an independent, publicly accountable grantmaking body that is controlled by community members, derives its funds from multiple sources – including individuals, governments, corporations and private foundations – and, through its grantmaking and leadership, seeks to enhance the quality of life in a specific geographic locale (Graddy and Morgan, 2006; Ostrower, 2007; Thompson, 2012). The core purpose of a community foundation can be expressed both philosophically and functionally as 'an institution that seeks to be a central, affirming element of the community, *foundational* to the places it seeks to serve' (Mazany and Perry, 2014: x). That 'service' is envisaged to cover a spectrum of ideas, including: being reflective of, and advocating for, a locality's philanthropic needs and preferences; responding to, seeking, and supporting multiple donors for that locality; stewarding and distributing funding for community needs; and building bridges among different groups within a community (Daly, 2008; Charles Stewart Mott Foundation, 2012). The way in which community foundations cast 'community' differs widely; it can range from very specific geographic locations, to more abstract ideas associated with 'belonging' and 'sense of place' (Jung *et al.*, 2013).

Originating in the US in a century ago, community foundations have experienced major global growth. This has been particularly noticeable over the last two decades: around 74 percent of community foundations were established within the last 25 years (Community Foundation Atlas, 2015). With around 1,800 community foundations currently in existence, they can be found in over 50 countries and cover every continent, except Antarctica (Charles Stewart Mott Foundation, 2012; Community Foundation Atlas, 2015). Notwithstanding the old stereotype that community foundations are the 'poor cousins' (Hodgson and Knight, 2010) in the family of philanthropic organizations, they are emerging as a major force: in the US, of the 100 biggest grantmaking foundations, 16 are community foundations (Sacks 2014); in the UK, community foundations are amongst the largest grantmakers to the nonprofit sector (Pharoah, 2011); while in Germany, where community foundations have only been around since 1996, they already have a combined endowment of €265 million (Initiative Bürgerstiftungen, 2014).

To illustrate and better understand community foundations, their roles and challenges, a number of metaphors have been applied. These range from 'agile servant' (Magat, 1989) and 'glue' (Rogers and Keenan, 1990), to 'matchmaker' (Daly, 2008; Graddy and Morgan, 2009), 'borderland institutions' (Ruesga and Knight, 2013), 'impact multipliers' (Rhodes, 2014), and 'anchors' of, and for, community (Perry and Mazany, 2014). Highlighting the diverse roles, hybrid nature, and evolving contexts of community foundations, these images point to the deep embeddedness of these organizations: their need to balance multiple purposes, the requirement to ensure that donors are well-served, that donor interests are aligned appropriately with community needs, and the potential of community foundations to act as vehicles of, and for, community cohesion and empowerment. The weight of these expectations, the ability to effectively balance multiple purposes and be adaptable to quite diverse, and often less than hospitable contexts, raises the question of whether the agile may also be fragile.

Our chapter critically reflects on these metaphors. After providing an overview of the emergence and growth of community foundations in the next section, we explore the ideas and implications of these metaphors and how community foundations engage with them. We particularly focus on the dual challenge and potential paradox inherent within the community foundation idea, the need to be philanthropy-led and community-responsive. While to date scholarship on community foundations has predominantly been US-centric, reflecting their US roots and popularity, we have tried to be as inclusive as possible of the limited research from other countries, particularly in considering recent developments.

Community foundations' growth: From model to movement

The first community foundation was established in 1914 in Cleveland, Ohio, by Frederick Harris Goff, a lawyer-turned-banker. Seeing the potential for greater efficiency in the management of bequests in a manner that could be directed for the betterment of community, part of Goff's vision was to sever 'the dead hand of the past', referring to the various wills and trusts that were frequently left to very specific charitable causes and, thereby, could not be easily redirected when causes became obsolete or when more pressing community priorities emerged (Grabowski, 2002). Consequently, the idea was to pool resources from a diversity of donors, not just the wealthy few, into permanent endowments. These would be under the control of citizen boards, focus on community needs as defined by the community, and exercise leadership in identifying new challenges and opportunities (Newman, 1989; Grønbjerg, 2006). The efficiency of this new philanthropic model came through the professionalization of grantmaking: while financial experts at banks would continue to manage the trust, the appointed citizen committees were to decide on their distribution, thereby moving from a focus on donor control towards one based on public representation (Sacks, 2006; Grønbjerg, 2006).

This model quickly spread across the US; by the end of the 1920s community foundations existed in most major American cities. As the model was transferred, some cities emphasized a community-responsive focus, often commissioning studies to identify the most urgent community needs, while others took a more donor-centric approach, initially concentrating on serving donor interests although many later assumed more reform-oriented agendas (Hammack, 1989; Grønbjerg, 2006). Subsequent expansion in the US was uneven: negligible in the 1930s, rapid growth in the 1950s, a new wave in the 1970s, and essentially flatlined since 2000 (WINGS, 2012).

From the US, the community foundation idea was quickly exported to Canada. With the central involvement of another banker, who knew of the Cleveland experiment and who made a substantial personal gift, Canada's first community foundation, the Winnipeg Foundation, was established in 1921. Through the next few decades, community foundations followed in major centres. A very active national infrastructure organization was founded in 1992, followed by 'explosive' growth in smaller centres since 2000 (Feurt and Sacks, 2000:25), with a current total of about 190 community foundations across the country (Community Foundations of Canada, 2015).

Outside of North America, community foundations were next to mature in the UK. Although they were not introduced until 1975 and remained poorly understood and underutilized for some (Leat, 2006), they eventually started 'hitting their stride' during the 1990s (Feurt and Sacks, ND). However, the size and role of community foundations varies greatly across the UK, with only one national community foundation in each of Scotland, Wales and Northern Ireland, and 44 quite different ones across England (Jung et al., 2013; Jung and Harrow, 2014). In England, many of those created after 2000 developed as grantmakers and managers for statutory funds. As such, they are much more reliant on state flow-through funding than the original model of a community foundation envisaged (Daly, 2008); they are not that dissimilar from other publicly funded voluntary organizations which have been seeking a revised resources base (Nevile, 2010). Notwithstanding the 'community' label, most English community foundations are not ground-level upwards organizations: they are better understood as an elite project driven by the global vision and ideas of major private US foundations on the one hand, and UK government actors interested in reducing state spending on the other (Leat, 2006; Vogel, 2006; Baroness Prashar, 2010; Jung and Harrow, 2014).

Since the mid-1990s, community foundations have established themselves worldwide. Their international growth continues unabated, growing by 86 percent from 2000 to 2010 (WINGS, 2010; Mott, 2012). Within Europe, the last decade has seen a six-fold increase in community foundations with a total of around 650 community foundations as of 2015 (Community Foundation Atlas, 2015). This expansion has been especially marked in Germany. Here, the number has risen from ten community foundations in 2000 to 275 by 2014 (Hellmann, 2010; Initiative Bürgerstiftungen, 2014). In Russia, there are now 43 community foundations (Charles Stewart Mott Foundation, 2012), and the idea is taking hold in Brazil, India, South Africa and China. Due to different philanthropic traditions, the limitations of legal frameworks that define the sector, and the agendas of governments for it, community foundations are, however, still a relative rarity in East Asia (Wang et al., 2011). While numbers for these areas are often uncertain, and expansion is affected by the increasingly blended and boundaryless approach to what constitutes a community foundation in the 'new public philanthropy' thinking, Asia and Africa are widely considered as regions for major future growth of that field.

The global expansion patterns of community foundations testify to the transferability of the idea: the very 'adaptability of the concept makes it possible for communities to mould it to their own circumstances' (Feurt and Sacks, 2000:17). As part of this, however, there seems to have been a shift from conceptualizing community foundations as a specific model towards a broader recasting of community foundations as a movement focused on social justice, giving voice and redefining place (e.g. Jung et al., 2013). This is especially prominent in the global 'new generation' of community foundations. Illustrated by Silicon Valley Community Foundation's (2015) mission to 'strengthen the common good locally and throughout the world', these 'glocal' community foundations – combining the global with the local – are representative of, and deeply embedded in, new forms of community philanthropy focusing on empowerment and social change. Many have common characteristics which they share with what might be called 'new public philanthropies', including women's funds, human rights and peace funds, as well as community foundations per se (WINGS, 2012: 23). The characteristics of public philanthropies include: raising money from the public rather than relying on endowments from private wealth accumulation; combining donors and beneficiaries in a group; taking an approach that is community-based and bottom-up rather than externally driven and top-down; focusing on correcting injustices in these communities; and activities being 'generally about more than money', such as community facilitation, technical assistance, advocacy and various degrees of activism (Hodgson and Knight, 2010: 8; WINGS, 2012: 23).

This willingness to be more political is nicely illustrated in Egypt, where it seems that they are 'better positioned than private foundations to support democratic transition and consolidation' (Herrold, 2012: 35). It also highlights that community foundations resist simple classifications alongside organizational types (Hodgson et al., 2012); there is a need to remember that this evolving philanthropic form requires a constant reiteration and reflection on what community foundations are and why they exist. Such redefining, or reminding, may, however, place community foundations in some settings at continuing disadvantage to other, 'easier', forms of philanthropy.

The drivers of transfer and the importance of intra-philanthropy mentoring

While direct emulation and a sense of opportunity (Hodgson and Knight, 2010) partly account for the diffusion of community foundations, critical, if not the critical, factors in this process have been the intra-philanthropic support by national or regional organizations (WINGS, 2010) and the financial support and technical assistance provided globally by leading private foundations. Some community foundations are, therefore, both benefactors – through their grantmaking on others' behalf – and beneficiaries within the wider philanthropic community. In Germany, for example, the founder of the Bertelsmann Foundation established the country's first community foundation, the Stadt Stiftung Gütersloh, in 1996 as 'an enthusiastic homage to the American community foundation model' (Spallek, ND). Development in southern Italy was fostered by the Fondazione per il Sud, a grantmaking foundation specifically intended to facilitate the creation of viable social infrastructure in the region (Bolognesi, 2012), while in Russia, supporting growth was a leading project for the Charities Aid Foundation (CAF) Russia (ND). In the UK, the Esmée Fairbairn Foundation was central to community foundations' initial growth during the 1970s (Daly, 2008) and it recently supported the 'Philanthropy Fellowships' network. Managed by the UK umbrella body, UK Community Foundations was aimed at inspiring 'a greater culture of philanthropy in the UK' (Breeze, 2014). In addition, the US-based Charles Stewart Mott Foundation has played a key role in helping UK community foundations at a critical time during their development in the early 1990s to build their endowments through challenge funding (Leat, 2006: 259). For over three decades, the Charles Stewart Mott Foundation (2012: 6) has also provided a prominent, sustaining, presence for the worldwide development of community foundations, concentrating its major geographic focus on Central/Eastern Europe, Russia, South Africa and the US.

While endowed foundations might, therefore, be understood as an essential and key strategic partners for community foundations (Graddy and Morgan, 2006), the transplantation of the community foundation idea, while not lessening the 'movement' claims, might create problematic dependencies; it certainly makes for contradictions. On one hand, community foundations through their focus on locality seek to project an identity of difference from the bulk of organized foundation philanthropy; on the other hand, as beneficiaries, they in some sense become its client, and through efforts at their own endowment-building, become its analogue.

The level of growth of a multifaceted philanthropic delivery form, at some odds with the overtly private, often single-donor style and substance of private foundations, points to community foundations being regarded collectively as a social movement. This social movement orientation is a strong central theme within the field's practitioner and leadership literature. The 2004 Berlin Symposium on the theme of 'a global movement', for example, emphasized that 'community foundations – and their donors – make a long-term commitment to their communities', and while 'many community foundations link their grantmaking to social justice ... even where this language is not used, their commitment is to the whole community' (Sacks, 2006: 5). For Canadian community foundations, achieving social justice perspectives on their work was articulated as among 'our toughest challenges', recognizing the importance of 'aiming at solving social problems rather than treating their symptoms over and over again' (Community Foundations of Canada, 2006: 2). Such commentaries accord with scholarship that stresses the significance of transnational social movements during transitional times (e.g. Smith and Wiest, 2012). However, research on community foundations' social movement credentials and characteristics is largely absent. The case that 'foundations can fund movements, not create them' (Masters and Osborn, 2010: 12) adds further complexity: can community foundations *become* a movement? Further research in this area, to accompany practitioner assertion, would be welcomed.

Whether regarded as model or movement, with both the terms 'community' and 'foundation' themselves open to contest and debate, the emerging picture is one of an institution necessarily in flux, needing to be dynamic in its multipurpose actions and increasingly fluid as it develops across time and location.

Matchmakers: Being both donor and community-facing

Research and professional practice, particularly in the US, has been dominated by a debate over the extent to which community foundations pursue, or should pursue, an approach that is donor-focused – seeking to raise and manage funds as an expression of individual philanthropy – versus one that is community-oriented – whereby the measure of success is the extent to which community needs are met (Carson, 2003; Guo and Brown, 2006). Although it is increasingly clear that community foundations 'aren't just one thing' (Kasper *et al.*, 2014: 6) and that successful leaders need to attend to both, the pressures of asset building, donor advised funds (DAFs) and public expectations of impact are creating new dynamics in the donor-community nexus.

In a US context, Guo and Brown (2006) set out to explore this dilemma for community foundations; they look at variations in the fiscal efficiency and grantmaking performance of community foundations and at some of the reasons behind those variations. They found that where there were a larger number of community foundations in a particular state, they were all better at attracting donations. This might be because of greater public awareness, and thereby perceived legitimacy, of the community foundation as a phenomenon. Conversely, in densely populated regions, community foundations appeared to be less efficient at grantmaking. This might be attributable to a 'crowd mentality', each assuming that others were meeting community needs (Guo and Brown, 2006: 281-2). Imbalances between raising funds and distributing funds may also occur, with continuing tensions around donor expectations, as well as those of communities. In some contexts, however, the dominance of, or preference for, donor-facing work is becoming increasingly clear.

Asset building, as an aspect of sustainability and as an expression of a donor serving orientation, remains a central concern of most community foundations. Sustainability is directly related to their ability to acquire and steward their assets and, as Guo and Brown (2006) note, only indirectly related to how well they manage their distribution of funds. A continued emphasis on asset development is also a legacy of a community foundation's history, particularly for those in their 'adolescent' years. In a US study, Millesen and Martin (2014: 841) observe that, in order to grow, many younger community foundations, i.e. those less than ten years old, had spent their start-up years aggressively attracting a variety of different types of funding; when they reached a more mature stage, they continued to do so while 'struggling to define a clear role for themselves in their communities'. In addition, by attracting a broad range of donors and a substantial amount of restricted, donor advised funding, many found themselves in a position in which they were expected to manage these funds without the administrative capacity to do so (Millesen and Martin, 2014).

Our research in the UK context (Jung *et al.*, 2013) also identifies a marked shift towards emphasis on internal endowment building, whether driven as a functionalist expression of making more certain getting the job done in a sustainable manner during difficult economic times, or as a means to secure and sustain long-term community leadership roles. A good illustration of a purposeful reorientation to more donor-facing work are the former Scottish Community Foundation's rebranding in 2012 as 'Foundation Scotland' and the Community Foundation for Greater Manchester's move towards its 'Forever Manchester' brand. As yet, it is difficult to assess whether such recasting – or abandonment – of the 'community foundation' title represents a move of building on, or away from, the community foundation as a known, valued institutional form. In effect, where increasing competition for limited resources and falling away of government flow-through funding had occurred, a necessary focus was developing on 'independence through endowment maximization and an emulation of private foundations' funding models' (Jung *et al.*, 2013: 420). From Foundation Scotland's perspective (2015), the benefit has been that, on behalf of its donors, it is able to continue to distribute around £3.5m a year, making it one of the largest funders of the voluntary sector in Scotland.

While asset building has enabled community foundations to make significant contribution to overall philanthropic grantmaking, an endowment emphasis points to a growing institutional paradox: endowment growth draws community foundations increasingly closely towards the private foundation model and to elite donors whereas their creation owed much to a distancing from such an emphatically nonpublic institutional form. The underpinning of large endowments, however, could to a great extent free community foundations from the pressures of a few donors' control so that 'independence for what' becomes a serious institutional and managerial challenge (Jung and Harrow, 2014).

A major question, however, is the extent to which community foundations have strategic control over their 'assets'. This question is becoming more pertinent with the growth of donor advised funds (DAFs). Pioneered in the 1930s, DAFs are contractual relationships between a donor and a public charity. In essence, the donor's contribution – which has provided a tax benefit where applicable – is held in a separate account. The donor retains the right to advise on when, to whom, and in what amounts distributions are to be made. The legal control over those contributions sits, however, with the charity i.e. community foundations. (Hussey, 2010).

For a high net worth (HNW) donor, DAFs offer a flexible philanthropic means of giving. They combine advice and administration from a trusted institution, knowledgeable about the 'community', without the complexity, costs, or control of setting up an individual foundation. Another factor appealing to donors might be the perpetuity of a DAF, especially in instances where a donor has doubts that his or her 'zeal and vision will be sustained by subsequent generations' (Hoffstein, 2007: 29). To a community foundation, DAFs provide valuable assets that might otherwise have been held with a commercial investment fund. The community foundation can offer advice and matchmaking with suitable projects in line with the donor's interest(s), and the management fees from DAFs can be a significant source of income. The extent to which community foundations actively link their priority projects to donor interests varies considerably. For example, the UK's largest community foundation, the Community Foundation Tyne & Wear and Northumberland (2013, 2014), reports being a very active matchmaker, directing donors to the priorities it has established and in so doing incurring the additional staff resources this entails, while many North American counterparts are more passive holders of DAFs.

The growth of DAFs over the last 10 years has been remarkable. In the US, for instance DAFs have grown more than 10 percent annually, and currently constitute more than 50 percent of contributions and grants from community foundations (CF Insights, 2012: 5). There are widespread aspirations among community foundations to grow DAFs further, to use them to strengthen the local impact and capture 'strategic value' (CF Insights, 2012: 6). Many are actively competing with financial institutions by advertizing their advantages for the management and uses of DAFs. The extent to which the importance of DAFs will grow as a both a hallmark of, and lever for, community foundation-led philanthropy beyond North America remains to be seen. So, too, is community foundations' capacity to compete with commercial DAF products.

The growing emphasis on DAFs has, however, drawn some sharp criticism. Leat (2006: 267), for example, argues that their disadvantages include 'raising legal issues, being expensive to administer, may lead to the community foundation being seen as little more than a club for the wealthy and most significant, may conflict with the pursuit of community benefit'. Notwithstanding that a strong emphasis on DAFs and similar instruments may position community foundations as essentially little more than charity banking institutions, the availability of DAFs can also be seen as sound evidence of community foundations' responsiveness to donor needs.

Closely related to this is another challenge leveled at community foundations: that they should move from simply growing DAFs and endowments towards putting them to use for a social, as well as a financial, return through impact investing (Cheney et al., 2013: 45). As community foundations see themselves as stewards of public funds, it is unsurprising that they have been cautious in venturing into program- and mission-related investing. In the US, about a dozen community foundations – mainly those in urban centres that have experience in managing complex assets – were involved in some form of impact investing in 2014, although the portion of assets used in that way is small, averaging one to two percent (Feuss et al., 2014: 5). Some, however, have set much higher targets. For instance, the Community Foundation of Ottawa (Canada) has an objective, as yet unrealized, of investing ten percent of its assets in impact investing. The main impediments in meeting such aspirations, once risk averse boards can be convinced, are that the charity markets in which to invest are only slowly emerging and still lacking in attractive opportunities. Furthermore, in many jurisdictions the regulatory frameworks are unclear or restrictive.

Community anchors: Embeddeness, representation and leadership

As institutions of place-based philanthropy, community foundations are necessarily embedded in community. Thus, community foundations present, or seek to adopt, strong local identities, thereby creating an action-orientated lever for philanthropists, capitalizing on existing feelings of belonging to a place and wishing to contribute to a place where one feels attached (Maclean et al., 2012). In turn, community foundations as an expression of beneficial localism may be a significant factor in developing successful community engagement and renewal (Easterling, 2008). This may be particularly true in places such as the North East of England, where Maclean and colleagues did their work, and generally in areas where there is a strong sense of regional distinctiveness and social cohesion. Elsewhere, the community foundation may play a part in supporting a sense of community pride, contributing to previously lacking community revitalization (Van Slyke and Newman, 2006) and being 'key to the geography of place and thereby "anchor" their communities in real and palpable ways' (Perry and Malzany, 2014: 4). As exemplifier of the philanthropy, as well as the geography of place (Glückler and Ries, 2012), community foundations offer an attractive combination, of a recognizable ideological basis, harnessed to a quasi-representative operating structure that is predicated on a collaborative purpose.

A geographic community is not a single economic, social or cultural entity, however. Place is a complex relational endeavour, yet community foundations are equally tasked with both reflecting it and exemplifying it as a transformative basis for philanthropy. A fundamental question then is: how well do community foundations understand, respond to and represent in their own governance the diversity of their locales? How well do they function as 'borderland institutions' (Ruesga, 2014) linking the grassroots, particularly marginalized groups, to the other parts of community, and to what extent are they strategic agents of change for social justice? The record, at least for the well-established community foundations, is mixed. There are, however, recent indications that many are beginning to assume more strategic leadership roles.

In spite of their potential, research suggests that community foundations have tended to be closely aligned to community elites and slow to respond to real problems. In their study of US community foundations, Millesen and Martin (2014: 845) find significant homogeneity of board composition and, although board members embraced the value of diversity of representation to reflect the community, they rarely practiced it. This was often justified on the basis that the work was important and required 'hard working people who can get the job done'. It appears that governance practices are changing, though, as many community foundations are experimenting with various mechanisms for engagement of different sets of stakeholders, with youth advisory committees becoming particularly popular.

Beyond mere representation of, and responsiveness to, various communities within place, public expectations and opportunities are driving community foundations to exercise strategic leadership for social change. The traditional means of leadership has been through grantmaking. In the interests of being responsive to an engaging the community at large, though, most community foundations took a 'peanut butter' approach: spreading small grants widely to a broad range of causes and recipients. As has occurred with private foundations, there is a growing trend among community foundations to be more strategic in their grantmaking, to identify two or three funding priorities and to direct a substantial portion of their unrestricted funding to these. The primacy of being community-based, however, provides less latitude than their private counterparts to become highly focused.

Grantmaking is not the only vehicle for influencing social change. Community foundations have distinctive opportunities as knowledge producers and brokers, as shapers of community discourses, as direct players in policy processes, and as convenors and facilitators of collaboration among multiple stakeholders to collectively address community problems (Hamilton *et al.*, 2004; Bernholz *et al.*, 2005; Kasper *et al.*, 2014). The exemplar of such a leadership record is the Community Foundation for Northern Ireland: it navigated the sectarian conflicts while remaining respected by all sides, serving as a major force for peacebuilding and improving the situation of the marginalized (Jung *et al.*, 2013). This kind of leadership has been quite rare, however. Indeed, community foundations have come under extensive criticism (Carson, 2003) in that they have not been more active in strategic leadership roles, particularly in taking on a 'social justice' agenda (recognizing the complications and debate over that particular term). Milleson and Martin's (2014: 846) examination of board practices reports, amidst some interesting examples of change making, considerable amounts of board behaviour focused towards maintaining 'the status quo', mainly for fear of alienating powerful community members with resource access, along with support for past, 'traditional', practices. Similarly, Wolfe (2006) found that only two percent of boards of US community foundations had a social change agenda, with 18 percent 'leaning' to some social change, and 44 percent seeing themselves as 'traditional' community leaders or having no leadership aspirations at all. Leadership practices, too, may be changing and various community foundations are taking different paths in ways that are reflective of their communities and that differentiate themselves from other philanthropic institutions.

One approach that has won international acceptance is the annual production of indicators of community well-being. These can be used to advocate for improved services and policy change. Begun by Toronto Community Foundation in 2001, the Vital Signs initiative serves as such an 'annual community check-up' (Patten and Lyons, 2009: 56). It does this by generating user-friendly 'report cards' on a range of nationally agreed upon key indicators of quality of life with the intent of animating conversations with the community and with policy makers. With around 26 annual reports now produced across Canada (Vital Signs, 2015a), this national program provides far more than a 'strategic perch' (Patten and Lyons, 2009): for community foundations it facilitates both local and national conversations about public policy, without taking a direct advocacy role, a role most community foundations avoid. The Vital Signs approach to 'taking the pulse' of local communities has now spread globally. Examples range from Australia to Bosnia, Brazil, Ireland, New Zealand, the UK, and the US (Vital Signs, 2015b). Yet, this initiative is not without its challenges. In particular, Vital Signs is resource intensive and given that it relies upon the media to 'carry its message', which may vary depending on the news cycle, its ultimate impact on connecting information to action and the donor responsiveness is not yet fully understood.

Overall, the exercise of leadership aimed at policy and social change by community foundations in developed countries is highly variable. What predicts whether a community foundation is likely to demonstrate such leadership? Life cycle is a partial explanation. Graddy and Morgan (2006) found that, controlling for asset size and community characteristics, community foundations generally follow a predictable pattern as they age. They move from an initial, necessary, focus on building donor resources towards a community leadership role. While evolving towards leadership, this was not guaranteed as less than 30 percent eventually assumed a leadership focus. In the UK, Jung and colleagues (2013) report that neither age nor size necessarily recalibrate a community foundation's focus towards leadership as there remains a prominence of endowment building by community foundations linked to the diminishing government flow-through funding. Others (Sacks, 2006) stress the essential ingredient of individual leadership: in Russia, as elsewhere, the success of community foundations is attributed to 'inspired and strong leaders' (Sacks, 2006: 17).

Finally, alignment with prevailing governmental agendas will be a factor in keeping community foundations in the public eye, and in prompting them to assume new kinds of leadership roles. With the growing global expectation that private finance will play a central part in solving social problems, some governments, perhaps most actively in the UK, are encouraging an expanded role for community foundations. This is occurring through matching funding, as well as through more contested means, such as proposed legislation to direct revenue from state-controlled gambling to community foundations (Sidel, 2010). While a good fit with public policy may benefit community foundations, it may also place very high expectations on them, thereby making them vulnerable to political changes, or implicating them in shifting government responsibilities relative to the nonprofit sector in a manner incompatible with their community focus (Vargas-Hernández and Noruzi, 2010). Furthermore, the very role of engaging communities in conversations and consultations may make local enemies, as well as friends. Wood (2012), for example, cites the US experience of Silicon Valley Community Foundation, encountering fierce opposition from 'Tea Party' members for being too closely aligned to central government (Wood, 2012).

For the 'new generation' of community foundations (Hodgson *et al.*, 2012), the story is quite different. Engagement in leadership in, and for, the community is integral to their work as most are operating in contexts in which relationships between citizens and the state are being reshaped and most seek to enhance the agency of citizens. For example, as Herrold (2012: 37) observes, Egypt's two community foundations, the Community Foundation for South Sinai and the Maadi Community Foundation, in supporting the aims of the revolution led their communities to become more civically and politically engaged. This was despite the risks posed by the legal environment of participating in such activities. Community foundations in developed countries are being urged, by the community foundation 'movement' and by key supporters such as the Mott and the Aga Khan Foundations, to learn from this new wave and to 'reimagine' their own value proposition to their communities as part of innovative approaches to community philanthropy (Bernholtz *et al.*, 2005; Knight, 2012; Kasper *et al.*, 2014: 12).

The agile servant: Reflections on research of model and movement

The community foundation model offers a philanthropic archetype, following its North American form as a typical original example, from which others have been copied. In the process of its worldwide spread, the community foundation model has proven to be highly agile, adapting to different contexts, power relationships and aspirations, so that many of its current forms are quite different from the original invention. Increasingly, as community foundations blend into a broader spectrum of community philanthropy, it is difficult to identify a 'simple formula' for what constitutes a community foundation (WINGS, 2012). Both the hybridity inherent in the community foundation model and the multiple ways in which it is evolving make research more complex, but more essential than ever.

If the institutionally-based core template is becoming substantially differentiated, it is likely that clusters of community foundation types are forming and are experiencing varying degrees of success. Most of the research, however, has been focused on the US with some international case studies (e.g. Hodgson *et al.*, 2012) and practitioner reflections (e.g. Sacks, 2006), but little comparative analysis. There is a clear need for stronger research that addresses the implications and outcomes of what 'context' means for the shifting nature or retention of a community foundation model and its relationship to, and possible competition with, other forms of community and place-based philanthropy. The latter including established forms, such as United Way, as well as emerging forms of collective action. Existing research has found community foundations wanting in their leadership roles, and there have been strong admonishments to step up to much greater change roles, but we actually know very little about the processes of, and factors that affect, the exercise of such leadership. Differentiation in interpretations of 'community leadership', with some overtly active, others appearing passive, is an important research topic in its own right; for example, where community foundations have found their leadership spaces through 'niche picking' that differentiates them from other philanthropic institutions (Phillips *et al.*, 2011: 9). This line of research includes the development and effects of philanthropy networks between community foundations and other foundations and trusts, the implications of competitor organizations, including those claiming the position of anchor institutions in communities, and the nature and effects of leadership systems and structures. Importantly, it also needs to address the nature and exercise of community foundations' power. This is a strong theme in literatures critiquing and challenging private foundations, but the examination of power, not only in a collaborative sense as 'convening power for' (Ruesga, 2014: 140) but in a more blatant sense of 'power over', is far less emphatic in community foundation studies.

Although the buzz in the literature in recent years has been on the community aspect of the model, we should not lose sight of the foundation aspects. As community foundations continue to build significant endowments, providing capacity that brings them into the operating space of private foundations, it will be important to understand more fully any differences in strategy, and in the ways in which – and whether – they do multiply impact. As DAFs grow, the latitude for unrestricted grantmaking, the outcomes of a quasi-commercial orientation, and outright competition with for-profit financial institutions may have significant effects on the management of community foundations.

Finally, research needs to address the movement, as well as the model. Although there is still a reluctance to embrace the idea of being a 'movement', the publication of the first global Community Foundation Atlas, funded by the Charles Stewart Mott Foundation, makes a direct claim for the existence of a movement and the implicit need for its strengthening:

> It is expected that the creation of an easily accessible, comprehensive information resource about the community foundation movement will build a sense of solidarity among members of the field who may not be aware of the existence of many of their counterparts abroad and the similarities of their concerns and the variations in their problem solving'.

(WINGS, 2013: NP)

This alone creates high expectation levels, and demanding tests for community foundations in their model and movement guises. It also presses home the importance of a strong comparative transnational research and learning agenda, in which typology and theory building form important parts, for this still rather unique philanthropic form.

References

Bernholz, L., Fulton, K. and Kasper, G. (2005) "On the Brink of a New Promise: The Future of U.S. Community Foundations". New York: Blue Print Research and Design and the Monitor Group.

Bolognesi, D. (2012) Strengthening Civil Society in Southern Italy. Can Community Foundations foster an innovation process?, International Society for Third Sector Research, International Research Conference, Siena, Italy, July.

Breeze, B. (ed) (2014) Great British Philanthropy, Growing a Fellowship of Donors to Support Local Communities, The Philanthropy Fellowship, http://i.emlfiles8.com/cmpdoc/0/8/7/8/7/files/257916_great-british-philanthropy-report-dec-2014.compressed.pdf?dm_i=1OSC,318HX,CFOVXQ,AWOM1,1 [Accessed 6 April 2015].

Carson, E. D. (2003) Making Waves to Build Community and Raise Assets: A 21st Century Strategy for Community Foundations, Keynote Address, Community Foundation Network Annual Meeting, 24 September. www.commfoundnet.plus.com/feature_articles/6.pdf

CF Insights (2012) Do More than Grow. Realizing the Potential of Community Foundation Donor-Advised Funds, Council on Foundations.

Charities Aid Foundation (CAF) Russia (ND) Development of Local Community Foundations, www.cafrussia.ru/eng/programs/fms_eng/.

Charles Stewart Mott Foundation (2012) Annual Report, Community Foundations – Rooted Locally, Growing Globally, www.mott.org/files/publications/AR2012.pdf.

Cheney, A. L., Merchant, K. E., and Killins, R. (2013) Impact Investing: A 21st Century Tool to Attract and Retain Donors. *The Foundation Review*, 4(4), 45–56.

Community Foundation Atlas (2015) Facts, www.communityfoundationatlas.org/facts/ [Accessed 27 May 2015].

Community Foundations of Canada (2006) Addressing our Toughest Challenges: A Social Justice Discussion Guide for Community Foundations, November. www.cfc-fcc.ca/documents/pf_4_SJ_Discussion_Guide.pdf [Accessed 14 December 2012].

Community Foundations of Canada (2015) About CFC, www.cfc-fcc.ca/about-cfc/index.cfm [Accessed 27 May 2012].

Community Foundation Tyne & Wear and Northumberland (2013) Strategy 2013–16: Summary, June 2013, www.communityfoundation.org.uk/wp-content/uploads/2010/09/Strategy-2013-16-FINAL-summary-for-publication.pdf [Accessed 27 May 2015].

Community Foundation Tyne & Wear and Northumberland (2014) Our Year 2014, www.communityfoundation.org.uk/wp-content/uploads/downloads/2014/11/CF-YEARBOOK-2014-FINAL.pdf [Accessed 27 May 2015].

Daly, S. (2008) Institutional Innovation in Philanthropy: Community Foundations in the UK. *Voluntas*, 19: 219–41.

Easterling, D. (2008) The Leadership Role of Community Foundations in Building Social Capital. *National Civic Review*, 97: 39–51.

Feurt, S. L. and Sacks, E. W. (2000) An International Perspective on the History, Development and Characteristics of Community Foundations, in P Walkenhorst (ed.), "Building Philanthropic and Social Capital: The Work of Community Foundations", Bertelsman Foundation Publishers, Gütersloh, Germany,15–39.

Feuss, B., Cutts, M. and Emerson, J. (2014) Driving Impact through Donor Advised Funds: Community Foundations as Catalysts for Impact Investing, Silicon Valley Community Foundation.

Foundation Scotland (2015) What We Do, www.foundationscotland.org.uk/about-us/what-we-do.aspx [Accessed 7 April 2005].

Glückler, J. and Ries, M. (2012) Why being There is Not Enough: Organized Proximity in Place-based Philanthropy. *The Service Industries Journal*, 32(4): 515–521.

Grabowski, J. J. (2002) "Frederick Harris Goff in Robert T. Grimm Jr. Notable American Philanthropists: Biographies of giving and volunteering". Westport CT: Greenwood Publishing Group.

Graddy, E. A. and Morgan, D. L. (2006) Community Foundations, Organizational Strategy, and Public Policy. *Nonprofit and Voluntary Sector Quarterly*, 35(4): 605–30.

Graddy, E. A. and Wang, L. (2009) Community Foundation Development and Social Capital. *Nonprofit and Voluntary Sector Quarterly*, 28(3): 392–412.

Grønbjerg, K. A. (2006) Foundation Legitimacy at the Community Level in the United States, in K. Prewitt, M. Dogan, S. Heydemann and S. Toepler (eds.) "The Legitimacy of Philanthropic Foundations", Russell Sage Foundation, 150–74.

Guo, C. and Brown, W. A. (2006) Community Foundation Performance: Bridging Community Resources and Needs. *Nonprofit and Voluntary Sector Quarterly*, 35 (2), June 2006, 267–87.

Hamilton, R., Parzen, J. and Brown, P. (2004) Community Change Makers: The Leadership Roles of Community Foundations. Chapin Hall Center for Children at the University of Chicago.

Hammack, D. (1989) Community Foundations: The Delicate Question of Purpose, in R. Magat (ed.), "An Agile Servant: Community Leadership by Community Foundations", The Foundation Center, The Council on Foundations.

Hellmann, B. (2010) The Challenge of Sustainability – How German Community Foundations Can Strengthen Their Financial and Organizational Stability. Paper prepared for the Center on Philanthropy and Civil Society, The City University of New York.

Herrold, C. E. (2012) Philanthropic Foundations in Egypt: Fueling Change or Safeguarding Status Quo?, Takaful 2012, Second Annual Conference on Arab Philanthropy and Civic Engagement, June 10–12, Cairo, Egypt, Selected Research, 34–53.

Hodgson, J. and Knight, B. (2010) More than the Poor Cousin? The Emergence of Community Foundations as a New Development Paradigm. The Global Fund for Community Foundations

Hodgson, J, Knight, B. and Mathie, A. (2012) The New Generation of Community Foundations, Global Fund for Community Foundations and International Development Research Centre, Canada.

Hoffstein, M. E. (2007) Private Foundations and Community Foundations, Canadian Tax Foundation Fifty-Ninth Annual Tax Conference November 25–27, 1–39. www.carters.ca/pub/article/charity/2007/meh1125.pdf.

Hussey, M. J. (2010) "Avoiding Misuse of Donor Advised Funds". Cleveland State. L. Rev., 58, 1, 59–96.

Initiative Bürgerstiftungen (2014) Bürgerstiftungen in Zahlen 2014, www.buergerstiftungen.org/fileadmin/ibs/de/8_Presse/2_Pressematerial/IBS_Faktenblatt_2014.pdf [Accessed 27 May 2015].

Jung, T. and Harrow, J. (2014) Cutting Off the Dead Past from the Living Present? A Critical Examination of Community Foundations in England, Paper presented at the 11th International Conference of the International Society for Third Sector Research, 22–25 July, Muenster, Germany.

Jung, T., Harrow, J. and Phillips, S. (2013) Developing a Better Understanding of Community Foundations in the UK's localisms. *Policy and Politics*. 41, 3, 409–27.

Kasper, G., Marcoux, J. and Ausinheiler, J. (2014) What's Next for Community Philanthropy: Making the Case for Change. Monitor Institute.

Knight, B. (2012) The Value Of Community Philanthropy, Aga Khan Foundation, Charles Stewart Mott Foundation.

Leat, D. (2006) Foundation Legitimacy at the Community Level in the United Kingdom, in K. Prewett, M. Dogan, S. Heydemann and S. Toepler (eds.), "Foundations and the Challenge of Legitimacy in Comparative Perspective", Russell Sage Foundation, New York, 252–270.

Maclean, M., Harvey, C. and Gordon, J. (2012) Social Innovation, Social Entrepreneurship and the Practice of Contemporary Entrepreneurial Philanthropy. *International Small Business Journal*, 31(7): 747–63.

Magat, R. (1989) "An Agile Servant: Community Leadership by Community Foundations", Foundation Center.

Masters, B. and Osborn, T. (2010) Social Movements and Philanthropy: How Foundations Can Support Movement Building. *The Foundation Review*, 2(2), 12–27.

Mazany, T. and Perry, D. C. (2014) "Here for Good: Community Foundations and the Challenges of the 21st Century", M. E. Sharpe, Armonk, New York, 95–106.

Millesen, J. L. and Martin, E. C. (2014) Community Foundation Strategy: Doing Good and the Moderating Effects of Fear, Tradition, and Serendipity, *Nonprofit and Voluntary Sector Quarterly*, vol. 43(5) 832–49.

Nevile, A. (2010) Drifting or Holding Firm? Public Funding and the Values of Third Sector Organisations. *Policy and Politics*, 38(4): 531–46.

Newman, B. L. (1989) Pioneers of the Community Foundation Movement, in R. Magat (ed.), "An Agile Servant: Community Leadership by Community Foundations", The Foundation Center, The Council on Foundations.

Ostrower, F. (2007) The Relativity of Foundation Effectiveness: The Case of Community Foundations. *Nonprofit and Voluntary Sector Quarterly*, 36(3), 521–27.

Patten, M. and Lyons, S. (2009) Vital Signs: Connecting Community Needs with Community Philanthropy in Canada. *The Philanthropist*, 22, 1, 56–61. www.thephilanthropist.ca/index.php/phil/issue/view/83.

Perry, D. C. and Mazany, T. (2014) The Second Century: Community Foundations as Foundations of Community, in T. Mazany and D.C Perry (eds.). "Here for Good: Community Foundations and the Challenges of the 21st Century", M. E. Sharpe, Armonk, New York, 3–26.

Pharaoh, C. (2011) "Charity Market Monitor". Caritas, London.

Phillips, S. D., Jung, T. and Harrow, J. (2011) Community Foundations as Community Leaders? Comparing Developments in Canada and the United Kingdom, Paper presented to the 40th Annual Conference of the Association for Research on Nonprofit Organizations and Voluntary Action (ARNOVA) November 17-19, Toronto, Canada www./carleton.ca/sppa/wp-content/uploads/Phillips-Jung-Harrow-ARNOVA2011_Community-foundations.pdf [Accessed 27 May 2015].

Prashar, Baroness, (2010) "On Philanthropy, Debate 2 December". House of Lords: c1626.

Rhodes, C. (2014) Community Foundations as Impact Multipliers, in T. Mazany and D. C. Perry (eds.), "Here for Good: Community Foundations and the Challenges of the 21st Century", M. E. Sharpe, Armonk, New York, 95–106.

Rogers, D. E. and Keenan, T. (1990) The Role of Foundations in American Society. *Health Affairs*, 9, no. 4: 186–194.

Ruesga, G. A. (2014) The Community Foundation as Borderland Institution, in T. Mazany and D. C. Perry (eds.), "Here for Good: Community Foundations and the Challenges of the 21st Century", M. E. Sharpe, Armonk, New York 131–43.

Ruesga, G. A., and Knight, B. (2013) The View from the Heights of Arnstein's Ladder: Resident Engagement by Community Foundations. *National Civic Review*, 102(3), 13–16.

Sacks, E. (2006) Community Foundations: Symposium on a Global Movement, Current Issues for the Global Community Foundation Movement, WINGS/European Foundation Centre, Brussels, Belgium.

Sacks, E. (2014) The Growing Importance of Community Foundations, Lilly Family School of Philanthropy.

Sidel, M. (2010) Recent Developments in Community Foundation Law: The Quest for Endowment Building. *Chicago-Kent Law Review*, 85: 657–82.

Silicon Valley Community Foundation (2015) About SVCF, www.siliconvalleycf.org/about-svcf [Accessed 27 May 2015].

Smith, J. and Wiest, D. (2012) "Social Movements in the World-System: The Politics of Crisis and Transformation". New York, NY: Russell Sage Foundation.

Spallek, N. (ND) Germany's First Community Foundation: Stadt Stiftung Gütersloh (City Foundation of Gütersloh), Wir für unsere Stadt (Our City, Our Responsibility): Time – Ideas – Money, Bertelsmann Foundation.

Thompson, V. (2012) African American Philanthropy: Community Foundations' Giving to Minority-Led Nonprofit Organizations. *SPNHA Review*, vol. 8, iss. 1, http://scholarworks.gvsu.edu/cgi/viewcontent.cgi?article=1020&context=spnhareview.

Van Slyke, D. M. and Newman, H. K. (2006) Venture Philanthropy and Social Entrepreneurship in Community Redevelopment. *Nonprofit Management and Leadership*, 16(3):345–72.

Vargas-Hernández, J. G. and Noruzi, M. R. (2010) An Exploration of Partnerships, Coalitions, Sole and Trans-organizational Systems and Community Partnerships Designing. *ŒCONOMICA* 1: 17–42.

Vital Signs (2015a) National Reports. Research Findings, www.vitalsignscanada.ca/en/findings [Accessed 27 May 2015].

Vital Signs (2015b) International Reports, www.vitalsignscanada.ca/en/international [Accessed 27 May 2015].

Vogel, A. (2006) Who's Making Global Civil Society: Philanthropy and US Empire in World Society. *British Journal of Sociology*, 57(4): 635–55.

Wang, L., Graddy, E., and Morgan, D. (2011) The Development of Community-Based Foundations in East Asia. *Public Management Review*, 13(8), 1155–78.

WINGS GLOBAL (2010) Status Report on Community Foundations 2010 www.wings-community-foundation-report.com/gsr_2010/gsr_theme_facts/global-growth.cfm [Accessed 27 May 2015].

WINGS (2012) Global Status Report on Community Foundations 2012 http://www.issuelab.org/click/download1/global_status_report_on_community_foundations_2012_update [Accessed 27 May 2015].

WINGS (2013) Community Foundation Atlas Will Commemorate Movement's 100th Year www.wingsweblog.wordpress.com/2013/11/19/community-foundations-atlas-will-commemorate-movements-100th-year/ [Accessed 27 May 2015].

Wolfe, R. (2006) "Community Foundations' Leadership – Traditional, Change Agent, or Nonexistent?" Stanford University.

Wood, E. (2012) Lessons in Building a Better Community, One Voice at a Time. *The Foundation Review* 4(4): 71–83.

20

Hybridity and philanthropy

Implications for policy and practice

Steven Rathgeb Smith

Private foundations hold a highly visible and quite unique place in a country: they benefit from generous tax advantages and exemptions; they are quite diverse in mission and orientation; and they have considerable autonomy over their programs and operations, especially compared with many other types of philanthropic and public institutions (Hammack and Anheier, 2013; Leat, Chapter 18). Yet, foundations face increased competition in terms of influence and support. In many countries, the giving options for individual donors have exploded; donors can give to a proliferating array of causes and organizations and create vehicles for giving, such as donor advised funds (DAFs) in the US, that depart from the traditional foundation model. The widespread interest in social entrepreneurship, social innovation, and social enterprise has tended to focus attention on programmatic outcomes and leveraging grant funds. Many foundations also experienced steep losses in their assets due to the financial crisis, leading them to be more attentive than ever to the allocation of their scarce grant monies. With increased competition to their influence and legitimacy, many foundations are innovating in their structure, investment strategies, giving patterns, and creating new alliances and partnerships (Salamon, 2014).

The result is substantially increased hybridity in the organization of foundations and their programs (Smith, 2010). In general, hybridity refers to organizations with more than one institutional logic (Hammack and Heydemann, 2009; Billis, 2010; Skelcher and Smith, 2014). Foundations, like other organizations, are guided by particular logics such as a community or family logic. Their control over resources has tended to offer foundations an opportunity to pursue particular institutional logics such as meeting local community needs or specific mission related priorities, such as supporting democracy. But foundations now face more demands for relevance and accountability, encouraging many to adopt new strategies to support their grantmaking activities. Consequently, many foundations are trying to balance new, and different, logics through new alliances with government, other foundations and nonprofits, and even for-profit social enterprises. In particular, community foundations need to balance individual donor goals for their donor advised funds with the broader needs of the community (Harrow *et al.*, Chapter 19). This shift to hybridity offers opportunities for enhancing impact, but also raises complicated dilemmas regarding mission and accountability. In the following pages, this chapter examines the growth of hybridity within organized philanthropy and its implications for foundations, their grantees, and public policy.

Philanthropic institutions and hybridity

Research on hybridity is quite extensive. For example, Koppell (2003) notes the existence of quasi-governmental organizations that do not fit traditional definitions of government agencies because they operate like a private corporation (Skelcher, 2004, 2009). Minkoff (2002) studies nonprofit organizations which combine features of two distinct organizational missions – in her case, national advocacy and service organizations. Thus, she is especially interested in nonprofit organizations that are committed to social change and have both a service and an advocacy mission. Relatedly, Joldersma and Winter (2002) suggest that hybrid organizations are public service organizations that serve government and other types of clients, including market-based clients. Yet another interpretation of hybridity is offered by Evers (2005; and Laville 2004) who argues that hybrid organizations reflect different logics and rationales within nonprofit organizations, thus, often highlighting the norms of the state, market, and community or civil society sectors (Brandsen *et al.*, 2005). Consequently, nonprofit organizations are inherently hybrid organizations. Yet, the works of Evers (2005) and Brandsen *et al.* (2005) do not adequately explain the marked shifts in organized philanthropy over the last few years, the changes in the mix of logics within many different types of foundations. These are evident across many policy fields.

Philanthropy's hybridity in relation to grantmaking and programme operations is nicely illustrated by the example of nonprofit social housing in the US. The federal government has implemented an important tax credit program to support low-income housing called the Low Income Housing Tax Credit (LIHTC). Basically, this program allows private investors (and equity funds) to pool their money in support of nonprofit social housing projects and receive a tax credit. Often, this tax credit funding is mixed with other public and philanthropic funds from foundations and corporations. In particular, national foundations including the Ford Foundation and the Enterprise Foundation (now called Enterprise Community Partners) have provided extensive support for specific projects and capacity building to help social housing programs which receive tax-credit financing to develop sound and effective business plans. Foundations and corporate giving programs have also been essential to the widespread enthusiasm and interest in social enterprises that mix nonprofit and for-profit characteristics (Dees, 1998; Alter, 2007). Foundations have often directly funded new social enterprises as shown by the case of Building Community Forge, a nonprofit social service agency based in Hartford, Connecticut. It operates a restaurant that employs disadvantaged individuals; the restaurant income is also used to subsidize social housing and other programs. The Mellon Foundation of Connecticut has provided substantial support for this program over the course of many years. Many other examples exist, including the noteworthy work of REDF, a California-based foundation that has promoted innovative social enterprises for the disabled and unemployed, and the Greyston Bakery in Yonkers, New York, a for-profit bakery that employs disadvantaged workers alongside an affiliated foundation that operates social service programs.

The turbulence of the organizational environment for philanthropy reflects significant shifts in citizen and donor attitudes. The United Way has instituted a policy of 'donor choice'. This offers donors much greater control over the destination of their donation than was previously the case. DAFs, often located within community foundations or commercial investment houses, are designed to give donors greater flexibility in their donations compared with private foundations (Harrow *et al.*, Chapter 19). Also, the venture philanthropy movement is predicated in part on the idea that donors should have much more direct engagement with their grantee organizations than is typical with traditional foundations (Letts *et al.*, 1999; Morino, 2011). More broadly, the movement for greater donor choice and engagement in grantmaking reflects the widespread concern among policymakers and philanthropic leaders that organized philanthropy needs to pay much greater heed to outcome evaluation and the performance of their grantees (Fleishman, 2007; Brest *et al.*, 2009). Large national foundations, such as the Edna McConnell Clark Foundation, the Annie E. Casey Foundation, and the Robert Woods Johnson Foundation, have invested millions of dollars in the evaluation of their grant programs and more broadly the dissemination of best practices regarding philanthropic grantmaking and programming. The Robin Hood Foundation in New York City has made evaluation and performance targets a central tenet of its grantmaking practices.

Importantly, this interest in impact and accountability has in turn led foundations to innovate in their funding and grantmaking strategies. Many foundations no longer exclusively rely upon short-term grants to donor agencies – the traditional form of grant-making. Instead, many foundations utilize a diverse mix of funding strategies including: longer-term grants, pre-development loans, planning grants, and loans for acquisition and construction. This shift is evident in new thinking on program-related investments (PRIs). In the Tax Reform Act (TRA) of 1969, Congress imposed heavy taxes on investments by foundations that were considered so speculative or risky as to jeopardize the foundation's tax-exempt purpose. However, TRA allowed higher risk investments if they met three key conditions: they had a charitable purpose; they did not have the production of income or property appreciation as their primary goal; and they were not connected in any way to lobbying or electioneering (Schmalbeck, 2004–2005; IRS, 2006; Grantcraft, 2011).

PRIs are part of a growing movement in philanthropy for mission-based investing which is the practice of using foundation assets for purposes that fit with the mission of the foundation, and simultaneously earning a financial return (Emerson, 2003; Cooch and Kramer, 2007; F. B. Heron Foundation, 2007; Swack, 2009; Lindblom, 2010; Lawrence and Mukai, 2011a; Wood *et al.*, 2012). Good illustrations of PRIs in action can be found in the work of the Packard Foundation. This foundation's Conserving California Landscape Initiative (CCLI) used a PRI strategy including loans to purchase or facilitate the purchase of land or conservation easements (Delfin and Shui-Yan, 2006). Packard also provided a PRI loan to a for-profit health company to supply needed drugs to developing countries. Overall, the Packard Foundation devoted over $450 million to PRI investments between 1980 and 2012 (David and Lucille Packard Foundation, 2014). The Ford Foundation (1991) has been using PRI investments extensively in its 'asset and community development' programs to fund land trusts, revolving loan funds, microfinance programs, loan guarantees, and sometimes equity investments in for-profit companies with a social mission. Since 1968, the Ford Foundation (2012a) has provided over $560 million in PRI investments to nonprofit and for-profit organizations. It has also supported a diverse set of innovative Community Development Financial Institutions (CDFIs), including the Self-Help Federal Credit Union with a PRI investment of over $30 million (Ford Foundation, 2012b; see also Mary Reynolds Babcock Foundation, 2011; Calvert Foundation, 2012; 2014). The Medina Foundation, a family foundation in Seattle, decided to dramatically shift its grant strategy and devote a substantial investment to the creation of the Express Credit Union, a for-profit community-based financial services organization that offers low-income families important financial products and an affiliated nonprofit entity to offer related social services and support (Medina Foundation, 2012). Several foundations also used PRI investments as a rapid response strategy to address the serious problems resulting from the financial crisis of 2008 and its aftermath. The MacArthur Foundation, for instance, committed $34 million in PRIs in response to the homeowner foreclosure crisis including a $15 million low-interest loan to ShoreBank in Chicago, a bank specializing in loans to disadvantaged individuals and communities (Lawrence, 2009).

PRIs are part of this movement for mission-based investing because they reflect a link between the overall goal of the foundation – helping communities in need – and their funding priorities and strategy. Thus, a foundation interested in helping low-income communities might invest its endowment in institutions or funding vehicles such as loans that benefit these same low-income communities. Or a foundation might invest part of its assets in a new for-profit start-up health firm in a developing country to further its mission of improving health. As a result, mission-based investing differs slightly from socially responsible investing which tends to focus on screening in an investment strategy to exclude certain types of industries such as tobacco or companies with poor labour practices (Swack, 2009).

Mission-based investing, including PRIs, pushes foundations to more explicitly manage different institutional logics within their organizations, since foundations are more likely to be engaged in various types of market-based activities. For example, instead of granting to a local nonprofit to promote community development, a foundation could invest in *linked deposits* at local banks so that local banks can provide low interest to local businesses (Cooch and Kramer, 2007, p. 26). The Rose Foundation of northern California bought stock in a lumber company in order to have the ability as a sizable shareholder to press the company to preserve an important expanse of redwood forest (Emerson, 2003). The investment of the Packard Foundation in the commercial health firm is another example. These investments also require foundations to manage different logics than is normally the case in more traditional foundation grants; in the case of the Packard grant for example, the Foundation must balance the market logic of the health firm with its own vision of community needs.

Concerned about impact and leveraging scarce grant dollars, many foundations are engaging in more formal types of collaboration with public and nonprofit entities that bring foundations into a closer relationship with government (Kania and Kramer, 2011). Foundations have, of course, funded projects of public policy significance for a very long time (Hammack and Anheier, 2013). But in recent years, foundations have forged complicated partnerships with government that require balancing public and foundation priorities on an ongoing basis. Examples abound. In 2006, the Gates and Rockefeller Foundations established a major partnership to develop new crops to help farmers in Africa called the Alliance for a Green Revolution in Africa (Rockefeller Foundation, 2008; AGRA, 2012). The Gates Foundation collaborates with numerous public, for-profit and nonprofit entities throughout the world in support of their initiatives. At the local level, countless foundations are collaborating in support of program innovation and reform, especially related to urgent social and health problems. For instance, a nationwide initiative called Funders Together to End Homelessness strives to bring together the resources and expertise of multiple funders in order to develop a more coordinated and effective strategy to end homelessness (Wertheimer, 2011). In Washington State, Thrive by Five was formed as a collaborative effort of several private foundations, corporate funders and the state of Washington to support early childhood education. In Minnesota, the Itasca Area Schools Collaborative is a joint project of local schools and the Blandin Foundation to support opportunities for improved success in school for all students regardless of income or background (Bielefeld, 2014). In the UK, the government has provided £80 million to support Community First, a program to help communities come together to identify their strengths and local priorities in order to plan for their future and become more resilient. It is managed by the Community Development Foundation as a partnership with the national government (Community Development Foundation, 2014).

These initiatives involve managing a mix of different logics: the community, the government, and often market imperatives. To be sure, some of these partnerships represent the agreement of the public sector to foundation priorities, but in many other cases, the mission and programmatic priorities are negotiated among the various partners. In this sense, these partnerships represent the increase in hybridity within organized philanthropy. In order to effectively manage these hybrid arrangements, foundations and their partners need to devise strategies that effectively manage potentially conflicting logics and expectations among donors, as well as their descendants, staff and volunteers.

The complex mix of logics within organized philanthropy is also illustrated by the growing interest in social impact bonds (SIBs) which require the joint production of a particular service by several public and nonprofit entities. SIBs essentially offer government the opportunity to define specific outcomes and then agree to pay an external organization if they meet the agreed-upon targets (Clifford and Jung, 2016). In Peterborough, England, social impact bonds were implemented through a new intermediary entity called One Service which included several service agencies and funders. Private funders, including leading foundations, invest in One Service and then receive repayment from the government (Ganguly, 2014; Social Finance, 2014) – indeed, the Rockefeller Foundations used a PRI investment to support the Peterborough program. SIBs have also been used in New York City to support an innovative jail recidivism program; the social impact bonds operate through a lead organization that works closely with other funders and an actual social service delivery agency (Preston, 2012). SIBs represent a shift among foundations and philanthropists to focus more specifically on impact and evaluation. The result is a mix of different logics that foundations and other partners need to manage.

Another example of hybridity – DAFs – represents new and more complicated balancing between individual goals of donors and the broader community interest and has seen rapid growth in the last 15 years. These funds are, at least for many wealthy individuals, an alternative to establishing a private foundation because they permit a donor to make a charitable gift and take an income tax deduction for that tax year and, at that time or later, advise which charities should receive the distribution. Further, DAFs are not required to file separate tax returns, file for tax-exempt status, or adhere to private foundation rules; thus, DAFs have many of the advantages of a private foundation, but without the higher transaction costs and ongoing administrative burdens (Bjorklund, 2003; General Accounting Office, 2006: 12; U. S. Department of Treasury, 2011).

A few other examples of the changes within organized philanthropy illustrate the turbulent organizational environment. First, more organizations are called foundations when in fact they are not private foundations as defined under federal law. Instead, they are typically a private 501(c)(3) public charity – a trend driven primarily by the pressure on nonprofit and public organizations to raise private donations. For instance, Tacoma (WA) Goodwill Industries, a social services agency, established the Goodwill Heritage Foundation as a 501(c)(3) public charity; its mission is to 'seek long-term funding to endow the programs of Tacoma Goodwill Industries'. Indeed, it has become quite common for larger 501(c)(3) public charities and churches to create affiliated foundations which are actually public charities, reflecting a prevalent assumption among development professionals and nonprofit executives that attracting private donations and foundation grants will be easier if a separate organizational entity focuses on the sustainability and long-term future of the parent organization. Donated funds can also be restricted to specific purposes and insulated from the ongoing uncertainties of the operating budget of the parent organization.

While this trend of creating 'foundations' which are actually not private foundations began in earnest with nonprofit, 501(c)(3), organizations, it has recently grown rapidly among governmental agencies, notably at the local level. For instance, in Seattle, foundations have been created in the last ten years by the following municipal agencies: Parks and Recreation, the Police, the Public Library, the School District, the Seattle Center (a multipurpose event area), the Pike Place Market Development Authority, the Zoo (a mixed public-nonprofit initiative), and Historic Seattle, a preservation organization. None of these foundations are private nonoperating foundations as defined by federal law; instead they are 501(c)(3) public charities raising money to augment the support the related organization receives (primarily from tax revenues). Native American tribes, which are considered sovereign nations, have also established similar foundations. These public foundations illustrate the interest of many philanthropists and foundations in supporting public-policy oriented initiatives; the affiliated foundations are a vehicle for attracting and channeling these donations. From the government's perspective, these affiliated foundations offer an opportunity to raise and spend funds with fewer restrictions and scrutiny than is typically the case with direct government appropriations.

This trend toward grantmaking public charities is also evident in the growth of 'donor giving circles'. In an era of greater emphasis on donor and consumer choice, donor giving circles are increasingly attractive (Layton, Chapter 8). Giving circles are typically structured as 501(c)(3) public charities, rather than as private foundations. Donors are members of these organizations and are expected to donate a minimum amount every year. Members are then expected to contribute volunteer time and their expertise to help nonprofit recipient agencies. In this sense, these new organizations are an effort to offer high engagement philanthropy where members are actively involved in the recipient organizations. Good examples include Social Venture Partners with many chapters around the country and the Washington Women's Foundation; both organizations are registered as public charities.

Greater complexity of organizational form and the potential for conflicting logics is also illustrated in the US by 'health conversion' foundations. During the 1980s and 1990s, many nonprofit hospitals and Blue Cross/Blue Shield firms (which were previously organized as nonprofit entities) were either sold to for-profit companies or were converted to for-profit status. In the process of the sale or the conversion, the charitable assets of the nonprofit entity were often converted into an entirely new private foundation, frequently with very substantial assets. Indeed, three of the largest foundations in California – the California Endowment, the California Healthcare Foundation, and the California Wellness Foundation – are health conversion foundations (*Health Affairs*, 1997; Ferris and Melnick, 2004). The logic of these conversion foundations is that the assets of the existing nonprofit should remain committed to charitable purposes and often restricted to use in the geographic region for the benefit of the state or community, rather than distributed to shareholders of the acquiring company throughout the world. The growth of conversion foundations has slowed considerably in recent years, partly due to frequent controversy and scandals involving these foundations. After the conversion, these new foundations can find themselves ensnared in multiple and conflicting demands from the community and the for-profit hospital. Many of the initial conversion foundations had ties to the for-profit hospital and were also expected to uphold promises made by the acquiring company to the local community on standards of care and levels of service. New conversions have tried to learn from past problems, but these foundations, nonetheless, present complicated management and governance challenges (Carlson, 2012).

Another type of foundation – corporate foundations – also embody this mix of different logics. Corporate foundation staff are frequently employees of the corporation and the corporation provides direct cash support and/or in-kind assistance such as office space and utilities. The boards of corporate foundations are typically controlled by the corporation. Predictably, the grantmaking policies of corporate foundations are closely tied to the priorities of the corporation. Many corporate foundations, such as the Starbucks Foundation and the Wal-Mart Foundation, depend upon annual allocations from the corporation; thus, they do not build assets or an endowment. Consequently, the grantmaking capacity of corporate foundations tends to be highly dependent upon the financial health of the corporation, a sharp contrast to many private nonoperating foundations which have substantial assets and strive to build their asset base to ensure the long-term sustainability of the foundation. To be sure, corporate foundations are not a new phenomenon, but the attraction of corporate social responsibility worldwide has prompted more engagement by corporations in various types of philanthropy including the establishment of affiliated foundations. But these foundations often need to manage different logics such as a market logic tied to the strategic direction of the company and the needs of the community or citizenry, broadly defined. Thus these foundations do not have the autonomy and independence of action of other types of foundations, especially foundations with sizable endowments. Many for-profit social enterprises such as the Greyston Bakery have also established similar affiliated foundations and also face the dilemma of managing market and community logics.

Policy and practice implications

Foundations, then, find themselves in a more complex operating environment. On the one hand, this is encouraging new initiatives and prompting the formation of different types of philanthropic instruments and organizations; on the other hand, foundations are facing pressure to be more outcome-oriented and to demonstrate impact for their investments. In part, this concern with outcomes and evaluation stems from the sheer amount of money that is now held by foundations and DAFs: in the US, private foundations held $590.2 billion in assets in 2009 and paid over $45.8 billion in grants (Roeger *et al.*, 2012); DAFs in sponsoring organizations had assets valued at $31.1 billion (U.S. Department of Treasury, 2011); with foundation's steady growth across Europe, European foundations held more than €200 billion in assets in 2008 (European Foundation Centre, 2008).

Moreover, the increase in hybridity within organizational philanthropy has raised new and nettlesome questions regarding the accountability of foundations and their affiliated entities. One persistent problem is that mismatch between the government regulatory structure and the larger and more diverse foundation universe. First, the staff capacity and resources of the federal and state regulatory agencies have not kept pace with the growth in foundations, indeed, the Internal Revenue Services (IRS) and some state agencies have reduced their staffing levels. Second and relatedly, the existing reporting system for foundations was designed for a more conventional and simpler philanthropic universe. For instance, organizations holding DAFs are required to include data on their organizational assets and record of charitable donations on their form 990-PF. However, DAFs do not need to be separately reported. Consequently, the complicated regulatory issues pertaining to DAFs, such as the relationship of the donor to the fund (and possibly levels of control) are very difficult for the IRS to discern. Similar issues arise with supporting organizations which are not required to provide information on 'payout' rate comparable to private foundations. The relationship between supporting organizations and their grant or loan recipient is frequently unclear (U.S. Department of Treasury, 2011).

Third, transparency is a more pronounced challenge for citizens due to the increased diversity of the foundation and philanthropic world. Many private, nonoperating foundations, especially larger foundations such as the Ford Foundation, the Gates Foundation, and the Rockefeller Foundation, have detailed reporting procedures that go well beyond that required by federal law. But many smaller foundations, especially family foundations, often do not provide easily accessible information on their grantmaking policies and awards. DAFs are a big component of the assets of community foundations but detailed information on these funds are often lacking.

To address the calls for more accountability, greater investment in self-regulation is occurring. For instance, the Council on Foundations (CoF) issued a 'Statement of Ethical Principles' that seeks to encourage greater accountability and self-regulation by foundations. Recently, CoF developed national standards and ethical principles for community, corporate, and independent foundations, and standards for international grantmaking. It has also initiated training programs focusing on best practices for foundation managers. CoF has also tried to promote best practices among community foundations (Council on Foundations, 2010). Reflecting the worldwide interest in self-regulation by foundations, the European Foundation Centre (2011) has also recently published a report on transparency and self-regulation among European foundations.

The challenge and opportunity of hybridity

Foundations face an uncertain environment that often requires them to manage multiple logics. Moreover, wealthy individuals and companies now have a wide array of charitable vehicles including donor-advised funds, supporting organizations, charitable remainder trusts, public charities and even for-profit companies. Indeed, in a widely-publicized move, Google's first philanthropic initiative was Google.org that was established as a unit within the corporation; under this structural umbrella, a more traditional philanthropic foundation was created. This hybrid structure is similar to the Omidyar Network, the philanthropic arm for the founders of eBay. In both cases, these philanthropic initiatives invest in nonprofit and for-profit entities (Fulton and Blau, 2006; Hafner, 2006; Boss, 2010).

Many foundations in previous decades tended to view their role as supporting innovation and program reform, with the expectation that government might choose to support worthy programs after they demonstrated their effectiveness. But more targeted and scarcer government funding has pressured foundations to adopt a different approach. Hence many foundations are striving to place more emphasis on impact, evaluation, and capacity building as a way of promoting greater effectiveness, especially as it pertains to complicated social problems such as homelessness, economic development, and mental health (Fleishman, 2007; Morino, 2011). Many United Way chapters and foundations, which previously distributed many relatively modest grants to a broad range of local nonprofit agencies, increasingly focus their unrestricted, nondonor designated grantmaking on just a few key priorities such as early childhood education and homelessness. Their grantmaking is also tied to the use of logic models and other evaluation tools by their grantees in order to enhance the impact of their grantmaking. So in this sense, the priorities of many foundations and United Way chapters, as well as their evaluation tools, are often quite similar to government, representing a marked departure from their previous funding policies that emphasized support of organizations rather than direct engagement in solving social problems. United Way chapters increasingly operate like community foundations and thus represent another important player in the organized philanthropic world at the local level.

This rethinking of roles and responsibilities and grantmaking can be conceptualized along a continuum. Some foundations will reinvent themselves and fundamentally rethink their roles and mission. The refocusing of the Edna McConnell Clark Foundation on low-income youth and outcome evaluation is just one high-profile example of this adaptation (Edna McConnell Clark Foundation, 2011). Other foundations are adopting more modest but nonetheless important strategies such as greater use of PRIs or multiyear grants; increased willingness to collaborate with other foundations, nonprofit organizations, and government; and more targeted investment strategies. In this context, foundations are often working together or with government and private sector partners, either directly or indirectly, to achieve an important public priority such as reducing homelessness or building a new wing to a local museum.

To respond to these emergent developments, many foundations have adopted new relationships in their community. Foundations now find themselves as partners in more horizontal networks with public and nonprofits entities. Many foundations supporting social enterprises also have complicated relationships with for-profit firms. These shifts require foundations to think creatively about the governance and accountability of these new initiatives and new approaches to their approach to accountability and results.

To be sure, foundations, especially smaller foundations will continue to fill particular market niches and may not necessarily engage in new more hybrid activities. However, small foundations will also be increasingly challenged in terms of their relevance by new models of philanthropy such as donor-advised funds and demands for greater impact.

This changing landscape for foundations is worldwide. Collaborative initiatives involving foundations are evident in many large-scale, as well as more modest initiatives in a wide variety of countries. The use of new tools of social finance and innovations such as social impact bonds have been to date more prominent in countries such as the US, the UK, Australia and New Zealand that have implemented more market-oriented strategies in public and nonprofit management. However, the ongoing restructuring of the welfare state in many countries suggests that even foundations in countries with less dramatic change in the public and private responsibilities for public policy are likely to experience pressure for change in their role and relationship to other foundations and local nonprofits and government.

Thus, foundations appear to be at an important moment in their historical development: in the crowded philanthropic marketplace, foundations will need to distinguish themselves in order to maintain the trust and support of the community and policymakers. The increase in the number of nonprofit organizations, the diversification of policy and philanthropic instruments, and the increasingly common public-private organizational models provide more opportunities for foundations to be engaged in addressing important public problems. This new landscape of organizations requires support if it is to be sustained, especially given the economic crisis and the competition for public and private grants. As a result, foundations will need to support the institutional infrastructure of nonprofit organizations. A sound business strategy and enhanced impact by nonprofit grantees requires an appropriate strategic vision, effective governance and a sustainable revenue plan. As part of this effort, foundations are likely to be more engaged in supporting or promoting mergers and significant collaborations among grantee organizations. In search of more leverage and more impact in a more complicated environment, foundations are likely to steadily increase their involvement with mission-based investing including the creative and innovative investments in nonprofit and for-profit organizations to achieve foundation goals.

These new investment strategies pose organizational risks, so foundations will need to balance the goals of impact and leverage with longstanding policies on the support of local community organizations and adequate investment returns. Nonprofit organizations, for their part, will continue to face a proliferating array of philanthropic options. Yet, these options are likely to be outcome-oriented and emphasize entrepreneurial management and programming. Nonprofit service agencies will need to invest in their own professional infrastructure to effectively cope with this more complex environment. Further, this evolving philanthropic culture will require that foundations and their nonprofit grantees be very assertive in advocating for the other important values expressed through local community organizations, including citizen engagement, social justice, and programmatic diversity.

Notes

The author would like to thank Staci Goldberg Belle, Beth Lovelady, Meghan McConaughey, Benjamina Menashe, and Skip Swenson for their excellent research assistance. The Nancy Bell Evans Center on Nonprofits & Philanthropy at the Evans School of Public Affairs at the University of Washington and the Department of Public Administration and Policy at American University provided important funding support. The author is also indebted to Putnam Barber, David Hammack, Jenny Harrow, Tobias Jung, Susan Phillips, and Mark Rosenman for comments on earlier versions of this paper.

References

Alliance for Green Revolution in Africa (AGRA) (2012) *AGRA Partnerships*. www.agra-alliance.org/section/links.

Alter, K. S. (2007) *Social Enterprise Typology*. www.virtueventures.com/files/setypology.pdf.

Bernholz, L., Fulton, K. and Gabriel, K. (2005) *On the Brink of New Promise: The Future of US Community Foundations*. San Francisco: Blueprint Research and Design and Monitor Institute. www.monitorinstitute.com/downloads/what-we-think/new-promise/On_the_Brink_of_New_Promise.pdf.

Bielefeld, W. (2014) 'Developing the Pathway to Student Success', *The Hubert Project E-Case*, Minneapolis: Humphrey Institute of Public Affairs, The University of Minnesota,. www.hubertproject.org/hubert-material/345/.

Billis, D. (ed) (2010) *Hybrid Organizations and the Third Sector: Challenges for Practice, Theory and Policy*, New York: Palgrave Macmillan.

Bjorklund, V. (2003) *Choosing Among the Private Foundation, Supporting Organization and Donor-Advised Fund*, New York: Simpson Thacher. www.simpsonthacher.com/siteContent.cfm?contentID=4&itemID=73&focusID=239.

Boss, S. (2010) 'Do No Evil', *Stanford Social Innovation Review* (Fall): 66–71.

Brandsen, T., Van de Donk, W. and Putters, K. (2005) 'Griffins or Chameleons? Hybridity as a Permanent and Inevitable Characteristic of the Third Sector', *International Journal of Public Administration*, 28(9/10): 749–66.

Brest, P., Harvey, H. and Low, K. (2009) 'Calculated Impact', *Stanford Social Innovation Review* (Winter): 50–6.

Calvert Foundation (2012) *Luring Capital towards Sustainable Fishing: Our Work with the Cape Cod Fisheries Trust*. Bethesda, MD: Calvert Foundation. www.calvertfoundation.org/blog/354-luring-capital-towards-sustainable-fishing-our-work-with-the-cape-cod-fisheries-trust.

—— (2014) *Calvert Foundation Announces Intention to Invest $20 Million in WIN-WIN Initiative*, Bethesda, MD: Calvert Foundation. www.calvertfoundation.org/press/releases/515-win-win-cgi.

Carlson, J. (2012) 'Past Discretions Lead to Tighter Rein on New and Future Conversion Foundations', *Modern Healthcare*. 11 February. www.modernhealthcare.com/article/20120211/MAGAZINE/302119972.

Clifford, J. and Jung, T. (2016) 'Social Impact Bonds: exploring and understanding an emerging funding approach', in O. Lehner (ed.) *The Routledge Handbook of Social and Sustainable Finance*, Routledge: London.

Community Development Foundation (2014) *Community First*. www.cdf.org.uk/content/funding-programmes/community-first.

Cooch, S. and Kramer, M. (2007) *Compounding Impact: Mission Investing by US Foundations*, Boston: FSG Social Impact Advisors. www.cdfifund.gov/Documents/Compounding%20Impact%20Mission%20Investing%20by%20US%20Foundations.pdf [Accessed 25 September 2015].

Council on Foundations (2010) *Centennial Plan: Strategies for a Strong Community Foundation Field, 2011–2014*. Washington, DC: Council on Foundations, www.philanthropynw.org/sites/default/files/resources/Centennial-Plan-Strategies-for-Strong-Community-Foundation-Field.pdf.

David and Lucille Packard Foundation (2014) *Program Related Investments*. www.packard.org/wp-content/uploads/2014/02/PRI-Program-Overview-FINAL.pdf.

Dees, J. G. (1998) 'Enterprising Nonprofits', *Harvard Business Review* (January-February): 55–67.

Delfin Jr., F, and Shui-Yan T. (2006) 'Strategic Philanthropy, Land Conservation Governance, and The Packard Foundation's Conserving California Landscape Initiative', *Nonprofit and Voluntary Sector Quarterly*, 35(3)(September): 405–29.

Edna McConnell Clark Foundation (2011) *A Good Thing Growing: 2000–2010, Citizen Schools/Harlem Children's Zone/Roca*, New York: Edna McConnell Clark Foundation. www.emcf.org/fileadmin/media/PDFs/emcf_goodthinggrowing.pdf.

Emerson, J (2003) 'Where Money Meets Mission: Breaking Down the Firewall Between Foundation Investments and Programming', *Stanford Social Innovation Review* (Summer): 38–47.

European Foundation Centre (2008) *Foundations of the European Union: Facts and Figures*. Brussels: European Foundation Centre. www.efc.be/programmes_services/resources/Documents/EFC-RTF_EU%20Foundations-Facts%20and%20Figures_2008.pdf.

European Foundation Centre (2011) *Exploring Transparency and Accountability: Regulation of Public-Benefit Foundations in Europe*. Brussels: European Foundation Centre. www.efc.be/programmes_services/resources/Documents/ExploringTransparencyAndAccountabilityRegulationOfPublicBenefitFoundationsInEurope_FINAL.pdf.

Evers, A. (2005) 'Mixed Welfare Systems and Hybrid Organizations: Changes in the Governance and Provision of Social Services', *International Journal of Public Administration*, 28(9/10): 737–48.

Evers, A. and Laville, J-L. (2004) 'Social Services by Social Enterprises. On the Possible Contributions of Hybrid Organisations and a Civil Society', in A. Evers and J-L. Laville (eds) *The Third Sector in Europe*, Cheltenham/Northampton: Edward Elgar.

F. B. Heron Foundation (2007) *Expanding Philanthropy: Mission Based Investing at the F. B. Heron Foundation*, www.missioninvestors.org/system/files/tools/case-study-expanding-philanthropy-mission-related-investing-at-the-fb-heron-foundation-michael-swack-jack-northrup-and-janet-prince-southern-new-hampshire-university-school-of-community-econ-devo.pdf.

Ferris, J. M. and Melnick, G. A. (2004) 'Improving the Health of Californians: Effective Public-Private Strategies for Challenging Times', *Health Affairs*, 23(1)(May/June): 257–61.

Fleishman, J. (2007) *The Foundation: The Great American Secret*, New York: Public Affairs.

Ford Foundation (1991) *Investing for Social Gain: Reflections on Two Decades of Program-Related Investments*, New York: Ford Foundation. www.fordfoundation.org/pdfs/library/Investing_For_Social_Gain.pdf.

—— (2012a) *Program Related Investments*, New York: Ford Foundation. www.fordfoundation.org/grants/program-related-investment.

—— (2012b) *Improving Access to Financial Services*, New York: Ford Foundation. www.fordfoundation.org/issues/economic-fairness/improving-access-to-financial-services.

Fulton, K. and Blau, A. (2006) *Looking Out for the Future: An Orientation for Twenty-First Century Philanthropists*. The Global Business Network and the Monitor Institute. www.futureofphilanthropy.org/files/finalreport.pdf [Accessed 25 September 2015].

Ganguly, B. (2014) *The Success of the Peterborough Social Impact Bond*, www.rockefellerfoundation.org/blog/success-peterborough-social-impact.

General Accounting Office (GAO) (2006) *Tax-Exempt Organizations: Collecting More Data on Donor Advised Funds and Supporting Organizations Could Help Address Compliance Challenges*. Washington, DC: GAO.

Grantcraft (2011) *Program-Related Investing: Skills and Strategies for New PRI Funders*, New York: Grantcraft. www.grantcraft.org/assets/content/resources/pri_guide.pdf.

Hafner, K. (2006) 'Philanthropy Google's Way: Not the Usual', *The New York Times*, 14 September.

Hammack, D. and Heydemann, S. (2009) *Globalization, Philanthropy and Civil Society: Projecting Institutional Logics Abroad* Bloomington, IN: Indiana University Press.

Hammack, D. and Anheier, H. (2013) *The Versatile Institution: The Changing Ideals and Realities of Philanthropic Foundations*, Washington, DC: Brookings.

Health Affairs (1997) 'Conversion Foundations: A Listing', *Health Affairs*, 16(3)(March/April): 238–42.

Internal Revenue Service (IRS) (2006) *Program Related Investments*, www.irs.gov/Charities-&-Non-Profits/Private-Foundations/Program-Related-Investments.

Joldersma, C. and Winter, V. (2002) 'Strategic Management in Hybrid Organizations', *Public Management Review* 4(1): 83–100.

Kania, J. and Kramer, M. (2011) 'Collective Impact,' *Stanford Social Innovation Review*, (Winter): 36–41.

Koppell, J. G. S. (2003) *The Politics of Quasi-Government: Hybrid Organizations and the Dynamics of Bureaucratic Control*, Cambridge: Cambridge University Press.

Lawrence, S. (2009) *A First Look at the Foundation and Corporate Response to the Economic Crisis*. New York: Foundation Center. www.foundationcenter.org/gainknowledge/research/pdf/researchadvisory_economy_200901.pdf.

Lawrence, S. and Mukai, R. (2011a) *Key Facts on Mission Investing*, New York: Foundation Center. www.foundationcenter.org/gainknowledge/research/pdf/keyfacts_missioninvesting2011.pdf.

Letts, C. W., William P. R., and Grossman, A. (1999) *High Performance Nonprofit Organizations*, New York: John Wiley.

Lindblom, L. (2010) *Changing Corporate Behavior through Shareholder Activism: The Nathan Cummings Foundation's Experience*. New York: The Nathan Cummings Foundation. www.nathancummings.org/sites/default/files/Changing%20Corporate%20Behavior%20thru%20Shareholder%20Activism.pdf [Accessed 25 September 2015].

Mary Reynolds Babcock Foundation (2011) *Community Development Financial Institutions: A Study on Growth and Sustainability*. Winston-Salem, NC: Mary Reynolds Babcock Foundation. www.missioninvestors.org/system/files/tools/community-development-financial-institutions-a-study-on-growth-and-sustainability-bethany-e-chaney-for-the-mary-reynolds-babcock-foundation.pdf.

Medina Foundation (2012) *Current Initiatives*, Seattle: Medina Foundation. www.medinafoundation.org/index.php?p=Economic_Opportunity&s=89.

Minkoff, D. (2002) 'The Emergence of Hybrid Organizational Forms: Combining Identity-Based Service Provision and Political Action', *Nonprofit and Voluntary Sector Quarterly*, 31: 377–401.

Morino, M. (2011) *Leap of Reason: Managing to Outcomes in an Era of Scarcity*, Washington, DC: Venture Philanthropy Partners.

Preston, C. (2012) 'Getting Back More Than A Warm Feeling,' *The New York Times*, 8 November 2012, www.nytimes.com/2012/11/09/giving/investors-profit-by-giving-through-social-impact-bonds.html?pagewanted=all.

Rockefeller Foundation (2008) *Alliance for a Green Revolution in Africa*. New York: Rockefeller Foundation, www.rockefellerfoundation.org/our-work/initiatives/alliance-for-a-green-revolution-in-africa/ [Accessed 25 September 2015].

Roeger, K. L., Blackwood, A. S., and Pettijohn, S. L. (2012) *The Nonprofit Almanac 2012*, Washington, DC: Urban Institute Press.

Salamon, L. M. (2014) *Leverage for Good: An Introduction to the New Frontiers of Philanthropy and Social Investment*, New York: Oxford University Press.

Schmalbeck, R. (2004–2005) 'Reconsidering Private Foundation Investment Limitations', *Tax Law Review*, 58: 59–110.

Skelcher, C. (2004) 'Public-Private Partnerships and Hybridity', in E. Fairlie, L. E. Lynn Jr. and C. Pollitt (eds.) *The Oxford Handbook of Public Management*, London: Oxford University Press.

—— (2009) 'What Do We Mean When We Talk About Hybrids?' Paper for network research workshop.

Skelcher, C. and Smith, S. R. (2014) 'Theorizing Hybridity: Institutional Logics, Complex Organizations, and Actor Identities: The Case Of Nonprofits', *Public Administration*, DOI: 10.1111/padm.12105.

Smith, S. R. (2010) 'Foundations and Public Policy', in H. K. Anheier and D. H. Hammack (eds.) *American Foundations: Roles and Responsibilities*, Washington, DC: Brookings.

Social Finance (2014) *Peterborough Social Impact Bond Reduces Re-Offending by 8.4%; Investors on Course for Repayment in 2016*. www.rockefellerfoundation.org/uploads/files/a5de37d9-f46d-40b8-859c-2dcbdbc6098f-peterborough.pdf.

Swack, M. (2009) *Expanding Philanthropy: Mission-Related Investing at the F. B. Heron Foundation*. New York: F. B. Heron Foundation. www.missioninvestors.org/system/files/tools/case-study-expanding-philanthropy-mission-related-investing-at-the-fb-heron-foundation-michael-swack-jack-northrup-and-janet-prince-southern-new-hampshire-university-school-of-community-econ-devo.pdf.

U.S. Department of Treasury (2011) *Report to Congress on Supporting Organizations and Donor Advised Funds*. www.treasury.gov/resource-center/tax-policy/Documents/Supporting-Organizations-and-Donor-Advised-Funds-12-5-11.pdf.

Wertheimer, D. (2011) 'Maximizing the Impact and Amplifying the Voice of Philanthropy', *Responsive Philanthropy* (Fall): 1–6. www.ncrp.org/files/rp-articles/Responsive%20Philanthropy_Fall11_Homelessness.pdf.

Wood, D., Thornley, B. and Grace, K. (2012) *Impact at Scale: Policy Innovation for Institutional Investment with Social and Environmental Benefit*, Insight at Pacific Community Ventures and the Initiative. www.rockefellerfoundation.org/news/publications/impact-scale-policy-innovation.

21

Entrepreneurial philanthropy

Jillian Gordon, Charles Harvey, Eleanor Shaw and Mairi Maclean

Wealthy entrepreneurs have long been involved in large-scale philanthropy (Bradley, 1987; Chernow, 1998; Nasaw, 2006; Fleishman, 2007; Harvey *et al.*, 2011). Individuals of historic stature, like Andrew Carnegie, Andrew Mellon and John D. Rockefeller, are remembered as much for their social innovations as their business prowess. More recently, research has suggested a revival in the engagement of super wealthy entrepreneurs in ambitious projects for social renewal (Schervish, 2003, 2005; Handy and Handy, 2006; Bishop and Green, 2008). Bill Gates and Warren Buffet have emerged as champions of the new wave of mega-philanthropy following their union in 2006 when Buffet gifted $31 billion to the Bill and Melinda Gates Foundation. The duo subsequently went on to create the Giving Pledge in 2010, declaring their intention to dispose of the greater part of their wealth philanthropically, and inviting others to pledge the same. All of this has encouraged the media to pay more attention to super wealthy individuals and their involvement in philanthropy. Indeed, these individuals now enjoy celebrity-like status (Bishop and Green, 2008). The academic discourse, in contrast, has, bar some exceptions, largely remained silent on the issue (Acs and Phillips, 2002; Schervish, 2003, 2005; Desai and Acs, 2007).

In this chapter, we focus on the philanthropic activities of high net worth (HNW) entrepreneurs who are involved in substantial acts of philanthropy, at home and abroad. Such individuals are referred to as 'entrepreneurial philanthropists'. Entrepreneurial philanthropy is defined as the 'pursuit by entrepreneurs on a nonprofit basis of big social objectives through active investment of their economic, cultural, social and symbolic resources' (Harvey *et al.*, 2011: 428). Importantly, entrepreneurial philanthropists do not view philanthropy simply as giving away their personal funds. Rather, they view philanthropy as a mechanism to invest excess wealth to orchestrate social change on a large scale; they envisage to achieve this through application of their business know-how and they aim for measurable social returns on investment. To achieve social change on that scale, entrepreneurial philanthropists operate within the extra-corporate networks that span the domains of business, politics, government, charities and philanthropy. Admission to such circles is related to, and dependent on, their power and standing within the economic domain.

The chapter begins with a discussion of the historical context of entrepreneurial philanthropy, focusing on the influential ideas and pioneering endeavours of Andrew Carnegie. This is followed by a theoretical discussion of the phenomenon of entrepreneurial philanthropy, in which entrepreneurial philanthropists are viewed as capital-rich, hyperagents (Schervish, 2003, 2005) with the wherewithal and capabilities needed to promote social change. As hyperagents, entrepreneurial philanthropists have access to the circuits of power that bind the upper echelons of society. This space is referred to within the academic discourse as the field of power (Bourdieu, 1996; Maclean *et al.*, 2010). We use Bourdieu's (1996) capital theory as a theoretical lens through which to view the different types of resources applied in entrepreneurial philanthropy. In addition, Schervish's (2003, 2005) hyperagency theory is drawn upon to explain the nature of the phenomenon. This is followed by an analysis of contemporary entrepreneurial philanthropy in the UK drawing on data, including personal interviews, with entrepreneurial philanthropists. The implications are then discussed and provisional conclusions drawn.

Historical context of entrepreneurial philanthropy

Entrepreneurial philanthropy is not new. One only has to look back and consider the exploits of Andrew Carnegie, John D. Rockefeller, Titus Salt, and William Hesketh Lever, to see that successful entrepreneurs may extend their reach from the economic to the social realm. It is therefore best viewed as an evolving phenomenon, with entrepreneurship and philanthropy firmly entwined, and wherein the values and dispositions associated with entrepreneurship permeate philanthropic practice.

The career of Andrew Carnegie is illustrative. Carnegie was a renowned industrialist and philanthropist from humble Scottish origins who had migrated with his family to the US as a young boy. The son of a handloom weaver, Carnegie progressed from bobbin boy in a cotton mill to telegraph operator, railways manager, bond salesman and founder of the market dominant steel company that, when sold to JP Morgan in 1901, became US Steel. Carnegie's meteoric career is already well-documented (Hendrick, 1932; Livesay, 1977; Nasaw, 2006). His vast wealth was secured through a strategy of growth through continuous reinvestment in an integrated cluster of businesses based around Pittsburgh. Large profits and the proceeds from the sale of the company funded his philanthropic ventures. While these expanded greatly in scale and scope between 1901 and 1914 (Nasaw, 2006; Harvey *et al.*, 2011), Carnegie's philanthropic activities had begun decades earlier in 1873, when he gifted an organ to his former church. This was followed in 1874 by the gift of swimming baths to Dunfermline, his hometown in Scotland. He went on to pay for thousands of church organs in the belief that music had a civilizing effect on society; he also built thousands of libraries for the masses across North America, Britain and the British Empire. In this, he was inspired by personal experience and the idea that access to books was a source of personal liberation and social advancement (Nasaw, 2006). He built and stocked libraries with the proviso that the municipal authorities paid for their upkeep, restocking and running costs, ensuring continuation once the capital he had provided was exhausted.

Carnegie was a gifted self-publicist, writing extensively about the relationship between wealth creation and philanthropy, most famously in the *Gospel of Wealth* (Carnegie, 2006). Through his writings, Carnegie acknowledged that economic progress had led to the means of productions being concentrated in the hands of the few, resulting in the growth of income inequality, which caused envy and threatened to undermine society. He viewed philanthropy as a mechanism that might help maintain social harmony (Karl and Katz, 1987). Carnegie's moral stance is captured in his famous dictum: 'The man who dies thus rich dies disgraced' (Carnegie, 2006: 12). Carnegie's worldview is one which contemporary philanthropists have embraced. Individuals like Sir Tom Hunter, Bill Gates and Warren Buffett have publicly expressed their wish to follow in the footsteps of Carnegie, disposing philanthropically of the majority of their fortunes whilst still living – giving rise to the slogan 'giving while living' and reference to them as 'Carnegie's children' (Bishop and Green, 2008).

Carnegie is thus viewed as a pioneer of entrepreneurial philanthropy, both as practitioner and moral philosopher (Harvey et al., 2011). Generally, he put more than money into his projects. His contribution to the international peace movement, for example, involved writing, public speaking, organizing high-profile events, pressing for legislative changes, negotiating international agreements and seeking the support of governments and heads of states (Harvey et al., 2011: 425). He was highly focused in his philanthropy and most often rejected unsolicited requests for help (Nasaw, 2006). Moreover, he responded to perceived social needs innovatively: he established Hero Funds to reward self-sacrifice on the part of ordinary men and women and pension funds to help attract talented people to teach in universities and colleges (Wall, 1970). His lasting legacy was the Carnegie Corporation of New York, established in 1911 to administer the remainder of his personal fortune, and to promote his long-term interests in higher education, libraries, research and international peace. Carnegie's approach to philanthropy serves in many respects as a model for the entrepreneurial philanthropists of today. He is estimated to have made philanthropic investments worth $9.12 billion (in 2010 prices) during his lifetime (Harvey et al., 2011: 427) and died true to his word, having relieved himself and his family of what he regarded as the ethical burden of trust that came with colossal wealth.

Theoretical perspectives on entrepreneurship, power and philanthropy

A necessary component of entrepreneurial philanthropy is access to considerable personal wealth, most typically amassed over the course of a business career. Often, such individuals have risen to become dominant actors within their industry; they have acquired considerable power stemming from command over substantial resources (Clegg et al., 2006). This elite category of entrepreneurs controls key technologies and know-how, and they pursue dominant business strategies frequently involving mergers and acquisitions (Chandler, 1977; Harvey et al., 2011). A distinguishing feature of such individuals is their capacity to learn quickly and respond flexibly to changing situations and opportunities; they demonstrate the 'knack' of correctly reading the future trajectory of industries and business sectors (Cope, 2005). The entrepreneurial businesses they create are fast changing and adapt continuously in response to interactions with customers, suppliers, competitors and partners (Chia, 2002; Tsoukas and Chia, 2002). Considering the extensive resources they command, and the power it confers on them, it is instructive to explore the different types of resources at their disposal.

To this end, Bourdieu's theory of capital serves as a useful theoretical framework. Bourdieu (1986) asserts that the most powerful members of society have an abundance of four forms of capital – economic, social, cultural and symbolic – which they use to maintain and extend their reach within society. He argues that economic capital is the most important: it can be converted readily into each of the other forms of capital. Figure 21.1 depicts each of the four forms of capital that elite entrepreneurs possess, and signifies their interaction, cash serving as the medium of exchange that facilitates capital conversion.

Economic capital includes both tangible and nontangible assets, such as buildings, plant and equipment, patents, organizational routines and the systems that facilitate production. Cultural capital refers to the knowledge, know-how and capabilities of the entrepreneur, their employees and business associates. Social capital refers to networks, contacts, relationships and alliances, which have a productive value. The fourth form of capital is symbolic, and refers to the reputation and status of the entrepreneur and their organizations, which facilitate trust in partners, suppliers, customers and regulators. Importantly, symbolic capital is a powerful silent resource that can be used

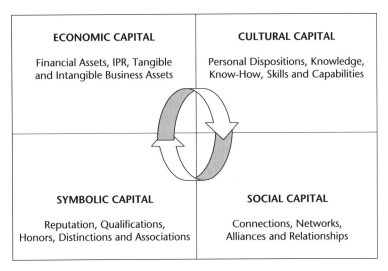

Figure 21.1 Forms of entrepreneurial capital and the accumulation process

Source: [Harvey *et al.*, 2011: 429]

to create belief within the business community and markets about the capabilities of entrepreneurs and firms (Maclean *et al.*, 2006; Harvey and Maclean, 2008).

The accumulation of different forms of capital is integral to the advancing fortunes of the most successful entrepreneurs. It is equally important to the practice of entrepreneurial philanthropy, which, rather than constituting a discrete life world, is best regarded as a natural extension of prior accumulative tendencies. Whilst there may be no direct economic return from engagement in philanthropy, as Figure 21.2 suggests, there may be positive returns with respect to social, cultural and symbolic capital, which indirectly might yield economic returns. The model helps to explain how capital can be accumulated and deployed in the process of entrepreneurial philanthropy (Bourdieu, 1986; Erikson, 2002; Firkin, 2003; Shaw *et al.*, 2008). It also helps to explain how entrepreneurial dispositions impact on philanthropic practices. Furthermore, and importantly, the notions of convertibility, accumulation and deployment lead us to the notion that capital and the exercise of power are fundamental to hyperagency.

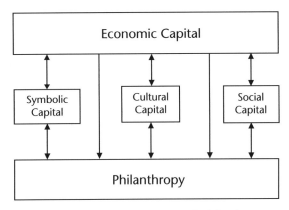

Figure 21.2 A capital theoretic model of entrepreneurial philanthropy

Source: [Harvey *et al.*, 2011: 432]

Building on Bourdieu's (1986) argument that the truly powerful in society have an abundance of all four forms of capital, the theoretical concept of hyperagency, posited by Schervish (2003, 2005), emphasizes the transformative potential of agents with command over significant resources. The transformative capacity of an individual is a function of personal wealth viewed broadly: 'Wealth holders are uniquely endowed with material resources and cognitive dispositions that enable them, both as a group and as individuals to fashion outcomes that they desire' (Schervish, 2003: 9). Given the ability of entrepreneurial philanthropists to draw on multiple forms of capital, it is suggested here that their ability to move seamlessly between the fields of business, politics and development is the hallmark of their status as hyperagents. This is exemplified by Sir Tom Hunter, a Scottish businessman who has partnered with former President Clinton on philanthropic projects in Rwanda and Malawi. The creation of the Clinton Hunter Development Initiative symbolizes the union of the distinctive resources of each partner, a powerful combination when striving to bring about widespread social and economic change:

> Partnering with President Clinton means we have been invited into these countries by their presidents, as guests and supporters of these countries. We call it Venture Philanthropy. We do see it as an investment. I don't see it as giving money away — I am a Scotsman after all! We do want a return on our investment but it's a different sort of return — in Africa the return is if we raise per capita GD.
>
> (*Sir Tom Hunter, The Financial Times, 7th December 2006*)

The Clinton Hunter initiative illustrates the workings of capital theory (Bourdieu, 1986) and hyperagency (Schervish, 2003; 2005); both are valuable tools for the exploration of contemporary entrepreneurial philanthropy, as demonstrated in the research findings reported below.

Researching entrepreneurial philanthropy

The findings presented here stem from a research project on entrepreneurial philanthropy that incorporates three main parts. The first is a database of 100 UK based entrepreneurs engaged in philanthropy. The data are drawn from seven discrete sources and relate to age, family, social class, religion, educational attainment, sources of wealth, philanthropic targets, philanthropic spend, networks and distinctions for the period of 2007–2010. Analysis of such data allows a picture to be built up of the different types of capital possessed by entrepreneurial philanthropists. Three criteria were applied to determine who should be included in the project database: first, individuals must have amassed their fortune through business; second, they had to have a minimum net worth of £10 million in 2007; third, their cumulative philanthropic spend must have been at least £1 million by 2007. The second part of the research is a series of life-history interviews conducted with 30 entrepreneurial philanthropists, 15 executives of philanthropic foundations, and 15 wealth managers and other experts in the field. The third part of the research is ten in-depth case studies based upon multiple sources of data: interviews, documents, websites, observation, and in two cases, participant observation. In adopting this three-part approach to gathering fieldwork data, we have endeavoured to examine the phenomenon of entrepreneurial phenomenon holistically, mapping out its form and extent while drilling down to consider questions relating to motivation, ideology and method. In what follows, we selectively present some indicative findings using capital theory as the organizing analytical device.

Foci of entrepreneurial philanthropy

It is near universal for entrepreneurs to focus their philanthropy on education, children and young people, healthcare, citizenship and the creation of economic opportunity. The emphasis geographically is on the UK and developing countries in Africa. In the UK there are numerous initiatives and programs to support young people aged between 16 and 24 to improve their job prospects by providing targeted education and training programs that might lead them to take up paid work. Entrepreneurs commonly believe that education can empower young people to aim higher. Significant philanthropic investments have been made in the development of school curricula that incorporate leadership and enterprise components. Leadership initiatives are not targeted solely at young people, but also at those who are charged with their education. A considerable number of entrepreneurial philanthropists target their efforts at strengthening the leadership skills of teachers and head teachers. Combining enterprise and leadership is intended as a means to getting more young people to embrace business as a career. They also aim to develop a sense of citizenship in young people. The overarching aim of such programmes is to encourage young people to strive to make a positive contribution to society. The following quote is illustrative:

> Our programmes are focussed on trying to enhance citizenship, trying to enhance young people's understanding of the problems in our society, what they can do to help, trying to enhance tolerance, to enable young kids to live in a non-prejudiced way and accepting people.
>
> *(EP, Case 1)*

The African continent attracts significant resources from UK-based entrepreneurial philanthropists. Eight out of the ten of our case study foundations have philanthropic interests in one or more African countries, only two are focused solely on the UK. The areas being targeted include poverty alleviation, healthcare, education, economic infrastructure, routes to market for local products, and creation employment opportunities, as illustrated by the following quote.

> Internationally, it is focussed on how can we help people help themselves … we try and create economic activity, try and create enterprise, try and create employment, try and give a family the ability to earn money to pay for the education of their children, to buy food for their kids and all the other things they should do.
>
> *(EP, Case 1)*

This resonates closely with the sentiments expressed in the earlier quote by Sir Tom Hunter about his philanthropic activities in Africa, where the emphasis is placed on achieving a return that equates to an increase in the GDP of the country. The themes of helping people to help themselves, and of empowerment, recur throughout each of the case studies. The philanthropists are piloting and funding programs across the spectrum, often in partnership with national governments, international organizations, private businesses, nongovernment organizations and local grassroots organizations. In taking such an approach, the entrepreneurial philanthropists are able to hold sway over policymakers and leverage resources beyond their own. The specific forms of capital deployed in entrepreneurial philanthropy are discussed further in what follows.

Deployment of economic capital

The voluntary transfer of economic capital is what most people identify as being at the heart of philanthropy (Fleishman, 2007). Yet, while much attention is lavished on the personal wealth

Table 21.1 Foundation expenditure and personal wealth

Case	Funding Model	*Spend in 2008	*Spend in 2009	**Estimated wealth in 2008
Case 1	Endowment	£7,009,321	£12,214,000	£890,000,000
Case 2	Endowment and funds retained in a venture capital fund until required	£11,443,749	£8,173,541	£1,000,000,000
Case 3	Foundation income derives from an investment vehicle income	£33,775, 210	£27,438,186	£110,000,000

Sources: *Foundation annual reports.**Sunday Times* Rich List 2008.

of successful entrepreneurs, less attention is given to the amount of money actually redistributed through philanthropy. Our research suggests that while the deployment of economic capital is very important, it is not always the most important form of capital brought to bear in entrepreneurial philanthropy. By their own testimony, entrepreneurial philanthropists place considerable emphasis on their know-how, connections, personal credentials and strategic ability. Nevertheless, the cash they invest in philanthropic projects is substantial. This can be seen in Table 21.1. This provides headline financial details for our three largest case study foundations, ranked by philanthropic spend: investments in individual programmes of between £250,000 and £6 million are typical.

Table 21.1 suggests that philanthropic spend relative to personal wealth has to date been relatively small for two of the three foundations. The exception is Case 3 for which the income of the foundation is linked to a corporate financial investment vehicle. The first case foundation by contrast is funded from endowment income. The founder made an initial investment of £50 million and intends to increase this in due course. The entrepreneur behind the second foundation has pursued a third course. In this case, the cash earmarked for philanthropic purposes is invested in the founder's venture capital fund, and income is drawn down into the foundation when required to fund specific projects.

Deployment of social capital

The importance of know-who is a prominent theme in the study. An analysis of our database of 100 UK entrepreneurs engaged in philanthropy reveals that, on average, each individual has three influential contacts. An influential contact is defined as someone who, within their circle, is in a position of significant power (Useem, 1979). Such influential contacts are spread across diverse fields, including politics, philanthropy, business, finance, media, sport, entertainment, education, the environment and the arts. Of particular interest are the names of influential individuals from the field of politics like Bill Clinton, Nelson Mandela, Kofi Anan and Tony Blair. Furthermore, the names of all three major UK political party leaders in 2010 are identified 24 times within the dataset, suggesting that ownership of political social capital is of particular relevance to this set of elite entrepreneurs. This implies that the entrepreneurs seek to accumulate social capital to strengthen their political power base and capacity for purposeful action. The interconnected symbolic dimension cannot be ignored; association with key political contacts enhances the symbolic capital of entrepreneur within the domain of philanthropy. The productive value of social capital is well established within the academic discourse (Burt, 1997; Jack *et al.*, 2004; Maclean, 2008; Jack, 2010), as Coleman states 'the function identified by the concept of social capital is the value of these aspects of the social structure to actors as resources that they can use to achieve their interests' (Coleman, 1988: 101). Another interesting aspect is that 19 of the 100 entrepreneurs share at least one influential contact confirming the density of the networks in which they are embedded. But how specifically is social capital deployed in pursuit of philanthropic ends?

The case studies suggest that the productive value of social capital is two-fold. First, social capital is applied to secure access to additional financial resources. In the third of our case studies, social capital has helped win additional funding for initiatives from business, charitable trusts and government agencies. In Case 2, political connections have proved valuable in securing additional funding to prolong the life of enterprise education programs in UK schools. Second, philanthropists use their social capital in order to gain access to knowledge and expertise relevant to the specific issues they are targeting. The following quotes are illustrative:

> Our understanding with governments is that if we take something on we agree what success looks like and if our independent evaluation says that has been achieved the government can take it on as policy.
>
> *(EP, Case 2)*

> (Name of person) is very accomplished; he has been a very successful government minister for the UK; we have had a number of conversations and the partners have had a number of conversations with them about embedding our programme.
>
> *(EP, Case 1)*

These quotes illustrate the important role that political capital plays in entrepreneurial philanthropy in attracting funding and influencing government policies. This suggests that the entrepreneurs are strategic networkers, who target potential contacts who might help realize their philanthropic vision. Importantly, this also suggests business practices, which have facilitated the growth of business ventures, are carried over and applied within the philanthropic domain.

Deployment of cultural capital

Cultural capital is described by Bourdieu (1986) as existing in three forms: embodied (personal disposition), objectified (cultural goods) and institutionalized (certifications and credentials). Analysis of our database demonstrates that entrepreneurial philanthropists are rich in institutionalized cultural capital. This is reflected in the array of educational qualifications listed in Table 21.2.

Analysis of the institutions awarding the qualifications reveals that a majority of the undergraduate-level degrees were awarded by institutions within the elite Russell Group of research intensive universities, as were all of the awards of doctorates. Likewise, all of the MBAs

Table 21.2 Educational qualifications of philanthropists

Highest Qualification	N=100
None	25
Undergraduate degree	52
Master of Business Administration	13
Other Master's degree	6
Doctor of Philosophy	4

Source: Shaw *et al.* (2011: 12)

were awarded by US Ivy League universities, with Harvard the pre-eminent source awarding seven degrees. This suggests that the philanthropists are rich in cultural capital and that this is likely to have been influential with respect to their subsequent engagement in philanthropy. Another interesting feature is the interrelation of cultural capital with the social capital and symbolic capital that derives from attending elite educational institutions.

In numerous publications, Bourdieu (1977, 1986, 1998) proposes that embodied social capital is acquired through *habitus*, of dispositions being formed through regular experience of practices within distinct fields. The idea is that the tendency to behave in stereotypical ways is a consequence of living and working within particular contexts, such as families and organizations that operate as structuring-structures. According to this view, it is unsurprising that entrepreneurial dispositions first manifested in business carry over into the philanthropic domain, as highlighted by the following quotes:

> What I am good at is the skills needed in running a business, dealing with people and trying to work a way around problems. I have no natural skills in philanthropy. I don't actually know what it means. I mean, a philanthropist is a person who tries to help other people. Yes, that is my intention; but I am doing it as a business person.
>
> *(EP, Case 1)*

> It is a business-like approach, it is determining at the outset what you want to achieve … agreeing what success looks like over a period of time and then breaking it into manageable chunks.
>
> *(EP, Case 2)*

> In applying business principles (to our philanthropy) we expect a return; we only want to do programmes that have the highest value.
>
> *(EP, Case 3)*

These quotes suggest that the practice of entrepreneurial philanthropy requires a level of engagement that moves beyond the traditional identification of philanthropy with the writing of large cheques; confirming the attraction of performance measurement and accountability as central to the practice of entrepreneurial philanthropy alongside the desire to achieve impact and transformational change.

Deployment of symbolic capital

Symbolic capital is the fourth type of capital deployed by entrepreneurial philanthropists. An analysis of the 100 UK entrepreneurs in our database shows, as displayed in Table 21.3, that there is significant ownership of symbolic capital.

This highlights the numerous types of symbolic capital possessed by the entrepreneurs. Overall, 40 have been awarded state honours and more than a half have been recognized by universities, most commonly through the award of an honorary doctorate. This is hardly coincidental as 51 of the 100 entrepreneurs have made education the main target of their philanthropy. In recognizing that there is a symbolic value attached to receiving awards and distinctions, the fact that over half of the sample has received business awards suggests that the philanthropists were already held in high esteem in businesses. In addition, eight have received awards for their philanthropy and three have received the Beacon Prize, the UK award celebrating giving that has had significant impact. Those interviewed confirmed their wish to be recognized for their

Table 21.3 Titles, honours and awards

Type of award	No.
Knighthood	13
Commander of the Order of British Empire (CBE)	11
Officer of the Order of the British Empire (OBE)	13
Member of the Order of the British Empire (MBE)	3
Honorary Doctorates	44
Russell Group Fellowships	10
Beacon Prize Winners	3
Business Awards	52
Awards for Philanthropy	8

Source: Shaw *et al.* (2011: 15)

philanthropy and not simply for being successful in business. One interviewee put it most succinctly:

> I think excessive consumption and excessive wealth are distasteful. If you have got excessive wealth and you are doing something with it then it becomes excusable ... Philanthropy has given me a second career; I wouldn't like to be part of this world and just thought of as (an entrepreneur). I mean when you are trying to be a bloody good entrepreneur, it sounds great, but when you are a bloody good entrepreneur it sounds a bit hollow when people ask you what you did with your life.
>
> *(Philanthropist 8)*

These comments suggest that for some, legitimacy depends on having done more than make a lot of money (Maclean *et al.*, 2012). The drive to create and accumulate wealth may remain important for these individuals, but this motivation gains in meaning and becomes a greater source of satisfaction when allied to a philanthropic purpose:

> Philanthropy is a very fulfilling engagement. Being able to change things for the better is hugely fulfilling and I suppose it has refocused our money making because I don't make money for the sake of making money. Those material goals have now been satisfied. I am making money now for the foundation, which is a great motivator and it has made us even more focused on making money.
>
> *(EP, Case 1)*

Discussion

Entrepreneurial philanthropy, we propose, is distinguished from large-scale charitable giving by wealthy individuals in three crucial respects. First, entrepreneurial philanthropists are not passive respondents to requests for support for a cause promoted by others. They are distinguished by identifying pressing social needs and devising innovative solutions. They seek, according to their own lights, to bring about beneficial social change that might be sustained in the long run. In other words, entrepreneurial philanthropists are would-be hyperagents who seek to fashion the world ideologically and practically in ways that seem desirable to them. Second, entrepreneurial philanthropy is not about relieving the symptoms of social problems but about addressing root causes such as disease, ignorance and lack of employment. The governing idea is the need to provide sustainable solutions to deep-seated economic and social problems. The preferred solutions invariably favoured by entrepreneurial philanthropists are those of the market and free enterprise. Their work is not designed to weaken, displace or compensate for the failings of capitalism, but to strengthen it at the grassroots level by fostering the conditions in which market economics might fully prosper. Hence, they insist in all their projects on the implementation of business practices, including that due emphasis is given to measurable outcomes, rates of return on investment, accountability and growth. They mean to make a difference for individuals, communities and nations rather than tinkering at the edges. Third, entrepreneurial philanthropists invest more than money in their projects. Financial resources are important in getting things off the ground and increasing the scale of activities, but at the same time, they invest knowledge, connections, and their reputation and high standing to bring projects to fruition.

The ethical and philosophical underpinnings of entrepreneurial philanthropy were first articulated by Andrew Carnegie in the *Gospel of Wealth* (2006). Carnegie, as we know from his biographer, David Nasaw (2006), was badly stung by the charge that he and other leading industrialists were 'Robber Barons' who, through the exercise of monopoly power, had kept prices high and wages low to the detriment of the common man. He, as a disciple of the Social Darwinist Herbert Spencer, saw it differently. He and his ilk had risen to the top not through monopoly but by competing aggressively in fast-changing markets. This had meant recognizing the need to employ the best technologies and increase the scale of production to drive down costs and prices, so expanding markets and benefiting society at large by distributing the fruits of rising productivity. As a consequence, production had become concentrated in the hands of fewer and fewer companies, like Carnegie Steel and Standard Oil; the owners of these enterprises had grown vastly rich. Such riches, Carnegie conceded, were not the product of individual genius and could not be ethically justified: they were an unjust side effect of a liberating and highly effective capitalist system. The remedy was not to destroy the system because it produced inordinately wealthy individuals, but for those entrepreneurs to deploy their financial resources and business acumen in the pursuit of ambitious social goals. By investing in education, health, culture and other socially desirable projects, entrepreneurial philanthropists might help renew and promote a more inclusive society: the logical and ethical presuppositions underpinning this vision apply just as much to the position of Microsoft and Bill Gates today as they did to Carnegie Steel and Carnegie in the later nineteenth century. Situation, solution and public utterances all bear a striking resemblance.

Entrepreneurial philanthropy plainly has arisen in the context of acute inequalities in income and wealth that result from capitalist economic development. On the one hand, power and resources become concentrated in the hands of the few to create the possibility of large-scale private intervention in social affairs (Desai and Acs, 2007; Harvey, 2010). On the other hand, the observable differences in life chances and living standards that result from economic inequality provoke in socially minded entrepreneurs the desire to make things better for others. This coming together of means and motivation induce the socially-minded to look to philanthropy as a means of putting something back into society (Lloyd, 2004). Tax advantages and normative pressures amongst peer groups of wealthy entrepreneurs lend momentum to the process such that in some societies entrepreneurial philanthropy has become established as a social movement. This can be seen across the US, more patchily in the UK and other parts of Europe, and is now evident, albeit selectively, in rapidly developing economies like India. What this movement stands for in essence is capitalism with a social conscience. Its values are those of free markets, free trade, individual liberty, efficiency, economic growth, and protection of property rights. The role of entrepreneurial philanthropy is ultimately to enable all members of society to enter the game, fulfil their potential, and make economic and social progress in life.

The idealism inherent in entrepreneurial philanthropy is evident, and there is no reason to believe that the majority of entrepreneurial philanthropists do not act in good faith. This fact should not disguise the downside, contradictions and limitations of the movement. The most obvious downside is that entrepreneurial philanthropy compounds elitism. In extending their reach from the economic to the social domain entrepreneurial philanthropists hold sway over public policy, and by seeking to augment their own resources by those of governments, they divert taxpayer resources to their own, albeit social rather than private, ends. The biggest contradiction is that when entrepreneurs become philanthropists, they are likely to gain personally from the investments they make. The cash and other resources they put into projects can yield significant returns in terms of cultural, social and symbolic capital, which in turn can benefit the businesses they own. The marginal utility of each additional unit of income may be near zero for the super wealthy who have reached the limits of consumption and craving for financial security, but, at the same time, the value placed on status, recognition and legitimacy rises in proportion to their degree of separation from the common man (Maclean et al., 2012). Herein lies a paradox: the seemingly invulnerable titans of capitalism are increasingly exposed to feelings of detachment from society and seek to legitimize their disproportionate share of power and resources by recognition of their social worth by others through receipt of state honours and other distinctions (Maclean et al., 2010). Beyond this, there are limits to the movement which empirical research has only recently begun to investigate. We do not know, for example, the ratio between the amount invested philanthropically by the super wealthy and the amount retained for private purposes. Relevant computations are made problematic by privacy laws and the fact that market movements cause asset values regularly to move upwards and downwards. Moreover, we do not know how many members of the super wealthy elite are actively engaged in large-scale philanthropy compared to the numbers who, if we accept philanthropy as a collective source of legitimacy (Maclean et al., 2012), benefit from their more munificent peers. These and other equally interesting questions await further research.

Conclusion

Entrepreneurial philanthropy is a research field which is currently underexplored and clearly undertheorized. But it is, we suggest, a topic which is vitally important in the present context of rising inequalities exacerbated by ever deeper cuts to government funding. The field demands further research in a number of critical areas. First, further study is needed to explore the impact that entrepreneurial philanthropy can have at a local level, investigating the positive role that it can play in helping to regenerate deprived communities through small-scale entrepreneurial projects of social benefit (Maclean et al., 2013). Second, more research is needed which examines entrepreneurial philanthropy from an international perspective, transcending national boundaries so that lessons learned do not remain hemmed in, within and confined to particular cultural contexts. Finally, further study is required to enhance understanding of historical perspectives on entrepreneurial philanthropy (Harvey et al., 2011) so that exemplars from the past may continue to enlighten us in the present and future.

References

Acs, Z. J. and Phillips, R. J. (2002) 'Entrepreneurship and philanthropy in American capitalism', *Small Business Economics*, 19(3): 189–204.

Bishop, M. and Green, M. (2008) *How the rich can save the world: Philanthro-capitalism*, New York: Bloomsbury.

Bourdieu, P. (1977) *Outline of a theory of practice*, Cambridge: Cambridge University Press.

—— (1986) 'The forms of capital', in J. Richardson (ed) *The handbook of theory and research for the sociology of education*, New York: Greenwood Press.

—— (1996) *The state nobility*, Cambridge: Polity.

—— (1998) *Practical reason – a theory of action*, Polity Press, Blackwell Publishers Ltd.

Bradley, I. C. (1987) *Enlightened entrepreneurs*, London: Weidenfeld & Nicholson.

Burt, R. S. (1997) 'The contingent value of social capital', *Administrative Science Quarterly*, 42(2): 339–65.

Carnegie, A. (2006) *The gospel of wealth essays and other writings*, D. Nasaw (ed), New York: Penguin.

Chandler, A. D. (1977) *The visible hand: The managerial revolution in American business*, Cambridge, MA: Harvard University Press.

Chernow, R. (1998) *Titan: The life of John D. Rockefeller*, New York: Random House.

Chia, R. (2002) 'Essay: Time, duration and simultaneity: Rethinking process and change in organizational analysis', *Organization Studies*, 23(6): 863–8.

Clegg, S. R., Courpasson, D. and Philips, N. (2006) *Power and organizations*, London: Sage.

Coleman, J. S. (1988) 'Social capital in the creation of human capital', *American Journal of Sociology*, 94: 95–120.

Cope, J. (2005) 'Towards a dynamic learning perspective of entrepreneurship', *Entrepreneurship Theory and Practice*, 29(4): 373–97.

Desai, S. and Acs, Z. J. (2007) 'Democratic capitalism and philanthropy in a global economy', in Z. J. Acs and R. R. Stough (eds) *Public policy in an entrepreneurial economics*, New York: Springer.

Erikson, T. (2002) 'Entrepreneurial capital: The emerging venture's most important asset and competitive advantage', *Journal of Business Venturing*, 17(3): 275–90.

Firkin, P. (2003) 'Entrepreneurial capital', in A. De Bruin and A. Dupuis (eds) *Entrepreneurship: New perspectives in a global age*, Aldershot: Ashgate Publishing.

Fleishman, J. (2007) *The foundation: A great American secret: How private wealth is changing the world*, New York: Perseus Book Group.

Handy, C. and Handy, E. (2006) *The new philanthropists: The new generosity*, London: William Heinemann.

Harvey, C. and Maclean, M. (2008) 'Capital theory and the dynamics of elite business networks in Britain and France', *The Sociological Review*, 56(S1): 105–20.

Harvey, C., Maclean, M., Gordon, J. and Shaw, E. (2011) 'Andrew Carnegie and the foundations of contemporary entrepreneurial philanthropy', *Business History*, 53(3): 425–50.

Harvey, D. (2010) *The enigma of capital and the crisis of capitalism*, London: Profile Books.

Hendrick, B. J. (1932) *The life of Andrew Carnegie (Vols 1 & 2)*, New York: Doubleday.

Jack, S. L. (2010) 'Approaches to studying networks: Implications and outcomes', *Journal of Business Venturing*, 25(1): 120–37.

Jack, S. L., Drakopoulou, D. S. and Anderson, A. R. (2004) 'Social structures and entrepreneurial networks: The strength of strong ties', *International Journal of Entrepreneurship and Innovation*, 5(2): 107–20.

Karl, B. D. and Katz, S. N. (1987) 'Foundations and ruling class elites', *Daedalus*, 116(1): 1–40.

Livesay, H. C. (1977) 'Entrepreneurial persistence through the bureaucratic age', *Business History Review*, 51(4): 415–43.

Lloyd, T. (2004) *Why rich people give*, London: Philanthropy UK, Association of Charitable Foundations.

Maclean, M. (2008) 'New rules – old games? Social capital and privatisation in France, 1986-1998', *Business History*, 50(6): 795–810.

Maclean, M., Harvey, C. and Press, J. (2006) *Business elites and corporate governance in France and the UK*, Basingstoke: Palgrave Macmillan.

Maclean, M., Harvey, C. and Chia, R. (2010) 'Dominant corporate agents and the power elite in France and Britain', *Organization Studies*, 31(3): 327–48.

—— (2012) 'Sensemaking, storytelling and the legitimization of elite business careers', *Human Relations*, 65(1): 17–40.

Maclean, M., Harvey, C. and Gordon, J. (2013) 'Social innovation, social entrepreneurship and the practice of contemporary entrepreneurial philanthropy', *International Small Business Journal*, forthcoming.

Nasaw, D. (2006) *Andrew Carnegie*, New York: Penguin.

Schervish, P. (2003) *Hyperagency and high tech donors: A new theory of the new philanthropists*, Boston, MA: Boston College Social Welfare Research Institute.

Schervish, P. (2005) Major motives major donors: 'The people and purposes behind major gifts', *New Directions for Philanthropic Fundraising*, 47: 49–87.

Shaw, E., Lam, W. and Carter, S. (2008) 'The role of entrepreneurial capital in building service reputation', *Service Industries Journal*, 28(7): 899–917.

Shaw, E., Harvey, C., Gordon, J. and Maclean, M. (2011) 'Exploring contemporary entrepreneurial philanthropy', *International Small Business Journal*, forthcoming.

Sunday Times (2008) *The Sunday Times* Rich List 2008.

The Financial Times (2006) 'The partnership with Bill Clinton', December 7: 16.

Tsoukas, H. and Chia, R. (2002) 'On organizational becoming: Rethinking organizational change', *Organization Science*, 13(5): 567–82.

Useem, M. (1979) 'The social organization of the American business elite and participation of corporate directors in the governance of American institutions', *American Sociological Review*, 44(4): 553–72.

Wall, J. F. (1970) *Andrew Carnegie*, New York: Oxford University Press.

Wei-Skillern, J., Austin, J. E., Leonard, H., and Stevenson, H. (2007) *Entrepreneurship in the Social Sector*, London: Sage Publications.

22

Venture philanthropy

When philanthropy meets social entrepreneurship

Jacques Defourny, Marthe Nyssens and Severine Thys

With the emergence and growth of 'venture philanthropy', the traditional, and very close, relationship between philanthropy and the nonprofit sector has seen major changes. Keen to break away from 'old fashioned' ways of philanthropy, venture philanthropists are seen as concentrating their support on innovative answers to social challenges. Rooted in the ideals of New Public Management, an approach first developed in the UK and focused on using 'knowledge and expertise acquired in business management and other disciplines to improve efficiency, effectiveness, and general performance of public services in modern bureaucracies' (Vigoda, 2003: 1; Van Haeperen, 2012), venture philanthropy tries to overcome the perceived weaknesses of traditional philanthropy and charitable actions. These are prominently spelled out in Salamon's (1987) critique of the field: 'voluntary failures', 'philanthropic amateurism and inefficiency', as well as 'philanthropic insufficiency', that is, an 'inability to generate resources on a scale that is both adequate enough and reliable enough to cope with the human service problem of an advanced industrial society' (Salamon, 1987: 111). Venture philanthropy, through its support of social enterprising claims to address some of these concerns. To this end, venture philanthropy specifically looks to, and borrows its practices and vocabulary from, the finance and venture capital field (Wei-Skillern *et al.*, 2007). As such, it moves beyond some of the ideas and ideals of entrepreneurial philanthropy discussed by Gordon and colleagues in Chapter 21.

Venture philanthropy has traditionally been seen as being closely intertwined with social enterprising: venture philanthropists look towards the activities of 'social entrepreneurs' with whom they desire to develop strong relationships and from whom they expect substantial social returns on investment (Wagner, 2002; Pepin, 2005). This is achieved through investing, not only money, but also time, skills, talent, expertise, strategic thinking and management experience (Wagner, 2002; Knott and McCarthy, 2007). Thereby, venture philanthropists focus on longer-term support for fewer projects, at times only one, launched by what they consider to be a highly promising social entrepreneur.

In this chapter, we explore the links and interactions, similarities and differences, between venture philanthropy and social enterprising. We question the often explicit and sometimes implicit overlap between venture philanthropy and social entrepreneurship. Consequently, the chapter refines our understanding of the interactions between the 'social enterprising' (SE) discourse on the one hand, consisting of theoretical approaches to, and empirical research on, social entrepreneurs, social entrepreneurship and social enterprises and venture philanthropy on the other.

The first section of the chapter is devoted to developing a more precise understanding of venture philanthropy. Thereafter, we look at the various conceptual SE approaches and assess the extent to which they give place, or perhaps even require, venture philanthropy as a major input. In the third part, we address the same question from a more pragmatic or technical point of view: in the evolution of organizations launched by social entrepreneurs, does the place and role of philanthropy vary according to actual phases of their development?

Venture philanthropy: Concepts and practices

Venture philanthropy was brought about by the arrival of a new set of actors in the philanthropy arena. Symbolized by the 'golden boys', individuals emerging from the US West Coast's IT boom or the East Coast's financial sector who had accumulated huge amounts of wealth in a relatively short timeframe, these philanthropists laid claim to a new way of giving. They refused 'old charity practices' and promoted a new philanthropy based on market principles, usually borrowed from the venture capital industry (Maximilian and John, 2007). According to Grenier (2006), the resulting perspective can be distilled into five overarching principles.

The first principle is to provide expertise alongside financial support. Venture philanthropy usually involves several resources to build institutional capacity of the beneficiary. It provides advice in a range of areas such as human management, accountability, and so on. This leads to the second focus of venture philanthropy: to promote organizational development before specific programs. This is an important difference from 'traditional charity', usually leaning more towards specific projects than on reinforcing institutional building. Another main characteristic of venture philanthropy is its focus on performance and impact assessment. Venture philanthropists want to assess the social impact of their action, looking for a social, and sometimes financial, return on their investment. For that, they try to develop methods and metrics to measure social impact, and calculate the cost benefits of their actions. In addition, venture philanthropists will usually develop long-term, and close, relationships with the supported organizations. A final, key, aspect of venture philanthropy is its 'exit strategy'. In the venture philanthropy framework, a supported organization must, in the end, become self-reliable. Venture philanthropy is, therefore, transitional, the goal being to achieve financial self-sufficiency. Financial engineering could be added to this list of venture philanthropy specificities, as many venture philanthropists try to go beyond pure grantmaking and to develop new financial tools specifically dedicated to nonprofits/social enterprises such as loan funding, shared equity and bonds, and so on (Grenier, 2006). Therefore, venture philanthropy can be defined as

> human resources and funding invested as donation in the charity by entrepreneurs, venture capitalists, trusts and corporations in search of a social return on their investment. It involves high engagement over many years with fixed milestones and tangible returns, and exit achieved by developing alternative, sustainable income.
>
> *(Pepin, 2005: 165)*

Within the venture philanthropy field, four groups of initiators can be identified (Grenier, 2006). The first of these is composed of wealthy individuals, usually enjoying new wealth from venture capital or finance backgrounds. The second is made up of nonprofits interested in fundraising for their own activities or for those of their individual or organizational members or associates. A third driving force can be companies or corporations that develop a venture philanthropy initiative aimed at supporting social causes. Finally, government departments or public agencies may initiate a venture philanthropy organization, but then they usually do it in partnership with others instigators. What is interesting here is the collaborative aspect of venture philanthropy; funds are often the results of several initiators who will try to attract further resources.

In addition, venture philanthropy can operate through three main channels. First, a venture philanthropist can provide direct financial and nonfinancial support, especially if his or her own offer in terms of specialized services and financial means is large enough and well suited to the needs of the supported organization. Second, when this is not the case, or when the investor or donor prefers not to play a direct active role, he or she can choose to provide funding and skills to a venture philanthropy organization which is generally set up as a foundation, a fund or a structure that incorporates both (as for instance, LGT Venture Philanthropy Foundation and Impetus Trust). Pulling together various financial sources and other inputs, the venture philanthropy organization becomes the major partner of the 'investee'. Third, it can happen that a venture philanthropist becomes a social entrepreneur himself or herself, for instance, when he or she realizes that partnerships at hands with existing social organizations and/or cooperation with public agencies do not lead to the undertaking or to the scale he or she is seeking (Van Slyke and Newman, 2006).

However, it must be underlined that the definitions and characteristics depicted above represent, in a Weberian sense, more an 'ideal-type' picture than what can be observed on the ground. This is particularly applicable to Europe, where the venture philanthropy field is still relatively young; it is a theoretical approach claimed by a new generation of philanthropists, it is certainly not always the result of empirical observations. In other words, there are possible gaps between vision and reality, between theory and empirical evidence, between project and concrete implementation. Second, venture philanthropy is only one new trend in the world of philanthropy, not the new rule. Moody's (2008) research in the US, emphasizes that not only has the construction and diffusion of the venture philanthropy field depended on opinion leaders who strategically defined, legitimated and advocated the new model, but also that, since its beginnings in the 1990s, 'its proponents are more modest'. What the proponents of venture philanthropy sometimes call 'Old Philanthropy' still exists and even still dominates the field. Moreover, it often keeps its legitimacy because venture philanthropy, as we will see, is not adapted to all kinds of nonprofits and social missions. Furthermore, as Cunningham outlines in Chapter 2, there are wider questions as to what constitutes 'new' and 'old' philanthropy.

Comparing SE with venture philanthropy

In order to explore the links between SE and venture philanthropy it is useful to focus on the three SE schools that have been put forward within the literature: the 'earned income' school of thought, the 'social innovation' school of thought and the EMES European approach of social enterprise (Defourny and Nyssens, 2010). This section outlines these three lenses and discusses their relationship with venture philanthropy.

Earned income

The first school of thought, the earned income one, is rooted in the US. It set the original ground for conceptions of social enterprise by mainly focusing on earned-income strategies. The bulk of early publications in this area are based on nonprofits' interest in becoming more commercial (Young and Salamon, 2002). As such, it is relatively prescriptive: many of the ideas were developed by consultancy firms and focused on strategies for starting a business that would earn income to support the social mission of a nonprofit organization and that could help diversify its funding base (Skloot, 1987). On that basis, the Social Enterprise Alliance in the late 1990s, a central player in the field, defined social enterprise as 'any earned-income business or strategy undertaken by a non-profit to generate revenue in support of its charitable mission'.

Within the earned income school of thought, a distinction between an earlier version, focusing on nonprofits and that embraces all forms of business initiatives can be made: the former can be seen as a 'commercial nonprofit approach', the latter as a 'mission–driven business approach' as it refers to the field of social purpose ventures as encompassing all organizations that trade for a social purpose, including for-profit companies (Austin *et al.*, 2006). It should also be noted that, relatively early, authors, such as Emerson and Twersky (1996), shifted the analysis from a sole market orientation to a broader vision of business methods as a path towards achieving increased effectiveness (and not just a better funding) of nonprofits. For this earned income school, social enterprise can be characterized as 'business solutions to social problems' (Grenier, 2009). This was picked up by venture philanthropists towards the end of the 1990s and combined this focus with the practices from venture capitalists for launching new businesses (Wei-Skillern *et al.* 2007: 67). Consequently, the connection between venture philanthropy and the SE earned income perspective is relatively straightforward as both place emphasis on both business tools and sustainability.

If venture philanthropy is viewed as a long-term relationship between the donor and the beneficiary organization, the goal is to ensure independence and financial sustainability of the initiative (Reis and Clohesey, 2001), not to engage in an indefinite dependence relationship. After staying involved over a specific time and once a project has achieved autonomy, efficiency and sustainability, there is usually a planned exit strategy for venture philanthropists (de Courcy Hero, 2001). Therefore, venture philanthropists are more likely to finance organizations that can, at least partially, earn income from their activities. Typically, organizations providing social services at a price below production cost or local businesses in underprivileged communities would be better partners for venture philanthropists than organizations just advocating for the rights of disadvantaged populations. However, it must be noted that venture philanthropy discourse about 'sustainability' does not necessarily imply supporting organizations which have to rely solely on earned incomes.

As part of its development, the net for venture philanthropy has broadened. Initially, nonprofit organizations were the main beneficiaries and venture philanthropy wanted to 'identify and support "social entrepreneurs" hungry to shake up the nonprofit work, and quantify their results' (Wagner, 2002: 347). Today, however, there is a clear tendency towards supporting any kind of organization, encompassing a wide variety of legal forms, as far as they are primarily driven by social goals, although corporate social responsibility (CSR) projects of conventional firms seem to be excluded from the spectrum of venture philanthropy put forward by the European Venture Philanthropy Association (EVPA) (Metz and Hehenberger, 2011). This then clearly places venture philanthropy in line with the mission–driven business approach of social enterprises at both conceptual and empirical levels; both put emphasis on social impact through business solutions and on sustainability. At a secondary level, however, venture philanthropists, and social enterprises looking for earned income, often realize that fulfilling social missions tends to require reliance on other types of resources that may prevent them from achieving self-sufficiency. Indeed, as acknowledged by EVPA (2010), organizations that are considered for investment by venture philanthropists actually range from charities relying on grants or a mix of grants and trading revenue, to social businesses only relying on sales income.

The social innovation school of thought

The second school, developed by the pioneering work of Young (1986), emphasizes the profile and behaviour of social entrepreneurs in a Schumpeterian way. Accordingly, entrepreneurs in the nonprofit sector are 'change makers'. They carry out 'new combinations' in at least one of the following ways: new services, new quality of services, new methods of production, new production factors, new forms of organizations or new markets. Social entrepreneurship may therefore be a question of outcomes rather than just a question of incomes. Moreover, the systemic nature of innovation brought about, and its impact at a broad societal level, is often underlined.

Within this perspective, the best known definition of social entrepreneurs is provided by Dees (1998: 4) who considers them to be

> playing the role of change agents in the social sector by adopting a mission to create and sustain social value, recognizing and relentlessly pursuing new opportunities to serve that mission, engaging in a process of continuous innovation, adaptation and learning, acting boldly without being limited by resources currently in hand, and finally exhibiting a heightened sense of accountability to the constituencies served and for the outcomes created.

In practice, this approach can be traced back to *Ashoka: Innovators for the Public*, the organization founded by Bill Drayton in 1980. The mission of Ashoka was, and still is, 'to find and support outstanding individuals with pattern setting ideas for social change' (Drayton and MacDonald, 1993: 1). Ashoka thus focuses on the profiles of very specific individuals, first referred to as public entrepreneurs, able to bring about social innovation in various fields, rather than on the forms of organization they might set up. Today, such social entrepreneurs are often portrayed as heroes of the modern times (Bornstein, 2004).

Venture philanthropy strongly resonates with this school of thought: such a social entrepreneur is often described as the 'natural' partner of venture philanthropists, the ideal form among the huge organizational diversity characterizing the third sector with whom to establish partnerships and cooperation. In other words, social entrepreneurs are the figure researched, and/or discovered by venture philanthropists; they are the one who fits with venture philanthropists' aspirations. There is also a reputational advantage: by involving themselves in the 'adventure', new philanthropists may themselves be perceived as social entrepreneurs.

Although Ashoka itself does not dwell on the notion of venture philanthropy, several of its key features mirror the discourse of most venture philanthropy organizations and platforms. First, the emphasis is put on financial as well as nonfinancial support. In a survey carried out by the EVPA (2011), its members consider that nonfinancial support is the key element for 58 percent of supported social organizations. This nonfinancial support is, in decreasing importance, of the following types: strategy consulting, coaching, networks, fundraising, governance, financial management and marketing. Second, the emphasis on the SE social mission and its social impact ('outcomes rather than incomes') as underlined by Dees and Anderson (2006) finds a clear correspondence in the venture philanthropy landscape: half of the responding venture philanthropy organizations in the above survey claim they focus on societal return only, and 38 percent seek both societal and financial returns with priority given to the former.

Despite such strikingly similar features, differences can be identified as to the place of social innovation. As such, venture philanthropy may be seen as an innovative methodology to support social organizations in the wide spectrum of philanthropic modes of action. Moreover, venture philanthropy itself witnesses the emergence of brand new instruments, as in the case of the Social Impact Bond in the UK. However, in the selection of social organizations to be supported, venture philanthropists look more for social or societal impact than for social innovation, i.e. the novelty of answers to social problems. More precisely, venture philanthropy will typically make social organizations stronger at all stages of their development to increase their societal impact, while the social innovation school of thought will focus more on the very conception and start-up phase of initiatives offering new systemic solutions to social challenges. Of course, such differences should not be overstated, neither from a conceptual nor from a practical point of view. In particular, the fast growing number of venture philanthropy organizations enlarges the spectrum of strategies and priorities among the latter and some of them claim explicitly their interest for social innovation.

The EMES school of thought

In Western Europe, the EMES European Research Network has developed the first theoretical and empirical milestones of social enterprise analysis. The EMES approach derives from extensive dialogue across several disciplines, including economics, sociology, political science and management, as well as across the various national traditions and sensitivities which coexist in the European Union.

To capture the SE phenomenon with its diverse expressions, the network, from the outset, preferred the identification of indicators over a concise and elegant definition. Such indicators were never intended to represent the set of conditions that an organization should meet to qualify as a social enterprise. Rather than constituting prescriptive criteria, they describe an 'ideal-type', i.e. an abstract construction that enables researchers to position themselves within the 'galaxy' of social enterprising. In other words, they constitute a tool, somewhat analogous to a compass, which helps analysts to locate the position of the observed entities relative to one another, and to eventually identify subsets of social enterprising that they want to study more deeply. Those indicators allow for the identification of brand new social enterprises, but they can also lead to the designation of older organizations being reshaped by new internal dynamics as 'social enterprises'. Within this perspective, three categories, each containing three criteria, provide a framework for exploring the SE field: economic and entrepreneurial dimensions, including a continuous activity producing goods and/or selling services, a significant level of economic risk, and a minimum amount of paid work; social dimensions, covering an explicit aim to benefit the community, an initiative launched by a group of citizens or civil society organizations, and a limited profit distribution; and participatory governance, referring to a high degree of autonomy, a decision-making power not based on capital ownership, and a participatory nature, which involves various parties affected by the activity.

Although resembling the other two schools of thought previously discussed in stressing a primary social objective embedded in an economic activity, the EMES approach differs from them mainly by stressing specific governance models (rather than the profile of individual social entrepreneurs) which are often found in European social enterprises. Such governance models could be seen as a channel to ensure the primacy of social aims and high levels of accountability as requested by venture philanthropy. First, a democratic control and/or a participatory involvement of stakeholders reflect a quest for more economic democracy inside the enterprise, in line with the tradition of cooperatives which represent a major component of the third sector/social economy in most European contexts. This generally means that the organization applies the principle of 'one member, one vote', or at least that the voting rights in the governing body that has the ultimate decision-making power is not distributed according to capital shares. Then, the ideal-typical social enterprise defined by EMES is based on a collective dynamics and the involvement of different stakeholders in the governance of the organization. The various categories of stakeholders may include beneficiaries, employees, volunteers, public authorities and donors, among others. They can be involved in the membership or in the board of the social enterprise, thereby creating a 'multi-stakeholder ownership' (Bacchiegga and Borzaga, 2003). The involvement of a diversity of stakeholders in the ownership structure of the organization can be a valuable asset. It can bring key resources to the organization in terms of skills, networks, political influence and financial resources as put forward by the literature on the board diversity in the nonprofit sector and its impact on organizations' performance (Cornforth, 2001; Brown, 2005). This is also a way to collectively build the social mission of an organization. By mobilizing different types of stakeholders concerned by the social mission, multiple stakeholder ownership can be a channel to unfold that mission and make it more explicit and precise (Laville and Nyssens, 2001). Therefore, combined with constraints on the distribution of profits, the participative governance can be viewed as a way to protect and strengthen the primacy of the social mission in the organization. This meets a concern of venture philanthropy, as it desires to work, foremost, to build stronger 'social purpose organizations' to primarily increase their social impact.

Second, those two combined guarantees also act as a 'signal' allowing other external funders including public bodies – not just philanthropists – to support social enterprises in various ways. Without such guarantees, often involving a strict non-distribution constraint, the risk would be greater that external support would simply induce more profits to be distributed among owners or managers. It is probably the same fear that leads authors to exclude traditional business, even CSR initiatives, from the venture philanthropy spectrum, as they are primarily, or ultimately, driven by the quest of financial return (Metz and Hehenberger, 2011). Moreover, financial support by public authorities and by venture philanthropists often allow social enterprises to avoid purely market-oriented strategies, which, in many cases, would lead them away from those who cannot afford market prices and nevertheless constitute the group that they target in accordance with their social mission.

This leads us to the issue of 'economic risk'. Social enterprises are generally viewed as organizations characterized by a significant level of economic risk. Such an economic risk even seems at the heart of social entrepreneurship as it reinforces the 'entrepreneurial flavour' of organizations pursuing social goals. In the EMES Network's perspective, however, instead of being mainly related to market sales and competition, the risk borne by social enterprises simply means that their financial viability depends on the efforts of their members to secure adequate resources for supporting the enterprise's social mission. These resources often have a hybrid character: they may come from trading activities, from public subsidies, or from philanthropy, including volunteering. In spite of the influence of business tools and market vocabulary upon venture philanthropy, such a broad conception of economic risk meets a key concern of venture philanthropy as part of the social organization resource mix. It even becomes a more prominent issue at the time of financial exit by the venture philanthropy organizations:

> Exit can create uncertainty, particularly for social purpose organizations with little or no earned income.... Depending on the profile of the next investor in line, issues such as potential social mission drift of the investee have to be taken into account. An exit in venture philanthropy can imply providing the social purpose organization with the necessary fundraising capabilities to be able to continue working towards its social mission without further venture philanthropy organizations involvement.
>
> *(Metz and Hehenberger, 2011: 18)*

Venture philanthropy tools and SE development stages

Taken together, the above outline the different issues to be addressed by venture philanthropy and SE. Let us now examine the various forms of interaction between venture philanthropy and SE that may be found at their different development stages.

Early-stage support

First, let us stress once more the 'proactive' overall attitude which characterizes venture philanthropy towards supporting certain initiatives: instead of just setting a few priorities in terms of fields of action and target groups, and then analyzing requests for grants from nonprofit organizations meeting such criteria, venture philanthropists will choose a smaller number of partners and provide multidimensional support. Using market-inspired competition among bids, venture philanthropists can, for instance, send a 'call for projects', give grants, and provide nonfinancial support to the most appealing parties with the highest expected impact/cost ratio. It is, therefore, the philanthropist who enhances the capabilities of the nonprofit organization, not the nonprofit who develops its project alone using philanthropic grants.

Such an ambitious involvement from the outset sometimes takes a form which is probably emblematic of early-stage support: the setting up of an incubator or more broadly the implementation of an incubating strategy for emerging social enterprises (although such initiatives may also be created by other private or public institutions without any venture philanthropy contribution). Beyond the diversity of their founders, these incubators may take different forms. Centralized incubators will be conceived as hubs, which physically host social entrepreneurs who get training, technical advice, and support in a dedicated setting where most services, including all types of administrative support, are mutualized. More decentralized incubators, or incubating strategies, will only organize a limited number of joint activities for their social entrepreneurs and send consulting firms and other advisers to places where the initiatives are taking shape.

Centralized incubators purely initiated by venture philanthropy are not easily found, as they have to cover a large range of services independently. In China, the Nonprofit Incubator (NPI), created in 2006 by a foundation and now established in four major cities, may be seen as a good example: NPI hosts leaders of emerging nonprofits which, in that country, can be seen as social enterprises as they represent innovative responses to social needs while raising alternative resources. Centralized incubators make particular sense within local development strategies, for instance in deprived urban areas to be regenerated. In such cases, however, they are generally the result of alliances among various local supporting institutions and venture philanthropy may just be one of them. In such settings, an incubated social enterprise may sometimes be conceived from the outset as a 'community enterprise', even involving various local stakeholders – volunteers, local firms, users, venture philanthropists, etc. – in the ownership structure of the enterprise. With such a 'multi-stakeholder ownership structure', the social enterprise can benefit from financial, knowledge, and intellectual capital on a long-term basis.

Social enterprise incubators involving venture philanthropy as a key driving force more commonly represent a combination of both centralized and decentralized operating strategies. Most prominent examples are provided by the increasing number of foundations, mainly based in the US, which have launched programs through which they select and support early-stage social entrepreneurs through fellowships. Organizations like Ashoka, Echoing Green, the Skoll Foundation, and the Schwab Foundation, among the best known, grant two- or three-year fellowships to emerging social entrepreneurs, and part of their support is designed and provided centrally. This may include joint training sessions, deep in-house interactions among fellows, promotion of a strong common identity and celebration of the greatest achievements. At the same time, these venture philanthropy organizations usually try to enlarge the range of partners able to provide financial or nonfinancial services; consulting companies, funds dedicated to the provision of seed money or credits, as well as other kinds of external tools frequently represent highly valuable partners. For example, another Chinese pioneering incubator, the China Social Enterprise Foundation, is currently developing various partnerships in the emerging and fast-growing field of philanthropy in that country.

In fewer, but quite interesting cases, venture philanthropy acts as a key actor from the outset to set up strong partnerships with the public authorities, even at very early stages, resulting in joint actions close to incubating strategies. In the mid-1990s, pilots projects experimenting with a new type of social enterprise, i.e. 'work integration social enterprises' (WISE), were selected and supported by a venture philanthropy program of the King Baudouin Foundation and the latter succeeded in mobilizing subsidies and seed money from the European Social Fund and from regional governments.

In some contexts, venture philanthropy does not play such a central role, but is involved in incubating strategies initiated by a major third sector organization, by an umbrella organization such as a federation of cooperatives (like 'SCOP enterprises' in some French regions), by partnerships between local communities and universities (for instance the Brazilian incubators of solidarity-based economic initiatives), or by a local authority like the incubator InVerso launched in the early 2000s by the City of Rome in a suburban area (Carrera, Meneguzzo and Messina 2006).

Project consolidation

Beyond its starting phase, the social enterprise has to find an economic model which is financially viable while targeting its social mission. When a social enterprise is solely conceived as a separate, earned-income strategy, developed to provide market income to another activity fully oriented towards social aims, the social enterprise's main concern is raising market income. However, although such a dual model is quite common in some contexts, our discussion here focuses on more integrated SE models, as the true novelty of social entrepreneurship is precisely to produce goods or services that meet otherwise unmet social needs while making production financially sustainable. In such cases, we can hypothesize that the social demand, if solvable, could have been detected and met by a for-profit company, and therefore the social enterprise operating model cannot generally rely only on market sales.

As a matter of fact, the viability of most social enterprises depends on the long-term capacity of their leaders to combine different kinds of resources, and these combinations will vary heavily according to the field and the assigned social mission. This generally means selling goods or services to the possible extent, as well as mobilizing traditional donations, venture philanthropy and volunteering and /or applying for public funding to compensate the organization for services provided for free or below the cost of production (Laville and Nyssens, 2001; Gardin, 2006).

There are many foundations which prefer not to get involved in the very early stages of social entrepreneurship and try to avoid dealing with the very diverse needs and challenges of an infant social enterprise. For instance, LGT Venture Philanthropy Foundation, among many others, clearly focuses on phases of maturity and social investments of a certain size. Consolidation may also be supported by some other private or public institutions providing risk capital, guarantees, or credit to social enterprises.

In terms of economic theory, the role played by philanthropy, as well as public redistribution may be explained by the social dimension of the production at stake. It is well-known by economists that the presence of collective benefits renders market-based financing inefficient. Indeed, market mechanisms do not generally internalize collective externalities or equity issues. Non-market intervention is then fully justifiable. In such a context, although inspired by business methods, venture philanthropy generally remains fundamentally a philanthropic and therefore a non-market resource for social enterprises.

As supported organizations grow, venture philanthropy tries to innovate, producing 'new public good' (Knott and McCarthy, 2007: 321) through new approaches to solve social issues, becoming a kind of 'incubator' of possibly new public policies or a large-scale private approach; or by financing research and lobbying activities. Then, inevitably, to improve SE effectiveness, venture philanthropists must cooperate with public agencies and other public institutions involved in the field that they choose to 'sponsor' (Van Slyke and Newman, 2006). Reis and Clohesy speak (2001: 111) about 'an emerging societal shift to a more entrepreneurial focus on the common good, resulting in new partnerships among the commercial, public, and nonprofit sector'. Challenging the 'old opposition' between public and private funding, they try to cooperate to maximize the efficiency of the programs, organizations or projects supported. In certain cases, foundations can even become a meeting, discussion and exchange platform between civil society organizations and public agents (Van Slyke and Newman, 2006; Pirotte, 2003).

Scaling up

Once a social innovation has been validated in a local context, the issue of its scaling up refers to the growth of the organization itself beyond a critical size or the development of other organizations for replication in different contexts. The main concern is then coming closer to a systemic change.

While the role of social enterprises in clearing up emerging social demands and in introducing innovative practices often supported by philanthropic resources is increasingly acknowledged, governments may sometimes consider the leadership of the scaling up phase to be their responsibility. A government takeover of funding might then suggest that the mobilization of philanthropy can weaken or even disappear over time. This may take place when public authorities backed by public opinion are particularly concerned with the limitations of traditional philanthropy and venture philanthropy. As listed by Salamon (1987), this could involve 'a philanthropic shortfall' (not enough resources), 'a philanthropic particularism' (trend to support specific groups or causes) and 'a philanthropic paternalism' (certain individuals are in a position to determine which services will be provided since they control the source of funding).

In the European context, the process of institutionalization of social enterprise has often been closely linked to the evolution of public policies (Defourny and Nyssens, 2011). In fact, social enterprises significantly influence their institutional environment and they contribute to shaping institutions including public policies. The sustainability and future growth of social enterprises can, therefore, be linked to recognition by government funding sources that social enterprises make a distinctive contribution to the community. The collective benefits associated with the delivery of certain services can, therefore, be produced by the introduction of new forms of redistributive policies from which all enterprises benefit in the more competitive context.

For example, following the pioneering Italian law adopted in 1991 about social cooperatives, several European countries introduced new legal forms reflecting the entrepreneurial approach adopted by this increasing number of nonprofit organizations, even though the term of social enterprise was not always used as such in the legislation (Defourny and Nyssens, 2008). So far,

16 new laws of this sort can be identified across European countries (Roelandts, 2009). In many European countries, besides the creation of new legal forms, the 1990s saw the development of specific public programs targeting social enterprise in the field of work integration. Indeed, Work Integration Social Enterprise (WISE) has increasingly represented a tool for implementing active labour market policies. In several countries, they have really become a 'conveyor belt' of such policies. In turn, legal frameworks tend to shape, at least in part, the objectives and practices of social enterprises. If this dynamic can be seen as a channel for the diffusion of social innovation, the key role of public bodies in some fields of social enterprises may also reduce them to instruments intended to achieve specific goals which are given priority on the political agenda, with a risk of bridling the dynamics of social innovation.

This issue, among others, has been analysed by the EMES Network in the field of work integration through a large empirical survey covering 160 social enterprises in 11 EU countries over four years (Nyssens, 2006). Analyses tend to show that a multi-stakeholder approach may be a resource to pursue a complex set of objectives and may consequently support the innovative capacity of social enterprises. The reliance on a variety of resources, both from the point of view of their origin (e.g. from private customers, from the business sector, from the public sector or from the third sector) and regarding the mode of resource allocation (e.g. sales of services, public subsidies, gifts and volunteering), also appears to be a key element to enabling social enterprises to fulfil their social mission. Keeping and managing such a hybridity nevertheless constitutes a daily challenge for social enterprise.

In the US context, the stronger reliance on private actors to achieve a large scale impact could result from a kind of implicitly shared confidence in market forces to solve an increasing part of social issues in modern societies. For Maier *et al.* (2014: 8), conducting a systematic review of literature on nonprofits becoming 'more business like', the application of venture capitalist methods to philanthropic funding produces in return philanthropists' high expectations regarding results and accountability. Even if various scholars stress the need to mobilize various types of resources, it is not impossible that the current wave of social entrepreneurship may act as a priority-setting process and a selection process of social challenges deserving to be addressed because of their potential in terms of earned income. This probably explains to a large extent why large segments of the nonprofit sector in the US, as well as the community and voluntary sector in the UK (Di Domenico *et al.*, 2009; Teasdale, 2010), express major fears of excessive confidence in market-oriented social enterprises on the part of both private organizations (foundations and major corporations within CSR strategies) or public policies seeking to combat social problems while reducing allocated budgets.

Past experience with some initiatives in the social economy has shown the following (Evers and Laville, 2004): when the distinctive features which characterize this 'third force' are downplayed over time, organizations tend to drift toward institutional isomorphism – a progressive loss of their inner characteristics under the pressure of legal frameworks or professional norms spilling over from the for-profit private or public sectors (DiMaggio and Powell, 1983). More precisely, some cooperatives have gradually come to resemble other forms of enterprise in the market economy. Similarly, certain mutual benefit societies, through their integration into the social welfare system, have turned into virtual copies of organizations in the public administration. To a significant degree, this kind of trajectory can reflect a mission drift.

Even if, on the one hand, governments provide funding for the production of the collective benefits, and on the other hand, earned income contributes to the sustainability of the social enterprise, experience shows that the mobilization of philanthropy and civic engagement can remain central to the creation of certain collective benefits in the long run. Social enterprises, by mobilizing volunteers, philanthropy and social networks, have a specific ability to strengthen social capital (Evers, 2001). In the same line, if stakeholders like workers and users get involved, this can create a capital of solid trust, so important for the provision of certain services.

Conclusion

We have highlighted how venture philanthropy can find echoes in the various SE schools of thought. For the earned-income school, venture philanthropy can help social enterprise adopting business methods and solutions to tackle social problems while building an operating model which exploits market opportunities to the larger possible extent. The social innovation school puts the emphasis on the profile, motivations and behaviour of social entrepreneurs who may often appear as ideal partners for venture philanthropists focused on innovative solutions and increased social impact. As to the EMES approach, it highlights specific governance models based on the involvement of stakeholders able to reflect converging, as well as diverging legitimate interests, as a major channel to ensure the primacy of social aims and high levels of accountability as requested by venture philanthropy.

Venture philanthropy often seeks to create a leverage effect which may contribute weakening the typical philanthropic shortfall and lead supported organizations toward a sustainable operating model. However, such a quest of sustainability in venture philanthropy discourses and actual practices does not necessarily mean looking mainly for market incomes. Such an open approach, more focused on outcomes than on types of incomes, tends to see sponsored organizations as hybrid ones which have to secure the best mix of resources to support their social mission. To a large extent, it seems close to the EMES conception of social enterprise, as well as the social innovation school of thought.

Being complementary to each other, the social enterprise's different types of resources can guarantee its autonomy – autonomy based on multiple linkages – and its economic viability. Hybridization not only means relying on different types of economic relations over a long period, it also means balancing these economic relations through negotiations with the various partners. Instead of imposing its own priorities and, therefore, bearing the risk of generating particularism, we would hypothesize that venture philanthropy at its best will probably find its very own place as one (important) partner among various stakeholders.

Along the same lines, the place and role of venture philanthropy, as well as its tools vary according to development stages of the supported organization. At each stage, venture philanthropy may contribute significantly to reducing amateurism through rigorous and well-designed modes of support. Here again, however, acknowledgement of the specific contribution of each type of financial and nonfinancial resources will help stakeholders converging to the social mission and reduce the risk of mission drift.

In a more fundamental perspective, what is at stake with the rise of venture philanthropy and SE is the need for many more efforts towards improving the appraisal of an organization's overall performance, the concept of performance being taken here as the capacity of an organization to achieve its objectives. This raises various key issues, which may be seen as major avenues for further research. How to capture social value is certainly one of those key issues. Indeed, SE and venture philanthropy are driven by social objectives and venture philanthropists want to assess the social impact of their investment. However, if methods to grasp social impact are flourishing, most often these measures are still confined to raw indicators of the volume of activities, which don't grasp the net effect (social return) of the investment. This is a major research challenge for the coming years.

In fields where research is still in its infancy, empirical evidence is of utmost importance. Too many discourses regarding SE and venture philanthropy can still be described as 'prescriptive', as they focus on strategies that a social entrepreneur or a venture philanthropist should adopt. As we have already underlined, there is a possible gap between wishes and reality. In such a context, case studies can provide relevant information about the dynamics underpinning SE and venture philanthropy, but databases on a large scale are needed to test more general hypotheses, thereby helping to provide the critical research underpinnings for this developing field.

References

Austin, J. E, Leonard, B., Reficco, E. and Wei-Skillern, J. (2006) 'Social Entrepreneurship: It's for Corporations too', in A. Nicholls (ed) *Social Entrepreneurship, New Models of Sustainable Social Change*, New York: Oxford University Press.
Bacchiegga, A. and Borzaga, C. (2001) 'Social Enterprises as Incentive Structures: an Economic Analysis', in C. Borzaga and J. Defourny (eds) *The Emergence of Social Enterprise*, London and New York: Routledge.
Bacchiegga, A. and Borzaga, C. (2003) 'The Economics of the Third Sector', in H. K. Anheier and A. Ben-Ner (eds) *The Study of the Nonprofit Enterprise, Theories and Approaches*, New York: Kluwer Academic/Plenum Publishers, 27–48.
Bornstein, D. (2004) *How to Change the World: Social Entrepreneurs and the Power of New Ideas*, New York: Oxford University Press.
Brown, W. A. (2005) 'Exploring the Association between Board and Organizational, Performance in Nonprofit Organizations', *Nonprofit Management and Leadership*, 15(3): 317–39.
Carrera, D., Menuguzzo, M. and Messina, A. (2006) *Social Enterprise Incubators: The Italian Experience*. Mimeo.
Cornforth, C. (2001) 'What Makes Boards Effective? An Examination of the Relationships between Board Inputs, Structures, Processes and Effectiveness in Nonprofit Organizations', *Corporate Governance: An International Review*, 9(3):217–27.
de Courcy Hero, P. (2001) 'Giving Back the Silicon Valley Way: Emerging Patterns of a New Philanthropy', *New Direction for Philanthropic Fundraising*, 32: 47–57.
Dees, J. G. (1998) *The Meaning of Social Entrepreneurship*, Stanford University: Mimeo.
Dees, J. G. and Anderson, B. B. (2006) 'Framing a Theory of Social Entrepreneurship: Building on Two Schools of Practice and Thought in Research on Social Entrepreneurship', *ARNOVA Occasional Paper Series*, 1(3): 39–66.
Defourny, J. and Nyssens, M. (2008) 'Social Enterprise in Europe: Recent Trends and Developments', *Social Enterprise Journal*, 4(3): 202–28.
—— (2010) 'Conceptions of Social Enterprise and Social Entrepreneurship in Europe and the United States: Convergences and Divergences', *Journal of Social Entrepreneurship*, 1(1): 32–53.
—— (2011) 'Approches européenne et américaine de l'entreprise sociale: une perspective comparative', *Revue internationale de l'économie sociale – RECMA*, 319: 18–36.
Di Domenico, M., Tracey, P. and Haugh, H. (2009) 'Social Economy Involvement in Public Service Delivery: Community Engagement and Accountability', *Regional Studies*, 43(7): 981–92.
DiMaggio, P. and Powell, W. W. (1983) 'The Iron Cage Revisited: Collective Rationality and Institutional Isomorphism in Organizational Fields', *American Sociological Review*, 48(2), 147–60.
Drayton, W. and MacDonald, S. (1993) *Leading Public Entrepreneurs*, Arlington: Ashoka, Innovators for the Public.
Emerson, J. and Twersky, F. (1996) *New Social Entrepreneurs: The Success, Challenge and Lessons of Nonprofit Enterprise Creation*, San Francisco: Roberts Foundation.
European Venture Philanthropy Association (2010) *European Venture Philanthropy Directory 2010–2011*, www.evpa.eu.com.
Evers, A. (2001) 'The Significance of Social Capital in the Multiple Goal and Resource Structure of Social Enterprise', in C. Borzaga and J. Defourny (eds) *The Emergence of Social Enterprise*, London and New York: Routledge.
Evers, A. and Laville, J.-L. (eds) (2004) *The Third Sector in Europe*, Cheltenham: Edward Elgar.
Gardin, L. (2006) 'A Variety of Resource Mixes inside Social Enterprises', in M. Nyssens (ed) *Social Enterprise – At the Crossroads of Market, Public Policies and Civil Society*, London and New York: Routledge, pp.111–36.

Grenier, P. (2006) *Venture Philanthropy in Europe: Obstacles and Opportunities*, European Venture Philanthropy Association (EVPA).

Grenier, P. (2009) 'Social Entrepreneurship in the UK: From Rhetoric to Reality?', in R. Ziegler (ed) *An introduction to Social Entrepreneurship: Voices, Preconditions, Contexts*, Cheltenham, UK: Edward Elgar.

Knott, J. H. and McCarthy, D. (2007) 'Policy Venture Capital. Foundations, Government, and Child Care Programs', *Administration and Society*, 39(3) 319–53.

Laville, J.-L. and Nyssens, M. (2001) 'The Social Enterprise: Towards a Theoretical Socio-Economic Approach', in C. Borzaga and J. Defourny (eds) *The Emergence of Social Enterprise*, London and New York: Routledge.

Maier, F., Meyer, M., and Steinbereithner, M. (2014) 'Nonprofit Organizations Becoming Business-Like A Systematic Review', *Nonprofit and Voluntary Sector Quarterly*, Published online before print December 12.

Maximilian, M. and John, R. (2007) 'Venture Philanthropy in Europe: Landscape and Driving Principles', in A.-K. Achleitner, R. Poellath and E. Stahl (eds) *Finanzierung von sozialunternehmern*, Schaeffer-Poeschel.

Metz Cummings, A. and Hehenberger, L. (2011) *A Guide to Venture Philanthropy for Venture Capital and Private Equity Investors*, EVPA Knowledge Centre.

Moody, M. (2008) 'Building a Culture: The Construction and Evolution of Venture Philanthropy as a New Organizational Field', *Nonprofit and Voluntary Sector Quarterly*, 37 (2) 324–52.

Nyssens, M. (ed) (2006) *Social Enterprise – At the Crossroads of Market, Public Policies and Civil Society*, London and New York: Routledge.

Pepin, J. (2005) 'Venture Capitalists and Entrepreneurs become Venture Philanthropists', *The International Journal of Nonprofit and Voluntary Sector Marketing*, 10: 165–73.

Pirotte, G. (2003) *Les fondations belges d'utilité publique: entre permanence et changements*, POLE-SUD/ Université de Liège.

Reis, T. K. and Clohesy, S. J. (2001) 'Unleashing New Resources and Entrepreneurship for the Common Good: A Philanthropic Renaissance', *New Directions for Philanthropic Fundraising*, 32: 109–143.

Roelants, B. (ed). (2009). *Cooperatives and Social Enterprises: Governance and Normative Frameworks*, Brussels: CECOP Publications.

Salamon, L. M. (1987) 'Partners in Public Service: The Scope and Theory of Government-Nonprofit Relations', in Walter W. Powel (ed) *The Nonprofit Sector. A Research Handbook*, New Haven, CT: Yale University Press.

Skloot, E. (1987) 'Enterprise and Commerce in Nonprofit Organizations', in W. W. Powell (ed) *The Nonprofit Sector: A Research Handbook*, New Haven, CT: Yale University Press.

Teasdale, S. (2010) 'What's in a Name? The Construction of Social Enterprise', *Working Paper 46*, Third Sector Research Centre, University of Birmingham.

Van Haeperen, B. (2012) 'Que sont les principes du New Public Management Devenus? Le cas de l'administration régionale wallonne', *Reflets et perspectives de la vie économique*, 2(Tome LI) : 83–99.

Van Slyke, D. M. and Newman, H. K. (2006) 'Venture Philanthropy and Social Entrepreneurship in Community Redevelopment', *Nonprofit Management and Leadership*, 16(3): 345–68.

Vigoda, E. (2003) 'New Public Management', in J. Rabin (ed) *Encyclopedia of Public Administration and Public Policy*, New York: Marcel Dekker.

Wagner, L. (2002) 'The "New" Donor: Creation or Evolution?', *International Journal of Nonprofit and Voluntary Sector Marketing*, 7(4): 343–52.

Wei-Skillern, J., Austin, J. E., Leonard, H., and Stevenson, H. (2007) *Entrepreneurship in the Social Sector*, London: Sage Publications.

Young, D. (1986) 'Entrepreneurship and the Behavior of Nonprofit Organizations: Elements of a Theory', in S. Rose-Ackerman (ed) *The Economics of Nonprofit Institutions*, New York: Oxford University Press.

Young, D. and Salamon, L. M. (2002) 'Commercialization, Social Ventures, and For-Profit Competition', in L. M. Salamon (ed) *The State of Nonprofit America*, Washington DC: Brookings Institution.

23
Financialization of philanthropy
The case of social investment

Ekkehard Thümler

Until very recently, the markets were widely regarded as the paradigm of a rational organization of society (Friedland and Robertson, 1990). Just like other sectors of society, philanthropy has extensively integrated economic methods and values into its structures and operations. As a result, an organizational field that was traditionally based on the logic of gift giving increasingly rejects the idea of an unconditional distribution of goods and embraces the rationales, techniques and language of markets. This development, known as the 'marketization' of the third sector, is characterized by a heightened emphasis on competition and earned income, the celebration of (social) entrepreneurship and the emergence of new actors, such as for-profit providers and donors (Salamon, 1993; Weisbrod, 1998; Eikenberry and Kluver, 2004).

Meanwhile, important changes have occurred in the economic sphere, as well as in society at large, that may require a modification of this perspective. In recent years, a growing body of scholarship has found that financial markets and the financial industry are increasingly overriding and dominating the real economy (Epstein, 2005; Windolf, 2005a; Krippner, 2011). Moreover, some researchers suggest that the logic of financial markets has spread through society at large (Martin, 2002; Epstein, 2005; Davis 2009). According to this perspective, finance has become the paradigm of a rational and value-maximizing type of social action and thus a generic 'model of how things are done' (Davis, 2009: xviii).

There is a long history of attempts to transfer economic tools and terminology to the field of philanthropy which is itself embedded in societal environments that are undergoing financialization processes so there are good reasons to assume that these seismic shifts have not left the charitable sector unaffected. The surge of interest in microcredits and, more recently, social impact bonds, are particularly prominent expressions of these developments, but they capture only the most visible aspects of what may turn out to be a much more profound transformation towards a 'social-purpose finance ecosystem' (Salamon, 2014: 6).

Approaching the concepts of finance and financialization from within an economic context, this chapter examines whether there is evidence for a process of financialization of philanthropy, what it consists of, and what it may entail. A comparison between structural characteristics of the financial sphere and of current developments towards a 'social investment' paradigm of philanthropy in Europe and the US provides numerous parallels, exemplifying the transformation of the charitable sector along financial templates. The chapter then argues that financialization is merely one part of a broader project of marketization, aimed at reshaping philanthropy in accordance with the paradigm of financial capitalism, thus completing and radicalizing previous processes of marketization. Finally, the chapter shows that the concept of financialization equips scholars with considerable analytical and theoretical leverage. In the first place, it provides a coherent blueprint of new actors, ideas and practices with a considerable potential to reshape the organizational field of philanthropy, as well as the very understanding of what it means to act in charitable ways. In addition, it helps to explain the emergence of social investment philanthropy and to predict the further course of events. In particular, it helps in assessing the possible consequences of this transformation, which at present are only addressed at the margins of academic and practical discourse.

Financialization and the financial sphere

Financialization, in a broad sense, means the 'increasing role of financial motives, financial markets, financial actors and financial institutions in the operation of the domestic and international economies' (Epstein, 2005: 3). The term has been used to designate a range of diverse phenomena, such as shifts in the dominant sources of economic revenue, the rise of the concept of stakeholder value as a dominant mode of corporate governance (Krippner, 2011) and changes in individual behaviour, including a rise of both private debt and private investments (Deutschmann, 2011). Importantly, processes of financialization are also spreading beyond the economic sphere. Scholars have diagnosed processes of financialization of the state (Davis, 2009) and of daily life (Martin, 2002; Davis, 2009). Recent analyses find evidence of financialization in domains as diverse as sustainability reporting (Hiss, 2013), infrastructure (O'Neill, 2013), microcredits (Mader, 2014) and the arts (Velthuis and Coslor, 2012).

These considerations suggest that financialization should be regarded as a broad and ongoing, yet uncoordinated and fragmented process, which may take different forms according to objectives and circumstances. The financialization of philanthropy is an overarching project that is not confined to more singular developments, such as the spread of microcredits. Rather, it denotes the comprehensive transformation of this field along the template of finance. Hence, gaining theoretical leverage over the phenomenon requires a better understanding of the underlying paradigm, that is, knowledge of the structures and processes which constitute the architecture of finance. The following section outlines the characteristic properties of this system and considers how it differs from the organization of the primary economy it allegedly transforms.

The characteristics of financialization

Finance is no longer regarded as the handmaiden of primary economy. Rather, it has evolved into a distinct 'sphere' (Knorr Cetina and Preda, 2012: 4) that is, a field of economic activity *sui generis*. The casting of it as a sphere, rather than an organizational field, is important in that it denotes a wider reach. While a field is confined to the actors and practice, institutions and logics which constitute the field (Scott, 2008), the former refers to a domain that exerts influence beyond its actual boundaries. The financial sphere can be distinguished from the three other economic spheres, namely production, consumption and exchange, by its particular function: to provide credit to the primary economy. Finance thus plays a crucial role in the process of production and serves as an important precondition for economic growth (Knorr Cetina, 2012: 119-122).

Finance centers around particular places and modes of activity, such as stock exchanges and the global system of digital over-the-counter markets (Knorr Cetina, 2012: 123). Compared to much of the exchange that takes place in the primary economy, financial markets have become separate 'transactional worlds' which rely in important ways on idiosyncratic technologies, flows of information and related practices (Knorr Cetina, 2012: 130).

New actors and activities in finance

The financial system is dominated by a new class of actors. In countries such as the US and the UK, the center of gravity has shifted from commercial banks to actors in the financial markets, such as investment banks, brokerage agencies and pension funds (Windolf, 2005a: 32–41; Davis, 2009). Banks as the traditional providers of credit have also changed and are now deeply involved in financial markets. As a result, clients' deposits now only account for a fraction of the money banks lend to their customers (Knorr Cetina and Preda, 2012: 2).

Rather than producing and trading commodities as the primary economy does, financial actors issue, develop, invest in and trade an increasing diversity of intangible financial products or assets, such as shares, bonds, interests or loans (Krippner, 2011). Unlike the primary economy with its broad range of activities and motivations, 'the core activities in financial markets … are investment and speculation' (Knorr Cetina, 2011: 121). The concept of investment is used in both economics and finance, albeit with slightly different meanings. In economics, investment denotes the purchase of material or immaterial goods, aimed at productivity growth and, hence, higher revenues. Financial actors invest in financial products with an expectation of future capital returns, such as dividends or interest (Wöhe, 1996; Busse von Colbe *et al.*, 2007; Springer Gabler, 2014).

Finance requires the support of intermediaries, namely analysts and rating agencies that convert uncertainty to risk, reduce complexity and thus provide investors with crucial operating knowledge. They use their own research to provide assessments of the overall creditworthiness of corporations, and of national states, prognoses of future performance, evaluation of compliance with legal and ethical standards, and general expectations of appropriate corporate behaviour (Windolf, 2005b: 44).

Environmental transformation of finance

Financial markets are not confined simply to the field of finance; they influence and transform their environments in important respects. First, financialization alters the cognitive framework of market participants. While financial markets rely on, and interact with, existing economic and noneconomic actors and structures, these are assigned new meanings, functions and relevance. For instance, Krippner (2012: 8) asserts that, under conditions of financialization, corporations are seen as flows of decomposable resources rather than stable entities. Moreover, financialization has led to an alternative understanding of the aims and outcomes of economic activity. Whereas an emphasis on growth was dominant in the big corporations of the 1960s, the focus has now shifted toward maximizing profit in terms of shareholder value (Windolf, 2005b: 24). At the same time, states have been portrayed as mere 'vendors of law' (Davis, 2009: 29), charged with supervizing markets, but abstaining from hard policy decisions on questions of distribution – a task that is now assigned to the markets (Krippner, 2011: 150). According to Davis, this process has also led to a new understanding of individuals and their roles in society. Formerly conceived as employees, citizens or voters, they have now become investors of human, social and political capital (Davis, 2009: 30). He characterizes this turn as the 'portfolio thinking' of private life. For instance, 'homeowners have been encouraged to see their homes as an investment asset rather than a durable tie to a community' (Davis, 2009: 30). Second, finance both draws on and triggers processes of globalization and standardization. For instance, credit used to be provided through a bank, in the context of an established and long-term relationship of mutual trust, as well as the bank's comprehensive, yet tacit and exclusive knowledge of the enterprise. Today, global investors have access to standardized information on corporations, enabling them to make investment decisions without any prior knowledge of the investee. For this reason, 'a Korean corporation evaluated as AAA is … as worthy of credit as a Canadian enterprise with the same ranking' (Windolf, 2005b: 46, author's translation). Finally, the rise of finance reconfigures power structures. Instead of peaceful coexistence for both new and old actors, it leads to an imbalance between corporations and financial investors. For instance, corporations need to adapt to the expectations of rating agencies and analysts to obtain the favourable ratings they need in order to attract money (Windolf, 2005b: 46).

While this list is far from complete, it provides an overview of the major characteristics of the financial sphere and, in particular, points to some well-established consequences of the growing importance and dominance of finance. The next section turns from finance to philanthropy, identifying similarities between the two realms with a view to providing evidence of the financialization of philanthropy.

Philanthropic action as social investment

Using the architecture of finance as an analytical lens to scrutinize recent developments in the philanthropic sector, a number of striking parallels may be observed. Since the advent of venture philanthropy in the US in the 1990s (Defourny et al., Chapter 22), the field of philanthropy has undergone a remarkably broad and profound process of change. In several important respects, this is oriented towards a financial paradigm. The concept of financialization is helpful in analyzing these developments as it illustrates the inner logic of what, at first glance, look like fragmented developments. Since the new approach comes under the heading of 'social investment' – or variants thereof, such as 'impact investing' (Weber and Scheck, 2012), or 'social-impact investing' (Salamon, 2014) – a close conceptual link to *the* major activity in finance is established. Over recent decades, the term has been used to describe a wide range of phenomena, some related to, and some beyond, the field of philanthropy. The latter include ethical and socially responsible types of capital investments (Bruyn, 1991), as well as more productive ways to provide public welfare (Giddens, 1998; Midgley, 1999). In a philanthropic context, social investment has been proposed as: a generic concept for third-sector research (Then and Kehl, 2012); a new model to provide financial assets for social purposes (Nicholls, 2010; Schröer and Sigmund, 2012); and a new way to conceive of philanthropic action, as, for instance, in the context of venture philanthropy (Letts et al., 1997).

The venture philanthropy approach has been particularly influential in introducing the social investment paradigm to the field of philanthropy. It is important for the present inquiry because, unlike the broader discourse on marketization, it has been explicitly oriented towards a financial paradigm, including its logic and methods, actors and practices. It aims to transform the practices of philanthropic foundations in imitation of the practices of venture capital firms. At its core lies the observation that traditional philanthropic approaches have proven inadequate to solve major social problems. To enhance the effectiveness of charitable giving, so the argument goes, philanthropists need to regard their practice as an investment of a particular – namely social – kind. Social investment, thus conceived, aims at establishing a long-term relationship with nonprofits in order to build the organizational capacity required for solving social problems on a large scale. Like their financial counterparts, venture philanthropists invest in a 'portfolio' of promising nonprofit organizations selected via processes of 'due diligence', based on explicit metrics of success. In this framework, all philanthropic action is oriented towards social impact as the ultimate 'social return of investment' (Letts et al., 1997; Frumkin, 2003).

In his 2003 review, Frumkin arrived at a rather sceptical verdict, however, on the achievements and transformative potential of venture philanthropy. Overall, he maintained, the approach merely results in a relabeling of philanthropic activity, without any substantial change in actual practice. As a result, Frumkin observed that 'many of the "investments" made by venture philanthropist [sic] look just like the 'grants' made by other donors' (Frumkin, 2003: 15). An important part of the problem was the fact that the old practice of philanthropy seemed to lag behind the newly invented language. Hence, Frumkin suggested, 'important breakthroughs in practices are needed that create real distance between venture philanthropy and traditional giving' (2003: 15).

In retrospect, what appeared to be simply a semantic change can now be regarded as a powerful generative metaphor (Schön, 1979). The shift from charitable giving to social investment triggered a development which actually *has* created 'real' distance. It seems the logic of social investment cannot easily be transferred to a philanthropic sector that is based on the logic of charitable gift giving. Recent decades have, therefore, seen a comprehensive attempt at creating both the structures and the conceptual framework appropriate to the financial sphere in a number of important respects.

As a result, Salamon's (2014) account of recent developments in philanthropy can be read as an immediate transposition of major elements of the financial sphere into the field of philanthropy. He diagnoses the emergence of a 'social-purpose finance ecosystem' (Salamon, 2014: 6), including new financial actors and entities, tools and products, as well as the redefinition of existing actors and their operating routines. His account is based on an overarching new narrative of philanthropy organized around the notion of 'social-impact investment'. This is a kind of philanthropy that takes a long-term view seeking to create social enterprises which are both economically viable and socially effective due to their ability to generate social *and* financial returns (Salamon, 2014: 5–6).

These developments mark a new concept of philanthropy that follows the financial model, and the next section points out the parallels between them. The analysis shows that financialized philanthropy replicates the technical architecture of the financial sector so as to perform similar production tasks in similar ways. Although this transformation is still in its early stages, and incomplete in important respects, it may ultimately result in the creation of a structural isomorphism (DiMaggio and Powell, 1991) that straddles the spheres of finance and philanthropy.

Parallels of finance and philanthropy

Financial themes and financial language have become ubiquitous today, both in the scholarship and the practice of philanthropy. Inadequate budgets due to the stagnation, or even the decline, of traditional sources of funding on one hand, and the enormous amount of free capital circulating in global financial markets, on the other, have created renewed interest in philanthropic finance. For instance, global financial stock was estimated at $212 trillion in 2010 (McKinsey 2011: 2). This leads to a greater awareness of new and alternative opportunities to mobilize these assets for social purposes, as well as the financial tools and transactions required to do so (Freireich and Fulton, 2009; Nicholls, 2010; Achleitner et al., 2011; Moore et al., 2012; Weber and Scheck, 2012; Salamon, 2014).

In the philanthropic sector, access to resources has traditionally been based on a direct relationship between funders and recipients. For the new logic to work, the exchange of resources needs to be organized in more indirect and market-like ways. While these developments are still in their early stages, a number of actors are experimenting with the establishment of social-purpose exchanges. Although they resemble their financial counterparts in terms of basic operations, their social mission distinguishes them from conventional platforms because they aim to attract investors who are in sympathy with the social objectives of the enterprises concerned. Examples include the NExT SSE (Breidenbach, 2011), the Social Stock Exchange Ltd in the UK and many others around the world (Shahnaz *et al.*, 2014).

New actors and activities in philanthropy

A number of new funders have emerged recently in the philanthropic field. These include venture philanthropists, as well as 'new donors' (Eikenberry and Kluver, 2004; Hess, 2005) – successful entrepreneurs who stress the 'investment' character of their giving. They are joined by nonprofit and for-profit investment funds, many of whom plan to maximize both the social and the financial return on their 'social impact investments' (Salamon, 2014: 18–20).

Microcredits are the most visible new financial tools of philanthropy. Particularly in developing countries, they are now provided by a genuine microfinance industry. Rapid growth has produced a credit volume of $US 89.4 billion assisting more than 200 million customers (Mader, 2014: 167). The rise of microfinance is highly relevant to the process of financialization, not only because these new tools are praised as being particularly effective in terms of poverty reduction, but also because they generate a particularly high return on investment (Mader, 2014). Recently, there has also been a surge of interest in social impact bonds. They are based on the idea that the state should encourage private investors to finance attempts to develop more effective solutions to social problems. Provided that public spending is actually reduced, the state pays dividends to the investors in return (Clifford and Jung, 2016).

Accordingly, rational nonprofit activity is no longer regarded as the mere giving away of gifts. In the new framework, philanthropic action ranges from traditional gift giving to profitable businesses championing a social cause. We are now seeing the emergence of an intermediary sector which eliminates the gap between nonprofit and for-profit action, creating a seamless continuum (Nicholls, 2010: 76). There are now two ways to measure returns in philanthropic practice. Social impact has become the universal 'currency' of these new practices however vague its meaning. As it is now widely acknowledged that the social economy may include profitable businesses, a financial return on investment has become a legitimate alternative measure of success (Nicholls, 2010; Salamon, 2014).

Similarly to finance, the new actors of financialized philanthropy are supported by specialist analysts and intermediary organizations. Nonprofit rating agencies, such as the American Charity Watch, the German Phineo or New Philanthropy Capital (NPC) in the UK, claim to provide donors with the objective, professional and in-depth knowledge of potential recipients that they need to make informed decisions on which organizations to support. Charity Watch adopts the big financial rating agencies' system by rating nonprofits from grades 'A+' to 'F,' (Lowell *et al.*, 2005). These organizations are complemented by a number of specialist microfinance rating agencies (Gutiérrez-Nieto, 2007), some of which have been founded by managers who had previously worked in finance (e.g. NPC in the UK), while others represent the interplay between new and old actors. In Germany, the rating agency Phineo has been established as a joint venture by the Bertelsmann Foundation and Deutsche Börse (German Stock Exchange Group). Beyond that, there are 'capital aggregators' and 'enterprise brokers' (Hagerman and Wood, 2014) who raise money from investors and provide liquidity to enterprises that have some kind of social mission (Richter, 2014). Again, they serve as experts with an intimate knowledge of underserved firms and markets. However, the extent to which these firms actually pursue a genuinely social rather than a straightforward for-profit agenda may often be difficult to determine.

Environmental transformation of philanthropy

As the financialization of philanthropy is still in its early stages, its broader impact has not yet been determined. However, attempts to redefine existing actors, tools and modes of operation in terms that are increasingly compatible with a financial paradigm are clearly visible today. The transformation from *philanthropic giving* along the lines of the gift economy (e.g. Adloff, 2010) to an example of *social investment* is the greatest change in this context. Others refer to new ways to conceive of established philanthropic organizations, notably philanthropic foundations. While they still have a role to play in the new scenario, albeit with different functions and under new labels, the more innovative foundations are now termed 'philanthropic banks' (Salamon and Burckart, 2014) in order to determine their place – if only in the second row – in the new financialized philanthropic environment.

In sum, the philanthropic sector is undergoing a profound and all-embracing process of change, the consequences of which are as yet unclear. Through financialization, we are seeing the transformation of the sector along the lines of the financial sphere, including its structures, processes and rationales. Table 23.1 below illustrates the close match between the emerging ecosystem of philanthropic social investment and the financial sphere.

Financialization as a completion of marketization

If indeed philanthropy is financialized, the following questions arise: Why does it happen and to what purpose? Some scholars suggest an explanation based on supply and demand. For instance, Salamon argues that an excess of financial assets leads financial actors to search for new profitable investment opportunities, while an increase in global social crises and the parallel growth of social entrepreneurship result in a rising interest in investment in social enterprises which may or may not generate their own revenues (Salamon, 2014). Yet, while these factors certainly have a role to play, there is an alternative explanation. This builds on the original diagnosis of a marketization of the third sector.

If marketization itself is not just transferring business methods to the charitable sector, but represents an attempt to structure philanthropic activity according to economic paradigms, financialization makes perfect sense. If finance is indeed an essential component of modern

Table 23.1 Structural parallels between finance and social investment philanthropy

	Finance	Social Investment Philanthropy
Function	Providing credit to the primary economy	Providing credit to social entrepreneurs
Benefits	Enabling economic growth	Enabling the growth of a social economy
Markets	Exchange traded and over-the-counter markets	Social stock exchanges
Actors	For-profit investors (investment banks, stock brokers, pension funds, etc.)	Nonprofit, for-profit and quasi-public investors (social investment funds, 'philanthropic banks')
Motives	Financial returns	Social and financial returns
Core activities	Investment and speculation	Social investment
Products	Diverse financial tools and products such as credits, bonds and others	New tools of socio-finance, such as microcredits or social impact bonds
Intermediaries	Rating agencies Financial analysts	Non-profit rating agencies Social impact analysts

capitalism, the marketization of philanthropy can only work successfully if it is complemented by a proprietary system of philanthropic finance. While there is certainly no explicit masterplan, the very idea of social investment urges actors to create the kind of ecosystem that is required if the project of marketization is to work at all, and to work well.

Viewed in this light, the financialization of philanthropy is not an independent phenomenon. Depending on one's point of view, it can be described either as the completion or the radicalization of marketization. Compared to earlier attempts to add economic tools to the philanthropic toolkit, the new developments have an entirely new dimension, aiming, as they do, at a fundamental reconstruction and re-evaluation of philanthropy. First, philanthropic activity is no longer portrayed as a type of action *sui generis* which is enhanced by the use of economic methods. Rather, rational philanthropic action *is* an investment in the proper sense of the word, which considerably reduces the scope for alternative practices. Second, the social investment paradigm is based on a coherent outlook on society. Proponents of social investment do not demand entirely new kinds of philanthropic action. Rather, they see charitable effectiveness as a *function* of investment-like behaviour, the effects of which can be enhanced if this aspect is strengthened. Accordingly, the social investment approach entails a straightforward normative programme. Its essence is expressed by the idea that philanthropic organizations *should* increasingly behave like social investors and that the sector as a whole needs to be rearranged to facilitate this shift.

Given these considerations, we might ask if it would be better for the concept of financialization to be replaced by a modified version of marketization that draws more on the paradigm of financial capitalism in the sense outlined above. Despite strong arguments for this position, financialization has an important role to play. First, it enables us to understand how the different, seemingly unrelated building blocks of this transformation are interconnected through their respective roles in the financial sector. This process, if successful, might have far-reaching consequences which are beyond the scope of the current debate (but see Nicholls, 2010: 87–93; Salamon, 2014: 93–94). Second, financialization provides scholars with the theoretical instruments required to explain events and assess the further course of developments, as well as possible consequences. This issue of consequences is addressed in the next section.

The consequences of financialization

Scholars and practitioners alike mostly emphasize the enormous opportunities inherent in attempts at redirecting a substantial share of global capital into the philanthropic sector. The risks of financialization play a merely peripheral role in this discussion (Salamon, 2014: 93–97). In fact, there are a number of potentially desirable effects, for example, increasing awareness of how to mobilize existing resources for philanthropic purposes, such as ethical or mission-related investments. Furthermore, the development of new financial products such as microcredits or social impact bonds may result in the emergence of a wholly new set of instruments in the philanthropic toolkit that might be effective in addressing a range of social problems that cannot be tackled by more conventional means (Salamon, 2014).

Given the events of the financial crisis of 2008–09, and its major societal consequences, however, unlimited faith in the power of finance to solve some of the very problems it has caused in the first place seems unwarranted. While the majority of economists maintain that financial markets generate desirable effects such as economic growth (Knorr Cetina, 2011: 112), many scholars of financialization point to a broad range of unintended and problematic results (Windolf, 2005a; Epstein and Jayadev, 2006; Davis, 2009; Krippner, 2012; Heires and Nölke, 2014), which suggests particular caution when it comes to making philanthropy safe for financial investors.

The next section highlight some of the more problematic and unintended consequences. Acknowledging that the list may be incomplete, the assumption is that where financialization of philanthropy is continuously occurring, more of the following issues will arise.

Alternative modes and rationales of resource allocation

According to Krippner, financialization can be explained as a political response to 'the inability of an affluent society to face the political challenges imposed by the end of affluence' (Krippner, 2011: 149). She contends that policymakers turned to the markets in order to avoid making hard decisions on the question of distribution. As a result, she observes 'eroding collective capacities to engage questions of economic justice' (Krippner, 2011: 150). If this assessment is correct, the financialization of philanthropy may lead to similar results. For instance, the measures employed by nonprofit rating agencies such as the German Phineo result in decisions on the allocation of scarce resources being based on largely non-normative criteria (Phineo, 2012). As a consequence, nonprofit organizations that operate in incommensurable situations and aim at furthering basically incommensurable values are subject to an identical evaluation regime. In this framework, projects that aim to save human lives are evaluated by the same methods and obtain the same ratings as projects aimed at saving frogs.

Another consequence is the fact that social impact as the alleged *raison d'être* of the new philanthropy is notoriously hard to define and measure (Ebrahim and Rangan, 2010; Liket, 2014). In contrast, determining the *financial* return of (social) businesses is a much more straightforward task. Hence, investors and intermediaries will have strong incentives to focus on maximum returns on investment, while treating social value more as a desirable by-product than as the proper purpose of social enterprises (cf. Gutiérrez-Nieto and Serrano-Cinca, 2007).

Corporate misbehaviour

The financial crisis of 2008–09 highlighted the undesirable side effects of the excessive deregulation of finance that has been identified as the cause of severe economic and political crises; at the same time, major actors in the financial industry have repeatedly been found guilty of corporate misbehaviour and fraud (Stiglitz, 2010; Roubini and Mihm, 2011). Similar problematic consequences are to be expected if the philanthropic sector simply opens the gates to financial actors without determining the rules of appropriate corporate behaviour. At the very minimum, the language of impact investment will increasingly only be used for reasons of legitimacy, thus erecting philanthropic facades behind which the quest for maximum financial returns rather than social purposes will be pursued. In the worst case, the impacts of financialization on the philanthropic sector will closely resemble the situation in the real economy. Critical analysts such as Mader (2014), who explores the dark side of the microfinance industry, point to very similar potential consequences, such as corporate misbehaviour and cyclical systemic crises leading to over-indebtedness and misery of debtors, as well as the widespread inclination to provide public subsidies intended to guarantee private profits.

A shift in power from social enterprise to finance

Disregard for the power of financial actors is another blind spot of current debates on the transformation of philanthropy. Financialization is mostly treated as a matter of technology; the implications of opening the field to the wealthy and powerful actors of the global financial markets, creating new forms of resource dependency, are neglected. This may be due to rather techno-cratic conceptions of finance as a merely functional part of modern economy. For instance, while Salamon (2014: 93) acknowledges that 'there will be winners and losers' of financial-ization, the modern revenue-generating, service-providing generation of social entrepreneurs should be expected to be positioned on the winning side of the new regime of accumulation (as opposed to advocacy or civil rights organizations). However, scholars of financialization shed doubts on these assumptions as they maintain that, rather than being the servant of the real economy, finance has become its master in important respects. For instance, Deutschmann (2011: 382) argues that, 'from a sociological view, financialization can be characterized as a hegemonic regime of rentiers over entrepreneurs'. The same development is likely to occur in the field of philanthropy. Under conditions of financialization, profitable social enterprises will increasingly be taken over by large investors (Shahnaz *et al.*, 2014: 144) or will face increasing pressure to deliver profits regardless of their social mission.

The rise of alternatives

While attempts to mobilize the assets of the financial industry for philanthropic purposes are at the heart of current debates, there is also resistance to financialization and experimentation with alternatives. Van der Zwan (2014: 121) points to 'promising new initiatives that go against the grain of the financial regime, both inside the realm of finance (peer-to-peer lending platforms, community cooperative banking), as well as outside (new forms of community ownership and systems of sharing)'. In the field of philanthropy, a number of more grassroots-oriented organi-zational forms have emerged as possible alternatives to industrial finance, such as giving circles, which pool financial, social and cultural capital to find new answers to the old insufficiency challenge (Eikenberry, 2006). Moreover, the concept of financialization in the context of phi-lanthropy may also sharpen focus when it comes to civil society initiatives that actively oppose these developments and advocate reining in the power of global finance rather than extending it (Fioramonti and Thümler, 2013).

Conclusion and outlook

The concept of financialization, if applied to the philanthropic sector, makes visible a broad transformation along the paradigm of the financial sphere. Its heuristic advantage lies in the potential to subsume different phenomena under one umbrella term and thus make visible the underlying template of seemingly unconnected developments. This chapter has argued that financialization should be discussed and understood in the wider context of a marketization of philanthropy along the lines of financial capitalism. This approach suggests new explanations for familiar phenomena and allows us to make predictions regarding the possible consequences.

It also creates a major puzzle, however, which cannot be solved in the context of this paper. The financial crisis of 2008–09 exposed the potentially dramatic consequences of deregulated financial markets that are now widely regarded as a major threat to the stability and welfare of contemporary societies. These events have triggered a highly critical public and political reaction towards the excesses of the financial industry, as well as comprehensive attempts to re-embed and re-regulate this sector (Fioramonti and Thümler, 2013).

Against this backdrop it comes as a surprise that civil society in general and philanthropy in particular have displayed an almost complete disregard vis-à-vis these developments, and there is little sign of initiatives to tackle their root causes (Fioramonti and Thümler, 2013; Scholte, 2013). An increasing number of scholars and practitioners aim to reshape the philanthropic sector according to the paradigm of those same financial markets, including calls for an active process of deregulation and intervention by the state to enable and accelerate these processes. Possible risks and unintended consequences are largely excluded from these considerations (Weber and Scheck, 2012; Salamon, 2014).

This raises the question of a possible connection between the two phenomena. Obviously, the project of tapping the assets of global finance is hardly compatible with attempts at opposing the power of the financial industry. Further investigations of the processes of financialization and marketization in the field of philanthropy should describe, trace and explain these developments and their interconnections more thoroughly. Finally, research should increasingly explore the political economy of financialization, taking a more systematic and realistic account of its actual and potential social and political consequences.

References

Achleitner, A.-K., Spiess-Knafl, W. and Volk, S. (2011) 'Finanzierung von Social Enterprises – Neue Herausforderungen für die Finanzmärkte.' In H. Hackenberg, S. Empter (eds): *Social Entrepreneuship – Social Business: Für die Gesellschaft unternehmen*. Wiesbaden: VS Verlag für Sozialwissenschaften, 269–86.

Adloff, F. (2010) 'Gift/Giving.' In H. K. Anheier and S. Toepler (eds): *International Encyclopaedia of Civil Society*. New York: Springer, NY, 756–59.

Breidenbach, S. (2011) 'Sozialbörsen zur Finanzierung von Social Businesses – Das Modell der NExT SSE.' In H. Hackenberg and S. Empter (eds.): *Social Entrepreneurship – Social Business: Für die Gesellschaft unternehmen*. VS Verlag für Sozialwissenschaften, 301–310.

Bruyn, S. (1991) *The Field of Social Investment*. Cambridge, New York: Cambridge University Press.

Busse von Colbe, W., Coenenberg, A. G., Kajuter, P., Linnoff, U., Pellens, B. (eds) (2007) *Betriebswirtschaftslehre für Führungskräfte. Eine Einführung für Ingenieure, Naturwissenschaftler, Juristen und Geisteswissenschaftler*. Stuttgart: Schäffer-Poeschl.

Clifford, J. and Jung, T. (2016) 'Social Impact Bonds: Exploring and Understanding an Emerging Funding Approach.' In O. Lehner (ed.): *The Routledge Handbook of Social and Sustainable Finance*. London: Routledge.

Davis, G. F. (2009) *Managed by the Markets. How Finance Reshaped America*. Oxford, New York: Oxford University Press.

Deutschmann, C. (2011) 'Limits to Financialization.' In *European Journal of Sociology* 52(3): 347–89.

DiMaggio, P. J. and Powell, W. W. (1991) 'The Iron Cage Revisited: Institutional Isomorphism and Collective Rationality in Organizational Fields.' In W. W. Powell, P. J. DiMaggio (eds): *The New Institutionalism in Organizational Analysis*. Chicago, London: The University of Chicago Press, 63–82.

Ebrahim, A. and Rangan, V. K. (2010) *The Limits of Nonprofit Impact: A Contingency Framework for Measuring Social Performance*. Harvard Business School (Harvard Business School General Management Unit Working Paper, 10–099).

Eikenberry, A. M. (2006) 'Giving Circles: Growing Grassroots Philanthropy.' In *Nonprofit and Voluntary Sector Quarterly* 35(3): 517–32.

Eikenberry, A. M. and Kluver, J. D. (2004) 'The Marketization of the Nonprofit Sector: Civil Society at Risk?.' In *Public Administration Review* 64(2): 132–40.

Epstein, G. A. (2005) 'Introduction: Financialization and the World Economy.' In G. A. Epstein (ed.): *Financialization and the World Economy*. Cheltenham: Edward Elgar Publishing, 3–16.

Epstein, G. A. and Jayadev, A. (2006) 'The Rise of Rentier Incomes in OECD Countries: Financialization, Central Bank Policy and Labor Solidarity.' In G. A. Epstein (ed.): *Financialization and the World Economy*. Cheltenham: Edward Elgar Publishing, 46–74.

Fioramonti, L. and Thümler, E. (2013) 'Accountability, Democracy, and Post-growth: Civil Society Rethinking Political Economy and Finance', in *Journal of Civil Society* 9(2): 117–28.

Freireich, J. and Fulton, K. (2009) *Investing for Social and Environmental Impact. A Design for Catalyzing an Emerging Industry*. Monitor Institute.

Friedland, R. and Robertson, A. F. (1990) 'Beyond the Marketplace.' In R. Friedland and A. F. Robertson (eds): *Beyond the Marketplace. Rethinking Economy and Society*. New York: Aldine de Gruyter, 3–51.

Frumkin, P. (2003) 'Inside Venture Philanthropy', In *Society* 40(4): 7–15.

Giddens, A. (1998) *The Third Way. The Renewal of Social Democracy*. Cambridge: Polity Press.

Gutiérrez-Nieto, B. and Serrano-Cinca, C. (2007) 'Factors Explaining the Rating of Microfinance Institutions.' In *Nonprofit and Voluntary Sector Quarterly* 36 (3): 439–64.

Hagerman, L. and Wood, D. (2014) 'Enterprise Brokers.' In L. M. Salamon (ed.): *New Frontiers of Philanthropy. A Guide to the New Tools and Actors Reshaping Global Philanthropy and Social Investing*. Oxford: Oxford University Press, 209–20.

Heires, M. and Nölke, A. (2014) 'Die Politische Ökonomie der Finanzialisierung.' In M. Heires (ed.): *Politische Ökonomie der Finanzialisierung*. Wiesbaden: Springer VS, 19–29.

Hess, F. M. (2005) 'Introduction.' In F. M. Hess (ed.): *With the Best of Intentions. How Philanthropy is Reshaping K-12 Education*. Cambridge, MA: Harvard Education Press, 1–17.

Hiss, S. (2013) 'The Politics of the Financialization of Sustainability.' In *Competition and Change* 17(3): 234–47.

Knorr Cetina, K. (2012) 'What is a Financial Market? Global Markets as Microinstitutional and Post-Traditional Social Forms.' In K. Knorr Cetina and A. Preda (eds): *The Oxford Handbook of the Sociology of Finance*. Oxford: Oxford University Press, 115–33.

Knorr Cetina, K. and Preda, A. (2012) 'Introduction.' In K. Knorr Cetina and A. Preda (eds): *The Oxford Handbook of the Sociology of Finance*. Oxford: Oxford University Press, 1–9.

Krippner, G. R. (2011) *Capitalizing on Crisis: The Political Origins of the Rise of Finance*. Cambridge, MA and London: Harvard University Press.

Letts, C. W., Ryan, W. P. and Grossman, A. (1997) 'Virtuous Capital: What Foundations Can Learn from Venture Capitalists.' In *Harvard Business Review* (75): 36–50.

Liket, K. (2014) 'Why Doing Good is Not Good Enough', Essays on Social Impact Measurement. Rotterdam, PhD Series in Research in Management No. 307.

Lowell, S., Trelstad, B. and Meehan, Bill (2005) 'The Ratings Game.' In *Stanford Social Innovation Review* 3: 38–45.

Mader, P. (2014) 'Mikrofinanz zwischen "Finanzieller Inklusion" und Finanzialisierung.' In M. Heires (ed.): *Politische Ökonomie der Finanzialisierung*. Wiesbaden: Springer VS, 163–77.

Martin, R. (2002) *Financialization of Daily Life*. Philadelphia: Temple University Press.

Midgley, J. (1999) 'Growth, Redistribution, and Welfare: Toward Social Investment.' In *Social Service Review* 73 (1): 3–21.

Moore, M.-L., Westley, F. R. and Nicholls, A. (2012) 'The Social Finance and Social Innovation Nexus.' In *Journal of Social Entrepreneurship* 3(2): 115–32.

Nicholls, A. (2010) 'The Institutionalization of Social Investment: The Interplay of Investment Logics and Investor Rationalities.' In *Journal of Social Entrepreneurship* 1 (1): 70–100.

O'Neill, P. M. (2013) 'The Financialisation of Infrastructure: The Role of Categorisation and Property Relations.' In *Cambridge Journal of Regions, Economy and Society* 6(3): 441–54.

Phineo (ed.) (2012) 'Engagement mit Wirkung.' Berlin. Online. Available www.phineo.org/downloads/PHINEO_Engagement_mit_Wirkung.pdf> [accessed 18 July 2014].

Richter, L. (2014) 'Capital Aggregators.' In L. M. Salamon (ed.): *New Frontiers of Philanthropy. A Guide to the New Tools and Actors Reshaping Global Philanthropy and Social Investing*. Oxford: Oxford University Press, 91–120.

Roubini, N. and Mihm, S. (2011) *Crisis Economics: A Crash Course in the Future of Finance*. New York: Penguin Books.

Salamon, L. M. (1993) 'The Marketization of Welfare: Changing Nonprofit and For Profit Roles in the American Welfare State.' In *Social Service Review* 67(1): 16–39.

——. (2014) *Leverage for Good. An Introduction to the New Frontiers of Philanthropy and Social Investment*. Oxford: Oxford University Press.

Salamon, L. M. and Burckart, W. (2014) 'Foundations as "Philanthropic Banks."' In Lester M. Salamon (ed.): *New Frontiers of Philanthropy. A Guide to the New Tools and Actors Reshaping Global Philanthropy and Social Investing*. Oxford: Oxford University Press, 165–208.

Scholte, J. A. (2013) 'Civil Society and Financial Markets: What is Not Happening and Why.' In *Journal of Civil Society* 9(2): 129–47.

Schön, D. A. (1979) 'Generative Metaphor: A Perspective on Problem-setting in Social Policy.' In A. Ortony (ed.): *Metaphor and Thought*. Cambridge. Cambridge University Press 254–283.

Schröer, A. and Sigmund, S. (2012) 'Soziale Investition–zur Multidimensionalität eines ökonomischen Konzepts.' In H. K. Anheier, A. Schröer and V. Then (eds): *Soziale Investitionen. Interdisziplinäre Perspektiven*. Wiesbaden: VS Verlag für Sozialwissenschaften, 87–114.

Scott, W. R. (2008) *Institutions and Organizations. Ideas and Interests*, 3rd ed., Thousand Oaus: Sage Publications.

Shahnaz, D., Kraybill, R. and Salamon, L. M. (2014) 'Social and Environmental Exchanges.' In L. M. Salamon (ed.): *New Frontiers of Philanthropy. A Guide to the New Tools and Actors Reshaping Global Philanthropy and Social Investing*. Oxford: Oxford University Press, 144–64.

Springer Gabler (ed.) (2014) 'Gabler Wirtschaftslexikon, Stichwort: Investition', Online. Available http://wirtschaftlex:non.gabler.de/Definition/investigation.html (accessed 6 January 2016).

Stiglitz, J. (2010) *Freefall: Free Markets and the Sinking of the Global Economy*. London: Penguin Books.

Then, V. and Kehl, K. (2012) 'Soziale Investitionen: ein konzeptioneller Entwurf.' In H. K. Anheier, A. Schröer and V. Then (eds): *Soziale Investitionen. Interdisziplinäre Perspektiven*. Wiesbaden: VS Verlag für Sozialwissenschaften, 39–86.

van der Zwan, N. (2014) 'Making Sense of Financialization.' In *Socio-Economic Review* 12(1): 99–129.

Velthuis, O. and Coslor, E. (2014) 'The Financialization of Art.' In K. Knorr Cetina and A. Preda (eds): *The Oxford Handbook of the Sociology of Finance*. Oxford: Oxford University Press, 471–87.

Weber, M. and Scheck, B. (2012) 'Impact Investing in Deutschland. Bestandsaufnahme und Handlungsanweisungen zur Weiterentwicklung. Impact in Motion', Online. Available www.impactin-motion.com/wp/wp-content/uploads/2013/05/Impact-Investing-in-Detschland_08052013.pdf> [accessed 11 September 2014].

Weisbrod, B. A. (ed) (1998) *To Profit or Not to Profit. The Commercial Transformation of the Nonprofit Sector*. Cambridge: Cambridge University Press.

Windolf, P. (2005a) 'Die neuen Eigentümer.' In Paul Windolf (ed.): *Finanzmarkt Kapitalismus. Analysen zum Wandel von Produktionsregimen*. Wiesbaden: VS Verlag für Sozialwissenschaften, 8–19.

Windolf, P. (2005b) 'Was ist Finanzmarkt-Kapitalismus?.' In Paul Windolf (ed.): *Finanzmarkt-Kapitalismus. Analysen zum Wandel von Produktionsregimen*. Wiesbaden: VS Verlag für Sozialwissenschaften, 20–57.

Wöhe, G. (1996) *Einführung in die Allgemeine Betriebswirtschaftslehre*, 19th ed., München, Vahlen.

24

The contested terrain of corporate philanthropy and social responsibility

Theories, approaches and challenges

Michael Moran and Elizabeth Branigan

The purpose of this chapter is to examine two distinct but closely related concepts: corporate philanthropy and corporate social responsibility (CSR). Both have seen increasing prominence over the last few years. This can be explained by reference to a range of contextual factors. First, the reconfiguration of the role of the state and the rising power of the firm within the economy and society has led to calls for firms to assume responsibilities beyond their traditional role as an engine of economic growth. Second, this has been coupled with increased demands from the nonprofit sector for resources, as the sector has grown and government funding has become more thinly spread and increasingly scarce. Third, external pressure from civil society organizations critical of corporate behaviour, combined with internal claims that corporate philanthropy and CSR can have tangible and intangible benefits to the firm, has precipitated a mainstreaming of such practices. Indeed calls for greater responsibility have become so ubiquitous that since the early 2000s corporate philanthropy and CSR have become a mainstream function of almost all large firms in industrialized states, albeit with varying degrees of integration, efficacy and authenticity.

Nonetheless, despite the ubiquity of the concepts of corporate philanthropy and CSR, they remain heavily contested: there is limited scholarly consensus on definitions; debates remain on instrumental questions including empirical debates over the utility of philanthropy to the firm and its shareholders; and there are questions about the so-called business case, and the legitimacy of philanthropy in a context still largely dominated by norms of shareholder primacy. Moreover, the financial crisis that began in 2008 was in part precipitated by firms that were considered, under many ostensibly objective metrics, to be among the most socially responsible and philanthropically generous, leading some to question corporate philanthropy's and CSR's effect on civilizing corporate behaviour.

This chapter begins by covering the basic definitional terrain, situating corporate philanthropy and CSR in historical context. Against this historical backdrop, we then explore the range of theories of corporate philanthropy and CSR that have emerged as tools to explain, and perhaps more appropriately structure, corporate behaviour. After this, we then outline the cases for corporate giving and responsibility, before briefly assessing current trends in corporate practice and measurement.

Historical development of the concepts of corporate philanthropy and corporate social responsibility

As this section will illustrate, CSR arose out of corporate philanthropy, before subsuming the latter as a subcategory. While CSR has been cast as a broader guiding framework for ethical business practice, and has been described in many ways and used in a wide range of applications, there is still no universally agreed definition of what it means. In a broad sense, CSR is a conceptualization of corporate power as extending beyond the market to the realms of politics, culture and society. As Wood (1991: 692) has argued 'the basic idea of corporate social responsibility is that business and society are interwoven rather than distinct entities'. The key deliberations that have emerged around this concept are concerned with the extent to which responsibility must be taken, to both ensure that this relationship creates positive social impact, and that any detrimental effects of this reach are moderated.

Here we offer an overview of the historical development of the definitions of CSR and of corporate philanthropy as one of its key constituent elements: two approaches that have been inextricably entwined in both theory and practice since their origins. We explore the changes in the conceptualisations of, and relationships between, these two concepts, our central argument being that they have transmuted in direct relation to a series of significant changes in the global political, social and economic environments throughout the twentieth and early twenty-first centuries. In analyzing these changes, we explore a range of challenges and responses to the questions of whether corporate philanthropy can genuinely be described as a legitimate form of philanthropy and/or whether it constitutes a central pillar of the CSR approach.

The 1920s to 1960s: Corporate philanthropy as social responsibility

CSR has a longer history in the US than in most other countries. It has its roots in the late 1920s, when it was broadly understood as 'social responsibility' (Berle, 1939; Dodd, 1932; and Donham, 1927, cited in Okoye, 2009 and Berle and Means, 1932, cited in Kemper and Martin, 2010: 231). This social responsibility was expressed through corporate philanthropy, leading some authors to define this period as the 'the philanthropic era' of CSR, where voluntary charitable contributions were the main form of social activity that firms undertook (Carroll, 2008: 25). This responsibility by corporates was, however, not really acknowledged and debates until the 1950s (Carroll, 1999, 2008; Carroll and Shabana, 2010; Kemper and Martin, 2010). Frederick (2008: 200) describes three significant features characterizing the thinking in the 1950s: the conceptualization of corporate managers as public trustees; an understanding of the need to balance competing claims to corporate resources; and the common perception of philanthropy as a representation of business support for society. Frederick (2008: 200) argues that at this time, the foundation of CSR continued to be philanthropy – 'the allocation of company funds to support worthy community projects' – which was seen as helping to reduce inequality and as being 'a responsibility, not to say a privilege, of public trusteeship.'

Carroll (1999, 2008), who has played an important role in documenting the development of corporate philanthropy and CSR, cites the publication of Howard R. Bowen's (1953) book *Social Responsibilities of the Businessman* as the origination of the modern literature on this topic. Carroll (1999: 269) notes that '[a]s the title of the [Bowen] book suggests, there were apparently no businesswomen during this period'. The use of the term 'businessman' is also important as it highlights the fact that at this time social responsibility was viewed as the responsibility of individuals, rather than the firm being perceived as a distinct entity with its own agency.

This individualized perspective dominated throughout the 1960s and is evident in works by theorists such as Davis (1960), McGuire (1963) and Davis and Blomstrom (1966). The critical shift of conceptualizing the corporation as agent in its own right began in the 1970s, yet the fundamental ambiguities that are inherent in a firm being both an individual legal entity and a group of people are still being debated decades on (Lorenzo-Molo *et al.*, 2012).

The 1970s: The rising power of the firm in society

The 1970s saw a significant shift in the definitional terrain as it ushered in the theories emerging from the Chicago School of Economics, which considered the idea of a corporate's social responsibility as misguided, as firms are entities that exist solely to maximize stakeholder value. In 1970, Milton Friedman mounted the now well-known argument that 'the only one responsibility of business towards society is the maximization of profits to the shareholders within the legal framework and the ethical custom of the country' (1970). Followers of Friedman, such as Fama, Jensen and Meckling, have further extrapolated on the view that a corporation's responsibility relates solely to its financial stakeholders (Fama, 1980; Fama and Jensen, 1983; Jensen and Meckling, 1976).

A significant contribution to the development of the corporate philanthropy and CSR concepts was made in 1971 by The Committee for Economic Development (CED). This positioned itself in direct contention with the Chicago view. In its 'Social Responsibilities of Business Corporations' CED observed that 'business functions by public consent and its basic purpose is to serve constructively the needs of society – to the satisfaction of society' (CED, 1971: 11, cited in Carroll, 1999: 274).

Around the same time, Votaw offered a very reflective description of CSR. As it captures the complex and contested nature of CSR, it is still widely cited today:

> The term ... means something, but not always the same thing to everybody. To some it conveys the idea of legal responsibility or liability; to others, it means social responsible behavior in the ethical sense; to still others, the meaning transmitted is that of "responsible for" in a causal mode; many simply equate it with a charitable contribution; some take it to mean socially conscious; many of those who embrace it most fervently see it as a mere synonym for legitimacy in the context of belonging or being proper or valid; a few see a sort of fiduciary duty imposing higher standards of behaviour on businessmen than on citizens at large.
>
> *(Votaw, 1973: 11, cited in Carroll, 1999: 280, 2008; Garriga and Melé, 2004: 52; and Okoye, 2009: 613, amongst others)*

The most significant contributions to developing the understanding of CSR in the decade to follow were Freeman's development of stakeholder theory, first presented in 1984, and Donaldson's (1982) work on social contract theory, which expounded the view that the firm was embedded in society. 'Instrumental theory', 'tied social responsibility research to the emerging dominant neoliberal economic paradigm as closely as possible' (Kemper and Martin, 2010: 234). All of these theories will be explored in greater depth throughout the argument to follow.

From the influence of the anti-corporate social movements in the 1980s, through the rapid acceleration of globalization in the 1990s, society's relationship with corporations and their social license to operate has been under constant review. During this period, understandings of CSR have expanded to include characteristics of both environmental sustainability and human rights. Following the 1992 United Nations Conference on the Environment and Development in Rio de Janeiro, known as the 'Earth Summit', the concept of sustainable development has been commonly used to describe the role played by business in environmental and many social issues. The emerging corporate goal of sustainability has subsequently become a key platform of many CSR approaches (Kemper and Martin, 2010).

Around the same time, CSR became a priority concept in human rights discourses and, in particular, for the United Nations, which delineated obligations on business with regard to the promotion and protection of human rights. Former United Nations Secretary-General Kofi Annan fostered the United Nations Global Compact, a framework that includes ten principles that companies are encouraged to uphold in the areas of human rights, labour standards, the environment and anti-corruption. The Global Compact was operationalized in 2000 and has since been adopted by a range of organizations globally, including The Business Leaders Initiative on Human Rights and the World Business Council for Sustainable Development. The United Nations Secretary-General has, furthermore, appointed a Special Representative on the Issue of Human Rights and Business, who developed the 'Protect, Respect, Remedy' framework in an attempt to regulate the deleterious impacts on social and human rights standards of the increasing number of companies that operate across national boundaries and thus beyond the reach of conventional corporate control mechanisms (Kell and Ruggie, 1999; Moir, 2001).

Corporate philanthropy as a key pillar of CSR

As outlined earlier, corporate philanthropy has had a critical role to play in the development of CSR: it provided the basis for CSR and now forms an integral element of many CSR strategies. Godfrey (2005) differentiates corporate philanthropy from CSR as being: first, a charitable and nonreciprocal transaction, i.e. made without the expectation of necessarily getting anything back, and second, voluntary and discretionary. Carroll positions corporate philanthropy as one of the four key pillars in a 'pyramid' model of CSR. This comprises: economic, legal, ethical aspects and voluntary/philanthropic contributions. In fact, Carroll revised this schema in 1991 to accord even greater priority to philanthropy as core to corporate citizenship. A strong argument has been made that corporate philanthropy can be used to generate nonfinancial benefits, such as: reputational capital; employee commitment, productivity and trust; positive social action; and constructive relationships with regulatory institutions or legislative bodies (Fombrun, 1996; Godfrey, 2005; Gan, 2006). Godfrey's (2005) work demonstrates the union between CSR as commercial strategy and CSR for moral and ethical legitimacy through philanthropy, arguing that good deeds earn social credits, as well as contributing to shareholder wealth. Godfrey (2005) has also made the critical distinction that only giving that is perceived to be a genuine expression of social responsiveness has this potential: if corporate philanthropy is understood to be an attempt to gain status or as a marketing strategy it can, instead, erode reputational capital.

In the twenty-first century, the most significant contribution to re-articulating corporate philanthropy has been Martin's (2002) and Porter and Kramer's (2002) popularization of the idea of 'strategic philanthropy', whereby it is argued that that corporate philanthropy has the potential to be successful across both business and social domains if social responsibilities are converted into business opportunities.

As outlined earlier, the intention here has been to provide a map of the evolving conceptual terrain in relation to changing global circumstances, rather than to determine working definitions of CSR and corporate philanthropy. It is clear from this overview that corporate philanthropy has a long history, as both a legitimate form of philanthropy and, often, as a central pillar in CSR approaches. In the section to follow, we will further interrogate the fundamental definitional constructs we have introduced here by outlining various theoretical approaches before we examine in greater depth the arguments for and against the practices of corporate philanthropy and CSR.

Theories of corporate philanthropy and corporate social responsibility

Not surprisingly, the theoretical and conceptual territory remains equally as contested as the definitional. Over the decades, various approaches to explaining the impetus, motives and intent for corporate philanthropy and CSR have developed from a range of disciplinary and ideological perspectives. This has led to a seeming cacophony of voices, some of which question whether corporations should indeed engage in corporate philanthropy at all. Nonetheless, as Melé (2008: 76) has aptly observed these should 'be understood as normative' in nature and treated as ideal types as they provide a useful lens to understand corporate behaviour from competing perspectives.

We identify four groups of corporate philanthropy and CSR theories. These include: agency theory and shareholder value; stakeholder and social contract theories; theories of corporate citizenship, and finally, critical theories. Illustrated in Figure 24.1, we address each of these in turn.

Agency theory and shareholder value

The emergence of the business and society push coincided with the economic crises of the early 1970s that precipitated the shift from Keynesianism to monetarism under the direction of the aforementioned Chicago school. As noted, its chief figurehead, Milton Friedman (1962), had early on challenged the legitimacy of noncore spending by firms. This was consistent with his long-held conviction and soon to be dominant view, that the principal objective of the firm is profit maximization. Kemper and Martin (2010: 231) maintain that this was 'no accident'. Citing Donaldson (1982), they argue that Friedman's interventions were in fact strategically geared toward stimulating a debate around the fundamental role of the firm within economy and society and confronting the concurrent attempts by early CSR proponents, for instance Davis (1960), to define the corporation in broader terms (Kemper and Martin, 2010: 231-33).

The students of the Chicago school advanced agent-centred theories that pivoted around three core assumptions – what Kemper and Martin (2010: 231) described as 'nested axia': the supremacy of shareholder value, as reflected in a firm's (short-term) share price; the centrality of the principal-agent problem to the modern firm, and finally, the utility of performance incentives for mitigating the agency dilemma, by according managers stock options to align their preferences with that of principals. These manifested in a range of cognate theories with roots in classical economics, including agency theory and the theory of the firm that takes as its starting point the position that humans are self-interested actors, driven primarily by utility maximization (Jensen, 1972; Jensen and Meckling, 1976; Fama, 1980).

Agency theory, and other theories that assume egoistic motives, have a number of clear implications for corporate philanthropy and CSR more broadly. First, corporate philanthropy is by definition a discretionary form of spending. Decisions regarding allocation are generally taken by management (or the agents) instead of owners (or the principals) – parties whose interests are not necessarily always aligned. This presents fertile grounds for principal-agent problems with decisions on recipients made by individuals using what are in effect other people's funds. Second, the most immediate gains are accrued to the managers, 'who reap the benefits', rather than the owners, who meet the costs, (Koehn and Ueng, 2009: 4) further exacerbating the dilemma. Benefits range from the intangible, such as public recognition, to access to elite networks, including invitations to opening nights etc. Agency theorists, therefore, see corporate philanthropy as a potentially

	Agency theory	Stakeholder and social contract theories	Corporate citizenship	Critical theories
Motive for CP/CSR	Self-interest/egoistic	Strategic/ contractarian	Contractarian/ altruistic/political	Political/ self-interested
Key rationale of CP/CSR	Maintaining shareholder value through strategic philanthropy – or avoid	Preserving shareholder value through active stakeholder management	Strengthening business contribution to society/ corporations as citizens	Maintaining business to preserve structural and ideational power of capital
Foundational theorists	Adam Smith; Milton Friedman	Adam Smith; John Locke; Jeremy Bentham	Charles Taylor; John Locke	Antonio Gramsci; Autoro Escobar; Michael Foucault; Jürgen Habermas
Contemporary exponents	Fama (1980); Jensen and Meckling (1976); Porter and Kramer (1999); Jensen (2001)	Davis (1960); Donaldson (1982); Freeman (1984); Carroll (1991); Donaldson and Dunfee (1999)	Bowen (1953); Kell and Ruggie (1999); Matten and Crane (2003)	Margolis and Walsh (2003); Levy and Kaplan (2008); Mitra (2008)
CSR/CP and firm performance	Negative – where undertaken for agent's (manager's) self-interest Positive – where undertaken strategically to shore-up reputation and reduce risk	Positive – effective management of diverse stakeholders' critical basis of firm performance	Positive – firm as citizens with associated responsibilities but bounded political rights	Positive – enable firms to co-opt critics and potential critics
Key strength	Goal clarity and lack of ambiguity – shareholder interests paramount and clear direction for agents (managers)	Integrates non-traditional risks – particularly environmental, social and governance risks	Embeds firm within society and as political actor within liberal democracy	Normative and post-positivist – challenges existing problem-solving/ positivist theories
Key weakness	Narrow fixation with owners – firm as purely an instrument of wealth creation	Ambiguity with respect to balancing interests of diverse stakeholders – that is, difficult to prioritize	Potentially vests too much power in firm's ability to adhere to norms	Highly normative – lack of clear reform program

Instrumental ←→ Rights-based

Figure 24.1 Theories of corporate philanthropy (CP) and corporate social responsibility (CSR)

problematic endeavour. It is open to gaming by agents who can use corporate philanthropy to their advantage due to information asymmetries. It also presents a potential breach of fiduciary duties as it is potentially a form of 'waste' (Shaw and Post, 1993: 747).

Nonetheless, while shareholder interests retain primacy, this does not preclude a firm from strategically oriented social investments (Shaw and Post, 1993: 747). Noncore contributions to the community that would 'produce an increase in shareholder value' are warranted and indeed encouraged (Garriga and Melé, 2004: 53). Agency theorists maintain that it is only those that incur a cost without a commensurate gain that should be avoided. More recent and nuanced conceptualizations of agency-theory, such as Jensen's (2001) 'enlightened value-maximization', have taken account of the rewards for the firm of taking heed of the interests of some classes of stakeholders, other shareholders, in maintaining market value over the long-term (Garriga and Melé, 2004: 53). In this reading, philanthropy remains in the long-term interests of shareholders and '[t]he agents of the firm (management) have great discretion in making choices regarding what constitutes best interests under a business charter' (Sasse and Trahan, 2007: 31).

Stakeholder and social contract theories

Another set of theories – which Kemper and Martin (2010: 233) observe rose as a direct 'reaction to Friedman's ideas' – can be broadly reconciled around their focus on the importance of a range of interest groups. 'Stakeholder theory' – a deliberate 'play on the word "stockholder"' (Freeman and McVea, 2001: 2) – was originally proposed by Emshoff and Freeman (1978) and subsequently extended by Freeman (1984). This approach theorized, that the complexity of the social, political, environmental and economic context in which modern organizations operate necessitates careful management of the expectations of a range of interest groups, including employees, customers, suppliers, lenders and, of course, shareholders. Freeman (1984: 46) defined a stakeholder broadly as 'any group or individual who can affect or is affected by the achievement of the organization's objectives'. A direct admonition of agency theory (Kemper and Martin, 2010: 233), stakeholder theory articulated how managers must carefully weigh up the importance of all actors affected by a firm's activities to inform decision-making, and was designed 'to broaden the concept of strategic management beyond its traditional economic roots' (Freeman and McVea, 2001: 2).

While it was not developed as a CSR theory per se, the concept of stakeholder management has proved highly influential on CSR thinking (and indeed practice) forming the conceptual foundations of many corporate philanthropy and CSR theories, as well as providing a rationale for extending strategy beyond the firm to include broader societal actors (Carroll, 1991: 43). Stakeholder theory has several obvious implications for corporate philanthropy and CSR. First, Carroll (1999: 290) has argued that the notion of stakeholders provides some 'specificity' to the most fuzzy and ambiguous aspect of CSR, the term 'social'. By doing so it 'personalizes … societal responsibilities by delineating the specific groups or persons business should consider in its CSR orientation and activities' (Carroll, 1999: 290). Second, it provides a 'defensive rationale for CSR: corporate philanthropy offers protection against the potential negative impacts the firm will cause any number of stakeholders' (Sasse and Trahan, 2007: 34) and, ergo, stakeholders to firms. Commonly characterized as 'insurance-like protection', it is argued that corporate philanthropy generates positive 'moral capital among communities' (Godfrey, 2005: 777-78) that can be drawn upon in times of crisis and to offset some forms of reputational damage. Finally, it supposedly offers a 'rejection of ethical egoism' that is ostensibly characteristic of agent-based approaches and argues philosophically that there is a 'compatibility of morality and capitalism' (Donaldson, 1999: 238).

Another variant of stakeholder theory is similarly contractarian in its orientation. First articulated by Donaldson (1982) in *Corporations and Morality*, this approach extends Lockean classical liberal ideas regarding the social contract to business ethics (Fort, 2000: 383). From this perspective the firm does not operate within a social and political vacuum. Rather, business retains 'indirect obligations' to the society (and environment) in which it operates (Jamali, 2008: 220). Articulated more extensively in Donaldson and Dunfee's (1999) 'integrated social contract theory' (ISCT), it illustrates how managers 'can make decisions in an ethical context' (Moir, 2001: 19). In explaining ISCT, they distinguish between the macrosocial contract – or the expectation that a firm will provide support for local communities within an overarching rules-based normative framework known as 'hyper-norms' – and the microsocial contract – or 'the explicit and implicit agreements that are binding within an identified community' (Garriga and Melé, 2004: 56). In doing so, contractarians are making an unequivocal case against 'untrammelled pursuit of profits, addressing Friedman's arguments directly' (Kemper and Martin, 2010: 233), in favour of a system-level analysis that sees the firm embedded within community through an intricately linked array of contracts which serve to legitimize capitalism. Philanthropy and social investment are one means by which these social contracts can be legitimized.

Corporate citizenship

Some scholars have seen contractarian ideas as providing a philosophical and moral basis for conceptualizing the firm as 'citizen' – or so-called corporate citizenship. Taking obvious cues from political science this set of theories similarly focuses 'on the interactions and connections between business and society' (Garriga and Melé, 2004: 55-56). As a consequence, these have been categorized as 'political theories' (Garriga and Melé, 2004: 55; Okoye, 2009: 615; Kemper and Martin, 2010: 234) in that they ascribe to business a place in power relations and sometimes deploy power-based analyses. Nonetheless, in problematizing the concept, Matten and Crane (2003) have observed that in many conceptualizations, corporate citizenship does not substantively differ from the other more *instrumental* understandings of corporate philanthropy and CSR, for example the shareholder and stakeholder approaches, in that these approaches portray philanthropy as a narrow function of reputational and stakeholder management. They term these the 'limited' and 'equivalent' types of corporate citizenship. In this sense, the use of the term is little more than a shift in nomenclature and the use of the idiom 'superficial' and atheoretical.

At the other end of the spectrum, though, what Matten and Crane (2003: 6) term the 'extended view' are rights-based approaches. These can be anchored in the broader literature on globalization that emerged in the 1990s as articulated by global governance theorists, such as Scholte (2000) and Falk (2000). In this reading, the rise of corporate influence and the corresponding decline of state power that has accompanied increased interdependence – perhaps more appropriately viewed as reconfiguration of the state's functions – has undermined the state's ability to act as 'guarantor' of 'social and political rights' as understood in the classical liberal tradition (Matten and Crane 2003: 10). Applying a 'more robust conception of citizenship drawn from political theory' Matten and Crane (2003: 14) argue that the management literature, which has dominated corporate philanthropy and CSR thinking, and its equivalent corporate citizenship, has misread liberal theory in equating corporations with citizens. Rather corporations are more appropriately likened to the state. In doing so they suggest that if the state's power has declined and the relative power of business has increased then business has commensurate responsibilities to citizens as 'facilitators of rights' (Matten and Crane 2003: 16) including through philanthropy.

Critical theories

The final set of approaches, perhaps better conceived as perspectives, share similarities with the 'extended' view in that they take as the starting point the position that there has been a fundamental reconfiguration of the distribution of power within contemporary capitalism. Generally omitted from the mainstream management literature, critical theories of CSR and corporate philanthropy can be loosely divided into those emerging out of political science – in a range of variants from the post-colonial (Ponte *et al.*, 2010; Mitra, 2011) to the neo-Gramscian (Levy and Kaplan, 2008) – to a growing body of work known as critical management studies (CMS) (Grice and Humphries, 1997; Banjeree, 2008). However while these perspectives share (the contestable) position that the corporation has achieved a position of almost governmental importance, they reject the normative position that corporations can be tamed.

While the diversity of views under the broad appellation of 'critical' makes the task of distilling the ideas challenging, and beyond the scope of this chapter, critical theories make a variety of shared claims regarding corporate philanthropy and CSR. These are worth briefly introducing as they offer a counter to the portrayal of philanthropy in many mainstream management texts. First, critical theorists question the authenticity of corporate responsibility and assert that corporate philanthropy is deigned to furnish corporate reputations to limit criticism. In this sense it is part of the marketing function and designed to counter civil society criticism of unethical corporate behaviour and malfeasance. Second, they argue that 'despite the emancipatory rhetoric' the discourses of CSR and corporate philanthropy 'are defined by narrow business interests and serve to curtail the interests of external stakeholders' (Banerjee, 2008: 51). In this reading, private funding for nonprofit organizations may also be used to co-opt critical voices by creating resource dependencies and shared interests and preferences. Finally, critical theories challenge the notion that the theoretical gulf between on the one hand shareholder capitalism and on the other stakeholder capitalism is substantive. They argue that the intellectual skirmish between the two approaches remains to some extent artificial due to the foundational, as well as clear ontological and epistemological similarities between the two approaches essentially grounded in neo-classical and neo-liberal economics.

Indeed this final point is worth exploring further. While stakeholder theory claims to provide 'guidance for CSR decisions' this does not substantively differ from what classical 'shareholder maximization adherents would suggest' (Sasse and Trahan, 2007: 34). This is particularly so when read against frameworks such as Jensen's (2001) enlightened stakeholder maximization. Moreover, such approaches are attempting to challenge 'economic versions of contractarianism' in an environment in which the 'shareholder maximization paradigm reigns' (Margolis and Walsh, 2003: 271-73). That is, organisational scholars, for example stakeholder theorists, are attempting to offer a 'rival theoretical model' but are operating within a hegemonic paradigm in which the maximisation purists, with their focus on performance, set the agenda. This has the perverse effect of focusing the debate on narrow metrics, such as financial performance, which serves to reinforce the 'economic contractarian model and accepts its assumptions' (Margolis and Walsh, 2003: 278). Putting these similarities aside, the debate between the two broad standpoints on the costs and benefits of corporate philanthropy has remained one of the most contested aspects of scholarly research on corporate philanthropy and CSR over the past four decades. This has manifested itself most clearly in the longstanding dispute over the business case for corporate philanthropy and CSR, and the even more contested debate regarding the relationship between corporate social and corporate financial performance. More recently, the terrain has shifted further. The debate has moved beyond whether corporate philanthropy and CSR is good for business to whether it has become either a basic function of compliance – the so-called 'new compliance agenda' (Elkington, 2011: 1) – or wholly integrated into core business, most clearly reflected in Porter and Kramer's (2011) concept of 'creating shared value' (CSV).

The business case

Shareholder capitalism and agent–centred approaches to corporate philanthropy and CSR can be categorized as holding a 'narrow view of the business case' in that it is 'only recognized when there is a clear [or direct] link to firm financial performance' (Carroll and Shabana, 2010: 93). By contrast the 'broad view [adopted variously by stakeholder and corporate citizenship approaches] … recognizes direct and indirect relationships between CSR and firm performance' and according to Carroll and Shabana (2010: 93 citing Berger *et al.*, 2007: 144) acts as 'a man-agement philosophy, an overarching approach to business'. However, the underlying logic – that strategic corporate philanthropy and CSR are good for the bottomline – is premised on a number of instrumental benefits that are broadly, although not equally, recognized.

Attracting and retaining high quality employees and staff

There are two principal ways that well executed and structured corporate philanthropy programs are seen as important for firms in 'yielding a competitive advantage in human resources' (Schmidt Albinger and Freeman, 2000: 250). First, corporate philanthropy can act 'as a signal to potential applicants that an organization is socially responsible and upholds ethical values' (Orlitzky, 2008: 120). This is said to lead to an increased ability to attract staff, an assertion that has been sup-ported by a range of studies. Early research by Turban and Greening (1997) has been reaffirmed by Backhaus *et al.* (2002: 309) who have shown that 'job seekers' consider a firm's social perfor-mance 'important at all stages of the job search, but most important when choosing whether to take the job offer'. Similarly Schmidt Albinger and Freeman (2000: 250) have found that

> organizations demonstrating higher levels of [corporate social performance] have an increased ability to attract employees … increasingly important when that organization seeks to attract highly educated applicants with a high level of job choice.

Second, it has also been shown that the corporate philanthropy and CSR are important for retaining staff, strengthening what Meyer and Allen (1997, cited in Godfrey, 2005: 786) have termed 'affective commitment' – or the 'employee's emotional attachment to, identification with, and involvement in' an organization. Employees ostensibly derive 'pride from their company's positive involvement in the community' and identify with employers that directly incorporate them into corporate philanthropy and CSR activities (Porter and Kramer, 2006: 7). Dutton *et al.* (1994) have demonstrated that employees are more committed to firms with a positive public image.

Enhanced reputation

Closely linked to the notion that employees favour firms with strong community investment programs – what can be termed 'supply-side' benefits – corporate philanthropy and CSR also generate 'demand-side' reputational benefits including increased 'brand value, which in turn, increases a company's [stock of] goodwill' (Falck and Heblich, 2007: 248). This happens in two ways, and among two different classes of stakeholders. First, corporate philan-thropy and CSR can act as ancillary function of traditional 'advertising' or marketing (Lev *et al.*,

2010: 185) targeted at *customers*. By enhancing a company's reputation, it is asserted that corporate philanthropy can lead to enhanced 'customer loyalty, thereby reducing the price elasticity of demand' (Lev *et al.*, 2010: 185). Lev *et al.* (2010: 198) find that this translates strongly in 'consumer sectors', notably financial services and retailing, with corporate philanthropy 'associated with increased sales growth'. This provides managers with a clear and persuasive argument for shareholders in favour of social investments. Second, reputational signals can also be important for attracting ethical and socially responsible investors (SRI) (Orlitzky, 2008: 118), as well institutional *investors*. While a comparatively small component of capital markets, the former class of investor is nonetheless of growing importance, while the latter class of investor is more inclined to favour corporate philanthropy and CSR for its risk management benefits, in line with the longer-term investment horizons of, for example, pension and superannuation funds (Lev *et al.*, 2010: 195).

Risk management

Stakeholder theorists have long posited that careful management of diverse, nontraditional, interests is a prudent mechanism of risk reduction through, for instance, the avoidance of litigation and legal costs (Orlitzky, 2008: 121). Over time, though, it has become increasingly commonplace to argue that managing broader environmental, social and governance (ESG) exposures, underpinned by sound ethical foundations, is a prudent mechanism for the reduction of systemic business risks. This view is widely shared by the abovementioned classes of SRI and institutional investors, which see ESG risk management as effective in maintaining value over the long-term. It is also a view held by regulators alarmed over corporate short-termism, revealed in high-profile examples of corporate malfeasance such as Enron and again during the bank-induced global financial crisis and the more recent Barclay's Libor scandal. Companies themselves have also 'awakened to these risks' (Porter and Kramer, 2006: 2). As Husted (2005: 175-76) notes, CSR as risk management strategy is 'fairly straightforward': simply put, companies that develop strategies to monitor and mitigate their environmental impact, maintain high labour standards and workplace practices, and engage proactively with the communities in which they operate should, ergo, 'anticipate and reduce business risks from sources such as potential government regulation, labour unrest or environmental damage'. Similar arguments have been put forward with respect to benefits of 'strategic philanthropy' as an 'insurance-like protection' (Godfrey, 2005: 777). A significant amount of research has been devoted to establishing causality, including by Orlitzky and Benjamin (2001: 388), which finds evidence that a 'higher reputation for corporate citizenship' is correlated with low business risk.

Corporate philanthropy and CSR as corporate strategy

The idea that firms can obtain a competitive advantage through strategic social investments is not new. As noted earlier, Porter and Kramer (2002) have long argued that firms that align philanthropic strategy with core business competencies can nurture a competitive edge over rivals. The problem is, they assert, that corporate philanthropy and CSR are rarely done correctly. It is generally diffuse, unstructured and fragmented and unrelated to broader organizational goals, which results in uncoordinated activities that are unlikely to yield long-term benefits for firms or communities (Porter and Kramer, 2002). To unlock 'long-term competitive potential' firms should 'apply their distinctive strengths' in their corporate philanthropy and CSR (Porter and Kramer, 2002: 15). This emerges from a fundamental recognition of the 'interdependence between a company and society' (Porter and Kramer, 2006: 6).

It is also underpinned by a belief that firms are in some instances better resourced, equipped and retain superior information than other institutional forms – including government – to tackle complex social and environmental problems in their area of expertise (Porter and Kramer, 2011). This does not obviate the role of government, which retains its own competitive (and comparative) advantages. Rather, firms have unique capacity to scale-up and innovate, which means they are ostensibly better equipped to address 'wicked problems' that cannot be resolved through traditional philanthropy or the state as the cost is simply too high. This has been most recently articulated in the concept of 'creating shared value' (CSV), which has emerged as the latest trend in sustainability discourse proffered by Porter and Kramer (2011). The idea of CSV combines the competencies of companies and NGOs to deliver products or service solutions with both commercial scale and positive social impact for customers, clients and communities more broadly. This accords closely with Carroll and Shabana's (2010) 'broad view' or Berger *et al.*'s (2007) 'syncretic model' but according to its growing band of proponents, CSV moves beyond strategic philanthropy and indeed CSR to a wholesale incorporation of social and environmental thinking into corporate strategy.

Corporate philanthropy in practice

In the twenty-first century there has been a surge of interest in CSR and corporate philanthropy as means of tackling some of the myriad challenges posed by globalization and financial austerity. A 2010 survey by Edelman, a public relations firm, showed that 69 percent of consumers globally now believe corporations are in a uniquely powerful position to make a positive impact on good causes (COF, 2012: 10). In turn, a range of high profile companies have begun to view corporate philanthropy as a critical part of their operations.

Companies engage in a variety of activities to meet their corporate philanthropy objectives including: direct cash contributions to charities and other nonprofit organisations; product and equipment donations; partnerships with nonprofit organisations or NGO organizations; cause-related marketing; employee matched giving programs; scholarship programs; contributions of employee labour or technical expertise; and the provision of in-kind services. When partnering with nonprofits or NGOs, affiliations are generally pursued with institutions that operate in the fields of education, health, the arts and cultural affairs. In international environments these may include development activities such as: education and medical interventions; the provision of community infrastructure; or training programs in an area of technical expertise relevant to the business (Genest, 2005: 315–316).

Implementation frameworks

The rise in interest in these practices has seen a concomitant demand for guides to and examples of implementation and measurement. Based in the US, the Committee Encouraging Corporate Philanthropy (CEcorporate philanthropy) is an international consortium of businesses that focuses on raising the level and quality of corporate philanthropy. The CEcorporate philanthropy developed the Corporate Giving Standard Benchmarking Tool, based on data collected through the annual Corporate Giving Standard (CGS) Survey, which has run since 2001. The 2011 survey included data from a total of 214 firms, including 62 of the top 100 companies in the Fortune 500, detailing philanthropic contributions across all respondents in excess of $19.9 billion in cash and product giving (CEcorporate philanthropy, 2012:1). In 2012, the CEcorporate philanthropy produced *The Global Guide to What Counts: A Defining Moment for Corporate Giving*, which aims to offer clear and simple guidance to undertaking corporate philanthropy. Also in the US in 2012, *The Council on Foundations*, a nonprofit organization that comprises over 1,700 grantmaking foundations and corporations, produced *Increasing Impact, Enhancing Value: A practitioner's guide to leading corporate philanthropy*.

The Guide to UK Company Giving has been produced annually since 2004. In 2011, it detailed more than 600 companies in the UK that made philanthropic contributions of around £762 million to voluntary and community organizations, including £512 million in cash donations. The company listings detail the nature of the company, its community giving policy, levels of giving (both cash and in-kind), details relating to employee and payroll giving, sponsorship and cause-related marketing, the company's charity of the year and partnerships. The guide offers advice for nonprofit organizations on what to be aware of when seeking corporate support, and help to attract a successful partnership or sponsor. All these frameworks seek to encourage innovation in, and expansion of, the corporate philanthropy field.

Measurement Tools

The development of effective measurement tools has emerged as a necessary priority in achieving successful corporate philanthropy implementation. The London Benchmarking Group (LGB) model is the best known and most widely used tool to measure the charitable contributions of companies. It takes its name from the group of UK-based companies that collaboratively developed the model. The Group in the UK numbered more than 100 member companies at the time of writing, and now has a global membership base that also includes companies from Europe, US, Middle East, Asia and Australia. The LBG model not only counts charitable cash donations, but also a broader range of corporate philanthropy community and business engagements such as employee volunteering, product donations and in-kind contributions of training and technical assistance. It also records the outputs and longer-term community and business impacts of corporate philanthropy projects and includes a range of case studies on its website (www.lbg-online.net/).

The LBG is run in conjunction with Business in Community's (BITC) voluntary benchmarking and incentive scheme. BITC is a business-led charity focused on promoting responsible business practice, which recognizes companies who make charitable contributions in excess of one percent of pre-tax profits with a certificate and the right to use the PerCent Club logo (www.bitc.org.uk/; Spence and Thomson, 2009: 374).

Conclusion

Over the past 50 years, there has been significant theoretical, conceptual and practical evolution in both corporate philanthropy and CSR. These changes rapidly gathered pace from the mid-1990s with the onset of accelerated globalization, subsequent civil society critique of corporate behaviour and ultimately the mainstreaming of CSR. Even those firms that were resistant or laggards to the corporate philanthropy and CSR agenda, now routinely report on social and environmental activities, mostly in separate sustainability reports, employ staff to oversee their programs and tend to genuinely believe that their philanthropic and CSR activities are core to business and beneficial to society. Still, the question must be asked: can firms be ethical and responsible? Are corporate philanthropy and CSR merely window-dressing? Given that the growth of the corporate philanthropy/CSR agenda has closely tracked a number of high-profile corporate failures, scandals, and finally, the global financial crisis would lead any rational observer to scepticism.

Nonetheless, over time there has been a growing understanding among firms of their obligations to society, as well as a growing sophistication of strategy among a minority of leaders.

In many ways the idea of the firm as purely an economic instrument of wealth creation as theorized in traditional shareholder capitalism has broken down, at least when seen through the narrow lens of Friedman. The enlightened stakeholder approach does not dramatically differ from other stakeholder and social contract theories and there is seemingly a reasonable degree of consensus that corporate philanthropy and CSR are good for the bottom line. Corporate citizenship and critical theories, which privilege political factors, offer a more sceptical reading, but ultimately it remains to be seen whether the corporate philanthropy and CSR movements, in particular in the current emphasis CSV incarnation, can lead to more sustainable business practices.

Similar trends can be observed with respect to research. While corporate philanthropy and CSR research was until relatively recently novel and indeed marginal area of scholarship, it is now firmly in the mainstream, featuring prominently in mainstream journals and universities. Long debated questions regarding, for example, the relationship between corporate philanthropy/CSR and firm performance continue to be debated, but as with the theoretical debates, there has been a recent turn away from whether corporate philanthropy/CSR are good for the bottom line to how they can best be executed to deliver both social and economic outcomes. In this sense, the CSV agenda, which is yet to be tested, offers perhaps the most fruitful and compelling research agenda.

References

Backhaus, K. B., Stone, B. A. and Heiner, K. (2002) 'Exploring the Relationship between Corporate Social Performance and Employer Attractiveness', *Business and Society*, 41(3), 292–318.

Banerjee, S. B. (2008) 'Corporate Social Responsibility: The Good, the Bad and the Ugly', *Critical Sociology*, 34(1): 51–79.

Berger, I. E., Cunningham, P. H. and Drumwright, M. E. (2007) 'Mainstreaming Corporate Social Responsibility: Developing Markets for Virtue', *California Management Review*, 49(4): 132–58.

Berle, A. A. and Means, G. C. (1932) *The Modern Corporation and Private Property*, New Jersey: Harcourt, Brace and World Inc.

Bowen, H. R. (1953) *Social Responsibilities of the Businessman*, New York: Harper.

Carroll, A. B. (1991) 'The Pyramid of Corporate Social Responsibility: Toward the Moral Management of Organizational Stakeholders', *Business Horizons*, 34(4): 39–48.

——. (1999) 'Corporate Social Responsibility: Evolution of a Definitional Construct', *Business and Society*, 38(3): 268–95.

——. (2008) 'A History of Corporate Social Responsibility: Concepts and Practices', in A. Crane *et al.*, eds. *The Oxford Handbook of Corporate Social Responsibility*, Oxford: Oxford University Press, 19–46.

Carroll, A. B. and Shabana, K. M. (2010) 'The Business Case for Corporate Social Responsibility: A Review of Concepts, Research and Practice', *International Journal of Management Reviews*, 12(1): 85–105.

CED (1971) *Social Responsibilities of Business Corporations*, New York: Committee for Economic Development.

Committee Encouraging Corporate Philanthropy (CEcorporate philanthropy) (2012) *Giving in Numbers: 2012 Edition*.

Council on Foundations (COF) (2012) *Increasing Impact, Enhancing Value: A Practitioner's Guide to Leading Corporate Philanthropy*, Council on Foundations, New York, NY.

Davis, K. (1960) 'Can Business Afford to Ignore Social Responsibilities?', *California Management Review*, 2(3): 70–6.

Davis, K. and Blomstrom, R. L. (1966) *Business and its Environment*, New York: McGraw-Hill.

Dodd, E. M. (1932) 'For whom are Corporate Managers Trustees?', *Harvard Law Review*, 44: 1145–63.

Donaldson, T. (1999) 'Response: Making Stakeholder Theory Whole', *The Academy of Management Review*, 24(2): 237.

——. (1982) *Corporations and Morality*, New York: Prentice-Hall.

Donaldson, T. and Dunfee, T. (1999) *The Ties That Bind: A Social Contracts Approach to Business Ethics*, Cambridge, MA: Harvard Business School Press.

Donham, W. B. (1927) 'The Social Significance of Business', *Harvard Business Review*, 5(4): 406–19.

Dutton, J. E., Dukerich, J. M. and Harquail, C. V. (1994) 'Organizational Images and Member Identification', *Administrative Science Quarterly*, 39(2): 239–63.

Elkington, J. (2011) Don't Abandon CSR for Creating Shared Value Just Yet, www.theguardian.com/sustainable-business/sustainability-with-john-elkington/corporate-social-resposibility-creating-shared-value [Accessed 10 October 2015].

Emshoff, J. R. and Freeman, R. E. (1978) *Stakeholder Management*, Philadelphia: The Wharton Applied Research Center.

Falck, O. and Heblich, S. (2007) 'Corporate Social Responsibility: Doing Well by Doing Good', *Business Horizons*, 50(3): 247–54.

Falk, R. (2000) 'The Decline of Citizenship in an Era of Globalization', *Citizenship Studies*, 4(1): 5–17.

Fama, E. F. (1980) 'Agency Problems and the Theory of the Firm', *The Journal of Political Economy*, 88(2): 288–307.

Fama, E. F. and Jensen, M. C. (1983) 'Separation of Ownership and Control', *Journal of Law and Economics*, 26(2): 301–25.

Fort, T. (2000) 'A Review of Donaldson and Dunfee's *Ties That Bind: A Social Contracts Approach to Business Ethics*', *Journal of Business Ethics*, 28(4): 383–7.

Frederick, W. C. (2008) 'Corporate Social Responsibility: Deep Roots, Flourishing Growth, Promising Future', in A. Crane *et al.*, eds. *The Oxford Handbook of Corporate Social Responsibility*, Oxford: Oxford University Press, 522–31.

Freeman, R. E. (1984) *Strategic Management: A Stakeholder*, Boston: Pitman Publishing.

Freeman, R. E. and McVea, J. (2001) *A Stakeholder Approach to Strategic Management*, Charlottesville, VA: Darden Graduate School of Business.

Friedman, M. (1962) *Capitalism and Freedom*, Chicago, IL: University of Chicago Press.

Fombrum, C. (1996) *Reputation*, Boston: Harvard Business School Press.

Gan, A. (2006) 'The Impact of Public Scrutiny on Corporate Philanthropy', *Journal of Business Ethics*, 69(3): 217–36.

Garriga, E. and Melé, D. (2004) 'Corporate Social Responsibility Theories: Mapping the Territory', *Journal of Business Ethics*, 53(1/2): 51–71.

Genest, C. M. (2005) 'Cultures, Organizations and Philanthropy', *Corporate Communications: An International Journal*, 10(4): 315–27.

Godfrey, P. C. (2005) 'The Relationship between Corporate Philanthropy and Shareholder Wealth: A Risk Management Perspective', *Academy of Management Review*, 30(4): 777–98.

Grice, S. and Humphries, M. (1997) 'Critical Management Studies in Postmodernity: Oxymorons in Outer Space?', *Journal of Organizational Change Management*, 10(5): 412–25.

Husted, B. W. (2005) 'Risk Management, Real Options, Corporate Social Responsibility', *Journal of Business Ethics*, 60(2): 175–83.

Jamali, D. (2008) 'A Stakeholder Approach to Corporate Social Responsibility: A Fresh Perspective into Theory and Practice', *Journal of Business Ethics*, 82(1): 213–31.

Jensen, M. C. (1972) 'Capital Markets: Theory and Evidence', *Bell Journal of Economics and Management Science*, 3(2): 357–98.

——. (2001) 'Value Maximization, Stakeholder Theory, and the Corporate Objective Function', *Journal of Applied Corporate Finance*, 12(1): 8–21.

Jensen, M. C. and Meckling, W. H. (1976) 'Theory of the Firm: Managerial Behavior, Agency Costs and Ownership Structure', *Journal of Financial Economics*, 3(4): 305–60.

Kell, G. and Ruggie, J. (1999) 'Global Markets and Social Legitimacy: The Case of the "Global Compact"', *Transnational Corporations*, 8 (December): 101–20.

Kemper, A. and Martin, R. (2010) 'After the Fall: The Global Financial Crisis as a Test of Corporate Social Responsibility', *European Management Review*, 7(4): 229–39.

Koehn, D. and Ueng, J. (2009) 'Is Philanthropy Being Used by Corporate Wrongdoers to Buy Good Will?', *Journal of Management and Governance*, 14(1): 1–16.

Lev, B., Petrovits, C. and Radhakrishnan, S. (2010) 'Is Doing Good Good for You? How Corporate Charitable Contributions Enhance Revenue Growth', *Strategic Management Journal*, 31(2010): 182–200.

Levy, D. L. and Kaplan, R. (2008) 'Corporate Social Responsibility and Theories of Global Governance: Strategic Contestation in Global Issue Arenas', in A. Crane *et al.*, eds. *The Oxford Handbook of Corporate Social Responsibility*, Oxford: Oxford University Press, 432–51.

Lorenzo-Molo, C. F. and Udani, Z. A. S. (2012) 'Bringing Back the Essence of the "S" and "R" to CSR: Understanding the Limitations of the Merchant Trade and the White Man's Burden', *Journal of Business Ethics*. In-press.

McGuire, J. W. (1963) *Business and Society*, New York: McGraw-Hill.

Margolis, J. D. and Walsh, J. P. (2003) 'Misery Loves Companies: Rethinking Social Initiatives by Business', *Administrative Science Quarterly*, 48(2): 268–305.

Martin, R. (2002) 'The Virtue Matrix: Calculating the Return on Corporate Responsibility', *Harvard Business Review*, (March 2002), pp. 69–75. Harvard Business School Publishing.

Matten, D. and Crane, A. (2003) *Corporate Citizenship: Towards an Extended Theoretical Conceptualization*, Nottingham: International Centre for Corporate Social Responsibility.

Melé, D. (2008) 'Corporate Social Responsibility Theories', in A. Crane *et al.*, eds. *The Oxford Handbook of Corporate Social Responsibility,* Oxford: Oxford University Press, 47–82.

Meyer, J. and Allen, N. (1997) *Commitment in the Workplace: Theory, Research, and Application*, Thousand Oaks, CA: Sage.

Mitra, R. (2011) 'Framing the Corporate Responsibility-reputation Linkage: The Case of Tata Motors in India', *Public Relations Review*, 37(4): 392–8.

Moir, L. (2001) 'What Do We Mean By Corporate Social Responsibility?', *Corporate Governance*, 1(2): 16–22.

Okoye, A. (2009) 'Theorising Corporate Social Responsibility as an Essentially Contested Concept: Is a Definition Necessary?', *Journal of Business Ethics*, 89(4): 613–27.

Orlitzky, M. (2008) 'Corporate Social Performance and Financial Performance', in A. Crane *et al.*, eds. *The Oxford Handbook of Corporate Social Responsibility,* Oxford: Oxford University Press, 113–34.

Orlitzky, M. and Benjamin, J. D. (2001) 'Corporate Social Performance and Firm Risk: A Meta-Analytic Review', *Business and Society*, 40(4): 369–96.

Ponte, S., Richey, L. A. and Baab, M. (2010) 'Bono's Product (RED) Initiative: Corporate Social Responsibility that Solves Problems of Distant Others', *Third World Quarterly*, 30(2): 301–17.

Porter, M. E. and Kramer, M. R. (2002) 'The Competitive Advantage of Corporate Philanthropy', *Harvard Business Review*, December, 5–16.

——. (2006) 'Strategy and Society: The Link between Competitive Advantage and Corporate Social Responsibility', *Harvard Business Review*, (December), 78–91.

——. (2011) 'Creating Shared Value', *Harvard Business Review*, (January–February), pp. 3–17.

Sasse, C. M. and Trahan, R. T. (2007) 'Rethinking the New Corporate Philanthropy', *Business Horizons*, 50(1): 29–38.

Schmidt Albinger, H. and Freeman, S. (2000) 'Corporate Social Performance and Attractiveness as an Employer to Different Job Seeking Populations', *Journal of Business Ethics*, 28(3): 243–53.

Scholte, J. A. (2000) *Globalization: A Critical Introduction*, Basingstoke: Palgrave Macmillan.

Shaw, B. and Post, F. R. (1993) 'A Moral Basis for Corporate Philanthropy', *Journal of Business Ethics*, 12(10): 745–51.

Spence, C. and Thomson, I. (2009) 'Resonance Tropes in Corporate Philanthropy Discourse', *Business Ethics: A European Review*, 18(4): 372–88.

Turban, D. B. and Greening, W. D. (1997) 'Corporate Social Performance and Organizational Attractiveness to Prospective Employees', *Academy of Management Journal*, 40(3): 658–72.

Votaw, D. (1973) 'Genius Becomes Rare', in D. Votaw and S. P. Sethi, eds. *The Corporate Dilemma: Traditional Values Versus Contemporary Problems*. New Jersey: Prentice Hall.

Wood, D. J. (1991) 'Corporate Social Performance Revisited', *Academy of Management Review*, 16(4): 691–718.

Part VI
The management of philanthropy

Vignette: The Management of Philanthropy

Parents and children together

Using social return on investment (SROI) to move from story-telling to strategic change and greater impact

Jim Clifford

Parents and Children Together (PACT) is a £4 million turnover charity supporting children and families based in Oxfordshire, UK. Founded in 1911 under the auspices of the Church of England, PACT undertakes a range of services: some are self-funded, using private donations and funds from the Diocese, some use a social enterprise approach, providing contracted-for social services funded by local or national government. In 2010, PACT faced growing pressures on its resources; with increasing social need, there was a challenge to grow funds to meet it. While its centenary celebrations in 2011 would provide an opportunity for fundraising and wider engagement, how could it tell a story that demonstrated the value that its work was creating?

PACT's Chief Financial Officer (CFO) had previously been looking at Social Return on Investment (SROI) to assess whether it held some value and could provide a useful approach. Overwhelmed with other priorities, though, and struggling to make sense of the working methodology, he was getting nowhere fast. Unexpectedly, however, an opportunity arose: Cass Business School at City University London, and advisers Baker Tilly agreed to participate in a wider piece of case study research. As part of this, and with academic support and professional assistance, SROI evaluations for three PACT projects would be produced as a by-product. These would focus on PACT's domestic adoption and fostering services, the Oxfordshire county-funded children's centres in Witney, and the Alana House project which supported women offenders to remove the chaos from their lives and avoid reoffending. In the words of PACT's CEO, Jan Fishwick: '… we couldn't say "no"!'.

From preliminary discussions, it was clear that a complex range of outcomes would need to be addressed in all three studies. Furthermore, the focus needed to be on enabling the three projects to tell their respective stories. Emphasis was to be given to the question of 'How do these projects make a difference to their respective communities?' rather than only focusing on the financial part of the SROI evaluation in itself. To this end, and departing from traditional approaches to SROI evaluations, the approach used was based on action research. This would enable the research to emerge as the managers of the three projects told and retold their stories in a group setting, challenged and supported by each other, with an external researcher and the

CFO as guide, challenger and report writer. Their collective learning would be supplemented by research data from third party studies, and from feedback from their own projects. This would lead to the formation of a more holistic picture of the differences PACT made in the selected areas and the ways in which this was achieved. Running counter to popular conceptions of SROI as being highly time intensive, each project manager committed around three days in total, and the researcher could manage to support the development of separate reports on three different areas of PACT's work in very little more than the time taken to do one.

The SROI reports were completed in three months. Despite their being tempered with conservatism, they showed striking results. Just one aspect of the Witney project (total centre budget of £300,000 per annum), the work on preschool healthy eating, was delivering over £5 million of value a year. Permanence for a child brought about through adoption was delivering some £800,000 per child against a cost of £27,000, with around £300,000 for fostering, the latter being lower because fostering is state-funded, whereas adoption is not. The work on the Alana House project was showing over £35 million a year of gains, against 'all-in' funding cost of £170,000. Staying true to the original ambition, these reports explained in some detail how the changes brought about by PACT were achieved in the lives of their communities and how those appeared to those affected. Each made a compelling story.

The action research approach meant that both project managers and the executive team engaged with the SROI evaluations, and with each other, as they shared and recorded their stories. They forged new relationships and were quick to support each other through the challenges of the project, but also out into their daily work. Uplifted by the results, they gained a new sense of the value of what they were doing: this was the 'wow!' to go with their conviction that they were 'doing what mattered'. The learning implicit in the approach enabled them to look again at how PACT's services were delivered. With these new insights, they realized they could change what they were doing to make it even more effective. In Witney, the preschool 'eating together as a family' work would be continued; with medical research showing that children built up, or avoided, a propensity to obesity during breastfeeding and weaning, the profile of work in these areas would be raised. The huge value being achieved in permanence for children demanded more focus: PACT acquired another financially-challenged agency to double its capacity.

Funders and partners were affected, too. An earlier public sector decision to stop funding Alana House and the other 47 similar centres was given a reprieve. Additional, partner and local authority engagement was seen in Witney. Perhaps the greatest effects, however, were seen in the adoption and fostering arena, where the high quality domestic service had tended to be overshadowed by PACT's much larger international adoption sister. The enthusiasm engendered in the organization spread rapidly to the Trustee Board. All embraced the SROI evaluation and used it to drive profile and fundraising around this service in PACT's centenary programme. The audience for this swiftly became national and pushed PACT, and its CEO, firmly into the limelight within an emerging UK-wide debate about how to change lives for children in care. Coinciding with this wider debate, and the screening of a landmark documentary on using therapeutic parenting to bring about change in the lives of very damaged children, 'A Home for Maisie' by BBC Cymru, the PACT report was used as a basis to produce a joint statement by 'the great and the good' stakeholders in the adoption and fostering fields on how to take UK adoption forward. This, thought to be the first time such a group had all pulled so obviously in the same direction, proved a key driver in a campaign for national change: at ministerial level, in the courts, and in all working to help such children towards a better future. What had started out as an important piece of work for PACT had brought a social return to a whole sector. The story, told through the SROI study, had become a national bestseller.

25

Good governance in philanthropy and nonprofits

M. Elena Romero-Merino and Íñigo García-Rodriguez

As philanthropy, and the nonprofit sector more generally, has grown in size and importance, questions of governance have become an ever more prominent concern. Various scandals, combined with a realization that 'the angelic' sector has a 'darker side', explored by Smith *et al.* in Chapter 17 of this volume, have led to increasing calls for novel perspectives on, and approaches to, governance research and practice within the field (Cornforth and Brown, 2014). Traditionally, work on governance within the nonprofit sector has focused on boards' performance, on their roles in fundraising and their linking to the community. Furthermore, such studies have tended to be descriptive, normative and lacking strong theoretical and empirical foundations (Miller-Millesen, 2003). When attempting to explain the complexities of nonprofit governance systems, and the contexts within which these operate, such an approach seems too narrow. Not only does it overlook the more holistic meaning of the word 'governance', from the Greek *kybernân*, 'steering a ship or a chariot', and the broader governing responsibilities derived therefrom, but it also ignores wider aspects of governance mechanisms relevant for philanthropic organizations.

This chapter provides a chronological journey through the most prominent theoretical perspectives relevant to philanthropic organizations' governance; it travels from traditional perspectives, such as the role of board size or independence, to seeking more dynamic and diverse governance mechanisms as key to understanding and increasing the effectiveness, and consequently the performance, of philanthropic organizations. While a number of perspectives have been proposed in relation to nonprofit governance, including signaling theory, which points to information asymmetries between different stakeholders (Spence, 1973; Marcus and Goodman, 1991), or stewardship theory, which focuses on the stewardship roles taken on by directors (Donaldson and Davis, 1991; Davis *et al.*, 1997; Van Puyvelde *et al.*, 2012), there are two underlying, fundamental, factors: resource dependency and agency. These two ideas also play a special role in the changing relationship dynamics between grantmakers and grantees that arise from a stronger focus on measuring impact in philanthropy (Schnurbein, Chapter 30). This chapter will therefore concentrate on the issues raised by resource dependency and by agency theory, and how their insights can, and should, be integrated with more recent ideas from cognitive perspectives.

Within the philanthropy arena, governance studies have tended to focus on private, grantmaking foundations. The argument has been that these display certain characteristics that make them distinct from other nonprofit organizations and their governance requirements. Such foundations: usually have a single donor and do not need to fundraise from a broader donor base; tend to spend the earnings from their capital investment; and fund other organizations to do their work (Stone, 1975). However, as the chapters by Leat and by Harrow *et al.* highlight, private foundations are only one set of players within the wider philanthropic foundation game. As such, it is important to acknowledge that some of the insights provided by the governance literature in general, and the one on nonprofit governance in particular, might not be applicable across the entire foundation field. Simultaneously, though, one should not take too narrow a perspective. With philanthropic foundations reinventing themselves in the social finance and social investment landscape, and some traditional grantmaking foundations reflecting on, and moving towards, fundraising approaches to counteract decreasing capital income and/or increasing social needs, broader nonprofit governance issues suddenly arise in, and become relevant to, this area. Consequently, this chapter takes a broad perspective; it draws on the wider insights that emerge on nonprofit governance and reflects how these relate to the composition of philanthropic foundations' boards.

Defining nonprofit corporate governance and governance mechanisms

Unlike in the private sector, where a variety of different, and at times conflicting, perspectives on corporate governance exist, specific definitions of governance for the nonprofit field have been less prominent (Ostrower and Stone, 2006; Cornforth, 2012). Instead, the focus has frequently been on simply transferring definitions from the corporate to the nonprofit field. This is illustrated in the writings of authors such as Jegers (2009) or Hyndman and McDonell (2009) who follow the corporate finance perspective on governance put forward by Shleifer and Vishny (1997: 741) when stating that 'governance deals with the ways in which suppliers of finance to corporations assure themselves of getting a return on their investment'. Such a direct transfer is, however, problematic. Notwithstanding the increasing discourse on 'social return on investment' and the financialization of philanthropy (Thümler, Chapter 23), it is not easy to translate the conceptual underpinnings of investment and financial perspectives to an environment where profit distribution has traditionally not been a priority.

This is not to say that there is no potential for drawing insights from the private sector literature. Charreaux (1997, cited in Charreaux, 2004: 2), for example argues that governance is 'the set of organizational and institutional mechanisms that define the powers and influence the managers' decisions, in other words, that "govern" their conduct and define their discretionary space'. In this line, Cornforth and Chambers (2010: 1) cast nonprofit governance as 'the systems and processes concerned with ensuring the overall direction, control and accountability of an organization'. This definition then follows the etymological roots of the governance concept, by referring to the ways in which the organization (and its managers) is guided and controlled. To do so, governance mechanisms must play a dual role. They must be able to act as both advisors to, and monitors of, the executive team. Governance, thereby, covers what has traditionally been referred to as 'service and control tasks' (Zahra and Pearce, 1989). Service tasks are related to the organization's guidance. It includes not only advice and counsel for managers, but also the provision of external legitimacy and networking (Hillman and Dalziel, 2003). The governance mechanisms can thus be considered as an active part, as playing a critical role in guiding management in strategic decision making processes (Andrews, 1980; Minichilli *et al.*, 2009). The control or monitoring task, on the other hand, supposes that managers are opportunistic. Consequently, the main task of governance mechanisms is to protect the resource contributors (shareholders in firms, or founders, funders and donors in philanthropic foundations) from managerial misappropriation. To do so, governance mechanisms must control the organization's performance, monitor its activities, and assess the management team or its philanthropic equivalent (Johnson *et al.*, 1996).

As part of this, the place and context of these mechanisms must be clarified. In the bulk of the nonprofit governance literature, this is considered to be the board. While the board is the most important governing part within a nonprofit, it is by no means the only one. Albeit less researched, other external, governance mechanisms include government, private donors, capital structures and financial disclosure or transparency arrangements of a foundation. As has been highlighted in other parts of this volume, governments are taking an increasingly strong interest, and role, in the foundation world (Healy and Donnelly-Cox, Chapter 12; Phillips and Smith, Chapter 13), a trend that extends to the wider nonprofit field: governments set standards for the configuration of the internal structure of nonprofits by encouraging professionalization (Guo, 2007) and by supporting only those organizations that meet codes of good governance requirements (Ostrower, 2007). Furthermore, governments decide the activities or projects they support by setting clear boundaries. This can influence the strategic plans and ambitions of these organizations and serve as an organizational control mechanism (Andrés-Alonso *et al.*, 2006). Within philanthropy, this is prominently reflected, for example, in the case of governmental flow-through funding for community foundations. This directive and control function is likely to increase as governments focus on 'impact' philanthropy. Finally, governments also act as regulators for the field through legislation, though the empirical evidence base in how far this translates to good governance warrants further development (Ostrower, 2007; Alexander *et al.*, 2008; Hyndman and McDonell, 2009). Mirroring governments, in the case of philanthropic foundations the founder(s), and/or the individuals or organizations providing the resources can similarly act as a guide and monitoring body. They can influence both the type of activities pursued by a foundation and the composition of its board.

As happens in firms, and especially with the wider move to venture philanthropy, social investment, and social finance (Salamon, 2014), capital structure can also act as a governance mechanism insofar as that a higher level of financial resources involved (either to the foundation or from the foundation) is likely to result in increased financial monitoring. Across the wider nonprofit field research on this topic is still in its infancy, but a number of studies have been emerging over the last few years (Jegers and Verschueren, 2006; Jegers, 2011). In addition, foundations can use accounting information and transparency in financial statements to monitor financial performance, especially by using external auditing to reduce uncertainty about the validity of the figures (Jegers, 2002). Thus, transparency and accountability measures can be considered as positive governance mechanisms for nonprofit organizations as in many countries these are open to public inspection (Boozang, 2007; Harrow, Chapter 31).

Finally, one should not forget boards of trustees as absolute protagonists in the nonprofit governance literature. Boards of trustees – the nonprofit equivalent of boards of directors – are responsible for protecting the interests of the founders, donors, beneficiaries and society in general by guiding the organization with care, skill and integrity (Andrés-Alonso *et al.* 2006, 2009). For many years, boards have been perceived in a relative narrow way. They were considered as mere fundraisers, cheerleaders or even as simply rubberstamping bodies. But, as will be seen throughout the rest of this chapter, boards play a far more active role in the nonprofit sector when compared to the corporate world (Coombes *et al.*, 2011).

The normative approach to nonprofit governance

During the 1990s, the majority of studies on nonprofit governance referred to the board as a unique governance mechanism and approached its workings from a predominantly normative viewpoint. Many authors produced manuals and reports with recommendations about the roles that boards should play and the activities that trustees had to develop (Houle, 1989; Carver, 1990; Chait *et al.*, 1991). Not only has this tendency continued (Cornforth, 2001; Miller-Millesen, 2003), but the spectrum of expectations has become increasingly wide. The board is expected to cover: strategic planning; selection and evaluation of managers; monitoring programs and services of the organization; managing and controlling financial resources; improving the public image of the organization; and selection and training of new trustees. As part of this, a plethora of self-assessment toolkits for board members has been developed by academics, consultants and umbrella organizations. Tools, such as the Board Self-Assessment Questionnaire (BSAQ) (Holland, 1991), the Board Self-Assessment Tool (McKinsey and Company ND), the Governance Self-Assessment Checklist (GSAC) (Gill *et al.*, 2005), the Good Governance Tool Kit (VicSport, ND), or the Charities Toolkit (Kingston Smith, 2013), are designed to assess the skillset of trustees and the degree of compliance of board members with essential tasks.

A number of criticisms have been raised with this approach. First of all, these tools and models frequently lack strong supporting empirical evidence (Jackson and Holland, 1998; Hough, 2006) and their prescriptions are rarely compared, and related, to actual board practices (Herman *et al.*, 1997; Zimmermann and Stevens, 2008; Ostrower and Stone, 2010). This lack of contextualization is further problematic in that proposed 'best practices' are indiscriminately applied across the wide range and characteristics of nonprofit organizations (Miller-Millesen, 2003; Parker, 2007): from small local charities and family trusts to international nonprofits and multimillion corporate foundations. Furthermore, by advocating 'ideal' board behaviours (Herman, 1989; Hall, 1990; Cornforth, 1996), the expectations promulgated within these tools might be unrealistic and, when boards fail to live up to these standards, demotivating. The extent to which these guides, or tools, are used is also unknown, as is the case when foundations' groups produce apparently tailored guides for their members (Jenkins, 2012). Finally, as studies give prominence to describing boards, or defining good practice, there is also a notable lack of theoretical underpinnings (Speckbacher, 2008). The next section will therefore outline key theoretical frameworks that can inform our understanding of nonprofit governance and assess the extent to which these perspectives are supported by empirical evidence.

The resource dependency approach to nonprofit corporate governance

For many years, the most influential theory in governance studies was 'resource dependency'. This perceives organizations as open systems, constrained by their context. As Pfeffer and Salancik (1978: 1) state, 'to understand the behaviour of an organization you must understand the context of that behaviour – that is, the ecology of the organization'. To reduce environmental uncertainty and dependency, an organization can accumulate power or control over vital resources (Ulrich and Barney, 1984; Hillman *et al.*, 2009). Within nonprofits, this was understood as a need to develop a strong board, one that includes trustees who are in a position to influence the outside world to the nonprofit's advantage (Callen *et al.*, 2010). Boards, thereby, are considered to function as resource catalysts: they provide linkages to necessary resources and act as 'boundary spanners' (Provan, 1980; Harlan and Saidel, 1994; Brown, 2005). Such boundary spanning can take various forms and cover numerous activities. Reflecting the notions of treasure, time and talent, these can range from fundraising activities, as for example required by community foundations, to developing a foundation's relationships with external stakeholders, such as government, public realtions (PR), or offering specific advice and counsel.

Within this school of thought, a board's boundary spanning activities is directly related to organizational performance as these help to reduce dependencies between the organization and external contingencies (Hillman and Dalziel, 2003). This relationship has been widely tested in the nonprofit field. The board's ability to provide resources is related to board size, linkage (interlocking) and diversity, as well as to individual features of the trustees, such as demographic characteristics, knowledge and skills. Early studies concentrated on the ability of the board to accumulate resources (Provan, 1980; Green and Griesinger, 1996; Herman and Renz, 2000), but soon a growing body of work emerged that recognized the strategic role of the board as a key factor in affecting nonprofit performance (Green and Griesinger, 1996; Herman *et al.*, 1997). As part of this, the notion of agency was introduced within nonprofit governance debates.

The agency theory approach to the nonprofit corporate governance

According to agency theory, an organization is a legal fiction, a nexus of contracts that allows individuals to develop an activity together (Jensen and Meckling, 1976). The main concerns of this perspective are the issues that arise between those who act (agents) on behalf of others (principals) while performing some service in the organization. This agency relationship requires that the principals delegate some decision-making authority to the agent, who usually has the knowledge and skills to act on behalf of the principal. However, the agent might not always act in line with the principal's expectations (Berle and Means, 1932). The resulting conflict of interests between principal and agent is the 'agency cost' and governance mechanisms are aimed at reducing this through monitoring the agent's behaviour.

This perspective of agency theory is the most widely used theoretical approach for the study of corporate governance (Dalton *et al.*, 1998). Similarly to the corporate setting, where differences between shareholders (as principals) and managers (as agents) might arise (Wellens and Jegers, 2013), the principal-agent argument has wider applicability; it is relevant to relationships between actors of any kind. Within a foundation, for example, the board is responsible for the effective use of resources and the avoidance of their expropriation: the principal is the donor and those administering and running the foundation are the agents (Fama and Jensen, 1983; Miller, 2002; Andrés-Alonso *et al.*, 2006). Nevertheless, as Harrow and Phillips (2013) contend, there is also ongoing debate within nonprofits as to who 'owns' them – in the case of foundations, the original funders or their descendants, the business which created them, the multiple donors and contributors in foundations which fundraise, or combinations of these groups, salaried employees and volunteers. For foundations seeking, or having, a specifically local presence, their community engagement decisions may include expansion of board membership to local 'voices', who are not themselves donors, whilst also not beneficiaries (Harrow, 2011).

There is then still some reluctance to apply traditional agency theory to both philanthropic and nonprofit settings, the argument being that without any profit to distribute to those who control these organizations' opportunistic behaviour by employees or managers is avoided (Hansmann, 1980; Brody, 1996). Although the constraints of nonprofit settings might eliminate the figure of a residual claimant, like a shareholder in firms, it does not reverse the incentives that other insiders could have to misappropriate the organization's resources (Fama and Jensen, 1983). Another argument by those challenging the appropriateness of agency theory for the nonprofit sector point out that it presumes the existence of a goal conflict between the donor and the management team. Miller (2002) shows that nonprofit board members do not expect conflict between staff and the purpose for which the organization was created. This, however, only indicates that board members are unaware, not that there is no conflict. As Jensen (1994: 49) notes, 'altruism … does not turn people into perfect agents who do the bidding of others'. There is plenty of opportunity for opportunistic behaviour and fraud across philanthropic contexts (Smith *et al.*, Chapter 17).

When studying the optimal board composition from an agency perspective, one usually finds one of the following areas as the central focus of research: the board size, its independence, or the presence of donors among its directors. With respect to size, agency theory considers that smaller boards reduce agency problems because they speed up decision-making, reduce potential free rider behaviours, and consequently cut down administrative costs (Jensen, 1993; Yermack, 1996). In the nonprofit field, though, boards are usually larger than their counterparts in for-profit organizations (Forbes and Milliken, 1999; Steane and Christie, 2001). Empirical data as to whether this has any negative effects on their performance is inconclusive (Dyl et al., 2000; Callen et al., 2003; O'Regan and Oster, 2005; Andrés-Alonso et al., 2006). On the subject of board independence, agency theory holds that the presence of outsiders on the board positively affects the performance of the organization (Fama and Jensen, 1983). The assumption is that out-siders provide greater objectivity and independence of perspectives, thus reducing the potential for opportunistic behaviour (Callen and Falk, 1993; Oster, 1995; Dyl et al., 2000; O'Regan and Oster, 2005; Andrés-Alonso et al., 2006; Brickley et al., 2010). While boards of trustees are gener-ally composed of a majority of outsiders (Oster, 1995), the effects on nonprofit performance are uncertain.

Agency theory also suggests that the involvement of donors or founders on the board enhances a board's effectiveness through increasing its motivation to monitor (Callen et al., 2003; Hough et al., 2005; Hyndman and McDonell, 2009; Jegers, 2009). But, again, the empiri-cal evidence-base is inconclusive. Although donors and founders might lack residual rights in some foundations, they do represent the organizational equivalent of a shareholder: they are concerned about the use of the resources they have provided to the organization. As Fama and Jensen (1983) posit, major donors monitor the organization better than donors on board. When the major donor is public, such as in the case of the Big Lottery Fund in the UK, a grantmak-ing trust whose income derives from the sale of national lottery tickets, that monitoring power appears to be even greater, although the sense of 'ownership' will also be diffused. Public donors may have enough power and access to information to become efficient monitors (Herman and Renz, 2000; O'Regan and Oster, 2002) because they usually demand detailed plans, financial budgets and information on each project they finance (Frumkin and Kim, 2001; Callen et al., 2003; Andrés-Alonso et al., 2006).

Finally, capital structure and nonprofit transparency have recently been introduced as gover-nance mechanisms in the nonprofit field. From an agency perspective, debt is considered as an indirect way to limit managerial behaviour (Jensen, 1986); managers are curtailed by debt and interest payment obligations and by the continuous screening of their lenders. While traditionally of less relevance to philanthropic foundations than the wider nonprofit sector, this might increase as some foundations recast themselves as foundations banks and social investors (Salamon, 2014). In this line, transparency supposes an increase in the exposure of managerial and board decisions to social screening. Although there is no empirical evidence of the direct effect of these two mechanisms on performance, they might be an effective disciplinary governance mechanism.

Taken together, only major donors, especially public ones, seem to have proven effective in monitoring the managerial team of nonprofits. Board features that have traditionally been studied only provide cursory support for shaping an effective governing body; there is not enough evidence of the effect of debt and transparency on nonprofits' performance. As these shortcomings are partly attributed to the limitations of trying to apply a private sector theory to the nonprofit field (Miller, 2002; Brown, 2005), there have been increasing calls to complement agency theory with other approaches to adequately capture all the implications for how corpo-rate governance can help nonprofits (Andrés-Alonso et al., 2010; Callen et al., 2010; Steinberg, 2010; Van Puyvelde et al., 2012).

Towards an extended model of nonprofit corporate governance

So far, efforts of building an extended model of governance for the nonprofit field have been geared towards effectively configuring a board of trustees. To this end, it is useful to combine the issues raised by agency theory with the underlying principles of resource dependency (Hillman and Dalziel, 2003; Miller-Millesen, 2003; Callen *et al.* 2010). To better understand the social processes that guide behaviours on boards, incorporating group/decision theories also seems relevant (Brown, 2005), while a cognitive approach helps to delve deeper into the processes involved in innovation and knowledge creation (Andrés-Alonso *et al.*, 2010). Some of these factors encourage monitoring while discouraging the board's strategic role and vice versa (Callen *et al.*, 2010; Ostrower and Stone, 2010). As such, it is necessary to reflect on the potential challenges and opportunities for bringing these perspectives together to inform research and practice.

The cognitive perspective is rooted in the work of Charreaux (2005). Based on evolutionary economics and organizational learning, it puts special emphasis on knowledge generation as an open and subjective element, resulting from the interpretation of the environment made by the multiple participants within an organization (Treichler, 1995). It points to the importance of trustees' diverse characteristics: each has a different set of experiences, knowledge, perceptions, interpretations and actions that partially reflects his or her own cognitive schema. These differences result in 'cognitive conflicts' which in turn improve the quality of strategic decision-making in uncertain environments through the consideration of more alternatives and evaluating these alternatives more carefully (Forbes and Milliken, 1999). Given board of trustees' commitment to strategic planning and effective decision-making, this approach seems to be especially suitable for nonprofit contexts (Bradshaw *et al.* 1992; Judge and Zeithmal, 1992) as it supplements the ideas of agency theory. On the one hand, the high level of information asymmetries and uncertainty that characterizes the nonprofit sector increases agency problems, and so the need for effective mechanisms of control; on the other hand, this high level of uncertainty links to the need for critical interactive decision processes to create value, which in turn is relevant to cognitive conflict and strategic decision-making (Andrés-Alonso *et al.*, 2010).

Relating this to practical questions surrounding board configuration, potential conflicts do, however, arise: board size and independence need to be considered, alongside board capital, board diversity, and the proactive character of the trustees and their group dynamics. While agency theory recommends smaller and more independent boards to reduce costs and increase objectivity in the monitoring activity, once the cognitive role of the board is included, the assumptions surrounding board size and board independence on the organization's performance are questioned: more board members, though slower in decision-making, would provide more information and cognitive resources (Bantel and Jackson, 1989; Olson, 2000), resulting in a positive effect on nonprofit performance (Abzug *et al.*, 1993; Ostrower, 2002; Ostrower and Stone, 2010; Aggarwal *et al.* 2012). Similarly, outsiders, although potentially more objective in monitoring proceedings, might lack specific knowledge to support innovation and creative decision-making, as well as the commitment and motivation of those more closely related to the cause. While we have not found empirical evidence to support a positive relationship between insiders and nonprofit performance, many authors maintain that trustees' motivation is a determinant of board effectiveness (Taylor *et al.*, 1991; Steane and Christie, 2001). Therefore, the influence of board size and independence on the organization's performance must be reconsidered in an extended model of governance.

Closely related to this is the notion of board capital. This combines human capital (expertise, experience and reputation) and relational/social capital (networks and linkages to external constituencies) (Hillman and Dalziel, 2003). Human capital gives trustees exposure to making complex managerial and financial decisions (Olson 2000); the board benefits from the accumulation of the different kinds of knowledge and skills that individual board members bring to the table (Ostrower and Stone, 2010; Vidovich and Currie, 2012). Social capital provides political engagement, connections to influential funders and social ties; it is essential for nonprofits to access key networks within their respective organizations and in the communities they serve (King, 2004). Taken together, these factors are also considered as determinant of board performance (Hillman and Dalziel, 2003; Preston and Brown, 2004; Brown, 2007; Brown et al., 2012) by both being cumulative, but also by offering another important factor: diversity.

Diversity strengthens the creativity of a board (Bantel and Jackson, 1989) and, thus, its strategic role. It relates to both observable attributes, such as ethnicity, age, or gender, and to less visible ones, such as education, technical abilities, functional and socioeconomic background, status, personality characteristics or values (Tsui et al., 1992; Milliken and Martins, 1996). Heterogeneous groups have a greater breadth of perspective to bring to decision-making and, as they can draw on a wider set of expertise, might arrive at more potential solutions to a problem (Hambrick and Mason, 1984; Van der Walt and Ingley, 2003). Diversity thus has a positive effect on board effectiveness and, consequently, on nonprofit performance, a view empirically supported by the work of Andrés-Alonso et al. (2010). Whether, as part of that, it is more important for board members to be proactive (Andrés-Alonso et al., 2010; Coombes et al., 2011; Brown et al., 2012) or for boards to act as a team (Nicholson et al., 2012) is unclear, with further research combining the two needed to examine board effectiveness and nonprofit performance.

In sum, by adding agency theory arguments and a cognitive approach, we reach a more complete perspective to understand nonprofit governance. At this juncture, the traditional board features, like size and independence, seem to lose some of their importance while other, new characteristics, like diversity, proactivity or strategic decision-making groups, gain weight in the governance literature. However, the search for an optimal board configuration requires a far more robust empirical support for this assessment before it can be used as guidance for good practice.

Conclusions and future lines of research on nonprofit corporate governance

Although theoretical approaches on nonprofit corporate governance have advanced greatly in recent decades, there is still a long way to go in terms of empirical testing. Especially in relation to 'good' governance for foundations and nonprofits in general, much more work is required. While this chapter has pointed to some of the key studies, a lot of them are derived from cross-sectional data from the US nonprofit sector: as Wellens and Jegers (2013) suggest, longitudinal and cross-country research is necessary to draw overall conclusions.

This line of research is difficult to implement, though, given the lack of structured databases of these organizations, especially outside the US. As such, researchers must currently develop their studies on the basis of primary data (surveys, interviews, case study), which makes it challenging to obtain cross-national or longitudinal samples. In addition, the latest theoretical advances introduce variables related to cognitive schemata and group thinking that require very specific information about individuals, reiterating the need for better and more overarching research approaches that can be applied across times and contexts.

Contextual factors are increasingly critical for scholars, as the foundation form itself demonstrates degrees of differentiation as well as similarity, arising from governmental intervention. Developments and decisions pertaining to the rise of the Italian banking foundations, with their governance structures reflecting a particular (legally enshrined) approach to the linkages between strategic and executive functions, and their funding drawn from public savings banks' assets rather than donations (Leardini *et al.*, 2014) is an important case in point. Varying foundation contexts will also create differentiations in the interactions between internal and external governance questions. Steen-Johnson *et al.* (2011: 556) argue that these two subfields of scholarship, in nonprofit governance generally, are importantly intertwined and need to be studied as such: 'the internal governance game shapes the conditions for the organization's positions and actions in the external government environment and vice versa'. For foundations, this intertwining will be especially relevant, for example, when they decide to collaborate with governments or fellow foundations.

Furthermore, there are other governance aspects to consider that are beyond the scope of this chapter. For example, the chapter has not given attention to endogeneity problems that may exist among the different kind of mechanisms or between the features (size, age, prestige) of a foundation and its governance requirements. These might relate to the power and influence of donors and funders to shape the selection of board members (Andrés-Alonso *et al.*, 2009) or to how transparency expectations lead to boards' configurations (Saxton *et al.*, 2012). While these have been touched upon in the nonprofit research literature (Abzug *et al.*, 1993; Moore and Whitt, 2000; Ostrower, 2002; Ostrower and Stone, 2010; Aggarwal *et al.*, 2012), the relationship between these and other governance factors have not been explored widely. While there is thus still no clear answer to the question of how to best configure an internal governance system, bringing together the insights from diverse theories and perspectives, to critically reflect on their complementarity and differences, as well as to consider the future research trajectories they highlight are important steps towards a more coherent understanding of the complex nonprofit governance landscape.

References

Abzug, R. *et al.* (1993) 'Variations in Trusteeship: Cases from Boston and Cleveland, 1925-1985', *Voluntas: International Journal of Voluntas and Nonprofit Organizations.* 4(3), 271–300.

Aggarwal, R. K., Evans, M. E. and Nanda, D. (2012) 'Nonprofit Boards: Size, Performance and Managerial Incentives', *Journal of Accounting and Economics.* 53(1-2), 466–87.

Alexander, J. A., Young, G. J., Weiner, B. J. and Hearld, L. R. (2008) 'Governance and Community Benefit: Are Nonprofit Hospitals Good Candidates for Sarbanes–Oxley Type Reforms?', *Journal of Health Politics, Policy and Law.* 33, 199–224.

Andrés-Alonso, P., Martín-Cruz, N. and Romero-Merino, M. E. (2006) 'The Governance of Nonprofit Organizations. Empirical Evidence from Nongovernmental Development Organizations in Spain', *Nonprofit and Voluntary Sector Quarterly.* 35 (4). 588–604.

Andrés-Alonso, P., Azofra-Palenzuela, V. and Romero-Merino, M. E. (2009) 'Determinants of Nonprofit Board Size and Composition. The Case of Spanish Foundations', *Nonprofit and Voluntary Sector Quarterly.* 38(5), 784–809.

Andrés-Alonso, P., Azofra-Palenzuela, V. and Romero-Merino, M. E. (2010) 'Beyond the Disciplinary Role of Governance: How Boards and Donors Add Value to Spanish Foundations', *British Journal of Management.* 21(1), 100–14.

Andrews, K. (1980) 'Directors Responsibility for Corporate Strategy', *Harvard Business Review.* November–December, 174–84.

Bantel, K. A. and Jackson, S. E. (1989) Top Management and Innovations in Banking: Does the Composition of the Top Team Make a Difference?', *Strategic Management Journal.* 10, 107–24.

Berle, A. and Means, G. (1932) *The Modern Corporation and Private Property.* New York: Macmillan.

Boozang, K. M. (2007) 'Does an Independent Board Improve Nonprofit Corporate Governance?', *Tennessee Law Review,* 75(1): 83–136.

Bradshaw, P., Murray, V. and Wolpin, J. (1992) 'Do Nonprofit Boards Make a Difference? An Exploration of the Relationships among Board Structure, Process, and Effectiveness', *Nonprofit and Voluntary Sector Quarterly.* 21(3), 227–49.

Brickley, J. A, Van Horn, R. L. and Wedig, G. J. (2010) 'Board Composition and Nonprofit Conduct: Evidence from Hospitals', *Journal Of Economic Behavior and Organization.* 76(2), 196–208.

Brody, E. (1996) 'Agents without Principals: The Economic Convergence of the Nonprofit and For-Profit Organizational Forms', *New York Law School Law Review.* 40, 457–528.

Brown, W. A. (2005) 'Exploring the Association between Board and Organizational Performance in Nonprofit Organizations', *Nonprofit Management and Leadership.* 15(3), 317–39.

Brown, W. A. (2007) 'Board Development Practices and Competent Board Members: Implications for Performance', *Nonprofit Management and Leadership.* 17(3), 301–17.

Brown, W. A, Hillman, A. J. and Okun, M. A. (2012) 'Factors that Influence Monitoring and Resource Provision among Nonprofit Board Members', *Nonprofit and Voluntary Sector Quarterly.* 41(1), 145–56.

Callen, J. L. and Falk, H. (1993) 'Agency and Efficiency in Nonprofit Organizations', *The Accounting Review.* 68(1), 48–65.

Callen, J. L., Klein, A. and Tinkelman, D. (2003) 'Board Composition Committees and Organizational Efficiency: The Case of Nonprofits', *Nonprofit and Voluntary Sector Quarterly.* 32(4), 493–520.

Callen, J. L., Klein, A. and Tinkelman, D. (2010) 'The Contextual Impact of Nonprofit Board Composition and Structure on Organizational Performance: Agency and Resource Dependence Perspectives', *Voluntas: International Journal of Voluntary and Nonprofit Organizations.* 21(1), 101–25.

Carver, J. (1990) *Boards that Make a Difference.* San Francisco: Jossey-Bass.

Chait, R. P., Holland, T. P. and Taylor, B. E. (1991) *The Effective Board of Trustees.* New York: Macmillan.

Charreaux, G. (2004) *Corporate Governance Theories: From Micro Theories to National Systems Theories.* Working Paper of Fargo N° 1040101. Université De Bourgogne.

Charreaux, G. (2005) 'Pur Une Governance D'entreprise 'Comportementale': Une Réflexion ('A Behavioural Corporate Governance Theory: An Exploratory View'). *Revue Française De Gestion.* 31, 215–38.

Coombes, S. M. T. *et al.* (2011) 'Orientations of Non-Profit Boards as a Factor in Entrepreneurial Performance: Does Governance Matter', *Journal of Management Studies.* 48(4). 829–56.

Cornforth, C. (1996) Governing Non-Profit Organisations: Heroic Myths and Human Tales. In *Researching the UK Voluntary Sector.* London: National Council for Voluntary Organisations.

Cornforth, C. (2001) 'What Makes Board Effective? An Examination of the Relationships between Board Inputs, Structures, Processes and Effectiveness in Non-Profit Organizations', *Corporate Governance: An International Review.* 9(3), 217–27.

Cornforth, C. (2012) 'Nonprofit Governance Research: Limitations of the Focus on Boards and Suggestions for New Directions', *Nonprofit and Voluntary Sector Quarterly.* 41(6), 16–1135.

Cornforth, C. and Chambers, N. (2010) 'The Role of Corporate Governance and Boards in Organisational Performance', in K. Walsh, G. Harvey and P. Jas (eds), *Connecting Knowledge and Performance in Public Services: From Knowing to Doing.* Cambridge: Cambridge University Press, 99–127.

Cornforth, C. and Brown, W.A. (eds) (2014) *Nonprofit Governance: Innovative Perspectives and Approaches.* Abingdon, Oxon: Routledge.

Dalton, D. R. *et al.* (1998) 'Meta-Analytic Reviews of Board Composition, Leadership Structure, and Financial Performance', *Strategic Management Journal.* 19(3), 269–90.

Davis, J. H., Schoorman, D. F. and Donaldson, L. (1997) 'Toward a Stewardship Theory of Management', *The Academy of Management Review.* 22(1), 20–47.

Donaldson, L. and Davis, J. H. (1991) 'Stewardship Theory or Agency Theory: CEO Governance and Shareholder Returns', *Australian Journal of Management.* 16(1), 49–65.

Dyl, E. A., Frant, H. L. and Stephenson, C. A. (2000) 'Governance and Funds Allocation in United States Medical Research Charities', *Financial Accountability and Management.* 16(4), 335–51.

Fama, E. and Jensen, M. C. (1983) 'Separation of Ownership and Control', *Journal of Law and Economics.* 26, 301–25.

Forbes, D. P. and Milliken, F. J. (1999) 'Cognition and Corporate Governance: Understanding Boards of Directors as Strategic Decision-making Groups', *Academy Of Management Review.* 24(3), 489–505.

Frumkin, P. and Kim, M. T. (2001) 'Strategic Positioning and The Financing of Nonprofit Organizations: Is Efficiency Rewarded in the Contributions Marketplace?', *Public Administration Review.* 61(3), 266–75.

Gill, M., Flynn, R. J. and Reissing, E. (2005) 'The Governance Self-Assessment Checklist: An Instrument for Assessing Board Effectiveness', *Nonprofit Management and Leadership.* 15(3), 271–94.

Green, J. C. and Griesinger, D. W. (1996) 'Board Performance and Organizational Effectiveness in Nonprofit Social Service Organizations', *Nonprofit Management and Leadership.* 6(4), 381–402.

Guo, C. (2007) 'When Government Becomes the Principal Philanthropist: The Effects of Public Funding on Patterns of Nonprofit Governance', *Public Administration Review.* 67(3), 458–73.

Hall, P. D. (1990) 'Conflicting Managerial Cultures in Nonprofit Organizations', *Nonprofit Management and Leadership*. 1(2), 153–65.

Hambrick, D. C. and Mason, P. A. (1984) 'Upper Echelons: The Organization as a Reflection of its Top Managers', *Academy of Management Review*. 9(2), 193–106.

Hansmann, H. B. (1980) 'The Role of Nonprofit Enterprise', *Yale Law Review*. 89, 835–99.

Harlan, S. L., and Saidel, J. R. (1994) 'Board Members' Influence on the Government – Nonprofit Relationship', *Nonprofit Management and Leadership*. 5 (2), 173–96.

Harrow, J. (2011) 'Governance and Isomorphism in Local Philanthropy: The Interplay of Issues among Foundations in Japan and the UK', *Public Management Review*. 13(1), 1–20.

Harrow, J. and Phillips, S. D. (2013) 'Corporate Governance in Nonprofits: Facing up to Hybridization and Homogenization', in M. Wright, D. S. Siegel, K. Keasey and I. Filatotchev (eds), *The Oxford Handbook of Corporate Governance*. Oxford: Oxford University Press, 603–33.

Herman, R. D. (1989) 'Concluding Thoughts on Closing the Board Gap', in R. Herman and J. Van Til (eds), *Nonprofit Boards of Directors: Analyses and Applications*. Brunswick, NJ: Transaction Books.

Herman, R. D. and Renz, D. O. (2000) 'Board Practices of Especially Effective and Less Effective Local Nonprofit Organizations', *American Review of Public Administration*. 30(2), 146–60.

Herman, R. D., Renz, D. O. and Heimovics, R. D. (1997) 'Board Practices and Board Effectiveness in Local Nonprofit Organizations', *Nonprofit Management and Leadership*. 7(4), 373–86.

Hillman, A. J. and Dalziel, T. (2003) 'Boards of Directors and Firm Performance: Integrating Agency and Resource Dependence Perspectives', *Academy of Management Review*. 28(3), 383–96.

Hillman, A. J., Withers, M. C. and Collins, B. J. (2009) 'Resource Dependence Theory: A Review', *Journal of Management*. 35(6). 1404–27.

Holland, T. P. (1991) 'Self-Assessment by Nonprofit Boards', *Nonprofit Management and Leadership*. 2(1), 25–36.

Hough, A. (2006) 'In Search of Board Effectiveness', *Nonprofit Management and Leadership*. 16(3), 373–7.

Hough, A., Mcgregor-Lowndes, M. and Ryan, C. (2005) *Theorizing about Board Governance of Nonprofit Organizations: Surveying the Landscape*. Conference Paper in 34th Annual Conference of the Association for Research on Nonprofit Organizations and Voluntary Action, November 17–19, Washington DC.

Houle, C. O. (1989) *Governing Bodies: Their Nature and Nurture*. San Francisco: Jossey-Bass.

Hyndman, N. and Mcdonell, P. (2009) 'Governance and Charities: An Exploration of Key Themes and the Development of a Research Agenda', *Financial Accountability and Management*. 25(1), 5–31.

Ingley, C. B. and Van Der Walt, N. T. (2001) 'The Strategic Board: The Changing Role of Directors in Developing and Maintaining Corporate Capability', *Corporate Governance: An International Review*. 9(3), 174–85.

Jackson, D. K. and Holland, T. P. (1998) 'Measuring the Effectiveness of Nonprofit Boards', *Nonprofit and Voluntary Sector Quarterly*. 27(2), 157–82.

Jegers, M. (2002) 'The Economics of Nonprofit Accounting and Auditing: Suggestions for a Research Agenda', *Annals of Public and Cooperative Economics*. 73, 429–51.

Jegers, M. (2009) 'Corporate Governance in Nonprofit Organizations', *Nonprofit Management and Leadership*. 20(2), 143–64.

Jegers, M. (2011) *Managerial Economics of Non-Profit Organizations*. Brussels: Vub Press.

Jegers, M. and Verschueren, I. (2006) 'On the Capital Structure of Non-Profit Organisations: An Empirical Study for Californian Organisations', *Financial Accountability and Management*. 22(4), 309–29.

Jenkins, R. (2012) *The Governance and Financial Management of Endowed Charitable Foundations*. London: Association of Charitable Foundations.

Jensen, M. C. (1986) 'The Takeover Controversy: Analysis and Evidence', *Midland Corporate Finance Journal*. 4(2), 6–32.

Jensen, M. C. (1993) 'The Modern Industrial Revolution, Exit, and the Failure of Internal Control Systems', *The Journal of Finance*. 48(3), 831–80.

Jensen, M. C. (1994) 'Self-Interest, Altruism, Incentives and Agency Theory', *Journal of Applied Corporate Finance*. 7(2), 40–5.

Jensen, M. C. and Meckling, W. H. (1976) 'Theory of the Firm: Managerial Behaviour, Agency Costs and Ownership Structure', *Journal of Finance Economics*. 3(4), 305–60.

Johnson, J. L., Daily, C. M. and Ellstrand, A. E. (1996) 'Board of Directors: A Review and Research Agenda', *Journal of Management*. 22(3), 409–38.

Judge, W. Q. and Zeithmal, C. P. (1992) 'Institutional and Strategic Choice Perspectives on Board Involvement in the Strategic Decision Process', *Academy Of Management Journal*. 35(4), 766–94.

King, N. K. (2004) 'Social Capital and Nonprofit Leaders', *Nonprofit Management and Leadership*. 14(4), 471–86.

Kingston Smith (2013) Charities Toolkit, www.kingstonsmith.co.uk/upload/pdf/Charties%20Governance%20Toolkit_Final.pdf [Accessed 13 June 2015].

Leardini, C., Rossi, G. and Moggi, S. (2014) *Board Governance in Bank Foundations: The Italian Experience*. Heidelberg: Springer.

McKinsey and Company (ND), Nonprofit Board Self Assessment Tool, www.linkingmissiontomoney.com/documents/McKinseyboardassessmenttool.pdf [Accessed 13 June 2015].

Manne, G. A. (1999) 'Agency Costs and Oversight of Charitable Organizations', *Wisconsin Law Review*. 227–72.

Marcus, A. A. and Goodman, R. S. (1991) 'Victims and Shareholders: The Dilemmas of Presenting Corporate Policy During a Crisis,' *The Academy of Management Journal*. 34(2), 281–305.

Miller, J. L. (2002) 'The Board as a Monitor of Organizational Activity', *Nonprofit Management and Leadership*. 12(4), 429–50.

Miller-Millesen, J. L. (2003) 'Understanding the Behavior of Nonprofit Boards of Directors: A Theory-Based Approach', *Nonprofit and Voluntary Sector Quarterly*. 32(4), 521–47.

Milliken, F. J. and Martins, L. L. (1996) 'Searching for Common Threads: Understanding the Multiple Effects of Diversity in Organizational Groups', *Academy Of Management Review*. 21(2), 402–33.

Minichilli, A., Zattoni, A. and Zona, F. (2009) 'Making Boards Effective: An Empirical Examination of Board Task Performance', *British Journal of Management*. 20(1), 55–74.

Moore, G. and Whitt, J. A. (2000) 'Gender and Networks in a Local Voluntary-Sector Elite', *Voluntas: International Journal of Voluntary and Nonprofit Organizations*. 11(4), 309–28.

Nicholson, G., Newton, C. and Mcgregor-Lowndes, M. (2012) 'The Nonprofit Board as a Team. Pilot Results and Initial Insights', *Nonprofit and Management Leadership*. 22(4), 461–81.

O'Regan, K. and Oster, S. (2002) 'Does Government Funding Alter Nonprofit Governance? Evidence from New York City Nonprofit Contractors', *Journal of Policy Analysis and Management*. 21(3), 359–79.

O'Regan, K. and Oster, S. (2005) 'Does the Structure and Composition of the Board Matter? The Case Of Nonprofit Organizations', *Journal Of Law, Economics and Organization*. 21, 205–27.

Olson, D. E. (2000) 'Agency Theory in the Not-For-Profit Sector: Its Role at Independent Colleges', *Nonprofit and Voluntary Sector Quarterly*. 29(2), 280–96.

Oster, S. (1995) *Strategic Management for Nonprofit Organizations*. New York: Oxford University Press.

Ostrower, F. (2002) *Trustees of Culture: Power, Wealth, and Status on Elite Arts Boards*. Chicago: University of Chicago Press.

Ostrower, F. (2007) *Nonprofit Governance in the United States: Findings on Performance and Accountability from the First Representative National Study*. Washington: Urban Institute Center on Nonprofits and Philanthropy.

Ostrower, F. and Stone, M. M. (2006) 'Boards of Nonprofit Organizations: Research Trends, Findings and Prospects for Future Research', in W. Powell and R. Steinberg (eds), *The Nonprofit Sector: A Research Handbook* (2nd Ed.). New Haven: Yale University Press.

Ostrower, F. and Stone, M. M. (2010) 'Moving Governance Research Forward: A Contingency-Based Framework and Data Application', *Nonprofit and Voluntary Sector Quarterly*. 39(5), 901–24.

Parker, L. D. (2007) 'Internal Governance in the Nonprofit Boardroom: A Participant Observer Study', *Corporate Governance: An International Review*. 15(5), 923–34.

Pfeffer, J. and Salancik, G. (1978) *The External Control Of Organizations: A Resource-Dependence Perspective*. New York: Harpercollins.

Preston, J. B. and Brown, W. A. (2004) 'Commitment and Performance of Nonprofit Board Members', *Nonprofit Management and Leadership*. 15 (2), 221–38.

Provan, K. G. (1980) 'Board Power and Organizational Effectiveness among Human Services Agencies', *Academy of Management Journal*. 23, 221–36.

Salamon, L. M. (2014) *New Frontiers of Philanthropy: A Guide to the New Tools and New Actors that are Reshaping Global Philanthropy and Social Investing*. Oxford: Oxford University Press.

Saxton, G. D., Kuo, J. S. and Ho, Y. C. (2012) 'The Determinants of Voluntary Financial Disclosure by Nonprofit Organizations', *Nonprofit and Voluntary Sector Quarterly*. 41(6), 1051–71.

Shleifer, A. and Vishny, R. W. (1997) 'A Survey of Corporate Governance', *Journal of Finance*. 52(2), 737–83.

Speckbacher, G. (2008) 'Nonprofit Versus Corporate Governance: An Economic Approach', *Nonprofit Management and Leadership*. 18(3), 295–320.

Spence, M. (1973) 'Job Market Signalling', *The Quarterly Journal of Economics* 87(3), 355–374.

Steane, P. D. and Christie, M. (2001) 'Nonprofit Boards in Australia: A Distinctive Governance Approach', *Corporate Governance: An International Review.* 9(1), 48–58.

Steen-Johnson, K., Eynaud, P. and Wijkström, F. (2011) 'On Civil Society Governance: An Emergent Research Field', *Voluntas: International Journal of Voluntary and Nonprofit Organizations.* 22(4), 555–65.

Steinberg, R. (2010) 'Principal–Agent Theory and Nonprofit Accountability', in K. J. Hopt and T. Von Hippel (eds), *Comparative Corporate Governance of Non-Profit Organizations.* Cambridge: Cambridge University Press.

Stone, L. M. (1975) 'The Charitable Foundation: Its Governance', *Law and Contemporary Problems*, 29(4): 57–74.

Taylor, B. E., Chait, R. P. and Holland, T. P. (1991) 'Trustee Motivation and Board Effectiveness', *Nonprofit and Voluntary Sector Quarterly.* 20(2), 207–24.

Treichler, C. M. (1995) 'Diversity of Board Members and Organizational Performance: An Integrative Perspective', *Corporate Governance: An International Review.* 3(4), 189–200.

Tsui, A. S., Egan. T. D. and O'Reilly, C. A. (1992) 'Being Different: Relational Demography and Organizational Attachment', *Administrative Science Quarterly.* 37(4), 549–79.

Ulrich, D. and Barney, J. B. (1984) 'Perspectives in Organizations: Resource Dependence, Efficiency, and Population', *Academy of Management Review.* 9, 471–81.

Van der Walt, N. and Ingley, C. (2003) 'Board Dynamics and the Influence of Professional Background, Gender and Ethnic Diversity Of Directors', *Corporate Governance: An International Review.* 11(3), 218–34.

Van Puyvelde, S. *et al.* (2012) 'The Governance of Nonprofit Organizations: Integrating Agency Theory with Stakeholder and Stewardships Theories', *Nonprofit and Voluntary Sector Quarterly.* 41(3), 431–51.

VicSport (ND), Good Governance Tool Kit, www.goodgovsport.eu/files/GGGS_WEB/Files/2_Good_governance_tool_kit_from_VicSport.pdf [Accessed 13 June 2015].

Vidovich, L. and Currie, J. (2012) 'Governance Networks. Interlocking Directorships of Corporate and Nonprofit Boards', *Nonprofit Management and Leadership.* 22(4), 507–23.

Wellens, L. and Jegers, M. (2013) 'Effective Governance in Nonprofit Organizations: A Literature Based Multiple Stakeholder Approach', *European Management Journal.* 32(2), 223–43.

Yermack, D. (1996) 'Higher Market Valuation of Companies with a Small Board of Directors', *Journal of Financial Economics.* 40(2), 185–211.

Zahra, S. and Pearce, J. (1989) 'Boards of Directors and Corporate Financial Performance: A Review and Integrative Model', *Journal of Management.* 15(2), 291–334.

Zimmermann, J. A. M. and Stevens, B. W. (2008) 'Best Practices in Board Governance. Evidence from South Carolina', *Nonprofit and Management Leadership.* 19(2), 189–202.

26

Achieving philanthropic mission
Directing and managing grantmaking

Peter Grant

Philanthropy is, in itself, an entirely unproductive process: philanthropic funds do nothing productive until they are transferred to a person or organization that puts them to use. Nonetheless, many mission statements from well-known grantmaking foundations claim or imply otherwise: 'to improve the health and health care of all Americans' or 'to improve the quality of life throughout the UK'. Such statements give the impression of philanthropic organizations being directly involved in social missions when they are, actually, conduits through which social missions can be met. The importance of a grant as a 'non-contractual one-way transfer of assets for a social purpose' (Grant, 2012: 12) lies in the fact it is a transfer with a use as its goal. The 'black box' nature of philanthropic foundations (Bethmann *et al.*, 2014), however, makes it difficult to understand the management and assess the achievements of their grantmaking and other ways in which they pursue their philanthropic missions.

To date, there has been minimal scholarship on the internal processes that characterize grantmaking. This might either be because these are seen as a secondary matter to philanthropy's grand design and a relatively unimportant aspect of philanthropic action, or simply because they are difficult to observe. Where this scholarship does exist, it concentrates on grantmaking decisions – that is, on what gets funded – rather than processes in full; it looks more to wider questions of accountability instead of management of these processes in their own right. This is illustrated by McCoy *et al.* (2009: 1650) who, in analyzing the Bill and Melinda Gates Foundation's grantmaking process, report that this 'seems to be largely managed through an informal system of personal networks and relationships rather than by a more transparent process based on independent and technical peer review'. Yet, in any organization, effective performance and achievement of organizational mission are based on a strong relationship between strategy and governance translated into a workable operational plan. In a philanthropic organization, that plan is often its grantmaking process.

The internal processes for directing and managing grantmaking in foundations are critical to achieving philanthropic mission: that this 'management of philanthropy' is an important area for advancing scholarship and practice in its own right. Foundations, which are in 'the funding business', have a responsibility 'to fund the work of others as efficiently and effectively as possible'(Grant, 2012: 85). The main problem of philanthropic management was defined well by Ostrower (2004) over a decade ago, when she concluded that foundations typically define effectiveness very generally, albeit with considerable variations among grantmakers, and that their effectiveness goals are often overshadowed by other priorities. A key challenge for foundations then is to clarify and specify what they believe it means to be effective, and have in place the appropriate governance systems and good grantmaking practices to achieve their goals. This entails not only focusing on the 'product' on offer to the end beneficiaries, but paying attention to their own internal workings as a funder. Increasingly, it also means looking beyond grants as the primary means of carrying out philanthropic missions.

This chapter examines the relationship between foundation governance, grantmaking, and strategy. To this end, it picks up some of the themes highlighted by Romero-Merino and Garcia-Rodriguez in Chapter 25. Rather than approaching the topic from governance theories, however, this chapter challenges some of the popular perspectives on governance and relates them specifically to the philanthropic grantmaking process. As such, the first part of the chapter focuses on questions surrounding governance within foundations in relation to grantmakers' boards and staff; the second part concentrates on practical questions about the management of grantmaking; and the third takes a critical look at 'strategic' philanthropy which is currently touted as the most effective means of achieving philanthropic missions.

'Good' governance in philanthropic organizations

Organizational 'governance' is the mechanism that translates the philanthropic mission into strategic directions and executes both through operational plans, as illustrated in Figure 26.1. Cornforth (2003: 17) defines organizational governance as 'the systems and processes concerned with ensuring the overall direction, effectiveness, supervision and accountability of an organization'. As a system, governance presents four imperatives: setting an organization's overall direction; ensuring its effectiveness; supervising its assets; and providing accountability to stakeholders. In the nonprofit sector, a veritable cottage industry has developed in producing guides and consulting on 'good' governance (Tickell, 2005; CIPFA, 2004; Panel on the Nonprofit Sector, 2007). As yet, there is minimal serious scholarship on governance in philanthropic foundations, although attention is developing in relation to corporate and family philanthropy and their particular governance dilemmas (Bartkus et al., 2002; Van Cranenburgh and Arenas, 2013).

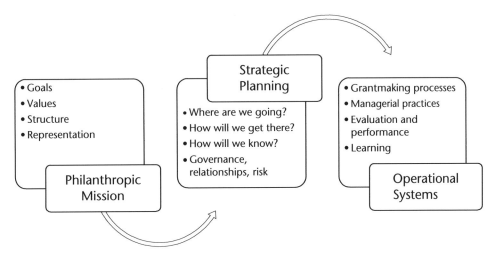

Figure 26.1 Governance, strategy and grantmaking

This literature points to three important factors that influence the quality of governance: the composition and role of the board; the foundation's relationships with stakeholders, particularly managing the power imbalance; and its approaches to risk.

The foundation board and staff

While the principles and specific practices of good governance may be debated, what is not contested is where responsibility for ensuring good governance lies within an organization. Its governing board is 'responsible for reviewing and approving the organization's mission and strategic direction, annual budget and key financial transactions, compensation practices and policies, and fiscal and governance policies' (Panel on the Nonprofit Sector, 2007: 13). There are some potential differences, however, in the key issues faced by boards of grantmaking foundations than those in the wider nonprofit sector that has been the subject of most of the extant research.

One important difference is source of funds and sense of 'ownership' (Harrow and Phillips, 2013) this entails. First, in the broader nonprofit world, the funding rarely comes from members of its own board or their close relatives. Particularly in family foundations, this is very common, however (Leat, Chapter 18). Second, most charities have to fundraise in order to survive, while private foundations have a permanent endowment, and so are relieved of this major task. Third, the stakeholders of most charities are clearly defined; they are the end beneficiaries of the charities' work. For philanthropic institutions, the stakeholders are more elusive. Are they just the recipients of their grants or the actual beneficiaries of those recipients? Where do the founders, if still active, or their families fit in? This can lead to a serious confusion over exactly 'whose money' it is that the foundation controls and in whose name the foundation holds its assets 'in trust'. As Richard Jenkins (2012: 25) points out:

> because their relationship with beneficiaries is mediated through their charitable objects, which may be fairly wide, and which may be clouded by ideas like "acting in the best interests of the charity", endowed charitable foundations can face the danger of running adrift through having a lack of clarity over why it is they exist.

In legal terms, there is no such confusion. Once an individual, group of people, or a company decides to establish a foundation, rather than simply making 'off the cuff' donations, they are legally relinquishing their personal control over the assets. 'Trustees gather not to represent their own interests, nor those of the founder, but solely those of the beneficiaries' (Jenkins, 2012: 25). As soon as philanthropists decide to adopt an organizational conduit for their benevolence, especially one that brings with it tax advantages, then they irrevocably lose the right to treat those assets as their own. Indeed, they have no greater entitlement to oversee the administration of those resources than any other person. By adopting a public face, philanthropy becomes, to a greater or lesser extent, a *public resource* (Young, 2000; Desai and Yetman, 2006). This is hotly contested by those who argue that if a person or donor has made the money in the first place, they retain a right to decide how and to whom it is allocated. This is a valid point while that money remains in the personal possession of the individual, but it is fatally weakened once that individual decides to adopt a public form for philanthropic giving. Therefore, it should make no difference whether the founder or members of their family sit on the board or not: the organization should be governed in exactly the same way with the interests of the end beneficiaries always paramount. Can the majority of philanthropic organizations swear that this is actually the case?

When we look to the composition of foundation boards, one might be sceptical about the degree of a public sense of ownership. The clearest way in which stakeholder involvement in an organization can be made manifest is by their direct representation in the governance of the organization (Cornforth, 2003; Hyndman and McDonnell, 2009). Diversity on nonprofit boards has also been shown to bring improved performance and accountability (Hallett, 1990; Coffey and Wang, 1998; Burbridge et al., 2002; Grosvold et al., 2007). In practice, there is often a lack of any stakeholder representation, or worse, lack of any diversity in foundation board representation. Much of the problem lies in the poor recruitment practices. Rather than going through a rigorous process of identifying gaps in knowledge or experience, producing detailed specifications for the roles and then adopting an open, public recruitment campaign, too many philanthropic organizations simply appoint a friend or business colleague of one or more of the existing board members. This leads to narrowly defined boards with few younger, less affluent or non-white members.

The boards of family foundations may intentionally lack diversity, as control remains with the founding family through many generations. In a study of 200 of the largest US independent foundations, Lungeanu and Ward (2012) find, as expected, that granting strategies are more narrowly focused in family than in nonfamily foundations when the family remains in control of the board. As new generations are included and as board size increases, however, family foundations become open to outside ideas and eventually become more diversified in what they support.

A related issue is that foundation boards often become far too involved in day-to-day, operational decisions. One of the first principles of good governance is for the board to remain focused on high level objectives or as one 'good governance code' puts it:

> trustees should focus on the strategic direction of their organization, and avoid becoming involved in day to day operational decisions and matters (except in the case of small organizations with few or no staff). Where trustees do need to become involved in operational matters, they should separate their strategic and operational roles.
>
> *(Tickell, 2005: 11)*

Nowhere in the nonprofit sector is this principle more ignored than in foundations, and there is a simple explanation that is strongly supported by empirical research (Andreoni, 1990; Rose-Ackerman, 1996; Hyndman and McDonnell, 2009; Breeze, 2010). The pleasure and satisfaction of the act of giving itself prompts board members to take active, operational roles. The greatest satisfaction for altruistic, volunteer board members of a philanthropic organization is making the actual grants, not the dull and dry accountability and supervisory roles they often perform in their professional lives (Grant, 2012: 86-7).

Many foundation boards also suffer from a fundamental misunderstanding about the actual business in which they are working. Philanthropists and philanthropic institutions facilitate social change or activity; they do not, except in specialized circumstances, carry it out themselves. When philanthropy is done through an organization, its board is in the *funding* business, with the task of funding the work of others as efficiently and effectively as possible. As Grant (2012: 92) advises board directors:

> You are not an educator, social worker or artist. Unless you want to be highly interventionist – and this requires very specialist forms of investment like venture philanthropy – you operate most effectively when you don't interfere too much with what the deliverers of the service are doing. If social investors think they are unique to their specialism, they will

concentrate too much on the wrong things – the 'quality' of the 'product' on offer to the end beneficiaries – and forget about their own internal workings as a 'funder.'

Taken together, and especially where governance styles and practices are understood as expressions of leadership, a key managerial message for philanthropy involves the quality of recruitment of professionals to foundations, both as board members and employees. In larger and the very largest foundations especially, 'who are the grantmakers' may be understood as the leading salaried employees, including chief executives. There is again minimal research on foundations' patterns, means and sources of recruitment to their staff or to their boards. Underlying commentaries suggest the predominance of relatively closed and thus preferential recruitment modes, particularly with family foundation boards 'giving' senior salaried roles to junior family members.

This very whiff of privilege, however, may do a disservice to the contributions and commitments of staff. Although succession planning among CEOs in the business world and research is widely understood to be a core test of organizations' leadership and management approach, its scrutiny in a foundation context barely occurs. An exception is the study of foundation CEOs by Santora and colleagues (1997) which reveals that none had experience with succession planning, and advocates 'the need to study the process of *grant awarding* (author's italics) to uncover additional aspects related to understanding power, leadership and influence in foundations' policies'(Santora *et al.*, 1997: 108). While scholarship on employment motivation and remuneration in nonprofits generally is limited (but growing), its attention is predominantly on fund seekers, rather than on the minority, the fund distributors. Thus, little is known about the managerial cohorts working in foundations, their levels of pay and education, gender, age and diversity, notwithstanding that these will vary according to national cultural and regulatory environments.

Stakeholder relationships

For foundations, stakeholder relationships are heavily influenced by the distribution of power within the philanthropic relationship, or rather its dangerous imbalance. Philanthropic institutions, especially grantmaking foundations endowed in perpetuity, are in immense positions of power over those who seek their resources. This power relationship was recognized by the economist Kenneth Boulding (1981) who defined grants as coming from two different motivations for gifts, arising out of 'love' and out of 'fear'. In some cases, the two motivations are mixed, but he concluded that 'the grants economy cannot be separated clearly into an integrative sector and a threat sector' (Boulding, 1981: vi). It requires great concentrations of will and control for philanthropists to overcome the temptations that come with this power. Because grantmakers are always in a position of power over their recipients, they will hardly ever hear what their stakeholders really think about them, unless they work hard to ensure they have a voice.

The problem of defining stakeholders in the first place can be inhibited in foundations with long-term asset bases. It is often forgotten that, unless the legal structure of a philanthropic organization specifically states that it is established in perpetuity, it has a duty to place the achievement of its philanthropic mission above that of preserving the value of its financial assets. In the UK, only 43 percent of endowed foundations are so constituted (Pharoah *et al.*, 2014). In the US, tax law stipulates that foundations must distribute five percent of their assets each year, but there is no such stipulation in the UK (Pharoah and Harrow, 2010). In both countries, there has been criticism that insufficient funds are being utilized for philanthropic purposes by some foundations and that certain boards see their power as being enhanced by the size of their endowments rather than the effectiveness of their programs.

The governance imperative of 'ensuring effectiveness', with its managerial implications, only works so far for foundations as it is not subject to shareholder challenge nor to market whims, except where their own investments are affected. Boards rarely hear what their stakeholders really think of them, and may suffer from lack of reliable feedback, and senior managers in foundations may well be in similar positions. The conservative critic, Martin Morse Wooster (2006: 19), states that 'the grantmaker usually finds himself surrounded by mendicants, courtiers, and flatterers. Faced with all this flattery, he naturally becomes more than a little full of himself'. For this reason, both the boards of philanthropic organizations and their senior managers need to find ways in which they can access reliable information about their own performance.

The extent to which this is addressed by grantee surveys of perceptions of foundations or grantees' opportunities to present their experiences within program or project evaluation for funders is unclear (Center for Effective Philanthropy, 2009). Experiments in improving stakeholder relationships are, however, becoming more evident and discussed, although practice rather than academic literature predominates. Such surveys offer increasingly detailed insights into the kinds of managerial learning that foundations need to adopt, and certainly do not create a uniform 'warm glow' of grantees towards their grantmakers. Buteau and Chu (2011: 1) for example, in a US based survey of more than 24,000 grantees about their views of 130 foundations find that grantees particularly value opportunities to discuss their reports and evaluation with foundations, yet nearly half of grantees reported that no such discussions occurred. Recognizing that foundations face their own constraints in their ability to have those discussions, Buteau and Chu (2011: 3) observe 'that foundations are more likely to discuss reports or evaluations with grantees when their staff are managing fewer active grants'. The dual emphasis that foundations give to these interactions − as a means of 'better understanding effectiveness' (their own, but as mediated by grantees) and 'streamlining (evaluation and reporting) processes' creates tensions. Buteau and Chu's (2011: 2) work emphasizes the central importance of 'strong funder-grantee relationships − the quality of interactions and clarity and consistency of communications'. All these processes necessitate particular managerial skills and expertise, while contributing centrally to the achievement of a foundation's goals and articulating its own values.

Combined with the feelings of power and prestige that permeate philanthropy is the fact that philanthropists face few external pressures to improve their efficiency or effectiveness. Despite their quibbling about regulations imposed by government, philanthropists and their institutions are not subject to review by shareholders, nor are they at the whims of a market. Thus they suffer from a lack of reliable feedback, and may become risk averse, even though in many respects they have greater latitude to take risks than do government funders.

Risk aversion

This chapter began with the contention that philanthropic organizations in themselves are unproductive bodies. It follows that if a philanthropic organization cannot define itself in relation to the achievements of those it funds, it must instead achieve its mission by adding value to the activity of philanthropic investment itself. Thus the achievement of effectiveness, one of the prime goals of good governance, needs to come through in some way.

There is also a temptation, stemming from the stewardship role over philanthropic assets, to be highly risk averse. But this is due to a misunderstanding of the true nature of risk in philanthropy. In 1987, Michael Hooker (1987: 139) wrote that 'caution rather than boldness ... guides foundations' selection of proposals ... they can be likened more to commercial bankers than to venture capitalists'. His interjection became one of the catalysts for one strand of philanthropy that endeavours to become more like venture capitalists (Defourny *et al.*, Chapter 22; Hebb with MacKinnin, Chapter 29). The comment also has credence for explaining the limited risk appetite of philanthropic organizations.

In spite of all the rhetoric about being catalysts and venture philanthropists, recent evidence indicates that grantmakers remain risk averse (Brick *et al.*, 2009; Jenkins, 2012). In part, this has to do with their misunderstanding of the most fundamental risks in philanthropy. Many of those engaged in philanthropy think of risk as being about the danger of their investments being misappropriated. This is one risk, but it is by no means the greatest. By far the biggest risk is that their investments do not have the effects anticipated. Inevitably, quite a substantial part of this is about financial risk, but not the key bit. Philanthropic organizations may well have highly efficient, low cost programs that create lots of outputs – staff employed, courses run, information produced, beneficiaries reached. But, these are of little use if they are not having the desired impact on the real beneficiaries – for example, improving their health or getting them jobs. The real risk in philanthropy, then, is not so much about money, but about effects. Boards, therefore, need to have information that provides them with good measurement of effects (von Schnurbein, Chapter 30). Effective governance is also not about minimizing or even necessarily about reducing risk; it is about properly calculating what the risks are and then taking known risks – with a plan in place for when things go wrong. Good governance, including a well-functioning board, informed and constructive relationships with stakeholders and quality information so as to manage risks, is essential for effective philanthropy. So, too, is the process and conditions for making grants, as examined in the next section.

Who and what defines 'good' grantmaking

The factors that constitute 'good' grantmaking have been well elucidated in the literature (GrantCraft, 2004; Liffman, 2004; Big Lottery Fund, 2005; AIGM, 2011; Harrow and Fitzmaurice, 2011; Directory of Social Change, ND; National Committee for Responsive Philanthropy, ND). The most comprehensive of these consider grantmaking from both sides of the transaction. Consistently, recipients identify several key actions to be the hallmarks of a 'good' funder as described in Table 26.1.

None of these practices ought to be difficult to achieve. If organizations find them hard, then either they are putting too few resources into the administration of their funding processes, or they fundamentally fail to understand how these processes work. But these are a set of simple guidelines that define the way funders should treat their grantees. They say nothing about the outcomes for the end beneficiaries and so, even if funders adopted them all, would they really be practising good, and more especially effective, grantmaking? Good grantmaking rationales and practices become fragile when grantmakers' own objectives are either less than clear, or, worse, are internally competitive. Thus Millesen and Martin (2013), exploring decision-making in US community foundations that are facing demands from donors, recipients and communities, find that decision-making is 'influenced by three powerful forces; fear, tradition, and serendipity'.

In the academic literature, 'good' grantmaking is treated primarily as a function of high quality and sustained communications between grantmakers and grantees. While much of this work concerns relationships with individual grantees, philanthropic organizations' use (or lack of use) of web-based communications arises as a further opportunity for encouraging the openness of communications that grantees seek. The general view is that foundations have not been particularly transparent: for instance, in 2010 only 29 percent of 11,000 US foundations had a website (Smith, 2010), and a recent study (Brock *et al.*, 2013) of nonprofits indicates that

Table 26.1 Hallmarks of good funding practice

Aspect	Hallmarks of good funding practice
Application process	Funders should make it absolutely clear what they won't fund and what they will with no jargon or resort to the current 'buzz words' of social theory.
	Everyone who is eligible to apply for the grant should be given the opportunity to do so.
	Relatively short application forms or information requirements should be used that can utilize existing information and all applications should be acknowledged.
	Where the relative chances of getting a grant are slim and more information will be required, a two-stage process should operate.
Decision criteria	Every grant should be awarded on the basis of clear, transparent and publicly accessible criteria.
	Every grant should be based on a coherent and plausible rationale.
Process and relationships	The applicant should be able to speak directly to someone at the funder, ideally receiving a personal visit before the funding decision is reached.
	There should be swift decision-making to a published timetable (no more than about 12 weeks).
	There should be clear reasons given for rejection if unsuccessful.
	Grantmakers should ensure that the process of grantmaking is fair, unbiased and transparent.
	Grantmakers should share the findings of their failures, as well as their successes.
Grant terms and conditions	Grantmakers should provide unrestricted funding or if 'outcomes' are sought, these should be fully agreed and the funding should be for the full costs incurred.
	Funds should always be released well in advance of need.
	Project-based revenue funding should be available for at least three, preferably at least five, years.
	Post-funding reporting should be straightforward and aligned to the recipients' existing reporting methods.

more than half of respondents want their funders to be much more transparent about what has worked in their grantmaking and what has not. This appears to be changing, however. Heredia's (2013) study of US foundations' use of social media breaks new ground, raising further questions around foundations' private nature. She finds the foundations in her study are active users of social media, engaging with an active audience online. She argues that 'foundations' use of social networks provides researchers and the public with a new avenue for learning about foundations' activities and providing feedback about foundations' theories, practices, and research' (Heredia, 2013: 86).

A truly effective grant maximizes its intended social return or impact (Grant, 2012: 17), which means that the nature of the philanthropic mission needs to be considered when assessing what constitutes good grantmaking. If that mission is focused on charitable beneficiaries then a 'good grant' is one that brings maximum benefit to these people. So defining what makes a good grant is in itself not difficult. To be productive, philanthropy must also add value to the transaction process. Linda Kelly of the (UK) Lloyds TSB Foundation suggests 'for us, good grantmaking isn't just about the funding: it has to add value to charities and their beneficiaries/ users through listening, learning and responding to their needs' (Kelly, ND). Such an approach to 'value added' offers two important insights. First, we need to consider the cumulative impact of a granting program: many grants can add up to more than the sum of their parts. Second, effective funding is more than grantmaking. The 'transformation' of resources from funder to recipient usually depends on the many things that the funder can do in addition to simply providing some cash.

Exactly how this kind of transformation can occur is a crucial aspect of understanding the process of philanthropy, particularly how it relates to the science of operations management, a relationship hitherto virtually unexplored in the literature. The way philanthropists manage their operational processes is not sufficiently understood and quite often leads to the trap of 'grantmaking by theoretical analysis' (Ellsworth *et al.*, 2002). As discussed later, this trap has led some commentators to attempt to describe a single approach or prescription for philanthropy and its delivery: 'venture' or 'strategic' philanthropy become *the* answer to most, if not all, problematic grantmaking decisions. A better understanding of the way philanthropy works suggests that there is no single 'best' approach, although there is an underlying logic that can be better understood from a brief study of operations management thinking. Table 26.2 identifies important aspects of developing and managing philanthropic action, from the perspective of operations management thinking.

As noted, strategic planning and management of the philanthropic process are important to achieving impact, but strategy is also being misused in contemporary philanthropy.

The use, and misuse, of strategy in philanthropy

The major goals and values in foundations present a continuing basis for academic study in philanthropy, while the managerial means of turning these into workable strategies remains far less examined. Paradoxically, both practitioners and scholars may support this division by their emphasis on what is often broadly cited as 'beyond grantmaking' whereby innovative foundations take action to add significant value for their grantees, in addition to 'the grant',

Table 26.2 Applying operations management to grantmaking

Element	Guide to practice
Purpose defined	From the start, the grantmaker needs to understand and communicate the purpose of the funding program and link strategy with strategic planning.
An integrated system	Decisions are interconnected: what to focus on; what sort of recipients, which geographic areas will impact other decisions. Any decision may limit choice in other areas.
Robust research	Achieving philanthropic mission entails being able to identify which projects and organizations are most likely to produce the desired outcomes. A robust, thoroughly researched and effective process – an analysis of facts to reach a reasoned conclusion about a potential future scenario – is essential.
Effective measurement	The outcomes sought are often complex, and require appropriate, different forms of measurement. What will success look like? Such measurement should be planned from the beginning, not an afterthought.
Outcomes lead process	The design of a funding process needs to start from the *end* – the outcomes and impacts – and work logically back to the start, including who to support and how.
Continued management, but not process for the sake of process	The granting process does not stop once recipients have the funding; post-decision management needs to be ongoing to ensure intended results are produced. Process should make the really important human decisions easier, but an over reliance on process can be enslaving. Its development should be not determined by a few internal 'experts', but informed by an understanding of the needs of potential recipients.

and so create roles as 'changemakers' (Greeley and Greeley, 2011) or as 'institutional entrepreneurs' (Quinn *et al.*, 2013). While adding distinctive value in grantmaker-grantseeker relations is important, the phraseology of 'beyond grantmaking' suggests that grantmaking itself is a practice that ideally needs to be 'moved on from'. It also may downgrade the work of the smaller foundations whose work is encapsulated in the further phrase, with its own implicit meaning, of 'conventional grantmaking'. How then is strategy developing in philanthropic contexts, and with what managerial practice models?

In its broad, well intentioned and, on its own, essentially unproductive persona, philanthropy may not appear to mix well with the thinking on strategy which seeks to distill and encapsulate organizational goal and values and set baselines for their achievement. For example, Jenkins (2012: 25) has assessed that

> because their relationship with beneficiaries is mediated through their charitable objects, which may be fairly wide, and which may be clouded by ideas like "acting in the best interests of the charity", endowed charitable foundations can face the danger of running adrift through having a lack of clarity over why it is they exist.

It may be for that very reason that the concept of 'strategic philanthropy' has become so popular in recent years.

Until the late 1980s, most of what was being written about strategy development depicted it as a very deliberate process with thinking, followed by planning, followed by action. Since then, commentators have questioned whether strategic *planning* was as critical a priority to business success as had been previously thought; a debate evolving as to whether strategy should be practised as art, science or a combination of both. Proponents of more integrative and emergent approaches (Mintzberg, 1987, 1994) argue that strategy should be practised mainly as an intuitive, creative and divergent thought process – strategy as art. For Mintzberg (1987) strategies could *form*, as well as be *formulated*, meaning that a realized strategy could emerge in response to an evolving situation, or be brought about deliberately, through a process of formulation followed by implementation (more recently, Kania *et al.*, 2014). Moreover, in demonstrating how the planning process itself can destroy commitment, narrow organizational vision and discourage change, Mintzberg concluded (1994) that 'strategic planning' is oxymoronic, as strategy cannot be 'planned', since planning is about analysis and strategy about synthesis.

Alongside those who continue to support the view that strategy is a rational, analytical, convergent thought process, others have argued that strategy should combine both approaches to achieve the best outcomes (Liedtke, 1998, 2000; Graetz, 2002). Much of this debate seems to have passed philanthropy by, and there has been much confusion about how strategy should be utilized in philanthropy.

Probably most philanthropists would want to be considered 'strategic' in the sense that their individual investments are more than just the sum of their parts. During the past ten years, however, strategy in philanthropy has been employed to describe what its proponents contend is an entirely new approach. Its leading impetus was Porter and Kramer's 1999 *Harvard Business Review* article, whereby strategic philanthropy entails doing four (somewhat overlapping) things: achieving (measurable) superior performance in a specific area; choosing a unique positioning; engaging in unique activities and forgoing some grantmaking opportunities in order to focus on others. Strategic philanthropy also entails deciding what *not* to do and this, they say, 'is the acid test of whether a foundation (or any organization for that matter) has a strategy' (Porter and Kramer, 1999: 127). Three elements of strategic philanthropy were subsequently identified (Kramer 2001: 44): 'identifying the change one hopes to bring about, clarifying internal values and strengths, and ascertaining external needs' and that 'it is only by undertaking all three simultaneously that a fully formed strategy, capable of evaluation, can be achieved.'

Such affirmation of strategic philanthropy would seem to turn limited research findings about its value and effectiveness into a supposed universal theory. It falls into what Ellsworth *et al.* (2002) call the 'theoretical analysis trap,' whereby the proponent goes beyond developing a theory of change that *might* explain how a particular social change could be brought about, and instead substitutes a supposed universal theory relevant to all circumstances. In a somewhat neglected, but richly rewarding critique of certain philanthropic approaches Ellsworth *et al.* (2002), caution against 'grantmaking by strategic planning'. While they admit that strategic plans establish a hierarchy of goals, objectives and indicators and are essential to all organizations, there is a danger in thinking that the strategic plan is an end in itself. Though the strategic approach is often promoted as being 'best practice', and it does establish a target for a philanthropist to aim at, its significant drawbacks include: easily becoming an imposed 'top down' donor-driven approach; becoming an internal obsession when philanthropic organizations should be externally focused; based more on theory than reality; and transforming into an over emphasis on bureaucratic rather than innovative approaches and the possibility that monitoring and evaluation of the plan itself is forgotten.

Empirical evidence, while minimal, tends to support the view that the approach taken to strategic planning in many philanthropic organizations is still in the pre-Mintzberg era. Research by the (US) Center for Effective Philanthropy (2009: 10) concluded that 'foundation leaders' conceptions of strategy overvalue the presence of a strategic plan and undervalue the logical connections necessary to have a strategy'. Supporting much of Mintzberg's analysis, this research reports that assessment of results against strategies remains a significant challenge for foundations; staff struggle to determine the right data to collect and how to collect them, and look for help from their boards in these efforts. The study concludes that 'having something that is labeled a "strategic plan" and having thought through the step-by-step logic of how specific resource and programmatic decisions will ultimately lead to impact are not one and the same' (Center for Effective Philanthropy 2009: 11). The work also confirmed the influence of agency theory within philanthropic organizations as 'only half of the CEOs in this study reported that there is a completely shared understanding among the board, CEO, and staff, of the goals the foundation is working to achieve' (Center for Effective Philanthropy, 2009: 15).

Critiques and some close analysis of the 'strategic philanthropy' case are also challenging its practice, and re-examining its logic, to further support philanthropy's development (see the debate in response to Brest, 2015). In terms of its ability to produce results, Schambra (2013) boldly argues that strategic philanthropy has 'failed to solve even one social problem once and for all, by penetrating to its root cause'. In addition, rhetoric has outpaced practice. For example, Patrizi and Heid Thompson (2011: 52) assert that 'many foundations have adopted only the veneer of strategic philanthropy' and identify its complex challenges, notably strategies developed in isolation from the grantees that execute them and foundation structures and processes that 'do not support strategic endeavours'. Boris and Kopczynski (2013) acknowledge the momentum among leading US foundations towards charting impact, but find that 'the approaches they use are diverse and the language is idiosyncratic', which has implications around convergence or divergence for those foundations' managers, as well as their directing boards. Bernstein (2011) challenges the assumption underlying the very phraseology of 'strategic philanthropy', that the donor not only knows the problem it seeks to help solve, but also how best to solve it; raising issues of the roles and contributions to problem solving of foundations' other insiders and outsiders, their staff, including junior staff and their beneficiaries. On a broader front, Boesso *et al.* (2014) return to the inextricable links between foundations' governance and strategies in aiming to empirically examine if and how different governance attributes associate with different philanthropic strategies. Studying 112 Italian foundations, they find the strength of boards' advisory roles are critical. 'Active' boards are expected to screen relevant public needs and properly invest foundations' resources in meritorious projects, while 'inert' boards risk pursuing private goals, camouflaged as public interest, and they dissipate resources by unconditionally financing unrelated grant requests. Again, this raises the question of the respective roles of foundations' staff in sustaining or ensuring 'active' or 'inert' boards. Notwithstanding strategy's frequent rebadging within philanthropy, the core question running through foundations' decision-making and management is 'who and what defines good grantmaking'.

Reflections

Our current degree of understanding of the interaction between good governance, effective strategic planning and good grantmaking processes is not extensive. There are, for example, many excellent evaluations available on individual grant programs but, as yet, very few wider studies of the effectiveness and impact of philanthropic institutions. There are a number of frameworks for assessing philanthropy's impact (Letts *et al.*, 1998; Flynn and Hodgkinson, 2001; Niven, 2003; Paton, 2003; Cutler, 2009; Center for Effective Philanthropy, ND; von Schnurbein, Chapter 30) and some pioneering attempts by foundations to achieve a measure of their own impact. But the interaction of the three elements of governance, grantmaking processes and strategy remains as elusive as it did when Ostrower (2004) defined the problem more than a decade ago: that too few foundations actually clarify and specify what they believe it means to be effective, and make effectiveness a priority. For many foundations the challenge of defining and achieving effectiveness is affected by their unique insulation from external forces. Ostrower's (2004: 2) advice – 'foundations must find ways to obtain fresh perspectives and objective data on their performance to serve as a "reality check" on their own perceptions' – remains critical. The professionalization of philanthropy, which has particular importance for foundations, is not the subject in any detail of this chapter, but it may hold a partial key to this reality check. This might occur informally, as staff move within the foundation world. Or, it might occur formally, if and where more junior staff are actively engaged in giving insights into their foundations' program directions, as in the US 'Caring to Change' project which 'drew on the wisdom of younger people, people of colour, and others in philanthropy and nonprofits not normally involved in setting foundation strategy' (Rosenman, 2010, 2). Alternatively, professionalization might serve to reinforce the sense of separation from the rest of nonprofits. Indeed it might be argued that an objective judgement cannot come from within the philanthropic community itself because the issues of power prohibit such self-analysis. Therefore, we need more objective, external analyses of the extent to which philanthropy is meeting its mission, to what extent there is a gap between the reality and its potential for instigating meaningful social change, and how management processes in philanthropic organizations are central to achieving this level of change.

References

Andreoni, J. (1990) 'Impure Altruism and Donations to Public Goods: A Theory of Warm Glow Giving', *Economic Journal*, 100: 464–77.

Australian Institute of Grants Management (AIGM) (2011) *Grantmaking Manifesto: Clear and Conspicuous Declaration of Intent, Policy and Aims*, Our Community Pty Ltd, Melbourne.

Bartkus, B. R., Morris, S. A. and Seifert, B. (2002) 'Governance and Corporate Philanthropy: Restraining Robin Hood?', *Business and Society*, 41: 319–44.

Bernstein, A. R. (2011) 'Metrics Mania: The Growing Corporatization of US Philanthropy', *Thought and Action*, 33.

Bethmann, S., von Schnurbein, G. and Studer, S. (2014) Governance Systems of Grant-making Foundations', *Voluntary Sector Review*, 5(1), 75–95.

Big Lottery Fund (2005) *A Discussion Paper on Risk and Good Grantmaking, Big Lottery Fund Research*, Issue 17, London.

Boesso, G. and Cerbioni, F. (2014) 'What Drives Good Philanthropy? The Relationship between Governance and Strategy in Foundations', in G. Luca, A. Hinna, F. Monteduro (eds) *Mechanisms, Roles and Consequences of Governance: Emerging Issues (Studies in Public and Non-Profit Governance, Volume 2)*, Emerald Group Publishing Limited, pp.159–180.

Boris, E. T. and Kopczynski Winkler, M. (2013) 'The Emergence of Performance Measurement as a Complement to Evaluation among US Foundations', *New Directions for Evaluation*, 2013(137), 69–80.

Boulding, K. E. (1981) *A Preface to Grants Economics: The Economy of Love and Fear*, Praeger, New York and.

Breeze, B. (2010) *How Donors Choose Charities. Occasional Paper 1. Findings of a Study of Donor Perceptions of the Nature and Distribution of Charitable Benefit*, Centre for Charitable Giving and Philanthropy, London.

Brest, P. (2015) 'Strategic Philanthropy and its Discontents', *Stanford Social Innovation Review* April 27. www.ssireview.org/up_for_debate/article/strategic_philanthropy_and_its_discontents [Accessed on 20 May 2015].

Brick, P., Kail, A., Jarvinen, J. and Fiennes, T. (2009) *Granting Success: Lessons from Funders and Charities*, New Philanthropy Capital, London.

Brock, A., Buteau, E. and Gopal, R. (2013) *Foundation Transparency: What Nonprofits Want*, Cambridge, MA: Center for Effective Philanthropy.

Burbridge, L. C., Diaz, W. A., Odendahl, T. and Shaw, A. (2002) *The Meaning and Impact of Board and Staff Diversity in the Philanthropic Field*, Joint Affinity Groups.

Buteau, E. and Chu, T. (2011) 'Grantees Report Back: Helpful and Evaluation Processes', Center on Philanthropy, USA. www.jhartfound.org/images/uploads/resources/CEP_DatainAction_GranteesReportBack.pdf [Accessed on 8 September 2015].

Center for Effective Philanthropy (ND) 'Assessment Tools', www.effectivephilanthropy.org/index.php?page=assessment-tools [Accessed on 14 December 2011].

Center for Effective Philanthropy (2009) *Essentials of Foundation Strategy*, Center for Effective Philanthropy, New York.

CIPFA: The Chartered Institute of Public Finance and Accountancy (2004) *Good Governance Standard for Public Services*, The Independent Commission on Good Governance in Public Services, London.

Coffey, B. S. and Wang, J. (1998), 'Board Diversity and Managerial Control as Predictors of Corporate Social Performance', *Journal of Business Ethics*, 17: 1595–1603.

Cornforth, C. (2003) *The Governance of Public and NonProfit Organisations. What do Boards do?*, Routledge, Taylor and Francis Group.

Cutler, D. (2009) *The Effective Foundation – A Literature Review*, Baring Foundation, London.

Davis, J., Schoorman, D. and Donaldson, L. (1997) 'Toward a Stewardship Theory of Management', *Academy of Management Review*, 22(1): 20–47.

Desai, M. A. and Yetman, R. J. (2006) 'Constraining Managers without Owners: Governance of the Not-for-Profit Enterprise', http://dev.wcfia.harvard.edu/sites/default/files/Desai_Constraining.pdf [Accessed on 8 September 2015].

Directory of Social Change (ND) 'What is Good Grantmaking?', www.dsc.org.uk/PolicyandResearch/News/Whatisgoodgrantmaking [Accessed on 14 December 2011].

Donaldson, L. and Davis, J. (1991) 'Stewardship Theory or Agency Theory: CEO Governance and Shareholder Returns', *Australian Journal of Management*, 16(1): 49–64.

Donaldson, T. and Preston, L. E. (1995) 'The Stakeholder Theory of the Corporation: Concepts, Evidence and Implications', *Academy of Management Review*, 20(1): 65–91.

Ellsworth, L., Duggan, W. and Orosz, J. (2002) *What-works Grantmaking: A Strategy for Effective Philanthropy*, Creative Strategy Group.

Flynn, P. and Hodgkinson, V. A. (eds) (2001) *Measuring the Impact of the Nonprofit Sector*, Kluwer Academic/Plenum, New York.

Graetz, F. (2002) 'Strategic Thinking versus Strategic Planning: Towards Understanding the Complementarities', *Management Decision*, 40(5): 456–62.

Grant, P. (2012) *The Business of Giving: The Theory and Practice of Philanthropy, Grantmaking and Social Investment*, Palgrave Macmillan, Basingstoke.

GrantCraft (2004) 'Saying Yes/Saying No to Applicants'. The Foundation Center/European Foundation Centre.

Greeley, S. and Greeley, B. (2011) 'Beyond the Grant: How the WK Kellogg Foundation went Beyond Grantmaking to Contribute to a Major Early Childhood Initiative', *The Foundation Review*, 2(3),8: 79–93.

Grosvold, J., Brammer, S. and Rayton, B. (2007) 'Board Diversity in the United Kingdom and Norway: An Exploratory Analysis', *Business Ethics: A European Review*, 16(4): 344–57.

Hallett, A. C. (1990) 'Grant Making, Continuity, and Diversity at the Wieboldt Foundation', *Family Business Review*, 3(4): 409–12.

Harrow, J. and Fitzmaurice, J. (2011) *The Art of Refusal: Promising Practice for Grant Makers and Grant Seekers*, Centre for Charity Effectiveness, London.

Harrow, J. and Phillips, S.D. (2013) 'Corporate Governance and Nonprofits: Facing up to Hybridisation and Homogenization', in M. Wright, D. S. Siegel, K. Keasey and I. Filatotchev (eds), *The Oxford Handbook of Corporate Governance*, Oxford University Press, Oxford.

Heredia, R. (2013) 'Grantmaking Foundations' Use of Social Media: A Comparison across Location, Age and Donation Structure', Honors Thesis in Urban Studies, Stanford University, California. https://urbanstudies.stanford.edu/sites/default/files/rachelherediathesis.pdf [Accessed on 8 September 2015].

Hooker, M. (1987) 'Moral Values and Private Philanthropy', *Social Philosophy and Policy*, 4(2): 128–41.

Hyndman, N. and McDonnell, P. (2009) 'Governance and Charities: An Exploration of Key Themes and the Development of Research Agenda', *Financial Accountability and Management*, 25(1): 5–31.

Jenkins, R. (2012) *The Governance and Financial Management of Endowed Charitable Foundations*, Association of Charitable Foundations, London.

Kania, J., Kramer, M., and Russell, P. (2014) 'Strategic Philanthropy for a Complex World', *Stanford Social Innovation Review*, 19 (Summer). www.ssireview.org/up_for_debate/article/strategic_philanthropy [Accessed on 1 June 2015].

Kelly, L. (ND) 'Good Grantmaking Series – Lloyds TSB Foundation for England and Wales', Directory of Social Change, www.dsc.org.uk/PolicyandResearch/news/goodgrantmakingserieslloydstsbfoundation forenglandandwales [Accessed on 14 December 2011].

Kramer, M. E. (2001) 'Strategic Confusion', *Foundation News and Commentary*, May/June.

Letts, C., Ryan, W. P. and Grossman, A. (1998) *High Performance Nonprofit Organisations*, Wiley, New York.

Liedtke, J. (1998) 'Strategic Thinking: Can it be Taught?', *Long Range Planning*, 31(1): 120–9.

Liedtke, J. (2000) 'Strategic Planning as a Contributor to Strategic Change: A Generative Model', *European Management Journal*, 18(12): 195–206.

Liffman, M. (2004) *The Challenge of (Good) Grantmaking: Presentation by Michael Liffman to Melbourne Community Foundation AGM, 12 October 2004*, Asia-Pacific centre for Philanthropy and Social Investment, Melbourne.

Lungeanu, R. and Ward, J. L. (2012) 'A Governance-based Typology of Family Foundations: The Effect of Generation Stage and Governance Structure on Family Philanthropic Activities', *Family Business Review*, 25(4): 409–24.

McCoy, D., Khembhavi, G., Patel, J. and Luintel, A. (2009) 'The Bill and Melinda Gates Foundation's Grant Making Programme for Global Health', *The Lancet*, 1645–53.

Millesen, J. L. and Martin, E. C. (2013) 'Community Foundation Strategy: Doing Good and the Moderating Effects of Fear, Tradition, and Serendipity', *Nonprofit and Voluntary Sector Quarterly*, Published online before print May 9, 2013.

Mintzberg, H. (1987) 'Crafting Strategy', *Harvard Business Review*, July/August, pp. 66–75.

Mintzberg, H. (1994) *The Rise and Fall of Strategic Planning*, Simon and Shuster, New York.

National Committee for Responsive Philanthropy, (ND) 'Encouraging Good Grantmaking Practices', www.ncrp.org/campaigns-research-policy/grantmaking [Accessed on 14 December 2011].

Niven, P. R. (2003) *The Balanced Scorecard Step-by-Step for Government and Nonprofit Agencies*, Wiley, New York.

Ostrower, F. (2004) *Foundation Effectiveness: Definitions and Challenges*, The Urban Institute.

Panel on the Nonprofit Sector (2007) *Principles for Good Governance and Ethical Practice: A Guide for Charities and Foundations*, Panel on the Nonprofit Sector.

Paton, R. (2003) *Managing and Measuring Social Enterprises*, Sage, London.

Patrizi, P. and Heid Thompson, E. (2011) 'Beyond the Veneer of Strategic Philanthropy', *The Foundation Review*, 2(3), 6.

Pharoah, C. and Harrow, J. (2010) *Payout with an English Accent: Exploring the Case for a Foundation "Distributon Quota" in the UK*. Paper presented to the ARNOVA annual conference, Alexandria, VA.

Pharoah, C., Jenkins, R. and Goddard, K. (2014) *Giving Trends – Top 300 Foundations: 2014 Report*, London, UK: Association of Charitable Foundations; Cass Business School, London.

Porter, M. E. and Kramer, M. E. (1999) 'Philanthropy's New Agenda: Creating Value', *Harvard Business Review*, November–December, pp. 121–31.

Quinn, R., Tompkins-Stange, M. and Meyerson, D. (2013) 'Beyond Grantmaking: Philanthropic Foundations as Agents of Change and Institutional Entrepreneurs', *Nonprofit and Voluntary Sector Quarterly*, Published online before print June 24, 2013.

Rose-Ackerman, S. (1996) 'Altruism, Nonprofits and Economic Theory', *Journal of Economic Literature*, 34(2): 701–28.

Rosenman, M. (2010) 'Caring to Change, Foundations for the Common Good, Caring to Change Project', www.p-sj.org/files/7.%20Caring%20to%20Change-Foundations%20for%20the%20Common%20Good.pdf [Accessed on].

Santora, J. C., Clemens, R. A. and Sarros, J. C. (1997) 'Views from the Top: Foundation CEOs Look at Leadership Succession', *Leadership and Organization Development Journal*, 18(2): 108–15.

Schambra, W. (2013) 'The problem of strategic philanthropy', *Nonprofit Quarterly*, 12 August. www.nonprofitquarterly.org/philanthropy/22729-the-problem-of-strategic-philanthropy.html [Accessed on 20 February 2015].

Smith, B. (2010) 'Philanthropy's Digital Divide', *Philanthropy News Digest*, 3 May. www.pndblog.typepad.com/pndblog/2010/05/philanthropys-digital-divide.html [Accessed on 27 May 2015].

Tickell, J. (2005) *Good Governance: A Code for the Voluntary and Community Sector*, ACEVO, Charity Trustee Networks, ICSA, NCVO on behalf of The National Hub of Expertise in Governance.

Van Cranenburgh, K. C. and Arenas, D. (2013) 'Strategic and Moral Dilemmas of Corporate Philanthropy in Developing Countries: Heineken in Sub-Saharan Africa', *Journal of Business Ethics*, 122(3), 523–36.

Wooster, M. M. (2006) *Great Philanthropic Mistakes*, Hudson Institute, Washington.

Young, D. R. (2000) 'Alternative Models of Government-Nonprofit Sector Relations: Theoretical and International Perspectives', *Nonprofit and Voluntary Sector Quarterly*, 29(1).

27

The current landscape of fundraising practice

Richard D. Waters

The practice of fundraising – contrary to the popular perception that it is focused on solicitations – is actually centred on the creation and cultivation of relationships. The professional practice literature on fundraising has frequent references to 'relationship building' (Nudd, 1991: 175), 'friend raising' (Mann, 2007: 43), and 'philanthropic partnerships' (Sagawa, 2001: 201) rather than centred strictly on asking for donations. Indeed, Greenfield (1991) calls fundraising a unique form of communication that is based on social scientific principles that produce healthy relationships between a nonprofit and its donors. Kelly (1998) echoes this by defining fundraising as 'the management function of relationships between a charitable organization and its donor publics' (1998: 8). This definition sets the tone for this chapter, where it is argued that fundraising is not a marketing function; it is a carefully developed communication process that aims to create mutually beneficial relationships. Unlike marketing, there is no *quid pro quo* relationship where an exchange results in both parties receiving a tangible asset. In fundraising, rarely does an interaction result in a donor receiving a product in exchange for a donation. Hibbert (Chapter 6), developing this communication theme and overarching purpose, with its implications for philanthropy across its range of forms, emphasizes the prime need to generate a sound and contemporary evidence-base on the features of such communications that both attract donors and help charities respond to dynamic environments. This chapter delves further into those aspects of fundraising communications which are especially salient for fundraising knowledge and practice: the continuing requirement to communicate the specific and overall societal value of people giving up their private resources for the public good (Pharoah, Chapter 4).

Theories of fundraising

The fundraising process has been explained from different social scientific perspectives. Social exchange theory, which is rooted in social psychology, focuses on the actual transfer of money from a donor to a nonprofit. It argues that their relationship is ultimately the result of a dual cost-benefit analysis and comparison of the alternatives if the transaction were not completed (Weerts and Ronca, 2007; Drezner, 2009). For example, an individual may consider the consequences (e.g. closing the organization or clients not receiving services) of not contributing to a nonprofit making a request, and decide that she can spare a monthly donation to avoid these outcomes. Resource dependency theory, which stems from the field of organizational management, argues that organizations are dependent on resources from the external environment. They must become dependent on assistance from various other entities in this environment to sustain themselves, while competing with similar organizations for the public's attention (Alexander, 2000). Nonprofits frequently face competition from other nonprofits working toward similar missions, thereby competing for the same donors, be they individuals, foundations, or corporations (Brown, 2005). The position is variable for foundations, some progressing from their original endowment to their own fundraising or combine both, while others raise no further funds, beyond their endowment.

While these theoretical perspectives help explain the fundraising function, they do not adequately consider the core concepts of relationships and communications. The relationship management paradigm from the field of public relations offers predictable and testable hypotheses that are better suited to the conceptual grounding of fundraising. As shown in Figure 27.1, some event establishes the relationship between a nonprofit and donors. This antecedent brings the two parties together for back-and-forth interactions which give the nonprofit the opportunity to demonstrate its professionalism and trustworthiness (Hon and Grunig, 1999). As a result of the interactions and associated relationship cultivation, relational outcomes are generated for the donors that include: trust in the nonprofit's staff and their ability to achieve the mission; satisfaction with the interactions with the staff and the accomplishments of the organization; commitment to the nonprofit's mission; and a feeling of balanced power between the donor and the nonprofit. In a study of nonprofit hospitals, for instance, Waters (2011) finds that how donors evaluate their relationship with them predicts both annual giving and major gifts. Similarly, with social service organizations, O'Neil (2007) found that the relationship management process predicts which donors are most involved with them.

Another public relations approach – the situational theory of publics – further helps fundraisers segment their audiences based on their level of engagement with the nonprofit (McKeever, 2013). The situational theory of publics uses three variables–problem recognition, constraint recognition, and involvement–to categorize donors into four groups, as indicated in Table 27.1. The first group is the 'nonpublic'. They will never contribute to a nonprofit organization because they do not consider the mission or issue to be important. Simply put, nonpublics have other

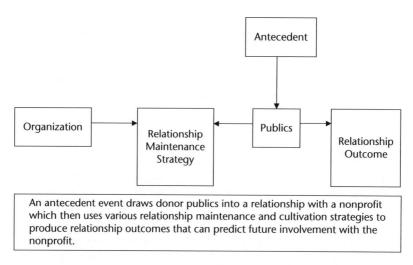

An antecedent event draws donor publics into a relationship with a nonprofit which then uses various relationship maintenance and cultivation strategies to produce relationship outcomes that can predict future involvement with the nonprofit.

Figure 27.1   The relationship management paradigm

Table 27.1 The situational theory of publics

Situation variable	Type of public			
	Non	*Latent*	*Aware*	*Active*
Problem recognition	Issue not important/ other priorities	Does not see personal impact of the issue	Recognize issue importance	Recognize issue importance
Constraint recognition	Not relevant	Not relevant	Strong	Constraints managed
Involvement	None	Potential	Potential – constraints impede	Motivated and involved
Communication strategy	None: will not engage on the issue	Education about the personal impact of the issue	Assist in removing constraints; change attitudes about constraints	Focus on benefiting donor and nonprofit

donating priorities. This is often difficult for fundraisers to accept because of their own connection to the organization's issue, and they waste too much effort trying to convert nonpublic donors. A second category is the 'latent public' that may not formally recognize that an issue is important because they do not appreciate how they are impacted by it. For example, people's health may be affected by environmental pollution, but they are not aware of how this impacts them personally. The challenge for fundraisers is to identify latent publics, and appropriately to educate them about the issue, before trying to change their behaviour. 'Aware publics' recognize that an issue is important, but typically have some type of constraint which prevents them from being more involved than they might be if the obstacles were removed. For instance, an individual who recently lost his job may recognize that an issue is worthy of philanthropic support, but lack of disposable income makes it difficult to contribute. The final group, the 'active public', is highly connected to the nonprofit's issue and easy to motivate into action because they have few obstacles in their way.

The style of communication required to reach these different types of audiences differs significantly. For latent publics, fundraisers should focus on the educational dimension of fundraising communication to show how they are impacted by the issue so they are motivated to become active. For aware publics, the strategy centres on attitude change: fundraisers need to illustrate how these individuals can remove the obstacles preventing higher levels of involvement. The active publics are easy to move to action, so messages to this group should demonstrate how best to benefit the organization. With this segmentation in mind, we consider how the fundraising process unfolds for the different donor publics.

The fundraising process

Fundraising centres on the creation and maintenance of positive relationships between a nonprofit and its donor publics. Although solicitation represents only a small percentage of the fundraisers' tasks, the focus on increasing gift revenue is vital to nonprofits which need to diversify and grow their donor bases. Thus, fundraisers should be advised against taking a pure marketing perspective with fundraising, and recognize the subtle differences between marketing and communication. With a marketing transaction, the customer ultimately receives a product in exchange for the money being given to the firm or nonprofit. For a donation, however, there is no tangible product normally being given in exchange, although it is important to acknowledge that there are times when a free coffee mug or other small scale premium is provided during annual giving campaigns.

Donor motivations

Why do individuals voluntarily give away their money to an organization without any personal benefit? Pharoah's (Chapter 4) review of the differing disciplinary perspectives emphasizes their multidisciplinarity both in relation to the impulse to give and giving behaviours. Kelly (1998), from a fundraising management perspective, discusses this phenomenon as the 'mixed-motive' giving model, recognizing that people have quite different reasons for giving. Boulding (1973: 4) argues that the donor may feel that the gift creates 'a sense of community, even if the community isn't as vague as the common humanity that unites the donor and the recipients'. This feeling of community development may cause the donor to feel good simply for having made the gift.

A positive 'warm glow', as described by Andreoni (1990), is not the only reason that people donate. Indeed, Mixer (1993) presents a comprehensive list of reasons for giving, grouped as being altruistic (internal) or egoistic (external), while Adloff (Chapter 3) provides an indepth examination of what constitutes altruism and its converse, drawing on the growing range of literatures contributing to our understanding.

Whether a nonprofit receives a gift out of altruistic or egoistic motivations should not be of concern to a fundraiser as long as the gift does not violate ethical boundaries or create a conflict of interest for organizations and individuals concerned. Nevertheless, the nuances of how ethical boundaries are drawn, and conflict of interests are determined, may be complex and shift over time, requiring fundraiser sensitivity (Dunn, 2010; Harrow and Pharoah, 2010). Jeavons (1991: 55) reminds us: 'mixed motives are the rule, not the exception, of our experiences in philanthropy'.

There has been substantial empirical research carried out on donor motivations in various disciplines in the academy (Webber, 2004; Gladden et al., 2005; Sargeant and Woodliffe, 2007). Of particular note is the comprehensive study on motivations for major gift donors conducted by Prince and File (1994) using qualitative and quantitative analyses for a cross section of nonprofits with a wide range of missions. Their analysis reveals seven distinct types of donors: communitarians; the devout; investors; socialites; altruists; repayers; and dynasts. The most common motivation for major gift donors is 'improvement of the community' (expressed by 26 percent of all donors) who Prince and File (1994) label 'communitarians': they give because doing so makes sense for the community, as well as for themselves. This group of donors is most often local business owners, so their involvement with nonprofits helps their businesses as well. They also tend to volunteer with nonprofits in addition to making financial contributions. Religious motivations (21 percent) are the second most common reason for major gifts. In essence, for the 'devout', giving is viewed as being God's will. These contributions tend to go to houses of worship rather than serving the broader nonprofit sector. The 'investor', in contrast, gives broadly to the sector. These donors, representing 15 percent of the sample, are motivated by personal gain, keeping one eye on the nonprofit cause and the other on personal benefit, whether that is through the effect on their taxes or receipt of some tangible benefit for their donation.

The final four categories of motivations each represent about ten percent of major gift donors. 'Socialites' give because the result of their gift – special events – allow them to expand their social networks; their gifts are directed primarily to arts and education, the two subsectors that most often throw galas and benefit dinners. The 'altruist' gives because it feels like it is the right thing to do: they make their donations selflessly and do not ask for much in return. 'Repayers' give to nonprofits because either they or someone they know has personally benefited from a nonprofit's programs or services. In essence, they feel that their donations allow them to give back to organizations that have helped them: this sense of loyalty largely benefits hospitals and education nonprofits. The final motivation defines a type of donor that Prince and File (1994) call the 'dynast'. These individuals donate because it is an expected family tradition; they have largely inherited their wealth and grown up with a family commitment to philanthropy. Over time, the specific issues supported by dynasts tend to shift as the next generation focuses their philanthropy on different causes than their parents and grandparents supported.

It is important to keep in mind that Prince and File's (1994) research was carried out on major gift donors, with 'major gift' normally considered to be a contribution of $10,000 or more (for a recent study, US Trust, 2014). Gifts of this size are of course important for nonprofits, although they are rare. Fundraisers acknowledge the Pareto principle, however: that 80 percent of donations come from 20 percent of donors (Tindall and Waters, 2010). It is increasingly argued that this proportion is shifting to a 90/10 split as an even larger percentage of dollars donated to charities are coming from the wealthy (Cowley et al., 2011; Zinsmeister, 2013).

These proportions of giving are reflected in the donor pyramid presented as Figure 27.2. A solid foundation is provided by many donors making small gifts at the base of the pyramid, a smaller portion of moderate size gifts creating its middle section, and a very small number of large value gifts at the top of the pyramid (for recent debate on the donor pyramid, see Polivy, 2014).

Although donor motivation research has tended to focus on major gifts, it is important to understand why donors who provide gifts in smaller amounts contribute. Their main motivations seem to be altruistic rather than egoistic. Bekkers and Wiepking (2011) report that these donors are most often giving out of an awareness of need, organizational reputations, effectiveness of the organization, and simply because they were asked with a well-crafted solicitation. While these donors may carry out a personal cost-benefit analysis to determine how much they can contribute, their gift is largely a result of altruistic reasons rather than any particular psychological or personal benefit.

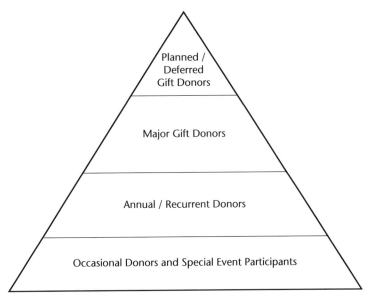

Figure 27.2   The donor pyramid

Motivations for donations by individuals are not the only ones that fundraisers must take time to research and understand. As shown in the Giving USA Foundation's report, corporations and foundations represented five percent and 15 percent, respectively, of gifts to the nonprofit sector in 2013 (Kalugyer, 2014). Foundations and corporations are not small players in the fundraising realm, and nonprofits must approach these organizations strategically, appreciating their funding rationales and priorities. For corporations, contributions to the nonprofit sector are often tied to how to improve their strategic position in the communities in which they work. Whilst some companies may not seek strong nonprofit connections to trigger gifts, Weeden (2011) notes that other corporations are more strategic in their giving and focus their contributions in ways that provide direct positive benefit for the company, for example through scholarship support. For fundraisers, the extent to which corporate philanthropy presents a complex and 'contested terrain' needs to be borne in mind (Moran and Branigan, Chapter 24), as well as the disbursement policies of foundations, both in jurisdictions with philanthropic foundations legally required to disburse particular percentages of assets annually, e.g. the US and Canada, and those without, broadly, the European experience. As part of that, strategies towards those foundations conversely running down and 'spending out' assets (Ostrower, 2009) need to be developed, and understanding of foundations' decisions on the time attached to the pursuance of certain philanthropic goals needs to be sought (Brest and Harvey, 2008).

Respecting donor rights

Whether the donation comes from an individual, corporation, or a foundation, the nonprofit sector has come to recognize that the donor has certain rights must be respected. In the US, a Donor Bill of Rights (see Table 27.2) was created by the Association of Fundraising Professionals (AFP), the Association for Healthcare Philanthropy, the Council for Advancement and Support of Education, and the Giving Institute in response to the growing level of concern about the management of the nonprofit sector, which was brought to the public's attention with the 1992 management scandal of the United Way. Created in 1993, the Donor Bill of Rights seeks to ensure that donors have confidence in the nonprofits they support and that fundraisers respect the philanthropic wishes of the general public. The code has earned the support of many nonprofits across the US and the three leading fundraising associations encourage their members to weave its principles into the culture of the organizations.

The Donor Bill of Rights appears to have had a positive effect on the public's confidence in the sector seems to be positive. O'Neill (2009) has noted that the adoption of these principles helped slow what appeared to be a decline in confidence, but much work remains for the sector to counter scandals and any mismanagement of the past. As technology's impact on fundraising continues to grow, AFP recognized that an E-Donor Bill of Rights was also needed to address online giving, which was not adequately covered in the original. Intended as complementary rather than as a replacement for the original, the E-Donor Bill of Rights provides more detailed guidance for how nonprofits engage in fundraising online.

Other countries have also recognized the need for ethical conduct and respect of donors, but have chosen different instruments (Breen, Chapter 14). Canada's peak association, for example, has initiated a rigorous system of voluntary, peer-reviewed accreditation of charities and nonprofits whose standards include good fundraising practices (Phillips, 2012). Following complaints of undue persistence by some fundraisers in England (Birkwood, 2015), the Institute of Fundraising (2015) recently moved from voluntary adherence to mandatory compliance with its code of conducts for member organizations raising funds.

Table 27.2 The US donor bill of rights

Donor Bill of Rights Principles	E-Donor Bill of Rights
Donors have the right to be informed of the organization's mission, the way the donations will be used and the organization's ability to use the donations effectively.	Donors should be clearly and immediately informed of the organization's name, nonprofit status, mission and purpose upon accessing the website.
Donors should be made aware of who is serving on the organization's governing board and should expect those individuals to exercise judgment in this leadership role.	Donors should have easy and clear access to contact information other than through the website.
Donors should have access to the nonprofit's most recent financial statements.	Donors should be assured that all third-party logos, sponsorships, and trustmarks are accurate, up-to-date and explained.
Donors should be assured that their contributions were used for the purposes for which they were given.	Donors should be informed whether a contribution entitles the donor to a tax deduction.
Donors should receive appropriate recognition and acknowledgement for their gifts.	Donors should be assured that all online contributions occur through a safe, secure system that protects their personal and financial information.
Donors should be assured that information about their donation is handled with respect and confidentiality to the extent provided by the law.	Donors should be clearly informed if the donation goes directly to the charity or is transferred through a third party.
Donors should expect all relationships with those representing the nonprofit organization will be professional in nature.	Donors should have easy access to the organization's privacy policy and be informed about what type of information is being collected about the donor and how that information will be used.
Donors should be informed whether those soliciting on behalf of the nonprofit are employees, volunteers or paid solicitors.	Donors should be provided with opportunities to opt out of lists that are sold, shared, rented or transferred to other organizations.
Donors should be allowed to remove their names and contact information from mailing lists the nonprofit may use or share with others.	Donors should not receive unsolicited communications unless they have decided to opt in to receive them.
Donors should be able to ask questions about the organization and receive timely, truthful answers to those questions.	

The ROPES process

As discussed, fundraisers must work in an environment that promotes ethical adherence to various codes while working with individuals, corporations, and foundations. A range of frameworks for encapsulating and guiding this work have been developed by scholars and practitioners. The 'ROPES' process provides a five stage framework for carrying out fundraising with these different donor publics (Kelly, 2001): Research; Objectives; Programming; Evaluation; and Stewardship. A development office of a larger nonprofit may be involved in any of these stages at any given time. Lindahl (2010) notes that the process is not linear due to the complexities of the fundraising function, although Kelly (1998) observes that the general nature of the ROPES process leads to a structured movement from one stage to the next during capital and annual giving campaigns.

In a study of AFP members, Kelly (1998) finds that fundraisers spend 30 percent of their time on programming, 20 percent on each of the research and stewardship stages, and 15 percent on each of the objectives, planning development, and evaluation stages. Although these numbers differ slightly from Wood's (1989) assessment of the fundraising process, certain themes are common in both studies. First, research is viewed as the most important part of the fundraising process even though it may not be the most time consuming task. Second, actual solicitation is a very small part of the fundraising program: less than five percent of a fundraiser's time is spent actually asking for donations (Woods, 1989). Both studies stress that the only way to be fully effective in the fundraising cycle is to have a strong stewardship component that demonstrates true gratitude to the donors.

Research

The research stage of fundraising sets the tone for a campaign, and often directly contributes to its success or failure. Research involves three key areas: the organization; the situation; and the donors. In terms of the organization, fundraisers need a solid understanding of its critical needs and funding priorities that have been established by the executive director and governing board. Waters and colleagues (2012) found that a large number of fundraisers operate independently of the rest of their organizations when developing a fundraising plan, and this introduces an environment where funds might be raised for programs and services that may not be priorities for the organization. Rather than working semi-autonomously, the fundraiser needs to be active throughout the organization to stay abreast of its current needs. Once needs are identified, the fundraising team must take time to understand their specific details by having conversations with program and service coordinators, volunteers, and clients. By listening to all of these voices, the fundraiser is in a better position to understand the situation and develop key messages around different elements of it. Fundraisers cannot simply receive general guidance from those connected to the programs; they must be proactive in researching the situation given that the interests of donors are varied, and using a one-size-fits-all approach for soliciting contributions will not be effective.

The final area of research focuses on the donors and potential prospects for the nonprofit. While donor research is most common in the health care and education subsectors, the Association of Professional Researchers for Advancement (APRA) offers insights into donor research for all nonprofits. Fundraisers are encouraged to use public information sources and the internet to gather information about potential donors, whether individuals, corporations, or foundations, for purposes of cultivation and stewardship. Donor 'research' is also carried out through the daily conversations that fundraisers have with existing and potential donors, including information about their motivations, and personal and professional lives that make it easier to identify areas of mutual concern for future solicitations.

Objectives

Successful fundraising involves a great deal of planning. Without a clear understanding of the organization's strategic plan, it is difficult for the fundraising team to develop a sound plan to secure external funding. Lindahl (2010) argues that a nonprofit which excludes the top development officer from involvement in is strategic planning is destined to fail because the organization has not recognized the need for a strategic approach to its fundraising efforts.

Once the overall direction and goals of the nonprofit are established, fundraisers must develop specific objectives to help advance the fundraising program. Recognizing that fundraising is a communication process and not simply a marketing exchange relationship, these objectives must align with communication processes which involve three stages: knowledge; attitude change; and behavioural change. Fundraisers cannot start the process by asking for a donation without having built a foundation for the solicitation appeal. Individuals, particularly those who are part of the latent or aware publics, must be educated about a particular need before their attitudes can be changed to perceive the need in the way the nonprofit wants them to see it. By jumping to the donation process prematurely, fundraisers will have skipped two important stages of communication.

Objectives must be created for each coordinated campaign, focusing on education and awareness, attitude change, and ultimately behaviours such as making a donation. These objectives must be specific, measurable, focused on a particular audience, actionable, and timely. For example, an awareness objective might be: 'increase awareness about the planned giving program among current donors aged 40–65 by 75 percent by January 30 of next year'. By constructing objectives in this manner, the fundraising team will be able to demonstrate through its evaluative research whether they were actually successful.

Programming

Fundraising programming largely consists of cultivation and solicitation. Regardless of the type of donor public, these two actions – particularly, cultivation – constitute the bulk of the fundraiser's time. Cultivation is closely linked to the notion of identification theory (Schervish, 1997), which for fundraising argues that the end goal is to bring the donor's identity and goals as close as possible to the organization's priorities. The communication literature outlines many different strategies for cultivating relationships with donors (Ki and Hon, 2008; Williams and Brunner, 2010; Gardner et al., 2015). These include: openness which focuses on the transparency of a nonprofit; networking which examines how well a nonprofit is connected in terms of cross-sector collaborations and working with other nonprofits; access, which looks at the extent to which donors have the ability to easily contact nonprofit staff; sharing of tasks, which assumes that nonprofit organizations work with volunteers and donors to deliver quality programming; assurance, which stresses that donor questions and concerns are legitimate and should be looked into by nonprofits; and positivity, which centres on the pleasantness and politeness of interactions with nonprofit representatives (Gardner et al., 2015). Cultivation is carried out on a daily basis through various means such as special events, social media conversations, meetings with clients and donors, phone calls, and direct mailings of the annual report and newsletter. In general, the more channels of communication that are used with donors, the greater the likelihood of having an engaged audience that will be responsive during solicitations.

Fundraising is most often equated with 'making the ask'. However, research has repeatedly shown that the actual ask constitutes the smallest percentage of a fundraiser's time (Woods, 1989; Kelly, 1998; Tindall and Waters, 2010). Yet, a fundraiser's ultimate measure of success is whether they were able to secure donations to the organization. The approach to solicitation varies considerably depending on the donor's history with the organization, research about the donor and his or her potential to give to the organization, and the donor's connection to individuals working for and with the nonprofit. The larger the gift that is being sought, the more personalized the solicitation will normally be. Revisiting the donor pyramid in Table 27.2, the large number of donors creating the base of the pyramid are most likely to receive direct mailings and other communications that have minimal level of personalization, although even within this group donors that have a long history of support for the organization and are giving somewhat larger gifts may receive phone calls from volunteers or fundraising staff encouraging an annual gift. In the middle of the pyramid, donors of moderate sized gifts are likely to have received personalized attention throughout the process; they may have been invited to special events or have received multiple phone calls during the year to keep them abreast of events at the nonprofit. Those few donors at the top of the pyramid usually receive high levels of personalized attention by being invited to luncheons and dinners to discuss their relationship with the organization and being asked for their opinion on what the nonprofit could be doing better.

For many fundraisers, this approach to personalized communication is incongruent with strategies for e-philanthropy that are touted by many consultants and marketing firms. Online fundraising has grown enormously over the past decade (Daniels and Narayanswamy, 2014), and certainly has its place within the programming stage of the ROPES process. But, fundraisers must think about the overall picture before deciding to spend significant amounts of time with their websites or social media platforms as online fundraising still reflects just 7.5 percent of overall giving (Grovum and Flandez, 2013). Based on numbers presented in the 2014 Giving USA Foundation report, that percentage translates into $US 20 billion, a mere fraction of the overall $US 269 billion donated by individuals.

Evaluation

Though 'evaluation' makes it sound as if the fundraiser waits until the end to assess the success of the campaign, evaluation should be occurring throughout the process. During the early stages of the campaign, fundraisers need to monitor response rates to direct mail pieces and follow up with donors who have failed to respond. If the message failed to resonate with potential donors, there may be time to change the solicitation before it is sent to others. Likewise, if an approach used in securing foundation grants or corporate sponsorships is turning these institutions away from the organization, the fundraiser needs to ask what could have made the request more attractive before going to other foundations and corporations. These evaluative techniques during the campaign can steer the campaign into more positive directions. Evaluation must also include an analysis of the overall efforts at the end of the campaign. Without looking at the entirety of the campaign, the fundraising staff cannot work on continuous improvements for future fundraising cycles. Post campaign evaluation should include both an assessment of giving at different levels of the donor pyramid and the cultivation strategies used with the different donor groups. Evaluation that connects back to the overall goals and objectives of the efforts also can be used as evidence that new hires are needed to grow the fundraising team.

Evaluation is one of the most neglected parts of the fundraising process (Lindahl, 2010), however, too many fundraisers think it is more efficient to simply focus on the stewardship stage. That said, fundraisers need to be good stewards of the donations that the nonprofit receives.

Stewardship

In a narrow sense, stewardship means that donations are used for the programs and services they were solicited. Kelly (1998) argues for a broader concept, outlining four proactive actions that help keep a donor connected to an organization and aware of what is happening with their donations. The first is 'reciprocity' which Gouldner (1960) views as a universal component of all moral codes. Donors have a choice of organizations when they wish to make a gift, and fundraisers should demonstrate appreciation that the donors chose their organization and that the gift is not taken for granted. This 'thank you' can take many forms ranging from a letter, acknowledgement email, telephone call, or special recognition event in the case of large gifts.

When fundraisers are soliciting funds, they frequently describe various programs and services. During the ask, if a donor signifies that he or she wants a donation to go to a specific program, the fundraiser has the obligation to ensure that the gift is used for that purpose. This stewardship strategy of keeping promises made is referred to as 'responsibility' by Kelly (1998). By keeping their word, nonprofits demonstrate through their actions that they are worthy of continued support. The third component highlights that it is not enough for nonprofits to be responsible, but they must also report back to the donors that they were true to their promises. Light (2008) notes that this 'reporting' strategy is a critical tool in meeting the increased calls for social and fiscal accountability. Whether nonprofits report back about their fundraising efforts and programs through newsletters and annual reports or over Facebook and Twitter, they must relay information about their internal operations so that they can build feelings of trust, satisfaction, and commitment among their supportive publics. The final stewardship dimension, 'relationship nurturing', creates an environment in which donors are told on a regular basis that they are cared about, their support is respected and appreciated, and that the organization wants them involved in more than just a donation capacity (Grace, 1991). Metrick (2005) argues that with proper care of the relationship, a donor may become a long-term, indeed, lifelong supporter of a nonprofit. This planned evolution of donors through a long-term fundraising program is examined in the next section.

Donor evolution

Fundraisers generally seek not only to retain donors, but over time transition them to higher levels of giving, as shown in Figure 27.3. Early gifts to a nonprofit often come from special events, such as walk-a-thons and fun runs, and occasional gifts that are made either in response to peer-to-peer requests through social media sites or casual giving made through mass marketed campaigns, such as public service announcements and billboard advertizing.

Annual giving donations are gifts made to organizations, generally in response to coordinated campaigns. In the US these are usually held in late spring, just after the personal income tax deadline, but before money is spent on May graduations and summer weddings, or in early

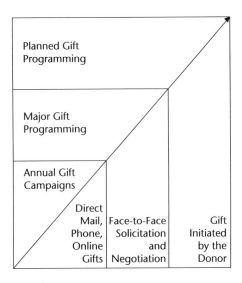

Figure 27.3   Donor progression

autumn when people begin annual reflections on the year, but before they spend money on winter holiday gifts. Elsewhere, campaigns may be more precisely coincidental with religious festivals of sacrifice or celebration. Annual gift solicitations are most often made through direct mail solicitations. In a content analysis of annual giving fundraising letters, Ritzenhein (1998) finds that the most common arguments are that: the nonprofit organization has quality programs; every individual's gift matters; and that the nonprofit organization addresses important community issues. Increasingly, nonprofits are phasing out the use of phone-a-thons, when volunteers telephone existing donors and make solicitation requests; radiothons, when nonprofits work with sponsoring radio stations to highlight their programs and services to raise funds from their listening audiences; and telethons, which are similar to radiothons, except appealing to television audiences. These forms of annual giving are being replaced by online giving techniques that are often managed through third party platforms that allow individuals to make one-time or recurring contributions automatically charged to credit cards. Mobile phone giving and text message-based giving is catching on in Western fundraising and mostly as a response to crisis situations and natural disasters (Kapucu, Chapter 11; however, it is a common form of fundraising in Japan, Korea and elsewhere (Smith, 2012; Bernholz, Chapter 28).

As a donor becomes a regular contributor to annual giving campaigns, fundraisers are likely to research their giving histories, personal finances, and professional lives even more closely to determine if they might be considered a major gift or planned gift prospect. Major gifts may be regular or one-time gifts of significant value that, in addition to cash contributions, are often made through the transfer of stock, securities, or assets. The major gift comes as a result of multiple visits or 'touchpoints' between a nonprofit and the potential donor, during which fundraisers learn about the donor's interests, and ultimately present a major gift proposal that outlines how a specified monetary contribution would be used to advance projects in line with the donor's interests. Given that the goal of the process is to reach the desired 'win-win zone' for both parties, fundraisers should not be afraid to negotiate with donors about the terms of major gifts (Swanger and Rodgers, 2013).

Planned gifts are the ultimate form of giving because they are not the result of a formal fundraising campaign. Instead, they are selfless gifts that come from supportive donors. Through complex estate planning with legal counsel, donors are able to set up a variety of giving mechanisms, including bequests, annuities, and trusts to benefit nonprofits after the donor's death. Even though planned giving costs very little for nonprofits to promote, Brown (2004) indicates that many did not have information readily available about planned giving options due to the complexity of the gift. Given the estimated value of the upcoming intergenerational transfer of $41 trillion wealth, however, nonprofits must embrace planned giving if they hope to receive a portion of the estates and assets (Lerner, 2011). Nevertheless, legacy giving, as a distinctive form of gift, raises fundraising challenges, both where organizations do set out to organize 'legacy giving' campaigns (for example in higher education), and where the interplay of 'giving while living' and 'bequesting' occurs (Wiepking et al., 2012). James and O'Boyle (2014: 355) propose that that bequest decision-making is analogous to visualizing the final chapter in one's autobiography, drawing attention to the fundraising challenge where 'due to inherent mortality salience, people may resist creating this final chapter'.

Conclusion

Fundraising focuses on the creation and maintenance of mutually beneficial relationships between a nonprofit and a variety of donor publics. Mutual benefit is key to this relationship as the nonprofit ultimately needs contributions to continue delivering its programs and services, but the donor must also feel satisfied with the altruistic and egoistic benefits they receive from the interaction. Continued, cyclical communication is at the core of fundraising. Programs that approach donors only when they need contributions will not succeed over the long run. Donors must be engaged multiple times in between solicitations, and they must be responded to and heard when they have questions and concerns.

While the amount of personalized attention a donor receives is largely connected to their giving history and size of previous donations, fundraisers have a variety of communication channels to provide the donor of even the smallest annual giving contribution some level of individual attention. Ultimately, it is the fundraiser's ability to keep donors involved with an organization that determines the success of the fundraising function. The overall goal of fundraising is not simply to raise funds, but it is to keep the relationships established with donors active and healthy by transitioning them up the levels of the donor pyramid. Some donors will not be able to move past the base of relatively small annual gifts; however, some will. Through donor research and cultivation, fundraisers can determine which donors have potential to transition from annual gift contributors to major gift and planned giving donors. This growth fuels the sophistication of the fundraising function while the nonprofit continues to expand its donor base by recruiting new donors. Communication, not marketing, is at the heart of fundraising success.

References

Alexander, J. (2000) Adaptive strategies of nonprofit human service organizations in an era of devolution and new public management, *Nonprofit Management and Leadership*, 10(3): 287–303.

Andreoni, A. (1990) Impure altruism and donations to public goods: A theory of warm-glow giving, *Economic Journal*, 100: 464–477.

Bekkers, R. and Wiepking, P. (2011) A literature review of empirical studies of philanthropy: Eight mechanisms that drive charitable giving, *Nonprofit and Voluntary Sector Quarterly*, 40(5): 924–73.

Birkwood, S. (2015) Fundraising Standards Board to investigate death of poppy seller Olive Cooke, says chief executive Alistair McLean, *Third Sector*, 18 May. www.thirdsector.co.uk/fundraising-standards-board-investigate-death-poppy-seller-olive-cooke-says-chief-executive-alistair-mclean/fundraising/article/1347535 [Accessed 11 June 2015].

Boulding, K. E. (1973) *The economy of love and fear: A preface to grants economics*. Belmont, CA: Wadsworth.

Brest, P. and Harvey, H. (2008) *Money well spent*. New York, NY: Bloomberg Press.

Brown, D. W. (2004) What research tells us about planned giving, *International Journal of Nonprofit and Voluntary Sector Marketing*, 9(1): 86–95.

Brown, W. A. (2005) Exploring the association between board and organizational performance in nonprofit organizations, *Nonprofit Management and Leadership*, 15(3): 317–39.

Cowley, E., McKenzie, T., Pharoah, C. and Smith, S. (2011) *The new state of donation: Three decades of household giving to charity 1978-2008*. London, UK: Centre for Charitable Giving and Philanthropy, Cass Business School City University London and CMPO, University of Bristol.

Daniels, A. and Narayanswamy, A. (2014) Online fundraising goes mainstream, *Chronicle of Philanthropy*, 18 May. www.philanthropy.com/article/Online-Fundraising-Goes/150539 [Accessed 29 May 2015].

Drezner, N. D. (2009) Why give? Exploring social exchange and organization identification theories in the promotion of philanthropic behaviours of African-American millennials at private-HBCUs, *International Journal of Educational Advancement*, 9: 147–65.

Dunn, P. (2010) Strategic responses by a nonprofit when a donor becomes tainted., *Nonprofit and Voluntary Sector Quarterly*, 39(1), 102–23.

Gardner, L., Seltzer, T., Phillips, A. L., and Page, R. E. (2015) The influence of message source and cultivation strategies in a nonprofit public relations context. In R. D. Waters (Ed.). *Public relations in the nonprofit sector: Theory and practice*. New York, NY: Routledge, 219–31.

Gladden, J. M, Mahony, D. F. and Apostolopoulou, A. (2005) Toward a better understanding of college athletic donors: What are the primary motives?, *Sports Marketing Quarterly*, 14: 18–30.

Gladden, J. M, Mahony, D. F. and Apostolopoulou, A. (2005) Toward a better understanding of college athletic donors: What are the primary motives?, *Sports Marketing Quarterly*, 14: 18–30.

Gouldner, A. W. (1960) The norm of reciprocity: A preliminary statement, *American Sociological Review*, 25(2): 161–78.

Gouldner, T., Phillips, A. L., and Page, R. E. (2015) The influence of message source and cultivation strategies in a nonprofit public relations context. In R. D. Waters (Ed.). *Public relations in the nonprofit sector: Theory and practice*. New York, NY: Routledge, 219–31.

Grace, K. S. (1991) Can we throw away the tin cup? In D. F. Burlingame and L. J. Hulse (Eds.). *Taking fund raising seriously: Advancing the profession and practice of raising money*. San Francisco, CA: Jossey-Bass.

Greenfield, J. (1991) *Fund-raising: Evaluating and managing the fund development process*. New York, NY: Wiley.

Grovum, E. C. and Flandez, R. (2013) The big boom in online giving, *Chronicle of Philanthropy*, 23 June. www.philanthropy.com/article/The-Big-Boom-in-Online-Giving/139965/ [Accessed 30 May 2015].

Harrow, J. and Pharoah, C. (2010) How do you ask difficult questions? Shared challenges and practice between fundraisers and researchers, CGAP Briefing Note 4, London: Centre for Charitable Giving and Philanthropy, Cass Business School, City University London.

Hon, L. C. and Grunig, J. E. (1999) *Guidelines for measuring relationships in public relations*. Gainesville, FL: Institute for Public Relations Research.

Institute of Fundraising. (2015) IoF Standards Committee takes action to strengthen charity fundraising practices, 11 June. www.frsb.org.uk/iof-takes-action-to-strengthen-charity-fundraising/ [Accessed 12 June 2015].

James, R. N., and O'Boyle, M. W. (2014) Charitable estate planning as visualized autobiography: An fMRI study of its neural correlates, *Nonprofit and Voluntary Sector Quarterly*, 43(2), 355–73.

Jeavons, T. H. (1991) A historical and moral analysis of religious fund raising. In D. F. Burlingame and L. J. Hulse (Eds.). *Taking fundraising seriously: Advancing the profession and practice of raising money*. San Francisco, CA: Jossey-Bass, 53–72.

Kelly, K. S. (1998) *Effective fund-raising management*. Mahwah, NJ: Lawrence Erlbaum Associates.

——. (2001) ROPES: A model of the fund-raising process. In J. M. Greenfield (Ed.). *The Nonprofit handbook: Fundraising*, 3rd edition. New York, NY: John Wiley & Sons, 96–116.

Ki, E.-J. and Hon, L. C. (2008) A measure of relationship cultivation strategies, *Journal of Public Relations Research*, 21(1): 1–24.

Lerner, S. (2011) Next-generation philanthropy: Examining a next-generation Jewish philanthropic network, *The Foundation Review*, 3(4): 82–95.

Light, P. C. (2008) *How Americans view charities: A report on charitable confidence, 2008*. Washington, DC: Brookings Institution.

Lilly Family School of Philanthropy, Indiana University. (2014) Giving USA: Americans gave $335.17 billion to charity in 2013; total approaches pre-recession peak, 17 June. www.philanthropy.iupui.edu/news-events/news-item.html?id=127 [Accessed 30 May 2015].

Lindahl, W. E. (2010) *Principles of fundraising: Theory and practice*. Sudbury, MA: Jones and Bartlett Publishers.

McKeever, B. W. (2013) From awareness to advocacy: Understanding nonprofit communication, participation, and support, *Journal of Public Relations Research*, 25(3): 307–28.

Mann, T. (2007) College fund raising using theoretical perspectives to understand donor motives, *International Journal of Educational Advancement*, 7(1): 35–45.

Metrick, L. A. (2005) Successful strategies for effective stewardship, *New Directions for Effective Stewardship*, 49: 29–41.

Mixer, J. R. (1993) *Principles of professional fundraising: Useful foundations for successful practice*. San Francisco, CA: Jossey-Bass.

Nudd, S. P. (1991) Thinking strategically about information. In H. A. Rosso and Associates (Eds.). *Achieving excellence in fund raising: A comprehensive guide to principles, strategies, and methods*. San Francisco, CA: Jossey-Bass.

O'Neil, J. (2007) The link between strong public relationships and donor support, *Public Relations Review*, 33(1): 99–102.

O'Neill, M. (2009) Public confidence in charitable nonprofits, *Nonprofit and Voluntary Sector Quarterly*, 38(2): 237–69.

Ostrower, F. (1995) *Why the wealthy give: The culture of elite philanthropy*. Princeton, NJ: Princeton University Press.

Phillips, S. D. (2012) Canadian leapfrog: From regulating charitable fundraising to co-regulating good governance, *Voluntas*, 23(3): 808–29.

Polivy, D. K. (2014) *Donor cultivation and the donor lifecycle map: A new framework for fundraising.* Hoboken, NJ: Wiley.

Prince, R. A. and File, K. M. (1994) *The seven faces of philanthropy.* San Francisco, CA: Jossey-Bass.

Ritzenhein, D. N. (1998) Content analysis of fundraising letters, *New Directions in Philanthropic Fundraising*, 22: 23–36.

Sagawa, S. (2001) New value partnerships: The lessons of Denny's/Save the Children partnership for building high-yielding cross-sector alliances, *International Journal of Nonprofit and Voluntary Sector Marketing*, 6(3): 199–214.

Sargeant, A. and Woodliffe, L. (2007) Gift giving: An interdisciplinary review, *International Journal of Nonprofit and Voluntary Sector Marketing*, 12(4): 275–307.

Schervish, P. G. (1997) Inclination, obligation, and association: What we know and what we need to learn about donor motivation. In D. F. Burlingame (Ed.). *Critical issues in fundraising.* New York, NY: John Wiley & Sons.

Smith, A. (2012) Real time charitable giving, Pew Research Center's Internet and American Life Project, www.pewinternet.org/mobilegiving [Accessed 29 May 2015].

Swanger, W. and Rodgers, S. (2013) Revisiting fundraising encroachment of public relations in light of the theory of donor relations, *Public Relations Review*, 39(5): 566–68.

Tindall, N. T. J. and Waters, R. D. (2010) The relationship between fundraising practice and job satisfaction at Historically Black Colleges and Universities, *International Journal of Educational Advancement*, 10(3): 198–215.

US Trust and Lilly Family School of Philanthropy. (2014) *The 2014 US Trust Study of high net worth philanthropy.* Boston, MA and Indianapolis, IN: US Trust and Lilly Family School of Philanthropy, Indiana University.

Waters, R. D. (2011) Increasing fundraising efficiency through evaluation: Applying communication theory to the nonprofit organization–donor relationship, *Nonprofit and Voluntary Sector Quarterly*, 40(3): 458–75.

——., Kelly, K. S., and Walker, M. L. (2012) Organizational roles enacted by healthcare fundraisers: A national study testing theory and assessing gender differences, *Journal of Communication Management*, 16(3): 244–63.

Webber, D. (2004) Understanding charity fundraising events, *International Journal of Nonprofit and Voluntary Sector Marketing*, 9(2): 122–34.

Weeden, C. (2011) *Smart giving is good business.* San Francisco, CA: Jossey-Bass.

Weerts, D. J. and Ronca, J. M. (2007) Profiles of supportive alumni: Donors, volunteers, and those who "do it all", *International Journal of Educational Advancement*, 7(1): 20–34.

Wiepking, P., Scaife, W. and McDonald, K. (2012) Motives and barriers to bequest giving, *Journal of Consumer Behaviour*, 11(1), 56–66.

Williams, K. D. and Brunner, B. R. (2010) Using cultivation strategies to manage public relationships: A content analysis of non-profit organisations' websites, *PRism* 7(2): 1–15. www.prismjournal.org/fileadmin/Praxis/Files/Journal_Files/Williams_Brunner.pdf [Accessed 2 June 2015].

Wood, E. W. (1989) The four R's of major gift solicitation, *Reid Report* (141), 1:6.

Zinsmeister, K. (2013) Donation: Which Americans give most to charity?, *Philanthropy Magazine*, Summer. www.philanthropyroundtable.org/topic/donor_intent/donation [Accessed 26 February 2015].

28

Wiring a new social economy

Reflections on philanthropy in the digital age

Lucy Bernholz

Digital technologies are not just changing philanthropy, they are creating a new social economy. For several decades, we have defined philanthropy as the formal interactions between certain institutions (community organizations) and certain revenue sources (charitable dollars). While national definitions and incentives vary, the essential equation is of a set of institutionally defined interactions framed as either non-governmental or not-for-profit. These organizations, and these funders, have become synonymous with civil society. Technology is changing that. Today we use private resources for public purposes in multiple and diverse ways, many of which are flourishing on the backs of new behaviours made possible by technology. As the activities, institutions, and resource flows that constitute philanthropy shift, eventually the policy boundaries of the sector itself will need to be redrawn.

Digital technologies facilitate a common set of behaviour changes, whether we look at their use in commerce, government, or the social sector. They expand and mobilize information access, facilitate the storage and use of massive datasets, and shift our expectations about to whom and what we can connect. Of course, people and institutions determine the extent and pace at which this progression unfolds, and there is currently great variation in the use of technology by non-governmental organizations around the world. It is evident, however, that many nonprofits struggle to keep up with the information technology investment curve. National policies on a wide range of issues, from telecommunications infrastructure to personal information storage to intellectual property, significantly influence the availability and use of technology's tools. Cultural preferences and the history of censorship or government surveillance also affect how willing individuals and organizations are to adopt communications tools, and which ones they prefer. For example, a 60 country study of digital media policy sponsored by the Open Society Foundation (2014) notes wide differences in proximal countries in national investment and cultural willingness to use digital broadband, blogging, social media, and social networking tools.

Disruptive innovation in all sectors tends to come from new players, those who are free to imagine a process or product anew rather than those using new tools to improve the old practices to which they are tethered. This continuous back and forth between new and old forms the story of technological adoption and new behaviour and enterprise creation. This process has reached the point where we need to draw new boundaries around the social sector.

This chapter aims to understand the role of technology in the social sector by examining its use from three perspectives. The first two views require a loose separation of organizations into the 'core' and the 'edge'. The bounds between the two groups are fluid, but in general the core group includes nonprofits and foundations created before digital networks became common. The problems these organizations focus on were largely defined in a pre-digital age and their solutions, organizational structures, and use of technology reflects this. The second group lives toward the edge of the sector. It includes enterprises that have been founded on digital networked technologies. The solutions that these organizations offer are unimaginable without global, digital, mobile connectivity. Their programs, missions, and organizational structures rely on access to cheap, scalable, reliable technology. Some offer global connections between peers or mobile phone based volunteer opportunities; some simply require cheap digital information storage and search in massive quantities.

Benkler (2006) describes a common characteristic of technology adoption by a sector or industry. Simply put: existing organizations and funders (the core) innovate with new technologies by using them to improve old practices and solve pre-defined problems faster or more cheaply. Newcomers (the edge) innovate by using new technologies to explicitly change the old practices and redefine the problem (Benkler, 2006). This leads to a dynamic exchange – indeed, a certain tension – between the 'insider innovators' and 'outsider innovators' in which both learn and change, and before long the edges of the sector have shifted. These interactions can be direct, such as the shared influence created by networks of technologists who serve both the edge and the core. More often the intersections are indirect, however, and arise from shifting norms and expectations. For example, as edge organizations publicly experiment with open and shared measures of performance the pressure rises for core organizations to do the same. Similarly, the success of core nonprofits in using social media and online platforms to raise money in tiny increments influences edge innovators to extend this practice to independent and commercial projects.

This dynamics of edge and core creates a third force that is changing the sector. When participants break through established structural norms or reach out to entirely new partners, it can redefine a whole industry. Thus, we see a music industry reshaped from record labels to tech companies and live performances or the publishing ecosystem of authors, editors, publishing houses and independent bookstores being broken apart by the nature of e-book distribution (Wasserman, 2012). This is precisely the moment we have reached in philanthropy as technology allows us to reach out to new capital and experiment with new enterprise structures. As the use of new technologies facilitates new organizational forms, we confront anew the tensions between private resource control and public accountability. Data and technology underpin the growing impact investing and social enterprise movements, which have also redrawn the boundaries of the social sector. In our age of big data, we see new tensions around intellectual property and in this era of global connectivity, we regularly confront transnational regulatory hurdles.

Technology, as we will see, is reshaping how we use private resources for public good. These new practices will need new governing requirements; both 'soft' industry standards and 'hard' regulations.

What technologies matter?

While it is the behaviours and expectations engendered by digital technologies that actually drive change, there is a short list of technologies that are responsible for most of the shifts currently unfolding. These include: large connected databases; online giving platforms; social media and social networks; and mobile phones and payment systems.

439

Underlying all of the front end technologies it is the general characteristics of digital information – namely its remixability, durability and resilience – that change behaviour, enterprises, and economies.

Digital data's key characteristics

Digital data can be mixed together in ways that static data stored on paper or non-networked technologies cannot. If the data are music, the *remixibility* allows for sampling of songs, streaming, and storing – all of which led to massive shifts in the recording industry. If the data are numeric information about population characteristics or revenue flows, they can be shown on a map, sampled, mined, and searched for patterns. They can be shown in comparison and contrast to other datasets, and can be analyzed and represented, misanalyzed and misrepresented by anyone with access to them.

Digital data are also *durable*: they are hard to remove or erase. Once stored on a server, copies can be made and stored elsewhere. If the server is owned by a separate enterprise, be it governmental or commercial, the initial users of the data may lose control over time of where the data are stored and how others use them. At the same time, storing data remotely allows users to access them anywhere and anytime. This virtual access shifts the physical boundaries of work, and these qualities have very different implications for human rights activists, health researchers, or law enforcement.

Finally, digital data are *resilient*: they can be used over and over again and never wear out. Our analog notion of 'originals' and 'copies' is fundamentally flawed in the digital era. There is no 'natural' limit to how many times these data can be used, only business models or legal considerations limit this. Such issues challenge old publishing models while sparking the imaginations of educators.

Philanthropic datasets

For more than a decade, data about giving opportunities have been moving online. The nonprofit sector has dedicated significant resources to developing online, searchable catalogues of tax and administrative information on nonprofit organizations. The GuideStar model in the US, UK, Israel, and India, TechSoup Global's NGO repository, and more than 100 online giving platforms in all parts of the world demonstrate the many uses for simple, searchable databases of organizations.

Whether in the form of scanned tax documents that provide an aggregate view of a nation's social organizations or through the carefully cleaned and curated data of all foundation grantmaking, there are now common, publicly available datasets of fundamental financial information about the philanthropic and nonprofit system. These datasets are richest in information about this core relationship – charitable giving and nonprofits. Additional datasets track social enterprises, impact investments, or government funding for social sector activity. Even though the data live in separate sets and in separate forms, the ability to bring the data together to see an encompassing view of all revenue to all organizations creating social goods is getting easier and easier.

In the US, independent third parties do the collation work. An entire ecosystem of monitoring, rating, and review sites has developed around the core information of what organizations exist and what revenue flows to them. A subset of these entities is working together to create standard data categories, application program interfaces (APIs) that allow data to be moved from one site to another, and ratings systems that complement each other. In just the last five years

GuideStar, Charity Navigator, Philanthropedia, Givewell, and Great Nonprofits, among others, have taken steps to deliberately cluster and use a shared set of data standards. Large US foundations are also experimenting with streaming their grants data in a common format. There are moves afoot to 'open' up the federally required tax data on all nonprofit organizations, which would make the core data available in truly digital forms. This has already been achieved in Canada where the federal regulator, the Canada Revenue Agency, provides the annual charity return as open data, downloadable from its website, and is moving toward e-filing of the return making the entire process fully digital.

There are at least 100 online giving platforms around the globe, each of which uses and/ or contributes to the digital data available about social organizations and their funding. Online giving is growing rapidly. This makes giving easy and instant, and is especially appealing to those giving small dollar gifts (which make up the vast majority of giving). One effect of this easy giving structure is to accelerate the phenomenon of matching the stated outcome to the size of the gift: organizations now commonly tout the 'results' that five, ten or twenty-five dollar gifts will enable.

These online giving sites are each powered by a dataset of giving opportunities. Add to these the growing availability of datasets from government funders on their spending (data.gov, data.gov.uk, and at least 30 other national and international sites) and we begin to see the raw material for a comprehensive digital understanding of organizations and revenues. In Canada, a commercial enterprise (ajah.ca) has built a single database of organizations, charitable giving, foundation grants, and government support – both grants and contracts – providing a more comprehensive view of the Canadian nonprofit sector than has been available (Lomax and Wharton, 2014).

The availability of data is a first step. Getting this information in standardized ways that allow users to intermingle and compare data from different datasets is the next step, and a danger is that in the enthusiasm for opening data, interest in standardization is lost. The technological elements of this step are not difficult, although ongoing maintenance is required and expensive in current models. What slows the implementation of such standardization, however, are the challenges that it poses to established business models or that it sets up for transparent interactions. These are not minor challenges. Being able to quickly and easily see aggregate foundation funding flows, compare organizational revenue, and track or map government spending to organizations draws attention that is not necessarily welcome by everyone in the sector. There are many in the sector, both funders and organizations, who do not welcome this level of transparency, many who do, and a majority that do not understand its implications.

These databases have fundamentally changed how we look for information on nonprofits. Personal recommendations or the insights of friends and colleagues remain important, even as we are all one click away from searchable, comparable information. However, these independent data sources do not appear to be the most meaningful sources of information to donors. A series of studies in the US found that less than 20 percent of donors regularly do any kind of research about the organizations they support, and most of what they look for is legitimacy information on individual organizations (GuideStar, ND; Ottenhoff and Ulrich, 2010).

Even before donors begin to adopt a more nuanced data analysis, broad easy access to verification data on organizations has changed the way donors interact with nonprofits. Because the overhead ratio is easy to calculate and compares numbers that fit all nonprofits, early vendors of charity ratings focused on it, even though they knew it was of limited actual value. It has become a standard that is hard to ignore, despite efforts within the sector and outside to move donors to more complex analyses. We are still in the collective search for widely available, meaningful measures of organizational effectiveness and social impact (von Schnurbein, Chapter 30).

For now, the marketplace is still in the creation stage between identifying and implementing measures that matter on a broad enough scale that donors and others can use them.

The relationship between databases and measurement is responsible, in a small but significant way, for the rise in impact investment. This movement, which seeks to draw financial return oriented capital toward enterprises that produce social goods, has many antecedents and champions. While its roots date back to the 1960s and socially responsible investing, and it is growing in a cultural moment that believes strongly in the power of market based solutions, the goal of measuring social impact requires the ability to crunch large quantities of meaningful, comparable data (Hebb, Chapter 29). The impact investment movement requires metrics, and comparable, sector-wide metrics require robust, connected databases. This will only become more evident as the impact investment movement to build online exchanges grows, and as the emergent efforts to match investors and enterprises in Asia, South America, and the Middle East expand.

Online databases of organizations that allow users to compare causes or actions also serve to blur the lines between nonprofits and other forms of enterprise. In just two years, the fundraising platform Kickstarter went from a niche market for art and cultural events to a system for raising millions of dollars for commercially viable products. The system's designers never limited the inventory of choices to nonprofit organizations: the original criteria for listing had only to do with an effort's artistic or cultural value. It quickly became clear that donors on the site cared about specific projects and not about the tax status of the particular endeavour. Kickstarter copycats, which allow anyone to post a project of any type and raise funds for it, have blurred the lines between commercial and nonprofit activities. This model of crowdfunding has proven so successful in the creative economy that the US passed a law in 2012 allowing companies to raise equity investments on similar sites.

When web-enabled databases first came online, community volunteer centres rushed to put their opportunities online for potential participants to search and choose. In 1998, VolunteerMatch, then a startup, took this approach a step further, combining volunteer opportunities from several sources and providing customized portals for corporate employee volunteer programs. Along the way, it became the norm for an interested citizen to go online, search by geography or type of activity and sign up to donate a few hours or an afternoon without any previous involvement with or outreach from a particular organization. As the ease of finding opportunities increased, so too did 'episodic volunteering'. Studies from the US, Australia, and the UK point to several reasons, including technology, to explain this (Corporation for National and Community Service, 2006; Bryen and Madden, 2006; NCVO, 2011).

Ten years later, two technologists carved up volunteering even further. By 2010, the rise in smart phone ownership and its pervasive reach shifted innovators' attention from computer desktops to mobile phones and tablets. These devices are particularly well suited to short term, discrete tasks – and this was the design focus behind micro-volunteering pioneers such as Sparked.com. The technology slices voluntary activities into tiny, digital components – tagging photographs, reviewing marketing text, or performing discrete online research tasks – and engages volunteers in completing them on their phones whenever they can. The people who use Sparked expect to find their volunteer opportunity online and finish it on their own timeline. The progression from VolunteerMatch to Sparked shows how technologies changed our understanding of volunteering itself. We are still learning what the parallel phenomenon of giving many small donations means for philanthropy.

Social networks and mobile tools

Digital databases of comparable information are clearly changing fundraising and volunteer recruitment. They also make it easier for organizations to tell their stories. Low cost digital video, mobile phone cameras, and online mapping software offer nonprofit organizations ready-made tools for storytelling. Perhaps the biggest change is not just how these tools change story-telling, but how they change *who* tells the stories. We have seen a shift from insiders to outsiders in terms of who can tell or carry an organization's message. The stories that reach the greatest numbers of people are those that get created and carried by an organization's community of supporters. Whether it is a video that goes globally viral or a message of protest against an orga-nizational policy, the communications and storytelling strategies in this technological landscape are about portability, engagement, and the use of many different media tools.

Social and mobile media are key accelerators of these changes. Mobile phones have been adopted faster and at a greater scale than any other technology (with the possible exception of early human's use of rocks as tools). In a world of over seven billion people, there are more than six billion cellular phone subscriptions, with India and China accounting for 30 percent of these (Meeker, 2012). This connectivity changes the way people act locally and globally. It enables innovations in banking, health care, disaster response, and education that few would have predicted would be linked to a telephone. And it exemplifies the fundamental shift from a scarcity of information to an abundance that will be at the core to the next round of social sector innovations.

Both mobile and social media shift the boundaries of philanthropy. Organizations are no longer the central source of information: individuals are (Rainie and Wellman, 2012). These individuals may be the beneficiaries of a social innovation, such as the Nigerian farmers who receive government subsidies on their mobile phones (Akinboro, 2014). Or they may be sup-porters of a cause, such as the hundreds of thousands of people who donate to charity via Twitter, or the millions who watch videos on their phones and pass on the word. Individuals become the carriers of the message about an issue and the fundraisers for it. We use phones to organize our own community and social change efforts, and alert others to our actions. While more than $50 million was raised via text message for relief efforts following the 2010 earth-quake in Haiti (Rogers, 2010; Kapucu, Chapter 11), one of the most notable characteristics of the mobile donors was the way they immediately told others about their action. They became not just donors but signalers to other donors (Smith 2012). When the donation tool and the communication tool are bundled together, as in mobile phones, giving becomes a much more social action.

The future impact of mobile phones on the social sector will come not just from their ubiquity, but also from their dual purpose as communication tools and payment systems. An estimated $US 600 billion was moved in 2013 by 200 million active users of mobile money services, with the most frequent use of mobile money payments being in African countries (Simpson, 2014; Smith *et al.*, 2012). For person-person remittance payments, one online website, Remitly, has had a 400 percent year-over-year rate of growth, with its diaspora customers now sending more than $100 million a year over their phones (Reuters, 2015). Clearly, remittances and micro-giving are already a big part of this phenomenon.

Nonprofit organizations have been particularly rapid adopters of low cost social media tools that require relatively small cash outlays, even if they require staff time to maintain and use, and are adopted much more quickly across all sizes of nonprofits than those that require large upfront costs. For instance, the rate of adoption for Facebook or Twitter by nonprofits is much faster than was the move to set up the most basic websites because the social media tools are free to use. Once on board with these tools, nonprofits tend to use them for operational purposes. A 2010 study of American nonprofits in all issue areas found that '92% of nonprofits use Facebook for marketing purposes and 46% use it for fundraising' (Nonprofit Technology Network, 2010) – an arc similar to that of the adoption of websites and email witnessed a decade ago. These uses are tools for running the organization, however, not for fundamentally reconsidering how services or programs are delivered. But, in the hands of individual supporters or those outside the organizations, these are tools for redrawing the boundaries of fundraising, communications, community mobilizing, and information access.

In sum, digital technologies have a supporting role in each of the major sector changes of the last decade, from impact investing to the kind of organizing that raged across North Africa in 2011 and fueled the Occupy movement. Aggregate data analyses of the sector and crowdfunding are only possible in an age of online communities. With digital technology as their starting point, these efforts are shifting the bounds of where social goods are produced and by whom.

What effect are these technologies having on philanthropy?

The application of technologies to our shared social problems is rewiring who, where, and how we use private resources to solve public problems. The old boundaries between markets and social purpose, individual donors and institutional foundations, and nonprofit organizations and informal communities of action are shifting. There are at least four ways digital technologies are helping pull philanthropy and nonprofits into a new social economy:

- Repackaging – facilitating the breaking down of institutional barriers and unbundling services long seen as inseparable;
- Revaluing – accelerating an emphasis on metrics and standardized data, and serving as the platform on which new forms of data constantly emerge;
- Redefining – creating new categories of action such as micro-volunteering; and
- Repositioning – as technologies make data and information accessible anywhere, we have more opportunities to use our professional skills and corporate structures to facilitate social good.

It is easiest to see these different levels of changes by looking through the lenses of the most familiar actors in the social sector – individuals, nonprofit organizations, foundations, and advisors.

Individuals at the centre

Individuals are the centre of gravity in the new social economy. People with smartphones have instant access to information, payment systems, and networks of other individuals, and they can patch together this mix in any way they choose. They can volunteer in brief moments for organizations they have never visited, using their phone as a tool to tag photographs of moon craters or identify park benches in need of repair (see ClickFix.com). They hear about a natural disaster within minutes of its occurrence on Facebook or Twitter, make donations via text message or a linked mobile transfer system, and alert their own networks of the event and their donation. They can organize small beach cleanups or global protest movements, check the legitimacy of an organization's tax exempt status, or voice their outrage and join others in changing both government and organizational policy. In just the first three months of 2012, Americans used social and mobile media to organize and join a national protest that led to changes in proposed legislation about internet piracy and forced an international nonprofit foundation, the Susan G. Komen Foundation, to change an announced funding policy (Kliff and Alzenman, 2012). They can raise money for projects or causes they care about with the ease and reach once available only to paid professionals.

Effects on nonprofits

Nonprofits are not only using technology, but are being used by it. A common challenge for nonprofits is keeping their listings up to date on all the online platforms that exist to raise funds. They face increasing demands for information from individual donors, foundations, and these third party platforms that provide external ratings and recommendations to donors. Social media appeal to many organizations because of their low capital costs. But as several high profile cases have shown, from social media backlash against the Susan G. Komen Foundation to funding scandals found through online databases, these tools set a bar for transparency and engagement that most nonprofits are ill equipped to meet.

Endowed foundations show the fewest signs of technological disruption so far (Smith, 2010). A few are taking steps to be much more visible and transparent – using social media and online communities to generate, fund, and share new ideas (Brock *et al.*, 2013). This is most common in the rise of 'innovation challenges,' which have become a standard part of the philanthropic landscape in the last decade through dedicated organizations such as the X Prize Foundation (xprize.org), shared platforms such as Innocentive (Schneider, 2013) or Ashoka's Changemakers (ashoka.org/changemakers). The website, glasspockets.org, launched by the Foundation Center in 2010 is intended to help foundations understand the value of transparency and be inspired to be more open in their communications; more broadly, the goal is to 'galvanize a transparency movement within philanthropy' (Camarena, 2011: 9).

Foundations are also using databases and shared data standards to facilitate some increased collaboration. For example, the WASH Funders portal (washfunders.org) at the Foundation Center is intended to map their grantmaking by issue and geography, making it easier (though not common) to generate shared strategies. Similarly, the pilot initiative Strategy Landscape from the Center on Effective Philanthropy and Monitor Deloitte was a data visualization tool to categorize and coordinate grantmaking strategies across funders; unfortunately, it failed because the demand was not as strong as anticipated and groups used the tool differently than expected, requiring greater technological flexibility than was feasible (Bolduc, 2013). Databases of shared metrics, such as those produced by the Center for Effective Philanthropy (effectivephilanthropy.org), have also facilitated benchmarking of performance by individual foundations and an industry-wide, at least in the US, discussion about best grantmaker practices. A small but influential number of foundations are using real-time grantmaking streams and databases, facilitated by open source grants management packages (FLUXX) or common taxonomies (IATI). Some community foundations have signed on to open source (e.g. Creative Commons) licenses that allow people to use and build upon the content of their published work so as to 'realize the full potential of the content we create, in ways we've never anticipated, and from allies we've never met' (McCort, 2015).

Digital tools make it as easy to collaborate with someone across the globe as with someone across the room. Social networks have helped us build communities of interest that range from cute cats in sinks to mobile health applications and micro lending. We can find – and work with – the people who share our interests or complement our skills, no matter if they work for the same organization – or kind of organization – that we do. This, along with demographic trend, employment statistics, and corporate practices feeds the creation of a fluid workforce. We have lower expectations about lifetime employment and few delusions of working for any one institution for a long time. Our professional networks cross organizational boundaries; we do not expect all of the skills or opportunities to exist within our own institutions. This goes beyond computer scientist Bill Joy's maxim that 'no matter where we work we should expect that the smartest people work elsewhere' (Lakhani and Panetta, 2007). Rather, it leads to working styles and institutional expectations that are more fluid, more collaborative, and more permeable.

There are two highly visible trends that exemplify this reality in philanthropy. The first is the rise of philanthropic prizes. As McKinsey and Company noted in its 2009 report, 'And the Winner is ...' the value of philanthropic prize competitions more than tripled in the 2000s (McKinsey & Co., 2009). Problem solving prizes, in which a reward or incentive is offered to whoever can solve 'x' problem are premised on the idea that the necessary expertise exists outside the funder's usual networks. That it may reside in an individual or a commercial venture is the assumption that drives so many such prizes to be 'ecumenical' about who can submit a solution. From agricultural innovation to fostering new types of journalism, there are increasing numbers of prizes, incentives, challenges, and grant dollars being used to attract social solutions from anywhere and anyone.

The permeability of institutional form is also seen in an increasing number of private/private partnerships in which the first is private philanthropy and the second private is commerce. The Bill and Melinda Gates and MacArthur foundations currently partner with private equity and venture capital investors to fund StartL.org, an incubator for digital education businesses. The Mozilla Foundation, a nonprofit that receives much of its earned income from commercial partnerships with search engines, is leading an effort (openbadges.org) to use online badges as certificates of accomplishment in the real world, not just in the games and virtual worlds from which they spring. These badges are meant to be signals of skills and accomplishments, such as diplomas and university degrees have been for centuries, which individuals would earn and use throughout their lives, expanding their skills and their job worthiness.

As in many other sectors, the real impact of technology is being felt at the edge. Although philanthropy advisors are not new, and established advisory services are not leading with technology, technology is drawing in a new form of advisor. The ecosystem of rating and review sites, for example, not only provide standalone data for independent analysis, they serve as a resource to independent advisors. Independent advisors who customize it to meet the interests of their clients often use the indepth research from Givewell.org or similar websites. Family offices, wealth management firms, and private banking advisory firms thrive on these third party data sites.

Peer-to-peer learning is a defining characteristic of the new collaborative economy, and giving circles – although not entirely new – are a prime illustration. While there are no universal statistics on giving circles, these peer groups seem to be one of the most pervasive forms of philanthropy learning (Eikenberry and Breeze, 2015). In less than two years, the Awesome Foundation expanded from ten friends in Massachusetts to more than 40 cities in eight countries (Awesome Foundation, 2012), the growth made possible by the group's native existence on social media sites and the internet.

The change in advisory services and peer-to-peer learning today is similar to the change that took place in philanthropy with the rise of donor advised funds (DAFs) two decades ago. These products, offered by major financial institutions, showed that the 'package' of staff expertise with financial management that foundations offered could be unbundled. Donors quickly created billions of dollars of DAFs and went without staff support. The rise of third party verification databases and recommendation and ratings sites now seems to be breaking apart the advisory side again. Peer networks allow individuals to assess the 'human capital' element of an organization or project – giving them access to trusted friends or colleagues from whom or with whom to assess the people behind an endeavour. The independent rating or legitimacy data from Guidestar provides enough objective data to assess the organization or see it in comparison to potential peers. These two types of information – credible independent data and subjective assessments of people and talent – have always been part of donors' decision-making. Technology is simply separating them into databases and social networks and allowing donors to mix them together as needed.

As data about nonprofits, issues, independent projects, social enterprises, revenue flows, other investors all becomes available, and people can activate or join networks with the phone in their pocket, many of the established sector behaviours start to blur. The issue of current interest – be it climate change, education, art, or activism about internet access – comes to the fore. With one device, individuals can give money, take action, rally support, and compare opportunities. The established lines between nonprofits, individuals and investing shift to the background, and the individual and his or her interest moves forward. Technology is not the only force, or even the primary motivation, for these shifting sector lines, but without it the change would be neither as fast nor as broad.

What new research do we need?

Technology – particularly the global, mobile and digital networks to which two-thirds of the global population is connected – changes not only how we solve problems but also how we define them. In what is likely to be a cycle of disruption and recombination, technology allows us to break down known existing institutions or industries into component parts and then combine them in new ways. Currently, we are at the breakdown stage: the current effect of technological tools on philanthropy has been to drive it toward ever smaller actions – think of text donations, micro-volunteering and gifts of nickels embedded into cash register purchases. Digital technologies have made it ever easier to give smaller and smaller amounts of money or time. Online databases, powerful because they are huge, are largely used to find small discrete bits of information. The big question is whether or not these little bits can be aggregated into big change.

Think of how private donors can now easily provide classroom supplies and field trips to individual classroom teachers. Does this turn their attention away from larger school policy issues? Online platforms make it possible for anyone with $25 to make a loan to entrepreneurs across the planet; does this shift how philanthropy addresses global poverty? These technologies help us break down complex problems into manageable bits and make it very easy for more people to participate.

A second step, however, is for size to become a factor in the power of the network. Making it easy to participate is one step, making the whole add up to more than the sum of its parts is the next step. Most of the research to date has taken our existing frameworks for donor motivation and behaviour, and looked for these online. A new research frame would begin with an understanding of the nature of online networks and see how these instruments are nudging behaviour or shaping attention.

Our technologies make it both possible – and necessary – for disparate projects in different places with different funders to be sorted, categorized, and displayed along common criteria. This, in turn, feeds the desire to be able to compare such programs along shared measures of outcomes, and again, the technology makes such a long sought after dream more possible than ever before. Thus we have commercial and nonprofit funders developing common standards and measures so they can compare and contrast nonprofit and commercial projects by a single set of standards. In the last few years alone, we've seen the launch of the Global Impact Investing Reporting Standards (GIIRS), the development and use of shared reporting standards for international aid (IATI), and the launch of online 'stock' exchanges for widely disparate programs, all of which need to report out against standardized sets of outcomes. What we may be moving toward is a better understanding of what types of money and enterprise are best suited for which kinds of social problem solving.

Finally, massive databases, search engines, mobile phones with cameras, social networks, and an internet on which anyone can write, report, and investigate their surroundings have changed how we share information. Low cost mobile phones with texting and camera capabilities make it easy to imagine tracking your dollars to their final place of use. Early examples of this can be seen in the clean water movement, where organizations that build water wells are using local residents as monitors of those wells: residents snap photos that get uploaded to websites and allow anyone to check in and make sure the well is still functioning. The tie between donor and beneficiary gets closer and a direct feedback loop is now possible. There is great potential for a new discipline of evaluation and design that fully incorporates this kind of feedback.

The new social economy

The more we examine the effects of technology on social good, the more we see that there is something bigger at work here than just the nature of smart phones, tablets, and server farms. What these devices do is store and share data. Every time we interact with them, we create more data; these data, in turn, become useful. These datasets – and the people who know how to build applications on top of them, use them to shape behaviour, feed them back to those who want them– are the links in the chains between the edge innovators and the core institutions. They become the currency of connection and of change.

Anyone who has ever shared a photo taken with their cell phone has changed the data archive of minor (and perhaps, major) news events. Anyone who has ever sent a donation by text message has changed the data landscape of giving. Everyone who signs the typical release form when they visit their doctor may contribute to the tissue database from which a cancer cure is found. Balancing an individual's right to privacy and right to one's private data with the potential public benefit that massive datasets can produce requires us to expand our 'real world' definition of the public sphere and public goods to include the world of online databases, cloud computing, and 'virtual' communities.

Data change how we think about solving shared social challenges. Medical breakthroughs are accelerated by data that are shared across research institutions. Data from emergency rooms and police stations helps homeless shelters better serve their clients. Foster care programs can help children stay in school during family transitions, and foundations are starting to share grant information so they can better align their strategies.

The combination of established institutions, new technologies to manage and mine data, and social change innovators constitutes the most fertile ground for change. It is here we see nonprofits such as the Public Library of Science disrupting scientific research and the universities and publishing houses that support it. It is here we see peer-to-peer market condition monitoring among rural farmers. And it is here that we see the use of Twitter to predict pandemics and mobile phone photography to monitor water wells. Each of these small acts races up the networks that makes them possible and challenges the basic assumptions about how to organize the work.

Conclusion: What new rules do we need?

The new social economy is built around data. How it moves, who owns it, what they can or cannot do with it – the technological rules for these activities – become pertinent faster than the legal rules can keep up. Three primary areas of regulatory concern in the new social economy include: issues of data ownership and transparency; the relationships between the new enterprise forms that data makes possible, including social/commercial hybrid, multinational NGOs and those organizations that 'donate' their data; and public accountability about public subsidized organizations in the new social economy.

Anything that can be digitized can become data. It is not just numbers but also photos, videos, cell phone calls, text messages, Facebook posts, and blog comments. Soon it will be three dimensional objects. Every time we interact with each other digitally, we leave a trail of information behind us that reveals where we were, whom we connected with, how often we looked at something, and what we did with the information we used. Data flows regardless of organizational structure. They allow a type of monitoring from the field – with photos or text messages – that has never before been possible. They allow people to connect with other people – with or without organizational intermediaries – in ways that are truly disruptive.

Nonprofit organizations and philanthropists face these concerns. Even as they push to put more information online, they must worry about security concerns. Some organizations, such as human rights advocates, child serving enterprises, or those that deal with domestic violence have high security needs. For political activists, in many parts of the world, the digital tools that make communication so easy are a real threat, as it makes them (and all of us) easily traceable. Experts from the Tactical Technology Collective, a Berlin-based technology training program for human rights activists, spend lots of time helping individuals and organizations understand and manage their 'digital shadows,' the trail of data we leave behind with every click, text, and call.

Tactical Technology Collective is one example of a new class of nonprofits – technology support organizations – that have developed in the last decade. From TechSoup Global, which has a presence in dozens of countries to local co-ops of 'techies' who work with nonprofits, this is an entire field of expertise and network of organizations born in the last two decades. Fast forward to the current day and we find similar networks of techies working together, through even looser affiliations such as GeeksWithoutBorders, Random Hacks of Kindness, and Campus Party. These individuals are acting on the same do-good impulses, but with all the benefits of 20 years of network building. They build and share free software, put open source tools such as Ushahidi to work, solve problems collectively and in 24 hour globally distributed ways.

These coders and hackers have become a force unto themselves. CrisisCamps built and distributed several no cost software tools during the Haiti earthquake. Networks of volunteers from one event will reassemble weeks or months later for the next opportunity to donate their skills for the benefit of a cause. These individuals, their networks and even their tech firm employers are becoming a vital part of the social economy.

There is another level at which data matters in the social economy. More than just an instrument of change, some datasets are also public goods. Consider all of the data collected over the years by government agencies – anonymous, massive datasets on our collective health, wealth, education, demographic makeup, and so on. Public access to these public datasets is driving major policy changes and major public technology investments. The current legal structures that define charitable activities or that privilege certain public goods with tax exemptions say nothing about data. They say nothing about any public good created digitally, such as open source software used for emergency response. They also say nothing about access to these resources. The old codes that regulate privately funded public goods – the rules that guide the social sector – will need to change.

What are the guiding principles, in the nonmarket, non-governmental space, for how these data are owned, used, and shared? Who needs to report out on what information? These questions cut into issues of ownership, transparency, and accountability. They are currently mediated by policies in the realm of telecommunications, intellectual property, privacy, and corporate governance. A new frame for how we want these resources made available for shared social good, while protecting the rights (and safety) of individuals, is needed. Balancing personal privacy with the public good that can be generated from aggregated information will be a defining legal and social question in the next decades.

449

References

Akinboro, B. (2014) Bringing mobile wallets for Nigerian farmers, Consultative Group to Assist the Poor. www.cgap.org/blog/bringing-mobile-wallets-nigerian-farmers [Accessed 31 May 2015].

Awesome Foundation. (2012) Home. www.awesomefoundation.org/ [Accessed 15 June 2014].

Benkler, Y. (2006) *The wealth of networks: How social production transforms markets and freedom.* New Haven, CT: Yale University Press.

Bolduc, K. (2013) Lessons from a risk taken. Center for Effective Philanthropy, 25 April. www.effectivephilanthropy.org/lessons-from-a-risk-taken/ [Accessed 20 May 2015].

Brock, A., Buteau, E. and Gopal, R. (2013) *Foundation transparency: What nonprofits want.* Cambridge, MA: Center for Effective Philanthropy.

Bryen, L. and Madden, K. (2006) Bounce-back of episodic volunteers: What makes episodic volunteers return. Working Paper CPNS 32. Brisbane: Queensland University of Technology.

Camarena, J. (2011) Advancing transparency in philanthropy, *Responsive Philanthropy*, Spring. www.ncrp.org/files/rp-articles/Responsive_Philanthropy_Spring2011-AdvancingTransparency.pdf [Accessed 26 May 2015].

Corporation for National and Community Service. (2006) *Issue brief: Volunteer growth – A review of trends since 1974.* www.nationalservice.gov/pdf/06_1203_volunteer_growth_factsheet.pdf [Accessed 20 June 2012].

Eikenberry, A. M. and Breeze, B. (2015) Growing philanthropy through collaboration: The landscape of giving circles in the United Kingdom and Ireland, *Voluntary Sector Forum*, 6(1): 41–59.

GuideStar. (No Date) *Money for good II.* www.multivu.com/players/English/52621-guidestar-and-hope-consulting-money-for-good-II/ [Accessed 16 June 2014].

Kliff, S. and Alzenman, N. C. (2012) Komen foundation revises funding policy, *Washington Post*, 3 February. www.washingtonpost.com/business/economy/komen-revises-funding-policy/2012/02/03/gIQAVRa3mQ_story.html [Accessed 29 May 2015].

Lahkani, K. and Panetta, J. (2007) Principles of distributed innovation, *Innovations: Technology, Governance, Globalization*, 2(3): 97–112.

Lomax, P. and Wharton, R. (2014) *10 innovations in global philanthropy.* London, UK: NPC. www.thinknpc.org/publications/10-innovations/ [Accessed 27 May 2015].

McCort, K. (2015) Open policies unlock our full potential, *Vancouver Foundation*, 6 May. www.vancouverfoundation.ca/whats-new/open-policies-unlock-our-full-potential [Accessed 26 May 2015].

McKinsey & Company. (2009) *And the winner is…. Capturing the promise of philanthropic prizes.* New York, NY: McKinsey & Co. www.mckinseyonsociety.com/capturing-the-promise-of-philanthropic-prizes/ [Accessed 20 June 2014].

Meeker, M. (2012) Internet Trends: D10 Conference, *All Things D*, May 30. www.allthingsd.com/20120530/mary-meekers-internet-trends-live-at-d10-slides/ [Accessed 21 June 2014].

National Council of Voluntary Organisations (NCVO). (2011) *Third sector foresight: Trends in volunteering.* www.ncvoforesight.org/drivers/trends-in-volunteering [Accessed 18 June 2014].

Nonprofit Technology Network. (2010) 2010 nonprofit social networking benchmarks report, *Nonprofit Technology Network*. www.nten.org/blog/2010/04/20/2010-nonprofit-social-network-benchmark-report [Accessed 25 June 2014].

Open Society Foundations. (2014) *Mapping Digital Media Project.* New York, NY: Open Society. www.opensocietyfoundations.org/sites/default/files/mapping-digital-media-overviews-20140828.pdf [Accessed 10 January 2015].

Ottenhoff, B. and Ulrich, G. (2010) *Money for good.* San Francisco: Hope Consulting. www.hopeconsulting.us/work/money-for-good. [Accessed 16 June 2014].

Rainie, L. and Wellman, B. (2012) *Networked: The new social operating system.* Cambridge, MA: MIT Press.

Reuters. (2015) Remitly raises $12.5 million to transform the way people send money globally. www.reuters.com/article/2015/03/19/idUSnMKWb3KwRa+1ca+MKW20150319 [Accessed 1 June 2015].

Rogers, K. (2010) Haiti donations, *The Nonprofit Times*, 1 April. www.thenonprofittimes.com/article/detail/haiti-donations-2519 [Accessed 20 April 2013].

Schneider, S. (2013) The power of the crowd, *Alliance*, 18(1): 24–5.

Simpson, R. (2014) *Mobile payments and consumer protection.* London, UK: Consumers International. www.consumersinternational.org/media/1439190/ci_mobilepaymentsbriefing_jan14_final.pdf [Accessed 1 June 2015].

Smith, A. (2012) Haiti text donors and their experiences giving to earthquake relief, Pew Research Center, 12 January. www.pewinternet.org/2012/01/12/haiti-text-donors-and-their-experiences-giving-to-earthquake-relief/ [Accessed 28 May 2015].

——., Anderson, J. and Rainie. L. (2012) The future of money in a mobile age, Pew Research Center. www.pewinternet.org/2012/04/17/the-future-of-money-in-a-mobile-age/ [Accessed 20 May 2015].

Smith, B. (2010) Philanthropy's digital divide, *Philanthropy News Digest*, 3 May. pn www.dblog.typepad.com/pndblog/2010/05/philanthropys-digital-divide.html [Accessed 27 May 2015].

Wasserman, S. (2012) The Amazon effect, *The Nation*, 18 June. www.thenation.com/article/168125/amazon-effect [Accessed 20 June 2014].

29

Building the market for impact

Tessa Hebb with Sean MacKinnon

The past decade has seen the emergence of new trends in strategic philanthropy. While traditionally a separation between the investment arm of a philanthropic organization – in charge of ensuring retention and growth of endowed capital – and its grantmaking activities – responsible for delivering organizational objectives and mission – was commonplace, strategic philanthropy tries to align all aspects of a philanthropic organization with its mission. Increasingly, constrained resources have played a central role in this development: particularly in the period following the 2008 financial crisis, philanthropic organizations began to ask why they should only concern themselves with the distribution of five percent of their resources, while the remaining 95 percent is invested without regard to mission (Godeke and Bauer, 2008). This simple question sparked philanthropic organizations to think more critically about the strategic use of all resources under their control in order to achieve their goals. As a result, many philanthropic organizations are no longer content to simply give grants to worthwhile causes: they want to utilize all their assets in alignment with their missions. Equally, they want to ensure that the outcomes generated from these approaches are meaningful and measurable. Such a shift replaces a grantmaking mentality with a new investment-driven paradigm.

Many terms have been used to capture the ideas inherent when assets are invested to achieve both positive financial returns and ancillary benefits. These terms include double and triple bottom line, mission-related investing, program-related investment, blended-value, impact investing, and social finance to name just a few (Emerson, 2003; Godeke and Bauer, 2008; Monitor Institute, 2009). Regardless of terminology, this new approach is seen as an important step in generating innovative ways to address social needs. For simplicity, we will use the term 'impact investing' in this chapter to describe the 'active investment of capital in businesses and funds that generate positive social and/or environmental impacts, as well as financial returns (from principal to above market rate) to the investor' (Monitor Institute, 2009).

The impact investment philosophy can unlock substantial capital to build a more sustainable and equitable global economy while also allowing for sound investment practices including diversification across geographies and asset classes (Bridges Ventures and The Parthenon Group, 2010). In fact, large financial institutions, such as J. P. Morgan (O'Donohoe et al., 2010), suggest that impact investing is a new and emerging asset class in, and of, itself with global investment opportunities of up to $1 trillion over the next ten years. A recent report *Accelerating*

Impact (E.T. Jackson and Associates, 2012) suggests that in 2011 alone, $4.4 billion of impact investments were made.

Impact investing has deep implications for the sector, both for philanthropic organizations and for recipients of these investments. The investment paradigm fundamentally alters the relationship between the two (Thümler, Chapter 23). For foundations, this model focuses their attention on the impact that results from their investment in the organization. Does the impact advance the goals of the foundation? Is it the best use of resources to achieve the aims of the foundation? Such questions lead to new approaches in grantmaking. For grantees, there is an equally fundamental shift brought about by these innovations. Rather than seeing themselves as defined solely by the good works they undertake, and in turn seeking others prepared to support their mission, recipient organizations begin to see their economic, social and environmental impacts as assets. They ask 'who else values these results?'.

Indeed, advocates of this approach suggest it has the ability to unlock entrepreneurial value creation across the sector, a key aspect of innovation (Bugg-Levine, 2013). Porter and Kramer (2011) go as far as to suggest that such models provide a new framework for capitalism, one based on shared value that includes social and environmental returns on investment in addition to financial returns.

In contrast, critics of this approach to philanthropy argue that there is a profound difference between using business-like techniques and becoming businesses (Edwards, 2010). They argue that one of the primary roles of civil society is to challenge the status quo. This stands in sharp contrast to the role of financial markets that protect, and in many cases profit, from our current social system. This deep divide separates those willing to exploit financial markets for the potential good they can deliver, and those who seek a more profound change in the unequal distribution financial markets create.

This chapter provides a critical assessment of the emerging methods and trends in impact investing by philanthropic organizations. Looking to the US, the UK, and Canada, it reviews the growing diversity of financial instruments and intermediaries available to philanthropic organizations, and their implications for the sector. These new instruments require appropriate regulatory frameworks if they are to grow and flourish. As such, the chapter looks at enabling policy environments across these three jurisdictions and traces the impact such environments have on financial innovation in the philanthropic sector. Conversely, outdated and outmoded regulation can create barriers to the growth of social finance. These are also explored, alongside other barriers to adoption of impact investing. The chapter concludes with reflections on the implications of impact investment for philanthropy.

Forms of impact investing

The conceptual framework that underpins impact investing is best captured by the 'Blended Value Proposition', first articulated by Jed Emerson in the early 2000s. This states

> that all organizations, whether for-profit or not, create value that consists of economic, social and environmental value components – and that investors (whether market-rate, charitable or some mix of the two) simultaneously generate all three forms of value through providing capital to organizations.
>
> *(Emerson, 2003)*

Understanding the concept of blended value is key to understanding the implications of impact investing for both the providers of capital and its recipients. Philanthropic organizations increasingly look for the blended value impact of their investment, whether it is a grant, loan, or equity position in the organization with no financial return, below-market financial return or market-rate financial return. As part of that, two overarching perspectives can be identified: 'impact first' and 'finance first'.

Those who seek social and environmental impact above financial return are called 'impact first investors (Monitor Institute, 2009). These are prepared to take lower returns on their capital in order to achieve the social and environmental impacts they seek. Such investors are generally found in the philanthropic sector. With a grant, for example, the donor seeks 100 percent social and/or environmental return with no financial return required. Despite the fact that there is no financial return, the blended value proposition argues that grants are an investment in the organization. Philanthropic organizations seek measurable outcomes that result from these investments, just as they do for any other financial instrument in the impact investing continuum, which is discussed later on. The shift toward 'investing' rather than 'giving' is key to understanding newly emerging trends in strategic philanthropy.

In contrast, a 'finance first' impact investor (Monitor Institute, 2009) is seeking a market rate risk-adjusted return on investment and is willing to take less social and environmental return to achieve this financial outcome. Often, the endowed capital of a philanthropic organization with a mandate to ensure the principal for perpetuity will seek 'finance first' impact investments with some positive social and environmental outcomes, but a greater emphasis on financial return. There is still an intentional investment of capital to achieve a positive social or environmental outcome, but the investment itself is more in tune with traditional investment approaches; financial return is not sacrificed to achieve this purpose, but rather an ancillary benefit is generated by the investment. A good example here is investment in market-rate mortgages that enable affordable housing projects to be built, or investment in clean technology firms that encourage a shift to renewable energy sources while providing a market rate of return to the investor. The investment is first judged on its financial return and appropriate asset class. Only when these are deemed acceptable is the additional social and/or environmental outcome factored into the investment selection (Hagerman and Hebb, 2009). This is illustrated in Figure 29.1.

As demonstrated above, impact investing by philanthropic organizations takes many forms. In some jurisdictions, monies can be leveraged from the grantmaking side of foundations in

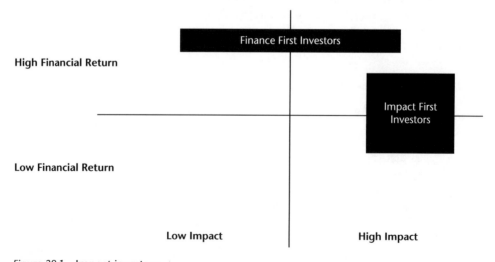

Figure 29.1 Impact investors

Source: Adapted from Monitor Institute (2009)

order to make investments in agencies, rather than simply offering them grants. This practice, common in the US and the UK, is known as Program Related Investment (PRI) and is recognized by both the US Government Internal Revenue Service and the UK Charity Commission of England and Wales.

In most philanthropic organizations, we find a firewall between the grantmaking and investing arms of the organization. Traditionally, within the US, the grantmaking arms of philanthropic organizations annually distribute roughly five percent of the capital in accordance with their missions, while investment committees have seen their role simply to preserve and grow endowed capital without regard to where or how this capital is invested, in order to ensure the viability of the organization in perpetuity. But notions of strategic philanthropy are breaking down the wall between the grantmaking arm and the investment arm of the organization. There is an increased awareness that both market-rate financial return and impact can be achieved when investment is deliberately targeted to mission.

The resulting continuum of financial instruments used by both 'impact first and 'finance first' impact investors is outlined in Figure 29.2. Impact first investors tend to use the investment tools and instruments found on the left hand side of the continuum. They seek blended value investments at below market rates that range from grants to organizations that deliver no financial returns and 100 percent social and or environmental returns, to below-market loans and equity positions that provide capital at a reduced rate to organizations while delivering some financial return back to the philanthropic organization. In these cases, the financial returns are below the amount the impact investor could have received with a comparable investment in traditional financial markets. These below-market financial tools are often used to make Program Related Investments, discussed later in this chapter. By establishing revolving funds that pay back at least the principal amount of the investment over time, these monies can be reinvested in new organizations, thus increasing their potential impact. In a period of scarce philanthropic resources, such instruments have proven effective in achieving this goal (Godeke and Bauer, 2012).

Below-market investments include loans, capped equity and quasi-equity investments that look for much lower financial returns with longer time horizons than those usually dictated by the market. In addition to these below-market instruments, philanthropic organizations can provide guarantees that enable investees to access a loan with a third party lender at acceptable rates. Often, these types of loans (particularly if the organization does not have collateral to back up the loan) would not be made with the backing of the philanthropic organization who agrees to pay back the principal if the organization fails to meet its obligations.

Below-market investments are often used to leverage additional investment in an organization. For example, the investee can use this below-market capital or guarantee to provide a first-loss guarantee that brings in additional market-rate investment. Anthony Bugg-Levine (2013), who helped pioneer impact investing through the work of the Rockefeller Foundation (2006–2011), has termed this multi-pronged approach 'complete capital', layering grants, below-market and market rate investment, social capital, and intellectual capital in order to achieve scale in addressing today's intractable problems.

In contrast, the right side of Figure 29.2 is dominated by financial instruments used by 'finance first' impact investors. These investors tend to represent the investment arm of philanthropic organizations that carry the responsibility to invest the endowed capital in a manner that maintains and enhances the funds over time. Such investors have a trust relationship or fiduciary duty to the funds and are not able or willing to sacrifice financial returns for social and/or environmental impacts. For most philanthropic organizations, the endowed capital represents the bulk of their resources, yet for many, these assets are invested without regard to the mission of the organization. With the realization that all the resources of the philanthropic organization

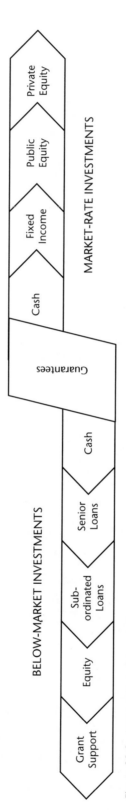

Figure 29.2 Impact investing continuum

Based on: F.B. Heron Foundation, www.heron.org

can be put to use effectively if investors deliberately seek market-rate investments that in addition to financial returns also generate positive social and or environmental returns, this has begun to change.

Examples of 'finance first' investing include cash deposits in community-based financial institutions (known as community development financial institutions in the US and UK and often associated with local community credit unions), investment in micro-finance institutions, and market-rate mortgages for affordable housing or building purchases by organizations. Often providing working capital or bridge financing for organizations comes with market-rate returns. Market-rate equity investment can be made through private equity or infrastructure investment and can include large investment opportunities such as enhanced transportation, sewage and water systems, as well as small investments such as those in social purpose businesses.

What is evident from the diagram above is that in order to make such investments, there must be a suite of financial instruments, an enabling regulatory regime, and a set of financial intermediaries with expertise in this particular market who facilitate the exchange of capital between the suppliers (philanthropic organizations) and the demand for that capital (third sector organizations). These three topics will be explored later in this chapter.

The impact investing marketplace: The US, UK and Canadian experience

Despite the lofty proclamations on the potential for this market, let us briefly examine the state of impact investing across each of the US, UK, and Canada.

The US impact investing environment

Impact investing in its various forms is further advanced in the US than in other countries. It has the benefit of over 40 years of experience to draw on. What is unique in this setting is that enabling public policy regimes have been used to unlock the potential of the large philanthropic assets that underpin the US sector, with only small amounts of government direct investment required. Recent estimates of the potential market size in the US for impact investing are as high as $120 billion (Hope Consulting, 2010).

While the bulk of impact investing in the US comes from private capital primarily driven by philanthropic investors, the US government has played a major role in encouraging targeted investment in communities through a framework of US government regulation combined with tax incentives that have been instrumental in leveraging private capital for community investment. Three key policy areas helped establish impact investing in the US: program-related investment (PRIs), the Community Reinvestment Act (CRA), and a network of Community Development Financial Institutions (CDFIs). We will look at each of these in turn.

Program Related Investments (PRIs) have long been encouraged in the US. The first PRIs were made as far back as 1969. Under an Internal Revenue Service ruling, US foundations and other philanthropic organizations are able to use part of their mandatory annual grant distribution to provide loans and other financial instruments to their grantees. The US PRIs are generally at below-market rates, but require the principal to be repaid. Such funds are then held in a separate account and used for subsequent PRIs. This tool enables philanthropic foundations to leverage their grantmaking dollars through a revolving fund structure that does not violate the principle that the grantor not gain a direct benefit from the grant. A 2007 report *Compounding Impact* (Cooch and Kramer, 2007) surveyed 92 philanthropic organizations and found that they had made $2.3 billion of impact investments over the past 40 years, with the bulk of that growth from 2002 on. PRIs have been able to amplify US philanthropic organizations' impact over time, they also helped changed the grantmaker and grantee relationship.

Equally important, CRA, established in 1977, requires US banks to invest in local community development. Prior to that time, it had been found that banks were engaged in 'red lining' certain low income areas in their region (a practice of refusing loans). As a result, the CRA required banks to make capital accessible in these neighbourhoods and publish reports on their loan portfolios. Banks in the US may satisfy this requirement either through direct investment in low-middle-income (LMI) communities or through investment in Community Development Finance Institutions and/or local credit unions with expertise in this arena. Significant investment in community finance has been generated as a direct result of the CRA and strengthened CDFIs across America.

The third element to the robust impact investing environment in the US is the development of CDFIs. First established by the US Department of Treasury in 1994, US CDFIs have leveraged approximately $1.2 billion of government funding in the CDFI Fund into $25 billion of investment at the community level. The US government also provides a variety of tax incentives such as the Low Income Housing Tax Credit and the New Market Tax Credit that support targeted impact investments and are often administered by CDFIs.

Building on this framework, the Rockefeller Foundation has been instrumental in encouraging impact investing, both in the US and internationally, through a multiyear, multimillion dollar initiative that helped generate a considerable depth for the impact investing market in that country. This includes support of numerous research initiatives including the 2009 Monitor Institute report, *Investing for Social and Environmental Impact*, referred to throughout this chapter. The Rockefeller Foundation also spawned the Global Impact Investing Network (GIIN), the Impact Reporting and Investment Standards (IRIS), and the Global Impact Investing Rating System (GIIRS). GIIN provides an internationally recognized platform to encourage impact investing from private sources around the world. Current membership stands at 80 plus with a range of philanthropic, private, and governmental investors interested in scalable, efficient investments designed to generate both financial and positive social and/or environmental impact. A major GIIN initiative is IRIS, a common framework for reporting the performance of impact investments. The lack of such a framework is often cited as one of the major barriers to the growth of impact investing. GIIRS is a rating system that utilizes the IRIS taxonomy to develop an external rating among impact investment opportunities. It functions as other standard rating systems, but utilizes social and environmental performance data, rather than financial. All three components are seen as key aspects of the infrastructure needed to develop this market.

The UK impact investing market

The UK has seen considerable advances in impact investing in the last ten years. This has been achieved through coordinated efforts between the UK Government, philanthropic organizations, and the third sector itself, in the development of a social finance and impact investing marketplace. However, with less of a track record in impact investing than we find in the US, and a smaller market including a smaller philanthropic sector, the UK government has had to put considerably more resources directly into this sector, in addition to a framework of enabling public policy in order to seed its growth and development.

Beginning in 2000, the UK government established a number of intermediaries, support systems and tax structures that encourage social finance. Building on the successful US model of Community Development Financial Institutions (CDFIs) detailed above, the UK government established CDFIs, created Community Investment Tax Relief (CITR) that provides a 25 percent tax credit (a similar structure to the US New Market Tax Credit), and a support system for these funds through the Community Development Funds Association. Much of this activity was galvanized through the Office of the Third Sector, a government department established in 2006 and renamed the Office for Civil Society in 2010.

The report *Social Investment Ten Years On* (Social Investment Task Force, 2010) describes the advances made over the decade in the UK, including the development of new intermediaries such as the UK Charity Bank specializing in loans for the third sector organizations, Bridges Ventures Fund for equity investments and the Triodos Social Enterprise Fund. In recent years, the UK has pioneered new impact investing instruments, including the social impact bond, explored in detail later in the chapter.

At the forefront of developments within the UK have been new regulatory innovations such as the Community Interest Company, a hybrid legal structure to enable investment in social enterprise, and also Big Society Capital, a social investment bank drawing on UK unclaimed bank deposits, 'a private sector body with a 'locked-in' social mission' (Pharoah, 2012: 94). These innovations have relied on government regulation to establish an enabling environment for impact investing in the UK.

Increasingly, UK charities and foundations are being encouraged to use impact investing strategies, including guidance from the England and Wales Charity Commission that outlines the legal framework of such approaches, as well as from consultancies and think tanks, such as New Philanthropy Capital (NPC). They provide extensive publications to assist charities on how to make social investments in the UK, further encouraging the 'investment' approach to philanthropy. Organizations such as the UK Social Investment Task Force, Philanthropy/UK and New Philanthropy Capital have helped further advance social finance and impact investing in the UK, with a recent report by the City of London (2013) estimating the UK's social investment market to be around £202 million in 2011/12.

The growing impact investing market in the UK is as a direct result of an enabling policy environment that encourages government, third sector, and philanthropic organizations to work together to build innovative investment infrastructure to address community needs. However, this approach has required significant government investment to become a sustainable marketplace.

The Canadian impact investing marketplace

In Canada, impact investing has been slower to materialize (Malhotra *et al.*, 2010; Jagelewski, 2011). In fact, the Canadian Task Force on Social Finance (2010) estimated that impact investments could yield as much as $30 billion for investment in social enterprises and more sustainable community organizations. Yet there has been a shortage of funding for social enterprises (Canadian Task Force on Social Finance, 2010; Malhotra *et al.*, 2010). Recent estimations of impact investing in Canada placed them in the region of $5 billion (Bragg, 2010), but there are indications that major changes are taking place (MaRS, 2014; Critchley, 2015).

One of the barriers to growth of impact investing in Canada has been the regulatory regime which, unlike the UK and US, has not tended to encourage impact investing. Program Related Investments made from philanthropic organizations' grantmaking arm were only made permissible in 2012. As a result, key components of this market have been slow to develop. Furthermore, tax-credit incentives for impact investing in Canada have been limited, most having been developed by provincial governments. The federal Canadian Government has invested directly in a series of Community Futures Development Corporations across Canada. While these structures have proven successful, they are only mandated to operate in rural settings. This leaves the urban centres in Canada with a patchwork of individual investment intermediaries operating at local community scale.

One of the few exceptions is the Fiducie du Chantier de l'économie sociale based in the Canadian province of Quebec. This fund initially received seed funding of roughly $30 million from the federal government in 2006 to develop a patient capital fund to meet the need for long-term investment by collective enterprises. Another large impact investor in Canada is Vancity Savings Credit Union based in British Columbia. With $16 billion of assets under management, their objective is to manage the funds in such a way that they return social, environmental and economic benefits to local communities. There is an option for the investor to receive either market interest rate or lower on their deposits. Additionally, Vancity has developed an equity investment fund, Resilient Capital, to provide impact investment opportunities.

However without strong government enabling policies and programs, the impact investing market in Canada remains small and underdeveloped.

Building the market for impact: Instruments, regulation and intermediaries

Three components are required if impact investing is to reach its full potential: a suite of instruments that enable the flow of capital into these investment opportunities, regulation and policy regimes that encourage the development of this market, and intermediaries with the necessary knowledge to facilitate investments that achieve the stated goals of impact first and finance first investors. We will examine each of these in turn.

Instruments

Key to building a successful impact investing marketplace is a suite of financial instruments by which to conduct the exchange of capital from supply to demand. Increasingly, we are seeing new social finance instruments that enable this capital flow. New instruments range from social impact bonds to new online trading platforms that encourage private capital to flow into civil society organizations.

In general, the social financing tools available to nonprofits are either equity or debt instruments (Brodhead, 2010; Handford, 2005; Kingston and Bolton, 2006; Wuttunee et al., 2008). Equity or the ownership interest of shareholders in business is one of the best instruments to deal with the start-up financing problem (Handford, 2005). To start a new business, for-profit organizations generally use equity to access working capital for their business (Kingston and Bolton, 2006). However, 'lack of access to equity finance is perceived by many in the social enterprise sector as a key barrier to growth and development' (Bank of England, 2003). Recently, there are examples of a few nonprofits that have been experimenting with various type of equity as a source of their finance (Strandberg, 2010).

Sometimes using equity structures can be controversial due to the potential conflict between shareholder interests, which are financial, and the social objectives of the nonprofit enterprise (Handford, 2005). Additionally, equity investors may want to be involved in the management of the business (Wuttunee et al., 2008) which may have the potential to dilute the social objectives.

Debt financing through loans and guarantees are another option available to philanthropic impact investors. Traditionally, nonprofits were unable to access the debt through mortgages, equipment loans, and lines of credit, due to lack of collateral (Phillips and Hebb, 2010). To solve collateral problems, many nonprofits have developed new innovative financial tools to access capital through debt financing (Kingston and Bolton, 2006; Mendell and Nogales, 2008). Many seek out new lending organizations or issue community bonds in order to access debt capital.

For example, Carrot Cache, a small local community economic development fund in Canada, provides loans to nonprofits by accepting multiple guarantors who pledged to support the loans if they go into arrears (Socialfinance.ca, 2011). Philanthropic organizations in Britain have been utilizing this approach for several years (UK Office of the Third Sector, 2010). An example of such UK practice is the Peabody Trust which deposited £500,000 with the Charity Bank who then lends these funds to nonprofits (Kingston and Bolton, 2006).

Community bonds are another example of innovative new financial instruments. Community bonds are securities issued by nonprofit organizations to raise debt-financing (Mendell and Nogales, 2011). These are binding commitments to pay the investor a set rate of interest over the life of the bond and to return their capital at the end of the term. One of the best known examples of community bonds is Calvert Community Investment Note offered in the US, which has leveraged $200M in assets over a 15-year-period (Calvert Foundation, 2012). Community Bonds can be very good sources for nonprofits to scale up their activities because they have deep relationships with their communities and constituencies. In Canada, The Center for Social Innovation (CSI) was able to raise $6.5 million to purchase real estate by issuing a five-year, four percent mortgage backed community bond (Mendell and Nogales, 2011).

Social Impact Bonds (SIBs) are another new innovative instrument in the impact investing toolbox. First developed in the UK, these are a form of 'pay for performance' that allow non-profits to be rewarded by government for success in achieving clearly identified goals. In turn, the nonprofit can monetize this reward through the sale of bonds to investors (usually philan-thropic organizations) who are paid when these milestones are achieved. First used in the UK, this model has seen international uptakes and is now used globally, including in the US, Australia and Canada (Clifford and Jung, 2016).

Regulatory frameworks: UK, US and Canada

Creating effective financial instruments requires enabling government policies and regulations that encourage this activity. As detailed above, both the US and UK have implemented a number of government programs designed to develop and strengthen impact investing. This approach has resulted in both countries having robust impact markets. In contrast, only in the past few years have we seen regulatory changes in Canada designed to stimulate this market.

Program Related Investments established by IRS ruling in 1969 first encouraged such investing in the US. As a result, new instruments, intermediaries and metrics have been able to take hold, primarily funded through the large US philanthropic sector. In addition to enabling government programs and incentives, the US draws on a number of self-regulatory bodies to develop this market. Notable is the Global Impact Investing Network (GIIN) with its approach to standard-ization of impact measurement by its members as key for a mature market. Additionally, the Mission Investors Exchange, a self-regulating network that includes the PRI Makers and More for Mission with over 200 US foundations and impact investing organizations. In addition, we find a number of self-regulating organizations within the large Community Development Finance Institutions' community.

In the UK, Programme Related Investments have also been encouraged by the UK govern-ment. Enabling legislation has been promoted by government through publications such as the Charity Commission's 2003 report *The Magic Roundabout*. The UK looked to the US sector as a public policy model and encouraged not just PRIs, but also direct investment in equity and loan funds designed to invest in positive community impact. While the enabling policies are similar between the two countries, the UK government has played a much more direct role than we find in the US in financing the sector through patient capital funds in order to achieve scale sufficient to attract private capital. As a result, impact investing in the UK is much more dependent on government interventions in the market than we find in the US.

The UK government went a step further than the US by creating the Office of the Third Sector beginning in 2006 through to 2010. Additionally, they developed the aforementioned Community Interest Company, a hybrid legal structure that enables the flow of capital more readily to social enterprise as many nonprofit organizations require new legal structures in order to offer shares in their organizations. This structure has been adapted to the US at the state level with the Limited Liability Company (L3c), but currently there is no comparable national legislation in the US. In 2012, the Canadian province of British Columbia announced plans to develop a new hybrid legal structure, the 'community contribution company', which combines socially beneficial purposes with a restricted ability to distribute profit to shareholders. This marked the first hybrid legal structure of this kind in Canada.

In general, the regulatory frameworks have been slow to develop in Canada. Traditionally, Canadians have depended on the government and community organizations to provide social services while private organizations, capital markets and the business sector have been the typical sources for financial returns (Phillips and Hebb, 2010; Mendell and Nogales, 2011). Governmental support has been lagging and has failed to develop frameworks to encourage more mainstream acceptance of impact investing (Phillips et al., 2010). Legislative barriers have hindered progress in the impact investment field with the structure of Canada's investment industry roughly divided: philanthropy on one end of the financing spectrum and profit-maximization at the other (Harji, 2009; Venture Deli, 2012). Canada's existing legislative, tax, legal and regulatory frameworks have been developed over generations in support of the traditional bifurcated philanthropic system which has raised the difficulty of establishing impact investing mechanisms in Canada (Social Finance Task Force, 2010).

Intermediaries

Financial intermediaries are essential to the advancement of the impact investment marketplace; they match available financial products to the specific needs of investors. Intermediaries require a certain sophistication to identify potential partners and structure creative deals that blend the various risk/reward expectations of different investors in a relatively seamless manner (Harji, 2009). Without intermediaries, impact investors are not able to calibrate risk and opportunity adequately, therefore, limiting the amount of available capital (Harji and Hebb, 2010; Hope Consulting, 2010). Conversely, social ventures are in need of capital and the lack of intermediaries acts as a barrier to growth (Malhotra et al., 2010).

Because of its longer history in the US, impact investing intermediaries have been able to grow in step with market demand. It is striking in the US context that while government provides an enabling policy environment through tax codes, tax credits and other incentives, it leaves the aggregation of capital to market forces. Intermediaries with specialized expertise in the market develop in tandem with both supply and demand of capital. All three are required in order for the market to grow and flourish. The US, with its large philanthropic sector and equally large community sector, has been able to support the growth of intermediaries to enable the adequate flow of capital between them.

We find a wide range of intermediaries such as community credit unions, CDFIs and large institutional investors like the pension fund TIAA-CREF that offers investors a community investment option and currently has a portfolio of $600 million in impact investments. We also find US-based intermediaries providing both loans and equity investments. The Community Development Venture Capital Association represents dozens of private equity impact investment funds across the US with over $2 billion of assets invested. While all of these intermediaries utilize government incentives, such as the Low Income Tax Credit or New Markets Tax Credit, they aggregate private capital for public good.

US intermediaries include the Calvert Foundation, with current investments of over $200 million dollars in communities throughout the US and around the world. Funded by philanthropic organizations, individuals and other institutional investors since 1988, this intermediary offers a range of investment notes at market and below market rates of return and in turn invests this money for high impact in communities.

In the UK, intermediaries have primarily relied on government funding in their early stages of growth. Bridges CDV fund launched in 2002 with £40 million is a case in point. The UK government's matching funds enabled this fund to start with a degree of scale it may have otherwise lacked. Similarly, the Futurebuilders Fund for the Third Sector was launched in 2004 with £125 million funded by the government. By 2006, the UK market was beginning to mature and the £75 million Bridges CDV Fund II was successfully launched without government-directed funding, as was the Triodos Opportunities Fund. By 2008, UK-based CDIFs' total investments had risen to £472 million. However, several intermediaries focused on investment in social enterprise still require direct government investment in order to become sustainable. Social enterprise, with its small scale and extensive due diligence, results in small payoffs that are not normally attractive to large investors, including many in the philanthropic sector.

In contrast to both the UK and US, the lack of intermediation in Canada has been at the forefront of the challenges facing the impact investment market (Emerson and Bonini, 2003; Ayton and Sarver, 2006; Jagelewski, 2011). The supply of capital does not always correspond to the needs of the enterprises and there has been significant misalignment between the demand and supply sides of social finance (Mendell and Nogales, 2008; Harji and Hebb, 2010). The sector continues to be undercapitalized relative to the needs and pressures placed on it (Harji, 2009) and can be described as an uncoordinated marketplace (Monitor Report, 2009).

Given the relatively small market in Canada, it is difficult for intermediaries to develop without a coordinated approach that includes ready investors, government incentives and a pipeline of available investment ready opportunities in the marketplace. To date, the Canadian government has not taken as active an approach to this market as we have seen in the US with its incentive systems, and the UK with its direct government involvement. In 2010, the Canadian Task Force on Social Finance Report made seven recommendations to facilitate this coordination. Several recommendations called on government action to clarify the rules surrounding impact investments, provide tax credit incentives for investors in the sector, and like the UK, to directly invest in patient capital impact investing funds in Canada. The task force also called on the philanthropic sector, recommending at least ten percent of all foundation assets be allocated to impact investments by 2020. Several Canadian philanthropic organizations have now made this recommendation to their members (Martin, 2012).

As detailed earlier in this chapter, some Canadian intermediaries have emerged in the past five years, most notably the Fiducie du Chantier de l'économie sociale, which benefited from an initial investment from government that has enabled the fund to leverage private dollars. The Chantier offers patient capital with a 15-year moratorium on repayment of the principal. Investments range from $50,000 to $1.5 million, not exceeding 35 percent of the project's cost. Because of the 15-year moratorium on repayment of principal, patient capital offered by the Fiducie can be leveraged to obtain more financing (Mendell and Nogales, 2011). Investors in this fund, which include many large Canadian institutional investors, receive a debenture with an eight percent annual return and a 15-year pay back on the principal. During these recent financially turbulent times, this financial intermediary has been a solid performer.

Following the release of the Task Force on Social Finance in Canada, several new intermediaries developed in Canada, signaling the growing interest and awareness in impact investing
in this county. These include the Cape Fund dedicated to investing in Canada's First Nations
businesses, the Royal Bank of Canada's Impact Investing Fund, Vancity's Resilient Capital
Fund and the Community Forward Fund. All are new intermediaries, seeded with private
dollars dedicated to impact investing in Canada. While several are underpinned by investment
from philanthropic organizations, all have developed in an uncoordinated manner with limited
government involvement.

The dearth of intermediaries in Canada has been attributed to the relatively new existence of
an impact investment marketplace and the smaller scale of deal making opportunities; economic
incentives for intermediaries have not been sufficient to attract new intermediaries to the sector
(Emerson and Spitzer, 2007). The level and scale of the impact investment market may be too
small and ad hoc in Canada resulting in reduced interest from large scale investors without a
more coordinated approach from all levels of government who see the benefit to communities
that is generated from impact investment.

Impact investing: Can it deliver on its promise?

Impact investing provides much needed capital to assist in addressing some of the world's most
pressing problems. Proponents suggest that governments around the world no longer have
the required resources to fully address these problems, but by unleashing the power of private
capital, seeking scale in solutions to social problems, and using innovative financial tools new
approaches can achieve the desired results and, in some cases, not only generate positive social
and environmental returns, but also financial returns. This is a persuasive logic and it is little
wonder that many governments around the world are encouraging, incentivizing and in some
cases directly investing in the impact investment market.

In the US, with its robust philanthropic sector, enabling policy regimes have encouraged
private philanthropic investment in communities. Over the past 40 years, they have used tax code
regulations and tax credits to seed this market. Private capital has done the rest, and currently the
US has the largest impact investing market in the world, both by absolute size and per capita.

In 2000, the UK government made a deliberate decision to emulate the US impact investing
model (termed social finance in the UK). But with a much smaller philanthropic sector, and
limited track record in this market, the UK government played a more direct role in enabling
the growth of impact investing than its US counterparts. The UK government developed
PRIs to encourage philanthropic organizations, passed similar tax credit legislation, but it also
established intermediaries with direct funding, developed networks to serve the sector and even
a government department, the Office of the Third Sector, to play a direct and active role in
developing impact investing into a viable opportunity in the UK.

In contrast to both the US and UK, the Canadian government has taken a laissez-faire
approach to the impact investing market in Canada. Early interest in leveraging private capital
for public good was shown by the Federal Liberal Government in the early 2000s. But a change
of government in 2006 found much of this work shelved and little encouragement at the
national level to develop this market. Some leading philanthropic organizations with an interest
in this area, a few provincial governments and a variety of other stakeholders have advanced
impact investing in Canada, but without a systematic national government interest it remains
fragmented at best.

Beyond the need for enabling policy environments, sources of capital, intermediaries, financial
instruments and a robust community sector that can put the capital to productive and impactful

use, there lies a more fundamental question at the heart of impact investing: Should social problems be addressed through market mechanisms? Michael Edwards (2010) and others use the expression 'philanthro-capitalism' to describe this model of solving the world's problems through private capital and benevolence. They dislike capital market motivations as a driver of the philanthropic sector (Edwards, 2010; The Nonprofiteer, 2012). This position stands in sharp contrast to the proponents of impact investing, who see an opportunity to leverage resources in innovative ways to address today's problems. Those who disagree with this approach suggest that seeking business solutions to social problems does not address the real issues facing the planet, particularly when the world's wealthiest individuals use their substantial clout to address problems of their choosing rather than through democratically-based institutions. Michael Edwards suggests that the very nature of civil society organizations (CSOs) is to challenge the status quo and achieve social transformation, while business conforms – and one might even say exploits – our current economic and political structures: 'Nonprofits must understand that the desire to earn income and the desire to use business to promote social change are two different and entirely incompatible objectives ... Don't mix your models' (Edwards, 2010: 46). For Edwards and others, one cannot serve social needs as a business opportunity.

But such views are in the minority, as impact investing is increasingly promoted as a way to leverage all available resources to address deep seated and often intractable social problems. Increasingly, innovative partnerships between governments, philanthropic organizations and civil society are demonstrating the effectiveness of this approach (E.T. Jackson and Associates, 2012).

Conclusion

One of the most striking developments in philanthropy has been the move to align all assets of a foundation, bringing together mission- and investment-related strategies. This has spawned a shift to an 'investment' rather than a 'giving' focus across the sector; grant mentality is being replaced with an investment mentality. While some authors raise concerns (Thümler, Chapter 23), the shift is profoundly positive: it unlocks innovative, entrepreneurial value for philanthropy as its constituent parts begin to think in terms of the blended value (Emerson, 2003) they bring to the table.

Blended value embodies the full range of social, environmental and economic impacts created by the organization and desired by the investor. When investments seek social, environmental and financial returns, such an approach is termed impact investing. Whether 'impact-first' or 'finance-first', impact investing offers an innovative approach to addressing today's social need. It has the ability to leverage new resources in a period of scarcity. But to date, it continues to be a relatively uncoordinated marketplace.

Connecting the supply of capital to the demand for capital remains a challenge. Three distinct areas have been identified for improvement if we are to advance impact investing. First, we need new and innovative financial instruments designed to meet the needs of this distinct marketplace, further pushing the 'new frontiers' of philanthropy that have started to emerge (Salamon, 2014). Second, we need enabling public policy that includes regulation and incentives to encourage private capital into this space. Third, we need an increase in intermediaries who bring the necessary expertise to the market required to close the information gap that exists between supply and demand.

Government regulation will continue to play a vital role in the development of the impact investing marketplace. Government policy is able to create the enabling environment for impact investing, particularly for strategic philanthropic partners, by encouraging and incentivizing this approach. In jurisdictions such as the US and UK, where government has played this role, impact investing has been able to leverage significant private dollars to address today's social needs. But more can be done.

In partnership with government and the third sector, strategic philanthropy is unlocking new and innovative ways to solve some of the world's most pressing problems. By focusing all its resources on its ultimate goals, strategic philanthropy is creating a market for impact.

Notes

I would like to thank Sean MacKinnon and Babita Bhatt of the Carleton Centre for Community Innovation, Carleton University for their contribution of the literature review for this chapter.

References

Ayton, R. and Sarver, S. (2006) 'Social Lending Today: Challenges Facing Social Finance Intermediaries,' Centre for the Development of Social Finance, Background Paper.

Bank of England (2003) *The Financing of Social Enterprises*, Special Report by the Bank of England, London: Bank of England.

Bragg, I. (2010) 'Impact Investing in Canada: A Survey of Assets', Social Investment Organization.

Bridges Ventures and The Parthenon Group (2010) 'Investing for Impact: Case Studies across Asset Classes', www.parthenon.com/GetFile.aspx?u=%2fLists%2fThoughtLeadership%2fAttachments%2f15%2fInvesting%2520for%2520Impact.pdf.

Brodhead, T. (2010) 'On Not Letting A Crisis Go To Waste: An Innovation Agenda for Canada's Community Sector', *The Philanthropist*, 1(23).

Bugg-Levine, A. (2013) 'Complete Capital', *Stanford Social Innovation Review*, Winter.

——. and Goldstein, J. (2009) 'Impact Investing: Harnessing Capital Markets to Solve Problems at Scale', *Community Development Investment Review*, 5(2): 30–41.

——. and Emerson, J. (2011) *Impact Investing: Transforming How We Make Money While Making a Difference*, New York: Jossey-Bass.

Calvert Foundation (2012) *Invest*, /www.calvertfoundation.org/invest.

Canadian Task Force on Social Finance. (2010) *Mobilizing Private Capital for Public Good*, www.marsdd.com/wp-content/uploads/2011/02/MaRSReport-socialfinance-taskforce.pdf.

City of London (2013) 'Growing the Social Investment Market: The Landscape and Economic Impact', Research Report, City of London Economic Development.

Clifford, J. and Jung, T. (2016) 'Social Impact Bonds: Exploring and Understanding an Emerging Funding Approach', in O. Lehner (ed.) *The Routledge Handbook of Social and Sustainable Finance*, Routledge: London.

Cooch S. and Kramer M. (2007) *Compounding Impact: Mission Investing by US Foundations*, FSG Social Impact Advisors, www.cdfifund.gov/what_we_do/resources/Compounding%20Impact%20Mission%20Investing%20by%20US%20Foundations.pdf.

Critchley, B. (2015) 'How Social Impact Investing is Playing Out in Canada', *Financial Post*, 11 June.

Edwards, M. (2010) *Small Change: Why Business Won't Save the World*, San Francisco: Berrett-Koehler.

Emerson, J. (2003) 'The Blended Value Proposition: Integrating Social and Financial Returns', *California Management Review*, 45(4): 35–51.

Emerson, J. and Bonini, S. (2003) 'The Blended Value Map: Tracking the Intersects and Opportunities of Economic, Social and Environmental Value Creation', Executive Summary, Blended Value, (Unpublished Mimeo).

Emerson, J. and Spitzer, J. (2007) 'From Fragmentation to Function: Critical Concepts and Writings on Social Capital Markets' Structure, Operation, and Innovation', Blended Value, www.blendedvalue.org/wp-content/uploads/2004/02/pdf-capital-markets-fragmentation.pdf.

E.T. Jackson and Associates (2012) *Accelerating Impact: Report for Rockefeller Foundation*, New York.

Godeke, S. and Bauer, D. (2008) *Philanthropy's New Passing Gear: Mission-Related Investing*, New York: Rockefeller Philanthropy Advisors.

Hagerman, L. and Hebb, T. (2009) 'Balancing Risk and Return in Urban Investing' in G. L. Clarke, A. D. Dixon and A. H. B. Monk (eds.) *Financial Risk Management: From the Global to the Local*, Oxford: Oxford University Press.

Handford P. (2005) *Guide to Financing for Social Enterprise*, Western Economic Diversification Canada, www.csef.ca/guidetofinance_june05_eng.pdf.

Harji, K. (2009) 'Delivering More Capital to Communities', *Making Waves*, 20(3): 5–12.

Harji, K. and Hebb, T. (2009) 'The Quest for Blended Value Returns: Investor Perspectives on Social Finance in Canada', Ottawa: Carleton Centre for Community Innovation.

———. (2010) 'Investing for Impact: Issues and Opportunities for Social Finance in Canada', Montréal: ANSER Conference.

Hope Consulting (2010) 'Money for Good: The US Market for Impact Investments and Charitable Gifts from Individual Donors and Investors', //www.thegiin.org/cgi-bin/iowa/resources/research/96.html.

Jagelewski, A. (2011) 'Social Impact Bonds: A Practical Social Innovation', Horizons Policy Research Initiative, http://impactinvesting.marsdd.com/knowledge-hub/resources/social-impact-bonds-a-practical-social-innovation/ [Accessed 8 October 2010].

Kingston J. and Bolton M. (2006) 'New approaches to funding not-for-profit organisations', *Journal of Nonprofit and Voluntary Sector Marketing*, 9(2): 112–21.

Malhotra, A., Laird, H. and Spence, A. (2010) *Social Finance Census*, Toronto: Social Venture Exchange and Ontario Nonprofit Network.

MaRS (2014) *Impact Investing in Canada: State of the Nation*, MaRS Centre for Impact Investing/Purpose Capital.

Martin, B. (2012) *Foundations as Catalysts for the Canadian Social Finance/Impact Investing Infrastructure: A Background Paper for HRSDC*, Ottawa: Community Foundations of Canada.

Mendell, M. and Nogales, R. (2008) *Social Enterprises in OECD Member Countries: What are the financial streams?*, Paris: Organisation for Economic Co-operation and Development.

———. (2011) 'Working Paper on Solidarity Finance,' FIESS, Montreal.

Monitor Institute (2009) 'Investing for Social and Environmental Impact', New York: Rockefeller Foundation. www.monitorinstitute.com/impactinvesting/.

Nonprofiteer (2012) 'Today's Oxymoron: Apolitical Economics,' *The Nonprofiteer*, www.nonprofiteer.net/2008/04/22/todays-oxymoron-apolitical-economics/.

O'Donohoe, N., Leijonhufvud, C. and Saltuk, Y. (2010) 'Impact Investments: An Emerging Asset Class,' New York: J.P. Morgan and Rockefeller Foundation. www.thegiin.org/cgi-bin/iowa/resources/research/151.html.

Pharoah, C. (2012) 'How Will Funding Play a Role in the Shaping of the Big Society?' in ESRC Centre for Charitable Giving and Philanthropy, Cass Business School, *Philanthropy and a Better Sociey*, London: Alliance Trust, 91–96.

Phillips, H. and North Investment Management (2010) 'An Overview of Impact Investing', RBC Global Asset Management Inc.

Phillips, S. and Hebb, T. (2010) 'Financing the Third Sector: Introduction', *Policy and Society*, 29(3): 181–7.

Porter M. E. and Kramer M. R. (2011) 'Creating Shared Value', *Harvard Business Review*, 89(1–2): 2–17.

Salamon, L. M. (2014) *Leverage for Good. An Introduction to the New Frontiers of Philanthropy and Social Investment*, Oxford and New York: Oxford University Press.

Socialfinance.ca (2011) 'Home,' www.socialfinance.ca.

Social Investment Task Force (2010) *Social Investment Ten Years On*, www.socialinvestmenttaskforce.org/downloads/SITF_10_year_review.pdf.

Strandberg, C. (2010) *The State of Community/Mission Investment of Canadian Foundations. Report*, www.corostrandberg.com/publications/community-investment/the-state-of-community-mission-investment-of-canadian-foundations#.

UK Office of the Third Sector (2010) 'Voluntary and Community Groups and Social Enterprises', www.webarchive.nationalarchives.gov.uk/+/cabinetoffice.gov.uk/voluntary-sector.aspx.

Venture Deli (2012) 'Home', www.venturedeli.com/.

Wuttunee, W., Chicilo, M., Rothney, R. and Gray, L. (2008) *Financing Social Enterprise: An Enterprise Perspective*, Social Enterprises Knowledgeable Economies and Sustainable Communities.

30

Measuring impact and recognizing success

Georg von Schnurbein

With external pressures on, and internal developments of, the philanthropy field, performance and impact measurement have become increasingly prominent themes across policy, practice, and research (Light, 2004; Zimmermann and Stevens, 2006; Carman, 2007). Driving factors include: a public interest in evaluation, better accountability, responsibility and success; the changing nature and characteristics of philanthropy brought about by philanthropreneurs, venture philanthropy, impact investment, and the financialization of philanthropy (Gordon *et al.*, Chapter 21; Defourny *et al.*, Chapter 22; Thümler, Chapter 23; Hebb and MacKinnon, Chapter 29); and, the hybridization of philanthropy itself (Smith, Chapter, 20). As such, there is a growing interest in understanding why, and how, things are done (Evers, 2005; Billis, 2010).

Defining success for, and of, philanthropy is, however, a difficult and complex, undertaking (Murray, 2010). As a core unit of the sector, nonprofits' organizational effectiveness has attracted a lot of research attention. The findings indicate that organizational performance is multidimensional with priority given to nonfinancial over financial criteria (Baruch and Ramalho, 2006). Thus, when trying to identify success, multiple indicators and approaches are necessary. Research also indicates that the perception of nonprofit success is socially constructed, and not consistently valued by different stakeholders (Herman and Renz, 2008). Thus, performance is always the result of a negotiation (Murray, 2010).

Furthermore, within the literature there is neither agreement, nor are there clear boundaries, on how performance and impact measurement should be approached, understood, and used (LeRoux and Wright, 2010). In general, performance measurement deals with the effectiveness of a nonprofit organization (Herman and Renz, 2008; Sowa *et al.*, 2004). Furthermore, performance measurement refers to the ongoing process of defining, monitoring, and using performance measures to improve organizational effectiveness in addressing public problems (Poister, 2003). As part of this process, impact measurement concentrates on the results, especially outcomes and impact, of nonprofit activities. Thus, in the context of philanthropy, impact measurement includes the relevant actions of the funder, the grantee, and the beneficiary (Leat, 2006; Thomson, 2010). However, the societal utility of philanthropic performance goes beyond the success of any single organization. Measuring impact draws attention to the results in society at large. Hence, this extension leads to even more complex evaluation situations (Anheier *et al.*, 2011).

This chapter discusses the complexities of impact measurement, including its underlying drivers, reasons, and relationships, and points to implications for further research. Special emphasis is placed on relationships between funders and grantees. As funders become more and more operationally involved, their part in the impact evaluation goes beyond giving money. Consequently, the question arises as to how the funder itself, as well as its actions, can be included in the evaluation of philanthropic activities (Langer, 2004). The following sections explore the drivers and reasons for impact measurement. The chapter then turns to the role of the funder and how impact measurement is utilized. It concludes with reflections on current research issues in relation to both theory-building and empirical analysis, as well as thoughts on future developments surrounding impact measurement in philanthropy.

Drivers and reasons for impact measurement

The focus on identifying impact is generally associated with measurement and quantification. In the context of nonprofit organizations and philanthropic services, different terms such as assessment, evaluation, or accountability are in use to describe more or less the same process: proving the successful provision of services and goods. Although the increased use of measurement has been perceived as a recent development (Frumkin, 2004), at least within the UK, it has been a longstanding issue for the nonprofit sector (Barman, 2007a). The reasons for measurement have, however, changed over time. Before performance measurement became the focus of funders and nonprofit leaders, measurement activities were targeted to the assessment of community need or pure financial efficiency. As Barman (2007a: 112) concludes, 'measurement emerges in moments of uncertainty and change ... [and] ... reflects larger debates and contestations over the appropriate purpose and nature of the voluntary sector'. Thus, the actual emphasis on impact measurement reflects a change in the perception of the philanthropic sector by society at large; it is of special relevance to philanthropic activities, where 'one party donates resources to another party for a charitable purpose or to better welfare of society' (Benjamin 2010: 385). What then are the driving forces for the growth and application of impact measurement? Key ones appear to be information asymmetries, risk preferences, isomorphism, and the idea of change.

Drivers of oversight and accountability

In philanthropic relationships, funders give resources to nonprofits as intermediaries linked with a mandate to provide goods or services to beneficiaries following the funders' purpose. Notwithstanding a thorough selection process of funded projects, funders and grantees have inherently different goals, interests, and motivations (Speckbacher, 2003). The intermediaries might misrepresent their capacities to funders in order to obtain a grant (adverse selection), or might try to elude conditions agreed upon (moral hazard). As a consequence, both funders and grantees are obliged to agree on arrangements of monitoring, measurements, and oversight systems (Van Slyke, 2007). Grantees are held accountable for their use of resources and to the outcomes they have produced assembling these resources (Carman, 2010). Murray (2010) differentiates between two basic forms of accountability: legal and moral. Legal accountability is based on formally, and officially, defined contracts that both parties accept. Moral accountability exists when 'reporting is legally not required but parties believe there is an obligation for one to be accountable to the other' (Murray, 2010: 347). A funder–grantee relationship is usually based on legally valid contracts. However, grantees often feel a moral accountability to other stakeholder groups such as beneficiaries or the community. Benjamin (2010) differentiates accountability relationships from philanthropic relationships by stating that in the former, one party mandates another party with the fulfilment of some desirable aim; in the latter, the funder donates resources for a charitable purpose. Thus, the use of impact measurement should reduce information asymmetries and strengthen the alignment of risk preferences.

Drivers of regulations and expectations

Leat (2006) emphasizes that grantmaking foundations and other institutional funders do not fulfil the basic assumptions of resource dependency and uncertainty usually supposed to nurture isomorphism in nonprofits (Romero-Merino and Garcia-Rodriguez, Chapter 25). Because of their endowed capital, and feeble legal requirements, these funders are relatively immune from external pressures. Leat (2006) rates the foundation sector as being a case of weak institutionalism explained by the considerable variability. However, one can argue that different forms of pressures can explain why impact measurement has become so important in the nonprofit world (Light, 2002).

In nearly all European countries, foundation law regulation has been revised in the past ten years (EFC, 2011). Thus, coercive isomorphism in the form of legal regulation has supported foundation professionalization, as well as anticipatory coercion in the form of governance codes (Dawson and Dunn, 2006; von Schnurbein and Stöckli, 2010). Additionally, open published toolboxes for performance and impact measurement, such as the Program Outcome Model (America, 1996), the Inspiring Impact Initiative (2015), or the Total Impact tool (Cabinet Office, 2014), have increased the pressure on funders to use these measurement tools. Mimetic isomorphism emerges from peer learning. Especially in the area of impact measurement, new approaches such as venture philanthropy or impact investing have changed the attitude towards impact measurement in many other institutional funding organizations. Procedures and vocabulary are borrowed from venture capitalists and transformed into the nonprofit sector (Defourny et al., Chapter 22; Hebb with MacKinnon, Chapter 29). Other factors of mimetic isomorphism are the growing number of conferences on philanthropy, a rising number of members in umbrella associations and the facilitation of communication through digital media (Leat, 2006). The most relevant forms of isomorphism on impact measurement seem to be the ones of normative isomorphism. Along with an increase of professionalism and bureaucracy came the wish to prove that funded projects are successful. New approaches of scaling up and creating leverage ask for impact measurement in order to define which projects are worth being multiplied. With the rising number of employed staff in foundations, information asymmetries between staff and trustees lead to a rising use of performance measurement tools because trustees do not have the same insights as staff members (Anheier and Leat, 2006). As a consequence, forms of isomorphism have nurtured the development of new standards and procedures in accounting and performance measurement (Murray, 2010).

Drivers of conceptualization

Social problems, as well as the envisaged solutions thereto, have become increasingly complex. As part of that, the expectations placed at the doors of private donors, or funding institutions, go far beyond the ethic principle of 'do no harm' (Wenar, 2010). Thus, philanthropic action requires well thought-out concepts that cover and align the interests of diverse stakeholders. In order to create real change, an underlying theory of change has to be developed and, afterwards, the goal attainment has to be measured. A theory of change stems from the assumption that 'programs are based on explicit or implicit theories about how and why the program will work'

(Weiss, 1995: 66). One can say that the theory of change is the fundamental philosophy behind the philanthropic actions of an institutional funder. It explains how the purpose of the foundation will be put in place by using a certain type of method or instrument and targeting a social problem in a specific way. Theories of change are usually based on logic models that explain in a causal chain how the resources invested are used and what kind of outputs or outcomes should be achieved (Carman 2010). Thus, only by measuring the contribution of the project to social change, the theory of change can be proven to be right. Accordingly, impact measurement is always oriented to the organization's mission, not only to aspects of effectiveness and efficiency (Sawhill and Williamson, 2001).

Drivers of multiplication and leverage

Despite the global growth of philanthropy, especially the foundation sectors, the economic potential of 'the good economy' is still perceived to be falling far behind public subsidies and investments. Being aware of the scarcity of philanthropic money, new ways of funding have developed (Salamon and Burckart, 2014). These highlight the importance of multiplication and leverage. As a consequence, the understanding of giving has transformed from alms and charity to finance and investment (Thümler, Chapter 23): strategies and techniques from venture capital have been adapted to the financing of social purpose organizations and the notion of investing and reinvesting has been introduced in philanthropy (Letts, Ryan, and Grossman, 1997). This development has been mirrored by an increase of hybrid organizations combining social and economic goals in favour of a better goal attainment (Billis, 2010; Smith, Chapter 20). The basic idea of hybrid organizations is to use economic value creation strategies to solve social problems and by this, increase the utility of the donated money. These new structures on both sides – social investors and social entrepreneurs – call for new forms of measurement that cover economic and social aims. However, the aim to define and measure blended value is a major challenge.

Driving forces

Several organizations have made great efforts to develop measurement tools for nonprofits and to disseminate the idea of impact measurement. In the US, United Way and the Roberts Enterprise Development Fund (REDF) are among the pioneers of this movement. In 1996, United Way published the handbook 'Measuring Program Outcomes: A Practical Approach'. This offered a step-by-step introduction to nonprofit performance measurement based on a logic model approach. The logic model follows a value chain approach including inputs, process, outputs, and outcomes (United Way of America, 1996; Murray, 2010). The aim is to describe a sequence of activities and results that are attributable to the focal intervention or to detect what else can affect the described outcomes. At the same time, REDF developed the Social Return on Investment (SROI) in order to make the value creation of social investments more visible to philanthropists. The innovative idea of the SROI was to monetize social impact in order to allow cost-benefit analyses that go beyond simple cash flows (Emerson *et al.*, 2000). This quickly was adopted and further developed internationally by organizations such as the New Economics Foundation and Social Value UK, formerly known as the SROI Network. While in the original version of SROI equal emphasis was placed on quantitative and qualitative aspects of the evaluation, subsequent developments, especially within the UK, have seen a shift of emphasis away from the qualitative towards the quantitative measurement aspect of the evaluation (Clifford and Jung, 2011).

Alongside the development of new tools and methods for performance measurement, funding organizations have played an important part in paving the way for impact measurement. For example, the Edna McConnell Clark Foundation changed its funding policy into a venture philanthropy approach, supporting organizations not only financially, but also in terms of capacity building and network creation. Additionally, specialized consultancies, such as Rockefeller Philanthropy Advisors and the Center for Effective Philanthropy, have focused on helping foundations and other funding organizations to develop impact measurement procedures for their funding programs, while, more recently, government agencies have started to take a more active, and steering, interest in the area (Harrow and Jung, 2015).

While the number of measurement tools is burgeoning (Mildenberger *et al.*, 2011), their implementation is still lacking behind. One major reason for this may be the specific nature of the relationship between funders and grantees.

The challenging role of the funder

Focusing on the value of nonprofit activities to society at large, impact measurement increases complexity across the nonprofit sector. This results from the fact that in philanthropic exchange processes the beneficiary usually does not pay the costs of the services received. Vice versa, the funder as 'creditor' does not expect any direct return for his or her donation. Hence, on both sides of a nonprofit interaction, incentives for higher involvement, and specific expectations on the service provided, are low. Funders often do not expect more than the good feeling of doing good; beneficiaries accept the way the service, as a gift, is provided and do not ask if it could be done better or differently. The nonprofit organization, as intermediary, can only refer to its own principal aims and assess the compliance of the service with these goals. This might be one of the reasons as to why, for some time, measuring nonprofit success did neither receive major attention by practitioners nor by researchers (Forbes, 1998). Since then, the theoretical discussion on nonprofit effectiveness has made vast progress (Greiling, 2009; Herman and Renz, 2008; Murray, 2010). Additionally, new funding approaches in practice have led to a new understanding of the role of the funder (Letts *et al.*, 1997). Strategic philanthropy or venture philanthropy puts the funder in the position to do more than just donating money (Frumkin, 2006): '[t]he relationship between the venture philanthropist and … the grantee, is more intensive, frequent, and engaging than traditional philanthropic relationships' (Van Slyke and Newman, 2006: 347). The core values of these new approaches are taken from the venture capitalist approaches prominent in early stage investments of enterprises (Defourny *et al.*, Chapter 22). Although differences between strategic, high-engagement, or venture philanthropy appear, the basic principles are more or less consistent: high engagement by the investor through financial, intellectual and social (networking) support, investment in capacity building, investments of three to five years with a clear exit strategy, goal definition and performance measurement (Letts *et al.*, 1997). In covering both the performance of the grantee and the goal attainment of the funder, associated impact measurement is of high complexity. On the one side, funding organizations, especially grant-making foundations, offer grants according to their purpose. However, by supporting another nonprofit organization, the foundation has no longer fulfilled its mission. The intended benefit will not be achieved until the grantee has established the service for the beneficiaries. On the other side, the grantee is accountable not only to the grantmaker, but to a wide range of stakeholders including government, individual donors, beneficiaries and the general public. This can lead to conflicts of interest that may have negative effects on the project outcomes (Wyser and von Schnurbein, 2011). Barman (2007b) states that funders' involvement, intentionally or unintentionally, influence the way that nonprofit organizations execute their projects and services.

Furthermore, in line with resource dependency theory, this approach means that the nonprofit organization is likely to act more in line with the interests of the funder with those of the beneficiaries (Whitman, 2008). In the search for programmatic improvement, funder and grantee have to make a joint effort for a process that combines the evaluation with the decision-making context (Mayhew, 2012).

Changing logics of the funder-grantee relationship

Mayhew (2012) describes the funder-grantee relationship as a strategic alliance that combines different organizational resources with accordant goals. Benjamin (2010) distinguishes philanthropic and accountability relationships, highlighting that greater accountability may complicate the ability of the funders to consider other philanthropic concerns.

Philanthropic relationship

As already defined, a philanthropic relationship is based on a donation of resources of the funder to a grantee for a charitable purpose. It is noteworthy that, the charitable purpose has to be in alignment with both the funder's (e.g. a foundation) and the nonprofit's core values and mission. Philanthropic action covers a wide spectrum that ranges from single donations to legacies or grants made by a foundation (Harrow, 2010). In the context of impact investing, prevalence is given to the activities of institutional funders that pursue specific, stated, goals. The funding decisions of these actors are dependent on governance structures, networks, and personal preferences (Frumkin, 1998). Thus, philanthropic funding is closely related to underlying values that funders want to see implemented in society, on their perspectives of deserving and undeserving causes (Schervish and Havens, 1997; Whitman, 2009; Harrow, 2010; Healy and Donnelly-Cox, Chapter 12). Based on the goals stated in a foundation's deed, potential fields of activities will be assessed, and ways of creating or supporting social change will be weighed up. This will result in a funding strategy on which basis grants will be made. Only those grant applications in line with the foundation's intended goals will be accepted and grants will be paid out on the basis of a contract that entails – among other issues – evaluation guidelines. A major distinction to other exchanges, such as political or commercial exchanges, is the fact that philanthropic exchanges are not conclusive. Thus, the funders do not get a market price adequate service or good for their donation (von Schnurbein and Bethmann, 2010) and, in order to accomplish its mission, a grantmaking foundation is reliant on the services of the grantee. As a consequence, the philanthropic relationship has shifted from a paternalistic, financial exchange to a partnership structure in which the funder is investor, consultant, and collaborator (Barman, 2007b; Harrow, 2010). This has led to increased expectations of accountability (Harrow, Chapter 31). Combined with this new approach to philanthropy, the notion of accountability has increased. Formerly, when grants were understood as gifts, evaluation was of low relevance. Now, as grants are perceived as investments, evaluation is a necessary part of grantmaking.

Accountability relationship

In an accountability relationship, one party delegates authority to another party for achievement of some desirable end (Jensen and Meckling, 1976). Following the underlying assumptions of agency theory – self-interest and information asymmetry – a funder has the obligation to overview the activities of the grantee in order to assure usage of the given grant that confirms with the mission. Hence, the accountability relationship is always based on a process of formal evaluations of past activities (Murray, 2010). Carman (2010) describes the underlying assumption of the 'accountability movement' as follows:

> If funders require nonprofit organizations to provide them with reports about performance information, and funders require that they engage in program evaluation, then nonprofit organizations will learn from this and, in turn, be able to provide more effective services in more efficient ways.
>
> *(2010: 5)*

Thus, the accountability relationship starts with the grantee receiving the grants and planning the activities. Based on the strategic planning, the goods and services are provided. Afterwards, the activities are evaluated. Finally, the grantee checks if the planned goals were accomplished and reports to the funder.

As discussed above, the founder-grantee relationship can be described from a philanthropic perspective and from an accountability perspective. Although there are similar participants and comparative actions, the underlying logics are different. As highlighted in Figure 30.1, the directions of processes are diametrical. In a philanthropic relationship, the process starts with the core values and mission goals of the funder and ends with the contribution of grants to the grantee (Leviton and Bickel, 2004); the accountability relationship begins with the resource demand of the grantee and ends with the contribution to the accomplishment of the funder's mission. Impact measurement consists of the methods, procedures, and instruments that add to the understanding of this final aspect of the accountability relationship. The different logics are critical for the way that impact measurement is executed. Funders that prioritize the philanthropic relationship may prefer qualitative data and storytelling that helps them determine how

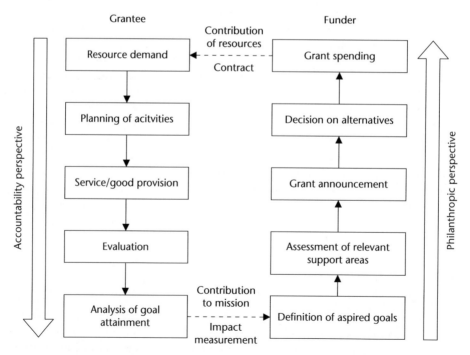

Figure 30.1 Diametrical logic of philanthropic and accountability relationship

a funded project served to fulfil their main purpose. Funders with an accountability perspective, though, may ask for quantitative data and scientifically proven explanations in order to measure cost–benefit relations.

Utilizing impact measurement

Given the problems of defining nonprofit effectiveness and the complexities of funder–grantee relationships, critics highlight the lack of objectivity, and question the sense, of any measurement that goes beyond assessing outputs (Campbell, 2002; Moxham, 2010). Easterling (2000) names three practical limitations of measuring outcomes. First, outcome evaluation is expensive as the assessment tools require additional efforts of staff and clients in nonprofit projects. Second, due to their socially constructed nature, the outcomes of nonprofit programs are elusive. Finally, grantees are resistant to outcome evaluation: it is associated with judgment, punishment, and cost reductions (Bass and Lemmon, 1998). On the other hand, some studies see potentially positive effectors of outcome and impact measurement, for both funders and grantees, especially in relation to strategic decision-making and goal attainment (Carman and Fredericks, 2008; LeRoux and Wright, 2010). Consequently, there have been calls for research to guide and improve evaluation systems (Murray, 2010). As impact measurement is cost-intensive and time consuming, it can only be justified if it has the right focus, verifies the intended goals, leads to a better understanding of the situation, and, finally, consolidates at least one of the funder's aims.

Clarifying the measurement range

Due to the fact that impact measurement deals with multiple dimensions, value prioritization, and convertibility over time, deciding on an appropriate measurement range is an essential prerequisite for any successful evaluation (Herman and Renz, 2008). From the funder's perspective, the standard scope of an evaluation is a single grant, and the associated activities paid for. However, as previously highlighted, there has been an increasing trend to move away from simple grants. In many cases – and especially in those of interest to impact measurement – funding is more complex; it ranges from perennial support and program funding to cooperations and multigrantee funds, but also to more nuanced support, such as organizational capacity building support, alongside the core grant (Cairns et al., 2011). Furthermore, the specification of the measurement range has implications for the people involved. Depending on the evaluation's focus, different people in the foundation and the nonprofit organization will be responsible to carry out the evaluation process. For a single project or program, the project or program manager will supervise and steer the process, whereas in a complex initiative with multiple grantees, the foundation's director or even the trustees will be integrated in the evaluation process. Taken together, these factors mean that, from the grantee's perspective, evaluation is a difficult balancing act; it is not always obvious which aspects and activities need to be included in any one evaluation. If only one project is funded by a foundation, why should the nonprofit organization as a whole be the focus of the evaluation? Hence, the assessment range must be wide enough to allow comprehensible and significant statements on the success of an intervention, yet narrow enough so as to reduce complexity and external factors to a manageable level (Mark and Beery, 2004). As such, a valid case can be made against a blanket approach to impact measurement: the process should be limited to larger grants, programs, and initiatives that play a major and important role in the strategic direction of the funder.

Verifying the intended goals

Funder and grantee may have related, but not always concordant goals. Thus, funder and grantee have to align the major aims of the intervention at the beginning. However, as philanthropic projects are often uncertain in their development, the initial goals may become partly obsolete or inappropriate. As a consequence, impact measurement only leads to a useful result if the goals are adjusted and still in alignment with the foundations mission (Leviton and Bickel, 2004). Additionally, the foundation has to check if the goals are measurable and applicable for the analyzed intervention (Sawhill and Williamson, 2001).

Breaking down complexity

Philanthropic action usually aims at the development of society at large. However, reducing or solving societal problems is never easy because many components and stakeholders are involved or affected by any one intervention; it is often difficult to identify and trace the full consequences of activities. In this respect, the underlying methods and instruments of impact measurement help to reduce complexity and to focus on core aspects. In this respect, logic modeling has established itself as a relevant and useful approach to impact measurement (Carman, 2010). From an institutional perspective, it serves as an instrument of normative isomorphism, stating that a successful logic model may be transferred onto other projects or scaled up to a larger program setting (Leat, 2006). Although there are a large number of different evaluation tools existing, only few of them have reached a larger attention in both theory and practice (Murray, 2010; Mildenberger et al., 2011).

The choice of the evaluation tool depends on various aspects, e.g. the defined goals, resource constraints, or the selected perspective onto the project. If the foundation wants to gain a broader understanding of the performance of an intervention, stakeholder-related analyses such as the Foundation Assessment Tools (CEP, 2002) are helpful to cover the different points of view. The aim of this tool is to cover the perceptions of different stakeholder groups and to benchmark the results with comparable projects. Primarily developed for business analysis, the balanced scorecard was also adapted to serve nonprofits for their performance evaluation (Kaplan, 2001). It covers financial and nonfinancial measures and is oriented to a long-term value (Murray, 2010). Patton (2003) further develops the approach by presenting a dashboard for social enterprises. A stronger focus on the outcome, instead of means, is offered by the aforementioned Program Outcome Model, developed by United Way (United Way, 1996). It follows a clear logic modeling approach and puts an emphasis on the implementation process. The tool suggests quantifying all results through the definition of specific and measurable indicators. Finally, Social Return on Investment (SROI) has gained a lot of attention (Kehl et al., 2012; nef, 2004). Based on a classical cost-benefit analysis, it not only tries to quantify results, but tries to monetize social outcomes; it emphasizes the fact that social projects provide more benefit than just the direct action. By monetizing the social investments, it offers a way to capture side effects and long-term social benefits. SROI's most compelling advantage is that it can present one final figure to picture nonprofit success. This, however, needs to be arrived at in a reliable and appropriate way, which, in the past, has not always happened. Hence, critics concentrate less on the general idea of SROI and more on the methodology (Lingane and Olson, 2004). Nevertheless, SROI is constantly developed and adopted in practice (Clifford and Jung, 2011; Kehl et al., 2012). Taken together, a central concern with these tools is that they always can only arrive at an approximation of impact, not a decisive impact statement. Consequently, foundations face the task of continually re-evaluating their methodological choices and practices, which in turn raises concerns about the longitudinal comparability of any impact assessment findings.

The effects of impact measurement

Ideally, impact measurement should play a positive role in philanthropy. First, it should improve the effectiveness of the philanthropic activities and leverage added value for any resources provided. Second, it should improve the funding process and the funder-grantee relationship. A good starting point for this is the counterfactual question 'what would have happened without the project?'. While impact measurement frequently ends with the presentation of achieved goals, its biggest potential is future advancement (Easterling, 2000). Thus, the primary aim of impact measurement should not be external pressures for legitimacy or accountability, but to develop learning capability (Buckmaster, 1999). Unfortunately, though, evaluation and decision-making are rarely ever linked (Stone et al., 1999). Only a limited set of studies focuses on the use of performance data for strategic decision making (Siciliano, 1997; Moynihan and Ingraham, 2004; Carman and Fredericks, 2008). Given empirical findings that performance measurement can have a positive effect on strategic decision-making (LeRoux and Wright, 2010), and the vision of evidence-based philanthropy that projects' funding should be decided on the basis of a scientific or research-based approach that has been tested in quasi-experimental designs or randomized control trials (Williams-Taylor, 2008), it becomes clear that funding is increasingly a consequence of antecedent experiences and requires systematic evaluation.

Consequences for the actors involved in any evaluated intervention, such as funder, grantee, and beneficiaries, are both positive and negative. On the one hand, an impact assessment approach provides funders with helpful guidance when faced with tough choices, such as when to cease supporting underperforming projects. At the same time, the grantee might learn to become more effective by gaining a better understanding of an issue's complexities, or find opportunities to scale up an outperforming project.

In any case, a precondition for the successful implementation of lessons learned is an open and constructive communication of the evaluation results. Mayhew (2012) shows that a more collaborative approach between funder and grantee to evaluation utilization leads to a higher performance. Given the difficulties associated with defining 'success' in the nonprofit field (Herman and Renz, 2008), guidance on how to recognize and reward nonprofit success is scarce (Sanger, 2008). Nonetheless, a couple of important themes can be identified. First and foremost, the success of philanthropy is always a means to an end, such as the well-being of beneficiaries or the achievement of the organization's major aim. Consequently, it is important to bear in mind that the outcomes of a funded project, or lack thereof, are rarely ever the achievements, or failures, of only one actor; they emerge from the collaboration and interaction of several constituents, at least the funder, the grantee, and the beneficiaries. Thus, the success of a project or program has to be shared with all parties involved; similarly, failure and the lessons it offers needs to be embraced and understood across all participants. Within this context, responsiveness and flexibility is paramount (Herman and Renz, 2008). To this end, and given the fluid nature of impact, benchmarking with other projects or comparisons over time means that the outcomes and impacts of a project or an organization become more visible and easier to interpret over time. To develop learning, documentation and communication about good examples create archetypes for other organizations to follow.

Similarly though, it is equally important to embrace failures. Various studies report that representatives of both funders and grantees tend to ignore or knowingly misinterpret negative evaluation results (Murray, 2010) or struggle with the contradictory pressures of legitimate organizational protection and the importance of sharing learning from *all* directions (Jung *et al.* 2012). While success stories are widely spread and communicated, projects that went wrong are rarely analyzed systematically. Instead, funders in particular should be interested to offer lessons learned from projects with negative outcomes in order to ameliorate resource allocation. Since nonprofits are lacking market pressures, improvement can only establish through oversight and accountability.

Outlook: Opportunities for future research

Impact measurement has become an essential task of nonprofit organizations and foundations. The notion of nonprofit performance has shifted from cost effectiveness and output orientation to outcomes and social impact. However, what one cannot measure, one cannot control. Thus, the question of social impact cannot be answered by reporting inputs and outputs. In the beginning of this chapter, several other drivers for impact measurement were presented. Another important aspect of impact measurement is the relationship between funder and grantee. The discussion showed the great variety of funders, and the specific complexities arising within the funder-grantee relationship. Especially, the goal alignment between the two actors in terms of social impact may be difficult. Despite the great improvements already achieved in the research on philanthropic impact, the importance of the topic calls for further, more scientific, work. Based on the preceeding discussion, major research gaps include: a better understanding of the role of the funder, operationalization of impact measurement, benefits and effects of impact measurement, and, most of all, how to recognize success. Mayhew (2012) states that the funder-grantee relationship has a strong influence on the success of evaluations. Thus, it is essential to better understand the ways that these relationships develop and the influence that the funders have on the project success. As funders become more actively involved, self-evaluations are not sufficient anymore. Additionally, difficulties remain in the operationalization and implementation of measurement and evaluation, relating to both timescales, as well as content. It is one core characteristic of nonprofit performance that it is not easy to measure; outcomes are difficult to define and have often long-term consequences. Not surprisingly, nonuse is still a major problem in practice (Fleischer and Christie, 2009). The current tendency towards an increased use of metrics facilitates the implementation of standardized tools. But, critics question whether quantification based on assumptions and estimations is really the right way to capture the multidimensional social benefit of nonprofit action. Additionally, more research on the benefits of measurement and evaluation for nonprofits has to be carried out. What are the consequences of impact measurement for the organization's management, future funding opportunities, or the greater community? Examples such as the studies of Millesen *et al.* (2010) and LeRoux and Wright (2010) offer promising starting points that show how measurement may help in developing the nonprofit sector. Referring to the thoughts on recognizing success, aspects of lessons learned and how to implement impact measurement results in daily practice offer a lot of space for future research. The issue of dealing with failures by funders and grantees is of high relevance, especially as new funding approaches emerge such as venture philanthropy.

Another promising field of future research on measurement is theory building. Most of the existing measurement tools are not embedded in a theory, but build on practical experience (Kehl *et al.*, 2011). Thus research should make attempts to develop a theory of impact measurement in order to develop a better foundation for further research. One possibility is the use of governance theories in order to capture the relationships informing evaluation situations. Additionally, further research should improve the understanding of nonprofit effectiveness (Herman and Renz, 2008).

Fueled by practical experience, impact investing is a new direction of research. As a consequence of the financial crisis since 2008, funders are more aware of the dormant capital invested in traditional economy instead of using it for their mission's purpose (Phillips, 2010). Combining impact investing with the existing literature on impact measurement might help develop better strategies to define indicators and reporting standards. From a practical point of view, many nonprofits and foundations lack experience in implementing impact measurement. Thus, a consequent and systematic use of measurement tools will help to improve the practicability and the informative value of the results conducted. Most of all, funders and grantees have to learn to better communicate amongst each other on focused goals and the processes to achieve these aims. A better collaboration and partnership among the actors will have the highest impact on the development and effectiveness of evaluation and measurement.

References

America, U. W. (1996) *Measuring Program Outcomes: A Practical Approach*, Alexandria, VA: United Way of America.

Anheier, H. K. and Leat, D. (2006) *Creative philanthropy: Towards a New Philanthropy for the Twenty-first Century*, London: Routledge.

Anheier, H. K. Schröer, A. and Then, V. (2011) *Soziale Investitionen*, Wiesbaden: VS Verlag.

Barman, E. (2007a) 'What is the Bottom Line for Nonprofit Organizations? A History of Measurement in the British Voluntary Sector', *Voluntas*, 18: 101–15.

Barman, E. (2007b) 'An Institutional Approach to Donor Control: From Dyadic Ties to a Field-Level Analysis', *American Journal of Sociology*, 112(5): 1416–58.

Baruch, Y. and Ramalho, N. (2006) 'Communalities and Distinctions in the Measurement of Organizational Performance and Effectiveness Across For-Profit and Nonprofit Sectors', *Nonprofit and Voluntary Sector Quarterly*, 35(1): 39–65.

Bass, G. and Lemmon, P. (1998) *Measuring the Measurers: A Nonprofit Assessment of the Government Performance and Results Act*: GPRA.

Benjamin, L. M. (2010) 'Funders as Principals', *Nonprofit Management and Leadership*, 20(4), 383–403.

Billis, D. (2010) *Hybrid Organizations and the Third Sector : Challenges for Practice, Theory and Policy*, Basingstoke, Hampshire: Palgrave Macmillan.

Buckmaster, N. (1999) 'Associations between Outcome Measurement, Accountability and Learning for Nonprofit Organisations', *International Journal of Public Sector Management*, 12(2): 186–97.

Cabinet Office (2014) Using a Total Impact Approach to Achieve Social Outcomes, www.gov.uk/government/publications/using-a-total-impact-approach-to-achieve-social-outcomes [Accessed 13 June 2015].

Cairns, B., Burkeman, S., Harker, A. and Buckley, E. (2011) *Beyond Money: A Study of Funding Plus in the UK*, London: Institute for Voluntary Action Research.

Campbell, D. (2002) 'Outcomes Assessment and the Paradox of Nonprofit Accountability', *Nonprofit Management and Leadership*, 12(3): 243.

Carman, J. (2010) 'The Accountability Movement. What's Wrong With This Theory of Change?' *Nonprofit and Voluntary Sector Quarterly*, 39(2): 256–74.

Carman, J. G. (2007) 'Evaluation Practice Among Community-Based Organizations: Research Into the Reality', *American Journal of Evaluation*, 28(1): 60–75.

Carman, J. G. and Fredericks, K. A. (2008) 'Nonprofits and Evaluation: Empirical Evidence from the Field', *New Directions for Evaluation*, 2008(119): 51–71.

CEP, C. f. E. P. (ed.) (2002) *Indicators for Effectiveness*, Boston: Center for Effective Philanthropy.

Clifford, J. and Jung, T. (2011) Social Return on Investment: Measuring the 'Un-measurable', Paper presented at the 40th Annual Conference of the Association for Research on Nonprofit Organizations and Voluntary Action (ARNOVA), Toronto, Canada, 17–19 November.

Dawson, I. and Dunn, A. (2006) 'Governance Codes of Practice in the Not-for-Profit Sector', *Corporate Governance*, 14(1): 33–42.

Easterling, D. (2000) 'Using Outcome Evaluation to Guide Grantmaking: Theory, Reality, and Possibilities', *Nonprofit and Voluntary Sector Quarterly*, 29(3): 482–6.

EFC, E.F.C. (2011) *Comparative Highlights of Foundation Laws – The Operating Environment of Foundations in Europe*, Brussels: EFC.

Emerson, J., Wachowicz, J. and Chun, S. (2000) Social Return on Investment: Exploring Aspects of Value Creation in the Nonprofit Sector, www.redf.org/wordpress/wp-content/uploads/2013/10/REDF-Box-Set-Vol.-2-SROI-Paper-2000.pdf [Accessed 10 October 2015].

Evers, A. (2005) 'Mixed Welfare Systems and Hybrid Organizations: Changes in the Governance and the Provision of Social Services', *International Journal of Public Administration*, 28: 737–48.

Fleischer, D. N., and Christie, C. A. (2009) 'Evaluation Use Results from a Survey of US American Evaluation Association Members', *American Journal of Evaluation*, 30(2): 158–75.

Forbes, D. (1998) 'Measuring the Unmeasurable: Empirical Studies of Nonprofit Organization Effectiveness from 1977 to 1997', *Nonprofit and Voluntary Sector Quarterly*, 27(2): 183–202.

Frumkin, P. (1998) 'The Long Recoil from Regulation Private Philanthropic Foundations and the Tax Reform Act of 1969', *The American Review of Public Administration*, 28(3): 266–86.

——. (2004) *Trouble in Foundationland: Looking Back, Looking Ahead*, Indianapolis, IN: Hudson Institute.

——. (2006) *Strategic Giving: The Art and Science of Philanthropy*, Chicago: University of Chicago Press.

Greiling, D. (2009) 'Erfolgsmassstäbe für Nonprofit-Organisationen', *Betriebswirtschaftliche Forschung und Praxis*, 61(1): 56–78.

Harrow, J. (2010) 'Philanthropy', in R. Taylor (ed.) *Third Sector Research*, New York: Springer.

Harrow, J. and Jung, T. (2015) 'Debate: Thou Shalt Have Impact, Total Impact – Government Involvement in Philanthropic Foundations' Decision-making', *Public Money and Management*, 35(3), 176–8.

Herman, R. D. and Renz, D. O. (2008) 'Advancing Nonprofit Organizational Effectiveness Research and Theory: Nine Theses', *Nonprofit Management and Leadership*, 18(4): 399–415.

Inspiring Impact Initiative (2015) Impact Hub, www.inspiringimpact.org/listings/ [Accessed 13 June 2015].

Jung, T., Harrow, J. and Pharoah, C. (2012) *Learning from Failure in the Nonprofit Sector?* Report on the ESRC Festival of Social Science Roundtable Discussion, Centre for Charitable Giving and Philanthropy, London.

Kaplan, R.S. (2001) 'Strategic Performance Measurement and Management in Nonprofit Organizations', *Nonprofit Management and Leadership*, 11(3): 353–70.

Kehl, K., Then, V. and Münscher, R. (2011) 'Social Return on Investment: auf dem Weg zu einem integrativen Ansatz der Wirkungsforschung', in H. K. Anheier, A. Schröer and K. Kehl (eds) *Soziale Investitionen*, Wiesbaden: VS Verlag für Sozialwissenschaften.

——. (2012) 'Social Return on Investment: auf dem Weg zu einem integrativen Ansatz der Wirkungsforschung', in H. K. Anheier, A. Schröer and K. Kehl (eds.) *Soziale Investitionen*, Wiesbaden: VS Verlag für Sozialwissenschaften.

Langer, A. (2004) 'Professionsökonomik, Verträge und Vertrauen. Zur Mikrofundierung Professioneller Dienstleistungen durch die Agenturtheorie am Beispiel der Sozialen Arbeit', *Zeitschrift für Wirtschafts- und Unternehmensethik*, 5(3): 284–311.

Leat, D. (2006) 'Grantmaking Foundations and Performance Measurement: Playing Pool?' *Public Policy and Administration*, 21(3): 25–37.

LeRoux, K. and Wright, N. S. (2010) 'Does Performance Measurement Improve Strategic Decision Making? Findings From a National Survey of Nonprofit Social Service Agencies', *Nonprofit and Voluntary Sector Quarterly*, 39(4): 571–87.

Letts, C., Ryan, W. and Grossman, A. (1997) 'Virtuous Capital: What Foundations Can Learn from Venture Capitalists', *Harvard Business Review*, 75(2): 36–and.

Leviton, L. C. and Bickel, W. (2004) 'Integrating Evaluation into Foundation Activity Cycles', in M. Braverman, J. K. Slater and N. Constantine (eds) *Foundations and Evaluation: Contexts and Practices for Effective Philanthropy*, San Francisco: Jossey-Bass.

Light, P. C. (2002) *Pathways to Nonprofit Excellence*, Washington, DC: The Brookings Institution.

——. (2004) *Sustaining Nonprofit Performance: The Case for Capacity Building and the Evidence to Support it*, Washington, DC: Brookings Institution Press.

Lingane, A. and Olson, S. (2004) 'Guidelines for Social Return on Investment', *California Management Review*, 46(3): 116–35.

Mark, M. and Beery, W. (2004) 'Making Judgements about What to Evaluate and How Intensely', in M. T. M. Braverman, J. Slater and N. Constantine (eds) *Foundations and Evaluation: Contexts and Practices for Effective Philanthropy*, San Francisco: Jossey-Bass.

Mayhew, F. (2012) 'Aligning for Impact: The Influence of the Funder-fundee Relationship on Evaluation Utilization', *Nonprofit Management and Leadership*, 23(2): 193–217.

Mildenberger, G., Münscher, R. and Schmitz, B. (2011) 'Dimensionen der Bewertung Gemeinnütziger Organisationen und Aktivitäten', in H. K. Anheier, V. Then and A. Schröer (eds) *Soziale Investitionen – Interdisziplinäre Perspektiven*. Wiesbaden: VS Verlag.

Millesen, J. L., Carman, J. and Bies, A. L. (2010) 'Why Engage? Understanding the Incentive to Build Nonprofit Capacity', *Nonprofit Management and Leadership*, 21(1): 5–20.

Moxham, C. (2010) 'Help or Hindrance? Examining the Role of Performance Measurement in UK Nonprofit Organizations', *Public Performance and Management Review*, 33(3): 342–54.

Moynihan, D., and Ingraham, R. (2004) 'Integrative Leadership in the Public Sector: A Model of Performance-information Use', *Administration and Society*, 36(4): 427–53.

Murray, V. (2010) 'Evaluating the Effectiveness of Nonprofit Organizations', in D. O. Renz and Associates (eds) *The Jossey-Bass Handbook of Nonprofit Leadership and Management*, 3 ed. San Francisco: Jossey-Bass.

nef. (2004) *Social Return on Investment: Valuing what matters*, London: nef.

Patton, M. Q. (2003) *Practical Evaluation*, Newbury Park, CA: Sage.

Phillips, S. T. H. (2010) 'Financing the Third Sector: Introduction', *Policy and Society*, 29: 181–7.

Poister, T. H. (2003) *Measuring Performance in Public and Nonprofit Organizations*, San Francisco: Jossey-Bass.

Salamon, L. M. and Burckart, W. (2014) 'Foundations as "Philanthropic Banks"', in Lester M. Salamon (ed.) *New Frontiers of Philanthropy. A Guide to the New Tools and Actors Reshaping Global Philanthropy and Social Investing*, Oxford: Oxford University Press, 165–208.

Sanger, M. B. (2008) 'From Measurement to Management: Breaking through the Barriers to State and Local Performance', *Public Administration Review*, 68: S70–S85.

Sawhill, J. C. and Williamson, D. (2001) 'Mission Impossible? Measuring Social Impact in Nonprofit Organizations', *Nonprofit Management and Leadership*, 11(3): 371.

Schervish, P. G. and Havens, J. J. (1997) 'Social Participation and Charitable Giving: A Multivariate Analysis', *Voluntas*, 8(3): 235–60.

Siciliano, J. (1997) 'The Relationship Between Formal Planning and Performance in Nonprofit Organizations', *Nonprofit Management and Leadership*, 7(4): 387–403.

Sowa, J. E., Coleman Seldon, S. and Sandfort, J. R. (2004) 'No Longer Unmeasurable? A Multidimensional Integrated Model of Nonprofit Organizational Effectiveness', *Nonprofit and Voluntary Sector Quarterly*, 33(4): 711–28.

Speckbacher, G. (2003) 'The Economics of Performance Management in Nonprofit Organizations', *Nonprofit Management and Leadership*, 13(3): 267.

Stone, M. M., Bigelow, B. and Crittenden, W. (1999) 'Research on Strategic Management of Nonprofit Organizations: Synthesis, Analysis, and Future Directions', *Administration and Society*, 31(3): 378–423.

Thomson, D. (2010) 'Exploring the Role of Funders' Performance Reporting Mandates in Nonprofit Performance Measurement', *Nonprofit and Voluntary Sector Quarterly*, 39(4): 611–29.

United Way of America (1996) Measuring Program Outcomes: A Practical Approach, www.nrpa.org/uploadedFiles/nrpa.org/Professional_Development/Accreditation/COAPRT/Measuring_Program_Outcomes-UW.pdf [Accessed 2 October 2015].

Van Slyke, D. M. (2007) 'Agents or Stewards: Using Theory to Understand the Government-Nonprofit Social Service Contracting Relationship', *Journal of Public Administration Research and Theory*, 17: 157–87.

Van Slyke, D. M. and Newman, H. K. (2006) 'Venture Philanthropy and Social Entrepreneurship in Community Redevelopment', *Nonprofit Management and Leadership*, 16(3): 345–72.

von Schnurbein, G. and Bethmann, S. (2010) 'Philanthropie in der Schweiz', *CEPS Forschung und Praxis – Band 01*, Basel: Centre for Philanthropy Studies (CEPS).

von Schnurbein, G. and Stöckli, S. (2010) 'Die Gestaltung von Nonprofit Governance Kodizes in Deutschland und der Schweiz', *Die Betriebswirtschaft*, 70(6): 495–512.

Weiss, C. H. (1995) 'Nothing as Practical as Good Theory: Exploring Theory-based Evaluation for Comprehensive Community Initiatives for Children and Families', in J. P. Connell, A. C. Kubish, L. B. Schorr and C. H. Weiss (eds) *New Approaches to Evaluating Community Initiatives, Vol. 1: Concepts, Methods, and Contexts*, Queenstown, MD: The Aspen Institute.

Wenar, L. (2010) 'Beyond Corporate Social Responsibility: Oil Multinationals and Social Challenges', *International Affairs*, 86(2): 548–9.

Whitman, J. R. (2008) 'Evaluating Philanthropic Foundations According to their Social Values', *Nonprofit Management and Leadership*, 18(4): 417–34.

——. (2009) 'Measuring Social Values in Philanthropic Foundations', *Nonprofit Management and Leadership*, 19(3).

Williams-Taylor, L. (2008) 'Why Are Performance-Based Programs So Important?', *Public Management* (May): 24–27.

Wyser, R. and von Schnurbein, G. (2011) 'Trilateral Evaluation Situation – A Theory-based Model', *ERNOP-Conference*. Vienna.

Zimmermann, J. A. M. and Stevens, B. W. (2006) 'The Use of Performance Measurement in South Carolina Nonprofits', *Nonprofit Management and Leadership*, 16(3): 315–27.

31

Accountability in 4-D

Changing approaches in contemporary philanthropy

Jenny Harrow

Accountability, both mandated and negotiated, is an evolving feature of philanthropic life. For foundations and other philanthropic actors, seeking to influence social change and needing to work with others, accountability and the legitimacy it brings, have become 'operational necessities' (Tomei, 2013: 403). Yet, philanthropy's varied forms, levels, directions and networks means that the forms and expressions of its accountability are in flux. The power asymmetries derived through private, discretionary gift making ensures growing external interest in – though not necessarily leverage over – philanthropy's accountability, both globally and locally. Such accruals of power, however, point to the greater importance of philanthropy's 'accountability by judgment' than its 'accountability by standards' (Stewart, 1984: 17). In particular, when foundations and other philanthropic actors' judgments lead them to seek 'transformational social change' (Partzsch and Fuchs, 2012), they become intertwined with governmental spheres, making them important policy actors, albeit not necessarily democratic ones (Jung and Harrow, 2013). This pushes them towards the more harsh accountability arenas, previously occupied only by public servants, including scrutiny of what organized philanthropy chooses *not* do, particularly in periods of prolonged austerity (Crowley, 2013). At the same time, increasing professionalism in the practice of philanthropy is producing higher expectations on the part of the public and within philanthropy itself.

How then is accountability within formal philanthropy and the foundation world changing, from whose perspectives and with what results? Why, how and to what extent is professionalization within philanthropy reinforcing and extending accountability thinking or adding a further oppositional layer, as it gives further credence to the active operation of discretion? These questions are considered in this chapter, beginning with three illustrations of the ways in which accountability in philanthropy is evolving and interpreted. It continues through examination of the definitions and dimensions of accountability, within and beyond nonprofit literatures, to consideration of contemporary philanthropy's characteristics, including professionalization as a potential engine of accountability. Changing practices in respect of accountability's dimensions are then reviewed and conclusions drawn on achievements and challenges and future directions for inquiry in the context of the intermingled private and public endeavour which philanthropy expresses.

Varieties of accountability in philanthropy: Some illustrations

Three illustrations, each of which recently attracted news media attention in different ways, reinforce awareness of accountability as a concept in motion, where its room for manoeuvre is variously constrained or wide ranging.

Case One: A former warehouse manager with the Toronto Salvation Army was arrested and charged with theft, possession of stolen property and criminal breach of trust in connection with CDN $2 million worth of donated toys that had gone missing over a period of two years. The stash of toys, enough to fill three tractor-trailers, was discovered in two rented warehouses; it included two bicycles, due for the Salvation Army's summer camps that had been donated by the province's Premier. The warehouse manager had been dismissed a week before the arrest and additional arrests were expected. After an inventory, all items were returned to the Salvation Army, and a spokesman confirmed that 'We will do everything in our power to ensure that something like this never happens again' (Canadian Broadcasting Company, 2012).

Case Two: Of the unprecedented USD $1.4 billion donated in the US in the wake of 9/11, nearly half was raised by the American Red Cross (ARC). Contributions were placed not in ARC's 'general fund' but in a separate 'Liberty Fund'. With one-third of the Fund spent on 9/11 victims, the ARC announced in October 2001 that more than enough money for victims' needs had been raised: ARC planned to spend over half the remaining money to build up blood supplies, improve telecommunications and prepare for possible future terrorist attacks. Victims, donors and members of Congress responded angrily. New York's Attorney General threatened legal action. Despite her vigorous defence of its action, ARC's president resigned, and in November 2001, the ARC announced the reversal of its decision, indicating it would direct the entire Fund to victims (Public Broadcasting Service, 2001).

Case Three: At a 'Nutrition for Growth' event in London in 2013, the Children's Investment Fund Foundation (CIFF) pledged funding of £517 million over seven years to reduce the incidence of undernutrition of children worldwide. The UK's nonprofit trade press reported this to be the biggest investment in undernutrition ever made by a private foundation (Mason, 2013). Set up by a 'hedge fund boss and his wife', CIFF had been steadily increasing its spending over recent years, despite sharply falling income from the hedge fund. Nutrition was one of its five strategic priority areas, together with neonatal mortality, deworming, early learning, and prevention of mother-to-child transmission of HIV/Aids. CIFF's co-founder told the meeting that its commitment outlined at the meeting represented an 'historic shift' as nutrition 'takes its place at the heart of the health, education and economic development agendas'. To support the CIFF initiative, £2.7 billion was committed by a range of donors, including £655 million from the UK government (Mason, 2013).

Together, these cases offer alternative insights into philanthropy's changing accountability: from answerability for failed procedures, to clear responsiveness to public pressures, through to leading responsibility for social impact. A shared theme of trust also exists. The first case reflects organizational trust of an untrustworthy employee and donors' looked for trust in an appropriate organizational response. The second case, in which media attention and political interests combined to provoke apparent problem-fixing redress, makes clear the sharpness of the donor market's response. Donors took no account of the broader infrastructure challenges faced by the American Red Cross, being determined to coerce the ARC's discretionary decision in another direction. Therrien (2011) assesses this situation as ARC being 'ethically stuck between accountability and development', and its final actions the result of having failed to 'choose the righter right' (Therrien, 2011: 1). Case three demonstrates accountability as proactive communications in the interests of social change. It hints at the alternative uses of apparent philanthropy 'league tables', however imperfectly constructed, pressing the case for philanthropy's promises to be respected, especially where they are part of a strategy, presented as coherent. Thus, accountability is expressed through openness demonstrating organizational depth of commitment, despite a falling asset base. Claims for the perceived 'historic shift' may yet make for hard comparisons with performance at a later date, together with uncertain comparisons with previous decades' responses to the 'global hunger challenge' (Margulis, 2013: 53).

Exploring definitions

Conceptually, accountability is discussed in a series of definitional whirlpools and from multiple directions (Conley and Doyle, 2011). The *public* nature of accountability is central to its meaning (Steffens, 2008), with questions of 'accountability to whom' and 'accountability for what' raising the ambiguity of public interest notions. Dichotomous understandings of accountability stress contrasts between: vertical and hierarchical accountabilities; to regulators and authorities; to partners and publics (Schillemans, 2011); and between accountability as mechanism and as virtue (Bovens, 2010: 949). Stewart's (1984: 17) earlier 'ladder of accountability' with its 'accountability of judgment' in topmost position, has acute relevance for philanthropy, despite its development for application to public officials and public servants.

Synthesising from Kearns (1996) and other literatures, Morrison and Salipante (2007) identify another paired concept: rule-based accountability (responding to explicit and objective standards of assessment) and negotiated accountability (responding to implicit and subjective standards of assessment). Achieving negotiated accountability requires 'more creativity, attention and skill on the part of leaders than do those for rule-based accountability' (Morrison and Salipante, 2007: 199). Negotiated accountability has special relevance for philanthropy because of its necessary incorporation of power and influence, although with varying outcomes, as the ARC case demonstrates. Further, from Morrison and Salipante's analysis, the different purposes of accountability are also evident, from accountability for control and assurance (rule-based) to accountability for learning and improvement (negotiated and discretionary). As philanthropy evolves so, too, do the pressures on different forms of accountability.

Philanthropy's changing characteristics

Three characteristics of contemporary philanthropy create challenges for accountability definitions, and have effects on its implementation, both rule-based and negotiated. These are: the relative diversity; hybridity; and professionalization of philanthropy. Philanthropy's diverse forms and self-descriptions – celebrity philanthropy, corporate philanthropy, entrepreneurial philanthropy, globalized and place-based dimensions, and virtual giving, among others – are all touched upon and discussed in other chapters of this *Companion*. This diversity entails multiple sets of stakeholders, often with different expectations and scales of accountability. For example, when women donors give for gender-based issues, such as combatting domestic violence, should their primary accountability be to other women, and not just those women supported through such programs? Does the accolade of entrepreneurial philanthropy create an allowance for increased failure, given entrepreneurship's association with risk-taking? This diversity also produces different authorities with formal mandates, or bodies claiming multiple reporting and regulatory or quasi-regulatory powers, including different levels of government, umbrella organizations with accreditation schemes, self-regulatory efforts and self-declared third party 'watchdogs', among which inter-organizational competition for public approval may occur.

These characteristics provide for varying interpretations of accountability rationales and practices. Diversity within faith communities, for example, given the complex associations between religious belief and giving may produce differing expectations regarding account-ability's content and focus. In addition, faith-based organizations vary in their own faith-accountability mechanisms, as noted in Jennings' (2013) matrix that divides faith based organizations into those belonging to an institutional hierarchy and those which are independent actors. Also, the implications for accountability in terms of the choice of gift recipient are complex in some areas of faith-led philanthropy, for instance where particular merit attaches to recipients marked by renunciation of wealth (Eck, 2013). In studying 'com-municated accountability' of Muslim and Christian charities in the UK, Yasmin and col-leagues (2013) found generally limited descriptive information rather than 'judgment-based information', with interview findings indicating as a key reason high donor trust and thus weak demand for the latter kind of accountability from stakeholders. Such high trust among donors may exist also in relation to secular giving contexts, for example in specialized areas, such as environmental concerns where donors and donees espouse particular shared values. However, while research continues to delineate an association between faith and giving propensity, there is no necessary guarantee that high trust will continue as an accountabil-ity shock-absorber or deflector in these organizations, especially when evidence appears of misplaced or abused trust.

Hybridization of philanthropic activity creates practical accountability dilemmas, particu-larly in public-private philanthropic partnerships and consortia relations among philanthropists and foundations, where vertical and horizontal forms of accountability often cross cut, and accountability trails become somewhat buried in the mixed domains of public and private social action. In addition, the underlying accountabilities – or their absence – of the public, private and nonprofit sectors that operate in such partnerships can create fundamental incompatibilities, often not initially recognized. For example, in the context of government-philanthropy poverty reduction partnerships in Turkey, Morvaridi (2013: 305)

Questions whether partnerships between the state and institutions that are not democrati-cally elected and do not fit within a robust accountability framework can fulfil (the state's) remit and responsibility (in terms of social protection and transformation).

A different set of challenges arise in corporate giving, where philanthropic effort may be simultaneously close to the firm (through its direct giving), and distinct from it (through the firm's foundation): the question of which entity is responsible for what may be opaque or contradictory. Givel (2013: 171), for example, examines a leading pharmaceutical firm with reported goals of no person anywhere being restricted from receiving essential and affordable medicines, yet with corporate responsibility programs that are 'discretionary and limited in scope and impact'.

Moreover, the hybridization *within* the wider nonprofit sector (Harrow and Phillips, 2013; Smith, Chapter 20) ensures that even where philanthropic action itself remains distinct, many of its funded organizations reflect degrees of boundary-blurring that make attribution of achieve-ment very difficult. Nevertheless, for independent philanthropy, it can be argued that 'robust-ness' is a self-defining feature, reaffirming accountability's subjective construction. A related source of hybridization occurs as a result of the collision, or merging, of different philanthropic cultures. For instance, Dar, (2013 NP) examining 'hybrid accountabilities, when western and non-western accountabilities collide' from the perspective of an Indian non-governmental organization (NGO), reports from ethnographic research that '(NGO) workers produce hybrid accounts in response to top-down reporting practices that intermingle donor and local trust-building practices.'

Contemporary philanthropy appears increasingly professionalized, leading to further expec-tations of professional practice, and greater sophistication in meeting stakeholder expectations.

For this chapter, a 'profession' is understood from a functional perspective, where its formally-educated occupants possess extensive knowledge and expertise important to society, gaining positions of significance and standing in that society and society-sanctioned powers in return for acting on their knowledge and protecting clients and/or the public. Professionalization is the process of gaining and consolidating that standing, primarily though knowledge transfer, reputation, self-regulation and exclusion (Saks, 2012). It is evident that 'the proliferation of foundations has created a class of grantmaking professionals' (Houston, 2010: 79), with grantmaking now commonly referred to as a 'profession' (Delgado *et al.*, 2001), with subfields such as 'development' philanthropy, becoming subdivided into their own 'professions' with their own 'curricula, professional association, credentials and support networks' (The Resource Alliance and Rockefeller Foundation, 2012: 38). Professionalism is also the operationalization of a profession's values, often through application of codes of conduct or ethical practice frameworks. It may also be seen as discourse, as in urging the importance of 'having the work done by professionals' (Evetts, 2012).

The question raised in response to these developments is: greater professionalization and consequent professionalism for whom? One underlying critique is that professionalization appears predominantly to support top-down accountability, working more evidently for donors, individuals and boards than for beneficiaries. Another is that professionalization creates stakeholder interests for philanthropy's employees. Conversely, given the disparities in size of philanthropic organizations, some might argue that philanthropy continues to be characterized by those whose instincts for help are either unsupported by timely knowledge, or driven by enthusiasm rather than expertise (Maas and Lickert, 2011). Nevertheless, assertions of professionalization in philanthropy predominate, alongside expanded professionalism in nonprofits generally. For example, see Gautier *et al.*'s (2013) analysis of 'philanthropic renewal in France after decades of distrust', developing in parallel with 'an increasingly professionalized French nonprofit sector'. These perspectives raise questions as to professionalism as an engine of philanthropic accountability, specifically the key roles it plays in reaching judgments and enhancing negotiated accountability.

Changing practices in accountability: Fourfold dimensions

In the light of these three characteristics, opportunities for, and expectations of, accountability in philanthropy occur in interactions between those giving and those receiving accounts, where the behaviour of the former is assessed by the latter in the light of possible consequences. In those interactions, four dimensions of accountability appear important. These are: *giving an account*, where the outcome and virtue is transparency; *fixing problems*, where the outcome and virtue is responsibility; *linking actions to values and public (often community) needs*, where the outcome and virtue is responsiveness; and *linking actions to results*, where the outcome and virtue is achievement or performance.

Giving an account: Transparency

The push for transparency within philanthropy derives from several sources, facilitated by expanding global technological capacity for information sharing, though accompanied by scepticism, if not cynicism, in societies around promises for social change. If philanthropy is seen as social actions involving the making and keeping of public promises for social betterment by private individuals and groups, then proactive information provision – contrasting with 'complying with' or 'surrendering' information to public regulators – has a role to play in demonstrating how, when, and where, promises are being kept, though mostly not *why* the promises were made in the first instance. Transparency, then, is a limited, if welcome, form of accountability.

The increase in greater disclosure requirements from regulators and by governments, the latter arising in part from anti-terrorist measures and the 'securitization' of civil society, also moves transparency to the fore, leaving other dimensions even more open to philanthropic discretion. That prominence is enhanced by arguments that transparency can be equated with 'good governance', and assessed transnationally as illustrated by the tool provided by Rey-Garcia *et al.* (2012: 77) for assessing foundation transparency internationally. Especially where organized philanthropy faces more than one regulator, with differing disclosure demands, as in the US with certain non-negotiable regulation at federal and state level, it is likely that a minimalist view of disclosure will dominate. This is particularly so in smaller organizations, where transparency costs matter.

Third party 'watchdogs', some with business and consulting interests among philanthropy givers and takers, might be expected to further enhance transparency. The extent of their influence is difficult to gauge, however, with influence likely confined to relatively closed circles of activist donors, financial and legal philanthropy advisers, and membership of particular networks. The online reports produced by the US Better Business Bureau Wise Giving Alliance, for instance, suggest considerable potential for indirect power over transparency matters. Its Standards for Charity Accountability offer to 'assist donors in making sound giving decisions and to foster public confidence in charitable organisations' (Better Business Bureau, 2013: NP). The value and credibility of such standards is nevertheless debated, as is the effect of such ratings on donor behaviour, and whether failure to meet standards have any consequences. Research findings are contradictory. Gordon and colleagues (2009), examining a group of charities rated by the intermediary Charity Navigator, report that rating changes do impact contributions: positive rating changes were associated with contributions increasing, and organizations with ratings decline were associated with decreased contributions. Szper and Prakash (2011), however, found that changes in charity ratings recorded on Charity Navigator in one US state tended not to affect those charities' donor support, reporting that charities believed donors to assess their trustworthiness from aspects such as word-of-mouth and community visibility, rather than from formal, mostly financial, information disclosure. This preference for more intuitive, personal-judgmental rather than formal account-giving by philanthropy is confirmed by Coyte *et al.* (2013) who studied how 'NGFs' (Non-Governmental Funders), account for their grantmaking decisions in an Australian context. They report that 'assurance is constructed as part of the decision-making process through a more socialising form of accountability, based on personal interaction, in contrast to a reliance on hierarchical accountability and transparency' (Coyte *et al.*, 2013: 397).

Other sources pressing philanthropy to increase transparency include affected individuals and groups (donors and beneficiaries) and the news media, with enlarged scrutiny of public institutions receiving philanthropic gifts. Universities may be prime targets of media scrutiny because of the size, sources and specificity of major gifts, although with varying effect. In the UK, compare the criticism of controversial gift acceptance at the London School of Economics, contributing to its director's resignation, (LSE, 2011), and that at the University of Cambridge, where a funded chair went ahead despite media reported protests in and beyond the University (Cambridge University Reporter, 2012). The phenomenon of the apparently tainted gift has transparency implications then for the givers, as well as receivers of gifts. So, too, does the growing interest in responsible investing by which foundations operate 'no-buy' lists for investments, disinvest in controversial, i.e. deemed unethical, commercial operations, and make public these investment decisions. Even so, disclosure of such decisions remains matters of choice, sometimes negotiation, but not necessity. Unusually, and ironically, some receivers of gifts are loathe to report their philanthropic sources. To illustrate: in a US study of corporate philanthropy with health advocacy organizations (HAOs), Rothman *et al.* (2011) examined Eli Lilly and Company's grant registry and HAO websites to determine grant-disclosure patterns. They concluded that 'only 25 percent of HAOs that received Lilly grants acknowledged Lilly's contributions on their websites, and only ten percent acknowledged Lilly as a grant event sponsor. No HAO disclosed the exact amount of a Lilly grant' (Rothman *et al.*, 2011: 606).

In spite of external pressures, there remains considerable reluctance about transparency within this sector (Breen, 2013; Cordery, 2013). A 2012 survey of Canadian nonprofits and foundations (Lasby and Barr, 2012: 224) is telling: both quite readily made available their annual reports and board composition, but only a third proactively disclosed their financial statements and fundraising information. Foundations were divided sharply between public foundations, which tend to be proactive in information sharing, and private ones, which are not likely to release much information at all (Lasby and Barr, 2012: 225). Nevertheless, there is some evidence that transparency practices are changing, especially among the largest philanthropic entities. This includes increased disclosure about detailed program data and about activities such as spending allocations and partnerships. The global health field offers multiple examples, with the Bill and Melinda Gates Foundation cited as not only the largest but most transparently operated (Moran and Stephenson, 2013). Yet, as McCoy *et al.* (2009: 407) note in attempting to track global health finances to discover who benefits, 'data on private sources of global health finance are inadequate but indicate a large and important role of private actors'.

Both voluntary and nonvoluntary disclosures of information have the potential – but not necessarily the effect – of opening up subsequent dialogue, particularly when used for impression management, or when there is fear that self-reported problems may prompt intense investigation. Although demands for more transparency in philanthropy appear difficult to fault, they need to be set against the argument that such pressures are inimical to the perception that philanthropy is at its best when it is anonymous, quiet and non-publicity-seeking. With giving in secret praised by many faiths, but culturally also seen as a confidential act in secular societies (Gautier *et al.*, 2013), the case for anonymity in giving encapsulates the ambiguity of philanthropy as a private action directed towards public gain, and points to barriers facing a blanket 'more transparency' call. Beyond faith and humility, those barriers will include desires for privacy and donor preference for maintaining private control of private spending. Thus, Scaife *et al.* (2012: 34–35) in exploring Australian philanthropists' perceptions of their giving, record both the recognition that

> when you put money in a foundation, when you have got your tax deduction, it's no longer your money" and the view that transparency demands are "ill advised", since "I don't want ... that kind of carping scrutiny of what we are doing ..."

The nature, form, and choices of transparency are important for philanthropy's accountability, but by no means sufficient for it. Meachen and Ward (2012, cited in Anderson 2013: 11)), also writing in an Australian context, make the case that 'transparency does not automatically increase accountability, and accountability can and does occur without total public transparency'.

Fixing problems: Responsibility

Taking responsibility for pre-empting and fixing problems emphasizes philanthropy's strengths and its capacity for learning. Examples of problem fixing carried out under a hostile public gaze, as in the ARC case, are relatively rare, but so are open discussions and public sharing about experiences in philanthropy that did not go according to plan. Here, the example of the Corston

Coalition, a group of 22 UK foundations, collaborating for the first time in direct advocacy, rather than funding existing advocacy groups, is an important exception. Urging government implementation of the government-commissioned (Corston) report on vulnerable women in the criminal justice system, this coalition undertook and published a review of its organizational learning, as well as its policy effects, with the intent of being useful to coalition members, future funder collaboratives and scholars (Kaufmann 2011: 7). The review is candid about the realities of moving from decision through to action as a collaboration among foundations that had never worked in this way or on this scale: it was a process marked by frustration and delay, with obstacles including members' boards and disagreements about the money and the manner of collaboration (Kaufmann 2011: 11). The review demonstrates that organizational problems were eventually 'fixed' (Jung *et al.*, 2013) and, as a learning document, it has strong potential to help future foundation collaborations, although its honesty in describing internal challenges may also create wariness among advocacy nonprofits and would-be foundation collaborators. This case, as Jung *et al.* (2013) underscore, also demonstrates the often transitory nature of problem-fixing and responsibility-taking as foundations move into and out of such coalitions, without explaining their exit strategies.

Both learning and responsibility-taking are supported by codes of practice and self-regulatory behaviour in philanthropy, especially where membership organizations act as 'accountability clubs', with ethical practice guidelines to which their members should adhere (Gugerty, 2009; Frumkin, 2010). For Frumkin (2010: 148), these vary considerably in their potential for enforcing compliance, ranging from those where operating principles are established, but without indication as to the consequences of failure to observe them, to others where principles are expected to be demonstrated, as well as adhered to by members. Relatively few foundations develop their own internal codes of conduct, and these, like the accountability club models, differ substantially in their capacity for enforcement. For example, the Skillman Foundation in Detroit describes its reasons for adopting a Code of Ethics in terms of the assurance it gives to 'grantees and the *general public*' that no staff or trustee will benefit from its grant funds, and no organization would gain an unfair advantage because of staff or trustee affiliation (Skillman Foundation, 2012). This appears as much a political as a professional (in the sense of trustworthy) form of responsibility. By comparison, the Ford Foundation's (2012) 'Staff Code of Conduct and Ethics' incorporates a strong element of compliance-based material. Ethics codes are not in themselves protection from ethical dilemmas in philanthropy, and suggest the existence of internal, as well as external accountability challenges. Nor will the existence of codes of conduct necessarily equate with ethical behaviour per se. In her scrutiny of 'the comfort of codes' in international philanthropy settings, Leat (2004: 20) stresses that 'the primary job of codes is to cut transaction costs – we replace trust in the organisation with trust in the code'.

The scale, as well as the nature, of philanthropic action points also to what public management literature calls 'professional accountability', that is placing control over organizational activities in the hands of employees with special skills or expertise to get the job done (Chan and Rosenbloom, 2010). The demand for highly quality staff, in part, explains the international burgeoning of graduate programs in nonprofit and philanthropic studies (Mirabella *et al.*, 2007; Mirabella and Young, 2012; Keidan *et al.*, 2014). As valuable as specialist philanthropy studies are, given the interventionist nature of philanthropic action, an expectation of professional behaviour will be high, but cannot be guaranteed. Although more professionalized, the philanthropy profession still lacks an authoritative professional body or bodies, controlling entry and exit as exist in other self-governing professions. Indeed, Damon (2006: 2) regards philanthropy as an exception among areas of 'highly consequential work' since its affairs are conducted without shared practices and or industry-wide codes. Similarly, Stauber (2010) finds that philanthropy as a profession is wanting, against classical tests, but argues that it should not become one, emphasizing the importance of wisdom as well as rigour in grantmaking.

Philanthropy is a highly contingent business, relying heavily on relationships. *Who* attempts to fix philanthropy's problems is then highly dependent on the context and nature of the philanthropic forms, scale and previous public persona, if any. Since philanthropy 'lacks the pragmatic must-do accountability' which other nonprofits face in relation to funders and clients (Lee, 2004: 169), openness about problem recognition, as well as problem-fixing tends to be discretionary. *'When does philanthropy apologize?'* is a question to which there are a potential range of answers. Board apology, in the form of resignation, is rare; only likely in damaging cases of internal fraud and theft. The very privacy of philanthropic decision-making, on, or beyond, boards, makes it impossible to assess the extent of philanthropy's being 'asleep on the job' or, alternatively, acutely active, monitoring and reviewing all actions in its name.

Longstanding exhortations exist for philanthropy to learn from its failures, notably Frumkin's (1998) authoritative case that distinguishes between constructive and unconstructive failure in grantmaking. Unconstructive failures, the more common kind, do not result in learning from failure, largely because no evaluation is conducted or is not communicated. Frumkin urged philanthropy to recover its 'diagnostic function' which has been impeded by the fact that it is far less glamorous than making 'prematurely optimistic' announcements of new programs (Frumkin, 1998). Yet, openly available accounts of such learning remain sparse. For Coffman *et al.* (2013: 38), the main challenge among US foundations 'is still how to increase evaluation use and the most common response is still to focus on the supply side'. However, for Boris and Kopczynski Winkler (2013: 69), 'American philanthropic foundations began to foster evaluation as a force for accountability and transparency in the 1980s', so that implicitly the 'problem fixing' aspect appears played down. Moreover, research on the experiences of professional field staff themselves conducting evaluations reports points to some facing ethical challenges, for example around the internal functioning of foundations and ownership and dissemination of evaluation (Morris, 2007.) Thus, debates as to whether evaluation within foundations is primarily an internal operations tool, or an external conduit for increasing openness and taking (or rejecting) responsibility, seem set to continue.

Linking actions to values and community needs: Responsiveness

Responsiveness within philanthropy may be expressed in terms of empathy with its beneficiary groups, developing cultural norms that shift towards social relations within giving relationships (Ostrander, 2007), and creating systems that demonstrate a disposition towards responsiveness, such as public meetings, governance structures, philanthropic appointments and grantee commentary. Formal mechanisms for responsiveness may be mandated by regulators (for instance, under incorporation legislation) and enshrined into an organization's own operating rules (for example, requirements for an annual open meeting with beneficiaries). As Hammack and Anheier (2013: 153) note, foundations have extensive discretion in this regard: they 'may embrace almost any minority cause, almost any approach to grantmaking'. Yet, underlying motivations for, and outcomes of, such practices vary immensely, from whole-hearted embracing of 'the other's' perspective to a 'going through the motions' attitude. As a practical matter, responsiveness in philanthropy is hard to assess if, and where, its expressions are unseen – and so much of relationship-building between grantmakers and grantees remains unreported, if not hidden. Where philanthropic values are explicit and understood widely to be consequential, those consequences may nevertheless be more complex and unexpected than initially believed. This is illustrated by Goss's (2007) examination of the role of philanthropic patrons in shaping gender politics and of foundations in influencing the women's movement in the US during the 1960s to 1980s. She argues that foundations played a critical part 'in segmenting U.S. womanhood into politically relevant subgroups', and that 'professional grantmakers have constituted a critical yet overlooked force behind the construction of US hyperpluralism, in the process diminishing the capacity of gender to unite women in common cause' (Goss, 2007: 1174).

For philanthropy generally, responsiveness in the public eye usually plays out through stakeholder engagement (Candler and Dumont, 2010), though privileging some stakeholders over others. Widening donor-stakeholder pools and engagement with weaker stakeholders (notably beneficiaries) appears more advocated than acted upon. For example, the International Network for Strategic Philanthropy study (Backer *et al.*, 2005) proposed that, especially in 'uncertain times', foundations should increase their interactions with stakeholders – taking the widest possible definition of stakeholders – by bringing them into decision-making. Rather than beneficiaries simply hearing *ex post facto* about philanthropic decisions, beneficiaries might be incorporated into the making of those decisions, thus empowering these organizations and communities. Indeed, McGinnis (2012), exploring 'participatory philanthropy' among six US funders that use community volunteer committees rather than traditional boards to allocate grants, found more congruence between grant decisions of these two approaches than the literatures suggest. Beyond concerns around conflicts of interest that such involvement might entail, the potential for co-optation has to be considered (Baur and Schmitz, 2012).

The trend for larger foundations to solicit 'grantee perception reports' can be cited as a limited (Watson and Manzione, 2010), but critical, form of responsiveness, although whether grantees' 'upwards reporting' then changes foundations' behaviour is unclear. The power to commission such reports remains with foundations, with findings apparently affecting strategy more generally than addressing (or redressing) specific grantee concerns. In the US, the Center on Effective Philanthropy's (CEP, 2012) Grantee Survey tool, with surveys conducted with over 52,000 grantees, is reported to have been used by over 190 funders in more than 87 countries. Although this might suggest the longer-term influence of comparative data among participating foundations, CEP reports that around 30 (around one-sixth) 'have made some parts or all of (these reports) public' (CEP, 2012). Over the longer term, nevertheless, grantees may yet increase their voice through this formal, invitational doorway.

Professionals' roles and attitudes play a part in growing mutual understanding between donor and recipient, although this, too, is open to interpretation, especially given the very limited research focusing on the experiences of philanthropy professionals. One example of concentration on staff roles is Kohl's (2008) research on relations between philanthropy, farmworker organizing and community development in California's Central Valley. This studied the philanthropy program officer's multiple field roles and experiences, where field staff helped frame funding applications to recognize that boards, predominantly made up of businessmen, 'will not touch strategies that imply holding "business" accountable' (Kohl, 2008: 22). The officers adopted roles, both proactive and political, as coaches, helping community organizations present their initiatives in language that resonated with the funding boards.

Responsiveness to whom is a question also being tempered by exertions of donor control, itself a function of the legal jurisdictions in which donation occurs. The donor intent challenge by donors' heirs, producing a six-year legal battle regarding Princeton University's use of a major gift dating from 1961 (Gary, 2010), is a prime example. Whether this comes to be seen over the longer term as a critical reverse-accountability trend, with donees forced to implement the top-down interpreted intent of deceased donors, or, more widely, as the outcome of some kind of secular philanthropic ancestor worship remains to be seen. Trends toward increased donor control (Harrow, 2010) are also evident in donor exclusivity arrangements, such as donor networks and giving circles, and through donor intermediaries where philanthropic advisers play key roles in funding choices and disbursement. In addition, the question of who sits at the (philanthropic) table to debate how decisions are made about the allocation of resources and actions, with an implication that newcomers would or should 'represent' receiving organizations or communities, and thus be able to *enforce* a degree of responsiveness, is becoming more fraught. This is most evident among community foundations where issues of representation of local populations is actively debated, and in publicized cases of intra-institutional accountability clashes, for example, when a foundation's major regeneration initiatives and spending in Detroit – and its reported 'foundation-knows-best attitude' – led to significant disagreement between the foundation and elected local government (Dolan, 2011).

Among philanthropy's severest critics, its *non*-responsiveness and suppression of views in favour of its own is its hallmark: this is tied to its privilege of privacy-making which is seen as nondemocratic (if not antidemocratic) (Hall, 2013). Thus Roelofs (2009: 930) expresses the view that though 'support from corporate or private foundations is essential to almost all civil rights, social justice or environmental movements that wish to be viable and visible, funders exercise control in so many ways. Freedom of speech and association … are thereby diminished'. In giving evidence to a 2012 parliamentary committee inquiry into UK foundations in international development, the Institute of Development Studies observed that there were 'serious issues around private foundations' lack of legitimacy, due to the private and undemocratic nature of their democratic processes' (House of Commons, 2012, 46). Similarly, Barnes (2005) is blunt in her examination of 'terror, oil and strategic philanthropy', where she argues that firms' community development initiatives in African contexts can, by the creation of dependence, create situations where the local public becomes accountable to them.

Philanthropy may be equally characterized as a friend of democracy, through its support of associational life and civil society, appropriately responsive to its societal settings and pressures. Here responsiveness occurs indirectly, as well as directly. The willingness of the largest foundations in western states to collaborate with governments in social projects (Wood, 2013) may also be seen as an accountable, responsive, act. Pennekamp and Focke (2013: 47), for example, examine one US foundation's attempt to provide a 'staging ground to build an independent, coherent response to a failing economy' in a Northern Californian town. Immediacy of philanthropic responses to major disasters provides a further analysis 'stage', as does work examining evidence of corporate philanthropy's 'social responsiveness' to catastrophes where firms had particular local interests or connections (Crampton and Patten, 2008). Fioramonti and Thümler (2011: NP) go even further to explore whether, given the lack of accountability in the international financial sector, foundations are 'using their resources to support a stronger civil society role in this field'.

Maintaining a balance regarding responsiveness is politically challenging, particularly in politically volatile settings. Both indigenous and transnational philanthropy often struggle to find the balance between politically responsible and socially responsible actions. This is, for example, highlighted by Silber's (2012) discussion of 'angry gifts' in relation to policy advocacy in Israel, and by Herrold's (2012) exploration of philanthropic foundations in Egypt: are they 'fueling change or safeguarding status quo?'. What counts as responsiveness on the accountability spectrum then appears as particularly elusive, subject to the geopolitical situations in which philanthropy operates. In contrast, accountability that seeks to link philanthropic action to results, broadly understood as philanthropic impact, looks initially to provide significant clarity in assessing philanthropy's achievements, as discussed in the next section.

Linking action to results: Impact

The centrality of demonstrating 'social impact' performance, as evidence of improving performance and positive effects for beneficiaries, runs throughout nonprofit literatures (Flynn and Hodgkinson, 2001; Polonsky and Grau, 2011). Rationales for impact measurement range from drives to increase nonprofit accountability as 'hollowed out states' increasingly rely on service provision by nonprofits (Alexander *et al.*, 2010) to the push from increasing citizen participation in policy processes with its 'how are we doing' question (Jun and Shiau, 2012). By applying sensemaking theory to funding relationships, Grimes (2010) finds performance measurement processes are not just a means of accountability, but also an organizational identity tool. Although the severe limitations on impact measurement have been well illustrated (Ebrahim and Rangan, 2010; Cosyns *et al.*, 2013: 287), the philosophical case for impact measurement and the managerial means of assessing impact through a variety of frameworks and tools are buttressed by the growth of consultancies, some being charities themselves, to support these drives.

Understanding, measuring and acting on impact knowledge in philanthropy for organizational improvement and learning is challenging in its own right (von Schnurbein, Chapter 30), but presents particular dilemmas when seen as a means of philanthropy's external accountability. Predominantly, it appears that impact is seen as a factor affecting philanthropy's own funding choices, but with the accountability sent downstream to the fundee, often within the somewhat self-congratulatory descriptor of 'high impact' or 'results-based' philanthropy – as if philanthropy might be likely to choose the converse. Yet, such descriptors also appear to push philanthropy increasingly towards time-limited social interventions, in seemingly less complex and bounded social problem areas; this stands in contrast to the enduring claim of much, and especially endowed, philanthropy that it can, and will, be there for the long-term.

In a related irony, for some foundations, impact-led approaches to funding decisions are perceived as preferable to 'responsive' approaches, where this is understood as reactive funding in accordance with incoming requests (Coon, 2013). Philanthropy professionals placing client-grantee interests uppermost recognize these pressures. In Kohl's study (2008: 30), for example, fieldworkers steered clients towards grant applications that reflected awareness that 'boards will not continue their reinvestment in long-term focused community building, without proof of measurable outcomes in the short term'. Further, from this perspective, philanthropy appears as an enforcer of other nonprofits' accountability, and then not necessarily systematically. For Bernstein (2011: 38) the 'growing corporatization' of philanthropy is exemplified by its 'metrics mania' that are associated with impact measurement and allied to moves that she describes as 'coercive accountability'. Buckley *et al.* (2012: 20) report effects on fundees of this impact-at-a-distance judgments by UK foundations: staff of one organization noted, 'we were asked to account for 95p underspend on a budget line. That kind of micromanagement comes when people don't really know what they are doing'; another observed that 'we often spend a lot of time reporting and then the funder simply says the cheque is in the post'.

For philanthropy, with its own impact necessarily bound up with its disbursement choices, particular accountability dilemmas occur around: the nature and forms of the impact reports it mandates; the problems of how philanthropy deals with poor results; the necessarily changing role of philanthropy vis-à-vis their fundees, with responsibility flowing back organizationally upstream; the effects of impact seeking on philanthropy boards; and the wider implications for philanthropy's influence, both their justification of priorities and their public policy impacts. An overarching factor in each of these areas is the extent and effects of professionalisation within philanthropy.

As the wider nonprofits literature emphasizes, the nature of 'impact' reporting being mandated by philanthropy often still pertains only to organizational inputs and outputs, with outcomes being a continual challenge (Ebrahim and Rangan, 2010), with the attribution questions as complex for philanthropy and their fundees as for public programs attempting to pinpoint 'success'. This may leave philanthropy operating with, at best, partial pictures from its fundees. An unexpected effect may be that, because the consequences of *not* achieving results may be more significant than in the past, fundees may omit to report where they have experienced a lack of success. Yet, such reporting of 'poor results' might itself be a critical learning area for the funder, for example arising from late approval of a grant or from its onerous demands for working collaboratively. Only in situations where the impact metrics to be collected, recorded and disseminated can be agreed between funder and fundee in a negotiated, rather than one-way, directive form does it seem likely that a degree of mutual impact-accountability can be built up. With Boris and Kopczynski Winkler (2013) arguing that, despite momentum and commitment to charting impact among some of the largest (US) foundations, their approaches are diverse and language idiosyncratic, negotiated discussion on the means of and uses of impact measurement will be hard to achieve.

To derive mutual learning advantage from impact accounting and reporting, a changing and enhanced role for funders relative to fundees is then looked for. This includes responsibility of the former to provide support which may range from technical assistance to increased feedback on their work. Contentiously, Buckley and colleagues (2012) explore the idea of a funders' 'duty of care' towards fundees, a phrase that carries an apparent subtext of professional behaviour. Impact and accountability questions are also raised by philanthropy's funding refusals. Harrow *et al.* (2011), studying UK foundations' communications strategies at the point of grant refusal, cite frustrated organizations seeking high levels of feedback on their failed applications and a wide range of funder practice, from detailed learning-directed support to no feedback whatsoever. In such a stand-off between internal and external accountability, pressures appear conflicting and taut. The effects of impact-seeking pressures on philanthropy boards remain generally uncertain. Equally, research on philanthropy's own impacts is mixed, capable of being both cautious and blunt as noted by the Corston Coalition review (Jung *et al.*, 2013).

The greatest extent of philanthropy's own impact assessment and reporting is found in medical research fields. For instance, in a retrospective impact analysis intended to future inform funding strategies, Asthma UK (Hanney *et al.*, 2013) stressed the value of 'increasingly ensuring people affected with asthma were meaningfully involved in reviewing all proposals for funding'. Although recognition of the importance of incorporating beneficiary/users within impact assessment rationales and frameworks is longstanding in the nonprofits literature (Wolpert, 2001), many areas of philanthropy still mostly continue to take the reports of the funded service delivery agencies as proxies for ultimate beneficiaries, while not themselves funding the costs of beneficiary impact review. Yet, none of these difficulties, nor the enthusiasm for impetus over impact, to 'just get on and get things done'(Harrow, 2013) exonerate philanthropy from turning the impact assessment lens upon itself. Paradoxically, in examination of the impact issues relating to philanthropy's public policy influence, Rogers' (2011) coinage of the notion of 'philanthro-policymaking' points to increasing growth in philanthropic power and influence, as an accompaniment to contemporary weak public accountability structures. However, Edwards' (2011: 389) commentary on Rogers' work emphasises that notwithstanding philanthrocapitalists' stress on 'getting the job done', 'impact and accountability are inseparable and must be viewed together'.

Conclusion

Accountability in philanthropy presents a concept and set of practices in motion, but with a presumption and predominance of facing 'accountability by judgment', that is, by its own standards rather than by those imposed by external organizations. Imbalance of attention to beneficiaries – yet willingness in claiming the impact 'prize' if fundees report significant success – may suggest philanthropy as an accountability freeloader, moving the risks and responsibilities of accountability reporting elsewhere. Yet, openness concerning philanthropy's decisions and funding choices, and clarity in reporting the limitations, as well as the gains, of its work may make philanthropy an accountability exemplar, retaining the confidence and power to publish its accountability-led learning because it wishes to, not because it has to.

Tracking between rule-based and negotiation-led accountability is important for philanthropy, but not a matter of 'either-or' choices. Accountability through impact reporting appears in its public guise to offer little negotiating scope and draws sharper, shriller lines between success and failure. However, there is little evidence about impact accountability when it is channeled inside philanthropic institutions, rather than being held at arms' length. Nor is the nature of negotiation as an internal accountability basis well understood.

In exploring philanthropy's changing characteristics as they relate to, and affect, its accountability practices and choices, it has been the thread of professionalization and professionalism as a behavioural benchmark that appears to make accountability a moving, rather than fixed, series of virtues and mechanisms. With the extent of professionalization within this sector more asserted than clearly demonstrated, it seems possible that in philanthropy we have professionalism of sorts, without a full, delineated and recognizable philanthropy profession. Professionalism alone, though, seems hard pressed to deliver accountabilities in its four different forms. What appears to give professionalism in philanthropy its momentum – the size and intricacy of the tasks it sets out to accomplish, the size of the sums on offer, its global as well as local reach – may also act to separate philanthropic endeavour and philanthropy's recipients. This may be expressed as a decline in empathy or new claims for autonomous self-regulation by 'philanthropy professionals'.

In the four forms of accountability discussed, opportunities for negotiating changes in accountability's content, style, and extent occur at various times, with such negotiating skills arguably a further aspect of professional activity. The extent of foundations' informal influences on each others' accountability practices remains unknown; it may extend beyond friendly copying of new trends in accountability, starting, but possibly also finishing, with transparency as the first, but insufficient accountability form. Questions of peer pressure between institutions, boards, individual donors and philanthropy staffs may all have accountability outcomes that cannot be wholly predicted. Research which is able to study these different forms of accountability negotiation over time is urgently needed.

In each of the three cases which began this chapter, accountability by judgment is a further theme, alongside that of trust, be it challenged, damaged or vindicated. Despite their publicly played-out narratives (two forced, one chosen) each offers a more nuanced set of accountabilities than media reports suggested. Respectively, these concern a judgment that a 'low key' apology/victim stance was appropriate, that the decision reversal would be sufficient for reputation defence and that an upfront public statement would confirm a leadership position, despite falling donations. All offer shifting understandings of accounting for their actions, and in the first two cases, there is the potential for the presumption of forgiveness – by no means a necessary outcome after sanctions of rule-based accountability – by future, if not current, donors. It seems possible that future donors to CIIF will be similarly forgiving, or insufficiently demanding, if the 'historic shift' towards nutrition cannot be subsequently demonstrated. Future research directions then include: the limits and operations of forgiveness when accountability as judgment is adhered to in philanthropy; the contributions of professionalization in philanthropy towards more rather than less discretion in its decision-making; and the extent to which the notion of negotiated philanthropy can continue to be on philanthropy's own terms, with improvisatory, as well as planned judgments in operation. Risks for philanthropy at all levels may include the pace of the wider 'impact' and 'what works' agenda in public as well, as nonprofit spaces. This may make accountability audiences less and less patient of nuanced and complex answers, pushing for sharper, more defined responses, and thus impatient with philanthropy's promises. Even though many philanthropists, both 'major' and 'minor', are likely at heart to be impatient for change, this may not bode well for negotiated accountabilities, which need time and trust to develop and grow with confidence.

References

Alexander, J. K., Brudney, J. L., and Yang, K. (2010) Introduction to the symposium: Accountability and performance measurement: The evolving role of nonprofits in the hollow state. *Nonprofit and Voluntary Sector Quarterly*, published online before print, May 21, 2010.

Anderson, G. (2013) *Where the money goes, private wealth for public good*, Centre for Social Impact, University of New South Wales, Australia.

Backer, T. E., Smith, R. and Barbell, I. (2005) Who comes to the table? Stakeholder interactions in philanthropy, *International Network on Strategic Philanthropy*, Bertelsmann Stiftung, www.csun.edu/sites/default/files/insp-paper.rtf_.pdf [Accessed 3 September 2015].

Barnes, S. T. (2005) Global flows: Terror, oil and strategic philanthropy, *Review of African Political Economy*, 32(104–105): 235–52.

Baur, D. and Schmitz, H. P. (2012) Corporations and NGOs: When accountability leads to co-optation, *Journal of Business Ethics*, 106(1): 9–21.

Benjamin, L. M. (2010) Funders as principals: Performance measurement in philanthropic relationships, *Nonprofit Management and Leadership*, 20(4): 383–403.

Bernstein, A. R. (2011) Metrics mania: The growing corporatization of US Philanthropy. Thought and action, *The NEA Higher Education Journal*, Fall, 33–41.

Better Business Bureau (2013) Standards for charitable accountability, www.bbb.org/new-york-city/charities-donors/standards-for-charity-accountability/ [Accessed 13 June 2015].

Boris, E. T. and Kopczynski Winkler, M. (2013) The emergence of performance measurement as a complement to evaluation among U.S. foundations, new directions for evaluation, *Special Issue: Performance Management and Evaluation*, 137, 69–80.

Bovens, M. (2010) Two concepts of accountability: Accountability as a virtue and accountability as a mechanism, *West European Politics*, 33(5): 946–67.

Breen, O. B. (2013) The disclosure panacea: A comparative perspective on charity financial reporting, *Voluntas: International Journal of Voluntary and Nonprofit Organizations*, 24(3): 852–80.

Buckley, E., Cairns, B., Harker, A. and Hutchison, R. (2012) *Duty of care: The role of trusts and foundations in supporting voluntary organisations through difficult times*, Institute for Voluntary Action Research, London.

Cambridge University Reporter (2012) 18 January, www.admin.cam.ac.uk/reporter/2011-12/weekly/6251/section7.shtml#heading2-15 [Accessed 13 June 2015].

Canadian Broadcasting Company (2012) Ex-Salvation Army executive charged in $2M toy heist, 26 November www.cbc.ca/news/canada/story/2012/11/26/can-salvation-army-theft-charge.html [Accessed 13 June 2015].

Candler, G. and Dumont, G. (2010) A nonprofit accountability framework, *Canadian Public Administration*, 53(2): 259–79.

Carman, J. C. (2010) The accountability movement, what's wrong with this theory of change?, *Nonprofit and Voluntary Sector Quarterly* 39(2): 246–74.

Center on Effective Philanthropy (2012) Grantee Perception Report, no pagination, www.effectivephilanthropy.org/assessment-tools/gpr-apr/ [Accessed 13 June 2015].

Chan, H. S. and Rosenbloom, D. H. (2010) Four challenges to accountability in contemporary public administration: Lessons from the United States and China, *Administration and Society*, 42(IS): 11S–33S.

Coffman, J., Beer, T., Patrizi, P. and Thompson, E. H. (2013) Benchmarking evaluation in foundations: Do we know what we are doing?, *Foundation Review*, 5(2)36–51.

Conley, L. and Doyle, M. (2011) Accountability and transparency: An annotated bibliography of selected web resources, Legal Resource Centre of Alberta. www.charitycentral.ca/docs/accountbiblio-en.pdf [Accessed 27 February 2012].

Coon, M. (2013) Toward a high-performance culture: From strategy to strategic human capital at The Rhode Island Foundation, *The Foundation Review*, 4(4): 57–70.

Cordery, C. J. (2013) Regulating small and medium charities: Does it improve transparency and accountability?, *Voluntas: International Journal of Voluntary and Nonprofit Organizations*, 24(3): 831–51.

Cosyns, H., Damme, P. V. and Wulf, R. D. (2013) Who views what? Impact assessment through the eyes of farmers, development organization staff and researchers, *International Journal of Sustainable Development and World Ecology*, 20(4): 287–301.

Coyte, R., Rooney, J. and Phua, B. (2013) The impossibility of philanthropic funding decisions: The Australian non-government funder experience, *Financial Accountability and Management*, 29(4): 397–418.

Crampton, W. and Patten, D. (2008) Social responsiveness, profitability and catastrophic events: Evidence on the corporate philanthropic response to 9/11, *Journal of Business Ethics*, 81(4): 863–73.

Crowley, N. (2013) Lost in austerity: Rethinking the community sector, *Community Development Journal*, 48(1): 151–7.

Damon, W. (2006) Introduction: Taking philanthropy seriously, in eds. W. Damon and S. Verducci, *Taking philanthropy seriously: Beyond noble intentions to responsible giving*, Indiana University Press, Bloomington, NY. 1–12.

Dar, S. (2013) Hybrid accountabilities: When western and non-western accountabilities collide. *Human Relations*. Published online before print June 20, 2013.

Delgado, L. T., Orellana-Damacela, L. E. and Zanoni, M. J. (2001) *Chicago philanthropy: A profile of the grantmaking profession*, Loyola University Chicago, Chicago, IL.

Dolan, M. (2011) Revival bid pits Detroit versus donor, *Wall Street Journal*, July 2.

Ebrahim, A. and Rangan, V. K. (2010) Putting the brakes on impact: A contingency framework for measuring social performance, Academy of Management Proceedings 2010. www.proceedings.aom. org/content/2010/1/1.237.short [Accessed on].

Eck, D. L. (2013) The religious gift: Hindu, Buddhist, and Jain perspectives on Dana, *Social Research: An International Quarterly, Special Issue, Giving: Caring for the Needs of Strangers*, 80(2): 359–79.

Edwards, M. (2011) Impact, accountability, and philanthrocapitalism, *Society*, 48(5): 389–90.

Evetts, J. (2012) Professionalism in turbulent times: Changes, challenges and opportunities, Propel International Conference, 9–11 May.

Fioramonti, L. and Thümler, E. (2011) The financial crisis and the nonprofit sector: Can philanthropic foundations support the creation of a civic watchdog of international finance?, *The International Journal of Not-For-Profit Law*, 13(3), June, no pagination. www.icnl.org/research/journal/vol13iss3/art_1.htm, [Accessed 13 June 2015].

Flynn, P. and Hodgkinson, V. A. (eds). (2001) *Measuring the impact of the nonprofit sector*, Springer, New York.

Ford Foundation (The) (2012) Staff Code of Conduct and Ethics, www.fordfoundation.org/pdfs/about/ Staff_Code_of_Conduct_and_Ethics.pdf [Accessed 13 June 2015].

Frumkin, P. (1998) Failure in philanthropy: Towards a new appreciation, *The Philanthropy Magazine*, July/ August, www.philanthropyroundtable.org/topic/excellence_in_philanthropy/failure_in_philanthropy [Accessed 13 June 2015].

Frumkin, P. (2010) *The essence of strategic giving: A practical guide for donors and fundraisers*, University of Chicago Press, Chicago, IL.

Gary, S. N. (2010) The problems with donor intent: Interpretation, enforcement and doing the right thing, *Chicago-Kent Law Review*, 997–1043.

Gautier, A., Pache, A. C. and Mossel, V. (2013) Giving in France: A philanthropic renewal after decades of distrust, Research Center, ESSEC Working Paper 1318, EEXEC Business School, www.hal.archives-ouvertes.fr/docs/00/91/48/05/PDF/WP1318.pdf, [Accessed 13 June 2015].

Givel, M. (2013) Modern neoliberal philanthropy: Motivations and impact of Pfizer Pharmaceutical's corporate social responsibility campaign, *Third World Quarterly*, 34(1): 171–82.

Gordon, T. P., Knock, C. L. and Neely, D. G. (2009) The role of rating agencies in the market for charitable contributions: An empirical test, *Journal of Accounting and Public Policy*, 28(6): 469–84.

Goss, K. A. (2007) Foundations of feminism: How philanthropic patrons shaped gender politics, *Social Science Quarterly*, 88(5): 1174–91.

Grimes, M. (2010) Strategic sensemaking within funding relationships: The effects of performance measurement on organizational identity in the social sector, *Entrepreneurship Theory and Practice*, 34(4): 763–83.

Gugerty, M. K. (2009) Signaling virtue: Voluntary accountability programs among nonprofit organizations, *Policy Sciences*, 42(3): 243–73.

Hall, P. D. (2013) Philanthropy, the nonprofit sector and the democratic dilemma, *Daedalus*, 142(2): 139–58. Posted Online April 11, 2013.

Hammack, D. C. and Anheier, H. K. (2013) *A versatile American institution: The changing ideals and realities of philanthropic foundations*, Brookings Institution Press, Washington, DC.

Hanney, S. R., Watt, A., Jones, T. H. and Metcalf, L. (2013) Conducting retrospective impact analysis to inform a medical research charity's funding strategies: The case of Asthma UK, *Allergy, Asthma and Clinical Immunology*, 9(1).

Harrow, J. (2010) Donor and donor intent, in Anheier, H. K. and Toepler, S. (eds)., *International Encyclopedia of Civil Society*, Springer, New York, 610–16.

Harrow, J. (2013) Impetus or impact – Implications for emerging philanthropy, Academy of Philanthropy and World Congress of Muslim Philanthropists Conference, Doha, Qatar. 5 March 2013.

Harrow, J. and Phillips, S. D. (2013) Corporate governance and nonprofits: Facing up to hybridization and homogenization, in M. Wright, D. S. Seigel, K. Keasey and I. Filatotchevv (eds)., *The Oxford Handbook of Corporate Governance*, Oxford University Press.

Harrow, J., Fitzmaurice, J., McKenzie, T. and Bogdanova, M. (2011) *The art of refusal*, Centre For Charity Effectiveness for the Charities Aid Foundation, London.

Herrold, C. (2012) Philanthropic foundations in Egypt; Fueling change or safeguarding status quo? Takaful 2012, Second Annual Conference on Arab Philanthropy and Civic Engagement, Selected Research, John D. Gerhard Center for Philanthropy and Civic Engagement, Cairo, June 10-12, 2012, no pagination.

House of Commons (2012) Thirteenth Report, International Development Committee: Private Foundations, 11 January 2012, www.publications.parliament.uk/pa/cm201012/cmselect/cmintdev/1557/155702.htm, [Accessed 13 June 2015].

Houston, S. (2010) Giving: celebrated, scrutinised, studied, *The Philanthropist*, 23(1): 79–82.

Hu, A. Gifts of money and gifts of time: Folk religion and civic involvement in a Chinese Society, *Review of Religious Research*, Published online 22 September.

Jennings, M. (2013) Do not turn away a poor man: Faith-based organisations and development, in M. Clarke (ed.), *Handbook of Research on Development and Religion*, Edward Elgar, Cheltenham, Glos, UK, 359–75.

Jun, K-N and Shiau, E. (2012) How are we doing? A multiple constituency approach to civic association effectiveness, *Nonprofit and Voluntary Sector Quarterly*, 41(4): 632–55.

Jung, T. and Harrow, J. (2013) Philanthropy and multi-level governance: Time for reflection, multi level governance: Scotland, England, Wales, Northern Ireland In europe Conference, Glasgow Caledonian University, JUC Public Administration Committee, and Political Studies Association, 13 February, Glasgow.

Jung, T., Kaufmann, J. and Harrow, J. (2013) When funders do direct advocacy: An exploration of the United Kingdom's Corston Independent Funders' Coalition, *Nonprofit and Voluntary Sector Quarterly*, Published online before print January 21, 2013.

Kaufmann, J. (2011) Funders in collaboration: A review of the Corston Independent Funders' Coalition (CIFC), Centre for Charity Effectiveness, Cass Business School, London.

Kearns, K. P. (1996) *Managing for accountability: Preserving the public trust in public and nonprofit organisations*, Jossey- Bass: San Francisco, CA.

Keidan, C., Pharoah, C. and Jung, T. (2014) Philanthropy education in UK and Continental Europe: Current provision, perceptions and opportunities, CGAP Occasional Paper, Centre for Charitable Giving and Philanthropy, Cass Business School, City University London and School of Management, University of St. Andrews.

Kohl, E. (2008) The program officer: Negotiating the politics of philanthropy, Institute for the Study of Societal Issues, ISSI Fellows Working Papers, University of California, Berkeley.

Lasby, D. and Barr, C. (2012) What the numbers say: Transparency among Canadian charities, *The Philanthropist*, 24(3): 223–6.

Leat, D. (2004) Domestic and international grantmaking: The comfort of codes, Centre of Philanthropy and Nonprofit Studies, Queensland University of Technology, Brisbane, Australia, Working Paper CPNS23.

Lee, M. (2004) Public reporting: A neglected aspect of nonprofit accountability, *Nonprofit Management and Leadership*, 15(2) 169–85.

London School of Economics (2011) LSE Director steps down, News Archives, www.lse.ac.uk/newsAndMedia/news/archives/2011/03/director_steps_down.aspx, [Accessed 13 June 2015].

McCoy, D., Chand, S. and Sridhar, D. (2009) Global health funding: How much, where it comes from and where it goes, *Health Policy and Planning*, 24(6): 407–17.

McGinnis, J. A. (2012) Participatory philanthropy: An analysis of community inputs impact on grantee selection, Phd Thesis, Department of Public Policy, Georgia Institute of Technology.

Maas, K. and Liket, K. (2011) Talk the walk: Measuring the impact of strategic philanthropy, *Journal of Business Ethics*, 10(3): 445–64.

Margulis, M. E. (2013) The regime complex for food security: Implications for the global hunger challenge, *Global Governance: A Review of Multilateralism and International Organizations*, 19(1): 53–67.

Mason, T. (2013) Hedge fund foundation to spend £517m tackling malnutrition, *Civil Society*, 10 June, www.civilsociety.co.uk/finance/news/content/15356/hedge_fund_foundation_to_spend_517m_tackling_malnutrition [Accessed 13 June 2015].

Mirabella, R. M., Gemelli, G., Malcolm, M. J. and Berger, G. (2007) Nonprofit and philanthropic studies: International overview of the field in Africa, Canada, Latin America, Asia, the Pacific, and Europe, *Nonprofit and Voluntary Sector Quarterly*, 36(4) supplement, 110S–135S.

Mirabella, R. and Young, D. R. (2012) The development of education for social entrepreneurship and nonprofit management: Diverging or converging paths?, *Nonprofit Management and Leadership*, 23(1): 43–57.

Moran, M. and Stevenson, M. (2013) Illumination and innovation: What philanthropic foundations bring to global health governance, *Global Society*, 27(2): 117–37.

Morris, M. (2007) Foundation officers, evaluation, and ethical problems: A pilot investigation, *Evaluation and Program Planning*,30(4): 410–15.

Morrison, J. B. and Salipante, P. (2007) Governance for broadened accountability: Blending deliberate and emergent strategizing, *Nonprofit and Voluntary Sector Quarterly*, 36(2): 195–217.

Morvaridi, B. (2013) The politics of philanthropy and welfare governance: The case of Turkey, *European Journal of Development Research*, 25(2): 305–21.

Ostrander, S. A. (2007) The growth of donor control: Revisiting the social relations of philanthropy, *Nonprofit and Voluntary Sector Quarterly*, 38(2): 358–72.

Partzsch, L. and Fuchs, D. (2012) Philanthropy: Power within international relations, *Journal of Political Power*, 5(3): 359–76.

Pennekamp, P. H. and Focke, A. (2013) Philanthropy and the regeneration of community democracy, *National Civic Review*, 102(3): 47–57.

Phillips, S. D. (2013) Shining light on charities or looking in the wrong place? Regulation-by-Transparency in Canada, *Voluntas: International Journal of Voluntary and Nonprofit Organizations*, 24(3): 1–25.

Polonsky, M. and Grau, S. L. (2011) Assessing the social impact of charitable organizations –four alternative approaches, *International Journal of Nonprofit and Voluntary Sector Marketing*, 16(2): 195–211.

Public Broadcasting Service (2001) Red Cross woes, 19 December, www.pbs.org/newshour/bb/business/july-dec01/redcross_12-19.html [Accessed 22 May 2013].

Rey-Garcia, M., Martin-Cavanna, J. and Alvarez-Gonzalez, L. I. (2012) Assessing and advancing foundation transparency: Corporate foundations as a case study, *The Foundation Review*, 4(3): 77–89.

Roelofs, J. (2009) Networks and democracy, it ain't necessarily so, *American Behavioral Scientist*, 52(7): 930–1005.

Rogers, R. (2011) Why philanthro-policymaking matters, *Society*, 48(5): 376–81.

Rosenman, M. (2010) Caring to change, *Voluntary Sector Review*, 1(2,):239–44.

Rothman, S. M., Raveis, V. H., Friedman, A. and Rothman, D. J. (2011) Health advocacy organizations and the pharmaceutical industry: An analysis of disclosure practices, *American Journal of Public Health*, 101(4): 602–9.

Saks, M. (2012) Defining a profession: The role of knowledge and expertise, *Professions and Professionalism*, 2(1): 1–10.

Scaife, W., Williamson, A., McDonald, K. and Smyllie, S. (2012) Foundations for giving: Why and how Australians structure their philanthropy. Australian Centre for Philanthropy and Nonprofit Studies, Queensland University of Technology, Brisbane, http://eprints.qut.edu.au/48801/1/48801.pdf, [Accessed 13 June 2015].

Schillemans, T. (2011) Does horizontal accountability work? Evaluating potential remedies for the accountability deficit of agencies, *Administration and Society*, 43(4): 387–416.

Silber, I. F. (2012) The angry gift: A neglected facet of philanthropy, *Current Sociology*, 80(3): 320–37.

Skillman Foundation, (2012) The Code of Ethics, www.skillman.org/About-Us/Code-of-Ethics, [Accessed 27 February 2012].

Stauber, K. (2010) Are we a profession? Should we be?, *The Foundation Review*, 2(1): 87–99.

Steffens, J. (2008) Public accountability and the public sphere of international governance, reconstituting democracy in Europe, RECON Working Paper, 2008/3.

Stewart, J. D. (1984) The role of public information in accountability, in A. Hopwood and C. Tomkins (eds), *Issues in Public Sector Accounting*, Philip Allen, Oxford, 15–34.

Szper, R. and Prakash, A. (2011). Charity watchdogs and the limits of information-based regulation, *Voluntas: International Journal of Voluntary and Nonprofit Organizations*, 22(1): 112–41.

The Resource Alliance (2012) Risk and philanthropy: Systematisation, education and professionalisation, October www.resource-alliance.org/data/files/medialibrary/2883/Risk-and-Philanthropy.pdf [Accessed 10 January 2013].

Therrien, M-C. (2011) The American Red Cross and the Liberty Fund: Ethically stuck between accountability and development, *International Business and Economics Research Journal*, 2(12): 1–9.

Tomei, A. (2013) Foundations: Accountability and legitimacy. *Voluntary Sector Review*, 4(3): 403–13.

Watson, D. and Manzione, T. (2010) Measuring grantee perception – Grantmaking, communications and impact, Paul Hamlyn Foundation (2010), Conference of the Association of Charitable Foundations, 22 September 2010, London.

Wolpert, J. (2001) The distributional impacts of nonprofits and philanthropy, in P. Flynn and V. A. Hodgkinson (eds), *Measuring the impact of the nonprofit sector*, Springer, New York. 123–36.

Wood, E. (2013) Lessons in building a better community, one voice at a time, *The Foundation Review*, 4(4): 71–8.

Wright, G. (1979) Professionalism in private philanthropy, *The Philanthropist*, 2(3): 1–11.

Yasmin, S., Haniffa, R. and Hudaib, M. (2013) Communicated accountability by faith-based charity organisations, *Journal of Business Ethics*, 1–21.

Part VII

Conclusion

The future for philanthropy research and practice

Vignette: Conclusion: The Future for Philanthropy Research and Practice

Reflections from a life as a philanthropist

Putnam Barber

I am not a wealthy person. I have not made much of a show of generosity – in cash or in kind – over the years. Yet, I claim the title of philanthropist: it is the best way to describe someone who believes, as I do, that private means should support public goods and who devotes time and attention – at whatever scale – to matching gifts to goals.

During my lifetime, the business of philanthropy has grown at an astonishing rate. It is not really surprising that those who seek to create public goods also seek out ways to encourage generosity among those who have the means to support their goals. I worry, though, about the scale and the character of those efforts. Drawing on my experiences over several decades, I have some advice to fellow philanthropists about how they might approach their giving and, in small ways, change the dynamic that draws attention to fund-seeking and away from commitment to goals.

Give early and seldom

Direct mail specialists will tell their clients not to give up asking until they have sent seven appeals. If you do not want to read, or bin without reading, six more requests from an organization you might support, respond the first time you are asked. Your response might be what I call a 49-cent donation, 49 cents being the current price of a first-class letter in the US. Write a note that declines, with polite regret, to make a gift, put it in an envelope with your own stamp on it, and drop it in the mail. My preferred text for these notes says, when it is true, 'Although I admire your work and wish you well, I have other priorities for my gifts and will not be able to provide support to your organization. Please do not send additional requests to this address'. It works pretty well. In addition, I must say my resolve grows stronger if I get further appeals from the same organization; not being able to honour that simple request suggests other things may be amiss in the outfit's management.

Alternatively, your response might well be a more generous gift. Your part in helping to achieve the goal is obviously larger when you do. There is a less personal reason for making larger gifts, though. It is inescapable that the costs of receiving, acknowledging, and depositing your cheque are exactly the same, whether the amount is $5 or $500. So, if you want to support the goals of the organization, you want to be sure your donation covers those costs with as much as possible to spare. For the same reason, it is also important to discourage repeated requests when you have sent support. It might even be more important: past donors are widely perceived as good prospects for future gifts. I always include a note asking that the recipient not exchange my name with other organizations and avoid addressing repeated requests to me. I ignore, while suppressing a sigh, the all-too-prevalent practice of enclosing with the thank you a self-addressed envelope with a big flap listing more gift opportunities.

When I follow my own advice in these ways, there can be some difficult moments. I often want to give in to my enthusiasm for a cause and send along a small gift just to 'show support'. As much as I know that gift would just lead to costs, and possible distraction, for the recipient, it is still tempting. I welcome the growing list of opportunities to announce such enthusiasms without a financial tie-in, such as 'liking' the organization online or sticking a good-old-fashioned bumper-strip on the car. I wish there were more, and easier, such ways to make gestures. More ticklish still is when the request for support comes not in the form of an envelope in the mail, but as an appeal from a neighbour, co-worker, or friend. There is a lot to balance in a moment or two when such a request is made. The best solutions I have found are not perfect. If the situation is right, I sometimes just hand some cash to the asker, saying 'please pass this along to the organization but leave my name out of it'. When the request is larger, or that option not open, I have to decide between saying something parallel to the 49¢ donation text or just acquiescing – perhaps in the hope of being able to make a reciprocal request on behalf of an organization I care about at some point in the future.

Giving early but seldom means two things – the donations I do make do more for the organizations that receive them, and I get fewer requests that I am not going to be able to honour. As a philanthropist, I welcome both outcomes.

Give freely and confidently

There is a nonprofit group that advises alumni about making gifts to their alma mater with restrictions designed to guarantee the recipient will always use the money just as the donor expected. In the welcome climate of freedom about what nonprofit groups can do, these advocates can of course offer assistance to anyone. My only response is to say I would never seek such advice. For me, the first question about any possible recipient of a gift is whether I have confidence that the organization is committed to a cause I believe in, and to doing its level best to focus its resources of time, money, and wisdom on serving that cause. I can see no valid reason for making a gift to an organization that fails that test.

With over a million nonprofits active in the US, it is hard to imagine there is not one that will responsibly advance any conceivable cause. For a donor to labour over setting restrictive conditions on a prospective gift not only diverts resources which might better be spent by a recipient, it also adds costs for accounting and other administration to the recipient organization for as long as the restriction lasts. In the worst case, the original goals may become 'impossible, inexpedient, or impractical', and the recipient may have to go to court for an order to remove the restrictions or redefine the goals in a way that comes as close as possible ('cy pres comme possible') under current conditions. Whatever else one might say about such an excursion into philosophical and philanthropic thickets, it is sure to be expensive, while not being guaranteed to match any ambitions of the recipient or of the original donor.

Luckily, institutions exist for no other purpose than to give attention to achieving this sort of purpose. With more than 700 community foundations active in the US, a donor who has a commitment to a particular goal or cause, and enough money to make a gift that will produce income well into the future, can arrange a dedicated fund with one, or more, of them to suit these purposes. A sensible gift agreement will include a clause that parallels the 'cy pres' standard, but puts the decision in the hands of the foundation's trustees, not some judge for whom philanthropy is but one of many difficult topics that require attention.

Pay attention

It is unfortunately true, that plausible sounding appeals for financial support show up all the time: in magazines, on television, on street corners, and in our mailboxes. Many of these are well-intentioned requests from hard working and reliable organizations. A few are prepared by opportunistic contractors employed by organizations that lack a commitment to service. A handful are simply bogus, offering nothing of value, except to the extent that they line the pockets of clever advocates.

Once you hear stories about how these scallywags pull at the heartstrings of vulnerable people, or hold out phony promises of special treatment or even chances to win fabulous prizes, it is natural to grow skeptical. How on earth can anyone tell the difference between the good guys and the crooks, or, more subtly, choose among the good guys to assure the greatest benefit from whatever gift is possible?

The simplest rule is 'Never give to strangers'. If I concentrate my giving on organizations where I have personal contact, I can be sure that their everyday affairs are conducted responsibly. If I have any reason for concern, I can compare my direct experience with the information about the organization and its work that is available online and through other sources. Of course, for many people and their causes, the opportunity to have direct everyday contact is not available. Important work, like fighting AIDS in Africa or ensuring supplies of clean water in Central America, needs, and deserves, support from donors in far-away places. Many of these donors will never have first-hand experience of the organization in action. What then?

Two strategies make sense: seek out trusted intermediaries, or choose large, well-known charities with strong reasons to protect their reputations. Trusted intermediaries can include a local service club whose members do travel to the far-away places to deliver aid and cash, or a religious network that assembles significant resources from large numbers of supporters. Asking around at work, in the neighbourhood, or other familiar places may turn up leads. Scanning the newspaper and searching online may also yield suggestions of groups to be contacted. The less direct the connection, of course, the more complex the process of gaining confidence is likely to be. It may be that the exact goals that got the search started do not match any organization that comes to light. One thing to remember is that many of the world's needs are broad and urgent, so being too particular about exactly how aid should be delivered may, in fact, represent an uncharitable limit of the help that might be given.

Then, of course, there are globally active aid and development organizations whose names are household words. They offer extensive information on their websites and in regular publications. They concentrate on urgent needs – some on disaster relief, some on disease prevention, some on education, some on health. The fact that a small donation looks tiny in comparison to the scope of their operations might seem discouraging. It should not. That scope is only possible because a legion of supporters – some equipped to give a lot, some eager to give a little – are engaged with these goals and gain satisfaction from being a part of an effort that would be impossible for any one of them acting alone.

Focus on the outcome

It is easy to find advice about giving. Some of it makes sense. A lot of it does not. In particular, the oft-repeated standards about how an organization's operating expenses should be classified and controlled can be damagingly misleading. As a donor, my goal is to do as much good as possible with my inevitably inadequate gifts. So, the questions I should be asking about the organizations I support are the same questions I would hope they are asking of themselves: What are you trying to do? How do you plan to do it? How do you know you can do that? How will you know you're succeeding? What is there left still to do? These are shorthand versions of the 'Five Questions' the Charting Impact Project invites organizations to examine closely.

Part of the answer to the 'how do you do it' question should be 'we will raise some money and we will manage the work with care'. Part of the answer to the 'are you succeeding' question will involve careful observation and evaluation. None of those tasks can be accomplished without expense. For donors to second-guess management about how those things get done and how much they should cost – especially if the donors' view is that they should be as cheap as possible – puts just the wrong sort of pressures on the organization. In response, managers may skimp on the things that would make the staff and volunteers more efficient and effective. Worse, they may stretch a point in the way they do their accounting to meet some rigid metric about the allocations of resources. I want to support organizations where the management cares about doing the job right and is candid with me about how much that costs. If I lose faith in their candour, it's hard for me to gain confidence in any other aspect of the work.

To look at this difficult question from another point of view, consider this. If I am giving money to an organization that presents itself as an intermediary, promising to deliver direct and immediate aid to particular people who suffer from deprivation that money can offset, then naturally I want the intermediary to pass along as much as is humanly possible. There will always be costs, of course, but resisting the temptation to let those costs grow at the expense of the beneficiaries is part of the job. However, the fact of the matter is that charity of that sort is rarely the focus of the organizations that come to us for support today. Even organizations whose mission is narrowly defined as fighting poverty have a broader view of what it will take to change economic conditions for people who are very poor. There are lots of different ideas about how that might be done, and some of them do not include handing over any cash to anyone. As a donor, I may choose among the methods, but it does not make sense to make that choice based on some sort of ratio calculated from the organization's financial reports. I need to be asking myself the harder questions about what course I believe holds the most promise of using my gift, and those of others, most effectively.

Examine your motives

No doubt about it. When I look at the list of organizations my family has supported over the past year, I experience what the psychologists have dubbed 'warm glow'. Though I seldom experience the results of their work first hand, there is a real, if vicarious, satisfaction in knowing we have been part of something larger than we ourselves could possibly have achieved alone. An important part of that is, though, more specific and idiosyncratic – we have chosen to support organizations and activities that seem to us deserving of greater effect than the mechanisms of politics or the marketplace are likely to make possible. In that sense, our gifts are not just financial transactions, they are also a form of voting for the sort of community – local and worldwide – we want to live in ourselves, and see sustained for our neighbours wherever they may live.

What you do not hear in that paragraph is any of the other motives for being charitable that are often invoked by cynics and doubters. The fact that I do not see myself in those terms is probably partly due to the simple fact that our donations are, in the scheme of things, at the low end of the gift pyramid. But that does not mean that I react with cynicism or doubt when I witness donor behaviour that suggests other motives are at play. The problem, in other words, is not that Mr. Megabucks or Ms. Moneybags want to see themselves pictured on the society pages, or their names over the door of an imposing building. The problems, if there are any, arise differently. Sometimes, eagerness to enjoy the ancillary benefits of largesse leads to irresponsible inattention to the question of whether anything worth doing is getting done with the proceeds; sometimes, people who demonstrate a willingness to make significant gifts turn into bullies – maybe without even knowing it – and expect that their whims about the way things should be done will be honoured in every particular. Even worse: sometimes they expect the recipient of their gifts to bend the rules in ways that are shameful – to be complicit in overvaluing a gift in kind; backdate a receipt to accommodate a tax-planning strategy; hire a relative; admit a stumbling nephew; exclude a rival, or a disfavoured group; lend the institution's name and reputation to a questionable idea or a disreputable cause.

It is hard, of course, for an organization to resist such pressures when it can see clearly how such a gift would enable expanding the work. It is especially hard when the boundaries are not so clear as my catalogue of temptations might suggest. But many do resist. Probably, more than we know, disputes between nonprofits and prospective donors rarely make the news. In the perfect world of my dreams, though, there would be more effective social sanctions that caused people to draw back, even when tempted in those shameful directions. The moral fabric of the charitable world should not have to depend on the willingness of organizational leaders to turn away from support that comes with unacceptable conditions attached.

Don't trust the government

Governments do many things well. But as allies for donors and prospective donors, government agencies fall short of what many wish for and might reasonably expect. The most reliable, broadly available, financial information about tax-exempt public charities and private foundations comes from an annual financial report that must be filed with the Internal Revenue Service. Because of the accounting rules, and the government's processing schedule, the most recent available report for any given organization is likely to cover a fiscal year that ended more than 12 months ago. Even though these documents are easily accessible to the public, the focus on documenting continued eligibility for exemption from corporate income taxes means that much of the information they contain is unlikely to help donors make wise choices. Moreover, the format certainly does not make navigating to the potentially useful sections a straightforward enterprise.

More deeply, though, the connection is weak between having tax-exempt status and assurance that the organization is well matched to a donor's goals. The standards for recognition that a group is organized and operated exclusively for one or more exempt purposes are necessarily broad and inclusive. Those who believe in the importance of civil society, as I do, welcome that breadth and accept that the result is far blurrier than any single citizen might be inclined to welcome. Further, once recognized as exempt, organizations seldom lose the status; when they do, it is more likely to be a result of failing to file the necessary reports than any other lapse or violation of standards. In short, the announcement that an organization is a '501(c)(3)' provides a prospective donor with little more than a promise that no part of any donation will be used to pay corporate income taxes. For those who are not familiar with the legal framework for charity in the US, '501(c)(3)' is the number of the section of the Internal Revenue Code [26 USC] that covers these matters in 133 words.

The annual information return filed by larger charities does include a 'statement of functional expenses'. This is designed to set forth in an orderly way the uses that the organization makes of its revenues. These are divided into familiar categories like salaries and advertising in one direction, and among program services, fundraising, and administration in the other. Careful observers of these matters persuasively report that these figures are unreliable with respect to one organization, and even less useful for comparing one with another. These disappointing results appear to stem from willful concealment of operating realities by some organizations, and from ignorance of the requirements by others. More respectable, perhaps, but no more encouraging is the fact that the established accounting rules that apply to the preparation of these figures allow for estimation of many key entries 'on any reasonable basis'. Finding out whether I agree that the methods used were, in fact, 'reasonable' from my point of view would take more work than I am likely to do, even if I could understand the explanation offered. It might be more likely that Internal Revenue Service (IRS) agents could derive useful information from such an investigation, but the fact is that the tax authorities examine less than one percent of the returns filed. Further, they have many more issues to concern themselves with than questioning the allocation of functional expenses.

Many states have regulations about fundraising practices. They often include financial reporting requirements in addition to setting limits on the ways organizations raise money, such as restrictions on the hours when telephone solicitation can occur. These financial reports are undoubtedly useful resources when the state regulators have reason to suspect that outright fraud is occurring. For one thing, misrepresenting financial performance in the reports is, often, itself a crime and an easier one to prove than that individual donors have been criminally misled. Many states also publish summary financial information about registered charitable organizations on an official website. The published figures vary from state to state. A safe generalization is that they are often designed to highlight high fundraising costs or a rough complement – a low ratio of program service expenditures to other costs. Sometimes these summary statistics are accompanied by explanations that quote standards-setting bodies as suggesting limits – 'no less than 65 percent of annual revenue should support program services', for example, or 'fundraising expenses of more than 15 percent of the amounts raised are considered excessive'.

This is not the place to argue the matter fully, and there are others who can do it more eloquently than I. I am, though, completely convinced that this sort of standard is not just misleading, but damaging. There are plenty of situations in which those standards simply do not apply. If prospective donors are persuaded not to support an organization that would, in fact, serve their goals well, much is lost on both sides. If organizations worry about being looked at askance as a result of a report of their expenditures, they may pay closer attention to such accounting devices as the estimation of cost allocations 'on any reasonable basis'. As a result, they end up with financial statements that are harder to use for their own internal management, not to mention less useful to outsiders. The states' presentations suffer, of course, from the same delays that affect the publication of the information in federal reports; in fact, many of them are based on extracting data from the federal forms either by the reporting organization itself or by state officials. At a more general level, the fact that the same organization shows up in multiple states' online listings with differing financial data can only worry a conscientious prospective donor who has not taken the time to look deeply into the methods the various states use to make these calculations.

Share the warm glow

If I cannot trust the government to help me choose among possible recipients of my donations, who does deserve my trust? For the most part, I find myself trusting the organizations I support. Over the years, I have turned away from a couple of groups, usually because they did such a stumbling job of handling the administration of my gifts that I lost confidence in their ability to manage the rest of their affairs. Of course, my goals have also changed with time, mostly in the direction of trying to make my contributions more useful by reducing the number of organizations I support and by increasing the size of the gifts I do make. The more I have learned over the years about the challenges of operating nonprofit organizations and the difficulty of raising the funds they need to do their work, the more I have come to trust the energy, dedication and intelligence of the people who are responsible for their successes.

Writing these notes has opened my eyes in another and, I think, important way. Because this project was much on my mind, I raised the topic of philanthropy for the first time with friends I have known for years. The subject had never before entered our conversations. In one case, I was immediately impressed with the depth and care with which my friend, who is childless, had thought about how to focus whatever wealth he may have accumulated by the end of his life on strengthening the parts of our community that have been important to him; in another, my friend and I found ourselves candidly explaining the ways we had selected organizations and causes to support over the years. Both conversations gave me new insight into the importance of philanthropy in clarifying strongly held values through making both choices and gifts.

It is ironic. Philanthropy is in a way a very outward-looking activity. Yet, it is often conducted in isolation. I sit alone, thinking about the things I care about and the organizations I might support in furtherance of those goals. Then I write cheques … or I go online and click a 'donate now' button. Later, I receive an acknowledgement and thank you in the mail. The conversations with my two friends taught me a valuable lesson: it is possible to talk about this critically important activity without vanity or sanctimony. And, it is well worth doing. I look forward to sharing the warm glow more widely from now on.

32

Concluding thoughts
The 'Ubers' of philanthropy and future disruptions

Susan D. Phillips and Tobias Jung

A sector that had few incentives to innovate, the taxi industry, was transformed in a remarkably short period by the smartphone car-service app Uber; this was done across the 58 countries in which Uber currently operates without owning a car or employing a cab driver. As an example, not an endorsement, of one of many agents producing change in disruptive, rather than incremental ways, Uber offers both metaphorical and practical insights for philanthropy in navigating an increasingly open, collaborative, data-driven economy. It also points to the advantages of being a first mover, while being strategic about potential backlashes from entrenched interests, and to the challenges for public policy in keeping pace with contemporary disruptions.

The Uber advantage for passengers is the ability to get a car, with choice of basic or luxury models, where, and when, needed, (usually) at a cheaper price than a regular taxi, with payment directly billed to a credit card and no tipping expected; drivers use an asset they already own, without expensive licensing, set their own hours, and make more money by driving to meet demand. Transparency, self-regulation and learning are built in: riders instantly rate their drivers, but drivers also rate their passengers, promoting a sense of accountability and safety for both. More than rides, Uber's product is data: by keeping a GPS record of every ride, driver and passenger, it knows patterns of demand and performance in a way that most taxi companies do not (Badger, 2014). It has also recognized opportunities that are closely related to taxi services, including delivering lunches and transporting puppies for playtime with downtown office workers, partnering with dog rescue nonprofits to raise awareness of shelter animals available for adoption. The ripple effects have been far reaching. Reportedly, they are changing patterns of car ownership, nightlife and locations of urban living (Ryzik, 2014). Not surprisingly, the owners of taxi medallions and licenses – rightly fearing the loss of value of these tightly regulated commodities – have vigorously resisted the entry of ridesharing operations. The response by governments has been described as 'whack-a-mole' (Johal and Zon, 2015) since these new players do not fit the old taxi rulebooks. Is Uber really a software company as it claims, or an unlicensed taxi business? Following demonstrations by taxi drivers on Paris streets, France banned Uber; so, too, have Germany, Thailand and many cities; some mounted sting operations to fine drivers, or imposed new rules on response times to make the service less convenient; others have tried to find means of coexistence between ridesharing and traditional taxis. For its part, Uber has been very selective in where, and how, it enters a new market, paying close attention to the 'unique topology of each new market' (Brown, 2013: NP) with place-centric launches, and favouring cities where its reception may be less hostile.

Our point in comparing ridesharing to philanthropy is not to glorify 'disruptive innovation' (Bower and Christensen, 1995) as an end in itself, but to offer five parallels to the changing dynamics of philanthropy as new tools, practices and organizations create different spaces alongside the continuing prominence of strategic, entrepreneurial, outcome- and investment-oriented approaches.

Attention to end users *and* suppliers

A key feature of the collaborative economy, embraced by Uber and other sharing platforms like Airbnb, is that they blend public and private – personal cars become 'taxis' and spare rooms double as 'hotel' rooms (Badger, 2014) – but do so in a manner that is built around the needs of customers while creating the right incentives for providers. So, too, must philanthropy. The rise of social media, cheaper communication, and the ability to reach episodic donors through crowdfunding, pushes philanthropy to redefine what a 'donor' is and the nature of their involvement. Ultimately, this forces greater transparency and accountability. Technology is already making payment systems frictionless, but this is only a small piece of the customization challenge. The entire philanthropic experience, including alignment with the right causes, the ease of conducting due diligence and ability to engage with organizations in different capacities, needs to be tailored more specifically and quite differently to different populations. In particular, young donors are reinventing philanthropy: they demonstrate the potential to get involved in new ways and on a global scale, for example through online viral campaigns and peer-peer microfinancing; hold a strong affinity for entrepreneurship; and seek to be engaged through meaningful action and in leadership capacities in addition to their financial contributions (Achieve, 2014). Most nonprofits, however, fail to adequately capture this; they still have an over reliance on traditional methods of attracting donors. Research agendas that provide much finer grained data about motivations, giving and engagement patterns so as to capture differentiations among population groups will be required, as well as better information about the use of the broad range of philanthropic tools that are now available.

Uber has also taught us to pay careful attention to the supply side, which for philanthropy involves not only individual and institutional donors, but a wide range of intermediaries. These include professional philanthropic advisors, fundraisers and gift planners, the institutions that manage Donor Advised Funds (DAFs) and impact investments, United Ways and federated funds, charity rating agencies, social exchange markets, the media that can so readily shape how different organizations and causes are perceived, and the nonprofits and charities through which philanthropy passes en route to public purposes. These intermediaries are taking on increased significance, serving as new instruments and asset classes, brokers, rating bodies, and learning systems. However, little is known about most of them. In the absence of evidence-based research, debates about the role of these intermediaries are waged primarily between entrenched, often polarized positions, as demonstrated by current discussions of DAFs. For proponents, these personal giving vehicles, often described as the poor donor's foundation, democratize philanthropy, encourage giving and disperse funds at a faster rate than private foundations (Cohen, 2014); their detractors argue that DAFs, particularly those held by corporate-affiliated gift funds, lack transparency, create an information buffer between nonprofits and donors, and divert funding from charities by sitting on contributions for indefinite periods, leading to calls for mandatory payout rates (Cantor, 2014; Madoff, 2014). As part of a broader debate about the value of perpetuity to philanthropy, DAFs merit much greater scrutiny, as do other intermediaries. Who are they serving and how well are they doing so? Indeed, questions of accountability – who is (or should be) accountable to whom and for what – have acquired a new saliency and become much more complicated in the collaborative economy.

Transparency, accountability and learning

A basic premise of why people trust nonprofits is information asymmetry: the 'contract failure' theory posits that when consumers have difficulty attaining full information about quality of services, they are more likely to trust nonprofits than providers with a profit motive (Hansmann, 1980). The transparency afforded by open, big data is rapidly reducing information asymmetries between service providers and consumers, and among donors, recipients and the public. The collaborative economy has become the *reputation* economy in which, as Unwin (2014: 22) notes, 'organisations will be judged by their connections as much as by their balance sheets, and will need to demonstrate they are open, and accountable, in the more complex, and more rewarding world.' Although this should create incentives to voluntarily be more forthcoming with information of all types, the philanthropic and nonprofit sector has not fully embraced such openness. Foundations are still seen to operate in 'stealth mode' (Camarena, 2013) and the financing and governance of many charities seems 'unfathomable' (Unwin, 2014: 21) to potential donors and the public. Competition for funding, and fear of losing funding if results are not as expected, has generally discouraged nonprofits from sharing information about innovations with each other and from reporting on their failures, as well as their successes.

With a lack of information about impact and results, the public, aided by third party rating agencies, has focused on inputs as a means of assessing effectiveness, particularly the wildly popular, but deeply misleading, notion that low ratios of administrative and fundraising costs are good measures of well-run organizations (Palotta, 2012). Technology and big, open, data are rapidly changing what is possible and expected (Bernholz, Chapter 28), enabling a variety of startups as well as established organizations to provide detailed assessments of the financing landscape, make 'grantmakers' data more useful' (Ajah, ND) and enable potential donors to make more informed decisions based on relevant information. The disruptive next step will be the use of this expanded transparency for purposes of learning and accountability.

The current learning systems for philanthropy fall short of their potential (Johnson and Remmer, 2008; US Trust, 2013), or at least research on them is so inadequate that their effectiveness cannot be assessed. With the importance of High Net Worth (HNW) individuals, impending intergenerational wealth transfers, and the creation of new pockets of wealth, the professional advisors to philanthropists are assuming more significant roles. Their ability to engage the values-based philanthropic conversations that extend beyond the mechanics of giving is reportedly improving, but still not fully serving their clients' learning needs and desires to involve the next generation (TPI, 2000; Scorpio Partnership 2008). The popularity of DAFs has compounded the challenges of advice seeking and giving. When DAFs are held by community foundations, the donors may benefit from extensive advice by the foundation staff, particularly for locally-based giving, and many community foundations are very actively marketing this advantage. In contrast, the money managers at corporate-affiliated gift funds are unlikely to endorse specific causes or charities, referring clients to standard third party sources and rating agencies (Nonprofit Quarterly, 2010), while recognizing that many donors do not seek or desire advice.

A distinctive feature of the collaborative economy is learning based on peer-to-peer networks and self-regulation, and attuned to end users. Peer-based learning is already occurring to some extent through a wide range of giving circles and networks of philanthropists or angel investors. Often these are informal and have an important social, as well as educational function (Eikenberry and Bearman, 2014). Some, such as Social Venture Partners (an affiliation of individuals who mentor each other about becoming better educated philanthropists while assisting community organizations to have more impactful projects), have become international in scale. As a formalized peer-to-peer system, more effective self-regulation has been advocated by several contributors to this volume (Phillips and Smith, Chapter 13; Breen, Chapter 14; Sidel, Chapter 16) as a mechanism for promoting accountability for purposes of learning in ways that rule-based state regulation does not.

Philanthropy has been widely criticized for its poor skills at listening to its 'customers' – specifically, its beneficiaries and its third sector intermediaries – and for neglecting to use such knowledge to improve performance (Shoemaker, 2015). The modus operandi of strategic philanthropy is a top-down approach led by a theory of change crafted by the donor (Anheier *et al.*, 2007; Brest *et al.*, 2015). This normalizes control by the funder, rather than promoting an injection of bottom-up perspectives that offer experiential knowledge to fit proposed solutions to user realities. As described in Part III of this volume, various communities, rather than waiting for philanthropic institutions to become more user sensitive, are mobilizing and experimenting with a wide range of 'horizontal,' community-led, initiatives. The private sector, which has been quicker to develop a user focus, is also filling some of this space, particularly in developing countries where it is working with those at the 'bottom of the pyramid', people living on $5 per day or less (Prahalad, 2004). Seeing this large segment of the population as both consumers and producers in a global market, and thus as a resource and opportunity rather than as a 'problem' for philanthropy to fix, many businesses are aggressively and controversially developing low cost services and making use of philanthropic tools, such as microfinance, to invest in these communities (Salamon, 2014: 56). Philanthropy's challenge, then, is to better integrate top-led and community-driven approaches, and in the process rework the power relationships that have discouraged two-way learning. This entails engaging and listening more actively to the recipient nonprofits, investing in their capacity to engage with, and learn from, the end users, and for donors to personally 'dig in' (Shoemaker, 2015) with the communities they are trying to assist, co-producing projects and programs in culturally competent ways. The point of such engagement is more than process, but is squarely focused on achieving impacts for improving lives and environments.

Investing in impact

The ability to have impact – to make a difference in people's lives – has become the new goalpost for philanthropy, replacing mere intentions of doing good (Harrow and Jung, 2015). If the search for impact is to remain credible, however, evidence of achievements is critical. The measurement of impact is unquestionably difficult, often requiring long-term horizons and plagued by issues of attribution (Edwards, 2014). Impact measurement has advanced in recent years, but has often gotten stuck on single indices such as Social Return on Investment (SROI); it is far from having solid indicators of blended or triple line investments (Trelstad, 2014). While stressing the importance of impact in their resource allocations (Brest, 2012; Bagwell *et al.*, 2013) philanthropic institutions and other funders have not assisted the development of better measurement to the extent they might. Many do not fund or provide technical assistance for performance assessment (Hall *et al.*, 2004; Kail *et al.*, 2013); they expect assessment over unreasonably short time periods (Edwards, 2014); and have a built in bias for measurement of the effects of services, rather than of infrastructure or advocacy (Salamon, 2014).

That philanthropy is underperforming on its impact agenda is, however, not solely due to the challenges of measurement. Adherence to an 'illusion of control' (Shoemaker, 2015: 7) is a major inhibiting factor. Affecting real change, particularly in difficult or complex environments, is a long-term proposition, but donors are reluctant to commit to long term funding horizons: they do not want the recipients to become dependent on them or they seek the flexibility to move on to new projects. Funding is increasingly of a restricted nature (Blackbaud, 2005), tied to a particular use or performance target, in order to adhere to a funder's strategy or an advisor's caution to sign only a very detailed gift agreement. As a result, the ability of recipients to be agile and adaptive as conditions change, or as they learn how to deliver more effectively, is impaired. Donors' reluctance to support organizational capacity building or advocacy also inhibits opportunities to scale up or to influence public policies that affect outcomes. In spite of the rhetoric around innovation, approaches to risk are cautious, and rarely are funds designated specifically for experimentation (Bagley, 2014). The public gives low ratings to how well nonprofits report on impact and, more generally, on how donations are used (Lasby and Barr, 2013; Wixley and Noble, 2014). In particular, acceptance of, and candour about, failure is still limited (Bishop and Green, 2014). While 'failure reports' are being advocated as a means of learning from things that do not work (Lomax and Wharton 2014; EVPA, 2015), thereby reinforcing the notion that some failures are an accepted part of risk taking and discouraging only positive reporting (DP Evaluation 2012; Shell Foundation, 2015), they are still a novelty and need to avoid becoming pro-forma rather than meaningful. A question remains of what difference better reporting alone would make because, in spite of the importance donors say they ascribe to impact, it appears to make little difference in their philanthropic decision-making (Cunningham and Ricks, 2004; Lasby and Barr, 2013). Relationships, reputation of recipients, being asked, warm glows, and a host of other factors still come into play, tempering or overriding any carefully calculated assessment of impact.

Finally, the drive toward impact tends to be a series of isolated journeys, with different philanthropists and institutions pursuing their own paths. Although the notion of working collaboratively for 'collective impact' – developing and acting on a shared agenda for solving specific problems – has become popular, if in some versions formulaic (Kania and Kramer, 2011), this admonishment is applied mainly to nonprofits, with individual and institutional philanthropists still tending to act alone.

While incremental progress toward better measurement and its use is likely to occur, larger scale disruption will come as impact goes 'retail'. Impact investing has become a major global asset class, promoted by international fund management firms, and has made the dimensions of risk, return, and impact the new standard of social investment. Nonprofits, large and small in all parts of the world, will need to show they have worthy projects in which to invest which creates pressures for standardized indicators (Thümler, Chapter 23). As Salamon (2014: 15) pointedly observes, rather than standardized (or necessarily sound) approaches, a plethora of impact measures has been created to support this market, and are 'so numerous that they begin to resemble those prizes in grade-school contests designed to ensure that every child comes home a winner'. In addition, the strong endorsement by many governments of social impact bonds, rooted in pay for success arrangements in which investors realize a return only if the nonprofits delivering the service meet assigned performance targets (Clifford and Jung, 2016), is making impact increasingly competitive. It puts new pressures on third sector organizations to be able to deliver. When combined with the integration of services and anticipation of collective impact, this then becomes very complex, and likely political in both a small 'p' and partisan sense. Academic research is just scratching the surface of this new world of impact investment and its politics, but will be vital to its future.

Engagement and collaboration

The collaborative economy by which consumers create, share and crowdsource goods and services, rather than purchasing them from traditional organizations, has opened unknown territory – not only for how we consume, but the expectations of engagement and collaboration that surround it. For individual philanthropists, a new meshing of giving with engagement is evident. Although volunteerism and donating have long been correlated – those who volunteer are more likely to give (Pharoah, Chapter 4) – they are increasingly being combined as part of a 'values-exchange' in which donors seek out, and participate in meaningful ways in, organizations that share their values (Rabin, 2014). This is particularly so for Millennials, women (TD Bank, 2014) and HNW donors who are all interested in using their heads by giving their distinctive talent in a leadership capacity, not just using their hands in conventional service roles. Instead of traditional fundraising, organizations thus need to be more attuned to 'resource raising' (Wilding, 2014: 28), managing and matching diverse kinds of talent.

At the organizational level, philanthropy has tended to be a solo, fragmented, competitive, and image-driven enterprise. Foundations hold financial and decision-making power over their grantees and protect their distinctive brands and reputations very carefully, rather like Uber itself which has been famously aggressive in poaching drivers. In an environment of scarce resources, successful nonprofits have also learned to excel at competition. Led by the rising influence of Millennials, a wide range of community-based experiments and individual philanthropists who have lost patience with unproductive competition, the future will increasingly demand greater collaboration among nonprofits, among philanthropic institutions and across sectors, as is already beginning to occur. Major foundations have demonstrated a willingness to work together on complex issues; regionally-based and cause-oriented (e.g. around environment or the arts) networks of grantmakers or investors have formed in many countries (e.g. the European Venture Philanthropy Association). The sustainability of many of these collaborations has been quite fragile, however, due to difficulties in maintaining the commitments, overcoming differences in organizational cultures, and matching institutional interests with those of their partners (Eikenberry and Bearman, 2014). In this regard, they have been fashioned as old-style power relationships among like kinds of organizations. A new type of collaboration percolating through the sharing economy reflects a 'new power' that, rather than being controlled by the few, is 'open, participatory, and peer-driven' (Heimans and Timms, 2014), involving a greater diversity of participants, each providing different kinds of resources. Radical transparency with a purpose of learning for improvement is a defining feature. Instead of emanating from formal evaluations, such learning comes from participation and peer-based sharing, giving participants a sense of agency and power (Heimans and Timms, 2014). The challenge will be to develop appropriate models of networked governance and horizontal accountability (to 'partners' rather than funders), suitable to a new power and empowerment (Jung and Harrow, 2015).

The corporate sector can be expected to be a major player in various types of partnerships and cross-sectoral collaborations, but less so in handing out cash than in providing skills, networks, infrastructure and other assets related to projects that advance firms' core business (Wilding 2014). In the field of human services, corporations are becoming leading players in pressing for intersectoral collaboration to fundamentally redesign, coordinate and integrate public services, many of which they already co-produce (KPMG, 2013), as a means to more stable and user-centred systems. In the absence of a strong evidence-base, the third sector has rightly tended to be deeply suspicious of such corporate partnerships, questioning the mutual benefit they generate and pointing to the uncertainty and risks they may entail. There is likely to be a growing divide among nonprofits: those willing to engage and exert their own 'new power' in these relationships on the one hand, and those who see such collaboration as greater marketization of philanthropy on the other. With heightened accountability, both within organizations and to a wide range of external stakeholders, with complex issues at play, and a problematic history of business engagement in other areas, such as the public sector, the challenges of making such cross-sector collaboration work should not be underestimated.

Place sensitive and policy relevant

A large part of what is seen to be exciting about contemporary philanthropy is its increased diversity that arises from an expanded range of tools for social investing, the invention of new forms of hybrid organizations and a 'big bang' of new actors (Salamon, 2014: 37). Place needs to be added to this list as a source of increased differentiation. As Uber recognized, what works in some places does not in others. The rapid growth of community foundations, which have doubled their numbers in the past 14 years to more than 1,800 and extended their reach globally (Knight, 2014), is the primary manifestation of greater place-sensitivity, and is changing the course of philanthropy in several ways. Community foundations are affecting the distribution of philanthropy in that, compared to individual giving, a very small percentage of their grantmaking goes to religion, with the bulk directed at education, human services, and arts and culture (Knight, 2014: 8). They are reporting success at catalyzing giving, sometimes through reviving traditional forms as Egypt's Maadi foundation has done with the *waqf*, but also in supporting community networking and innovation (Knight, 2014: 18). What distinguishes community foundations from other philanthropic institutions is that grantmaking is not the only, or necessarily the most important, thing they do: rather they provide the 'architecture for solving social problems' (Knight, 2014: 18) by promoting collaboration, convening conversations, building capacity among community organizations, supporting leadership development, and being knowledge centres (Harrow, Jung and Phillips, Chapter 19). Their success is related to an ability to work in the open, participatory, and context-specific, new power of collaborative economies. The rise of the middle class in the Global South is likely to produce a new spurt of growth (and funding) of community foundations and of other local initiatives directed by local communities. When coupled with greater transborder flows of money, talent and ideas, their diffusion can be expected to reshape more established forms of philanthropy across many countries.

The potential of these new developments will rely upon a receptive and enabling policy and regulatory environment. The ability of public policies and regulation to enhance and shape the instruments of philanthropy is clear: for example, new regulations in the mid-1990s encouraged commercial banks to invest in community development in the US (Sagawa, 2014); when Canadian tax rules allowed donation of public securities to charities in 2006, revenues jumped dramatically; the creation of the UK's Big Society Capital injected significant capital for innovation; and if a European Foundation Statute were ever enacted, cross-border philanthropy would be greatly facilitated. The Uber analogy reveals how resistant to change public policy can be, particularly when governments try to force new phenomena into old regulatory boxes, rather than creating more flexible, suitable ones. Poorly fitting public policy that is the legacy of an era when the main goal was to oversee administration of tax benefits, and has been left to drift since (Phillips and Smith, Chapter 13), is a major impediment to evolving practices of philanthropy in a transnational environment. In spite of increasing domestic pockets of wealth, many developing countries are caught between motives to contain philanthropy, particularly foreign funding directed at advocacy, and to encourage expansion of private giving (Sidel, Chapter 16).

At root is the problem that governments know very little about the needs, challenges, and potential of philanthropy, in part because there is rarely an institutionalized access point, comparable to the voice of business in industry departments that makes at least one department (other than a tax agency) responsible and receptive. Thus, the current relationship of governments and the philanthropic and nonprofit sector is at best underperforming (Healy and Donnelly-Cox, Chapter 12). This sector is still treated mainly as an invisible social safety net, assumed to be willing to supplement public spending. At worst, the relationship has become increasingly politicized for partisan purposes that are disconnected from an interest in policies for more effective and accountable philanthropy (Phillips and Smith, 2014). Rather than continuing to drift on outdated assumptions, governments need to animate some serious and extended public conversations about policies for philanthropy and the sectors it serves. The agenda could be a lengthy one. Central items could include: policies for transborder giving, mechanisms of accountability and transparency, tax benefits and their redistributional effects, payout rates on foundations and DAFs, regulations on program-related and impact investing, roles of the new hybrids, and means of promoting social innovation, etc.

Conclusion: Research for a disrupted philanthropy

Philanthropy is undergoing constructive reinvention and redesign, with the extent of its multiplier effects on existing institutions and practices still to be properly assessed. The once inelastic concept of philanthropy has been stretched, aided by an array of new philanthropic tools and intermediaries, into a continuum that ranges from traditional charitable giving to social investment. The strategic, entrepreneurial and impact-oriented philanthropy that was declared new more than a decade ago is likely to remain firmly planted along it. Approaches that are more collaborative, community-oriented and place-based are on the rise, coexisting alongside strategic and venture philanthropy. The creative uses of technology, effects of democratized participation and roles of hybrid, blended-value, organizations are just beginning to take hold. The combined result will be an even more diverse and adaptable philanthropic landscape. Its geographies will shift and its scale will be both more local and more global.

The main challenges will be for public policy and academic research to keep up. Across the spectrum of topics covered in this *Companion*, from philanthropy's impetus through its implementation to its impact, the authors have identified gaps and suggested research agendas. They point to the need for case studies of philanthropy's recent innovations, but also systematic quantitative and comparative research. Extant research has focused mainly on either individual giving or the major institutions paying little attention to the diverse set of philanthropic intermediaries. The black boxes of individual decision-making and of the internal management of philanthropic institutions and network governance need to be opened. A collaborative bent for philanthropy would also value research on philanthropy's facets that we have talked about least in this volume – time and talent rather than treasure, and the interaction of volunteer engagement with giving. Questions of redistribution and impact imply a greater interest in how philanthropy affects its intended beneficiaries.

Two questions that permeate the *Companion* are whether philanthropy needs to 'up its game' in being more effective, and whether it is doing so. The conclusions that are threaded through the various dimensions and expressions of philanthropy in the volume are yes, and yes: there is much to be done to enhance philanthropy's potential, and much that is positive in taking it in this direction. Our intent is that these chapters have provided a variety of ideas as to how research can do the same.

References

Achieve. (2014) *2014 Millennial Impact Report*. Washington, DC: Case Foundation.

Ajah (No Date) PoweredbyData, www.poweredbydata.org/ [Accessed 15 April 2015].

Anheier, H. K., Simmons, A. and Winder, D. (2007) *Innovations in strategic philanthropy: Local and global perspectives*. New York, NY: Springer.

Badger, E. (2014) Taxi medallions have been the best investment in America for years. Now Uber may be changing that, *Washington Post*, 20 June. www.washingtonpost.com/blogs/wonkblog/wp/2014/06/20/taxi-medallions-have-been-the-best-investment-in-america-for-years-now-uber-may-be-changing-that/ [Accessed 10 January 2015].

Bagley, K. (2014) We need to unlock social capital and invest in innovation. In C. Slococ. (ed.), *Making good: The future of the voluntary sector, a collection of essays by voluntary sector leaders*. London: Civil Exchange, 44–6.

Bagwell, S., de las Casas, L., van Poortvliet, M. and Abercrombie, R. (2013) *Money for good UK: Understanding donor motivations and behaviour*. London: NPC.

Bishop, M. and Green, M. (2014) Who gains, who loses? Distributional impacts of the new philanthropy – Part B: Who gains. In L. M. Salamon (ed.), *New frontiers of philanthropy: A guide to the new tools and actors reshaping global philanthropy and social investing*. New York, NY: Oxford University Press, 550–61.

Blackbaud Inc. (2005) *Restricted gifts on the rise – New funding challenges for nonprofits*. Charleston, SC: Blackbaud.

Bower, J. L. and Christensen, C. M. (1995) Disruptive technologies: Catching the wave, *Harvard Business Review*, 73(1): 43–53.

Brest, P. (2012) A decade of outcome-oriented philanthropy, *Stanford Social Innovation Review*, 10(2): 42–7.

Brest. P. with responses (2015) Strategic philanthropy and its discontents, *Stanford Social Innovation Review*. www.ssireview.org/articles/entry/strategic_philanthropy_and_its_discontents [Accessed 14 May 2015].

Brown, M. (2013) Uber – What's fueling Uber's growth engine?, *GrowthHackers*. www.growthhackers.com/companies/uber/ [Accessed 9 February 2015].

Camarena, J. (2013) Meet the new glasspockets website, Foundation Center. www.blog.glasspockets.org/2013/11/camarena-20131114.html?_ga=1.169250786.256283547.1424533531 [Accessed 14 January 2015].

Cantor, A. (2014) Donor-advised funds let Wall Street steer charitable donations, *Chronicle of Philanthropy*, 28 October. www.philanthropy.com/article/Donor-Advised-Funds-Let-Wall/152337#disqus_thread [Accessed 15 January 2015].

Clifford, J. and Jung, T (2016), Social impact bonds: Exploring and understanding an emerging funding approach. In O. Lehner (ed.), *The Routledge handbook of social and sustainable finance*. Routledge: London.

Cohen, R. (2014) Corporate-originated charitable funds. In L. M. Salamon (ed.). *New frontiers of philanthropy: A Guide to the new tools and actors reshaping global philanthropy and social investing*. New York, NY: Oxford University Press, 255–90.

Cunningham, K. and Ricks, M. (2004) Why Measure? Nonprofits use metrics to show that they are efficient. But what if donors don't care? *Stanford Social Innovation Review*, 2(1). www.ssireview.org/articles/entry/why_measure [Accessed 16 January 2015].

DP Evaluation. (2012) A funder conundrum: Choices that funders face in bringing about positive social change. London, The Diana, Princess of Wales Memorial Fund/Association of Charitable Foundations.

Edwards, M. (2014) Who gains, who loses? Distributional impacts of the new philanthropy – Part A: Who loses. In L. M. Salamon (ed.), *New frontiers of philanthropy: A guide to the new tools and actors reshaping global philanthropy and social investing*. New York, NY: Oxford University Press, 539–49.

Eikenberry, A. M. and Bearman, J. (2014) Funding collaboratives. In L. M. Salamon (ed.), *New frontiers of philanthropy: A guide to the new tools and actors reshaping global philanthropy and social investing*. New York, NY: Oxford University Press, 291–308.

EVPA. (2015) *Learning from failures in venture philanthropy and social investment*. Brussels: European Venture Philanthropy Association.

Hall, M. H., Phillips, S. D., Meillat, C., and Pickering, D. (2004) *Assessing performance: Evaluation practices and perspectives in Canada's voluntary sector*. Toronto and Ottawa: Canadian Centre for Philanthropy and Centre for Voluntary Sector Research and Development, Carleton University.

Hansmann, H. (1980) The role of nonprofit enterprise, *Yale Law Journal*, 89: 835–901.

Harrow, J and Jung, T (2015) Debate: Thou shalt have impact, total impact – government involvement in philanthropic foundations' decision-making, *Public Money and Management*, May: 176–8.

Heimans, J. and Timms, H. (2014) Understanding the 'New Power', *Harvard Business Review*, 92(12): 49–57.

Johal, S. and Zon, N. (2015) *Policy making for the sharing economy: Beyond whack-a-mole*. Toronto: Mowat Centre.

Johnson, S. and Remmer, E. (2008) What's a donor to do now? *Alliance Magazine*, June. www.alliancemagazine.org/feature/what-s-a-donor-to-do-now/ [Accessed 12 January 2015].

Jung, T. and Harrow, J. (2015) New development: Philanthropy in networked governance – treading with care, *Public Money and Management*, January: 47–51.

Kail, A., van Vliet, A. and Baumgartner, L. (2013) *Funding impact: Funding impact practices in the UK*. London: NPC.

Kania, J. and Kramer, M. (2011) Collective impact, *Stanford Social Innovation Review*, 9(1): 36–41.

Knight, B. (2014). *Community Foundation atlas – Dimensions of the field*. Community Foundation Atlas. www.communityfoundationatlas.org/ [Accessed 10 February 2015].

KPMG. (2013) *The integration imperative: Reshaping the delivery of human and social services*. Toronto.

Lasby, D. and Barr, C. (2013) *Talking about charities*. Edmonton, AB: Muttart Foundation.

Lomax, P. and Wharton, C. (2014) *10 Innovations in Global Philanthropy*. New Philanthropy Capital: London.

Madoff, R. (2014) 5 myths about payout rules for donor-advised funds, *Chronicle of Philanthropy*, 13 January. www.philanthropy.com/article/5-Myths-About-Payout-Rules-for/153809 [Accessed 18 January 2015].

Nonprofit Quarterly. (2010) The myths and realities of commercial gift funds. *Nonprofit Quarterly*, 21 September. www.nonprofitquarterly.org/philanthropy/8196-the-myths-and-the-realities-of-the-commercial-gift-funds.html [Accessed 20 January 2015].

Palotta, D. (2012) *Charity case: How the nonprofit community can stand up for itself and really change the world*. San Francisco, CA: Jossey-Bass.

Phillips, S. D. and Smith, S. R. (2014) A dawn of policy convergence? Third sector policy and regulatory change among the 'Anglo-Saxon' cluster, *Public Management Review*, 16(8): 1141–63.

Prahalad, C. K. (2004) *The Fortune at the bottom of the pyramid*. Philadelphia: Wharton School Publishing.

Rabin, S. (2014) *Age of opportunity: Putting the ageing society of tomorrow on the agenda of the voluntary sector today*. London: Commission on the Voluntary Sector and Ageing.

Ryzik, M. (2014) How Uber is changing night life in Los Angeles, *The New York Times*, 31 October. www.nytimes.com/2014/11/02/fashion/how-uber-is-changing-night-life-in-los-angeles.html?_r=1 [Accessed 10 January, 2015].

Sagawa, S. (2014) A policy agenda for the new frontiers of philanthropy. In L. M. Salamon (ed.), *New frontiers of philanthropy: A guide to the new tools and actors reshaping global philanthropy and social investing*. New York, NY: Oxford University Press, 636–53.

Salamon, L. M. (2014) The revolution on the frontiers of philanthropy: An introduction. In L. M. Salamon (ed.), *New frontiers of philanthropy: A guide to the new tools and actors reshaping global philanthropy and social investing*. New York, NY: Oxford University Press, 3–88.

Scorpio Partnership. (2008) The role of wealth advisors in offering philanthropy services to high-net-worth clients. New Philanthropy Capital, Wise Partnership, Bertelsmann Stiftung: London.

Shell Foundation. (2015) *Shell Foundations 'lessons learned' series*. www.shellfoundation.org/Latest-Shell-Foundation-Reports.aspx [Accessed 24 May 2015].

Shoemaker, P. (2015) Reconstructive philanthropy from the outside in, *Stanford Social Innovation Review*. www.ssireview.org/blog/entry/reconstructing_philanthropy_from_the_outside_in [Accessed 25 February 2015].

TD Bank. (2014) *Time, treasure, talent: Canadian women and philanthropy*. Toronto: TD Bank.

TPI – The Philanthropic Initiative. (2000) *Doing well by doing good: Improving client service, increasing philanthropic capital: The legal and financial advisor's role*. Boston, MA: The Philanthropic Initiative.

Trelstad, B. (2014) The elusive quest for impact: The evolving practice of social-impact measurement. In L. M. Salamon (ed.), *New frontiers of philanthropy: A guide to the new tools and actors reshaping global philanthropy and social investing*. New York, NY: Oxford University Press, 583–603.

Unwin, J. (2014) The voluntary sector needs to reclaim its identity and set its own course. In C. Slocock (ed.), *Making good: The future of the voluntary sector, a collection of essays by voluntary sector leaders*. London: Civil Exchange, 19–22.

US Trust. (2013) *The U.S. Trust study of the philanthropic conversation: Understanding advisor approaches and client expectations*. New York, NYC: U.S. Trust.

Wilding, K. (2014) The voluntary sector should face the future with confidence. In Slocock, C. (ed.), *Making good: The future of the voluntary sector, a collection of essays by voluntary sector leaders*. London: Civil Exchange, 27–9.

Wixley, S. and Noble, J. (2014) *Mind the gap: What the public thinks about charities*. London: NPC. www.thinknpc.org/publications/mind-the-gap/ [Accessed 1 April 2015].

Index

Page reference for tables are **bold**; page references for figures are *italic*.

For Product Safety Concerns and Information please contact our EU
representative GPSR@taylorandfrancis.com Taylor & Francis Verlag GmbH,
Kaufingerstraße 24, 80331 München, Germany

Printed and bound by CPI Group (UK) Ltd, Croydon, CR0 4YY

10/05/2025

01866288-0001